Information Literacy Instruction

THEORY AND PRACTICE

Second Edition

Esther S. Grassian and Joan R. Kaplowitz

Neal-Schuman Publishers, Inc.
New York London

Published by Neal-Schuman Publishers, Inc.
100 William St., Suite 2004
New York, NY 10038

Printed and bound in the United States of America.

The paper used in this publication meets the minimum requirements of American National Standard for Information Sciences—Permanence of Paper for Printed Library Materials, ANSI Z39.48-1992.

Library of Congress Cataloging-in-Publication Data

Grassian, Esther S.
Information literacy instruction : theory and practice / Esther S. Grassian and Joan R. Kaplowitz. — 2nd ed.
p. cm.
Includes bibliographical references and index.
ISBN 978-1-55570-666-1 (alk. paper)
1. Information literacy—Study and teaching. 2. Information retrieval—Study and teaching. I. Kaplowitz, Joan R. II. Title.

ZA3075.G73 2009
025.5'24'071—dc22

2009023647

Dedications

I dedicate my portions of this book to you, dear readers, in the hope that you will teach your learners and learn from them, joyously, with caring and with heart.

—Esther S. Grassian

This book is dedicated to all the teachers who have touched my life and who believed in me long before I believed in myself; to my many students who asked me interesting and challenging questions and helped push me outside my comfort zone; to my friends both personal and professional who were always there when I needed them with a pep talk, a shoulder to lean on, and as many hugs as necessary; to my cats who always knew when I needed a cuddle and a purr; and finally to my wonderful family (Hillary, Greg, and Mike) who seem to be as proud of me as I have always been of them.

—Joan R. Kaplowitz

Contents

List of Figures

CD-ROM Contents

SUPPORT MATERIALS

SEARCHABLE AND LIVE LINKS FILES

Foreword

When we think of information literacy, there are two names that always come to mind—Esther Grassian and Joan Kaplowitz. Together, they have continued to advance our knowledge of the field of information literacy. Before the information literacy movement swept across the libraries of the nation, they were already writing and teaching about it. At every turning point in the practice of information literacy, they were already ahead of us, guiding us toward new directions and new approaches.

Now, these two scholar–practitioners have issued a second edition of their popular book, *Information Literacy Instruction: Theory and Practice*. Refreshed and updated, this book is very worthy of another reading. It is comprehensive in scope and turns a spotlight onto such dimensions as planning, instructional modes, copyright, new technologies, library anxiety, and assessment. For those new to the field, Esther Grassian and Joan Kaplowitz include clear definitions and a history of information literacy. Very useful also are chapters on how students learn and how students can become fully engaged in the learning process.

Reading through this book, I was struck again with the importance and urgency of teaching information literacy. Information is so abundant now and technology so pervasive that information literacy only continues to increase as a critical foundational skill. For this reason, librarians have to keep information literacy in the forefront of any educational process; this means that we, ourselves, must keep learning about this important skill.

It is easy to learn from this book. Written in their personal and comfortable style, this book is loaded with practical illustrations and examples. Esther Grassian and Joan Kaplowitz move easily between the theoretical and the practical as they lead us through every aspect of information literacy instruction.

The audience for this book is wide—librarians starting their careers, librarians who wish to increase their knowledge of information literacy, faculty who are teaching information literacy, and library administrators interested in program growth and resource needs can all benefit from this comprehensive book. This book can easily serve as a textbook or as a desk manual kept handy for any situation.

I have enjoyed and have benefited greatly by everything that Esther Grassian and Joan Kaplowitz have ever written. I have always admired their unparalleled depth and range of understanding about information literacy. All I can say is that they have worked their magic again, and I know that you will think that reading this valuable, important, and insightful book was time very well-spent.

Susan Carol Curzon, PhD
Dean, University Library
California State University, Northridge

Preface

Imagine, if you will, the following scenarios . . .

Scenario 1: The phone rings off the hook, 15 voicemail, instant messages (IMs), or text messages wait for an answer, and e-mail never seems to end. Administrators press for experimental pilot projects using new, untested, or difficult-to-use products. They insist on complete statistics, fully trained staff, and frequent progress reports. Meanwhile, instructional staff worry about being overloaded, having too little time to prepare, and looking foolish trying to teach without full understanding of, or comfort with, a broad range of instructional modes—not to mention an endless parade of new equipment, hardware, and applications. Instruction schedules need to be set up for ongoing programs; equipment checked and maintained; and examples, handouts, and Web sites, even virtual world sims and objects, created or updated.

Scenario 2: Your phone is silent. Your e-mail messages are mostly from listservs, colleagues, and friends. You rarely get requests for information literacy instruction (ILI), and very few people attend library workshops or visit your instructional Web pages. You wonder where all the learners have gone. You also wonder how they are evaluating the quality of online tools and materials they find, and if they even know about your library's licensed databases, much less how to use them effectively.

Four basic questions—what to do, how to do it, when to do it, and how to measure success—weigh most heavily on all librarians involved in ILI. *Information Literacy Instruction: Theory and Practice* is designed for anyone involved or interested in ILI, whether your situation falls under Scenario 1, Scenario 2, or somewhere in between or whether you are a library school/information studies student, a new librarian, or a seasoned professional.

Librarians have always taught people how to use libraries and information sources. Over the past 40–50 years, instruction has grown in importance in libraries and other information settings, even eclipsing traditional reference service. As computers entered library settings, training became an expected part of the librarian's job. Until relatively recently, though, few library schools have supported this role through either full-length credit courses or continuing education. In comparison to technology training and education, few opportunities for in-depth continuing education in ILI exist either. As was the case for the first edition, we intend this newer edition to fill a dual need by serving as both a textbook for library school ILI courses and a support and self-education tool for practicing instruction librarians by deepening their background knowledge and expanding their instructional skills.

We have been instruction librarians and instruction coordinators for many years. We proposed a User Education/Bibliographic Instruction course to the UCLA library school in 1989, and, when it was approved, we designed and taught it together the first time it was offered. Since 1990, we have alternated teaching this course each year at the UCLA Graduate School of Education and Information Studies, Department of Information Studies. We have based this book on our course, on our own practical instructional planning and delivery experiences, on our educations, and on our intensive studies of publications and other materials in information literacy and related fields, such as psychology, education, management, and technology.

We have designed this second edition of *Information Literacy Instruction* to include both theoretical underpinnings and practical applications that may be adapted or used as they are in a variety of settings, in all types of libraries and information arenas, wherever librarians help people learn. The material covered in each chapter was gathered from a wide variety of sources. Many excellent books, articles, and Web sites are available that offer more in-depth analysis of the material covered in our book. A selection of these works is included in the "Read More About It" sections at the end of each chapter. To acquire a thorough understanding of the theory and practice of ILI, we recommend reading this entire book. To take you even deeper into the topic, we suggest our companion volume, *Learning to Lead and Manage Information Literacy Instruction* (2005), which covers topics such as leadership, management, collaboration, research and grant writing, marketing, and managing technology. To gain the most out of these books, we recommend sampling additional suggested readings and trying out the exercises that are included at the end of each chapter.

ORGANIZATION

We have arranged the chapters of *Information Literacy Instruction: Theory and Practice* in the order in which we feel those new to ILI should learn about it. In Part I, Information Literacy Instruction Background, we begin by discussing definitions in Chapter 1 and then present the history of library instruction/bibliographic instruction/information literacy in Chapter 2. In Chapter 2, we also introduce the concepts of "synchronous" and "asynchronous" instruction used in many of the following chapters to mean, respectively, simultaneous and in real-time, for two or more individuals, as opposed to nonsimultaneous, any time/any place instruction for a single person.

We continue in Part II, Information Literacy Instruction Building Blocks, with a solid grounding in learning theory and styles and the application of theory to the practice of ILI (Chapters 3 and 4), followed by in-depth discussion of library anxiety, mental models, and conceptual change (Chapter 5) and then critical thinking and active learning (Chapter 6).

Parts I and II provide an essential foundation for all instructional planning and development. With this foundation on which to build, in Part III, Planning & Developing Information Literacy Instruction, we move on to Needs Assessment and goal-setting (Chapter 7), followed by principles for selecting instructional modes with pros and cons, as well as tips for effective use for each (Chapter 8). We do not, however, recommend specific modes of instruction, or even combinations of modes, as many different factors may influence your mode selection decision. Instead, we recommend offering a range of modes to meet a variety of learning styles and needs.

Part III of *Information Literacy Instruction* then moves on to Chapter 9, "Basic Copyright and Design Issues." Chapter 10 continues this theme by focusing on design of specific instructional modes and materials. Chapter 11 delves into the theories and practices of assessing, evaluating, and revising to round out the cycle of planning, designing, and developing ILI programs.

As Part III illustrates, planning, developing, assessing, and revising effective ILI programs takes time and effort. It also takes time and effort to prepare and deliver instruction for a variety of groups in different environments and under different physical and technological circumstances. Part IV will help you do just that. Chapter 12 is devoted to learner-centered teaching for synchronous and asynchronous formats (face-to-face or online), followed by four more chapters that are closely related: how to teach diverse groups (Chapter 13), how to develop instruction for particular library environments (Chapter 14), how to use technology to support pedagogy (Chapter 15), and how to approach teaching online tools and resources (Chapter 16). The final part of *Information Literacy Instruction*, The Future of ILI, is our view of what the future may hold for the topic (Chapter 17).

The accompanying CD-ROM offers a great variety of useful support material and information. Materials include a sample PowerPoint presentation slide show, a sample one-shot class/workshop outline, a table that describes a variety of learning styles, a table that discusses different types of assessment tools, an example of minimalist documentation, a snapshot of a Second Life (virtual world) ILI example, and a Two-minute Yoga exercise that can be used as a relaxation technique for instructors and as a stretch break during face-to-face sessions. We have also included a "Read More About It" list for each chapter of the book, as well as the complete book bibliography, both with live links. For a complete list of items on the CD-ROM, see the CD-ROM Contents list.

Information Literacy Instruction: Theory and Practice, 2nd edition, is intended to give you a basic grounding in ILI. *Learning to Lead and Manage Information Literacy In-*

struction (2005) builds on that base and takes you further into the topic, helping you acquire skills that will enable you to move on to a leadership and management role in ILI. We see these two books as a two-part publication, with *Information Literacy Instruction: Theory and Practice* as the first part and *Learning to Lead and Manage Information Literacy Instruction* (2005), as the second. We hope that after reading this updated edition you will understand the current range of instructional choices available and be able to plan, prepare, evaluate, and revise ILI programs in any environment, for a variety of audiences, utilizing emerging and traditional tools and resources as the need and circumstances warrant.

We may not have supplied answers to all of your ILI questions, but we hope this second edition of *Information Literacy Instruction: Theory and Practice*, along with its companion volume, *Learning to Lead and Manage Information Literacy Instruction,* will provide sufficient background, support, and guidance so that you will be able to ask the right questions and explore possible solutions and new technologies in support of teaching and learning. We also hope that you will reach out to others within and beyond librarianship for ideas and information sharing, as well as collaboration and partnership, and that both books will serve as support and stepping stones to your success in information literacy instruction.

Acknowledgments

From Esther Grassian

On a personal note, I thank my family for their extraordinary patience in putting up with the years of researching, writing, and endless rewriting I have spent on yet another book. I could not have done it without the love and support of my wonderful husband, Howard Cowan, not to mention his fabulous cooking, though he did keep asking me when that book would be done. . . . Yes, Howard, we can celebrate—it's finally done! My dear sons, David and Daniel, and my dear mother, Ann Stampfer, deserve thanks, too, for once again putting up with a distracted mother and daughter for several years. My colleague and co-author, Joan Kaplowitz, also deserves much thanks and gratitude for her cheer, her enthusiasm, her superb writing and teaching, and her expertise regarding psychology-related topics. It has been a privilege and a pleasure to work with her on all three books and on many presentations.

I also want to acknowledge and thank those who have inspired me most throughout my career, the greats in a long history of teaching and learning related to libraries—Mimi Dudley, Mary Reichel, Cerise Oberman, Sharon Hogan, Ilene Rockman, and Evan Farber. These dedicated librarians most of all focused on helping people become empowered by learning underlying concepts, as well as the mechanics of using libraries, information tools, and resources for current and lifelong learning. Their worthy endeavors began long before there were computers in libraries, when we all used paper, pencils, pens, books, card catalogs, printed reference tools (e.g., periodical indexes, book catalogs), workbooks, classes, and reference interactions to guide users in learning how to locate, examine, and utilize information tools and materials for themselves.

Today, many carry this torch forward in real life (RL), in virtual worlds like Second Life (SL), globally in many countries, and internationally through IFLA and UNESCO. I humbly acknowledge and stand in awe of your many creative efforts, as you extend a hand and your help to people at all levels, in all sorts of environments and circumstances, using new media as well as traditional means. You have inspired me to write, to share what I have learned, and to continue to learn in the hope that it will support you in your efforts to reach out and empower your learners.

From Joan Kaplowitz

On the surface, writing seems to be a solitary endeavor. However, every author will tell you that it cannot be done alone. I was lucky enough to have built a wonderful support system over the years who cheered me on, let me vent, brainstormed ideas with me, and generally kept me going through the long and sometimes lonely months of writing this book. I would especially like to thank my family, Greg, Hillary, and Mike, who cleverly decided to pursue careers in graphics, instructional, and Web design, respectively, and so became my very own homegrown design team. My collaborations and discussions with them have greatly enhanced the quality of my teaching and my publications—both written and online. I would also like to thank all my former students, interns, and reference desk assistants who have kept in touch with me over the years—especially since my retirement. They keep me current and up-to-date on everything that is impacting the profession. A big thanks also goes out to the members of the Southern California Instruction Librarians, whose programs and meetings help me stay connected to my wonderful California librarian colleagues and the amazing things they are accomplishing. My Santa Monica Yoga community also deserves some thanks. Although they may not have been aware of it, spending time and practicing in their company kept me grounded, centered, and sane during the gestation and birthing period for this book. And last but certainly not least, I will forever be grateful to my co-author, Esther Grassian, whose insightful comments and stimulating discussions of my chapters always made me think, view my work from a different perspective, and in the end helped me improve my work. Thank you Esther for all the years of collaboration on this and so many other projects.

Introduction

The more things change, the more they stay the same.

This aphorism comes to mind in connection with teaching information literacy. At first thought, it might seem that nothing has stayed the same: technology has transformed how people search for and find information, as well as how we teach. Our students in no way resemble those serious, dedicated students from days of yore, who were committed to the search for knowledge. Our classrooms don't resemble those of the past (and when they do, we lament the fact). The lecture is passé; student-centered learning is the only way to go. In fact, we may not see our students at all, as they may be remote learners. Even the terms used to describe the instruction we engage in have changed over time. How could it be that things have stayed the same?

LIBRARIANS

Let us start with the librarians who teach information literacy. Their attributes have, mostly, stayed constant. They need to be flexible, a Jack or Jill of all trades, committed to helping students understand the intricacies connected with finding, evaluating, and successfully using information. They are aided by knowledge of educational psychology and educational theory. Empathy and an understanding of students' tribulations during the research process are vital. Instruction librarians have always, I expect, felt strongly that students need to be empowered in their search for information, even if that term is of relatively recent vintage. They are eager to collaborate with faculty members and educational support units, fully understanding the close interrelationships between what each is teaching. School library media specialists are actively engaged in teaching information literacy skills, and librarians at public libraries are becoming adept at making opportunities to teach their constituencies as well.

TEACHING CONCEPTS

Librarians have always taught concepts. Although some of these concepts may have changed (the evaluation of information and information sources has become more complex in recent years), many of the basic mental models connected to information literacy instruction are timeless—students still need to differentiate popular from scholarly sources and to understand the publication cycle or what a database is. Today's publication cycle might include more options than in the past, but the general concept remains the same.

STUDENTS

We have an idealized notion of students from the past. They were reverent. They were scholars. They were knowledge seekers. They all wanted to learn! Truly? Today's more diverse student population may have a much broader range of factors motivating them to learn. We all have plenty of students in our classrooms who want to learn, who have aha! moments, who get excited when they make connections and when they understand something tricky. This has not changed. Nor have students' research anxieties and frustrations. The newly released "What Today's College Students Say About Conducting Research in the Digital Age" (Head and Eisenberg, 2009) reports on focus group discussions with students on seven U.S. campuses. The authors found that,

> In general, students reported being challenged, confused, and frustrated by the research process, despite the convenience, relative ease, or ubiquity of the Internet. In our sessions, frustrations included the effects of information overload and being inundated with resources, but more. Participants also reported having particular difficulty traversing a vast and ever-changing information landscape. Specifically, participants [sic] greatest challenges were related to finding the materials they desired, knew existed, and needed on a "just in time" basis. (Head and Eisenberg, 2009: 13)

CHANGES

To be sure, there have been changes. Twenty-five years ago, the technology that teaching librarians struggled with in the classroom might have been an overhead projector for transparencies or a slide projector. Information was found in books and periodicals, without a technological interface. Books, particularly reference books, showed up in library classrooms far more frequently than they do now. Although the resources librarians work with are different, and may not be nearly as tangible as they once were (try grabbing hold of an e-book), the essentials have not changed.

We may not even be teaching in a classroom, but rather in virtual space. This adds an additional layer of complexity to the teaching situation, but basic good teaching skills remain vital. Technology has changed our conception of the boundaries of what might constitute teaching situations, and, while our horizons have been widened, they still have fixed points.

Active learning and teaching techniques may be more ubiquitous now than in the past. Whether teaching students in person or online, the value of direct student interaction with the material is unquestioned. Student-centered learning is an important ideal, both in educational institutions generally as well as in library settings. Librarians both model and teach critical thinking skills. While the abilities to analyze and evaluate information and the sources from which it is available have always been important, this is particularly true in today's environment, where anyone can be an author or a publisher, and it often seems as if everyone is.

Technology has changed how students learn and how students find information. Librarians realize that, although students see themselves as adept at searching the Web, their skills are often rudimentary and in great need of refinement. Students often don't know about important online resources, and many, if not most, may completely ignore print in favor of electronic.

Clearly, the role of instruction librarians is not endangered. We have an arsenal of information and strategies that will help students in their quest for information and for developing effective information-seeking techniques. These skills for finding information will be put to the test not only during their academic years but throughout their lives.

Indeed, a recent national workplace survey reports that "more than seven in ten American white collar workers feel inundated with information at their workplace, while more than two in five feel that they are headed for an information 'breaking point'" (LexisNexis, 2008: online). In regard to specifically collecting information, it was found that "white collar workers spend an average of 2.3 hours daily conducting online research, with one in ten spending four hours or more on an average day" (LexisNexis, 2008: online). Students, now more than ever, need to learn how to find their way through the ever-burgeoning mass of information available to them. Absolutely critical is the evaluation of information and its sources. While information seekers often have a rudimentary sense of the need to determine if information is credible, they need a robust framework for making these decisions. Librarians continue to play a critical role in teaching these skills, one that complements what students are learning in their disciplines.

Assessment is a vital component of information literacy instruction, whereas in the past it might have been regarded as a desirable, though not crucial, add-on. This mirrors the evolving focus of education more broadly. Indeed, integration of the instruction we do into the broader educational endeavor has made great strides. While there were institutions where it was folded seamlessly into the broader educational mission—Earlham College springs quickly to mind—it has been a slower process at most institutions. But the broader acknowledgement of the need for information literacy skills allowed Ilene Rockman to state unequivocally, "Information literacy is no longer just a library issue. It is *the* critical campuswide issue for the twenty-first century, of keen importance to all educational stakeholders. . ." (Rockman, 2004: 1).

The field is maturing. Teaching librarians have more support than in the past. The Association of College and Research Libraries' Information Literacy Standards and a number of discipline-based standards provide excellent guidance for librarians developing or revising smaller instruction units or broad-based programs. Directives from accrediting agencies recognize the importance of information literacy skills and serve to highlight their importance on campus. The Institute for Information Literacy and programs and panels at conferences, indeed entire conferences, dedicated to instruction-related issues are a boon for librarians seeking to learn more. The literature of the field has developed and has, to our benefit, crossed boundaries into education, psychology, and other affiliated disciplines.

CONCLUSION

A solid grounding in the myriad aspects of how to be a good teacher is critical for librarians who would like to become effective teachers or who would like to refresh their pedagogical skills. Many of the pieces of the teaching puzzle are timeless, whereas others are just emerging. A firm foundation provides a basis on which one can implement proven techniques while accepting and embracing the new. To become accomplished, flexible, come-what-may teachers, we need excellent resources. You are holding one in your hands.

I used the first edition of this book over numerous semesters when teaching a graduate level information literacy instruction course. Its coverage of the fundamentals of the field was broad and to the point, and my students enjoyed reading it. When I received the manuscript for this second edition, I was immediately struck by the incredible amount of work the authors undertook to update it. They have done all readers a great service by being aware of, and sifting through, a great deal of new information gleaned from research, presentations, and the literature of numerous fields in the areas they covered before, in order to present the most important information. But beyond this, they have addressed new topics, such as the social, political, and economic aspects of information; the impact of users as information creators as well as information consumers; the move to learner-centered teaching and authentic assessment in education; and how to deal with changes in the information and instructional technology landscape and ways to incorporate these changes into the information literacy instruction that we do. This new edition of the book is once again cutting-edge and a critical resource for those new to teaching or interested in enhancing their skills.

Trudi E. Jacobson
Head of User Education Programs
University Libraries
University at Albany
Albany, NY

REFERENCES

Head, Alison J. and Michael B. Eisenberg. "Finding Context: What Today's College Students Say About Conducting Research in the Digital Age" (February 4, 2009). Available: http://projectinfolit.org/pdfs/PIL_ProgressReport_2_2009.pdf (accessed February 9, 2009).

LexisNexis. "National Workplace Survey Reveals American Professionals Overwhelmed, Headed for 'Breaking Point.'" Press release, February 26, 2008. Available: www.lexis-nexis.com/media/press-release.aspx?id=1041.asp (accessed February 16, 2009).

Rockman, Ilene F. and Associates. 2004. *Integrating Information Literacy Into the Higher Education Curriculum: Practical Models for Transformation.* San Francisco: Jossey-Bass.

Part I

Information Literacy Instruction Background

Chapter 1

Information Literacy Instruction: What Is It?

The more I learn, the more I realize I don't know.
—Albert Einstein

A ROSE BY ANY OTHER NAME—OR IS IT? WHAT IS INFORMATION LITERACY?

Welcome to the wonderful world of information literacy instruction (ILI). In the following chapters we will introduce you to the various theories, methodologies, and techniques that will help you in your ILI endeavors. But before we begin, we need to ask (and attempt to answer) the question, "What is information literacy (IL) anyway?"

The instruction part of ILI is easy. Librarianship has a long history of instructing users. Library orientation, library instruction, bibliographic instruction (or BI), and user education have been part of our vocabulary and our professional lives for many years. What if anything is unique about the term *IL*? A seemingly simple question, but if the literature is any indication, not one to which there is a simple or easy answer.

What's in a Name?

Words have power. In some cultures, when you name something (or someone) you gain control over that person or thing. In short, you own it. That might explain the library profession's longstanding quest to understand (and hopefully agree upon) what we mean by the term *IL* and the proliferation of material published on the subject. As we debate the definition, we gain more insight not only into its definition but also into the parameters that delineate the concept.

Developing this insight is crucial to our decisions about what and how we will teach and the ways in which we talk about the concept with people outside of our profession. Although some may feel the debate is just an exercise in semantics, defining what we mean by IL is central to our task as instructors. If we do not know exactly what IL is, then how do we teach it and, even more important, how do we know if we have succeeded in our instructional endeavors (Arp, 1990; Bruce, 1997; Maybee, 2006; Snavely and Cooper, 1997)?

Interestingly enough, the term *IL* is not as new as some might think. Paul G. Zurkowski first coined the phrase in 1974. According to Zurkowski (1974), an information literate individual is anyone who has learned to use a wide range of information sources in order to solve problems at work and in his or her daily life. Zurkowski's definition continues to have validity over 35 years later. Although the term did not catch on immediately, the concepts underlying it certainly did. Many terms were used to describe the concept over the years, but it was not until the mid-1980s that the term *IL* returned to the forefront.

INFORMATION LITERACY IN THE 1980S AND 1990S

The modern IL movement of the 1980s and 1990s acknowledged and built upon the rich history of BI begun in the late 1960s. (See Chapter 2 for more on the history of library instruction and BI and on the contributions made by the pioneers of the movement in the 1960s, 1970s, and the early

1980s.) However, the use of the term *IL* and the subsequent discussions of what that term meant really began in the mid-1980s. In 1985, Patricia S. Breivik described IL as an integrated set of skills and the knowledge of tools and resources. In her view, IL is developed through persistence, an attention to detail, and a critical, evaluative view of the material found. Breivik (1985) also depicted IL as a problem-solving activity. The American Library Association (ALA) Presidential Committee on Information Literacy's Final Report published in 1989 further endorsed the term and Breivik's definition, describing the information literate individual as someone who has the ability to recognize an information need, and can locate, evaluate, and use information effectively. The emphasis is on preparing people for lifelong learning: "Ultimately information literate people are those who have learned how to learn" (ALA. Presidential Committee on Information Literacy, 1989, p. 1).

The American Association of School Librarians' (AASL) Association for Educational Communications and Technology (AECT) also aligned with this view and defined the information literate student as one who accesses information efficiently and effectively, critically evaluates the information, and uses it accurately and creatively. There is an emphasis on independent learning and also an element of social responsibility. The information literate individual is someone who contributes positively to the learning community and to society. Underlying this definition is the belief that an information literate populace is the cornerstone of democracy (ALA. AASL. AECT, 1988, 1998).

As other librarians explored the concept of IL, additional aspects were added to its description. Carol C. Kuhlthau agreed with Breivik on the need for persistence, attention to detail, and caution in accepting information. She pointed out that one of the most important aspects of IL is an understanding of the amount of time and work involved in information seeking and use. The information literate individual must be aware that information gathering is not linear. It is a complex process in which questions change and evolve as new information is gathered and thought about (Kuhlthau, 1989, 1990). Susanne Bjorner contributed a few more attitudinal or personality traits to the mix. She included not only recognizing but also accepting a need for information. The information literate individual responds positively to the need for investigation, constructs a variety of strategies to reduce the information gap, evaluates and selects the most appropriate strategy, and assesses the effectiveness of the chosen strategy. Finally, the information literate individual not only uses the information now, he or she also stores it for future use (Bjorner, 1991). Hannelore B. Rader discussed the information literate individual as someone who can survive and be successful in a rapidly changing information environment. Being information literate allows one to lead a productive and satisfying life in a democratic society and to ensure a better future for coming generations (Rader, 1991).

Christina S. Doyle used the Delphi method to identify elements experts in the field associated with IL. Her research characterized an information literate individual as someone who recognizes an information need and acknowledges that accurate and complete information is the basis for decision making. These information literate people can formulate questions based on this information need, develop appropriate search strategies, and access information from a variety of sources. Furthermore, the information literate individual must be able to organize information and to use it in critical thinking and problem solving (Doyle, 1996).

Then we have Christine Bruce's description of an information literate person as one who engages in independent, self-directed learning using a variety of resources (print and electronic). Bruce's viewpoint criticizes what she and others like her call the "list of skills approach" as being a limited view of the information literate individual. Rather than looking at a skill set, Bruce and her followers examine how learners interact with information, how they value information and its use, the ways in which they critically examine information sources and information-gathering strategies, and how they developed a personal information style (Bruce, 1997; Maybee, 2006; Purdue, 2003). IL is described as a construct developed by the information literate individual in the course of his or her experiences. Such an individual creates a specific relationship with information in which he or she interacts with it in a way that provides personal meaning.

There seems to be no end to the descriptions of the term *IL*. We can even see some commonalities among the various definitions. So what is the problem? Although both ALA and AASL have adopted the term *IL* and continued to work on solidifying its parameters, especially through the development of the Association of College and Research Libraries (ACRL)'s "Information Literacy Competency Standards for Higher Education" (ALA. ACRL, 2000) and AASL's publication of *Information Power* (ALA. AASL, 2006; ALA. AASL, AECT, 1988, 1998), people both inside and outside the profession persisted in having difficulty understanding what IL meant. In part the problem arose because the term was developed by and for librarians and as such was not intuitively understood by those outside the profession. Furthermore, as IL was explored and examined in different environments, variations on the theme began to develop.

As we have already seen, IL has been described over the years as a process, a skill set, a competence, an attitudinal or a personality trait, a set of abilities, a way to help people contribute positively to the learning community and to society, and a construct that is created by the ways in which a person interacts with information. Critical thinking and evaluation as well as the ethical use of information have all been cited as being as integral to IL as they were to BI in the past (ALA. AASL, 2006; ALA. AASL, AECT, 1998; Bjorner, 1991; Bruce, 1997; Doyle, 1996; Kapitzke, 2001; Kuhlthau, 1993, 1990; NFIL (accessed 2008b); Neeley, 2002; Rader, 1990, 1991, 1993, 2003). Moreover, in an attempt to make the concept more understandable and applicable in a range of settings, variations on the term (such as *information fluency* and *information competency*) have been coined, thus muddying the "naming" waters even more (Associated Colleges of the South, 2003; California State University. Information Competence Assessment, 2002; Curzon, 1995; Gibson, 2008; Rader, 2004; Sharkey, 2006; Somerville et al., 2007; Stripling, 2007; Wilson, 2001).

Despite the issues surrounding what to call IL and how to describe it, the elements that make up the concept seem to be more or less consistent. Most descriptions include references to lifelong learning, critical thinking, problem solving, and, more recently, resource-based learning. In their 1992 examination of several IL descriptions, Michael Eisenberg and Michael Brown identified six common themes. The information literate individual recognizes a need for information; engages in information seeking behavior; explores, accesses, and locates material; interacts with the information to formulate hypotheses; synthesizes, interprets, and organizes the information; and finally evaluates the results (Eisenberg and Brown, 1992). The abilities to use information ethically and to apply that information to the individual's life are also considered to be crucial elements of IL.

Concepts associated with information fluency and computer literacy, such as being able to navigate the often confusing technology-mediated environment, use information technology effectively for research purposes, and manage, evaluate, and create information, are all recognized as necessary IL elements as well. In short, IL is viewed as the ability not only to locate and use information in a variety of formats but also includes an intellectual component—that of evaluating the quality and worthiness of the information found. IL is considered essential if people are to successfully adapt to the rapid social and technological changes that will continue to be part of our ever-evolving information world (Candy, 2000; Gibson, 2008; Pawley, 2003). Some library and information science professionals have even gone so far as to argue that IL is such an important concept that it should be considered a field of study in and of itself (Badke, 2005).

No matter what it is called, the primary advocates for the concept continue to be librarians. Unfortunately, the marginalization of the profession in many environments has made it difficult for us to "sell" the idea to others—especially when the phrase *IL* seems to be controversial even within the profession itself (Purdue, 2003). How can we expect others to understand the term when we cannot seem to agree among ourselves what we mean by it? The rise of the Internet with all its opportunities and challenges has also created issues for the term, which for the most part originated in the pre-Internet–based world.

The librarians who wrote about and researched the topic during the 1980s and 1990s grew up in a print-based world. Their view of what was then called *BI* was greatly influenced by how people searched for and used information in the print environment located in the physical library location. Although critical thinking skills, the teaching of concepts, and the transfer of learning to different environments were all included, examples were of necessity only those found in the library in which they were teaching. Furthermore, librarians' personal experiences in organizing and controlling access to information within the physical place known as the "library" played a large part in how BI and later IL were envisioned and taught. Prior to the year 2000 there was very little in the way of remote access to library materials. As we approached the twenty-first century, people began to gain the ability to "dial" into the library's catalog and databases, but they still had to come to the library to obtain the material they needed.

The rise of the Web expanded access to more and more of the actual material, and the linking and networking capability of the Web started to influence how people interacted with information and with each other (Kapitzke, 2001; Luke and Kapitzke, 1999). Ironically, although librarians were among the earliest adopters of these new information technologies, many clung to the traditional, hierarchical view of information structure. Presented with a chaotic universe, the overwhelming reaction of the profession in the early days of the Internet was to try to impose order on this chaos. There was many an attempt to apply cataloging and classification schemes to Internet resources. Librarians reviewed Internet-provided resources for quality and made recommendations to their users. However, the nonlinear nature of hypertext and the ephemeral and hybrid nature of digital environments as well as the development of search interfaces such as the Google (2008) search box made these efforts counterintuitive to users (Bodi, 2002; Kapitzke, 2001, 2003; Pawley, 2003; Wallis, 2003). Searchers, liberated by the ease of searching for information on the "net" and by the ability to move from resource to resource through the magic of hyperlinks, preferred to go their own way (Warlick, 2004; Williams, G., 2007; Williams, P., 2006). And as librarians themselves became more engaged in the Internet environment, and more cognizant of how users were interacting with information on the Internet, their views of what they should be teaching under the guise of IL began to evolve and expand, with the emphasis on teaching critical thinking and concepts becoming even more important.

WHERE DO WE GO FROM HERE? INFORMATION LITERACY IN THE TWENTY-FIRST CENTURY

Recent trends in higher education and librarianship as well as the enormous changes in information technology that have occurred over the past 10 or so years have also called into question the viability of the commonly accepted definitions for IL. What constitutes information and the nature of information as a commodity are being explored (Rader, 2004) as are the economic, legal, public policy, and social issues surrounding the use of information and the technological infrastructure that supports it (Curzon, 2002; IFLA. High Level Colloquium on Information Literacy and Lifelong Learning, 2005; Stoffle, 1998). Access to information bestows social capital. In a world so thoroughly dependent upon finding fast, if not always accurate, answers to all of life's questions, being information literate can give people (and nations) the competitive edge (Curzon, 1995; Neeley, 2002; Reidling, 2004; Stoffle, 1998; Town, 2003). Furthermore, users are no longer content to be mere passive consumers of information. Advances in technology allow them to be creators as well. This dual role of consumer and creator impacts not only how we view IL but also how we teach it (Lorenzo and Dziuban, 2006; Reidling, 2004).

Reports from the United States Chamber of Commerce, the National Conference Board, and the National Center on Education and the Economy express concern about how well our educational systems are preparing students for their role in an information-based economy. *Greater Expectations* from the American Association of Colleges and Universities (2002) and the report from the Partnership for 21st Century Skills (2003) both address the need to develop intentional, self-directed, and technologically savvy learners (ALA. ACRL, 2002). With the "No Child Left Behind" legislature coming up for review, education at all levels is under scrutiny. The call for educational reform resounds from all sides (Abell and Oxbrow, 2001; Kaleba, 2007; National Center for Education and the Economy, 2007). New modes of information delivery have empowered people to become perpetual learners. Futurists predict that by 2125 more than 50 percent of Americans will seek to continue their education beyond college (U.S. Department of Education. Institute of Education Sciences. IES National Center for Education Statistics, 2007; Von Holzen, 2005). Librarians must expand their roles in such an environment beyond face-to-face (F2F) classroom encounters and examine IL's place in a world in which distance and online education is becoming more and more a common occurrence (Lorenzen, 2001b). Furthermore, the current emphasis on learner-centered teaching, resource-based education, problem-based learning, accountability, assessment, and student learning outcomes offers us the opportunity to attract more attention to our IL endeavors, but only if we explore the concept in terms of this new educational, economic, technological, and information reality.

There has never been a better time for IL librarians to make themselves heard. All six higher education regional accreditation agencies have included reference to IL or terms that relate to the concept, such as acquisition of knowledge, evaluation of information, and the ethical or responsible use of information, in their standards for accreditation. Most descriptions align with those delineated in ACRL's "Information Literacy Competency Standards for Higher Education" (ALA. ACRL, 2000; Middle States Commission on Higher Education, 2006; New England Association of Schools and Colleges—Commission on Institutions of Higher Education, 2001; North Central Association of Colleges and Schools, accessed 2007; North West Commission on Colleges and Universities, accessed 2007; Southern Association of Colleges and Schools, accessed 2007; Saunders, 2007; Western Association of Schools and Colleges, 2001). However, the methods to implement and assess these IL standards are not well defined. Though the need for collaboration between classroom faculty and librarians is implied, the ways to do so are not clearly articulated (Saunders, 2007). Despite these drawbacks, there seems to be a consensus among these accreditation agencies about IL's role as a lifelong necessity. The endorsement of IL by these agencies has placed demands on schools, colleges, and universities to reexamine their curricula for evidence that IL is being addressed (Lorenzen, 2001b). Furthermore, the National Council for Accreditation of Teacher Education has included IL as part of its standards (National Council for the Accreditation of Teacher Education, 2002). This opens the door for proactive IL librarians to form coalitions with teachers, faculty, and educators and to collaborate with them to incorporate IL at all levels of the educational system. Worldwide interest in the subject has also grown, offering opportunities for librarians to advocate for IL around the globe (Chartered Institute of Library and Information Professionals, 2008; IFLA, 2008; IFLA. High Level Colloquium on Information Literacy and Lifelong Learning, 2005; Jacobs, 2008; U.S. NCLIS and NFIL, 2003; UNESCO, 2008b). For more on collaborations, see Chapter 14.

FINAL REMARKS

Despite all of these positive trends and some semblance of agreement about what constitutes IL (if not what precise term to use), controversies still exist about how to apply and teach the concept in the current educational climate and technological age. Questions of authority, access, and the very nature of information itself (who created it and why it was created) abound in the literature (Swanson, 2004). Critical thinking and evaluation are even more important to teach than ever before (Thompson, 2003). But we must also encourage our users to go beyond just thinking about the type of resources they are using to retrieve their information. To be truly information literate, one must first understand how information works as a social, political, and cultural force (Elmborg, 2006) and furthermore that our interactions with information contributes to these forces (Luke and Kapitzke, 1999; Pawley, 2003; Reed and Stravreva, 2006).

Clearly all of this challenges the ways in which we teach IL. One thing is certain. We need to leave our print-based ideas behind us and teach in a way that is relevant to the world in which our users find themselves. It is no longer enough to provide our learners with the skills to search library catalogs and proprietary databases. And we can no longer afford to spend the few precious moments we have with our learners in a fruitless attempt to convince them to start their searches somewhere other than Google. We need to accept their reality and go from there. We need to explore ways to teach people to be critical consumers and producers of information no matter where they find it and to thoroughly understand the powerful and political nature of the information commodity. IL must be viewed in context, and the ways in which it is being taught must take into account how and why certain types of information and knowledge matter within specific communities and environments. In short, our learners need to understand that information has value and that what people know is less important than what they are empowered to do with the information they possess (Kapitzke, 2001, 2003; Lloyd, 2006; Norgaard, 2003; Warlick, 2004). We need to go beyond the traditional steps in the research process approach and begin to teach IL in a broader, more conceptual way. In an era of rapid change, being information literate becomes an even more critical skill.

So how does one teach IL in a way that is relevant and realistic in today's complex world and that empowers learners to be competitive in a fast-moving, intricate, information-based global economy? In the end it is up to each one of you to reach out to others in your communities in order to formulate a definition of IL that is personally meaningful and that works in your specific environment. You and those you work with in this endeavor will then have taken ownership of the concept. You will be able to use that ownership to help define your own teaching and direct your instructional endeavors. No matter what you include in your individual conceptual framework for IL, the material in this book will help you, as an individual, develop and refine your skills as an IL instructor. What you pick as your content, where you choose to present it, the learning outcomes you expect your learners to attain, and how you decide to teach it will all be up to you. The following chapters will give you the framework. But you will have to provide the particulars.

EXERCISES

1. List three characteristics that describe an information literate individual to you. How would you design instruction that would develop each of these characteristics?
2. Describe the ways in which print handouts, workbooks, guided exercises, and/or Web-based tutorials could promote IL skills.
3. Create an activity that would help learners understand the social, cultural, and political contexts in which information is created and disseminated.

READ MORE ABOUT IT

ALA. AASL. 1998. *Information Power: Building Partnerships for Learning*. Chicago: ALA.

ALA. ACRL. "Information Literacy Competency Standards for Higher Education" (2000). Available: www.ala.org/ala/acrl/acrlstandards/informationliteracycompetency.htm (accessed April 20, 2009).

ALA. Presidential Committee on Information Literacy. "Final Report" (January 10. 1989). Available: www.ala.org/ala/mgrps/divs/acrl/publications/whitepapers/presidential.cfm (accessed April 22, 2009).

———. "A Progress Report on Information Literacy" (1998). Available: www.ala.org/ala/mgrps/divs/acrl/publications/whitepapers/progressreport.cfm (accessed December 23, 2008).

Curzon, Susan and Lynn Lampert, eds. 2007. *Proven Strategies for Building an Information Literacy Program*. New York: Neal-Schuman.

Gibson, Craig. 2008. "The History of Information Literacy." In *Information Literacy Handbook* (pp. 10–23), edited by Christopher N. Cox and Elizabeth Blakesley Lindsay. Chicago: ALA. ACRL.

Jacobs, Heidi L.M. 2008. "Information Literacy and Reflective Pedagogical Praxis." *Journal of Academic Librarianship* 34, no. 3: 256–262.

Lorenzo, George and Charles Dziuban. "Ensuring the Net Generation Is Net Savvy (White Paper)." Educause Learning Initiative (2006). Available: http://connect.educause.edu/Library/ELI/EnsuringtheNetGenerationI/39340 (accessed September 8 2008).

Rockman, Ilene, ed. 2004. *Integrating Information Literacy into the Higher Education Curriculum*. San Francisco: Jossey-Bass.

Chapter 2

History of Information Literacy Instruction

I have always imagined that Paradise will be a kind of library.

—Jorge Luis Borges (1899–1986)

LIBRARIES AND LIBRARIANS: WHERE DO THEY FIT?

Happily, negative images of libraries and librarians are fading. Many now see libraries and librarians at the heart of the university, the college, the community, and even the corporation, organization, and research entity. Increasingly complex technology has placed the library at center stage as staff, faculty, administrators, students, other user groups, and even accrediting agencies in the United States have begun to recognize the importance of being competent, literate, and, ultimately, fluent in information identification, location, evaluation, and use (ALA. ACRL, 2006a).

What does this mean for instruction in the use of libraries and library resources, for information literacy (IL) and for those who teach it—information literacy instruction (ILI) librarians? In some ways it means too much for librarians—too much work, too much effort, too many demands, and too many classes and instruction-related products to design, develop, test, revise, redesign, implement, evaluate, redesign, etc. It means making tremendous efforts to work broadly from the top down, building IL into accreditation standards and raising consciousness about its importance among non-ILI librarians, administrators, and other higher ups. It is a frantic world, quickly evolving, mutating—one blink, one breath, and it seems to have passed us by.

Some have questioned the end we are trying to serve (Gorman, 1991); others have questioned the means (Eadie, 1990; Wilder, 2005). Let us look at the gifts the past offers us, acknowledge the long and difficult path to the current state of ILI and those who took it, and consider whether the end and the means are justified (Grassian, 2005).

ROOTS OF INSTRUCTION AND INFORMATION LITERACY IN LIBRARIES

The modern library instruction movement began in U.S. academic libraries in the early 1960s and in Europe in the late 1960s and early 1970s, but library instruction is not new. At the first American Library Association (ALA) Conference in 1876, Melvil Dewey said, "the library is a school, and the librarian is in the highest sense a teacher. . . . " (1876). Surprisingly to some, "between 1876 and 1910 . . . some twenty institutions in the U.S. gave credit courses in library research, and forty offered noncredit courses in library use" (Roberts and Blandy, 1989: 2). In an 1880 essay, for example, Otis Robinson firmly states, "So important do we regard a good library education, that special instruction is given on libraries and the method of using them." He goes on to say that he himself "is accustomed, as librarian, to give . . . lectures from time to time to freshman and sophomore classes, to make them understand the great advantage of the use of a library, to explain in general terms the nature and use of the devices for finding what one wants, to show how they may supplement their course of study at every point by reading the authors and subjects studied. . . . But it is in the library itself that most of this instruction is given" (Robinson, 1880: 21).

Tucker (1980), Hardesty and Tucker (1989), and Farber (1995a) provide additional details on early library instruction efforts within the context of educational movements and historical periods since the nineteenth century. They note that libraries of all kinds have been involved in this effort for decades and that academic librarians have been doing research and writing about the need for library instruction since the late 1880s, beginning with Justin Winsor (University Librarian at Harvard University in the 1870s and 1880s) and Otis Robinson, mentioned above. They have tried to appeal to faculty and administrators at particular institutions, as well as to the academic community at large, and have used a variety of technological means to do so, attempting to differentiate between "information" and "instruction," between service and education, between giving a man a fish and teaching him how to fish (Tucker, 1980).

School libraries in the United States, first established in 1918, have been involved in library instruction since about 1938, when Alexander developed suggested library instruction for different grade levels, including general criteria such as "Each elementary grade (or room) should have a list of specific library knowledges [sic] and skills needed by the pupils in the work of that grade and in their outside life" and "All teachers in any elementary school should, in all their instruction, give reasonable attention to creating lifelike situations requiring library knowledges [sic] and skills" (Alexander, 1939: 271; Bonn, 1960). Since then, school librarians (now called *school library media specialists*) have worked with teachers to plan, develop, and implement numerous programs for all grades, from kindergarten through high school (Fargo, 1939; Kuhlthau, 1981; Craver, 1986). Public libraries and special libraries have traditionally focused on fact finding and information delivery, many providing informal individualized instruction rather than formal programs or courses. Beginning in the 1980s, driven by a technological tidal wave and efforts to redefine "library instruction" as "information literacy," public and special libraries have joined academic libraries and school libraries in developing and expanding more formalized instructional efforts for their users at all levels (Lubans, 1983). Many more now offer classes and in-person and virtual homework centers, as well as other online help (Mediavilla, 2001, 2003). Examples include the Brooklyn Public Library in New York (2008), the St. Paul, Minnesota Public Library (2009), the Multnomah County Library in Oregon (2008), and the Thousand Oaks Library in California (2009). Interestingly, the frequently sited homework help center B.J. Pinchbeck's (2007) "Homework Helper" Reference category links to a number of library sites, including virtual reference. Public libraries, like the Thousand Oaks Library, add value to free Web sites developed and maintained by nonlibrarians, like Pinchbeck's and many others, by providing remote and in-library access to licensed databases commonly used by high school and college students alike, such as Literature Resource Center (Thousand Oaks [CA] Library, 2008). (See Chapter 14 for more on this topic.) Where and how did this modern instruction movement begin in libraries?

During the 1960s, GI Bill veterans entered graduate school in large numbers, and increased educational pressures brought on by competition with Russia's Sputnik program as well as President John F. Kennedy's higher education initiative "opened the door to universal access to higher education" (Churchwell, 2007:105). In this context, Patricia Knapp's research at Monteith College Library in the early 1960s sparked the modern-day library instruction movement in the United States. Monteith was one of eleven colleges that made up Wayne State University. In the period from 1959 to 1962, Monteith College enrolled 300 to 700 students and had 15 to 30 faculty members. In this small college setting, Knapp (1966) conducted a research study to test out elements of Louis Shores's library/college concept. Shores saw higher education revolving around the library, where increasingly students would learn by using what he presciently called "'wet' carrels," with increasingly higher tech products, individualized to each student's needs and interests (Knapp, 1966: 166). As he put it, "When a college is a library, and a library is a college, it is a Library-College" (Shores, 1970: 159).

Knapp envisioned the library as the center of the higher educational experience. She came up with a number of different assignments to help improve the quality of undergraduate research papers, including "Library Competency Testing," "Using Surface Clues to Evaluate Books," and "The Independence Assignment" (Knapp, 1966: 66). The latter combined workbook-type questions for 250 students related to specific reference tools with a pre-assignment visit to the class by a librarian and a post-assignment one-hour class discussion with the librarian. She noted then, as we do today, that "Students tend to be uncritical in their choices of sources of information. . . . [T]hey tend to be content with 'something on' the subject, regardless of its validity" (Knapp, 1966: 41). To counteract this problem, she designed a number of assignments, one of which required students to select entries from the card catalog from among many on a single topic and provide reasons for their selections. ILI librarians continue to reinvent critical thinking exercises similar to hers but with a technological twist, for example, "Hoax? Scholarly Research? Personal Opinion? You Decide!" (Grassian and Zwemer, 2008). For more on critical thinking, see Chapter 6.

DEVELOPMENT OF MODERN LIBRARY INSTRUCTION MOVEMENTS

Bibliographic Instruction

Knapp's efforts are at the root of the modern library instruction "tree," which first developed two main branches. One focused on intensive integration of library instruction into the entire academic curriculum, course by course, in a "synchronous" (real-time) face-to-face (F2F) group instruction mode (Farber, 1974, 2007). The other branch focused on an almost entirely self-paced, hands-on, "asynchronous" (any time, any place) approach (Dudley, 1978). Both Farber and Dudley launched their approaches prior to the existence of public access computers in libraries.

Synchronous and Asynchronous Instruction

Synchronous and asynchronous are terms commonly used in discussing distance education, online learning, and e-learning at all educational levels and ages, though they may also apply to other sorts of instruction. The *Oxford English Dictionary* defines "synchronous" as "Existing or happening at the same time;... simultaneous" (1989: v.17: 483). It defines "asynchronous" as "Not coinciding in time" (1989: v.1: 738). Johnson (2008) calls synchronous instruction "real time" and asynchronous instruction "delayed time." Bedord (2007: 18) says that synchronous instruction means "in a group environment, allowing for live interactions, either face to face or online," while asynchronous instruction means students "[choose] to access learning materials on their own schedules fitted within the deadlines and structure of the class."

You may see other definitions, but, for this publication, we will use broad definitions, which include both in-person and online instruction and may or may not be technology mediated. Synchronous instruction, then, is simultaneous, in real time, with two or more individuals, and may be F2F or online. This includes traditional instruction in a classroom or a workshop held in a library training room. It also includes chat reference, online courses, and Webinars. Asynchronous instruction, on the other hand, may occur any time, any place, and remotely for a single individual, either online or through other formats, such as paper. An example of asynchronous use would be a learner in a physical library referring to a paper point-of-use guide on her or his own while sitting at a computer. Another example would be an individual using an online ILI tutorial or posting a message on a class discussion board.

These examples may seem clear, but you can also use some instructional materials either synchronously or asynchronously. For instance, you can have an entire group use a paper point-of-use guide as an outline to follow during an F2F workshop or class. Or, you can show a video to a group that is meeting online and have a discussion about it. So, in the end, how you use an item will determine whether it will be labeled "synchronous" or "asynchronous." Understanding these two concepts can also help us better grasp the value of and differences between the two historically significant approaches to instruction related to what we now call ILI.

F2F Group Instruction (Synchronous)

Evan Farber (1974) developed a fully course-integrated model library instruction program beginning in 1964 at Earlham College, modeled on traditional in-person college courses. For 35 or more years, Earlham College librarians and teaching faculty together have done an outstanding job of integrating ILI into the entire curriculum. Class by class, teaching faculty and librarians develop syllabi and assignments together in a synchronized, sequential approach to library instruction, beginning with "placement tests" and continuing through increasingly more complex instruction (Earlham College, 2008). For many years Farber (1974, 1993, 1995b) has also spoken about, written, and held workshops describing this approach. In 1987, he received the ALA Association of College and Research Libraries' (ACRL) Instruction Section's (IS) "Instruction Librarian of the Year Award" for his many efforts and achievements in promoting library instruction. This completely integrated and intensive approach has succeeded at Earlham and in numerous other institutions primarily because of their small size and higher ratio of librarians to students. Faculty status for librarians is another contributing factor to the success of this approach. Librarians who have faculty status are able to serve on academic senate committees, especially curriculum committees. Even in larger institutions, such curriculum committee service provides an opportunity to raise consciousness about IL among faculty and to lobby for its inclusion, at least in undergraduate general education courses (California State University, San Marcos Library, accessed 2008; Jacobson and Germain, 2004).

However, librarians at many large institutions do not have faculty status, have minimal contact with faculty, at least on the curriculum development level, and have low ratios of librarians to students. Fully scaling the Earlham librarian/faculty teaching model to large institutions seemed difficult, if not impossible, in the 1960s and 1970s. As a response to this perceived problem, another branch developed on the library instruction tree.

Self-paced Workbooks (Asynchronous)

In the early 1970s, amid much resistance from administrators and reference staff, Miriam Dudley at UCLA developed a highly successful learner-centered, self-paced library skills workbook (Dudley, 1978). This simply designed, asynchronous workbook was utilized by thousands of UCLA students, individually, over a ten-year period and adapted by libraries and librarians worldwide (Fjallbrant and Malley, 1984). It required students to use 20 different types of reference tools in order to answer a series of questions. For example, in the Almanacs section, students would need to find out who was Pope in a particular year and select the correct multiple-choice answer. Each type of reference tool had its own "module," and students could skip around to different modules or complete the workbook in the search strategy order in which it was printed. Workbooks were then corrected, and students with wrong answers were coached and encouraged to obtain correct answers. This approach worked best for large institutions with low ratios of librarians to students but also was adopted widely by smaller institutions with limited staff across the United States and in other countries.

Relationship to Reference

Dudley and Farber were farsighted pioneers, but many other pioneering librarians and organizations have written or edited significant library instruction–related works over the past 35 or more years, including Beaubien, Hogan, and George (1982), Oberman and Strauch (1982), Fjallbrant and Malley (1984), Mellon (1987), Reichel and Ramey (1987), Svinicki and Schwartz (1988), Breivik and Gee (1989), Fink (1989), Roberts and Blandy (1989), Brottman and Loe (1990), ALA. ACRL. BIS (1991, 1993a, 1993b), Shonrock (1996), Bruce (1997), and Grassian and Kaplowitz (2001, 2005, forthcoming). These works and many others, documented annually in the *Reference Services Review: RSR* column on ILI publications (Johnson, Jent, and Reynolds, 2007) and in Library Instruction Round Table's (LIRT) top 20 instruction articles of the year (ALA. LIRT, 2008b), have defined and enhanced librarians' efforts to teach, introducing us to user-centered approaches, outreach, and learning outcomes assessment, as well as other education and instructional technology skills, concepts, and techniques. Other chapters in this book and in *Learning to Lead and Manage Information Literacy Instruction* also address these issues. (See Chapters 11, 12, 15, and 16 of this book, respectively, regarding assessment, learner-centered teaching, and technology as it relates to ILI; see Grassian and Kaplowitz, 2005, Chapter 3, "Embracing Cooperation and Change" for more on outreach.)

The purpose of all of these instructional efforts was not necessarily to cut down on the total *number* of questions asked at reference desks but to raise the level of complexity of questions that remain following instruction in basic IL skills. So, instead of getting 50 questions a day on how to look up a book using the online catalog, you might get 10 of those questions plus another 20 on how to select among various electronic and print resources and how to construct an effective search strategy for the most appropriate ones. The more effective ILI is, then, the fewer basic reference questions you may encounter. Does this mean that reference librarians are less busy than they used to be? Actually, they are busier than ever, but in different ways, as the number, scope, and complexity of reference sources available even to the smallest, most isolated library have grown enormously. Statistics that keep track of the length and complexity of reference questions may be quite revealing to administrators who are used to relying on numbers of reference interactions alone to gauge reference desk workload. Furthermore, much of direct reference work with the public these days, in many types of libraries, has to do with teaching or helping people learn to make effective use of a myriad of sources, and not just finding the answers to their questions for them.

In the modern library instruction movement, beginning in the late 1960s and early 1970s, instruction librarians were quite foresighted as they tried to raise awareness of the great need for user aid in the form of teaching. Because most librarians were not trained to teach, they struggled mightily to learn from one another, attending workshops, programs, and conferences and devouring library instruction materials, articles, and eventually books. Many fought a difficult battle for acceptance against those who felt that library instruction was a frill and was taking librarians' time away from their real work, answering reference questions at the reference desk.

Today there is much administrative and colleague support for ILI in all sorts of libraries. In fact, in many types of libraries, ILI is a given, particularly for reference librarians. Interestingly enough, some are even recasting the workbook concept for the Web, particularly as interactive self-paced tutorials and exercises, but also as full courses. James Madison University's (2008a) "Go for the Gold" and Appalachian State University's (2007) "Library Research Tutorial," for example, even begin with a tour of the physical library and services, just as Miriam Dudley's (1978) *Library Instruction Workbook* did.

Beyond Farber and Dudley

Many other offshoots of both approaches have developed and grown over the years, notably workbooks or course-related or course-integrated one-shot sessions affiliated with a particular discipline or department, as well as independent standalone, library-initiated workshops or classes and various technology-based efforts. The underlying goals of both the Farber and Dudley branches were to help users learn about library resources and information tools and develop effective strategies for using them, for the purpose of lifelong learning. For example, Dudley's (1978) *Library Instruction Workbook*, modeled by hundreds of libraries in the United States and elsewhere, was structured in a search strategy approach, beginning with basic sources such as dictionaries and encyclopedias and moving to more specialized sources later. Each segment was self-contained, so users could use the workbook in a linear or in a modular fashion.

In the 1960s, 1970s, and early 1980s, little did instruction librarians know that their many efforts would one day sit at center stage in libraries, as technology entered the technical side of the library world and then the public arena. During the 1980s and 1990s, as technology made major impacts on libraries, faculty increasingly called on librarians to do "library orientations" or "library presentations" for their classes. Librarians began to mirror the teaching faculty's lecture mode, though often as guest lecturers who met with a class only once. As a result, librarians labeled these sorts of guest sessions as "one shots." One-shot ILI sessions have become popular and commonplace, particularly in academic libraries, partly because they emulate a familiar model in academia—a guest session, often to a synchronous, in-person class. Scalability of one shots remains a problem in large institutions, however, due to limited librarian staff and large user populations. Sometimes this is addressed by training instructors, who, in turn, teach ILI to their own students (Jacobson, 2004; Rockman, 2004d). During the 1980s and 1990s, many librarians enthusiastically researched and embraced educational theories and techniques as a substitute for the teacher training and education they did not receive in library school. After much research, study, and practice, library instructional theory matured and evolved. Some 30 years after Knapp's research, following the steady growth of both the Dudley and the Farber branches, a new shoot developed that ultimately has encompassed all forms of library-related and information research–related instruction—information literacy (IL).

Information Literacy

In the 1980s, as technology was beginning to show its public face in libraries, librarians involved in instruction suggested teaching/learning approaches that went beyond the basic need for orientation and introduction to research tools provided within a search strategy framework, like workbooks. They offered significant conceptual, disciplinary, and political approaches to what was then called *bibliographic instruction* (BI), by publishing important books. They also established *Research Strategies* (1983–2005), the first peer-reviewed journal completely devoted to BI (Oberman and Strauch,

1982; Bechtel, 1986; Fink, 1989; Reichel and Ramey, 1987).

Patricia Breivik reconceptualized the concepts and goals of library instructional efforts as *information literacy*. She chaired the ALA Presidential Committee on Information Literacy, whose 1989 definition of the phrase is still widely in use today. This group saw IL broadly, not limited to library resources but applying to all sorts of information sources. According to this view, if you need to know something for educational, personal, business, or any other reason, and if you can identify, locate, evaluate, and use that information effectively, then you are information literate.

National Forum on Information Literacy

Patricia Breivik has written and spoken widely on the issue of IL and also established the National Forum on Information Literacy (NFIL), an organization of national and international associations devoted to spreading the word on the need for IL at all levels and in all environments (NFIL, 2008a). The NFIL encourages and lists important new developments in IL in a variety of organizations, including the American Association for Higher Education (AAHE) and the National Education Association (NEA). In 2003, with UNESCO support, the U.S. National Commission on Library and Information Science and NFIL held an international IL meeting that resulted in the Prague Declaration of support for IL worldwide (U.S. NCLIS and NFIL, 2003). NFIL, UNESCO, and the International Federation of Library Associations (IFLA) sponsored a 2005 International Colloquium on Information Literacy and Lifelong Learning that resulted in the "Alexandria Proclamation on Information Literacy and Lifelong Learning," urging governments and national organizations to support IL for lifelong learning (NFIL, UNESCO, and IFLA, 2005).

More ILI Developments

As the NFIL helped this process along among organizations globally, Eisenberg and Berkowitz developed and pressed for implementation of "The Big6™ Library Skills" approach for K–12 in 1990. In 2008, The Big6™ Web site stated that it is "the most widely-known and widely-used approach to teaching information and technology skills in the world . . . implemented in thousands of schools—K through higher education" (Eisenberg and Berkowitz, 2008).

In 1998, ALA's American Association of School Librarians (AASL) published a critical and timely document, the first IL standards for K–12. These detailed and well-written standards had an enormous impact on school libraries and school library media specialists. AASL's 2007 update of these standards, "Standards for the 21st-century Learner," promises to have an equally significant impact (ALA. AASL, 2007b). As we noted, debate raged fiercely over the meaning, application, standards, and, particularly, the expected learning outcomes of the concept of "IL" from its introduction to librarians in 1989 through the early 2000s (Arp, 1990; Snavely and Cooper, 1997; Virkus, 2003). ALA, ACRL's "Information Literacy Competency Standards for Higher Education" (2000), ACRL, IS's "Objectives for Information Literacy Instruction by Academic Librarians" (2001), ALA, AASL's *Information Power* (1998b) IL standards for K–12, *Information Literacy Standards for Student Learning* (1998a), and "Standards for the 21st-century Learner" (2007b), as well as standards developed in other countries (Virkus, 2003) have all gone a long way toward answering some of these questions and, thus, taming the debate.

Both ACRL's and AASL's standards are purposely generic enough to accommodate the communication, research, and publication processes inherent in many different disciplines and they have even been translated into seven other languages and are used in countries around the world (ALA. ACRL, 2008c). For instance, the ALA, ACRL (2000) Standards include Standard 2 and its objectives a and b:

> Standard 2: The information literate student identifies a variety of types and formats of potential sources for information,
>
> Objective a, Knows how information is formally and informally produced, organized, and disseminated,
>
> Objective b, Recognizes that knowledge can be organized into disciplines that influence the way information is accessed.

The AASL (2007b) standards include the following:

> Skills 1.1.1, Follow an inquiry-based process in seeking knowledge in curricular subjects. . . . "
>
> Dispositions in Action, 1.2.5, Demonstrate adaptability by changing the inquiry focus, questions,

resources, or strategies when necessary to achieve success.

In an interesting twist, however, at least one critique of the ALA, ACRL (2000) "Information Literacy Competency Standards for Higher Education" contends that its generic nature wrongly places it outside of the context of specific disciplines. The argument contends that IL is best understood within a discipline rather than as a means of seeking an "answer" or a "unified 'truth'" (Simmons, 2005).

In the 2000s, ILI librarians in academic libraries have, in fact, taken further steps to delineate ILI for various disciplines by developing IL competency standards for those disciplines based on the ACRL Standards and to write a number of publications about IL for disciplines as well as for interdisciplinary majors (Baker and Curry, 2004; Brown and Krumholz, 2002; Grafstein, 2002; Jacobs, Rosenfeld, and Haber, 2003; Rockman, 2003b; *Teaching Information Literacy Skills to Social Sciences Students and Practitioners: A Casebook of Applications*, 2006). For example, standards have been developed for science and engineering/technology (ALA ACRL. STS, 2009) and for anthropology and sociology (ALA. ACRL. ANSS, 2008). Quite notably, ACRL's Anthropology and Sociology Section developed the latter through collaborative efforts with faculty in anthropology and sociology, and with the American Sociological Association (see Chapter 3 in Grassian and Kaplowitz, 2005). However, Simmons, Grafstein, and other ILI librarians who have published on the topic of IL in the disciplines, unfortunately, did not seem to be aware of important publications from the 1980s that offered conceptual approaches and frameworks for teaching and learning IL within various disciplines, as well as means of raising awareness of the political nature of information gathering, information access, and information use (Oberman and Strauch, 1982; Bechtel, 1986; Reichel and Ramey, 1987; Fink, 1989; Grafstein, 2002; Simmons, 2005).

A different but related debate also arose among academic librarians during the 2000s. This debate focused on the issue of whether or not ILI should be considered a discipline in and of itself and taught independently of other disciplines (Johnston and Webber, 2005) or whether it should be taught as its own credit course embedded within different departments (Badke, 2003, 2005). The debate also included the issue of whether or not IL should continue to be integrated into courses taught in traditional academic disciplines as "one-shot" guest sessions or standalone workshops (Byerly, Downey, and Ramin, 2006; Houlson, 2007).

Are these mutually exclusive scenarios for ILI? Ideally, any sort of ILI should be transferable to new situations and circumstances. When faced with these new situations and circumstances, learners should be able to apply what they have learned from course-integrated or standalone instruction, synchronous or asynchronous. In institutions where librarians have faculty status and where the library is considered an academic department, ILI may have a better chance of being established as its own discipline, with credit courses taught by librarians, while in others it may be quite difficult to establish such courses. We must keep in mind, though, that the ILI menu includes credit courses and many other formats. Any of these formats may be useful and best suited to specific circumstances and environments at a given point in time. Instead of debating whether or not one is better than another or more useful, we need to focus on expanding our ILI menus so that we can offer more options to our learners.

All of this serves to illustrate the fact that what is now called *information literacy* is firmly grounded in what used to be called *library instruction*, *bibliographic instruction*, and other terms utilized over many decades (Grassian, 2004a). Although *Research Strategies* ceased publication in 2005, other peer-reviewed journals focused on IL were established in the 2000s, including *SIMILE* (2001-) and the open access journals *Journal of Information Literacy* (2007-) and *Communications in Information Literacy* (2007-). Other established journals like *Reference Services Review* (1973-), *College & Research Libraries* (1939-), and *Journal of Academic Librarianship* (1975-), as well as *portal: Libraries and the Academy* (2001-) and the open access journal *Evidence-based Library and Information Practice* (2006-), greatly increased publication of IL-related articles. In 2006, the "SOS for Information Literacy" project began publishing the freely available *Educators' Spotlight Digest*, an online magazine primarily for K–12 school library media specialists. This magazine also has a "College Connections" column, however, reflecting a growing awareness of the importance of collaboration and sequential IL among various library environments ("SOS for Information Literacy," 2006; see also Chapter 12 and Grassian and Kaplowitz,

2005, Chapter 3, "Embracing Cooperation and Change," for more on this topic). The forthcoming *Encyclopedia of Library and Information Science*, too, will include an article on ILI (Grassian and Kaplowitz, forthcoming).

Indeed, the phrase *information literacy* finally seems to have caught on, as technology has permeated work and personal lives globally and greatly increased access to and consciousness of the power of information and information sources. Purdue University (2005) has established an endowed chair in IL. A number of libraries, and even institutions as a whole, have mission statements that include key IL elements, although they may not be labeled "information literacy." The ACRL Instruction Section's Library School Outreach Task Force identified eight examples of institutional mission statements that "reference information literacy in their student outcomes" and fifteen library mission statements that "reference information literacy or elements of a basic definition, including the ability to identify, locate, evaluate and use information effectively and ethically" (ALA. ACRL. IS, Library School Outreach Task Force, 2007b). (See the CD-ROM that accompanies this book for sample library and institutional mission statements.)

Governments, organizations, and individuals around the world use this phrase frequently and often use it correctly in terms of its key elements—information researching and critical thinking. However, some confusion between *information literacy* and *computer literacy* still remains among nonlibrarians, going back at least to 1996 (Shapiro and Hughes, 1996; UNESCO, 2007). Rockman (2004a) expressed concern, too, that as we focus increasingly on e-learning and emerging technologies and as research tools proliferate and become increasingly complex, librarians will be seen as technologists and nothing more. How do we get the message across to the general public and to our own constituencies and also work together to clarify and continue to define our role as well as expected learning outcomes for ILI?

Information Competency and Information Fluency

Defining IL has been a rather long and difficult process, as librarians and others have coined variant phrases since "information literacy" was first introduced, including "information competency" and "information fluency." (See Chapter 1 for more on this topic.) Maricopa County Community College (1994) was among the first to attempt to define IL competencies in what became known as "The Ocotillo Report." In 1997, the Wisconsin Association of Academic Librarians (1998) developed an Information Literacy Competency list and criteria for academic libraries in that state, as State University of New York (SUNY, 2000) soon did for that state. The California State University (2007) system developed a major information competency initiative in 1995 that aims to integrate IL into the curricula of all 23 of its campuses. California community college libraries have also lobbied for an "Information Competency Plan for systemwide implementation, training and evaluation" since 1998 (California Community Colleges, Board of Governors, 1998). Smalley (2008: online) reports that this initiative

> ...went to the Board of Governors (BOG) of the California Community Colleges. Title 5 language to make Information Competency a requirement for an AA or AS degree in the California Community Colleges was on the Consent Agenda . . . for the September 2002 meeting. . . . Just prior to the meeting, the item was pulled—the Department of Finance declared it was an unfunded mandate.

Despite this setback, Smalley (2008) goes on to document the scope of ILI in California community colleges by providing a long list of the institutions that offer IL courses. Sixteen of them have an IL competency graduation requirement.

Quite apart from libraries, in 1999, the U.S. National Academy of the Sciences published an important document defining the concept of "information fluency." The report, "Being Fluent with Information Technology," posited three components of "Fluency with Information Technology" or "FITness":

- Contemporary skills, the ability to use today's computer applications, enable people to apply information technology immediately
- Foundational concepts, the basic principles and ideas of computers, networks, and information
- Intellectual capabilities, the ability to apply information technology in complex and sustained situations, encapsulate higher-level thinking in the context of information technology. (U.S. National Academy of Sciences, Executive Summary, 1999: online)

The report described similarities between IL and FITness. However, it also placed information technology fluency on a higher plane than IL while largely ignoring a large body of IL theoretical knowledge and practical expertise.

Ten years ago, the FITness report illustrated that the phrase *information literacy* had reached national consciousness in the United States beyond librarianship. Indeed, *information literacy* is now used commonly in other countries and internationally (as we discuss later in this chapter), although some still confuse IL with computer or technology literacy (PIA Information Services, 2006; UNESCO, 2007). Despite this lasting confusion among some, the IL approach seems to be growing stronger daily. It is a phrase and a concept that has become more familiar and more comfortable just as more and more complex technology has become familiar and comfortable to many librarians. As mentioned earlier, AASL's, and subsequently ACRL's, IL standards have had an enormous impact worldwide, within and beyond libraries. In addition to direct usage of these standards, researchers are studying both application of all or portions of them and their relationships to other forms of assessment, such as the student self-reporting National Survey on Student Engagement (NSSE) (Boruff-Jones and Mark, 2003; Gratch-Lindauer, 2005, 2007; NSSE, 2008). Clearly, too, IL competency in the technological age requires fluency with information technology. In turn, skilled users of information technologies must gain or improve IL skills so that they will know which sorts of questions to ask and how to think critically about the technologies they utilize and the information they gather through those technologies.

DIGITAL DIVIDE AND INFORMATION LITERACY DIVIDE

Are our users as familiar and comfortable with computer technology as we have become? Many have; however, there is still a digital divide and an "IL divide." Many define the digital divide in relation to access to technology, particularly the Internet. Access is necessary, of course, but in and of itself is an insufficient condition for IL (Lorence and Park, 2008). People who have Internet access may still be on the wrong side of an IL divide, as even technologically sophisticated users may be unaware of or unable to think critically about and evaluate the vast array of information now so easily available to them (van Dijk, 2006).

In the United States, government efforts in the public schools have helped enormously in bridging the physical access digital divide in the school arena. The U.S. government instituted a telecommunications discount program run by the Federal Communications Commission (FCC) as part of the Telecommunications Act of 1996. This "E-Rate" program, part of the U.S. government's Universal Service program, supports discounted costs for wiring for Internet connectivity and Internet access, as well as other telecommunications costs in schools and libraries. The FCC established the Universal Service Administrative Company (USAC) to manage the process of applying for and approving grant applications for these funding discounts. USAC posts a "discount matrix" ranging from 20 to 90 percent that helps determine the discount percentage for each school or library applicant. The size of the discount depends on several factors, including the community poverty level and whether or not it is a rural or urban community (USAC, 2008). Funds for the E-Rate program come from telecommunication fees and total up to $2.25 billion annually in discounts (Simba Information, 2007). E-Rate funding for physical access can be extremely beneficial, at least for K–12 public school students, provided, that is, that schools are able and willing to take the time and energy to apply for these grants. (See Grassian and Kaplowitz, 2005, Chapter 6, "Grantwriting and Grants," for more on issues of when, why, and how to apply for and write grant applications.)

Physical access to computers represents a first step in bridging the digital divide. Public libraries have also contributed greatly to easing this problem, although demand for usage in public libraries may necessitate signups and long waiting periods. In addition, filtering, often required in public libraries for computers utilized by those under 18, also can pose a problem for high school students wanting to conduct research on topics like "breast cancer" that include often-filtered words like "breast."

In addition to public and school libraries' efforts to provide physical access, there are a growing number of community technology centers and organizations in the United States that are working on similar efforts (Long, 2008). For instance, MOUSE (Making Opportunities for Upgrading Schools & Education), established in 1997, is a nonprofit voluntary organization in New York City that connects high-tech professionals, corporations, and their resources with public schools (MOUSE, Inc., 2008). Computers for Communities, Inc., recruits students and prisoners to learn how to refurbish computers and then sells those computers for nominal sums ($40) or gives them away. In addition to making low-cost computers available to low-income people, prisoners who participate in this program learn an employable skill—how to repair and refurbish used computers (Computers for Communities, Inc., 2008). The One Economy Corporation has launched a "Bring IT Home America" campaign to provide home Internet access and computer training to low-income people in the United States (Gross, 2008). Microsoft has joined One Laptop Per Child (OLPC) efforts to provide poor children all over the world with low-cost laptops (Microsoft, 2008a). The Digital Divide Network (DDN) is operated by the international organization TakingITGlobal. DDN offers an information storehouse and community environment "for those working on eliminating the Digital Divide" (Digital Divide Network, accessed 2008).

All of these groups emphasize coalition building or partnering with others to help achieve universal access and computer literacy. Despite these efforts, however, the digital divide first documented in 1999 still exists, at least in terms of usage skills (U.S. Department of Commerce and National Telecommunications and Information Administration, 1999; Cooper, 2000). The Pew Internet & American Life Project (2007) reports that as of December 2007, just 37 percent of those 65 and older use the Internet; 38 percent of those with less than a high school education do so, as do just 56 percent of non-Hispanic African Americans.

HISTORY AND ROLE OF LIBRARY INSTRUCTION ORGANIZATIONS, PUBLICATIONS, AND OTHER SUPPORT GROUPS

Access to computers and Internet connections is a necessary but insufficient condition for an information literate populace. An IL divide still exists, even as Internet access barriers ease and as the general population becomes more familiar with computers. The volunteer group of library workers and library school students "Radical Reference" (2008) takes a proactive stance to helping activists and independent journalists, regardless of their political leanings, by using open source tools to answer their reference questions for free, via e-mail. Their social justice perspective includes a desire to empower people by "supply[ing] the public with search strategies and skills for finding valuable information on their own" (Friedman and Morrone, 2008: online). This is an example of where reference and ILI meet and clearly illustrates the fact that reference service fits quite well into the ILI continuum.

What else can we do to help? Libraries of all kinds should be natural partners of these groups, helping them expand their goals from access to effective identification, location, evaluation, and use—universal IL competency. Increasingly, ILI librarians and library organizations are reaching out to each other from within different types of libraries, and to government groups like those mentioned earlier, in order to have a national and even international impact. Library organizations have developed a number of IL competency standards. These standards serve as milestones in this endeavor. Further evidence for increased awareness of the significance of IL lies in the fact that all six higher education accrediting agencies in the United States now include IL among their standards, although some may identify the elements of IL, such as critical thinking, without calling it IL (Saunders, 2007). The ACRL Information Literacy, Accreditation site provides IL-related quotes from and links to these agencies (ALA. ACRL, 2006a). This is encouraging. However, librarians may still need to draw the attention of administrators to the fact that librarians can help institutions meet these standards (Saunders, 2007). Librarians with faculty status may find it easier to accomplish this than those who do not have faculty status by raising their profiles through participation on curriculum committees and other campus groups (Jacobson and Germain, 2004). If you do not have faculty status, you can ask for an ex-officio spot on a committee when it is permissible and when there is a receptive climate both among library administrators and among faculty and campus administrators. If you are not sure, ask, and keep asking. Find ways to get to know who is on these committees and try to approach them individually. Just serving on such committees may help you at least see where IL can be inserted into new curricula as they are planned and developed. When accreditation comes up for an educational institution at any level, take proactive steps to contact responsible individuals to point out IL-related issues in accreditation standards, even if they are not labeled as such, and what the library can contribute.

The ILI organizations we depend on and value so much did not spring magically to life. They developed in the early to mid-1970s because of a growing social consciousness and the grassroots organizing efforts of librarians who were mostly on the front line of reference. At that time, increasing numbers of older returning students, international students, underrepresented minorities, and other users labeled "nontraditional" were asking very basic questions at reference desks. Reference librarians were having a difficult time addressing their needs, as well as those of the populations that traditionally asked for help at reference desks. These problems were not limited to one portion of a country or even to a single country but seemed to be universal issues encountered in libraries worldwide.

Regional Instruction Organizations

In the United States, librarians who were struggling to develop and deliver instruction banded together in the 1970s to talk and share ideas and approaches to teaching and learning. They mounted grassroots efforts to establish organizations at the local, regional, and national levels that would support them with education, training, networking, and publications to keep them up to date, including the ACRL New England Chapter's New England Bibliographic Instruction Committee (NEBIC), now called New England Library Instruction Group (NELIG) (ALA. ACRL. NELIG, 2008). In 1974, for instance, under the impetus of Miriam Dudley and others, the California Clearinghouse on Library Instruction (CCLI) started life as a subcommittee of the California Library Association's (CLA) Reference and Information Services Chapter (RISC). In 1975, with over 200 members, CCLI dwarfed RISC, established itself as a separate CLA chapter, and broke into Northern and Southern Steering Committees. When CLA reorganized in 1991, both CCLI steering committees left CLA and became separate organizations in their own right. Since 1975, both CCLI groups' missions have been to serve as a forum for librarians interested in instruction; to share information and materials by means of a clearinghouse of paper, audio, video, and other materials; and to provide continuing education for its members by means of workshops, programs, a semiannual newsletter, and other publications. In 2000, CCLI South morphed into a California ACRL Chapter interest group, now called SCIL (Southern California Instruction Librarians). To this day, CCLI North and SCIL continue these efforts (California Clearinghouse on Library Instruction, North, 2005; ALA. ACRL. CARL. SCIL, 2008). Both organizations have been and continue to be wonderful sources of networking and aid for California librarians interested in instruction in all environments.

Library Orientation and EXchange

The year 1975 was astoundingly productive in terms of library instruction–related organizations. CCLI, BIS, and LIRT were established and so was another highly significant organization—Library Orientation and EXchange (LOEX, 2005). LOEX began as a 1971 conference at Eastern Michigan University. In the early 1970s, Eastern Michigan University received a grant from the Council on Library Resources and the National Endowment for the Humanities for a "library outreach" office, which was called LOEX for "Library Orientation and EXchange." Its functions then, as now, were to serve as a national library instruction clearinghouse, a central depository for all formats of library instruction materials, and to educate instruction librarians. Under the able leadership of a number of directors, LOEX has surpassed all hopes to become a model national information literacy depository, now focused more on online materials, and an educational "institution." Its annual conferences are always overbooked with lengthy waiting lists and have even been mimicked by others. A LOEX of the West (accessed 2008) conference is also offered every other year. These conferences are significant arenas for all of us to learn from each other about new and exciting developments in instruction. Annual LOEX conference proceedings are chock full of fascinating IL materials, copies of handouts, and other useful information. The 2007 conference, for instance, was titled "Uncharted Waters: Tapping the Depths of Our Community to Enhance Learning" (LOEX, 2007b).

ALA ACRL Bibliographic Instruction Section/ Instruction Section and ALA Library Instruction Round Table

Miriam Dudley was instrumental in establishing the ALA's ACRL Bibliographic Instruction Section (BIS) and played a part, as well, in establishing the ALA Library Instruction Round Table (LIRT). It was a hard fought battle, as she went to three different ALA presidents trying to persuade them to establish instruction organizations within ALA. Finally, in 1975, at the same time that CCLI was started in California and LOEX was established as a national clearinghouse, ACRL agreed to establish BIS, and ALA established LIRT (Dudley, 2000). As a section of ACRL, BIS—now called simply the "Instruction Section" (or IS)—is geared to the needs of academic librarians, while LIRT serves librarians interested in instruction regardless of their library environment (ALA. ACRL. IS, 2008c; ALA. LIRT, 2008a).

Since 1975, IS and LIRT have put on ALA conference programs and preconferences, published semiannual newsletters and numerous other significant items related to library instruction, established and maintained highly useful Web sites, and grown in stature and importance. As of late 2007, IS was the second largest ACRL section, with over 4,600 members worldwide. LIRT had over 1,600 members in 2007 and provides important linkages among instruction librarians and programs in widely varying school, academic, public, and special library environments.

IS has published both practical and theoretical works, including *Evaluating Bibliographic Instruction: A Handbook* (ALA. ACRL. BIS, 1983), the 1987 "Model Statement of Objectives for Academic Bibliographic Instruction," as well as a guide to its use, *Read This First: An Owner's Guide to the New Model Statement of Objectives for Academic Bibliographic Instruction* (ALA. ACRL. BIS, 1991). The organization has published other items to help novice and experienced instruction librarians alike, such as *Learning to Teach* (ALA, ACRL. BIS, 1993a), *The Sourcebook for Bibliographic Instruction* (ALA, ACRL. BIS, 1993b), *Designs for Active Learning* (Gradowski, Snavely, and Dempsey, 1998), and *Information Literacy Instruction Handbook* (Cox and Lindsay, 2008). The IS also reviews instructional materials online for its PRIMO database, has developed proficiency standards for instruction librarians and coordinators, keeps track of IL publications related to many academic disciplines, and offers a highly useful site that includes a number of checklists and links for analyzing instructional environments, as well as digests of discussions held at ALA conferences (ALA. ACRL. IS, 2007a, 2008a, 2008b, 2008e). IS committees also contribute an enormous amount of useful information, some, unfortunately, buried more deeply in the Web site, such as its Research and Scholarship Committee's "Research Agenda for Library Instruction and Information Literacy" (ALA. ACRL. IS, 2002).

ALA's LIRT has published a number of highly useful instruction works as well, carefully designed to meet the needs of instruction librarians in all sorts of environments, including Brottman and Loe's (1990) *LIRT Library Instruction Handbook*, *Information for a New Age: Redefining the Librarian*, put together by LIRT's Fifteenth Anniversary Task Force (ALA. LIRT, 1995), and Shonrock's (1996) *Evaluating Library Instruction.*

ACRL and Broader Information Literacy Initiatives

Continuing education for ILI is extremely important, but it presupposes that a person has already learned something on which to build. This is not always the case when it comes to teaching ILI. A number of library schools/information studies departments, pushed and pulled by many different constituencies and demands both internal and external, have offered ILI training or support to all interested MLIS students intermittently, despite the fact that almost all librarians teach and/or train users, staff, and others. A growing number offer full-credit courses in library instruction or ILI; however, many are offered irregularly and as electives or are geared to School Library Media Specialists (ALA. ACRL. IS., Professional Education Committee 2008f). As a result, librarians in many types of libraries who are new to instruction are still floundering, more than 30 years after the major library instruction organizations were formed in response to vast grassroots demand.

In 1997, Cerise Oberman decided that she had waited long enough for library schools to get around to the important task of preparing new librarians for instruction responsibilities. She proposed establishing IL immersion programs to help meet this basic need and to help prepare experienced instruction librarians to serve as IL change agents (Shirato, 1999). ACRL heeded her call and generously funded development of the Institute for Information Literacy (IIL) as continuing education in order to fill the ILI gap not addressed fully by library schools and information studies departments. The Institute began with three main goals: developing and offering an IL immersion program, investigating best practices in IL, and supporting the development of sequential instruction programs for school, public, and academic libraries. ACRL established the first Immersion Program in 1999. The ACRL Institute continues to focus primarily on educating librarians for instructional roles via annual IL immersion programs, now available in four tracks: Teacher Track, Program Track, Intentional Teacher Track, and Assessment Immersion Track (ALA. ACRL. Institute for Information Literacy, 2008).

These immersion programs have become highly popular and significant educational and continuing education venues for ILI librarians; however, they serve primarily academic librarians. Those in other types of libraries may desire programs that are geared to their own library environments but also attempt to bridge type-of-library silos through networking, outreach, and collaborative projects among all types of libraries.

In 2003, the IIL institutional "Best Practices in Information Literacy" initiative, spearheaded by Tom Kirk, identified institutions that offer model IL programs with exemplary characteristics (ALA. ACRL, Institute for Information Literacy, 2008). The ACRL IS' Information Literacy Best Practices Committee is now in charge of this effort and is working to update this project (ALA. ACRL. IS. Information Literacy Best Practices Committee, 2009).

IIL's third mission was to support development of sequential instruction programs for school, public, and academic libraries. At the time, AASL's 1998 IL standards promised to offer impetus to this effort (ALA. AASL, 1998a). Despite the best of intentions, development of a Web site with interesting examples, and well-attended meetings at some ALA conferences, however, the Institute's third goal has not yet been realized. Although IIL did not accomplish this mission, there are trends in this direction, including outreach efforts and collaborations between academic libraries and secondary school libraries, as well as expanding partnerships among libraries of many types, to further the goal of an information literate populace.

An ACRL Task Force also developed the *Information Literacy Competency Standards* mentioned earlier. ACRL has put the standards and other related materials on a highly useful IL Web site (ALA. ACRL, 2008b). The organization has also published two Internet Resources columns on IL (Grassian and Clark, 1999; Grassian and Oppenheim, 2005) and offers a venue for many IL-related articles in *College & Research Libraries News* and *College & Research Libraries.*

International Federation of Library Associations

The International Federation of Library Associations' (IFLA) Round Table on User Education was established in 1993 as a formal group after three years as a working group of this international organization. The Round Table's purpose was "to foster international cooperation in the development of user education in all types of libraries." Among its goals, the Round Table aimed to hold sessions on user education topics at IFLA conferences, disseminate information about user education projects and programs, and monitor education and training for user education librarians. In 2002, the Round Table morphed into the User Education Section and then into the Information Literacy Section (IFLA, 2008), and, in addition to its former goals, aimed to work with UNESCO to develop a database of IL materials from all over the world, "InfoLit Global." The database offers librarians, educators, and information professionals worldwide the opportunity to contribute IL materials for the benefit of all. The database is divided into five sections: Communication, IL Products for Users, Organizations, Publications, and Training the Trainers (IFLA and UNESCO, accessed 2008).

In 2000, UNESCO established the "Information for All Programme," or IFAP, a global intergovernmental endeavor (UNESCO, 2008a). UNESCO and IFLA established an alliance in 2006 so that they could help implement library-related portions of the Geneva Plan of Action adopted by the 2003 World Summit on the Information Society (WSIS) and endorsed in Tunis in 2005 (WSIS, 2008). The two organizations also developed several versions of the "IFLA/UNESCO Public Library Manifesto," the most recent in 1994 (IFLA and UNESCO, 1994), and the "IFLA/UNESCO School Library Manifesto" in 2000, revised in 2006 (IFLA and UNESCO, 2006), as well as a draft of "Information Literacy: An International State-of-the-Art Report." The draft is a lengthy and important document detailing IL in Australia, French-speaking countries, Latin America, Nordic countries, Russian Federation, Spain, sub-Saharan Africa, United Kingdom and Ireland, United States and Canada, and South Africa (UNESCO and IFLA, 2007). IFAP now has three main priorities: information literacy, "ethical, legal and societal implications of ICTs [information and communication technologies]," and information preservation (UNESCO, 2008a). In 2008, IFAP launched a series of 11 "Training the Trainers" regional workshops, to be offered in many different countries. The expectation is that those who take these workshops will, in turn, train others in their countries in basic information literacy skills, including effective use of information and critical thinking about it (UNESCO, 2008c). This is a welcome development and one to watch in terms of impact worldwide.

This increased attention to IL on the part of large international organizations calls attention to the fact that IL has been addressed for decades around the world for various types of libraries, at least as far back as 1970 at the International Association of Technological University Libraries' (IATUL) 4th Triennial Meeting, called "Educating the Library User" (IATUL, 1970). ILI, under a variety of names, has continued to develop and expand in many types of libraries and in many countries in Asia, Oceania, Africa, and Europe, including China, Singapore, Australia, New Zealand, Nigeria, the United Kingdom, Spain, Denmark, Finland, Norway, and Sweden ("U. K. Clearinghouse for Materials Related to Education of Library Users," 1977; Lubans, 1983; Fjallbrant and Malley, 1984; Fjallbrant, 1988; Swensen and Garrison-Terry, 1994; Bruce, 2000; Bruce and Candy, 2000; Lorenzen, 2003; Virkus, 2003; Grassian and Kaplowitz, forthcoming). Bruce's (1997) work merits particular recognition, particularly her research into the nature of IL. National and international conferences, workshops, programs, research, and publications attest to this, including annual conferences on IL in Mexico, France, Canada, and Australia (Universidad Autonoma de Ciudad Juarez, 2008; Formist, accessed 2008; WILU, accessed 2008; Lifelong Learning Conference, 2007). The University of Sheffield has even established an InfoLit iSchool in the virtual world Second Life (InfoLit iSchool, accessed 2008). Such focus on IL worldwide has also led to a call for training and education in ILI for librarians around the world (Julien, 2005).

Bibliographic Instruction Listserv and ILI-L

Instruction librarians reached a major milestone in 1990 when Martin Raish established the Bibliographic Instruction Listserv (BI-L), a moderated listserv for all librarians interested in instruction. Since then, under his able direction, BI-L has played a significant role as an outstanding source of help, inspiration, communication, and even continuing education for practicing ILI librarians, and Information Literacy Instruction Listserv (ILI-L) now provides the same valuable service. It serves as a kind of current bibliography, cum help desk, cum ongoing conference of ILI efforts and queries, reflecting the unending creativity and dedication of ILI librarians. However, dedication and creativity in and of themselves are not enough to make for effective instruction. Basic background in instructional theory and practice, especially as related to libraries and information resources, is essential, with continuing education as an important follow up.

WHAT ROLE SHOULD LIBRARIANS TAKE NOW AND IN THE FUTURE?

CCLI North and SCIL, IS, LIRT, and LOEX are prominent institutions now, with lengthy histories. They publish important works—both theoretical and practical—hold conference programs, workshops, and other events, and generally provide and bolster professional development for instruction librarians. Since 1993, both the IFLA Roundtable on User Education and BI-L/ILI-L have also served to raise consciousness about the importance of ILI in many countries. All of these groups, plus IL blogs like Information Literacy Weblog (Webber and Boon, accessed 2008) and Information Literacy Land of Confusion (Lorenzen, 2008), as well as the BI-L/ILI-L community, have thrived because they have filled a major need for community and continuing education among IL librarians.

Furthermore, ILI librarians in all sorts of environments, and with many different types of constituencies, realize that IL is a lifelong learning goal and effort requiring different sorts of help and instruction depending on information needs at particular points in a lifetime. Coordinated and sequential ILI at all levels may best meet these needs effectively and efficiently. Southern Illinois University's Edwardsville campus librarians Jackson and Hansen reached out to high school librarians in their area in a highly supportive fashion. They reported spending an entire year getting to know these high school librarians, visiting their schools, and offering them continuing education as first steps toward establishing collaborating IL partnerships (Jackson and Hansen 2006; 2007, in press). Going beyond academic/high school outreach, the LILi (Lifelong Information Literacy) Group in California consists of librarians from all types of libraries, investigating ILI in that state, in order to develop sequential ILI for lifelong learning (LILi, 2008).

These are just two examples of a strong movement among librarians to reach out to and help other librarians at different levels, and in many types of libraries, for the benefit of all of our users (see also Chapter 14 for more on this topic). In the United States, "SOS for Information Literacy's" selected database of reviewed materials and InfoLIT-L support and encourage outreach and collaboration among school and academic libraries. This effort extends globally as illustrated by Global InfoLit, IFLA's and UNESCO's joint database of instructional materials, contributed to individually by librarians from around the world (IFLA, 2008). The Partnership for 21st Century Skills (2008) is reaching out to many stakeholders in education, including K–12 schools, businesses, and policymakers at many levels. Their aim is to work together to update K–12 curricula for skills needed in a new technology-oriented world, such as information and communication skills, among others.

FINAL REMARKS

These exciting collaborative trends will certainly be beneficial in the long run, although questions do remain regarding the role of the librarian. As we move forward to expand and explore diverse avenues for offering and promoting ILI, we would do well to examine contributions from our IL past with an eye toward utilizing or adapting whatever remains applicable to the present.

EXERCISES

1. What benefits and problems do you see with each of the three major branches of the modern library instruction movement: Farber, Dudley, and Breivik?
2. What lessons have been learned, positive and negative, from past library instruction programs and individual efforts?
3. Do organizations (ILI, library and information science, accrediting bodies, community organizations), private groups, and government agencies have a role to play in the evolution of ILI and in self-teaching and professional development for ILI librarians? If so, what sort of role should they play, how, and why?
4. What is it that ILI librarians do? What is or should be the role of the librarian in teaching or training for IL, and how does it fit with the role and activities of others at various levels who teach or train in your institution or organization?

READ MORE ABOUT IT

ALA. AASL. "Standards for the 21st -century Learner" (2007). Available: www.ala.org/ala/aasl/aaslproftools/learning-standards/AASL_LearningStandards.pdf (accessed December 22, 2008).

ALA. ACRL. "Information Literacy" (September 16, 2008). Available: www.ala.org/ala/mgrps/divs/acrl/issues/infolit/index.cfm (accessed April 7, 2009).

ALA. ACRL. IS. "Instruction Section" (2008). Available: www.ala.org/ala/mgrps/divs/acrl/about/sections/is/homepage.cfm (accessed December 22, 2008).

ALA. LIRT. "Library Instruction Round Table" (2008). Available: www3.baylor.edu/LIRT (accessed December 22, 2008).

ALA. Presidential Committee on Information Literacy. "Final Report" (January 10, 1989). Aailable. www.ala.org/ala/mgrps/divs/acrl/publications/whitepapers/presidential.cfm (accessed April 27, 2009).

Dudley, Miriam. 1978. *Library Instruction Workbook*. Los Angeles: University of California Library.

Farber, Evan Ira. 1974. "Library Instruction Throughout the Curriculum: Earlham College Program." In *Educating the Library User*, edited by John Lubans, Jr. New York: Bowker.

Fjallbrant, Nancy and Ian Malley. 1984. *User Education in Libraries*. London: Clive Bingley, Limited.

Grassian, Esther. 2004. "Building on Bibliographic Instruction: Our Strong BI Foundation Supports a Promising IL Future." *American Libraries* 35, no. 9: 51–53.

IFLA. "Information Literacy Section" (October 23, 2008). Available: www.ifla.org/VII/s42/index.htm (accessed December 22, 2008).

Knapp, Patricia B. 1966. *The Monteith College Library Experiment*. Metuchen, NJ: Scarecrow.

LOEX. "Clearinghouse for Library Instruction" (2005). Available: www.emich.edu/public/loex/loex.html (accessed December 22, 2008).

Oberman, Cerise and Katina Strauch. 1982. *Theories of Bibliographic Education: Designs for Teaching*. New York: Bowker.

Reichel, Mary and Mary Ann Ramey, eds. 1987. *Conceptual Frameworks for Bibliographic Education: Theory into Practice*. Littleton, CO: Libraries Unlimited.

Research Strategies. 1983–2005. Ann Arbor, MI: Mountainside Publishing.

Smalley, Topsy. "Information Competency in the California Community Colleges" (2008). Available: www.topsy.org/infocomp.html (accessed December 22, 2008).

Virkus, Sirje. (2003) "Information Literacy in Europe: A Literature Review." Information Research 8, no. 4. Available: http://informationr.net/ir/8-4/paper159.html (accessed December 22, 2008).

Part II

Information Literacy Instruction Building Blocks

Chapter 3

The Psychology of Learning: The Theory Behind the Practice

A crank is a man with a new idea—until it catches on.

—Mark Twain

WHY PSYCHOLOGY?

Whether you have been involved in information literacy instruction (ILI) for 20 years or more or have never taught an ILI session in your life, you are more knowledgeable than you might think regarding the psychology of learning. How can this be? It is because life is full of learning experiences. Whether you are working toward earning a degree, becoming skilled at a craft, or improving your athletic ability, you are experiencing learning from the learners' perspective. And every time you help a colleague, friend, or family member try to improve his or her professional or recreational skills, you are acting as a teacher. As both a learner and a teacher, you know very well when teaching is effective and when it is not. What you do not know is the "why" that differentiates a successful learning experience from a failed one. That is where the psychology of learning enters the picture. Knowing the theory behind the practice of teaching will encourage us to improve our current material and help us to develop new and effective instructional approaches that incorporate sound educational psychology principles. A basic grounding in psychological learning theory will allow us to create learning environments that enable all of our learners to get the most out of their instructional experiences.

The most effective information literacy (IL) instructors are those who are familiar with a variety of learning theories and the teaching techniques that are based on those theories. Effective instructors remain flexible and are willing to mix and match various techniques as needed. The knowledgeable, skilled teacher can move easily among techniques, is familiar with a variety of options, and can select the technique or combination of techniques that is most appropriate for each situation. These teachers focus on both the content of what they are trying to get across and the differing needs of their learners. This chapter provides a basic overview of the concepts, terminology, techniques, and prominent figures in the area of psychological learning theory. Chapter 4 will put that theory into practice—showing you how you can use what educational psychologists have discovered about learning in your day-to-day ILI efforts.

PSYCHOLOGY OF LEARNING SCHOOLS: DOING, THINKING, AND FEELING

Massive amounts of books, articles, and research papers have been written over the years about how learning happens. There are probably as many different theories of learning as there are researchers and writers in the field. This quantity of information can be overwhelming and may be less than helpful to the IL instructor who is trying to make sense of often confusing and contradictory material. However, an examination of how these theories have evolved over time leads to a possible conceptual framework for dealing with them. Upon closer scrutiny, learning theories seem to fall into three major categories or schools of thought—*doing, thinking,* and *feeling*. If we look at the theories this way, we not only have a way to organize them, but we can see what each category of theories has to contribute to the instructional endeavor (Kaplowitz, 2008).

Although there can be wide variations among the predominant themes within each school, the basic underlying principles remain constant. Keep in mind that no school can be considered entirely right or totally wrong. Each has made major contributions to our understanding of learning, and as a result each offers suggestions about how to improve our teaching. Furthermore, if you consider behavior as a whole, including actions, thoughts, and feelings, you can see how each of the three schools has advanced our thinking about learning. Although staunch supporters of each school consider them independent, you may notice that the schools actually share several beliefs (Glasser, 1992). As you read the following material, try to keep an open mind and look for ideas that inspire you to try something new. Ideas for applying these theories to your ILI practice are covered in Chapter 4.

DOING—THE BEHAVIORIST MODEL

The oldest of the theories falls into the *doing* school of thought and is generally referred to as *behaviorism*. In many ways behaviorism was a product of its time and place in the history of psychology. Psychology in the late 1800s was just beginning to establish itself as an independent and more scientific discipline. The field was moving away from its parent discipline of philosophy and was embracing the scientific method as a means to study and understand behavior (Bransford et al., 1999b; Slavin, 2006). In *Origin of the Species*, Charles Darwin (1859) postulated a continuum between man and the animal kingdom. This opened up the possibilities of using animals in experiments the results of which could then be generalized to human behavior.

In 1879, Wilhelm Wundt established the first recognized laboratory specializing in the study of psychology in Leipzig, Germany (Haynie, 1994). Researchers studied human behavior using a method called *introspection* that relied on subjects describing their own personal experiences. Behaviorism as a theoretical school developed in part as a reaction to the subjective nature of these self-reports. It was an attempt to create a more scientific approach for the study of behavior and was greatly influenced by the rise of the scientific method in the late 1800s. Ironically it was Ivan Petrovovich Pavlov's (1927, 1928) work on the physiology of digestion that really marks the beginnings of this school of thought (Amsel, 1989; Burton, Moore, and Magliaro, 2004; Elliott et al., 2000; Slavin, 2006).

Based on Pavlov's work with the salivation reflex in dogs, the behaviorists developed a theory of learning that relied on the links or associations between stimulus and response. Many theorists and researchers are associated with behaviorism—such as Edward L. Thorndike, Edward Chace Tolman, John Watson, and, probably best known of all, B.F. Skinner (Cruickshank, Jenkins, and Metcalf, 2003; Slavin, 2006). Each contributed to the development of the school and its associated theories. Thorndike (1913) expanded Pavlov's work on conditioning and introduced such concepts for successful learning as readiness to learn, the value of repeating the behavior to be learned, and the relationship between the behavior and subsequent events. Tolman's (1932) *Purposive Behavior in Animals and Men* identified the principle of reinforcement by postulating that activities that are followed by a successful outcome or some other reward are more likely to be repeated than those that were not. John Watson expanded the notion of conditioning to human emotional behavior with his famous (or infamous) Albert and the White Rabbit experiment. In this study, a loud noise was associated with the sight of a small furry animal to create a conditioned emotional response in a young child (Watson and Rayner, 1920). Fortunately for Albert, this negative emotional response was reversed also through conditioning techniques, although the long-term effects of this experiment are unknown. Obviously this type of experiment defies current protection of human subject practice (Grassian and Kaplowitz, 2005). However, it did show that humans are as subject to conditioning as rats, birds, and monkeys. Clearly the concepts being discussed by the behaviorists were not restricted to animal behavior.

But it was B.F. Skinner, with his over 50 years of research and writing, who did the most not only to expand the knowledge base in this area but to also develop links between his theoretical hypotheses and practical classroom applications. It is through Skinner's work that the principles of active learning, immediate feedback, programmed instruction, task analysis, allowing learners to move at their own pace, and, of course, the value of reward and reinforcement of desired behaviors have been applied to education (Skinner, 1938, 1968, 1974, 1983). Skinner's emphases on teaching to individual differences and allowing learners to progress at their own pace also have had great implications for the study of learning styles, a topic we shall return to later in this chapter.

General Characteristics

- Behaviorists deal with observable behavior.
- Behaviorists view environmental factors in terms of stimuli and resultant behavior in terms of responses.
- Behaviorists attempt to demonstrate that every behavior is environmentally controlled and is based on each behavior being externally rewarded or reinforced.
- Immediate reinforcement/feedback must follow desired behavior for the behavior to be learned.
- Improvements or steps in the right direction should be reinforced, as should the final completed task, in order to help learners proceed at a faster pace.
- Undesirable behavior should never be reinforced.
- Active participation is crucial to learning.
- Learners should be allowed to move at their own pace.
- Learners should be tested for mastery at each stage of learning and should not be allowed to proceed to the next level until they have mastered preceding ones.

Educational Applications of Behaviorism

The behaviorist believes that people interact with the world through a process of trial and error. Any action or behavior that receives positive reinforcement during this trial and error exchange will be repeated in the future—in other words, that behavior has been learned. Acknowledging that much of human learning goes beyond the simple kind of "pressing a bar to receive food" experiments done with animals, behaviorists developed applications based on animal learning models that they felt could be extrapolated to the human arena (Kaplowitz, 2008; McGregor, 1999; Tennant, 2006). These applications include the following.

Active Participation

A major component of behaviorism is that the learner must be actively engaged in the process. Learners do not learn by watching. They learn by interacting with the material itself. In other words, they learn by doing. Furthermore, behaviorists measure learning through observable changes in behavior. So learners must perform in order to prove they have learned the material at hand. The notion of having our learners engage in hands-on activities and other active learning exercises during instruction is based on this behaviorist idea. Setting observable and measurable learning objectives/outcomes and assessing learning through observable behavior are both outgrowths of the idea that learning requires active participation or doing (Burton, Moore, and Magliaro, 2004; Cruickshank, Jenkins, and Metcalf, 2003).

Shaping, Successive Approximations, and Task Analysis

Shaping relies on the behavioral principles of reinforcement and training through successive approximations to reach the desired behavior. The technique starts with describing what you want the learner ultimately to do and breaking down complex skills into component parts—otherwise known as task analysis. Each successive approximation of the desired end product is then reinforced. In the early stages of learning very rough approximations are reinforced. The standard is raised as learning progresses so that more complex levels of behavior are required for reinforcement to occur. The learner gets closer to the intended learning outcome with each successive attempt. Reinforcement is used as a means to move the learner in the right direction toward the final desired behavior. Improvements as well as perfection are reinforced to encourage progress (Elliott et al., 2000; Mager, 1997a; Slavin, 2006).

Mastery Learning

Benjamin Bloom added one more layer to the task analysis idea. Material to be learned is still broken down into small units with clearly specified learning objectives. But mastery of each small unit must be demonstrated before the learner can proceed. Diagnostic progress tests are administered at the end of each learning unit to determine whether each student has mastered the content of that unit. Procedures to assist learners who do not achieve mastery at any level are also developed. A final test is administrated after mastery has been exhibited on all of the subunits to ensure that the full task has been learned (Bloom, 1981; Cruickshank, Jenkins, and Metcalf, 2003; Elliott et al., 2000; Skinner, 1968). Chunking a topic into easily digestible segments that are covered in sequence is a direct application of this shaping idea and as been applied not only in the classroom but in computer-based instruction as well.

Programmed Instruction

Programmed instruction is a self-instruction package that presents a topic in a carefully planned sequence. It requires that the learner respond to questions or statements by filling in blanks, selecting from a series of answers, or solving a problem. Programmed instruction packages can be presented either in print or via computer. This technique relies on many of the main principles of behaviorism. Learners proceed at their own pace, are actively involved in the learning process, get immediate feedback on their responses, and receive reinforcement as they succeed with each step of the program. Those who advocate programmed instruction stress that it improves classroom learning by presenting even the most difficult subjects in small steps so that learners can proceed at their own rates. This technique builds on the concepts of task analysis and shaping by successive approximations (Cruickshank, Jenkins, and Metcalf, 2003; Elliott et al., 2000; Skinner, 1968, 1984).

Modeling

Modeling can be defined as learning through imitation rather than direct instruction. It seems to be based on what psychologists refer to as *vicarious reinforcement*: We observe the pleasure that a behavior gives to the model, and we want that pleasure for ourselves. Advertising success is predicated on this principle. Much of our early learning is based on our parents' modeling of appropriate behaviors. Modeling is also a very useful technique to use when the task to be learned involves some kind of danger or risk. For example, modeling how to drive a car before actually allowing the learner to try is probably a much safer approach than just handing the learner the keys and letting him or her try to learn by trial and error. In teaching by modeling, the instructor demonstrates how to perform the task or skill. The learner observes the behavior and then attempts to imitate the instructor or model. Modeling enables the student to learn complete sequences of behavior in a much shorter time than by successive approximations and shaping (Bandura, 1977a, 1986; Burton, Moore, and Magliaro, 2004; Elliott et al., 2000; Slavin, 2006).

Behavior Modification

Behaviorists offer several methods for modifying inappropriate or undesirable classroom behavior. One such approach is the reinforcement of competing behavior. The key to this technique is the successful strengthening of a desirable behavior that will compete with and eventually replace the undesirable one. For example, selectively reinforcing the desired behavior of sitting still and raising one's hand to be called on while ignoring the inappropriate behavior of jumping up and speaking out of turn should decrease the instances of this undesirable behavior. It is important to be consistent when using this technique. Always reinforce the desired behavior and ignore the undesired ones (Cruickshank, Jenkins, and Metcalf, 2003; Elliott et al., 2000; Kazdin, 1994; Slavin, 2006).

THINKING—THE COGNITIVE MODEL

The second set of theories deal with thinking. Just as behaviorism was a reaction to the subjective and introspective approach to the study of learning that preceded it, these "thinking" theories were developed as a response to what they viewed as the mechanistic or simplistic view of learning described by the behaviorists. Heavily influenced by Gestalt psychology's studies in perception, early cognitive psychologists were interested in how people perceive, organize, interact with, and respond to elements in their environment by determining how elements, ideas, concepts, and topics relate to one another. They felt that people respond to patterns or whole situations, not to individual stimuli (Kaplowitz, 2008).

Many findings from these early Gestalt psychology perception experiments were difficult to explain in terms of accepted behaviorist principles. For example, Max Wertheimer, an early cognitive psychology researcher, discovered that when two lights are turned off and on at a definite rate, human subjects report the perception of a single light moving back and forth. This report cannot be readily explained in terms of the stimulus–response model (Wertheimer, 1912). Known as the *phi phenomenon*, this behavior implies that when processing the stimulus input humans add something to this incoming sensory data that results in the perception of movement. Something is happening between the stimulus and the reported result, something that the cognitive psychologists felt needed explanation. In short, we seem to be motivated to impose order on our experiences even if at first glance none seems to exist (Arp, 1993; Bigge and Shermis, 1999; Dembo, 1988b; Driscoll, 1994; Elliott et al., 2000; Slavin, 2006; Svinicki, 1994).

Cognitive psychologists theorized that the behaviorist model of learning was too limited in scope. In their view much of human learning occurs beyond the narrow focus of trial and error, successive approximations, and reinforcement of observable behavior (Winn, 2004). For example, insight, also referred to as the "aha" phenomenon, is a form of learning that takes place without practice. Here the learner solves a problem without practice by thinking about and determining a pattern or relationship between the aspects of the problem to develop the solution.

Wolfgang Köhler's famous experiment illustrates this point (Köhler and Winter, 1925). Monkeys were placed in a room with a bunch of bananas suspended from the ceiling just out of reach. The only other objects in the room were a couple of cardboard boxes. Monkeys in this situation tended to sit quietly for a time, just looking around the room. They then quite suddenly got up and moved the boxes under the bananas and piled them high enough so that the boxes could be used as a means of reaching the bananas. According to the cognitive psychologists, this behavior cannot be explained by a trial and error approach. There were no incorrect and thus unreinforced behaviors and no possibility for reinforcement of successive approximations of the solution to the problem. There was, however, a sudden perception of the relationship between the boxes and the bananas that resulted in the solution to the problem.

So, how do cognitive psychologists explain this behavior? In keeping with their roots in perceptual research, they discuss learning as it relates to patterns. Learners (in this case banana-deprived monkeys) look for order and patterns in their world. If perceived patterns are consistent with their current worldview, these patterns serve to reinforce that worldview. If, however, situations or experiences are at odds with an individual's current ways of perceiving and/or thinking about the world (often referred to as *mental models*), a tension or ambiguity results. Learners (human and monkeys alike) have a strong desire to reduce this tension. Faced with a disconnect between new experiences and old mental models, learners feel the need to reexamine or reconstruct their worldview in order to incorporate the new information. If successful, a revised worldview is developed, and the information becomes part of the learners' new mental model. In the case of those hungry monkeys, the cardboard boxes' basic function was revised to create a ladder to reach the bananas. Extrapolating this result to human learning, cognitive psychologists theorized that learning occurs when people reconsider input in new and creative ways in order to solve problems presented to them (Driscoll, 1994; Kaplowitz, 2008; Piaget, 1954; Slavin, 2006).

Exactly how mental models come to be reconstructed has been the subject of much research and discussion. Two particular viewpoints have had the most impact on educational psychology. Both deal with the growth and development of thinking, and both offer explanations about how knowledge is acquired and how information is perceived, organized, stored, and retrieved. However, the mechanisms behind those processes differ. One, most notably associated with the works of Jean Piaget and his associates, explains the process in terms of stages of development or maturation. The alternative explanation, known as *constructivism*, concentrates on the idea that learners actively build, create, or construct new mental models as a result of their interactions and experiences.

Both have their roots in the basic principles of cognitive psychology. It is the interpretation of how these principles apply to learning that differs. The strict Piagetian developmental model postulates that children move from concrete to abstract thinking in a precise chronological order. Constructivists counter that learning is more dependent upon the types of opportunities or experiences offered than on the learners' maturational stage of development. Learning for the constructivist is viewed as a process in which learners construct meaning rather than merely take in ideas and memorize them (Barr and Tagg, 1995; Bransford et al., 1999a; Gatten, 2004; Kaplowitz, 2008; Magolda, 2006; Oberg, 1999). The constructivist model depends quite a bit on social interactions that allow learners to test their understandings against those of others. Social construction of knowledge occurs when communities of learners collaborate to formulate ideas and test the validity of those ideas (Burton,

Moore, and Magliaro, 2004; Copperstein and Kocevar-Weidinger, 2004; Fister, 1990; Kaplowitz, 2008; Kelly, 1963; Lowyck and Poysa, 2001; Slavin 2006; Vygotsky and Cole, 1978). A closer examination of the two lines of research will help us understand the commonalities and differences between them.

Cognitive Development According to Piaget

Jean Piaget and his collaborators (Inhelder and Piaget, 1958; Piaget, 1952, 1954) were interested in exploring the ways children think at various steps or stages in their development. The sequence of stages is said to be the same for all children, although the ages when a child passes from one stage to the next can vary somewhat. Progress through the stages is one from concrete, irreversibility, and subjective egocentrism (viewing everything from one's own perspective) to the ability to think abstractly, be independent of the here and now, and view the world through multiple perspectives—that is, to see the world as others see it. Furthermore, a person's stage of cognitive development sets limits for the type of learning that can take place. We will return to this idea when we discuss the concept of learning readiness later in this chapter.

Piaget studied the ways children extract rules from their interactions with objects in the world and how they build mental models that can be used to interpret, organize, and make predictions about future interactions. Once built, these models are assimilated or incorporated into the child's worldview and used to make sense of other experiences. The driving force behind this model building is accommodation. New experiences that do not fit into the old worldview create a feeling of disequilibrium and discomfort in the learner. In cognitive psychology language, this is referred to as *ambiguity*. This feeling of discomfort drives the learner to rethink his or her understanding of the world in order to accommodate the new information. Once new mental models are developed to account for the mismatch between current knowledge and new information, a new assimilation framework is developed that will be used until the learner experiences the next mismatch or ambiguity between knowledge and information. This continually recurring cycle between assimilation and accommodation accounts for the development of more complex modes of thinking (Fenwick, 2000; Johnson and Cooper, 2007; Piaget, 1952).

William Perry expanded and extended this work by examining cognitive development in college students. His research showed that development continues during these young adult years. Students typically enter college with the idea that all knowledge is certain and rely on their professors and on their textbooks to share this knowledge with them. As they progress through college, students learn to question this view. They evolve from what Perry called *dualistic* (right/wrong) thinking to one in which they acknowledge different perspectives and learn to evaluate these perspectives in a relativistic world (Boud, 1988; Magolda, 2006; Perry, 1981, 1988).

Cognitive Development—The Constructivist Approach

Studies beginning in the 1960s on how children think and learn have resulted in constructivism, a variation on the Piagetian themes. Although retaining the idea of stages of cognitive development, the constructivist theories stress experience over maturation as the impetus for moving through these stages. The constructivist view, with its emphasis on learning in context, has called into question the Piagetian notion that cognitive growth is unidirectional moving from the concrete to the abstract (Ackerman, 1996). It does, however, owe much to another aspect of Piagetian theory—assimilation and accommodation.

Although both the constructivist and Piagetian theorists agree on the importance of the assimilation/accommodation cycle, they disagree on how this cycle affects the development of thinking and thus how people learn. To Piaget and his followers, the process is one of maturation. More complex assimilations occur at different stages in the child's growth and development. To the constructivist, however, change occurs solely as a result of interactions with the environment and can happen at any age or level of development. Knowledge is not viewed as simply passing from teacher to learner; knowledge is actually constructed in the learner's mind, thus the name *constructivism*. The learner does not get ideas; he or she makes ideas. Learners are thought to actively construct and reconstruct knowledge out of their experiences in the world (Driscoll, 1994; Freilberg and Driscoll, 2005). Constructivists propose that learners are particularly likely to develop new ideas when they are actively involved in making some kind of external artifact like a poem or a computer program that causes them to reflect upon what they are learning and share that learning with others.

Constructivists stress the role of affect or feelings as well as cognition in their principles. Learners are more likely to become intellectually engaged when they are working on something that has personal meaning to them. This idea also appears in the humanist approach to learning, which is covered later in this chapter. The constructivist and the humanist approaches both contend that creating new ways of connecting to the material is as important as forming new mental representations of it. In addition, both of these schools of learning emphasize diversity of approaches to learning. They recognize that learners can make connections with knowledge in many different ways and encourage multiple approaches to the presentation of the information so as to accommodate this diversity (Kafai and Resnick, 1996). The notion that variations exist in how people learn is also tied to the research into learning styles that are discussed in more detail later in this chapter.

General Characteristics

- Cognitive psychology is interested in the organization of information.
- The cognitive psychologist delves into the internal processes by which an individual tries to deal with the complexity of his or her environment.
- The cognitive psychologist studies the ways in which a person perceives and conceptualizes his or her physical and social world.
- The cognitive psychologist organizes learning into patterns, not parts. He or she is interested in how various elements, ideas, and topics relate to one another.
- Behavior is based on cognition, which is defined as the act of knowing about the situation in which behavior occurs.
- Insight and the motivation to reduce ambiguity are viewed as underlying learning rather than the building up of stimulus–response connections proposed by behaviorists.
- Cognitive psychologists who adhere to the work of Jean Piaget examine development of thinking across the life span. Those working in this area stress that different types of thinking accompany different stages of development.
- The constructivists counter that mismatches between new experiences and the learner's current mental models force the learner to develop more complex modes of thinking.

Educational Applications of Cognitive Psychology

Readiness

Readiness, an outgrowth of Piaget's work, proposes that learning cannot occur unless a person is at the appropriate stage of cognitive development. According to Piaget, children pass through four major stages of development (Piaget and Inhelder, 1969):

1. The sensorimotor period (birth to 18–24 months)
2. The preoperational period (2–7 years)
3. The concrete operational period (7–11 years)
4. The formal operational period (over 11 years)

Each child passes through these stages in order; however, the age at which a child enters a particular stage might vary. Particular types of thinking are associated with each stage of cognitive development. For example, the child in the sensorimotor period does not have a sense of object permanence; so, to the sensorimotor child, out of sight is really out of mind. That is why the peek-a-boo game works so well with very young children. When they cover their eyes and you are no longer in their line of sight, you actually have disappeared for this child.

The preoperational child has begun to use symbols but is not yet able to mentally manipulate these symbols. So, when water is poured from a tall, thin glass into a short, fat one, the preoperational child believes that the amount of water has changed in some fashion. He or she is totally dependent on concrete examples and cannot extrapolate beyond these examples to alternative solutions to problems.

In the concrete operational stage, the child develops the ability to mentally manipulate symbols. But he or she can do this with only concrete, tangible objects. The child in this stage can put objects into order by size or sort them into categories by shape and understands that the amount of water in the previous example remains constant regardless of the shape of the container into which it is poured. However, working with abstract concepts remains difficult. Thus, solving word problems is beyond the grasp of the concrete operational child.

The fourth stage, formal operational, is associated with the ability to think abstractly and is the beginning of adult thinking patterns. The child no longer is dependent on concrete manipulation of objects. He or she can use mental imagery and can consider a variety of possible solutions to problems, even those that may seem improbable or impossible. The formal operational child can now deal with the "what if" and is not totally dependent on the "here and now." Children at this stage can try out various solutions in their minds, determine possible outcomes, weigh the relative merits of the solutions, and then select the best ones. A major characteristic of this stage is the ability to accept the fact that there can be multiple solutions to a problem and to deal with these options in a logical and systematic manner.

According to Piagetian theory, no amount of teaching will cause the child to change his or her perceptions and ways of thinking until he or she reaches the appropriate stage of cognitive development. Teachers must take the child's cognitive developmental stage into account when attempting to present new concepts and ideas.

The constructivist also talks about readiness but does not tie it to maturation. Instead, readiness is a result of an accumulation of experiences. Children simply acquire more and more information about the world through their interactions with it and as a consequence are better able to apply that knowledge to the problems at hand. Studies based on this experience view have shown that if children are shown simple versions of problems they are quite capable of the types of thinking that Piaget thought developed only at later stages (Fox, 1995). Although the means of developing more complex ways of thinking differ in these two approaches, proponents of both viewpoints agree that learning cannot occur until the child is in the appropriate state of readiness. Regardless of how we define readiness, it cannot be ignored without great risk. Anyone who is pressed to learn something for which he or she is not ready will fail and thus lose interest in the process. Learners may even become so frustrated that they will avoid the subject in the future.

Relevance

The cognitive psychologist further postulates that the more engaged learners are with their environment, the more motivated they will be to deal with any ambiguities between the experience and their worldview. This will lead to active problem solving in an attempt to incorporate what they are experiencing into their worldview. Learners will be more engaged if they can relate to their experiences in some way. Learners are more apt to work on problems that have some relevance or significance to them. The notion of authentic instruction, and problem- or case-based learning can be seen as having its foundations in this concept of relevance (Cruickshank, Jenkins, and Metcalf, 2003; Elliott et al., 2000; Slavin, 2006).

The Discovery Method

Just as B.F. Skinner helped to shape the behaviorist view of teaching, Jerome S. Bruner provided major insight into how the cognitive perspective can be applied in the classroom. Bruner emphasizes the role of discovery in learning. In this approach, the instructor offers learners opportunities to discover solutions to problems and by extension the concepts, skills, or strategies needed to formulate these solutions. Learners are allowed to try different solutions and possibilities. The teacher who uses this method acts as a catalyst, letting learners find their own meanings. As learners interact with the problems or situations presented to them, they learn how to organize problems rather than attacking them in a hit and miss fashion. Discovery emphasizes intrinsic motivation (the learner's own desire to learn without the need for external reward). Self-fulfillment is the reinforcer here rather than any extrinsic or external reward from others (Bruner, 1963; Driscoll, 1994; Elliott et al., 2000; Kaplowitz, 2008; Postman and Weingarten, 1971).

Teachers who use this technique need to redefine themselves. This means they must be willing to step back from center stage and allow learners to find their own ways to solutions. The success or failure of this approach depends on the teacher creating situations that allow learners to interact with the material in a way that will facilitate the "discovery" of the solution. Teachers help guide learners through the process by asking thought-provoking questions or providing illustrative examples, thus shifting the role of the teacher from that of leader to one of facilitator (Bruner, 1966; Mayer, 2004).

Using the discovery method means letting go of a measure of control during instruction and allowing learners to move through the material in ways that are meaningful to them. However, the teacher is still in control in the sense that the use of this method requires a lot of planning and coordination. The development of effective discovery experiences requires that teachers be observant and flexible in order to continually monitor learners' progress and offer alternative approaches and gentle guidance if learners seem to be bogged down in the process. Teachers must also accept that the discovery method of teaching frequently takes more time than the traditional teacher-centric approach. However, the time is well spent, as this method offers learners the opportunity to incorporate their learning discoveries into their individual mental models and thereby own what they have learned in a real way. Furthermore, because the information is stored in a way that is meaningful to the learner, it is more likely that learners will be able to retrieve this information in the future when it is needed.

Small group exercises and class discussions are especially suited to the discovery method (see also Chapter 6 for more on active learning approaches). The teacher sets the stage, describes the problem, and perhaps offers some possible methods for its solution. The learners, either as the entire group or split into subgroups, work on the problem for a set period of time. The teacher acts as a facilitator for these discussions rather than as an expert who has all the answers.

Cerise Oberman and Rebecca Linton's (1982) work on the guided design method is a good example of the application of the discovery method to the field of ILI. This method uses an open-ended, problem-solving exercise, consisting of seven stages that lead the learners through the information-gathering research process. However, be warned that, if you plan to do the guided design exercise with your learners, it can take an hour or more to complete.

Expository Teaching and Advance Organizers

How do we teach concepts that seem too complex for learners to discover on their own? David Ausubel's idea of Advance Organizers addresses this concern. Advance Organizers offer a general overview of the information to be presented in advance of the learning experience and so provide a framework into which the learner can fit new information or material. Advance Organizers are most effective when they serve as a bridge between what is known—that is, what is already a part of the learner's worldview—and the new knowledge, skill, or strategy being presented (Ausubel, 1960; Ausubel, Novak, and Hanesion, 1978; Ausubel and Robinson, 1969; Elliott et al., 2000; Kaplowitz, 2008; Richards, 1978). These Organizers, sometimes referred to as *conceptual frameworks*, offer the learner a way to structure the new material in a meaningful way and places new information into a context to which the learner can relate.

To help your learners acquire meaning, identify relevant anchoring ideas that your learners already possess. In other words, relate new, potentially meaningful material to some topic with which they are already familiar. In the case of ILI, comparing the similarities and differences between resources already familiar to the learner and the new ones being introduced can help provide a framework for the instruction.

Although Ausubel promoted the idea of introducing the Organizer before presenting new material, Organizers can be placed at almost any point in the session. Organizers can also be used as a way of pulling material together after it has been presented. The Organizer then serves as a summary of the material rather than an introduction to it. The placement of the Organizer has implications for learning styles theory. Learners who prefer getting the big picture first will appreciate an advanced look at the structure of the material. Those who like to build the big picture for themselves will prefer having the organization presented after the fact.

Advance Organizers or conceptual framework techniques are most effective for assisting learners in what Ausubel called the *reception learning process*, best represented by the lecture and textbook approach of instruction. The key to successful reception learning is to encourage learners to go beyond rote memorization to real meaningful learning. It is up to the teacher to organize and present this information in such a way that learners are helped to make these connections. Information being presented either via the lecture method or in readings must be tied to what the learner already knows. The ability to relate new information to ideas already possessed by the learner is crucial for retention. The structure imposed on the information by the writer or the framework in which the instructor presents the information will allow the learner to make these crucial connections (Ausubel, 1960; Cruickshank, Jenkins, and Metcalf, 2003). Many frameworks exist in ILI. The publication sequence, controlled versus natural language searching, primary versus secondary sources, or popular versus scholarly sources are just a few examples of how Advance Organizers or conceptual frameworks have been used to teach IL. Chapter 5 further discusses conceptual frameworks and mental models.

Ausubel also promoted the use of what he called *expository techniques* to enhance learning. These techniques include asking meaningful questions as material is presented, pausing for learners to reflect on material, having them share their thoughts with their neighbors, and requiring learners to paraphrase what has just been presented. All these methods avoid the trap of rote learning by causing learners to continually put new ideas into their own words (Ausubel, 1977; Cruickshank, Jenkins, and Metcalf, 2003). One technique that can be used to check for comprehension and encourage the learner's meaningful incorporation of new ideas is the one-minute paper. Just prior to instruction the teacher tells the group they will be asked to respond to the following two questions at the end of the session (Angelo and Cross, 1993): What were the main points of this session? What is your main unanswered question? This might be done verbally or in writing. The one-minute paper serves as a summary of the important points covered during the session and highlights what concepts seem to be most meaningful and relevant to the learners. It can also serve as an informal assessment of the session. See Chapter 11 for more information on this technique.

Metacognition

The concept of metacognition—or thinking about thinking—plays an important role in the cognitive approach to learning. In order to really learn, individuals must not only interact with the material to be learned but they must also reflect on the learning process itself (Marzano et al., 1988). Reflection empowers learners to develop strategies for learning how to learn in addition to learning the material that is being presented.

The cognitive approach places great emphasis on the learning process itself. Successful learners are able to manage their own learning. To help learners acquire these self-management skills, teachers might wish to model the process. Teachers should present examples of a variety of strategies and provide time during the learning experience for people to reflect on their own learning as well as on the content being presented (Bransford et al., 1999a; Svinicki, 1994). Requiring learners to write about the process in some kind of research journal can also help them acquire the necessary skills. Virginia Rankin's (1988) article presents an excellent example of incorporating a metacognitive approach to ILI. The one-minute paper and other classroom assessment techniques (CATs), when used as a means of summarizing the learning experience, can also be viewed within this framework. They provide learners with an opportunity to reflect upon and reorganize their thinking based on the material that was presented (Angelo and Cross, 1993; Copperstein and Kocevar-Weidinger, 2004; Driscoll, 1994; Kaplowitz, 2008). See Chapter 6 for more on metacognition.

FEELING—THE HUMANIST MODEL

This brings us to the last of our main theories of learning—the humanist model. Rooted in the free-spirited, "express yourself" nature of the 1960s, the humanist approach looked at learning from a different perspective than its predecessors and examined the affective side of learning. The humanist emphasized that we must teach to the whole person and stressed the importance of recognizing that our learners' emotional, affective, or feeling states influence their educational successes. How learners feel about themselves and the material to be learned is as important as what they think about that material. Along with the cognitive psychologist, those following the humanist path insist that material must have personal meaning or it will not be learned (Dembo, 1988a; Elliott et al., 2000; Kaplowitz, 2008; Rogers, 1969; Tennant, 2006).

With its strong emphasis on the affective side of learning, it is not surprising that humanist psychology is extremely concerned with what motivates people to learn. The key player here is Abraham Maslow, who developed what he called the *hierarchy of needs* to help explain human motivation. Basic needs in this hierarchy are food, shelter, and sex. Next come needs such as safety, love, belonging, and self-esteem. Self-actualization, a person's ability to maximize his or her potential, is at the highest level of needs in this paradigm. According to Maslow, needs lower in the hierarchy must be satisfied before the individual can be motivated to address higher ones. Because learning seems to be motivated by self-actualization needs, Maslow suggested that learning does not occur until those needs that are lower on the hierarchy are met. It is easy to see how being hungry or sick might interfere with a person's ability to learn. But the idea that feelings of love, belonging, and esteem can affect learning was a new and somewhat revolutionary idea that greatly influenced ideas about teaching and learning (Driscoll, 1994; Kaplowitz, 2008; Maslow, 1987; Slavin, 2006; Tennant, 2006).

Because how people feel about themselves is the cornerstone of the humanist approach to learning, it comes as no surprise that the work of Albert Bandura also played an important role in the development of this model. Bandura's work on self-efficacy, or an individual's belief in his or her own possibility for success, was particularly influential. To the humanist, encouraging learners to believe in themselves should be an integral part of the educational process (Bandura, 1977b, 1982; Candy, 1990; Driscoll, 1994; Slavin, 2006).

The humanists endorse the creation of a different kind of learning environment in which learners are encouraged to believe in themselves, are given opportunities to succeed, and are treated with respect. In this environment teachers exhibit by words and deeds that they believe everyone can succeed. These teachers do not grade on a curve because this pits learner against learner. They are supportive of all their learners and promote collaboration and cooperation. Humanist teachers believe in their learners, and, as a result, learners begin to believe in themselves and their feelings of self-confidence and self-efficacy grow (Cruickshank, Jenkins, and Metcalf, 2003; Kaplowitz, 2008; McGregor, 1999). Furthermore, Kuhlthau's (1988) work indicates that learners become more confident and comfortable with the information search process when their teachers help them to acknowledge that feelings of uncertainty and anxiety are a natural part of research and not a reflection of their own abilities.

General Characteristics

The humanist school is concerned with the affective side of learning:

- Feelings and concerns are as important as thinking and behaving.
- Basic needs must be satisfied before self-actualization or working to the learner's full potential can be accomplished.
- The educational environment should foster self-development and understanding, which will lead to self-actualization.
- The humanist psychologist believes that people are determiners of their own behavior. They are not merely acted upon by the environment. People are free to make choices about the quality of their lives.
- Learning situations should be learner centered and oriented toward developing self-efficacy.
- Material must have personal meaning or relevance for the learners in order to be learned.
- Learners are thought to be intrinsically motivated rather than working for external rewards.

Educational Applications of Humanist Psychology

Self-directed or Self-regulated Learning

With humanism's emphasis on the affective side of learning, it is not surprising that humanists wish to encourage a self-reflective attitude in learners. For the humanist, it is not enough to learn the material. Learners are encouraged to examine how they feel about the material they are studying and how the learning experience has impacted their attitudes and values. This approach not only stresses the acquisition of knowledge about the subject matter but also encourages learners to examine their own work habits, perceptions, values, and potential. Learners are encouraged to gain a better understanding of themselves and others as learners and to take control of their own lives and destinies. Instructors involved in self-directed learning help learners use a variety of strategies and perceptual skills so that they can direct or regulate their own learning and gain insight into that learning as it takes place (Areglado, Bradley, and Lane, 1996; Boud, 1988; Slavin, 2006; Sternberg and Grigorenka, 2002, 2004).

In some ways this idea is reminiscent of the cognitive psychology idea of metacognition. However, the humanists are interested in learners developing a better understanding of their own feelings, attitudes, and values associated with learning as well as understanding the cognitive processes related to it. Furthermore, humanist teachers want their learners to reflect upon the learning process itself. How did they go about learning? Were certain types of learning experiences more enjoyable and productive than others? To the humanist, the more we understand about our own learning preferences, the better we can frame our learning experiences and increase our possibilities for success. The research on learning styles, which is discussed in a later section of this chapter, is a direct outgrowth of this idea. Know thyself and your learning preferences, and you can become a more successful learner.

Although we cannot always control our learning experiences, knowing how we learn best can help us relate better to any learning experiences in which we find ourselves. And some things are actually under our control. For example, if you know that you are a "morning person," you can try to schedule classes or work on projects in the early hours of the day. If, on the other hand, you work best later on in the day, sleep in (if possible) and do your heavy thinking/learning during the late afternoon or evening. If you are truly a "night person," you may find you do your best work after dark.

Knowing what works best for you can also help you adjust to learning experiences that do not suit you. If you are someone who likes active involvement but you are in a lecture-intensive situation, try to develop some active note-taking and self-reflection techniques that help you stay engaged even though the learning situation is mostly a passive one. See some of the techniques in the next chapter for more about turning passive learning experiences into more active ones.

Self-directed learners set goals and achievement standards for themselves, so the material to be learned becomes highly meaningful and relevant to them. The instructor's role becomes one of support, offering suggestions about how learners can reach their goals in the most effective way possible. This can require a good deal of advanced planning and a high degree of flexibility in dealing with the learners. Instructors who wish to teach in this fashion must be willing to view situations from their learners' perspectives. They must develop a high degree of empathy for their learners' feelings and points of view, and they must always treat their learners with respect. This approach flourishes when both learner and teacher see one another not only as mutually helpful human beings with resources to share but also as self-reliant human beings who care for themselves and others. Educators who work in this type of environment act as models, coaches, and mentors who validate learning and encourage the development of self-confidence on the part of the learner.

Learner-centered Teaching

The movement toward a more learner-centered approach to teaching is a natural outgrowth of humanist ideas about learning. In the learner-centered teaching environment, learning is viewed as a shared responsibility with the teacher cast in the role of facilitator rather than lecturer. Humanist teachers rely on many of the same techniques supported by their cognitive counterpoints. They, too, wish to create experiences in which the learners can interact with the material on their own and discover, create, or construct personal meanings. As a result, behavior is intrinsically (for learning's sake) motivated rather than based on extrinsic (external) rewards. Learners are interacting with the material in their own ways and in order to please themselves (Areglado, Bradley, and Lane, 1996; Fister, 1990; Kaplowitz, 2008).

Humanists, however, go a step further with this idea. In the humanist learning environment, learners are given choices in how they will interact with the material to be learned. They also might be given a say in how their learning will be assessed or graded. Learners could choose between taking a test on the material, writing a paper on a topic, creating a Web page or video, or making a live presentation. In some cases learners may even be allowed to decide how much each of their assignments will count toward a total grade. They may also be invited to assess their own or their fellow learners' work. Learning contracts are an outgrowth of this idea and allow learners to take responsibility for their own learning and to feel a sense of ownership in the process. Whenever we let learners pick their own topics for in-class exercises or for papers and projects, we are following the humanist approach to teaching. Using the humanist approach requires quite a leap of faith on the part of the teacher. It asks us to believe that, if given the chance, learners will both take charge of their own learning and be able to succeed in achieving their goals (Barr and Tagg, 1995; Boud, 1988; Candy, 1990; Cornwall, 1988; Kaplowitz, 2008; Weimer, 2003; Zimmerman, 1990).

A learner-centered approach to teaching may or may not result in self-directed learners. Although both approaches give learners more responsibility for and control over their learning, the self-directed learning environment actively promotes the idea of self-reflection and an examination of the more affective side to learning. It asks learners to examine why they interacted with the material in the way in which they did and how that interaction might impact them in the future. The learner-centered teaching approach gives the learner more freedom in deciding how to learn. It lets learners apply what they learned from their self-directed learning–inspired reflection to craft learning situations that offer the greatest opportunities for success.

PSYCHOLOGY OF LEARNING SCHOOLS: COMMON THREADS

Now that we have examined each school independently, it might be useful to look for common threads or themes among the three schools. Although each school seems to have been developed in part to refute its predecessors, a closer look at the principles associated with each school points out some interesting congruencies.

For example, both behaviorists and cognitive/constructivists view active participation as crucial to the learning process. The difference lies in how each explains the necessity of that active participation. The behaviorist would say that active participation increases the opportunity to "stumble" upon the correct solution through trial and error and gives the instructor the chance to shape behavior in the desired direction via positive reinforcement and immediate feedback. The cognitive psychologist (especially one who supports the constructivist model) says active participation is an opportunity for learners to discover new ways of knowing and enables learners to construct or reconstruct mental models. External reinforcement does not have a role here. The learner is internally or intrinsically motivated to fit new knowledge into his or her world. If this assimilation fails, the learner is driven to change his or her view of the world to accommodate the new information. Therefore, the result of active engagement with the data is that the learner constructs mental models that are consistent with this new information. The Piagetian or maturational model also supports active participation, because children need to experience disconnects between their current stage of development and their experiences in the world in order to stimulate the movement into the next, more complex or abstract stage of development (Kaplowitz, 2008; Sparks-Langer, 2000).

Next there is the concept of readiness. Behaviorists discuss readiness in terms of mastery and cautions teachers against moving learners to more complex concepts until they have mastered the more basic ones or, in other words, not until they are ready to do so. Although the cognitive psychologist agrees, readiness from this perspective is based on the level of complexity in the learners' mental models rather than the mastery of concepts. Both Piagetian theorists and constructivists agree that trying to force learners to acquire knowledge, skills, or abilities before they are ready to do so is doomed to fail (Kaplowitz, 2008). The humanist would also agree with this idea of readiness and with the types of techniques that allow learners to move through material at their own pace. Furthermore, the heavy emphasis on the importance of feedback that is seen in both the cognitive/constructivist and humanist ideas harkens back to the behaviorists' principle of reinforcement.

The cognitive/constructivists have other ideas in common with their humanist counterparts. Metacognition is a major component of both schools of thought. However, while the cognitive/constructivist is interested in learners reflecting on the cognitive aspects of their learning, the humanist encourages learners to think about their learning from a more affective angle. Theorists from both persuasions would agree that, in order to really learn, learners must not only interact with the material to be learned but they must also reflect on the learning process itself. This empowers them to develop strategies for learning how to learn in addition to learning the material that is being presented.

Because some of the basic tenets of becoming information literate include learning how to learn and becoming lifelong learners, the ideas of metacognition and self-reflection should really resonate with the IL instructor. Learners can be encouraged to think about their learning process through being asked to reflect upon their experiences. Instructors may wish to document the learning process by asking the learners to develop research journals in which they discuss how they looked for and retrieved the information they needed for their projects or papers and how they felt about the process itself. As previously mentioned, the one-minute paper and other CATs can also provide learners with opportunities to reflect on the material (Angelo and Cross, 1993; Kaplowitz, 2008).

Both humanists and cognitive/constructivists support the idea of relevance and personal meaning as crucial to the learning process. Each approach advocates offering learners the opportunity to actively experiment with the material to be learned and, in the case of the humanist, the ways in which they interact with it. Learners are encouraged to seek out their own answers to questions and/or problems. Authentic, real-life, meaningful, and relevant examples are utilized in order to really engage and motivate the learner. Abstract concepts become meaningful, transferable, and retained through active engagement with problems that matter to the learner (Kaplowitz, 2008; Woodard, 2003).

Humanist and cognitive/constructivists alike endorse the move from "sage on the stage" to "guide on the side." The instructor acts as a facilitator who orchestrates learning experiences in order to assist the learner to discover his or her own truth. Because the social nature of learning is also a prominent feature of both approaches, experiences, collaborative learning, and group work tend to be favored as teaching techniques. Learners are given time to exchange ideas. Together they formulate questions and look for ways of answering these questions. Teachers support the process by asking questions that challenge the learners, arouse their curiosity, and move them forward. Educational trends that emphasize shifting responsibility for learning from the teacher to the learner are consistent with this aspect of both humanist and cognitive/constructivist thinking (Barr and Tagg, 1995; Higgs, 1988; Kaplowitz, 2008; McGregor, 1999; Oberg, 1999; Weimer, 2002, 2003).

LEARNING STYLES: THE LEARNERS' PERSPECTIVE

Becoming familiar with the tenets of the three schools of learning is an important first step to improving our instructional endeavors. This familiarity can help us understand what lies behind the various techniques we use in our teaching. However, learners are far from a homogenous bunch and vary greatly in the ways in which they prefer to learn. If we wish to be effective, we must try to understand these variations so that we can design instructional experiences that will help us reach and teach everyone. Furthermore, we need to become familiar with our own style so that we can move beyond it and reach out to those with styles different from our own. We must try to avoid the very human tendency of only teaching in our own favored style. We tend to gravitate toward the teaching methods that reflect how we most like to learn. Consciously or unconsciously, we feel that "if it is good for me, it must also be good for you." However, when we stick to our own style we end up disenfranchising at least some of our learners (Kaplowitz, 2008; Keefe, 1982).

The literature on learning styles is rich and abundant. Teachers are often overwhelmed and wonder how they could possibly address all of these styles in their teaching when they are first introduced to this concept and to the multitude of styles that seem to exist. One way to deal with all this is to look at styles as falling into three fairly unique categories: physiological, cognitive, and affective (Keefe, 1982). Furthermore, these three categories can be seen as reminiscent of the doing, thinking, feeling paradigm used earlier to discuss the three models or schools of thought regarding learning. Physiological learning styles are "doing" styles that deal with how learners interact with or behave in relation to the material to be learned. These styles, therefore, are most aligned with behaviorist ideas about learning. Cognitive styles with their emphasis on how learners perceive, think about, organize, and retain the material seem connected to the cognitive/constructivist or "thinking" model. Finally, affective styles, which deal with how learners feel about the material to be learned, can be linked to the humanist school of thought (Kaplowitz, 2008).

The massive amount of literature that has appeared on learning styles over the years goes beyond the scope of this book. Therefore, the following is a very brief, cursory overview of the topic. Readers who want a more detailed description of the various styles and references to additional readings can refer to "A Brief Overview of Learning Styles" on the CD-ROM that accompanies this publication. One thing to keep in mind as you delve into this topic is that styles represent a preference for learning. They do not describe aptitude, personality traits, or values. Although an individual may prefer one way of learning to another, most of us learn to cope with nonpreferred modes when circumstances demand it. However, we may not be at our best if we are forced to work in a nonpreferred manner and may have to expend additional effort to gain from the experience. It may take longer to absorb the material under these circumstances as we try to take in material that is being presented in a way that does not fit in to how we think. Furthermore, unless we can figure out how to reorganize the material so that it does fit with our mental models, we may have difficulty retaining the material for very long.

Physiological Styles—How Learners Interact with the World

Physiological styles describe the ways that learners react to the world around them. These styles describe variations in tolerance for learning under varying environmental conditions such as illumination, temperature, and noise levels. They also deal with issues of health and nutrition—people's tolerance for working when hungry, tired, or ill. Mobility needs, how often a person needs to get up and move around during learning, falls into this style category. Finally, we have "time of day" preferences. Some people seem to be at their learning best early in the day, while others prefer the evening or even nighttime hours.

Although discussions of gender differences in learning and the idea that people may be either right or left brained would both fall into this category, the research surrounding these topics is quite controversial and has come under question. In terms of gender differences, if they do exist, it is unclear if they are innate or develop through socialization. Current advances in the ability to measure brain functions during learning have led researchers to question whether there really is, in fact, evidence to support the right/left brain differential. Furthermore, some researchers now hypothesize that characteristics traditionally associated with gender and hemispheric differences seem more connected to cognitive and affective styles (Berninger and Richards, 2002; Cruickshank, Jenkins, and Metcalf, 2003; Winn, 2004).

Cognitive Styles—How Learners Think About the World

Cognitive styles deal with information-processing habits. In other words, they relate to the ways people observe, think, problem solve, and remember, and they describe how learners prefer to perceive, organize, and retain information. The most well known is commonly referred to as *perceptual modality preference* or the way a person prefers to absorb information—visually through reading, aurally through hearing, and kinesthetically through doing (Barbe and Milone, 1982; Barbe and Swassing, 1988; Keefe, 1987; Messick, 1978).

Cognitive styles also deal with the bottom-up versus top-down approaches to learning. Some learners like to start with the broad, holistic, or abstract view of the topic, while others prefer to begin with a more narrow, specific, and focused approach that relies heavily on specific examples (Cruickshank, Jenkins, and Metcalf, 2003; Messick, 1978; Rayner and Riding, 1997; Riding and Cheema, 1991; Witkin, 1978; Witkin et al., 1977).

People can also differ in their decision-making speed and how fast they respond to input. Some learners are described as "impulsives," who are quick to process and respond to information. They are all about speed, being done first, and moving quickly to the next new thing—often at the cost of accuracy in their responses. "Reflectives" prefer a slow pace. They want to be given time to absorb and think about new material (Cruickshank, Jenkins, and Metcalf, 2003; Kagan, 1966; Messick, 1978). They tend to be the quiet ones in your classroom and can be overwhelmed by the behavior of their more impulsive classmates. However, keep in mind that they are still engaged in the learning process. It is just that they are not ready to respond as quickly as the more impulsive learners.

Affective Styles—How Learners Feel About the World

Finally, we come to those styles that deal with feelings or the emotional aspects of learning. These "affective" styles focus on how we relate to and value information. Curiosity, perseverance, risk taking, and competition/cooperation fall into this category, as do styles relating to motivation, attention, structural needs, and tolerance for frustration (Gaines and Coursey, 1974; Keefe, 1987). Also included in this category is the style known as *internal/external locus of control*. Internal-oriented people feel they are responsible for the consequences of their own actions, while external-oriented individuals see circumstances as beyond their control (Rotter, 1971, 1975). Having an internal locus of control would probably be associated with learners who are intrinsically motivated (learn for learning's sake), while those who have a more external locus would more likely be extrinsically motivated (work for external rewards). For more on motivation, see Chapter 4.

MEASURING LEARNING STYLES

It is clear that people vary widely in the ways they like to learn, but how does all this information help us teach? How can we possibly vary our teaching in order to appeal to all these different types of learners? And how do we even know the types of learners we are dealing with? A practical application of this research has been the development of various instruments to determine an individual's learning style. The early literature concentrated on individual styles such as impulsive/reflective, abstract/concrete, and locus of control. However, it soon became apparent that it would be more useful to take a broader, more global look at styles. With this in mind, several researchers developed inventories that measure groupings of styles—rather than individual ones. The two inventories discussed here characterize learners in terms of sets of behaviors. Each set includes elements of physiological, cognitive, and affective styles.

The most famous and widely used inventory is David Kolb's experiential learning model measured by the Learning Style Inventory (LSI). The inventory looks at learning behaviors in terms of two pairs of polar opposites or dimensions—*concrete/abstract* and *active experimentation/reflective* observation. The concrete/abstract dimension refers to how the learner prefers to process information. The active experimentation/reflective refers to how the learner prefers to interact with information and how he or she feels about that interaction. In order to get the full picture of someone's style, it is necessary to measure where he or she falls on each of these axes. Once this is done, the learner can be described in terms of four possible combinations or styles: Divergers (concrete and reflective), Convergers (abstract and active), Assimilators (abstract and reflective), and Accommodators (concrete and active) (Kolb, 1976, 1984; Kolb and Fry, 1975; Wilcoxson and Prosser, 1996).

Kolb goes on to offer suggestions about how to model instruction that can create opportunities for each type of learner. The method consists of four stages: concrete experience, reflective observation, abstract conceptualization, and active experimentation. Kolb's LSI and his experiential learning model have gained a great deal of popularity in instructional circles. However, the inventory itself is somewhat difficult to administer and score. Furthermore, the terminology used to describe the four style types is not that easy to understand. People can find it difficult to relate to such words as diverger, converger, accommodator, and assimilator. In addition, although Kolb's experiential learning method stresses the necessity of integrating all four experiences, some researchers question whether this model is necessary in all types of learning situations (Kaplowitz, 2008; Tennant, 2006).

The Learning Styles Questionnaire (LSQ) developed by Peter Honey and Alan Mumford (accessed 2008) offers an alternative approach. This questionnaire differs from LSI in both terminology and methodology. Learning styles are referred to as activists, reflectors, theorists, and pragmatists—a far more understandable set of categories. Furthermore, as opposed to the Kolb single-style approach, the LSQ provides not one score, but a score in each of the four styles. While one or two might stand out as having the highest score, a complete picture of the learner develops as he or she reviews how much or how little of each style contributes to the overall picture (Kaplowitz, 2008). We will discuss how to use both the Kolb and the Honey-Mumford learning styles perspective in an instructional setting Chapter 4.

FINAL REMARKS

So what did this excursion into the psychology of learning and learning styles tell us? All of the theories and research discussed have influenced the education process and have served to inform us about how people learn. No one single researcher or theorist can be singled out as having the complete, right answer. Each offers something for the IL instructor to think about and use. If we approach instruction with a grounding in, and appreciation for, the theoretical basis for teaching and learning, we will gain a greater understanding of the many practical applications that are used in educational settings.

Familiarity with a variety of methods and the theories behind those methods can give us insight into experiences that will appeal to different types of learners. The more familiar we are with our instructional options, the more prepared we are to create a varied instructional experience that has the best chance of appealing to all our learners. Providing varied learning opportunities within the classroom as well as in our online environment enhances the usefulness of these experiences. Combining in-person with virtual instruction broadens our reach and our effectiveness. Creating instruction that appeals to various learning styles also has another benefit. This type of instruction with its mix of methods and techniques tends to result in a more dynamic and interesting experience for both the learner and the teacher (Bligh, 2000; Holmes, 2002; Kaplowitz, 2008). In the next chapter, we will go into more detail about how to put these theoretical principles into practice.

Having a firm understanding of the theory behind

the practice will also allow instructors to be more flexible and effective teachers, who are quick on their feet and can adjust their methodologies and approaches on the spot if things are not going well. The most thorough and well-prepared IL instructor in the world can discover that what he or she had planned for a particular in-person situation or a virtual instructional experience is just not playing out as expected. Understanding why the plan is not working and having one—if not more—backup plans based on different theoretical approaches that consider our learners' potential stylistic differences allows the IL instructor to turn an unsuccessful situation into a triumph.

EXERCISES

1. Start with an ILI topic that you have been responsible for teaching. If you have not had this responsibility yet, use some situation in which you have been the learner.

   Analyze the experience by looking at all the different types of instruction that were used during the training. Some possibilities would be lectures, hands-on practice, self-paced workbooks or worksheets, readings, projects or papers, group work, journals, role-playing, and brainstorming.

   Match each technique that was used to one of the approaches to learning described in this chapter. Explain why that technique belongs in that approach and what principles the technique illustrates. If a technique seems to illustrate principles from a variety of theorists or schools, explain how the technique fits into all appropriate theoretical frameworks.
2. Think about training someone in an IL skill, such as searching a database or finding biographical information about a living person. Design an instructional experience that incorporates an example of one technique for each of the following approaches to learning: behaviorist, cognitive, and humanist. Explain how each example illustrates the theoretical principle associated with a particular theory or theorist.
3. Do a bit of self-reflection. What type of learner are you? You can decide based on the results of a learning styles instrument, or just think about what types of learning experiences are most effective for you. Now examine the ways you teach. Do you tend to teach in a way that is most like the way you like to learn? If so, try to develop some alternative approaches that move you out of your own comfort zone for learning.

Note: Keep in mind that although you might not find some of these techniques appealing as a learner, you need to include opportunities in your instruction that will appeal to all learners—those like you and those who learn in ways that are different from your own favored approach. Also be aware that learning styles instruments that are freely available on the Internet may not be completely reliable or valid. For more on validity and reliability, see Chapter 11.

READ MORE ABOUT IT

Bransford, John D., Ann L. Brown, Rodney R. Cocking, and National Research Council, eds. 1999. *How People Learn: Brain, Mind, Experience and School*. Washington, DC: National Academies Press.

Burton, John K., David M. Moore, and Susan G. Magliaro. 2004. "Behaviorism and Instructional Technology." In *Handbook of Research in Educational Communications and Technology* (pp. 3–36), edited by David H. Jonassen. Mahwah, NJ: Erlbaum.

Dembo, Myron H. 1988. *Teaching for Learning: Applying Educational Psychology in the Classroom*. Santa Monica, CA: Goodyear.

Elliott, Stephen N., Thomas R. Kratochwill, Joan Littlefield Cook, and John F. Travers. 2000. *Educational Psychology: Effective Teaching, Effective Learning*, 3rd ed. Boston: McGraw-Hill.

Honey, Peter and Alan Mumford. "Honey Mumford Learning Styles Questionnaire—LSQ." Available: www.peterhoney.com (accessed December 22, 2008).

Kaplowitz, Joan. 2008. "The Psychology of Learning: Connecting Theory to Practice." In *Information Literacy Instruction Handbook* (pp. 26–49), edited by Christopher N. Cox and Elizabeth Blakesley Lindsay. Chicago: ALA.

Keefe, James W. 1987. *Learning Style: Theory and Practice*. Reston, VA: National Association of Secondary School Principals.

Kolb, David A. 1984. *Experiential Learning: Experience as the Source of Learning and Development*. Englewood Cliffs, NJ: Prentice-Hall.

Riding, Richard and Indra Cheema. 1991. "Cognitive Styles: An Overview and Integration." *Educational Psychology* 11, no. 3: 193–215.

Slavin, Robert E. 2006. *Educational Psychology: Theory into Practice*, 8th ed. Boston: Allyn & Bacon.

Wilcoxson, Lesley and Michael Prosser. 1996. "Kolb's Learning Style Inventory (1985): Review and Further Study of Validity and Reliability." *British Journal of Educational Psychology* 66, no. 3: 247–257.

Winn, William. 2004. "Cognitive Perspectives in Psychology." In *Handbook of Research in Educational Communications and Technology* (pp. 79–112), edited by David H. Jonassen. Mahwah, NJ: Erlbaum.

Chapter 4

Psychology of Learning: Putting Theory into Practice

> *If a man does not keep pace with his companions, perhaps it is because he hears a different drummer. Let him step to the music he hears, however measured or far away.*
>
> —Henry David Thoreau

MAKING PSYCHOLOGY WORK FOR YOU

Hopefully the previous chapter has given you a basic understanding of what psychologists have to say about learning. But understanding the theory is only the first step toward transforming your teaching. Next you must incorporate that theory into your teaching practice and use what you have learned to increase the effectiveness of your instructional endeavors. Let us begin by looking at what each of the learning models has to say about the act of teaching. Figure 4.1 illustrates teaching principles and practices from each of the three perspectives.

APPLYING PSYCHOLOGICAL THEORY TO INFORMATION LITERACY INSTRUCTION

Each of the principles and teaching practices that underlies the three theories or models of learning has something to offer the information literacy (IL) instructor. We can mix and match from all three models to create the most effective instructional environment possible. Although we may resonate with certain ideas more than with others, the learning styles research reminds us that not everyone learns in the same way as we do. If we are to be truly effective, we must step outside our own personal comfort zone and vary our ways of interacting with our learners. This does not mean we have to give up our favorite methods completely and teach only in ways that match those of our learners. For one thing, it is often difficult to obtain information on our learners' preferred styles. Furthermore, any group of learners will probably have a variety of different preferences. Trying to match teaching methods to learners' styles can be very difficult and has not been clearly shown to be more effective than mixing methods. Moreover, mixing methods in order to reach everyone and giving learners as much option as possible is just good pedagogy. In order to create this variety, we need to listen to what each of the models has to tell us and combine ideas, principles, and techniques as we design our instruction. So what do the models have to offer?

Applying the Behaviorist Model

From the behaviorist model we get the notions of chunking, feedback, mastery, and reinforcement. We all know that presenting too much information in any format can result in overload and can actually interfere with learning. Furthermore, overwhelming the learner can lead to library and/or technology anxiety, which is also detrimental to learning and retention (see Chapter 5 for more on this topic). Add to this the idea of active learning, which seems to be a feature in all three models of learning in some way, and you end up with instructional endeavors (face to face [F2F] or online) that are broken up into manageable chunks and are interspersed with hands-on practice and other types of active learning experiences that allow for feedback about and reinforcement of correct efforts. An added bonus is that the practice periods give the learner time to process information and move it from short- to long-term memory storage. Guided practice followed by more free form, hands-on practice is a good way to incorporate

Figure 4.1. Three Perspectives on Teaching

Behaviorist **Principles and Practices**	**Cognitive/Constructivist** **Principles and Practices**	**Humanist** **Principles and Practices**
Principles: • Task analysis • Mastery • Moving at own pace **Teaching Practices:** • Breaks material into small units • Teaches each unit • Tests for mastery at each level • Offers help to reach mastery if necessary • Does not let learners proceed to the next level if they have not mastered preceding ones • Performs final check for mastery of complete task	**Principles:** • Assimilation and accommodation to reduce ambiguity • Knowledge construction • Relevance/personal meaning • Discovery learning **Teaching Practices:** • Emphasizes the active role of the learner • Views teacher as catalyst, facilitator, or guide who sets the stage for learning to occur. De-emphasizes lecture mode and transmission of information • Emphasizes learning through self-discovery • Creates situations in which learners can experiment with new material without previous instruction • Creates opportunities for interacting with the material that are unstructured enough to allow for self-exploration but that have specific goals so that learners can have a feeling of accomplishment • Allows learners to try things out and see what will happen, manipulate symbols, pose questions, and seek their own answers	**Principles:** • Importance of affective aspects of learning **Teaching Practices:** • Creates comfortable, safe, and encouraging learning environment • Projects a warm and welcoming teaching persona in order to satisfy the learner's basic emotional needs • Emphasizes the development of positive attitudes toward what is being learned as well as the acquisition of skills, knowledge, and abilities

Figure 4.1. Three Perspectives on Teaching *(Continued)*

Behaviorist **Principles and Practices**	**Cognitive/Constructivist** **Principles and Practices**	**Humanist** **Principles and Practices**
Principle: • Active participation **Teaching Practices:** • Uses guided exercises plus hands-on practice • Includes active question and answer periods • Uses problem-solving experiences	**Principles:** • Conceptualizing the world based on personal experience • Organizing experiences into meaningful patterns • Metacognition • Social nature of learning **Teaching Practices:** • Encourages learners to compare experiences, to reconcile what is found from one situation to the next one, and to compare experiences with other learners • Allows for sharing of results. Promotes idea of learner as discoverer who becomes an expert and then shares his or her new knowledge with the rest of the group	**Principles:** • Learner-centered teaching • Self-actualization • Self-efficacy **Teaching Practices:** • Views teacher as facilitator or coach who advises learners on how to develop to their full potential • Encourages learners to progress toward self-actualization
Principle: • Immediate feedback **Teaching Practices:** • Provides immediate feedback for all responses (quizzes, homework, in-class exercises, etc.) • Allows for discussion of results and questions generated by activities	**Principle:** • Readiness **Teaching Practices:** • Attends to learner's state of readiness for a particular learning task • Watches for evidence of interest in or frustration with a task • Persists only as long as the learner is interested, engaged, and is making reasonable progress toward the desired goal • Rethinks approach if learners stop making progress; a different, simpler approach may be called for • Views disinterest as sign of lack of readiness that should not be ignored	**Principles:** • Self-directed/regulated learning • Relevance/personal meaning **Teaching Practices:** • Gives learners a role in determining their own goals and objectives, and in deciding when they want to work on certain tasks • Gives learners options about how to approach and learn about new material

(continued)

Figure 4.1. Three Perspectives on Teaching *(Continued)*

Behaviorist **Principles and Practices**	**Cognitive/Constructivist** **Principles and Practices**	**Humanist** **Principles and Practices**
Principle: • Reinforcement **Teaching Practices:** • Praises learners for correct answers, proper study habits, and other desirable behavior through supportive verbal or written comments, gestures, and body language • Allows learners time to think and respond • Do not praise indiscriminately or it will lose its effectiveness • Is specific with praise so that learner understands what is being reinforced by the praise • Lets learners do something they like as an inducement or reinforcement for learning some other task	**Principles:** • Advance organizers • Conceptual frameworks • Expository teaching • Metacognition • Reflection **Teaching Practices:** • Provides structure or framework for material in advance of presenting material, when using lecture mode or assigning textbook readings • Includes focused questioning, discussion, and reflection opportunities during lectures	**Principles:** • Learner-centered teaching • Self-directed/regulated learning • Intrinsic motivation • Self-efficacy **Teaching Practices:** • Allows learners to participate in evaluation of own work • Provides learners with self-paced, self-correcting exercises, so that learners can determine when they have accomplished the designated task
Principle: • Successive approximations **Teaching Practice:** • Praises learners who attempt to answer questions as well as those who answer correctly, thus encouraging learners to continue to try, respond, and become more actively involved in the process	**Principles:** • Metacognition • Knowledge construction • Relevance/personal meaning • Learner-centered teaching **Teaching Practices:** • Places as much emphasis on how people learn as on the content material they are studying • Encourages learners to develop metacognitive skills through modeling, assignments, and self-reflective activities	**Principles:** • Self-directed/regulated learning • Reflection **Teaching Practices:** • Encourages people to learn more about themselves and how they relate to others in order to prepare for their role in society • Asks learners to think for themselves and to make their own decisions

Figure 4.1. Three Perspectives on Teaching *(Continued)*

Behaviorist **Principles and Practices**	**Cognitive/Constructivist** **Principles and Practices**	**Humanist** **Principles and Practices**
Principle: • Modeling **Teaching Practices:** • Models desired behavior • Sets a good example for the learners in all your interactions with them • Pays attention to learners' questions and comments so that they will pay attention to what is being demonstrated • Indicates by word and deed interest in learners' responses and respects their opinions to create an atmosphere that encourages full and complete participation		**Principles:** • Self-efficacy • Self-actualization **Teaching Practices:** • Believes that given enough time and support everyone has the ability to learn • Maintains positive outlook that underlies all interactions in the learning situation
		Principle: • Relevance/personal meaning **Teaching Practices:** • Believes that learning involves both the acquisition of new information and the individual personalization of this material • Believes teacher has responsibility for highlighting relevance of material to be learned

these ideas into IL instruction (ILI) (Clark and Feldon, 2005; Clark and Taylor, 1994; Mayer, 2004; Mayer and Moreno, 2003; Veldof, 2006). It is important to motivate learners and keep them engaged during these practice periods by reinforcing their behaviors through praise and encouragement. Remember that vocal tone, body language, and gestures as well as written and spoken communication are all powerful ways to reinforce learners' behaviors.

In keeping with the behaviorist principle of mastery, make sure you stop for a comprehension check after each segment or chunk. Hands-on exercises can help here. Once you have modeled the desired behavior or strategy, let learners try it out. Watching them try to apply what you have taught can give you a real sense of what has and has not been mastered. You can also use the classroom assessment techniques (Angelo and Cross, 1993) referred to elsewhere in this book. Another way to check for mastery is to stop and ask for questions. Make sure that you do this in such a way that shows you really mean it. Ask "What questions do you have for me now?" to show both that it is okay to have questions and that you really want to address those questions. Another type of comprehension check would be to pose focused questions that would allow you to see if the learners "got" or mastered what has just been covered (Freilberg and Driscoll, 2005; Rovai, 2004).

When asking questions in a F2F situation, make sure you give learners time to think and reply. Asking and then immediately answering your own questions sends the message that you really are not interested in their responses. Rather than reinforcing question-asking behavior, you will be discouraging it and thus will not be able to use this approach to check for mastery. Hard as it might be—wait out the silences that will often follow your questions. If too much time goes by, try rephrasing the question, offer some hints, or put the question in context to help the learners see what you are trying to get at. If learners cannot correctly respond at this point, they have not mastered the material and you need to review it again before you can allow them to move on to the next chunk.

Inserting questions or quizzes at intervals in your online instructional material also acts as tests for comprehension and mastery. For asynchronous material such as stand-alone tutorials, the quizzes can be self-correcting or the results can be e-mailed to you for feedback. In either case, it is helpful to offer some way to review the material if mastery has not been achieved on a particular topic.

Applying the Cognitive/Constructivist Model

The cognitive/constructivist model also endorses the idea of active involvement—in this case in order to help learners "own" the material. These interactions enable learners to create their own understanding or knowledge of the material and relate it to previous knowledge. As a result, what has been learned has great personal meaning or relevance to the learner. Including some fairly unstructured exercises or problems that allow learners to find (or "discover") their own answers would be a feature of active involvement from the cognitive/constructivist point of view (Cruickshank, Jenkins, and Metcalf, 2003; Jonassen, 1997). You can apply this discovery principle in your ILI by just turning your learners loose on a problem before you engage in any kind of formal instruction. Let them try to solve the problem individually or, even better, in groups. Then ask your learners to reflect upon the experience to encourage some metacognitive thinking. What did they find? Where did they find it? Was the experience difficult or easy? Were they satisfied with the results? If you are working with learners in real time (F2F or online) this can lead to a lively discussion and can be far more engaging to your learners than having you just present the material to be learned. The discovery approach can even work in asynchronous learning situations by combining online exercises with a blog, wiki, or discussion board format in which learners can share their experiences with you and with one another.

Because social learning also plays an important part in this approach, cognitive/constructivists emphasize cooperative or collaborative learning. Whenever we allow our learners to work together on projects or interact in groups, we are creating a social learning experience. Learners can do this in a synchronous F2F environment through the use of group exercises and problem-solving activities. If learning is taking place virtually, learners can interact online by posting projects or papers for review and critique on a course management system and/or by using discussion boards, blogs, or wikis to exchange ideas as described earlier. Learners can compare their own mental models and perspectives with their colleagues, learn from one another, and collaborate to develop the most appropriate solution to the problem or issue at hand. Thus collaboration allows for diversity of thinking and encourages the development of a community of learners.

Follow the cognitive/constructivist example of encouraging learners to relate new learning to old by offering outlines, conceptual frameworks, and other "scaffolding" support. Many conceptual frameworks and analogies have been developed for teaching IL, such as the publication sequence, scholarly communication, and primary versus secondary literature. For more on this topic, see "Active Learning" in Chapter 6.

Giving the learners a bare bones outline with just the main points provided and asking them to add their own notes encourages them to be more active note takers. When using this approach, make sure you build in some writing/reflecting/note-taking catch-up time. This is especially true if you are working in an online environment, as it is harder to judge if your audience is keeping up with you. In a F2F situation have learners swap and compare notes to enhance the experience (Biggs, 1999a; Bligh, 2000; Freilberg and Driscoll, 2005; Johnson and Cooper, 2007). If you use presentation software like PowerPoint or Keynote, provide learners with handouts of your presentation that include your slides along with room for notes.

Applying the Humanist Model

The humanist approach is very much one of learner empowerment. It is an especially nurturing approach with its view that everyone can succeed if given the right support, opportunities, and encouragement. Humanists, with their strong belief that every learner has the ability to succeed, encourage us to create the type of warm and welcoming atmosphere that goes a long way toward reducing library and technology anxiety and promotes learning (Stemler et al., 2006).

Humanists invite us to listen to and respect our learners. Allowing learners to, in some way, participate in the design and direction of the learning experience demonstrates this idea of shared responsibility. The learner-centered teaching and self-directed/regulated learning approaches referred to both in the previous chapter and later in this chapter can help you to introduce this sense of shared responsibility into your teaching.

Humanists see the learner as a creative and dynamic person who has the capacity to deal with all problems successfully. Sharing your own experiences in learning the material and showing what you personally went through can serve as an example of this positive attitude. It demonstrates that everyone has to start somewhere but that you believe that if you can learn they can as well. Allowing everyone to move at his or her own pace—an idea shared with behaviorists—also reinforces this idea. Not every learner gets a concept instantaneously, but given enough time and effort everyone can learn any concept.

The principles of relevance and personal meaning are important to cognitive/constructivists and humanists alike. Because meaning is not necessarily inherent in what is being presented, the learners may have to instill this personal meaning into the subject matter themselves. Although it may seem self-evident to the instructor that the material being presented will be of use to the learner, the instructor needs to demonstrate that relevance to help learners make that connection (Freilberg and Driscoll, 2005). Showing the learners how the resource can help them find a job, get into graduate school, or get information about recreational activities, as well as demonstrating its educational merit, can go a long way in capturing the learner's attention. No matter how well organized the material may be, learners will not learn it unless it has personal significance to them. Instructors can help learners derive this personal meaning during F2F discussions of the topics under examination or through illustrative examples and descriptions in online modes of delivery. Once the IL instructor demonstrates to the learners how what is being presented will be beneficial to them, it is then up to the learners to decide whether or not they wish to acquire this knowledge.

Varying the Mix

The most effective IL instructor mixes and matches techniques from all three of the models. These instructors not only incorporate a variety of methods and techniques into their instructional endeavors, they also closely monitor learners' progress and adjust the teaching methods they use as appropriate. They might even decide to try a different approach if it appears that their first idea is not working. This is, of course, easier to do in a F2F situation than in either synchronous or asynchronous online instruction. On the other hand, online modes of delivery may be able to offer more learning options that the learners can mix and match themselves.

See the discussion of the instructional café in Chapter 8 for more on this idea. For additional information on online instruction, see Chapter 15.

Keep in mind that in order to effectively apply these theory-based principles to our ILI practice we must learn to let go in our teaching endeavors. We must move out of the spotlight and concentrate on doing more than just providing information to a hopefully rapt and possibly captive audience. Instead, we should concentrate on creating opportunities for people to take control of and be responsible for their own learning. In doing so, we will be encouraging them both to develop their own strategies for learning and to become information literate individuals who are lifelong learners.

TEACHING WITH THEORY IN MIND

Pulling the relevant parts of each of these theories together into a coherent and useful package may seem a bit daunting to the ILI teacher. Fortunately, a number of teaching paradigms, frameworks, and models have been developed that do just this. The following is a discussion of six models that incorporate elements of behaviorist, cognitive/constructivist, and humanist principles and also acknowledge the importance of dealing with variations in learning styles.

Learner-centered Teaching Model

Of all of the various frameworks for teaching that have developed over the years, the learner-centered teaching (LCT) model seems to represent a true melding of the three major psychological learning theories. In the LCT environment, learners are expected to be active participants in the process (as supported by all three theories), to take responsibility for their own learning in the humanist tradition, and to construct their own knowledge according to the cognitive/constructivist view of learning. Teachers monitor learning for mastery, provide encouragement, reinforce correct responses, and offer constructive feedback and suggestions to promote further learning (all behaviorist principles). Learners are given a great deal of say in how they will approach learning and how that learning will be assessed (in adherence to the humanist tradition). Furthermore, learners are often allowed to pick their own topics, thereby increasing the personal meaning of the material being studied (thus supporting the cognitive/constructivist and humanist principle of relevance). Self-reflection is generally a feature of this approach, as learners are expected not only to learn the material at hand but also to consider how they learned it and how that learning affects them personally. This self-reflection encourages the development of metacognitive abilities—a fundamental principle of both the cognitive/constructivists and the humanist instructional approaches.

LCT emphasizes the collaborative learning, group work, and authentic assignments/assessment teaching approaches suggested by both the cognitive/constructivist and humanist theories. LCT teachers encourage discovery and exploration, set the stage for problem solving, and act as a resource to support learning. Learner–teacher communication tends to be multidirectional (both teacher to learner and learner to learner) in the form of active questioning or interactive discussions. Traditional lecturing tends to be avoided. When included, lectures tend to be short and followed by some more interactive exchange (Bligh, 2000; Keyser, 2000; Weimer, 2002). For more on how to vary techniques, see Chapter 12.

So, how would we bring LCT into our ILI? If we have the luxury of teaching a full-term credit course (F2F or online), we can easily apply LCT approaches to our teaching. Topics can be approached from a problem-solving perspective. Learners can be placed into groups in order to solve these problems or address issues collaboratively during individual class sessions. Larger projects can also be assigned that require learners to work independently—alone or in groups—outside of class time. In these larger projects, the problems to be solved can be somewhat unstructured so that multiple solutions are possible. Learners then can attack the problem from many angles and go about solving it in ways that fit their own learning styles. Learners can be asked to grapple with the big IL issues such as censorship, free access to information, privacy of personal information, and impact of information in a global society. Allowing for sharing of the results of these projects with the entire group reinforces the LCT notion that learners are responsible not only for their own learning but also for that of their fellow learners.

But what happens if our contact time is limited to one or two 50- to 90-minute F2F encounters? How can we apply LCT approaches in this setting while still giving our learners a quality experience? The first thing we need to do in order to get into the LCT mode is to give up the idea that we have to be the ones driving the instruction.

We often feel that we have so much we need to get across that the only way to do so is to pour that information into the learners' heads. However, cramming more and more material into our instructional endeavors does not lead to lasting learning. Plus, it tends to overwhelm our learners and causes them to tune out or create feelings of inadequacy because they cannot possible learn all of this material (Fink, 2003; King, 1993).

What do we do? We have so much to cover and so little time to do it. How can we "cover" it all if we let our learners loose to work on their own? First, if you are in a synchronous (F2F or online) situation with limited contact time, keep in mind that less is more as you develop your instruction. If we feel we have to talk at top speed for the entire session in order to "cover" all the material, maybe we are trying to do too much. Perhaps we can put some of this content into handouts or post it on an easily accessible Web page. Once you have done that, you can concentrate on the most important elements of the content that you feel need to be addressed in the F2F or synchronous online setting (Clark and Taylor, 1994). If you are planning for asynchronous instruction, you still want to make sure you are not including more material than can be reasonably absorbed. Make sure that each segment or "chunk" is short enough to hold the interest of the learner, and incorporate "tests for mastery" activities to serve as breaks between each segment or "chunk."

Second, keep in mind that people pay attention to only what matters to them personally. Asking your learners to write down their questions as they enter the classroom and organizing your session around these questions really exhibits your commitment to making sure you are presenting relevant and useful material. Or you can list possible topics on the board and ask the group to vote on which ones they want you to cover. You can use these techniques in a synchronous online session as well by using online chat or instant messaging technologies that are often available in course management systems or desktop lecturing software. In an asynchronous setting, you can allow learners the option of picking and choosing among a variety of topics—letting them work on the ones that are of most relevance to them—and possibly the order in which they work on these topics.

Blogs and wikis are another way to involve your learners when teaching in an asynchronous environment. Learners can submit their questions, and you can offer your instruction in response. Furthermore, this interactive Q and A approach can allow people to learn from one another as participants contribute their own ideas and experiences. These technologies (and others like them) can be used by themselves or as part of other types of online instruction. They can be included at the end of an online tutorial or pathfinder, for example, as a way for learners to continue to interact with the material and with you.

Third, keep in mind that people learn and retain better if they actively interact with the material in some way. Look at the learning outcomes you expect your learners to attain and see how your "lecture" might be turned into a more active experience. Instead of demonstrating the features of a number of relevant databases, have learners explore these databases in small groups and then report back to the full group in some fashion. They can even be asked to create posters that would help "sell" their database to others. You do not have to supply a lot of elaborate supplies, although the more you can offer the more fun it can be. Poster board or flip chart paper can serve as the basis. Pens, crayons, stickers, scissors, colored paper or cards, and glue are all useful. Go wild as long as you stay within your budget. This "poster session" idea could also be done in an online environment by asking learners to develop PowerPoint or other presentation software "shows" to be posted on a course site. Asynchronous online instruction should also be planned with interactivity in mind. A little creative thinking can go a long way to making your online material engaging and an active learning experience. See Chapter 6 for other active learning ideas, Chapter 12 for more on LCT examples, and Chapter 15 for more suggestions about using technology to support pedagogy.

Finally, make sure you leave time for learners to think about and reflect on what has happened in the instruction. If possible, do this in a way that allows them to share with others to increase the efficacy of this reflection. In the F2F format, simply asking learners to share one thing they learned—either in writing or verbally—reinforces the LCT approach as you are asking them to review the material rather than you doing it for them. This can be done via chat in the synchronous online environment. If you are offering asynchronous instruction of some kind, you could end your material with a segment that asks learners to summarize what they have learned. Even if you have no way of collecting this information, the act of summarizing can increase learners' grasp of the material. If you can collect this material, responding to the learners in some way would increase the effectiveness of this technique. Responses can be to individuals or summarized to the group and posted where the learners can easily access them.

Moving to a more LTC approach may seem scary at first. It is okay to go slow. Just review what you are trying to teach and examine it from the LCT perspective. Pick one or two things you could incorporate into your instruction that would reflect this approach and experiment with these ideas based on the constraints and characteristics of your mode of delivery (F2F, online, synchronous, or asynchronous). You can add more LCT ideas in future endeavors. You might find that reconsidering your teaching from the LCT viewpoint will end up reenergizing your teaching and make the experience more engaging for both you and your learners.

Self-directed/regulated Learning Model

One of the goals of self-directed/regulated learning (SDL) is to help learners develop self-awareness about their own learning process (Areglado, Bradley, and Lane, 1996; Boud, 1988; Higgs, 1988; Taylor, 1987). As such, this method has close ties to LCT. Both deal with giving learners options and more control over and responsibility for their own learning. However, LCT seems more focused on the cognitive side of the equation, while SDL is more concerned with the affective aspects of learning. It is important to keep in mind that allowing learners to work at their own pace is not the same as encouraging an SDL approach. Being self-directed is a characteristic of the learner, not a characteristic of the methodology being used. A self-directed learner, for example, would be someone who looks for supplemental material to help him or her understand the material to be learned. The self-directed learner would take the time to rewrite and paraphrase material presented by the instructor or in the reading material. He or she would also determine the approach for reviewing and studying the material that is personally relevant and effective. In other words, the self-directed learner figures out how to monitor and organize his or her own habits in order to enhance learning (Dalsgaard and Godsk, 2007).

Teachers must pay special attention to metacognition and reflection experiences during learning in order to encourage learners to develop these SDL habits. Whereas the LCT teacher might ask learners to reflect on the content of the learning, the SDL teacher would ask questions that encourage learners to think about how they related to the content and to the learning experience. Learners should consider how they felt while learning this material, think about which teaching and learning methods were most useful to them, and reflect on what, if any, value the content had for them. In an ILI endeavor we would ask learners to consider the ways in which gaining IL expertise empowers them. Or we could ask them how they feel about information and the information gathering experience. SDL teachers would be very concerned with library anxiety issues and would try to include some way for learners to express their feelings about these issues.

Both the LCT and SDL models put much of the responsibility for learning in the hands of the learner. Options play a big part in both models. Although each tries to give learners some choice about how to engage with material, the SDL teacher wants to encourage learners to make their decisions based on personal preference in terms of learning styles. Just like the LCT teacher, the SDL teacher would also endorse group work but for a slightly different reason. Whereas the LCT teacher is doing so for its social learning benefit, the SDL teacher views group work as a way for individuals to approach the topic in their own way—that is, according to their own learning style preference. The more trial-and-error, impulsive, concrete learner will probably be the one who does the keying when the group is exploring a new IL resource. The more abstract, reflective, inner-directed person might be happy observing, recording, and synthesizing the material. The global thinkers might wish to be given the opportunity to report their findings back to the larger group. For more on learning styles, see Chapter 3.

Although it is easy to see how a SDL environment can be encouraged in the F2F delivery mode, some of the online synchronous and asynchronous examples described in the LCT section could be adapted for the SDL model. Opportunities that encourage "virtual" reflection and the development of metacognition skills have already been addressed. Group work/projects that allow for individuals to contribute according to their preferred styles are often a part of online asynchronous courses. Offering options in asynchronous delivery formats (i.e., an online tutorial, slideshow, or print workbook) would also allow learners to be self-directed and select the approach that is most appealing to them. If you have the resources, you might even allow learners to choose between an online (synchronous or asynchronous) and a F2F version of the instruction. While these later two suggestions up the ante on the cost (in time, money, and effort) of delivering the instruction, they would definitely support SDL principles by allowing learners to find their own way through the subject matter and select the approach that is most efficacious for them. The various options do not all have to be developed simultaneously. You might start with one or two options and add more as time and circumstances permit. Keep in mind that you will need to factor in maintenance and updating of any material you develop.

The Information-seeking Process Model

Kuhlthau's information-seeking process (ISP) model is a direct application of theory to ILI practice. Her extensive research has enlightened us on the steps most learners go through as they pursue a research topic. One of the fundamental tenets of this approach is that if we share the process with our learners, they will be better able to cope with the cognitive and affective challenges involved at each step. Learners will discover they are not alone when they feel anxiety or frustration at the beginning of the process—nor will they think they are doing something wrong when they discover they need to backtrack on their research if they have taken a wrong turn or need more information to support their ideas (Kuhlthau, 1985, 1988, 2004).

The ISP model considers both the affective and the cognitive sides of learning. However, this approach looks at how the affective aspects contribute to or detract from learners' abilities to perform in the behavioral and cognitive realms of learning. The ISP model with its emphasis on the feelings associated with information seeking has strong connections to humanist principles such as relevance, self-actualization, and self-efficacy. The approach encourages the use of reflection and the development of metacognitive skills throughout the process—thus aligning it to the cognitive/constructivist as well as to the humanist approach. Furthermore, learners using the ISP model are expected to be active participants in the process as per the tenets of behaviorist theory. Teachers who structure their instruction along ISP lines often model the steps in the process—another behaviorist practice. Furthermore, the six steps outlined in the ISP can be viewed as a way of breaking the entire process into manageable "chunks" as per the behaviorist tradition.

Cunningham and Carr provide a model for applying this approach to a full-term ILI course. They introduce the ISP conceptual framework at the beginning of the course and then use it to structure the week-to-week sessions. Learners in both Kuhlthau's research and those who experienced the Cunningham and Carr approach report an increase in satisfaction and comfort level with doing information-gathering research (Cunningham and Carr, 2008; Kuhlthau, 1989, 2004).

Given a little thought we can also see how we can use this model in our so-called one shots. For example, we could start our session by asking our learners how they feel when they are given an assignment that requires gathering information on a topic. You could ask them to write down their feelings on Post-it notes and then let them paste their notes on the board. If they see other notes that are similar to their own, tell them to put them together. The resultant clusters of responses should help learners understand that it is okay to feel some anxiety and other negative feelings at the beginning of a project.

Or you could try a concept map exercise in which people just call out words or phrases they associate with the information-gathering process. You can then ask them to group these words and phrases into clusters and perhaps ask them to gather clusters into "How I feel at the beginning, middle, and end of the process" categories. The end result should come close to the feeling attached to each stage of the ISP. If you are working in an online environment, you could collect this information from the participants ahead of time via some kind of anonymous surveying product or at the very beginning of the instruction through polling software.

Attention, Relevance, Confidence, Satisfaction Model

John Keller's Attention, Relevance, Confidence, Satisfaction (ARCS) model offers another technique for structuring the instructional experience in a way that maximizes the learners' opportunities to develop the self-confidence and self-efficacy associated with humanist approaches. It can be seen as incorporating elements of behaviorist and cognitive/constructivist theories of learning as well. Both cognitive/constructivists and humanists would applaud ARCS's emphasis on personal meaning and relevance. Behaviorists would appreciate the elements of active learning and hands-on practice that provide instructors with opportunities to offer constructive feedback and reinforcement (Driscoll, 1994; Kaplowitz, 2008; Keller, 1987).

The ARCS educational experience emphasizes the capturing and sustaining of attention, incorporating relevant and diverse examples into the process, building confidence by creating opportunities for success, and creating satisfaction as the learners acquire new skills and abilities. When you start your instruction with some thought-provoking quote or an attention- getting video, you are applying the Attention part of the ARCS methodology. Follow that with opportunities for learners to work on topics of their own choice and you are employing Relevance. Using a variety of examples that reflect various cultural, ethnic, gender, and age differences in your learners also enhances the Relevance of the learning experience. Confidence and Satisfaction can occur through allowing learners some hands-on practice time in which they can demonstrate their newly developed skills and receive constructive feedback and reinforcement. Using the ARCS methodology in this manner can help us incorporate many of the principles associated with psychological learning into our instructional endeavors (Kaplowitz, 2008).

Experience–Practice–Application Model

The goal of the Experience–Practice–Application (EPA) model is to encourage curiosity and creativity through the use of authentic problem solving, active learning, and collaboration. Again, we can see elements of all three theories of learning represented in this approach. EPA emphasizes varying how learners interact with information through thinking, talking, listening, hands-on activities, and individual and group work, thus making use of techniques associated with each of the theories. EPA starts with exploring what learners already know or have experienced and then asks them to build on this prior knowledge as per cognitive/constructivist principles. EPA instructors use humanist techniques such as reflective writing, finding analogies, and directed question and answer sessions to get at this information and to help learners see how what they already know can apply to the new material they are trying to learn as well as to highlight the relevance of the material. Instructors can model these applications (a behaviorist practice), lead discussions on how to connect old knowledge to new, or create an exercise in which learners, individually or in groups, try to figure out how what they know might be applied to what they are trying to learn how to do.

Next learners are invited to try out (practice) the ideas generated by the previous discussions, demonstrations, or group work so that they can build a sense of personal confidence in their newly acquired skills, thus combining the humanist principle of self-efficacy with the cognitive/constructivist principles of metacognition and construction of new knowledge. Finally, EPA teachers can help learners transfer these skills to different situations by giving them a chance to apply what they have learned to something new and by providing feedback at various points in the instruction so that learners know how well they are doing. The hands-on characteristics of the practice and application steps certainly align with behaviorist principles of reinforcement and active involvement in learning (Hensley, 2004; Kaplowitz, 2008; Sparks-Langer, 2000; Veldof, 2006).

In an ILI setting, you can start the experience segment by asking learners what types of information they looked for recently. They might come up with weather forecasts, movie reviews, class schedules, definitions, and maybe even information on a topic. Then ask how they went about finding that information. Next lead a discussion of the pros and cons of the methods used and how those methods might be appropriate or inappropriate for academic-type information gathering. As the group settles on possible approaches, you can either demonstrate them yourself or ask the learners to try out the different approaches and report back to the whole group. The more effective approaches should begin to emerge from this exercise/discussion. Once these approaches are identified, you can give the learners the opportunity to try them out—perhaps on topics of their own choice. Finally, you can set a new problem for them to see if they can transfer learning to a new situation. For example, if you have spent time having them search a certain database, can they apply what they learned from that to a new, never before seen database? Or if they have identified appropriate resources for a science topic, can they now do the same for one that has a more historical focus?

Presentation–Application–Feedback Model

Although similar to the EPA approach, the Presentation–Application–Feedback (PAF) model emphasizes the importance of "doing" or the application portion of instruction. Most of the instructional content is placed in the hands of the learner as he or she tries to apply what has been learned. Thus this approach also resonates with the LCT model. The PAF approach starts with some kind of instructor-lead presentation or demonstration as per the behaviorist principle of modeling. This portion could include any of the questioning and discussion techniques described earlier. An important characteristic of the Presentation segment is that at this point in the instruction the instructor is doing the bulk of the work. However, a second characteristic is that this segment is as brief as possible—only long enough for learners to gain enough information to be able to start working on their own. No more than one-third of the session should be spent in the Presentation mode.

The Application segment is where actual learning takes place as learners are asked to perform. They are given the opportunity to try out their new skills in a variety of situations and to demonstrate that they have indeed "gotten it." Instructors and assistants answer questions and offer guidance as needed. Worksheets are often provided for learners to complete as they work on the various tasks assigned to them. The Application segment clearly emphasizes the learning-by-doing behaviorist approach. However, the Feedback element combines behaviorist reinforcement principles with cognitive/constructivist and humanist ideas of self-efficacy and reflection, as learners are encouraged to think about and celebrate their successful completion of the application activities.

Feedback occurs both during Application activities and at the end of instruction. During Application activities instructors can praise (reinforce) those who are performing well and help clear up confusion for those who are going off track. Instructors can also offer suggestions to all learners about how they can improve their performance as they observe learning in action as per the teacher-as-facilitator aspect of both cognitive/constructivist and humanist approaches. Reflection activities such as the one-minute paper can act as a review of the material and also provide feedback to both the learners and the instructor. The Feedback element of the PAF model also offers opportunities for instructors to see how well learners are succeeding at attaining the learning objectives set out for the instruction (Veldof, 2006).

All six of these models can be adapted for use in synchronous F2F or online situations as well as for asynchronous modes of teaching. Although online teaching may be less familiar to the IL instructor than F2F approaches, the models, techniques, and methods that have been developed from the psychological learning theory literature can be adapted for use in online settings. While it may be easier for us to see how to apply theory to our F2F instruction, applying theory to practice in an online setting is worth exploring. Some examples of using learning theory principles in online settings have already been discussed, especially in connection with LCT and SDL. The following are just a few brief ideas about how to apply theory to practice in an online teaching situation.

If you teach in a synchronous online environment, you can easily replicate some of the in-person ideas we have discussed. Using examples that are relevant to your learners is as important in this environment as it is in F2F instruction. Discussions can be multidirectional as learners engage with one another as well as with you through chat or discussion boards. As mentioned already, multidirectional discussions highlight diversity of thinking and also contribute to metacognition and reflection as learners make their ideas visible to all (Fink, 2003; Lowyck and Poysa, 2001; Rovai, 2004). Options can be given about how to interact with material—by reading, listening to audio material, viewing animated content, and so on. Learners can interact in groups or learn on their own. Projects can be assigned that replicate real-world experiences, allowing learners to work on authentic problems. Learners can be assigned exercises to work on during the synchronous period and then report back on their experiences as in an F2F class. If you are "meeting" with them for more than one session, learners can be asked to explore on their own time and report back at a later date. In many ways online instruction experiences offer multiple opportunities to apply learning principles because you have more available to you than what is physically present in the classroom. They support LCT approaches and can be appealing to more self-directed, independent learners (Diaz and Cartnal, 1999; Doherty and Maddux, 2002; Heller-Ross, 2000; Mestre, 2006; Sullivan, 2004; Weimer, 2002; Yi, 2005).

Asynchronous online experiences can provide much of the same variety and options as those in a synchronous online environment. Although you lose the opportunity to have live conversations and group discussions, you can make use of e-mail, discussion boards, blogs, and other social networking or virtual world technologies to increase contact between you and the learners and among the learners themselves. Interactive technologies make it easier to create online environments that allow learners to learn by doing, to receive feedback, to refine their understanding, and to build new mental models (Bonk and Graham, 2006; Bransford et al., 1999a; Fink, 2003; Gordon and Stephens, 2006; Heintzelman et al., 2007; Lowyck and Poysa, 2001; Mayer, 2005a; Olgren, 2000; Sullivan, 2004). With a little thought and some creative experimentation, your online instruction can allow learners to actively interact with material, receive feedback from you on their work, construct their own knowledge, relate personally to the material being learned, and even be asked to reflect on their own learning. Keep in mind that the same ideas you might have for "stand-alone" technology-based asynchronous instruction might be useful as a means to extend your contact time with your synchronous F2F or online learners (Chickering and Ehrmann, 1996; Dewald, 1999a, 1999b; Dewald et al., 2000; Freilberg and Driscoll, 2005; Lage, Platt, and Treglia, 2000; Yi, 2005). For more on using technology to support pedagogy, see Chapter 15.

TEACHING WITH STYLE

Another approach to applying theory to practice is to see what the learning styles literature has to offer us. As discussed in Chapter 3, learning styles research looks at how our learners vary rather than starting from the perspective of the different models or theories of learning. However, if we look at how some of this research has been applied in the teaching environment, we can see that these approaches rely heavily on principles already discussed in relation to the three major theories or models of learning.

Making Your Instruction Styles-friendly

One way to look at the styles research is to examine individual styles and then try to include various activities and ideas that will appeal to a cross section for different learners. For example, make sure your topics are relevant to your learners, use attention-getting examples when you model resources and strategies, and offer a variety of learning experiences that will appeal to the competitor, the cooperative learner, the intrinsically or the extrinsically motivated individual in order to reach various types of affective learners. Offer conceptual frameworks or Advance Organizers to help those learners with high structural needs and provide exploration and discovery opportunities for those with low structural needs (Dunn, 2000; Dunn and Griggs, 2000; Kaplowitz, 2008). Here are a few more suggestions about some specific style variations.

Mobility Needs

To allow for variations in mobility needs when teaching in a F2F or an online synchronous situation allow for breaks in instruction and incorporate different types of activities. This will give learners the freedom to move around and stretch if they wish. Asynchronous instruction opportunities can be particularly appealing to those with high mobility needs, especially if they allow learners some latitude in how long they work at one stretch. Online tutorials or print worksheets or books that allow learners to take a break and return at a later time have a great deal of appeal for high mobility needs learners.

For a F2F setting, try to design your classrooms so that furniture can be moved into various configurations to accommodate a variety of activities. This has the double benefit of dealing with mobility issues and also supports more active learning experiences. Placing learners at tables rather than in rows encourages learner-to-learner interactions. Learners seated in circles speak more to those seated across from them than to those seated beside them. When you are speaking to the entire class remember that those who are seated in the front or in the middle of the room tend to be those who are more inclined to be involved in the class. Make an extra effort to include those who are in the back or along the sides by moving around the room and engaging in eye contact with these more reluctant learners (Cruickshank, Jenkins, and Metcalf, 2003).

Time of Day Preferences

Although we may not have much control over when a class is scheduled or have the luxury of scheduling multiple classes at different times, we should still be aware of time of day preferences and see if we can offer some alternatives that might assist those learners trapped in a nonpreferred situation. Obviously, differences in the "time of day preferences" style are most relevant for synchronous (F2F or online) learning environments. One of the biggest appeals of asynchronous learning approaches is that learners can utilize them at their own convenience and therefore at their most optimal time of day for learning.

Modality Preferences

When teaching in the F2F setting, using a combination of lecture/demonstration, written handouts, and hands-on exercises increases the instructional appeal to aural, visual, and kinesthetic learners. Aural learners benefit most from the lecture and descriptions that accompany the demonstration. Visual learners appreciate modeling and demonstrations but are delighted to have handouts (or Web pages) that they can read and refer to at a later time. Kinesthetic learners enjoy any opportunity that allows them to actively interact with the material to be learned.

Online offerings (synchronous or asynchronous) should be developed with this mixing of formats idea in mind as well. Combining text with graphics and/or animation can increase the appeal of this material as can the appropriate addition of voice-over narration. Exercises, quizzes, and other interactive opportunities can also be built into online offerings for more kinesthetic learners.

Impulsives/Reflectives

Include times of quiet refection during instruction to assist the "reflectives" in your F2F or online synchronous classes. If possible, provide a mechanism in which learning goes on beyond the F2F synchronous experience to allow for further reflection. The "impulsives" in your group will like any fast-paced activity, such as brainstorming exercises and competitive problem-solving games, and will even enjoy quizzes to some extent. If possible, make use of instructional technology and course-management systems that allow everyone to express their opinions and exhibit their grasp of the material in their own time and in their own way. Offer some options for learning and responding in order to reach those with these different approaches to learning.

Asynchronous learning environments that allow for learning at one's own pace really address differences in this style. Each learner can choose the rate at which he or she will interact with the material and can either speed through or take as long as he or she wishes to reflect on it.

The techniques described to address individual styles can be useful to the ILI teacher, but none of these is sufficient to deal with the broader issues associated with the learning styles literature. Incorporating any of these approaches will address the needs of only some of your learners. A more global approach can be achieved if we consider the two learning styles instruments described in Chapter 3. Each offers ideas about how to create a more inclusive instructional experience that will appeal to a cross section of learners.

Kolb's Experiential Learning Model

Although literature exists that discusses how to vary instruction to reach people with different cognitive, affective, or physiological styles, David Kolb took this idea one step further. Kolb not only offered us a way to identify different types of learners through his Learning Styles Inventory (LSI), he also developed a teaching paradigm that creates opportunities for each type of learner. The method consists of four stages (Kolb and Fry, 1975). Let's look at each of these in turn.

Concrete Experience

During the concrete experience portion of the instruction, learners are offered concrete examples and are allowed to interact with them in order to develop their own generalizations. The discovery method and other types of hands-on experiences would fall into this category. If there is not enough time for the discovery method or if you do not have a hands-on facility, you can accomplish concrete experience through demonstrations and examples. Demonstrating what you wish people to learn and encouraging them to formulate ideas about what they are seeing is a form of concrete experience.

Reflective Observation

In reflective observation, learners are encouraged to observe their experiences and reflect upon them in order to form their own explanations of these experiences. Providing opportunities for learners to gather their thoughts about these demonstrations and/or their own experiences in the form of a research journal would qualify as reflective observation. Research journals can also be seen as a way for learners to develop metacognition skills, because they are encouraged to reflect upon their thinking during the research process (McGregor, 1999). Reflective observation can also be done through in-class or online discussions as well as classroom assessment techniques such as the one-minute paper (Angelo and Cross, 1993).

Abstract Conceptualization

Abstract conceptualization is the theory-building stage during which learners are actively involved in testing out their ideas. Group activities can be valuable at this stage as individual learners compare their ideas and test out assumptions in order to develop their final theoretical framework. Writing research papers, using analogies during discussions, or developing models or frameworks all appeal to the abstract conceptualizer.

Active Experimentation

During active experimentation, learners apply their theories to real-life situations. This is the realm of problem- or case-based exercises where practical applications are tested out to see how well theories hold up. Fieldwork or laboratory experimentation also falls into this category.

Each of these stages appeals to a different type of learner and offers each the opportunity to interact with the material in a preferred manner. Although the stages have been presented in a particular order, it is not necessary to always follow that order. However, according to Kolb, the learner must go through all four stages in order for learning to be complete. The value of this approach is that somewhere during the instruction, each learner is given the opportunity to shine—that is, to work within his or her preferred style.

To see how this plays out for ILI, take a look at Sonia Bodi's classic 1990 article. In this application of Kolb's experiential learning method, Bodi illustrates how you can vary your instruction even in a 50- to 70-minute session. The instruction includes a lecture/demo accompanied by sample material. Learners then complete a worksheet and develop a partially annotated bibliography on a topic of their choice following the lecture. Learners are required to meet with the instructor to discuss their progress after they have reflected on their experiences. Finally, learners must write a five-page research paper based on the gathered information. Each of the four learning styles is addressed by this methodology, thereby increasing the likelihood that learners will interact with the material in a way that matches their style. Note that this method expands the learning experience beyond the actual F2F contact time. Kolb's experiential learning method continues to have relevance as an ILI approach even 30 years after Bodi published her work on this subject (Train and Elkin, 2001).

Although Bodi's (1990) scenario relies heavily on F2F experiences, the current instructional technology environment would allow for many of these interactions to occur virtually instead (Gooler, 1990; Mayer, 2003; Mestre, 2006). For example, learners could discuss progress with the instructor via e-mail. Video conferencing can allow for collaborative work in real time. Webcasts can assist the visual learner. Worksheets could be translated into interactive online exercises to offer some hands-on practice opportunities. Feedback on these exercises could be built into the online experience directly, or the exercises could be sent to the instructor for review. Technology not only has expanded our reach but also has offered us more opportunities to create experiences that appeal to different types of learners. A blended learning environment that combines synchronous meetings with asynchronous online learning experiences can offer even more variety for our learners (Bonk and Graham, 2006). See Chapters 6 and 15 for more on this topic.

The Learning Styles Questionnaire Approach

Although the developers of the Learning Styles Questionnaire (LSQ) (Honey and Mumford, accessed 2008) did not create an overall teaching scenario to address the four styles identified by their questionnaire, if we look at each of the learning types, we can come up with an instructional experience similar to Kolb's experiential learning model that would address this issue. If we wish to appeal to each of the four LSQ learners, we should again have a variety of experiences in our instruction as described later (Kaplowitz, 2008; Train and Elkin, 2001). Keep in mind that the LSQ gives the learner scores in each of the four categories and so allows for a combination of styles, as opposed to Kolb's LSI, which categorizes the learner as one of the four types included in that inventory. Also remember that although we may each have a preferred style (or combination of styles) the most successful learners can adapt to any situation as needed. However, operating in a nonpreferred mode is more difficult and time consuming for learners as they must not only learn the material but also must try to translate the way it is being taught into something to which they can relate.

Activists

Activists like the thrill of discovery and enjoy new experiences. They bore easily and like fast-paced instruction, with lots of opportunities to try new things. They are also very social in their approach and so like opportunities to interact with other learners. Activists are concerned with "what's next?" or "what's new?" Activities that let learners try things out on their own appeal to this type of learner, as does any kind of brainstorming exercise. *Caution:* Although they like to work in groups, activists can be a bit overbearing and intolerant of learners who like to take their time to reflect on and discuss new information. It is helpful to offer guidelines to the groups before they begin work to try to keep this tendency in check. You can also monitor group interactions during the activity and intercede if it seems necessary.

Reflectors

To appeal to the reflectors, we need to offer opportunities to stand back and review experiences from different perspectives. Reflectors tend to be more cautious and do not jump to conclusions. They enjoy observing others in action and so the use of demonstrations is particularly good with this type of learner. Reflectors are interested in the "whys" and need time to think about things. Think/pair/share exercises are good for this type of learner, because they include time for individual reflection followed by sharing with just one other person before general group discussion takes place. Reflectors will probably be the observers and recorders when working with others in a group situation. Care must be given to allow reflectors the opportunity to participate in discussions. Let impulsives respond to your questions or contribute to your discussion topic first. They will want to do so anyway. Then ask for input from anyone else who has not spoken up as yet. This gives your reflectors time to gather their thoughts and offers them an opportunity to contribute as well.

Theorists

Theorists enjoy developing theories, principles, models, and systems. They tend to be logical, detached, and analytical. Subjective or ambiguous situations can be disturbing for the theorist who focuses on the "what" behind the situation. The theorists will enjoy pulling it all together after exercises or discussion periods. These learners will be enthusiastic about exercises and discussions that focus on reviewing and summing up what has been learned. They may offer their own ideas about the content—some of which might be surprising and offer new insight. These are the learners that make you go "Wow—I never thought of that before!"

Pragmatists

Finally, pragmatists like to apply theory to practice. They look for new ideas and approaches that they can experiment with and apply to their particular situation. Pragmatists like to work with situations that have a clear purpose and outcome. These learners ask, "How can I use that in my environment?" Pragmatists like to work on real-world scenarios. Case- or problem-based, authentic exercises or assignments have great appeal to them. Letting them work on problems of their own design is also a good approach with pragmatists.

Although the LSI and the LSQ use different terms and idiosyncratic terminology to describe the various learning styles being measured, they both point to the fact that we all learn in different ways. As teachers we must take this idea seriously if we expect to reach all of our learners successfully. Whether we think about learners in terms of divergers, convergers, adaptors, and assimilators or as activists, pragmatists, theorists, and reflectors, the bottom line is that we must offer our learners a variety of experiences during our synchronous or asynchronous instructional endeavors in order to be effective teachers. Fortunately, the three theories or models of learning offer us a rich body of techniques and scenarios to pick from as we design our instruction. As we examine the various principles associated with these schools, and the approaches that have grown from them, we can select and combine techniques so that we are appealing to and engaging learners with the widest variety of learning styles preferences possible.

MOTIVATION—GETTING OUR LEARNERS TO WANT TO LEARN

To paraphrase an old adage, "You can lead someone to instruction, but you cannot make him or her learn."

Creating a varied and dynamic instructional environment is only part of the battle. Learners must be willing to do the work involved and to accept the importance of that work. Learners will do quality work only if they believe the work they are being asked to do will satisfy their needs (Glasser, 1992; Marzano et al., 1988). They need to know "what is in it for them" before they will commit to the experience. In other words, they must be motivated to learn.

Motivation is a key element in all three theories or models of learning. Learning does not take place unless learners are there with you in the experience. So, how do we motivate our learners in our ILI? We may not have had a long-term connection with our learners that would help build trust and rapport. Nor do we have any power to bestow extrinsic rewards such as grades unless we are teaching for-credit courses. This is where many of the ideas related to teaching as facilitation rather than direction comes into play. If we engage in two-way conversations with our learners in our F2F or synchronous online encounters instead of just spewing information at them, they are bound to pay more attention and be more motivated to learn. Even better, encourage multi-way conversations so that learners are talking to one another as well as to you as the teacher (Bligh, 2000). Giving people responsibility for their own and their colleagues' learning will also increase motivation. Cooperative or collaborative learning methods can be very motivating, as they appeal to people's desires to belong as described by Maslow's hierarchy of needs (Glasser, 1992; Maslow, 1954). Furthermore, in an age when social networking plays such an important role in day-to-day living, group experiences in which knowledge is constructed collectively has a great deal of natural appeal.

Online environments offer many opportunities for learners to collaborate, synchronously or asynchronously, on projects, exercises, and other assignments and to exchange ideas via online discussions. Moving to a more facilitator role is as important in online instructional environments as it is in F2F ones. Teachers make themselves available to answer questions and support collaborative efforts, but they allow learners to make their own way through the assignment. Ground rules for working in teams should be established early to ensure successful collaborative efforts. Rules for exchanges via discussion boards should stress courtesy and the value of everyone's contributions. Teachers should monitor these boards to make sure the rules are being followed, answer questions as needed and offer constructive comments on postings that will help guide the discussion. But teachers must avoid taking over the conversation. Teachers should comment cautiously, as learners will view their comments as expert information (Vrasidas and McIssac, 2000). One approach is for teachers to wait until the discussion is over before posting their comments and opinions on the topic. See Chapter 15 for more on this topic.

Learning by doing, constructing one's own knowledge, and finding personal meaning in that which is being learned all contribute to the motivational aspect of instruction. Allowing learners to manipulate experiences to meet their own needs and/or interests and to relate to and find personal relevance in the experience is far more motivating than our telling them that what we have to say is good for them. Furthermore, allowing learners to interact with material each in his or her own preferred ways not only shows respect for our different learners but also makes the experience more comfortable and engaging for everyone. Learners' motivations increase because they are not being forced to try and fit themselves into someone else's learning stylistic shoes.

Using analogies or other ways of showing learners how what they already know can help them in this new learning experience also has motivational benefits. It helps learners see that what is being taught is not strange or alien and thus reduces anxiety—the enemy of motivation. Using learners' own examples, asking them to talk about their feelings about information gathering, and using topics that are currently in the news are all ways to capture learners' attention and help to point out what they stand to gain by participating in the learning experience.

And, of course, we cannot forget the motivational potential inherent in the ways we interact with our learners. Smiling, nodding, and offering verbal praise all go a long way to help learners feel good about themselves and the progress they are making. Providing timely feedback to questions, comments, and assignments in both synchronous and asynchronous online learning environments is also an important way to help learners sustain their interest in and motivation for the material being studied. A warm, supportive, and welcoming environment is a motivating one. Talk to your learners—not at them. Listen carefully to what they have to say. Show respect for and interest in your learners, and they will be more motivated to actively participate in the experience.

FINAL REMARKS

Research into learning styles tells us that we need to vary our approaches in order to reach all of our learners. Theories of learning offer us many options for how to design our instruction. Understanding the principles associated with psychological learning theories helps us make informed decisions about the ways we can mix and match methods in order to create instructional experiences that are appropriate for the material being taught and the audience we are trying to reach (Powis and Webb, 2005).

Flexibility, self-awareness, and open-mindedness are the keys to instructional effectiveness. Your willingness to try new approaches, especially ones that may not be compatible with your own personal preferences, and your ability to take risks in your teaching will allow you to reach a variety of learners. And your capacity to change approaches even in the middle of a session, if you sense you are losing your audience, will increase the likelihood that each person will have a positive learning experience regardless of his or her learning style preference.

Moving into new teaching territory takes courage and reflection. Think about the teaching methods you tend to use. Do they seem to fall into the behaviorist, cognitive/constructivist, or humanist approach? Are there some methods that you rarely or never use? Do those methods make you feel a bit uncomfortable? Can you get over that discomfort and try to include some of these "outside your comfort zone" methods so that you can reach learners who may have learning preferences that differ from yours? It might help to start small. Do one new and different thing. Reflect on the results both from your perspective and from that of the learners. If it seemed to work well, keep it in your teaching arsenal. If not, think about how to improve it or if necessary replace it with some other new and different idea. Keep experimenting with new ideas. It will keep your teaching fresh and interesting for you and your learners.

Do not rely just on what is written about psychological learning theory. Increase your awareness of how others teach as well. Cultivate the traits of the critical observer. When you watch someone else teach, see if you can identify methods that relate to different learning theories. Think about how those methods might help your instructional endeavors appeal to a variety of learners with different learning styles. If some of these methods do not appeal to you completely, consider how you could modify them so that they could be incorporated into your instructional efforts.

To further enhance your self-reflection, take one of the many learning styles instruments that have been developed. The major ones are usually fee based, but you can also find some freely available on the Internet. Keep in mind that these free instruments may not be as reliable or valid as the ones for which you have to pay. However, if used cautiously, they might provide you with some idea about your personal learning style. Reflect upon what you discover about yourself to help you decide if you seem to be focusing on methods that appeal primarily to your own style. Learn as much as you can about the other styles and try to think of ways to develop approaches that would appeal to these other types of learners. Challenge yourself to try something new and even difficult for you. Look at styles that are most different from your own. These tend to be the hardest ones for us to deal with. But to ignore them puts you at risk of disenfranchising at least some of your learners.

Remember the humanist credo that everyone is capable of learning. It is up to us to present the material in a way that will appeal to our learners. Variety is the key. While we may not be able to identify the style of each and every learner we encounter, varying the techniques in our instructional endeavors and offering as much choice as possible increases the likelihood of reaching most if not all of them. Learning style preference research points out the ways people can vary. Learning theories and their practical applications offer us a variety of approaches that we can use in an attempt to accommodate these variations.

EXERCISES

1. Review the various approaches described in this chapter, such as LCT, SDL, ISP, ARCS, EPA, the experiential learning method, and the LSQ approach. What are the similarities and differences among these approaches? Do some of them appeal to you more than others? Reflect on why this might be so. Pay special attention to those that do not seem to appeal

to you and consider what is bothering you about these approaches.

Try to design an instructional experience that reflects the framework that most appeals to you. Then redesign the experience using one of the frameworks that holds less of an appeal and compare the results. Would it be possible for you to combine your two designs into one that reflects aspects of both frameworks?

2. Read more about the styles discussed in the Kolb LSI, the Honey-Mumford LSQ, or another learning styles test of your own choosing. If possible, actually take the test yourself. Then design an instructional situation that would accommodate people who differ according to the styles mentioned in the inventory you have selected.

   What types of activities and teaching methods would you use in order to appeal to all the types of learners identified on the questionnaire or inventory you used? Keep in mind that many of our encounters with learners are limited to 50–70 minutes. However, you are not limited to these F2F experiences. Try to think of alternative modes of instruction that may not require F2F contact with the learner. Many of our learners benefit from these "on-their-own" interactions with the topics to be learned.

3. Describe motivation from the behaviorist, cognitive/constructivist, and humanist perspectives. What techniques are suggested by each of the three theories to help motivate learners?

   Reflect on your own teaching endeavors. Do you include ways to motivate your learners? If so, which of the theories of learning support your methods? If not, how would you revise your methods to help motivate your learners?

READ MORE ABOUT IT

Biggs, John B. 1999. *Teaching for Quality Learning at the University.* Buckingham, Great Britain: Open University Press.

Bligh, Donald A. 2000. *What's the Use of Lectures?* San Francisco: Jossey-Bass.

Bodi, Sonia. 1990. "Teaching Effectiveness and Bibliographic Instruction: The Relevance of Learning Styles." *College & Research Libraries* 51, no. 2: 113–119.

Chickering, Arthur W. and Stephen C. Ehrmann. "Implementing the Seven Principles: Technology as a Lever" (1996). Available: www.tltgroup.org/programs/seven.html (accessed December 27, 2008).

Cruickshank, Donald R., Deborah Bainer Jenkins, and Kim K. Metcalf. 2003. *The Act of Teaching,* 3rd ed. New York: McGraw-Hill.

Dunn, Rita S. and Shirley Griggs. 2000. "Practical Approaches to Using Learning Styles in Higher Education." In *Practical Approaches to Using Learning Styles in Higher Education* (pp. 19–32), edited by Rita S. Dunn and Shirley Griggs. Westport, CT: Bergin and Garvey.

Fink, L. Dee. 2003. *Creating Significant Learning Experiences: An Integrated Approach.* San Francisco: Jossey-Bass.

Freilberg, H. Jerome and Amy Driscoll. 2005. *Universal Teaching Strategies.* Boston: Allyn & Bacon.

Glasser, William. 1992. *The Quality School: Managing Students Without Coercion.* New York: Harper Perennial.

Hensley, Randall Burke. 2004. "Curiosity and Creativity as Attributes of Information Literacy." *Reference & User Services Quarterly* 44, no. 1: 31–36.

Kaplowitz, Joan. 2008. "The Psychology of Learning: Connecting Theory to Practice." In *Information Literacy Instruction Handbook* (pp. 26–49), edited by Christopher N. Cox and Elizabeth Blakesley Lindsay. Chicago: ALA.

Keller, John M. 1987. "Strategies for Stimulating the Motivation to Learn." *Performance and Instruction Journal* 26, no. 8: 1–7.

Kuhlthau, Carol Collier. 2004. *Seeking Meaning,* 2nd ed. Westport, CT: Libraries Unlimited.

Powis, Chris and Jo Webb. "Start with the Learner." CILIP: Chartered Institute of Library and Information Professionals (2005). Available: www.cilip.org.uk/publications/updatemagazinerchiverchive2005/janfeb/webbpow.htm (accessed July 31, 2008).

Stemler, Steven E., Julan G. Elliott, Elena L. Grigorenka, and Robert Sternberg. 2006. "There Is More to Teaching Than Instruction: Seven Strategies for Dealing with the Practical Side of Teaching." *Educational Studies* 32, no. 1: 101–118.

Weimer, Mary Ellen. 2002. *Learner-centered Teaching: Five Key Changes to Practice.* San Francisco: Jossey-Bass.

Chapter 5

Library Anxiety, Mental Models, and Conceptual Change

> *The Library defends itself, immeasurable as the truth it houses, deceitful as the falsehood it preserves. A spiritual labyrinth, it is also a terrestrial labyrinth. You might enter and you might not emerge. . . .*
>
> —UMBERTO ECO, *THE NAME OF THE ROSE*

LIBRARY ANXIETY: WHAT AND WHY?

Fear, unease, apprehension, panic—these are words long used to describe feelings about using libraries and library resources. Why? What could be better, more useful, and more rewarding than using a library and its resources to identify and locate information? Lots of things, as it turns out. For the many regular Internet users, Google, Yahoo, and Wikipedia offer quick and easy information, although in many cases unquestioned, regarding authority, currency, accuracy, and completeness. Library Web sites, on the other hand, present anxiety-producing barriers, such as menus with many choices and submenus, some mysteriously labeled as "Article Databases" or "Remote Databases." Even when called simply "Catalog," users may be thrown off if they are used to search engines. Some even call library databases of all kinds "search engines," including the library's catalog. Although we do not mean them to be barriers, libraries offer many complex means of getting to, selecting, utilizing, and interpreting results from multiple "search engines" and then locating materials, online or in print. All of this, including identifying known library materials and their locations, now requires computer use in just about every type of library, from school library media centers to public libraries, academic libraries, and special libraries.

As a result, for those who are not regular Internet or even computer users, library anxiety has increased with the proliferation of online information-researching tools, including library catalogs, melding into anxiety about computers and technology in general. In addition, library Web sites and the physical library itself both remain an overwhelming maze to many users. This is particularly true for large libraries with vast online and print collections, spread out in arrangements that seem confusing and very different from the categories used in physical and online bookstores. It is no wonder that using libraries and information-researching tools can make people feel anxious, as they still do (Bostick, 1992;Grassian, 1998; Antell, 2004; Jiao and Onwuegbuzie, 2004; Onwuegbuzie, Jiao, and Bostick, 2004; Carlile, 2007; Kwon, Onwuegbuzie and Alexander, 2007; Mizrachi, forthcoming).

In her 1986 study of library anxiety, Connie Mellon (1986) stated that 75–85 percent of library users she studied felt anxious when using the library. She reported that library size, lack of knowledge of physical locations, and not knowing where to begin or what to do were significant factors in determining levels of library anxiety. Three key points emerged from her study:

> 1) students generally feel that their own library-use skills are inadequate, while the skills of other students are adequate,
> 2) their inadequacy is shameful and should be hidden, and
> 3) their inadequacy would be revealed by asking questions. (Mellon, 1986: 160)

Keefer's 1993 research reinforced Mellon's findings, indicating that "details" or physical logistics such as call numbers and stacks with rows of materials can also throw users and add to anxiety levels (Keefer, 1993: 336–337). The results of Bostick's 1992 study, which included development and usage of the Library Anxiety Scale (LAS), indicated that library anxiety was an ongoing problem. Unfortunately, while considered highly reliable (Carlile, 2007; Mizrachi, forthcoming), LAS questions convey a negative tone. Could this negativity in itself increase library anxiety among those completing it? It is worth asking these questions, at a minimum, in order to sensitize ourselves to the emotional impact of written wording as well as oral. Setting aside the question of positive versus negative wording, researchers have uncovered useful information about library anxiety by utilizing the LAS, and one suggests adding questions that measure computer attitudes as well (Jiao and Onwuegbuzie, 2004).

Who or what is to blame for library anxiety, and what can be done about it? The term *librarian* was first used in 1713 to mean "the keeper or custodian of a library." That is, a "guardian," someone who watches carefully over an item and may or may not let others near it (*Oxford English Dictionary,* 1989). Today, information literacy instruction (ILI) librarians work hard to get across to users that we are guides and helpers and that libraries are incredible gateways to knowledge. Contrast the positive image of Giles, the high school librarian in the television show *Buffy the Vampire Slayer* (DeCandido, 1999), with Malachi, the librarian in *The Name of the Rose* (Eco, 1983). Malachi was an extreme caricature of a book custodian. He alone knew all of the library's secrets, which books it contained, what was in each book, and where the books were located. It was in his best interest that few knew how to read and that he had the authority to decide who could read which books, for information was power then as it is now. Giles, on the other hand, was Buffy's protector. His job was to teach her what she needed to know in order to kill vampires and other creatures, and he figured out what to tell her by reading library books.

This was a major improvement in the image of the librarian in 1999. But even before technology "mutated" them, libraries still seemed like secretive, mysterious, and anxiety-producing places. As the detective, William of Baskerville, did in *The Name of the Rose*, the general public has had to locate a series of confusing codes, decipher them, and then wend their way through mazes, going around or backtracking when reaching "blank walls" or "mirrors." They needed a lot of help navigating the "system" even then and often had trouble understanding and remembering underlying principles and structures. Users have encountered similar problems with card catalogs since Otis Hall Robinson first devised a model for them in the late nineteenth century, although they may not have realized what they were missing as they searched (*Encyclopedia of Library and Information Science*, 1978b).

Card catalogs were deceptively simple to use and seemed very similar to one another. Subject headings were often typed in red or capital letters on cards in card catalogs, and some card catalogs were even divided into subject catalogs and author/title catalogs. As users saw them, library catalogs simply required the ability to read, to know the alphabet, to flip through cards, and to find either known items by author or title or matches to topics (search by subject). However, one study of both academic and public library card catalog users found that "almost half the users who failed in their first attempt [to find a known item] gave up the search" (Tagliacozzo and Kochen, 1970: 375). About 75 percent of card catalog subject searches were successful, although the authors defined "successful" as an exact or a partial match to the query term. This meant that one-quarter of the time, users were not finding any matches and that some unknown number of the 75 percent success rate were only partial matches. Tagliacozzo and Kochen (1970: 374) went so far as to say that "at times the user's behavior appeared to be more the result of trial and error than of accurate planning." These are good indications that while some may have fully grasped concepts such as controlled vocabulary and chronological catalog card filing of historical topics, for others it was blind luck that they were able to use a card catalog at all to identify desired library materials.

For online systems, users try to apply what they know about searching using search engines, even when using online library catalogs. Often, they look for a search box and a search button and expect to see a list of results similar to what they find by using Google, Yahoo, or other search engines (Nielsen, 2007, cited in Mi and Weng, 2008: 7). This, in itself, constitutes a mental model of how searching works in general, yet users may be frustrated and face challenges in using library catalogs effectively (Mi and Weng, 2008). Online library catalogs and other information-researching tools like article databases offer few clues to alert the user to the existence of a conceptual scheme underlying "subjects," that is, the idea of controlled vocabularies that draw together like items regardless of their titles or even of words used in the complete text of items. Today, in contrast, many sites offer users the option of creating "tags" for items they find online, topic words that have meaning to the user. Some sites offer displays of "tag clouds" (sets of tags for specific items, with commonly used tags in larger fonts). Tag clouds are also called "folksonomies" (collections or taxonomies of user-generated tags), which, in theory, can help users find items again according to their own personal labeling system or concept map. How does this relate to library anxiety and information literacy (IL)?

In 2007, Rethlefsen reported on a number of different libraries that use tagging and social bookmarking for library-related resources in innovative ways. The Thunder Bay Public Library in Ontario, Canada (2008) and the Nashville Public Library (2008) use del.icio.us to allow their users to bookmark and tag their Internet links. They also post tag clouds made up of those del.icio.us tags. The Bibliothèques de l'Université Paris–Sorbonne (accessed 2008) bundles its del.icio.us tags into categories, including top ten tags, disciplines, and time periods. The University of Pennsylvania (2005) has even developed its own social bookmarking tool for academic library tags, "PennTags." Viewing tags created by others can help alleviate anxiety by allowing users to develop communities of interest and expand concept maps. Tagging, in and of itself, offers users the opportunity to participate actively in the social environment of a library catalog and other library resources, along with other library users, rather than restricting their use to individual, more passive information researching. So, tagging, tag clouds, and folksonomies can serve a social networking function in addition to a means of expanding one's own mental models (Spiteri, 2007). In schools, students at many levels can use del.icio.us to bookmark and tag sites of interest for group ILI projects. You can also use tags and even the Google Image Labeler (2007) game to illustrate the importance of controlled vocabularies.

Use of sites like LibraryThing (accessed 2008), where users can tag their own book collections, can expand this potential through the power of pooled tags that could be applied by users of many catalogs. In fact, some libraries are already doing this by including a LibraryThing widget on individual catalog Web pages (Wenzler, 2007). This can be highly useful as terminology and labeling change over time both in literary works and in nonfiction publications, even those that are available and searchable online in full text (Garrett, 2007). In everyday usage, too, labeling and language can change over time. Examples include "Gulf War," to describe the 1991 U.S. Iraq war, and "swiftboating," a reference to a political attack waged against U.S. presidential candidate John Kerry in the 2004 campaign by a group calling itself "Swift Boat Veterans for Truth," later turned into a verb. This is important in ILI as we help people learn to identify terms and ideas related to their information needs in order to reduce frustration and library anxiety.

Tags and Controlled Vocabularies

Valuable as they may be for individual recall and for social networking purposes, however, tagging and tag clouds do not take the place of controlled vocabularies. Rather, they can enhance controlled vocabularies with newer and more informal language that is meaningful to those who use those tags as descriptive identifiers. Controlled vocabularies provide conceptual frameworks for topics. They help learners grasp the scope of a topic and its relationship with other broader, narrower, and related topics. They also help establish conceptual frameworks for the organization of books on the shelves of libraries and provide for serendipitous intellectual and physical discovery of both topic areas and related materials.

Flickr (2008), an image sharing site, offers a case in point. The Library of Congress has worked with Flickr to establish a special site within Flickr for library image collections. Each image comes with a link labeled "No known copyright restrictions," detailing what the library can determine regarding usage rights. Some of these images come with Library of Congress subject headings and are labeled "Subjects." Images can be downloaded and used freely, and users may tag images. The U.S. Library of Congress (2008) may examine these tags as it considers how they may apply to or influence its controlled vocabulary.

How do people search for information, and why are cataloging and controlled vocabularies under attack by some at higher administrative levels, including the Library of Congress? One argument revolves around the fact that it takes time to do a good job of descriptive and subject cataloging and that time amounts to lots of money—$44 million a year, according to Deanna Marcum (2005), Associate Librarian of Congress. Because transaction analyses of library catalog usage generally indicate declining direct use of subject searching and increasingly widespread use of keyword searching, why spend limited funds on continuing to catalog materials so carefully and thoroughly? In other words, why do we still need subject headings and controlled vocabularies?

The Google one-box search-all approach, default keyword searching in library catalogs and many other databases, and even ILI that focuses on starting with keyword searches all have contributed to the widespread adoption of quick and easy searching methods. Some have said that categorization is too rigid, arguing that there can be many aspects to what may seem to be specific topics. According to Weinberger (2007: 230), for instance, "A topic is not a domain with edges." This leads to the assumption that keyword or full-text searching is best and is all we need in order to locate items as efficiently and effectively as we need to. Many do not realize, however, that most keyword searches vary in the kinds of data they search. Many keyword searches also search subject headings, and some library catalogs even include links to cross-references as possible additional search terms (Brigham Young University Library, 2005). So, in an invisible fashion, controlled vocabularies contribute to the success of keyword searches.

Subject headings and controlled vocabularies also help us bring together all items on a topic regardless of their "visible" or more commonly known labels and regardless of the language in which they are written (Beall, 2007). Searching for "Los Angeles" as a keyword, for instance, will not retrieve items that utilize "L.A." or "LA." Instead, keyword searching simply instructs a computer to find a match to what has been entered, character by character, including spaces. One study of University of Pittsburgh catalog searching concluded that users would not find almost 36 percent of hits if there were no subject terms in the catalog. The same study found that 100 percent of hits on the keywords *airplanes military parts* and 98.8 percent of hits on the keyword *businesswomen* contained subject headings, so almost none of those hits would be retrieved if there were no subject headings in the catalog (Gross and Taylor, 2005). Another example of the importance of subject headings is the problem of evolving language to describe historical events. AIDS was first labeled in several different ways: *Kaposi's Sarcoma and Opportunistic Infections* (*KOSI*) and *AID* (*acquired immunodeficiency disease*), and it was identified only in mid-1982 under the now commonly used term *AIDS* (*Acquired Immune Deficiency Syndrome*) (AVERT, 2008). If there were no subject headings, searching under any of the former terms would not retrieve anything published after the time the disease was called AIDS. This is a common occurrence. As events unfold, or even much later in time, they may be labeled differently.

Furthermore, those who are knowledgeable about a field may be familiar with its vocabulary. Those who are new to that field or topic, however, may not be and probably would not know of or be able to grasp the "network of relationships" embodied in controlled vocabularies like the Library of Congress Subject Headings (LCSH) through decades of hard work by knowledgeable and skilled catalogers (Mann, 2007). ILI librarians try to get learners to brainstorm these kinds of relationships for their own research topics by working through any number of active learning exercises and through modeling. Many of these exercises are designed to help learners practice brainstorming and mental mapping in order to come up with an expanded list of search words related to a given topic. Sharing examples from controlled vocabularies like LCSH, Dewey subject headings, or Medical Subject Headings (MESH) can also help get this idea across. Unfortunately, our users are not always aware of these important benefits of subject headings and controlled vocabularies. As ILI librarians, we need to help learners see the value of using subject headings (Antell and Huang, 2008) as a means of alleviating library anxiety.

Has the incidence of library anxiety decreased? Or has it just been driven underground by increased remote access? Because fewer people are visiting the physical library, there is less opportunity for direct observation of this problem, but it is still a problem, as researchers have discovered, even for "millenials," those born in and after 1982 and considered members of the "Net generation" (Jiao and Onwuegbuzie, 2004; Carlile, 2007; Kwon, 2008; Mizrachi, forthcoming).

Relationship to Technophobia

Since Mellon's study, and increasingly since Bostick's development of the LAS in 1992 and Keefer's 1993 study, technology has had an enormous impact on society in general and on libraries. This has greatly exacerbated the problem of library anxiety by making libraries and their researching tools much less standardized, much more complex in terms of navigating various formats of materials, and therefore even more anxiety-provoking than before. Difficult as the information-seeking process may have seemed at the time, few people suffered from "card-catalog-phobia," as card catalogs seemed fairly similar in most libraries. Online library catalogs and other online information-researching tools, on the other hand, are more likely to seem different from one another rather than similar, especially to naive users, and this adds the dimension of "computer anxiety" to existing library anxiety.

Technophobia and Empowering Users

Fear of technology, especially of "the computer," cuts across gender, age, ethnicity, and cultural groups. Weil and Rosen's 16-year-long research study of computerphobia, published in 1997, revealed that in any group of the 20,000 subjects studied, 25–50 percent were computerphobic. In addition, contrary to popular opinion, age and gender made no difference, as computerphobic people were "just as likely to be young as old, and were equally divided between men and women" (Weil and Rosen, 1997: 12).

The same researchers identified three broad categories of technology users, called "TechnoTypes": "Eager Adopters" (10–15 percent of the population), "Hesitant 'Prove-Its'" (50–60 percent of the population), and "Resisters" (30–40 percent of the population). Eager Adopters generally expect to have problems with computers and enjoy solving them. Hesitant Prove-Its also expect problems with technology, but they do not enjoy solving these problems and think they themselves have caused these problems to occur. Resisters generally try to avoid technology altogether because it makes them feel intimidated, embarrassed, or stupid, and they are sure they will break anything they touch. "User-hostile" error messages and the fear of one's privacy being invaded also contribute to technostress and computer avoidance (McGrath, 1999).

It is bad enough when you are a Hesitant Prove-It and have to wend your way through an enormous number and variety of information tools and resources just to identify and locate a book or an article—how much more so if you happen to be a Resister? Add to these initial fears the lack of interface standardization in library systems and differing search command terminology and syntax, even with Web-based systems. To make matters even worse, the struggle to learn one system may very well need to be repeated for most other systems. So, even if anxious library users learn how to use some library resources, especially if their mental models for using these systems are sketchy or minimal, when systems are upgraded or replaced by others with different interfaces or command structure the poor user is back to square one. Resisters may very well just give up as learning obstacles may seem insurmountable, and even Hesitants may be loathe to venture into the physical or virtual library world.

It is important to understand why this computerphobia exists and to take a kind, gentle, and encouraging approach to helping people feel more comfortable about using computers. You might begin by helping users acknowledge and learn about their own "TechnoType" so that they will see they are not alone. Weil and Rosen (1997) offer a "TechnoType Quiz" to help people self-identify, and they recommend a ten-step approach to learning new technology, including "Press the keys yourself," "Learn to expect problems with technology," and "You don't have to learn it all." At one time, the Thousand Oaks Library in California (a public library) offered computer classes to senior citizens that began by familiarizing attendees with the parts of the keyboard. Keyboards were removed from workstations and brought into a separate room where learners could manipulate them and learn the functions of the various keys before they were hooked up to workstations. This is an excellent way to help Weil and Rosen's Resisters overcome their computerphobia.

Another important way to make technology understandable is to provide pressure-free practice times and locations where people will begin to understand the basic rules of the system so that, ideally, they will be able to look for similar rules in other systems. Research indicates that there is hope, even for the most technologically inexperienced or computerphobic. The more people actually use computers, the more they get used to them and the less anxious many tend to feel.

An international study of teachers who taught in two languages indicated that the more general computer use they had, the less anxious they were, as long as the training they received encouraged them to make use of computers rather than fear them (Yaghi and Abu-Saba, 1998). By extension, ILI librarians hope that the same will be true even for the most library- and information-research inexperienced.

Are people still as anxious about technology as they were in the 1980s and 1990s? A 2007 review of three decades worth of studies indicates that they still are, with "between a quarter and a half of those sampled report[ing] some level of anxiety when faced with information technology." In fact, fear of information technology is a persistent phenomenon, affecting people of all ages, genders, and walks of life in the United States, Europe, the Middle East, and the Far East (Thorpe and Brosnan, 2007: 1259).

This technophobia adds a layer of dread and distress, as well as fear of social embarrassment, to the angst many people already feel when attempting to use library resources in person or virtually and can discourage use of libraries and library resources more than ever. Now, in addition to the factors noted earlier, library anxiety can be caused by feelings of being overwhelmed by the size and number of online information resources available via the library, feelings of inadequacy in knowing about likely sources of information to meet needs, and feelings of low self-esteem due to unintentional (or intentional) intimidation by library staff or being ignored or treated condescendingly, impatiently, or dismissively because of low levels of computer skills that may seem obvious to those accustomed to the fact that using library resources now entails use of technology.

Users in almost any type of library must now use primarily Web-based online catalogs and other online databases just to find a book or a periodical article, both physical and electronic. This means they must be able to use a mouse or a trackpad and to know how to scroll, how to move around on a Web page, what links are and how to use them to move around within the Web, what the location bar is on a Web page, and what a URL is. They must also know how to get to library research tools like the library catalog, databases that provide access to articles, book chapters, dissertations, and more, as well as online reference sources like dictionaries and encyclopedias. And this does not even begin to address the issue of widely varying database interfaces, how to search, how to limit, how to display results, and how to get copies of materials identified through these searches. When the Web, computer anxiety, and fear of technology are added to the library anxiety mix, when, as Clifford Lynch (1998: 18) puts it, "The information seeker is faced with an assault by an overwhelmingly rich array of incoherent information and events," anxiety levels can reach a point of no return where users simply give up and leave the library or the system in frustration and/or despair.

Does it help to know how to use technologies like cell phones, iPods, and digital cameras? What if you are skilled at using Google and Wikipedia? Yes, it helps. But, technology skills, while valuable, if not essential, do not equal the ability to recognize an information need and then identify, locate, evaluate, and use information effectively and ethically. The vast quantities of information now available in many different forms means that even technologically sophisticated users, such as the "Google Generation" (born after 1993), tend to spend a lot of time just getting to library resources before they ever have a chance to use them and in a way different from the way in which scholars traditionally conduct research. They engage in what one report calls "information seeking behaviour . . . [that is] horizontal, bouncing, checking and viewing in nature" (British Library and JSIC, 2008: 9). It is not much of a stretch to say that these users, too, may become anxious and impatient and avoid libraries because of the difficulties they face in navigating ("bouncing around") large and cumbersome library Web sites, with an increasing number and diversity of databases and interfaces, assuming they even know about and can find those databases through the library's Web site.

In these circumstances, it is not surprising that some former library users may turn to bookstores to meet their needs instead, if they can afford to do so and bookstores are located in fairly close proximity, or if they have easy Internet access to online bookstores and a credit card as well as trust in the security of online transactions. This could be one explanation for the appearance of an *American Libraries* article in the late 1990s favorably comparing bookstores to libraries (Coffman, 1998). After all, when you need to find something in a physical bookstore, although some have self-help computers where you can look up or even download books (Fialkoff,

2008), you do not need to look up a book yourself. You can ask at an information desk, and someone else will look it up for you. Often a bookstore employee will also get the book for you or take you right to it, or order it for you, assuming the book is still in print.

If you use an online bookstore, you can get recommendations tied to book titles you search. Of course, you are quite limited in selection to books still in print, and bookstores of all kinds generally do not make efforts to acquire materials representing a variety of viewpoints. Their primary goal is simply to sell as many books as they can, as quickly as possible. In order to do so, bookstores try to make their physical environments comfortable, attractive, and low key. Shelves are labeled with large signs, and materials are often grouped in broad general categories. Online bookstores, too, try to make searching easy by providing search categories, single-box searching, book cover displays that you can click on to get to more information about a book, searching within a book, suggestions for other books that might be of interest (purchased by users who bought the book you are considering buying), and reviews, as well as the opportunity for users to review books themselves. Libraries, on the other hand, utilize call numbers to group like items together on shelves. Controlled vocabularies and call number classification allow libraries to categorize materials into more focused topics and subtopics, as opposed to the bookstore's primarily general categories. However, many libraries require users to identify materials and call numbers through an online catalog and then find those books on the shelves on their own. This can be quite anxiety provoking for those who are not fully computer literate and frustrating as well for those who do not understand how call numbers work or what they mean, not to mention how to locate materials on library shelves. In addition, many library catalogs are essentially "omnidirectional." They do not allow users to comment on, tag, or review materials, although many library Web sites do provide e-mail, chat, and other means of asking questions remotely.

What Can We Do to Alleviate Library Anxiety?

Do you remember how it felt to be anxious about using a library and its resources? How can we help people feel empowered and less anxious about using libraries and library resources? Effective teaching requires an understanding of the learners' knowledge of technology, "technology-readiness," and affective state of mind. It can be useful for ILI librarians to relive the insecure and fearful feelings common to those exposed to new devices, new technologies, or new ways of doing things. Cerise Oberman's (1980) "Petals Around a Rose" problem-solving exercise, while intended to teach problem solving, can also serve as a reminder of the feelings that arise when one does not know where to begin or what to do. Some people figure out where to begin or what to do quickly in order to solve the problem posed, while for others it becomes a panicky and embarrassing situation as they become stressed and anxious and see themselves as dumb or lagging behind everyone else. In fact, Kuhlthau (1985) says we all go through progressive stages in performing library-related research, beginning with uncertainty.

These are the very same feelings people seem to have when they cannot figure out how to use libraries and computerized library systems. How do we help alleviate anxiety about using library resources and technology? Mellon's (1986: 163) study of the literature indicated that "acknowledging the anxiety and its legitimacy, and then providing successful experiences to counteract the anxiety, is the most effective method for treatment." Weil and Rosen (1997: 15–17) affirm this recommendation by asking readers of their book to self-identify their "TechnoType" and their feelings about technology and then exercise their own control over technology in their lives and to make the most of it. Brosnan (1998a) suggests that those who are anxious about using computers practice general simple and routine tasks first to build confidence. An interesting 1998 research study by Levine and Donitsa-Schmidt (1998) showed that "Computer experience was . . . found to have a significant effect on computer confidence" and that this effect increased when users were exposed to computers both in school and at home. The same study found that people tend to become more self-confident and have more positive attitudes about computers when they are in control, when they can proceed at their own pace, and when they can work from simpler to more complex programs (Levine and Donitsa-Schmidt, 1998: 139). Another study concluded that the more people use computers, the better they feel about them, and this, in turn, results in decreased library anxiety (Mizrachi and Shoham, 2004). Other researchers claim that library anxiety is temporary and "situation specific" (Onwuegbuzie, Jiao, and Bos-

Marketing

tick, 2004: 261). Anxiety about libraries also extends to anxiety about asking for help at a reference desk, where fear of asking "dumb questions" or embarrassing oneself may make people avoid reference desks or even online references altogether (Fister, 2002). Computer anxiety, too, seems to be more of a social phobia, related to one's own perceptions of one's ability to cope with computer-related situations that may seem threatening (Thorpe and Brosnan, 2007). All of this says much for the value of staged, sequenced, self-paced, and self-selected ILI, with frequent positive reinforcement, that is, providing anxious and less computer-savvy learners with the option of linear, increasingly complex ILI, while at the same time acknowledging that many people experience library anxiety as well as computer anxiety.

Whatever the approach, the instructor's attitude and manner are all important. Intimidating or condescending trainers can have a negative effect on anxiety levels of computer users who are even slightly technophobic. It is important for technophobes to find friendly trainers, to work in pairs, not to be embarrassed about asking questions, and to be able to repeat tasks before moving on (Brosnan, 1998a). Keefer (1993), too, states that it is important for the instruction librarian to acknowledge a library user's anxiety and to make it clear that such anxiety is common. As she puts it, "Lectures and instruction programs that let students know that everybody experiences anxiety and that asking for help is an important part of the search process can go a long way toward making students' initial library experiences less stressful" (Keefer, 1993: 337).

In group instruction, one way to help decrease library anxiety is to write on a board or flipchart or to use a PowerPoint presentation to show the progressive information search process stages that Kuhlthau (1985) says we all go through in performing library-related research: uncertainty, optimism, confusion/frustration/doubt, clarity, sense of direction/confidence, and relief/sense of satisfaction or dissatisfaction. If you ask for a show of hands for each stage and acknowledge having the same feelings yourself, learners will see that they are not the only ones who feel anxious about doing research. In fact, quite often learners will then visibly relax and seem able to absorb skills and concepts more readily. A study of two types of videos used to teach physics concepts supports this approach. One video taught quantum mechanics using a lecture format, while another, more effective video taught the same concepts through dialogue between a tutor and a student. Students who viewed the second video felt validated by seeing other students have difficulty with or ask questions about a topic, thus relieving their anxiety (Muller et al., 2007). Fister (2002) also suggests a number of ways that instructors can help alleviate library anxiety, in addition to scheduling in-person group instruction. These include renaming the library catalog as "search for books" and collaborating with instructors on assignments that require learners to ask questions at a reference desk. On a more basic level, a friendly smile, encouragement, and reassurance can also go a long way toward alleviating this sort of anxiety. With some tweaking, much of this can be done in synchronous or asynchronous online instruction as well as in person.

Signage, too, can have a positive or negative effect on library anxiety. Kupersmith (1987) suggests that positive, friendly signage with good use of graphics and color schemes can help alleviate anxiety. Instead of a sign that reads "No loud noise!" or "Shh," Kupersmith recommends using a sign that says "Quiet, please." In addition to relieving anxiety, this friendlier approach can also help in counteracting the negative image of the librarian as guardian of materials and of the physical plant (Kupersmith, 1984). To extend this friendly concept further, libraries could label the beginning of each call number area in their book stacks with some broad subject categories, for example, "BF = Psychology," and label the sections of their Web sites in welcoming, easy to understand language. (See Chapters 9 and 10 for more on this topic.) Libraries could also post enlarged copies of the broad classification scheme in key areas in their book stacks and on the library Web site (for viewing both on a computer and on mobile devices). User-friendly point-of-use guides, handouts, online tutorials, podcasts, blogs, videos posted on sites like YouTube or on the library's Web site, and self-paced workbooks or exercises can also help people feel more comfortable about using a library and its resources. If you can offer many different learning choices, with a variety of means of utilizing them, learners will be able to pick and choose whichever format suits their needs at that moment and their preferred learning style.

In general, our goal is to alleviate library anxiety, to make the library and information tools and resources more understandable so that the research process becomes more efficient and effective, and less frustrating. This is certainly more of a challenge than it used to be, as people increasingly shift to remote use of online resources. How can librarians help? Should we use instant messaging, chat, Facebook, Second Life, YouTube, blogs, and wikis? Should we continue to create help materials in tried and true paper form as well as online forms? Should we mount our paper point-of-use guides, pathfinders, and bibliographies online? Should we adapt them to an online, social networking environment, inviting comments, ratings, and tags? Should we redesign our library Web sites so that they will be warm, welcoming, and easy to use? Should we continue to meet and greet our users in person, as well as remotely, with a friendly, warm smile and with words of encouragement? The answer to all of these is a hearty Yes! We should be trying anything we can to help make learners feel comfortable and welcome in using library resources and getting help in and through the library, including warmth and supportive humor (Walker, 2006).

An effective way to do this is to help learners think critically and systematically about the library and its resources. Research has shown that library anxiety is fairly common, and those who are anxious about the library tend to have a poor critical thinking disposition, meaning they believe themselves to be lacking in critical thinking skills. However, as learners use libraries and conduct information research, library anxiety decreases as they gain confidence. As they gain confidence, their critical thinking dispositions improve, and they are better able to use critical thinking skills in information searching and retrieval. ILI librarians can help this process along by being positive and encouraging (Kwon, Onwuegbuzie, and Alexander, 2007; Kwon, 2008).

MENTAL MODELS, CONCEPTUAL FRAMEWORKS, AND CONCEPTUAL CHANGE

What do learners really know about information resources and libraries and how they operate? How much do they know about research strategies, and, in fact, how much do they need to know in order to make effective and efficient use of information resources in the search and evaluation process? What is the best way to help learners understand and assimilate abstract concepts and apply them to new situations? These perennial questions have bedeviled teachers and trainers at all levels and in many different disciplines.

As we noted in Chapter 3, there is evidence to support the cognitive psychology view that it is easier for people to learn something new if the teacher relates it to something they already know (Ausubel, 1960, 1977; Ausubel, Novak, and Hanesion, 1978). For instance, externally presented conceptual frameworks like controlled vocabularies can help explain what experts or designers had in mind in constructing systems and products. Mental models research can unearth users' internal views—the ways that users view the operation of these same systems and products. Sometimes this sort of research reveals that external conceptual and internal mental models for the same process can be worlds apart.

What are "mental models"? The phrase "mental model" is somewhat ambiguous, according to the *Encyclopedia of Psychology*, as the word *model* in this phrase can have two different meanings: "a model as a miniature of a real-world object or system . . . and a model as a theory that generates predictions" (American Psychological Association, 2000: 191). Successful ILI can help people make sense of information researching by helping them construct their own more accurate mental models of real-world information systems and processes, like search engines and database collections or "federated searching." Accurate mental models for information systems and processes can help information seekers effectively select among and use information-researching tools and also develop alternative approaches to information researching. In addition, understanding these mental models can help in improving system design and ILI (Westbrook, 2006). See Chapters 9, 10, and 16 for approaches to improving information-researching tools and IL help in order to address common mental models related to information seeking.

Altering Mental Models

Users of libraries and information resources operate under many misconceptions or incorrect mental models. Do people's mental models change, and, if so, how difficult is it to help the process along? According to some researchers, mental models can and do evolve quite naturally. However, according to others mental models may be quite resistant to change, or individuals may be unable to describe their mental models easily or may be totally unaware of the fact that they should even consider conceptual change (Kruger and Dunning, 1999; Westbrook, 2006). Donald Norman (1983: 7), a psychologist who has worked with the Apple Corporation on user interface design, states that, "A person, through interaction with the system, will continue to modify the mental model in order to get to a workable result." According to Norman, it is fairly common for mental models to be technically inaccurate and for people to forget the details of systems if they use them infrequently, to confuse similar devices and operations with one another, and to do extra physical work in order to avoid extra mental effort that would save physical work in the long run. It is not surprising, therefore, that ILI may not seem to "take" completely in group instruction, at a reference desk, or in remote learning situations. One study found that children under 13 and adults over 46 often have problems constructing effective searches and evaluating the results. The same study found that children do not understand how search engines work, have trouble using search queries as opposed to natural language, and fail to use synonyms and related terms, while older adults may not have a mental map of how the Internet works (British Library and JSIC, 2008: 22). In any case, the first step in altering incorrect mental models is recognizing that the model is incorrect, that there is some sort of contradiction, and therefore that the model needs to be changed (Jonassen, Strobel, and Gottdenker, 2005: 30). How do you get learners to identify their own mental models when often they are not even aware of them (Kruger and Dunning, 1999)?

Concern about this problem is not limited to ILI. A study of college physics students indicated that many had preconceptions about basic aspects of mechanics, such as the relationship between force and motion, and that these misconceptions often persisted following instruction. The author of this study saw this not as an obstacle, however, but as an advantage. He commended the fact that students had at least thought about the problem enough to construct their own "micro-theories" that actually worked in some cases, even though they were basically inaccurate. He saw this as an opportunity to get the learners to alter their theories on their own and accomplished this alteration in group instruction by posing questions asking students to predict the outcome of certain actions or by pairing students to discuss and together make predictions (Clement, 1983). Another study of college physics students, mentioned earlier in this chapter, compared the results of using two videos to teach quantum mechanics, one through a lecture approach and the other through a tutor–student dialogue. In addition to relieving anxiety, the second video seemed more effective at drawing out the students' prior knowledge of physics (Muller et al., 2007). Clement's techniques for altering incorrect mental models, and other techniques such as Muller's dialogue video, can be highly useful in ILI as well. For more on teaching techniques in group settings, see Chapter 12.

Some instructors ask their students to draw pictures of concepts as a way of getting them to think about their mental models and be able to express them, even visually. One study has shown that students do better on problem-solving tests if they draw their own pictures after reading a textual description of how something works as opposed to simply reading text alone or even reading text with accompanying pictures drawn by experts (Hall, Bailey, and Tillman, 1997). Annotating your own drawings or even developing multiple choice questions related to them requires additional metacognitive effort and can contribute to retention or "durability" of learning, even at the elementary school level (Georghiades, 2004; Pillsbury, 2006). Concept mapping can also help learners understand linkages and hierarchies among concepts. While learners may draw concept maps by hand, utilizing software like Mindomo (2008) and Inspiration (2008) to develop visual graphic organizers showing spatial or hierarchical relationships can be more effective, easier, and quicker for many different age groups. In addition to visual concept maps, Inspiration offers the option of adding links to Web pages, videos, and files, as well as a toggle between text-only outlines and graphic layouts of various kinds, similar to those utilized in brainstorming and mind mapping (Royer and Royer, 2004).

A literature review of collaborative concept mapping studies revealed that a group approach can be more useful than individual concept mapping. Learners first describe their own mental model to others in their group, engaging them verbally and/or pictorially. This process of discussion and interaction with others often results in transformed mental models, as group members come to agreement on the group's concept map, albeit with exceptions based on culture, knowledge, and experience. The same review reported both positive and negative findings for using concept mapping. Positive results include improved pretest/posttest results, and negative findings include unchallenged incorrect reasoning or assumptions incorporated into the final product. The study's authors conclude that there are many possible reasons for these mixed findings, including learning style preferences, learning context, process, and group composition. To minimize negative results, they recommend several approaches, including a variation on the think–pair–share approach, with individuals assigned to develop some concept maps of their own before working with others in the group. They also recommend using this technique synchronously in online learning and using "conversation scaffolds," like posing the beginning of a question or statement and asking learners to complete it (Gao et al., 2007).

Another study cautions against cognitive overload, including too much "learning by doing," warning that too much "extraneous processing" not directly related to achieving intended learning outcomes may actually hinder learning ("cognitive load theory"). In this study, students did better on a test after reading material containing prepared graphic organizers than when they were asked to prepare their own graphic organizers (Stull and Mayer, 2007). All of this leads to the conclusion that a balanced and flexible approach is essential, particularly when encountering learners' incorrect mental models in a range of library, media, and information center environments.

At the reference desk, librarians sometimes encounter users who think that "RM" at the beginning of a Library of Congress call number stands for "Room" and that the number that follows is a room number. Other users may search for periodical articles in an online library catalog or in a separate list of periodical title subscriptions rather than an article index, thinking that the catalog search box is the library's "search engine," meaning that it will search the contents of everything that library owns or to which that library has access. One user even asked a reference librarian, "Do you have a list of all the books I've ever read?" (Jeng, accessed 2000). While you may discover some faulty mental models through reference questions, pretesting prior to instruction can be more effective in revealing misconceptions and faulty mental models. An objective-type pretest question might ask where to look up scholarly articles on the topic of "interracial dating," with five alternative choices including "Sociological Abstracts" and the library's catalog. If learners pick the library catalog instead of "Sociological Abstracts," they probably think, incorrectly, that scholarly articles are listed in the catalog.

Once muddled mental models like this have been identified, the next step is to help users alter their misconceptions by focusing instruction on areas of greatest confusion. One effective approach is to identify broad stroke conceptual frameworks and use analogies to describe and explain them (Dagher, 1995). The research process lends itself quite well to this approach, for, despite the red herring generated by massive and unfiltered Web information overload and other new forms of communication, basic ILI research procedures and underlying structures and methods still remain remarkably similar to those used for decades.

Example: Basic Research Process

Generally, people conduct research for the purpose of scholarly investigation, for creation of information, for business, organization, and government needs, or for personal interest. Almost anything can be the subject of research. It can include printed, computerized, audio, and video images or daily life functions; music, animals, plants, and physical structures such as sculptures, paintings, and buildings; cognitive structures or activities including learning, thinking, memorizing, evaluating, writing, and speaking; or social networking through formats like blogs and wikis or virtual worlds. Even garbage has been the subject of research (Cote, McCullough, and Reilly, 1985). Research "publications" can be divided roughly into original, primary works (including empirical research studies, raw data, and personal "vanity" items), secondary studies or materials (about primary works), or some mixture of the two. Different disciplines, of course, may define "primary" and "secondary" differently, and avenues of "publication" or creation of primary and secondary resources, as well as access, may differ (Oberman and Strauch, 1982; Reichel and Ramey, 1987; Grafstein, 2002; Pace, 2004). However they are defined, these materials now appear in a larger variety of formats, including print and electronic. Electronic materials themselves may be broken down into numerous subsets, such as video, audio, static and interactive Web sites, databases, e-journals, images, and more. Whatever the format, the process of IL-related research still follows these steps, for the most part, though often recursively rather than in a strictly linear fashion, repeating some steps as the research takes different directions during the information researching process:

The researcher . . .

1. Becomes interested in and selects a topic, broad or narrow
2. Attempts to identify relevant information by using a variety of information resources, including search engines like Google, people, and citation trails, as well as other more traditional researching tools
3. Attempts to locate some or all of the information identified in step 2
4. May adjust or abandon her or his topic in favor of a new or modified one
5. Attempts to absorb, analyze, or review some or all of the information located in step 3
6. Again, may adjust or abandon her or his topic in favor of a new or modified one
7. Attempts to review, analyze, reflect upon, and utilize some or all of this information to answer an information need
8. May present findings to others in any of a variety of formats or utilize them for her or his own purposes

Related to this is the fact that in higher education students may be unaware at first that research and critical thinking approaches may differ from one discipline to another and that experts in a field have generally absorbed and adopted the thinking mode of a particular discipline in the process of becoming an expert in that discipline. This confusion can be quite problematic for college and university students, as they invariably take courses in a variety of disciplines and therefore may need to conduct information research for assignments in quite different ways. One way to counteract this problem is to help the disciplinary experts understand its scope and break it down into learning steps for those new to a discipline. Pace and Middendorf suggest a seven-step approach for faculty to help students learn how to think critically in any discipline:

1. Determine the learning "bottleneck," i.e., what is usually difficult for students in a particular discipline to grasp.
2. Determine the experts' thinking steps in moving through this bottleneck.
3. Model those steps for students.
4. Engage students in trying out and practicing these steps in groups and then individually.
5. Implement effective means of motivating students to do this.
6. Assess student achievement of expected learning outcomes.
7. Share with faculty colleagues. (*Decoding the Disciplines*, 2004: 3)

ILI librarians who are liaisons to academic departments and conduct ILI for those departments may wish to discuss this with the faculty in those departments as a means of helping students in those disciplines understand the different researching methodologies and mental models of differing disciplines. Reichel and Ramey's 1987 *Conceptual Frameworks for Bibliographic Education* described these sorts of disciplinary ways of thinking in specific disciplines in the social sciences, humanities, and sciences, and others (e.g., Grafstein, 2002) have followed in later years. How do you help learners effectively grasp these conceptual frameworks and develop correct mental models?

Using Analogies for Conceptual Frameworks

Understanding externally presented conceptual frameworks can help researchers save time and effort and uncover important and relevant information. For example, when researchers understand what controlled vocabulary is and how it works in research tools, they can search more efficiently and effectively by making use of subject headings or descriptors and thesauri. How can the use of analogies help in this process?

In 1981, Kobelski and Reichel provided a brief history of the use of conceptual frameworks that helped learners understand underlying structures and identified seven types of concepts that would lend themselves to analogies useful in library instruction. In 12 chapters of Reichel and Ramey's 1987 book, contributors identified conceptual frameworks useful in teaching library instruction for specific disciplines. The goal was to teach at a higher level by focusing on underlying concepts both for reference sources and for research in various disciplines rather than what was commonplace at the time, teaching the mechanics of using general and specific reference sources.

In 1987, the idea of teaching conceptual frameworks and using analogies to do so was quite a revolutionary intellectual leap for the field of library instruction and has had enormous impact on ILI ever since, as analogies have increasingly been used to get these concepts across. Analogies are sprinkled throughout the ACRL Instruction Section's *Designs for Active Learning* (Gradowski, Snavely, and Dempsey, 1998). Randy Burke Hensley and Elizabeth Hanson's (1998: 55–56) "Question Analysis for Autobiography" uses "the analogy of human memory as a database . . . to teach students how to develop a controlled vocabulary. . . . " Loanne Snavely's (1998) "Teaching Boolean Operators in a Flash Using a Deck of Cards" is another good example of this technique. Listserv queries regarding analogies have also generated a number of responses, including a reference to Shelley McKibbon's list of many IL-related analogies, and active learning exercises utilizing analogies (Grassian, 2008b; McKibbon, 2008; Nowakowski, 2008).

Most of the analogies described in these publications and in listserv messages are verbal or written and describe concrete activities or processes, but effective conceptual models can be visual as well. The known item "research pyramid" is a visual representation of one approach that reference librarians use to help locate materials. They begin by searching the local library catalog or other licensed databases, then proceed to a broader regional library catalog (e.g., the University of California's California Digital Library "MELVYL™ Catalog"), and from there to an even broader national catalog (e.g., OCLC's "WorldCat").

The search strategy hourglass is another graphic representation of a concept. It starts with an unfocused topic, proceeds through the resource-filtering process to a narrowed topic, then broadens to examine selected materials more closely, and, finally, broadens further to develop and communicate results (Kennedy, 1974). The hourglass depicts a series of steps in the research process, from topic selection, topic modification, and data collection to synthesis and presentation or submission of research results. Coincidentally, this hourglass diagram also meets Tufte's (1983) criteria for excellent graphic representation of data, as in and of itself the hourglass clearly conveys the message that research is a process and that it takes time to complete. For more on design of instructional materials, see Chapter 10.

Interestingly, analogies have been used in teaching all kinds of concepts in many different fields, especially in science education for children. For example, Mason's (1994) study used cake making as an analogy for photosynthesis. Newby conducted two controlled studies of the use of instructional analogies in teaching advanced physiological concepts. Results of his first study of 161 college students "indicate, first and foremost, that the use of analogies may significantly improve learners' ability to identify and comprehend the application of concepts" (Newby, 1995: 12) and also showed that recall and recognition of new concepts improved when analogies were used.

Components of Effective Analogical Reasoning

Teaching and learning by means of analogies, graphics, or text sounds like a quick, easy, and attention-getting means of helping people alter inaccurate mental models. There is more to this process, however, than first meets the eye. Researchers have identified seven independent components of analogical reasoning, most important of which are "encoding" (understanding the terms and attributes of "each end" of the analogy), "inference" (discovering the relationship between the main subjects of the analogy), and "application" (applying what they learned in the "inference" stage in order to "solve" the analogy) (Dagher, 1995). In other words, researchers caution us first to make sure that everyone understands what the supposedly familiar end of the analogy is and which features of it you will be focusing on before using it to explain a new abstract concept at the other end (Iding, 1997; Mason, 1994). So, for instance, if you are using the analogy of original versions of songs as opposed to "cover versions" to explain the difference between primary and secondary sources, you will need to make sure that everyone understands that "cover versions" are songs sung by an artist other than the original artist and released at a later date. In other words, they "interpret" the original songs.

Second, you need to be careful to help users understand the relationships you are trying to establish through analogies (Bishop, 2006). For example, learners may need a bit of explanation or introduction before understanding the analogy of product grouping in supermarkets (produce, dairy, fresh meats, fish, etc.)

as compared to controlled vocabularies used in article indexes. If you use this analogy, you would ask the learners to tell you where supermarkets put yogurt and milk. The answer is the "dairy" section. Why? Supermarkets try to make it easier for customers to find products by grouping like items together so that they will not have to guess where an item is and wander all over the store looking for it. Similarly, controlled vocabularies group similar items together to save you time and to help you identify useful items on the same or related topics. The Yellow Pages phone directory offers a similar analogy. Companies that produce these directories pick from among synonyms like "lawyer" and "attorney," and some provide indexes that cross-reference these synonyms (Wilson, 2008). Of course, these sorts of analogies presume that your learners have been to supermarkets, have looked for items there, and recognize that supermarkets use product groupings, or that they have used print Yellow Pages phone directories. Other analogies, like open air markets where jewelry stalls or stalls of household goods are located near each other, may work better in areas where mental models of these kinds of markets are more familiar to the general populace than supermarkets (Westbrook, 2006). Similarly, Craigslist allows you to find recommended items, people, services, etc., listed in preset categories, like "automotive," rather than "cars." If the market analogy or the Yellow Pages analogy does not apply for your learner group, it may be useful and enlightening to engage the learners by describing what it is you are trying to get across and then asking them to come up with examples from their own experience that would fit that concept (Sutherland and Winters, 2001).

Once you have described or demonstrated a concept, either with or without using an analogy, you may want to ask learners to write or draw pictures of their understanding of that concept. You may need to prepare them first by talking about what an analogy is, providing an engaging example, and then checking for understanding. According to one study, this approach can serve as an effective means of assessing whether or not learners have grasped concepts or have misunderstandings, as they will need to draw upon existing or prior knowledge in order to represent new knowledge to themselves and others (Pittman, 1999). In any case, you must also be sure to gear your analogies to the age level of your learners and to their life experiences.

Third, research indicates that thinking about the process of using a concrete analogy to understand an abstract concept and then discussing it in an interactive small group setting or "constructivist learning environment" where learners build or construct their own meaning based on their own life experiences, within social contexts (Gerstenmaier and Mandi, 2004), can be highly effective. In other words, using metacognition, "the inner awareness or ability to reflect on what and when, how and why, one knows" (Mason, 1994: 268), in a give-and-take synchronous environment helps learners understand how an analogy can help or hinder their understanding of a concept and can help them alter their own internal mental models, thereby integrating the new information. Hofstadter goes so far as to say that all human learning is based on analogy. Babies slowly build frames of reference, chunking experiences and comparing new experiences to older ones. Older people categorize or chunk experiences more quickly, because they have more prior experiences with which to compare a new experience (Hofstadter, 2000).

In ILI, in fact, small- and large-group exercises constitute an important means of learning new concepts by analogy. Do conceptual frameworks still constitute an effective means of helping users adopt correct mental models about IL tools and approaches? What are some effective means of utilizing a variety of conceptual models?

Conceptual Frameworks and Analogies

Publication Sequence

ILI librarians have used many of Kobelski and Reichel's concepts effectively since their publication in 1981. Some, like "Publication Sequence," have translated quite well to the Web. The "Flow of Information" Web site is based on Sharon Hogan's 1980 concept that describes how events are documented in stages through various forms of "publication," beginning with the first occurrence and proceeding through discussion, analysis, and summary or condensed reporting (Five Colleges of Ohio, 2000; Zwemer, 2000). Only time will tell if this concept will continue to serve as a valid instructional approach, however, given scholarly communication efforts to bypass traditional journal publishers in favor of direct publishing on the Web, exemplified by SPARC (The Scholarly Publishing and Academic Resources

Coalition, 2008), the DOAJ (Directory of Open Access Journals, 2008), and PLoS (Public Library of Science, 2008). Under these circumstances, ILI becomes even more important, as learners will need to take the time to think critically about the materials they find to a much greater extent in order to weed out those they might not have encountered if they had simply relied on established peer review processes to filter materials for them. You can teach the flow of information in an interactive large group exercise, in person, and then refer learners to the Web site for reinforcement. This approach is valuable for teaching learners where to start searching for information on a topic. For recent topics, blogs, online news sites, newspapers, and magazines may be more fruitful than journal articles or books.

Types of Reference Tools and Resources

The University of California, Santa Cruz's NetTrail is an example of how to use the Web to teach an instructional concept based on the analogy of a bicycle or hiking trail (Murphy et al., 2004), reflecting Kobelski and Reichel's (1981) "Type of Reference Tool" concept. This approach helps learners distinguish among reference tools like encyclopedias and periodical index databases, as well as types of periodicals like magazines and journals. Sites like these can be effective, especially if designed as independent modules where learners can "test out of" specific segments and can skip around, picking and choosing what they want to learn. Self-paced workbooks, both paper and electronic, often take a reference tools approach and also allow learners to skip around and select what they want to learn when they want to learn it.

Research as a Linear Process

Some wonder whether or not we should teach information research as a linear process (Kobelski and Reichel's [1981] "Systematic Literature Searching") often described in terms of the following steps:

1. Define terms.
2. Use encyclopedias to locate overviews.
3. Use catalogs and bibliographies to find books.
4. Use article indexes to identify and locate current information.
5. Use Web search tools to find additional current information.
6. Review materials, evaluate, and then write paper.

Online or paper workbooks and many general online IL tutorials, such as the "Road to Research" (Grassian et al., 2008), follow an outline of the elements reflected in the 1989 ALA definition of IL, often presented in a linear order, although not always using these exact terms: identify, locate, evaluate, and use effectively, with the added element of ethical or responsible use reflected in a number of later IL standards (ALA. Presidential Committee on Information Literacy, 1989, 1998; Picasso and Booth, 2007; ALA. AASL, 1998a, 1998b, 2007; ALA, ACRL, 2008a, 2008c; Goldenstein, et al., 2008; Wright, 2008;). Most of these tutorials allow learners to skip around to different sections or subsections.

1. "Citation Pearl-Growing" suggests that by utilizing descriptors of just a few useful citations as you search you can build a valuable "pearl" of search terms and additional citations relevant to your research topic (Markey and Cochrane, 1981).
2. "Berrypicking" describes real-life information searching as "an evolving search," similar to picking berries in a forest—one by one rather than in a bunch. When searching for information on a topic, users often shift their approach, rather than finding and using only a single set of results that perfectly matches their query within a particular system. Instead, researchers gather citations here and there as they go and may use a number of other searching techniques and sources as well (Bates, 1989).
3. Searching for and then selecting among your results takes time and thought, like shopping for jeans. You may pick up a lot of different pairs, take them to the dressing room, and try them on in order to pick the best ones. Similarly, you may identify a large number of articles, e-mail them to yourself, and then choose the ones that "fit" best (Williams, 2008).

Informal versus Formal Networks

ILI librarians have also applied a number of other important concepts in ILI. Greenfield's (1987) informal versus formal networks concept describes scholarly communication in the form of personal contacts and information shared at conferences, programs, meetings, and otherwise, as opposed to published scholarly materials that have been reviewed. Informal "networks" that utilize e-mail, listservs, newsgroups, chat, instant messaging, class discussion boards, RSS feeds, wikis, blogs, podcasts, videos, virtual worlds, and other new technologies, as they are developed, now constitute an important, although informal, part of the information development sequence. Social networks like MySpace, Facebook, Flickr, del.icio.us, Ning, Twitter, and Second Life all offer ILI opportunities, and some researchers are already experimenting with them (Centre for Information Literacy Research, 2008; Classroom Instruction in Facebook, 2008; Information Literacy Instruction Through Social Software, 2008; Greenhill, accessed 2009).

1. You can help people understand the concept of a social network by comparing it to gossip during coffee breaks as opposed to official announcements by administrators or government officials and then actually use social networks with your own ILI learners.
2. "Conversation" can be a useful analogy for scholarly communication. Some academic conversations or arguments take place at conferences, in the form of paper presentations, followed by questions and answers. Others are silent, published in journals. All are supported by references (evidence), selected by those who are presenting the argument. Scholars may critique the selection of evidence, the interpretation of that evidence, and/or the argument(s) (Bechtel, 1986). Some conversations, like Talmudic commentaries, go on for generations, and an author's references are like conversations with those who came before (Simon, 2008).

Popular versus Scholarly Articles

Learners are still confused about the differences between popular and scholarly articles, another important teaching/learning concept (Greenfield, 1987). Analogies useful to get this concept across include the following:

1. Help learners understand the intellectual "conversation" that constitutes higher education by understanding what the various conversations are, who is participating in them, how to evaluate the quality of their participation, and how to "make a significant comment on the issue or problem" (Bechtel, 1986: 223). Popular magazine articles, then, are similar to an informal conversation between two people who simply express their opinions on a topic. Journal articles, on the other hand, have a particular structure and support their "conversations" or "arguments" with evidence in the form of research data, studies, and other publications (Bechtel, 1986).
2. Baseball, too, is an effective analogy for popular versus scholarly materials, using a pyramid as a visual analogy. T-ball is at the bottom, as many people play it with few skills, and everyone wins. The next level is high school baseball. You must have some skills, so fewer people play, and although you may be interested in it, it is a hobby. The minor leagues are at the third level, with many fewer, but skilled people paid to play. Finally, the major leagues are at the smallest top part of the pyramid, with few, but highly skilled players who make a living out of playing baseball. Similarly, popular publications, written and read by many, appear at the bottom of a pyramid. Scholarly publications appear at the top, written by highly skilled experts and read by a select audience, mostly of other experts in the same field (Francis, 2008).

Mechanics of Use

In 1987, Lippincott identified a number of important conceptual frameworks for ILI, including mechanics of use. As we add new information tools and upgrade to new versions of existing tools, teaching the basic mechanics of use increases in importance. The problem is that we are drowning not only in tools (and the information itself) but also in unique interfaces to those tools. We cannot possibly help everyone learn all aspects of every information tool, so we must step back and teach common features using a few examples of the bare basics. Teach concepts, but also mechanics, to illustrate those concepts, and try to incorporate critical thinking throughout. The following analogies may help:

1. Watching someone else drive is useful, but you cannot learn to drive just by watching. You have to drive a car yourself, but driving a car and trying a new database can be really scary at first. After a while it becomes second nature, except

when driving a car you have never driven before or using a database that is new to you. It helps to know that, like cars, databases perform many similar functions. Once you know the basics, it just takes a little extra time to figure out how a particular car or a particular database works (Chudnick, 2008).

2. You can listen to 15- to 30-second music snippets before deciding to download music from an online store like iTunes. These snippets are somewhat analogous to abstracts. At a music download site, you must take another step to get the whole song. You have to pay for it. To get an entire article, you may need to click on a separate link for it, with a number of different possible alternatives, including using authentication through a proxy server, using a link resolver to locate the full text in another database (Daugherty, 2008), or retrieving a catalog record and going to a physical library in order to find a copy of the article.
3. Gamers may feel more comfortable experimenting with using a complex subject-specific periodical index database if they approach it the way they learn a new videogame. They need a strategy and repeated practice. They also need to remember that few people get it right the first time, and most people learn from their mistakes (Fick, 2008).

Sets

Lippincott (1987) described four other useful teaching concepts: "Sets," "Bibliographic Record," "Controlled Vocabulary/Free Text Terms," and "Boolean Operators." Each of these concepts has grown in importance in the technological age, and you can use analogies to teach them all. For example, the concept of "Sets" helps people learn how to divide a topic into component parts in order to develop an effective search strategy or to narrow or broaden a search. Useful analogies for this concept include the following:

1. You learn how to bake a cake by following a recipe that groups certain activities together—for example, sift the flour with the salt; cream butter and sugar together; add eggs to creamed mixture; measure liquid; and then alternate adding flour and liquid to egg mixture, one third at a time.
2. The building blocks approach breaks a topic into its parts, searches each part separately, and then puts various parts together to "build" a search that will provide the most relevant results (Markey and Cochrane, 1981).
3. The successive fractions analogy takes an approach opposite to the building blocks analogy. You keep limiting a broad search until you end up with a "fraction" of your first search, which consists of those results most relevant to your topic (Markey and Cochrane, 1981).

Boolean Operators/Connectors

Some learners grasp the idea of Boolean operators like "and," "or," and "not" fairly quickly if you use intersecting Venn diagrams to illustrate these concepts. This is particularly effective if you draw two or three intersecting Venn diagram circles on a board, label each circle, and ask as group to tell you what to color in, in order to represent each of the three main connectors.

1. Use food combinations like a peanut butter sandwich, a jelly sandwich, and a peanut butter and jelly sandwich. You could even use Goober Grape, a jar of peanut butter combined with jelly, to create a peanut butter and jelly sandwich. You could also refine this example further by saying that you do not want crunchy peanut butter (Oswald, 2008).
2. Ask learners to pick from a deck of playing cards those that represent certain characteristics, like black and King, or (number card or Queen) and (black). Use these to explain both Boolean operators and nesting (Snavely, 1998).

Milking the Bibliographic Record

Lippincott's (1987) "Bibliographic Record" concept helps people learn about the types of information provided about single items and how they may be "milked" in order to evaluate or filter for the most useful materials, as well as about how to find additional materials on the same topic.

1. You *can* tell some things about a book by its cover. If you look closely at the author, publisher, title, and publication dates in a citation, as well as the length of an item, you may be able to identify which sources would be the most promising in

a list of citations. Books published by university presses tend to be quite scholarly, for instance.

2. If you open the book and read the introduction, or use a Google Books search or Amazon's search within the book, you can probably shrink the number of promising results. In milking the bibliographic record, the equivalent would be reading the abstract for an item, if an abstract is provided.
3. Look at the table of contents of a book or examine the subject headings in the bibliographic record to determine if the item is on target for your information need and to focus your search.
4. Use the "TRACE" search tactic, taking another look at your previous searches to find additional search works, an analogy to retracing your steps (Bates, 1979).

Databases, Online Databases, Online Systems/Vendors

Does your library subscribe to 10, 20, or 100 or more databases or systems, provided by different vendors, many with their own interfaces? If so, learning to differentiate among them can help learners become powerful information users rather than people tossing around here and there in the information gale.

1. Put quite simply, a database is an organized collection of information, like the Yellow Pages or a baseball card collection organized by team. Placing a database's content into a computer's memory (with a means of searching and displaying results) turns it into an online database.
2. Online systems are collections of online databases, like file cabinets with folders, which in turn may contain more folders. These folders, then, contain papers on specific topics.
3. Car manufacturers/car models are like database vendors and individual databases (Daugherty, 2008).

The Right Information Source/Tool for the Right Purpose

Picking among a myriad of Web search tools, licensed and unlicensed online databases, and print information sources can be an overwhelming task. Web search tools alone can differ widely from one another, particularly in their means of gathering, organizing, searching, and displaying data. They may also differ in terms of the behind-the-scenes relevancy rankings (algorithms) that they utilize, as well as in their commercial nature. For example, a *Los Angeles Times* article published in October 2000 revealed that AltaVista "charg[es] fees for prominently displayed listings in search results . . . [and] has about 1,000 license agreements worth an average of $100,000 apiece" (Liedtke, 2000: 8). Useful analogies for this concept include the following:

1. Wal-Mart may have some types of items at reasonable prices, but the best selections may be at specialty stories, like Bike Barn for bikes and Linens 'n Things for housewares, or even the pharmacy within Wal-Mart for specific types of items (Hollingsworth, 2008; Williams, 2008).
2. Doing all of your research using free Web resources is like doing all of your grocery shopping at 7-11. They have food, but lots of it is not good for you and you have to check the ingredients carefully. On the other hand, using library subscription databases is like shopping at Whole Foods. There are many more healthy selections. "Shopping" at general search engines like Google means you are missing "nutritious" information formats (Aydelott, 2008).

The Caveat Emptor Approach

Empowering the learner is the essence of ILI, and what better way to achieve this goal than to help people become critical users of information and information sources? We need to encourage a healthy questioning attitude toward information products by helping them learn to pose a series of questions, such as: "Who is the audience?" "What is the purpose of the item?" "Who sponsored, developed, and wrote the item?" and "How accurate, complete, and up to date is it?"

1. Do you take the salesperson's word on reliability, drivability, and long-term value when buying a car? Or do you do research ahead of time and then take it for a test drive before purchasing?
2. Often, you can find Web site reviews of digital cameras or other products. Can you trust these sites? Who sponsors the site? Do they take advertising, and does this influence their reviews?

This is similar to critical thinking about research tools and the items retrieved by using those tools (Boyd, 2008).

Placement of Conceptual Frameworks

The analogies discussed are examples of conceptual frameworks and related analogies that can be used in whole or in part in various ILI situations, utilizing a variety of formats, and placed at different points in the learning process continuum. In fact, there has been debate about the point at which to introduce conceptual models such as these. Should they be used as text or as graphic "advance organizers" (prior to instruction), as "embedded activators" (during instruction), or as "post synthesizers" (following instruction) (Ausubel, 1960; Kools et al., 2006)? One large study of analogies used in textbooks found that a majority (76 percent) appeared as embedded activators during instruction, when the content became more difficult or abstract (Curtis and Reigeluth, 1984). Other findings from the same study included that 84 percent of the analogies used were verbal only (used no accompanying pictures), 82 percent used a concrete vehicle to explain an abstract topic, and 81 percent used "enriched analogies" (stated the grounds for the analogy and possibly the limitations). Questions arise here as to the effectiveness of analogies in learning, retention, and transfer, particularly in learning abstract concepts. According to Mayer (1979: 382), advance organizers "seem to have their strongest positive effects not on measures of retention, but rather on measures of transfer." This speaks strongly in support of using analogies in ILI, as the transfer of learning through learning how to learn is really what we are after.

The Cumulative Effect on Learning

Despite the questions and the debate about where to place analogies within a teaching/learning context, learners at all levels seem to grasp new abstract concepts such as controlled vocabularies better when they are compared to well-understood concrete analogies. Moreover, as with group concept mapping, when learners think about and discuss the analogies themselves as tools for understanding concepts—that is, when they engage in metacognition, or looking at their own thinking and learning process, especially in a small group setting—the effect can be multiplied (Hacker, Dunlovsky, and Graesser, 1998; Unger, 1996; Mason, 1994; Gao, et al., 2007).

Conceptual models like these, the use of analogies, and metacognitive exercises regarding analogy use can help users construct more accurate mental models as they begin to understand the ever-more complex, information-laden world. They encourage learners to step back and think about the resources they use and various ways of searching for and organizing information. This sort of critical thinking helps make the information-seeking process a manipulatable tool under the control of the user rather than an obstacle to be overcome or even an end in itself.

FINAL REMARKS

Many people are anxious about libraries and library resources. Some avoid libraries because libraries seem overwhelming and confusing, particularly with their many diverse and complex online "search engines." Some people are afraid to ask questions or even try to use library technologies (hardware or software) out of fear of technology or because of the potential for embarrassment. We must continue to work hard to demystify libraries and to help people alter incorrect mental models of information tools. We need to be empathetic and help people by simplifying and clarifying the information-seeking process, tools, and products. Adding affective elements to our information literacy standards would help us keep this in mind and also address these issues in our ILI (Cahoy, 2004). We have come a long way ourselves in learning to live with, if not anticipate, the new and changing face of libraries and information-researching tools. Now we must work harder to help bring our users along with us.

EXERCISES

1. Develop two active learning exercises using tagging and examples from controlled vocabularies to help learners understand the differences between them and the value of each.
2. Think of some modern-day analogies you might use to help people learn concepts that may be new to them, such as Web search tools versus licensed databases.
3. Review a Web-based tutorial that does not use an analogy—for example, Pennsylvania State University's "Information Literacy & You" (Wright, 2008)—and

come up with an analogy that would work with that site's approach.

READ MORE ABOUT IT

British Library and JSIC. "Information Behaviour of the Researcher of the Future" (January 11, 2008). Available: www.twine.com/_b/download/1y8bplft-4x/b0bsl79jx59rwtw7lr978psshbdk7tsxlb1w4wlpmfhprmt/1y8bplft-4x/b0bsl79jx59rwtw7lr978psshbdk7-tsxlb1w4wlpmfhprmt/gg_final_keynote_11012008.pdf (accessed December 22, 2008).

Carlile, Heather. 2007. "The Implications of Library Anxiety for Academic Reference Services: A Review of the Literature." *Australian Academic and Research Libraries* 38, no. 2: 129–147.

Gao, Hong et al. 2007. "A Review of Studies on Collaborative Concept Mapping: What Have We Learned About the Technique and What Is Next?" *Journal of Interactive Learning Research* 18, no. 4: 479–492.

Keefer, Jane. 1993. "The Hungry Rats Syndrome: Library Anxiety, Information Literacy, and the Academic Reference Process." *RQ* 32, no. 3: 333–339.

Kuhlthau, Carol C. 1985. "A Process Approach to Library Skills Instruction: An Investigation Into the Design of the Library Research Process." *School Library Media Quarterly* 13: 35–40.

McKibbon, Shelley. "Using Analogies to Get the Message Across" (April 2, 2008). Available: http://libguides.library.dal.ca/data/files/2983/Analogies.pdf (accessed December 23, 2008).

Mellon, Constance A. 1986. "Library Anxiety: A Grounded Theory and Its Development." *College & Research Libraries* 47, no. 2: 160–165.

Mizrachi, Diane. Forthcoming. "Library Anxiety." In *Encyclopedia of Library and Information Science,* edited by Marcia J. Bates and Mary Maack. New York: Taylor & Francis.

Onwuegbuzie, Anthony J., Qun G. Jiao, and Sharon L. Bostick. 2004. *Library Anxiety: Theory, Research, and Applications.* Lanham, MD: Scarecrow Press.

Reichel, Mary and Mary Ann Ramey, eds. 1987. *Conceptual Frameworks for Bibliographic Education: Theory into Practice.* Littleton, CO: Libraries Unlimited.

Spiteri, Louise F. 2007. "The Structure and Form of Folksonomy Tags: The Road to the Public Library Catalog." *Information Technology and Libraries* 26, no. 3: 13–25.

Weil, Michelle M. and Larry D. Rosen. 1997. *Technostress: Coping With Technology @Work @Home @Play*. New York: Wiley & Sons.

Westbrook, Lynn. 2006. "Mental Models: A Theoretical Overview and Preliminary Study." *Journal of Information Science* 32, no. 6: 563–579.

Chapter 6

Critical Thinking and Active Learning

If 50 million people say a foolish thing, it is still a foolish thing.

—Anatole France

CRITICAL THINKING

Learning to think critically is one of the most important goals of lifelong learning for all learners. Like the term *information literacy* (IL), however, *critical thinking* has been defined in many ways, to suit many different circumstances. Other terms and phrases for "critical thinking" include "critical inquiry," "good thinking," "critical reasoning," "analytic reflection," and "metacognitive ability." Popular publications and research studies abound on cognitive development (see Chapters 3 and 4), stages in the development of reasoning skills, metacognition, and how to teach critical thinking—in many disciplines and at various educational and age levels. Books on critical thinking include popular publications such as *Don't Believe Everything You Think* (Kida, 2006) and "What Was I Thinking" (Kolbert, 2008), as well as more scholarly treatments like "Critical Thinking: An Extended Definition" (Petress, 2004), "Critical Thinking in Education: A Review" (Pithers and Soden, 2000), and others (Hall, 2002; *Critical Thinking: Unfinished Business*, 2005; Willingham, 2007).

Why all of this attention to critical thinking? We are now able to get to information textually, orally, and visually almost anywhere. We carry communication and information access devices with us or wear them, or even embed them in our clothing for research, personal, and health-related purposes (Lukowicz, 2008; International Symposium on Wearable Computers, 2008). (See Chapter 15 for more on this topic.) And we are collaborating with and relying upon many others around the world, in exciting and innovative ways, as we connect globally and socially through the evolving Web (Tapscott and Williams, 2006). As we get used to faster and faster access to textual, oral/audio, and visual information, however, we may be relying too much on speedy access, on visual attractiveness, and on mass opinions (Rawlings, 2007). Both we and our learners need to be thinking critically more than ever about how information is generated, what it is we are accessing, who is responsible for it, what its purpose is, how we can search for it, and how it is presented to us. The key question then becomes who should teach people about these sorts of questions and how to find answers to them, above and beyond the mechanics of searching for information?

Relation to Information Literacy

In a frequently cited information literacy instruction (ILI)-related essay, Mona McCormick reminds us that it is not the process of finding information that is important, but what people do with it once they have found it. She defines critical thinking as the ability to distinguish fact from fiction, to notice opinion, and actually to think about whether information seekers will accept the "facts" and agree with the opinions to which they may or may not lead (McCormick, 1983). McCormick is referring to thinking critically about individual items we may find in searching for information, such as an article, a book, or a statistical table. However, critical thinking can be broader or narrower than that, depending on the definition of the phrase and on how one wishes to apply it. In fact, the definition of critical thinking and how it is applied lie at the heart of the debate over who should be teaching critical thinking, with some arguing for the ILI librarian and others for the content or subject matter expert—most often teachers or faculty at schools, colleges, or universities.

Willingham (2007) and Pithers and Soden (2000) claim that there are no generic critical thinking skills that can be applied independently to a variety of situations. Moreover, they claim that in order to think critically, one must have adequate knowledge of the content, subject matter, or "domain" and teach critical thinking only within a discipline. If this is so, then the teacher or faculty member would indeed be the best person to teach critical thinking, and such critical thinking could vary from one discipline to another. However, Willingham's argument regarding the nonexistence of generic critical thinking skills does not really relate to novices. Simmons (2005) calls novices "apprentices," learners new to a discipline and newly exposed to a topic, a concept, an article, or a book in that discipline. For naive learners like these, learning to pose basic generic questions is really the first step needed prior to critical thinking on a deeper level regarding a specific topic area or a discipline. Teaching these generic ways of thinking critically need not be limited to experts in particular disciplines. Miri, Ben-Chaim, and Zoller's (2007) longitudinal case study of high school science students supports this contention. They discovered that three main teaching strategies for higher-order thinking skills led to "students statistically significant pre–post improvement on their disposition toward truth seeking, open-mindedness, CT [critical thinking]-self confidence, and maturity . . . as well as, on their CT skills, particularly on the evaluation and inference categories. . . ." (Miri, Ben-Chaim, and Zoller, 2007: 363). These teaching strategies are: "(a) dealing with interdisciplinary real-world cases; (b) encouraging open-ended class discussions; and (c) fostering short inquiry experiments to be performed in groups" (Miri, Ben-Chaim, and Zoller 2007: 363). They go on to say that results of standardized critical thinking tests, like the California Critical Thinking Disposition Inventory (Insight Assessment, 2008a) and the California Critical Thinking Skills Test (Insight Assessment 2008b), indicated that these students were able to transfer their newly acquired critical thinking skills across domains.

All of this leads to the conclusion that librarians can do much to help the critical thinking process become a routine and natural part of each step of the information-seeking process at various age and skill levels and in varying environments. To do this effectively we must focus on bare-bones basics and then work with subject experts to provide additional evaluative criteria and detail for those who want it, as related to specific subject areas or disciplines.

Simmons (2005) supports and extends this conclusion through her analysis of the important role of ILI, particularly as "critical information literacy" in relation to the process of communication, research, and publication and how they differ among disciplines. She contends quite rightly that librarians are interdisciplinary, as they need to be aware of these disciplinary differences in order to do effective collection development for them. She contends further that information literacy is analogous to the "Writing Across the Curriculum" pedagogy, that ILI librarians have a similar role to play, and indeed can collaborate quite well with writing programs in joint writing/IL instruction. She goes on to critique the ACRL Information Literacy Competency Standards as focused too much on guiding learners to discover a "unified 'truth'" outside of a disciplinary context and urges librarians to move to a new role, utilizing genre theory to focus more on critical thinking in relation to specific disciplines (Simmons, 2005).

While all of this is true, it is not new, although it seems to have been forgotten both by Simmons (2005) and by Grafstein (2002), the latter in an often-cited article on ILI in the disciplines. In the 1980s, Oberman and Strauch (1982) and Reichel and Ramey (1987) included essays on teaching library researching and conceptual frameworks within the context of disciplines in the sciences, social sciences, and humanities, including chemistry, health sciences, psychology, sociology, design, and literary research. They offered practical approaches to teaching many important concepts that went far beyond simply teaching the mechanics of using research tools.

Bechtel, too, offered a highly useful and more generic model for teaching communication, research and publication in a variety of disciplines in the mid-1980s. She posited a model of "academic conversation" whereby those new to a discipline learn first that there are "conversations" or "arguments" regarding topics within a discipline and that these conversations occur orally at conferences, in hallways, in meetings, and in writing in the form of conference papers, articles, letters to the editor, and books. The conversants provide and interpret evidence to support all of the arguments. This evidence takes the form of footnotes and bibliographies. The main conversants and arguments in a discipline are well known to those who are experts in that discipline, including faculty and researchers, although they may not be recognizable to those who are new to the discipline. By researching, learning about, and offering their own interpretations of arguments and evidence, new learners are joining that academic conversation (Bechtel, 1986). Boettcher (2006) updated the scholarly communication process 20 years later regarding open access and the concept of the "scholar's choice," the idea that researchers control the content and can decide where they will submit their manuscripts for publication. However, Bechtel's basic generic model still applies and can be highly useful as a foundation for ILI regarding scholarly communication and the peer review process. In 1989, Fink also offered many significant insights into the politics of what was then called "bibliographic instruction" both generically and within different disciplines.

As we see increased movement among ILI librarians to address IL within disciplines today, we need to look back at discipline-focused work from the 1980s that may lay the groundwork for learners to apply discipline-specific critical thinking at many levels and in a variety of library environments. A look back at the literature also illustrates the fact that under all of its many previous names, including "library instruction" and "bibliographic instruction," IL has always included critical thinking and the teaching of transferable concepts. For more on the history of these concepts, see Chapter 2.

Information Literacy Instruction Organizations Provide Direction

In 1989, the ALA Presidential Committee on Information Literacy (1989: online) stated that "To be information literate, a person must be able to recognize when information is needed and have the ability to locate, evaluate and use effectively the needed information. . . . Ultimately, information literate people are those who have learned how to learn." "Evaluating" and "using effectively" comprise the critical thinking elements of this definition. Building on this definition, in the early 1990s, ACRL IS' Model Statement of Objectives for Academic Library Instruction spelled this out in detail for academic libraries as a tool for instruction librarians (ALA. ACRL. BIS, 1991).

In 2000, ALA's ACRL identified specific "competencies" that learners should have in order to become critical thinking information literate individuals. "Information Literacy Competencies for Higher Education" contains five standards along with detailed "Performance Indicators" for each standard and even more detailed "Measurable Outcomes" for each Performance Indicator. The guiding principles of this document state that evaluation was incorporated into various sections of the document, as appropriate, to reflect the fact that evaluation should occur throughout the research process. For example, The Introduction to the revised ACRL IS's "Objectives for Information Literacy Instruction by Academic Librarians" reiterates support for the librarian's role in helping people learn critical thinking and evaluation skills:

> Many of the outcomes from the *Competency Standards* that deal explicitly with evaluation are primarily the teaching responsibility of the course instructor in collaboration with the librarian. For example, the course instructor can address the quality of the content of an information source once it is retrieved; the librarian helps people learn how to interpret information in the sources that can be used for evaluating information during the research process. As reliance on Internet sources increases, the librarian's objectivity and expertise in evaluating information and information sources become invaluable. (ALA. ACRL. IS, 2001: 4)

This document provides a number of possible objectives that librarians can address to meet these Standards. To meet Standard 3, Performance Indicator 3.2.c. ("Recognizes prejudice, deception, or manipulation"), for instance, you could address the following objective: "Demonstrates an understanding that information in any format reflects an author's sponsor's and/or publisher's point of view" (ALA. ACRL. IS, 2001: online). All of these documents are available on a single ACRL IL page, arranged in categories along with other useful links: Overview, Standards & Guidelines, Resources & Ideas, and Professional Activity (ALA. ACRL, 2008b).

The Information Literacy Instruction Librarian's Job: To "Save the Time of the Reader"

These important publications, particularly ACRL's *Information Literacy Competency Standards*, now translated into other languages and recognized worldwide (ALA. ACRL, 2008c), indicate that IL promotes self-reflective thinking about how to identify, locate, evaluate, and use information. As we have seen in Chapter 2, the IL movement's focus on evaluation and critical thinking carries forward Patricia Knapp's ideals from the 1960s. Yet, for the most part, people really do not think much about how they search for information and often settle for whatever they can get quickly and without too much trouble. They may feel too shy or embarrassed to ask for help even when they cannot find the information they need. They may just settle for the complete text of articles or Web pages that are tangential to their topics rather than take the time to locate periodicals in a physical library and photocopy the articles, even if they are much more suited to the topic or of higher quality. This natural tendency reflects a corollary to Ranganathan's fourth law: "Save the time of the reader, or the reader will save her/his own time by taking the shortest route to information, regardless of its quality" (*Encyclopedia of Library and Information Science*, 1978a). Mann (1993) expressed this corollary as "The Principle of Least Effort." This means that users will do whatever takes less time and energy, even it means more effort later or if it means they end up with poorer quality information. This is assuming, of course, that people even know that there is relevant information available through means other than Google and Yahoo, often an "information epiphany" as Hall (2002) puts it.

What Should Librarians Teach?

In the pre-Web world, information was largely filtered before it ever got to users. Librarians selected books by reading book reviews written by reviewers hired by publishers or editors of magazines, newspapers, and journals. Many books were not reviewed, and, with limited budgets, librarians had to pick and choose for their collections even among those that were reviewed, trying, of course, to develop and maintain collections balanced by differing viewpoints. Articles published in most kinds of media, including newspapers, were reviewed by an editorial board and/or by peers. Self-published materials were often suspect and thought to be of poor quality. Compare that situation to the current open Web environment. Today, anyone or any group can self-publish on the Web in the form of Web sites, blogs, wikis, videos posted on YouTube, and so on. In addition, publishers and publications with solid reputations also publish on, or through, the Web, using it as a delivery mechanism.

Critical Thinking About Information Researching Tools

Instead of filtering materials before they ever get to the user, librarians now need to help users learn to pose questions and filter on their own. This means that ILI librarians in all types of libraries have important roles to play in teaching basic, generic, critical thinking skills applicable to almost any form or format of information. ILI librarians can help people learn to examine information-researching tools for sponsorship or authorship, timeliness, form of publication, and coverage or scope in comparison to other tools in the same field, regardless of the format. This includes general Web search engines like Google and Yahoo, as well as Web 2.0 tools and others as they are developed (Rawlings, 2007; Cohen and Jacobson, 2008; Grassian, 2008c).

Why should we teach critical thinking about general Web search engines? Web search tools like Google and Yahoo are a mystery to most Internet users. Many people think that all Web search tools search the entire Web, if not the entire world of knowledge, and then bring it all back free of charge. They are unaware of the fact that Web search tools collect information and store it in their own databases. Some search tools, like Yahoo!, select Web sites to include in their database rather than just gathering in all that they can find. Yahoo! offers a general search and focused search services, like "Green" and "Widgets," small programs you access through an icon you place on your desktop, like weather forecast or a chat service (TechTerms.com, 2008b). Yahoo! also offers a "Directory," Web sites listed in category menus. The "Librarians Internet Index" (LII) is a highly selective site that includes reviews of Web sites, also categorized in menus and searchable (LII, 2008). Both of these sites act as filters by selecting Web sites and then categorizing them. On the other hand, Google sends out "robots" to collect as many pages as possible for its database. Type your search words in its single search box and press Enter, and Google will provide a ranked list of results. How and why Google ranks its results is a closely guarded trade secret. Other free Web search tools and metasearch tools like Clusty (2008) and Dogpile (2008) also keep their ranking algorithms a secret.

Questions about these sorts of tools include: How do these sites differ, and when might you want to use one as opposed to the other? How do Yahoo! and LII decide what to include in their databases? What operation is Google performing behind the scenes before displaying the results of a search? For how long will Google keep cached copies of Web pages? Is there a limit to the number of items Yahoo! will include in its database? LII clearly states its selection criteria. How does Yahoo! decide which categories to use, which labels to use for these categories, and how to apply them? LII provides one or more Library of Congress subject headings for each site they include. Does Yahoo! list multidisciplinary sites under more than one category? Is there a limit to the number of different categories Yahoo! may use for a particular site? What time period do all of these tools cover?

We also need to help people learn to question other free research tools, like Google Scholar (2008). Useful as they are, like all research tools, the free ones have their limitations. For instance, as with general Google searching, Google Scholar's ranking algorithm is a mystery and will very likely remain a trade secret. We do not know Google Scholar's scope in terms of topics covered, time period covered, types and specific publications indexed, and how it determines numbers of "cited by" publications. These are all decisions made by Google administrators and not shared publicly. The exercise described in Figure 6.1 and UCLA Library's (2005) fairly simple exercise comparing Google Scholar and a licensed database illustrate all of this quite clearly.

This confusing state of affairs means that ILI librarians need to help learners to step back, think, and pose questions about all kinds of research tools before they even begin to use those tools to search for materials. If you start off with critical thinking about familiar tools like Google, it will be easier for learners to ask similar questions about other search tools. In turn, these questions can help our learners understand that database vendors also make important decisions that can impact what and how we search and the sorts of information we can retrieve by using those databases. These decisions include the following:

- Which materials to index
- What time period to cover
- Which words to use as descriptors
- Which descriptors to attach to each item indexed
- How one can search for materials
- How results will be displayed

Asking critical thinking questions related to these points shines a light on some of the political decisions that database vendors make, particularly regarding which materials to index and how to label items—i.e., which words to use as descriptors or subjects. Alt-PressWatch and Ethnic NewsWatch, for instance, index many publications that are not indexed in more mainstream general research tools like Academic Search Complete or Gale's General OneFile. Who is making these indexing decisions and why? What are they including, and what are they leaving out? Which subject areas does a given database cover? What types of materials does it index or list? What time period does it cover? Which words does a particular research tool use to describe items it indexes, lists, or provides, or does it avoid controlled vocabularies completely in favor of keyword searching? How have assigned "subjects" or "descriptors" changed over time? The MLA Bibliography uses subjects like "Women Politicians" and "African American Women Politicians," but not "Men Politicians" or "African Ameri-

Figure 6.1 Individual Exercise (Optional: Report Back to Entire Group)

1. Ask learners to look up a topic of their choice using Google and Google Scholar and note the first item listed in the results.
2. Then ask them to look up the same topic in the Librarian's Internet Index to see if the items they found using Google and Google Scholar appear here.
3. Ask what, if anything, this says about these Web-based resources and the items they list.

can Men Politicians." How do decisions like these help or hinder the user seeking information on a topic? And how do users distinguish among the various databases available through the library, including library catalogs, as opposed to licensed databases or freely available Web search tools? Often, libraries also contract with commercial library catalog vendors. Who are these vendors? What sorts of design decisions have they made? How do these decisions affect the user's access and ease of use? Do they offer "federated" and/or "faceted" searching?

"Federated" searching enables users to search across databases in an effort to simplify the search and find process. While this approach does streamline searching, it can add conceptual problems of its own. Users may not care where information comes from or its quality, reliability, and currency as long as they can get something quickly and easily. This is not especially admirable, and it is not really new; it is simply a fact of life. When libraries had only print periodical indexes, users took the first few items they could find, and the same was true when CD-ROM indexes were introduced. The quick and easy route is often the one most traveled and may serve some information needs. Quick and easy federated searching offers us great critical thinking opportunities, however, as learners are often unaware of what they are searching and of differences among controlled vocabularies from one database to another. Intermingled results and slow response rates can add to the problem (Wrubel and Schmidt, 2007). Figure 6.2 illustrates two ways of helping learners grasp the concept of a federated search.

"Faceted" searching improves upon federated searching by adding a variety of categories and subcategories with which to refine a search without returning to the original search screen. North Carolina State University's (NCSU) Endeca Catalog includes refinement categories such as format, call number location, and region of the world as "facets" or aspects of search results. Following a search, these categories appear as links in the left-hand column, with the numbers of results listed for each category (NCSU Libraries, accessed 2008). However, the refinement categories the user sees will vary, depending on her or his search. Using the "advanced search" option allows learners to see all of the possible categories, yet many people do not notice or use an advanced search, even when using the most popular general search engine, Google. As you help learners grasp these mechanics of use, it is also important to get them to step back and think about the information-researching tools they are using, what they search, how they search, how results are displayed, and why they may or may not get the kinds of results they expect or want. Are we layering more complexity on top of the databases over which we have most control, our library catalogs, rather than making it easier to use our catalogs? Should we, instead, work with general Web search engines like Google, and even use Google Scholar, for instance, as our library catalog

Figure 6.2 Teaching Federated Searching and Critical Thinking: Two Methods

1. Native Mode Database → Federated Searching
   a. Begin by selecting an appropriate database, including use of three evaluative criteria: topics covered, materials indexed or provided, and time period covered.
   b. Briefly model use of a database, including basic mechanics and critical thinking about search terms, retrievals, controlled vocabulary, Boolean, and truncation. Ideally, learners would follow along on their own computers, learning by doing.
   c. Model use of federated searching, describing it as a way to save time and possibly get some unexpectedly useful results by searching across many different databases simultaneously in a simple manner.
2. Federated Searching → Native Mode Database
   a. Begin with federated searching.
   b. Pose questions to the learners regarding the results, particularly the subject matter, types of materials listed or provided, time periods covered, authenticity, and completeness.
   c. Challenge learners to try more advanced searching in a single database in order to identify advantages of this type of searching as opposed to federated searching (often limited to basic keyword searching).

search engine, if not integrate wholly with it? These are questions we should consider. They are questions our users may answer for us, as they vote for "search engines" with their eyeballs.

Learning to look for limitations in all research tools, as well as in information materials, is an essential part of the critical thinking process. Librarians can play a key role here, as we use many different databases and other research tools in many formats. As a result, we encounter many distinctive differences in interfaces, in coverage of materials indexed, in time periods covered, in subject/descriptor vocabulary, in labeling, in search options, in displays of results, and in help offered by vendors.

Critical Thinking About Materials Retrieved

Why is it important to help people learn to pose critical thinking questions about Web pages, blogs, articles, books, and other materials? The answer revolves around the issue of filtered information. All of us filter information through our own experiences and knowledge. Many of us have forgotten Paddy Chayefsky's (1976) warning in the 1976 movie *Network* to be critical of typical information sources such as newspapers and television network news. What would Chayefsky have thought of the Web, blogs, and other information tools and resources that did not exist in 1976? What does the average person think about them? Research has shown that those who are the least skilled and knowledgeable tend to have the highest opinions of their own intellectual abilities (Kruger and Dunning, 1999). Yet these are the very people who most need to get in the habit of asking basic critical thinking questions about the materials they find, such as the following:

- What is the purpose?
- Who is the audience?
- Who is the author or sponsor?
- What sort of expertise does the author or sponsor have related to this topic?
- How accurate is it?
- How up to date is it?
- How complete is it in comparison to other materials on the topic? (Beck, 2008; Cohen and Jacobson, 2008; Grassian, 1995)

ILI librarians can also help people learn that they need to look for and examine evidence provided to support arguments of all kinds—for politicians, for products, for research studies. Learners need to be aware of the fact that opinions posted publicly on blogs and elsewhere may be bought and sold, as well (Honan, 2008). So, sometimes even knowing who an author is does not tell you about his or her motivation for writing. Amazon.com and many other dot com Web sites have advertising on many of their pages. Does the Expedia travel Web site list airfares for all airlines or just particular ones? Which listings come to the top of their results pages? Who pays to provide this service free of charge to users, and why? Authorship and sponsorship are not always obvious or easy to determine, and yet we need to know who authors and sponsors are, as well as their expertise and biases, so we can make our own judgments about the reliability and quality of a particular Web site or other information tool. Learners can practice these skills on their own or in groups by using exercises like "Hoax? Personal Opinion? Scholarly Research? You Decide!" (Grassian and Zwemer, 2008).

Once learners are sensitized to watch for these criteria and to look for and examine supporting evidence, experts can help them hone these skills and focus them on the discipline, the issue, or the product at hand (Frick, 1975; Bodi, 1988; Rankin, 1988; Kida, 2006). Specifically, subject matter experts can step in to provide their informed opinions as to the authority of the sponsor or writer, the reputation of the publication or publisher, and the depth and breadth as well as accuracy of the information itself and the evidence supplied in its support.

ILI librarians are not alone in their efforts to help their users learn to think critically about information resources. Numerous educators have expanded on the notion of teaching critical thinking, identified successful ways of teaching it, and provided detailed practical frameworks for teachers (Beyer, 1985a, 1985b; Munro and Slater, 1985; Pithers and Soden, 2000). In academic libraries, librarians often work with course instructors in teaching critical thinking as related to course syllabi and assignments, through one-shot face-to-face (F2F) group instruction and many other forms of ILI. The Widener University Library's Web site evaluation materials include a tutorial and exercise as well as links to the original evaluation materials developed by Alexander and Tate (1996). School libraries and public libraries are also helping their user populations learn to think critically about information resources through ILI-related workshops, classes, and handouts. The Nashua Public Library (2008: online), for instance, includes "evaluating web sites and online information" in its two-hour Internet class. The San Diego Public Library offers a workshop and an annotated handout on medical information on the Internet (Martin, accessed 2008). The Lexington (MA) Public Schools Libraries' (2008: online) Web site offers a set of Web evaluation questions for elementary school students, as does Kathy Schrock's (2008a, 2008b) "Guide for Educators" site. Outreach efforts to different types of libraries can also help librarians help their learners improve their information researching and critical thinking skills in order to better prepare them for higher level research (LILi, 2008). For more examples of critical thinking materials developed by librarians, check "InfoLit Global" (IFLA and UNESCO, 2008), "SOS for Information Literacy" (2006), "PRIMO" (ALA. ACRL. IS, 2008e), and A.N.T.S. (2008).

All of this may help you as you engage in this effort yourself, and from the earlier discussion we may be able to agree that critical thinking is an essential element of IL. We may also be able to agree that we need to figure out clear, simple, and effective ways to draw people's attention to and help them learn to practice these evaluative skills. In the words of a well-known bumper sticker, our users need to get in the "Question Authority" habit, and we can help them learn which questions to pose. However, to do so effectively, we need to distinguish both critical thinking and IL from computer literacy and technology literacy.

Information Literacy or Technology Literacy?

Does technology literacy include critical thinking, and is technology literacy distinct from and more important than IL? Shapiro and Hughes tried to take the concept of critical thinking a step further by including the categories of "Critical Literacy" and "Resource Literacy" among the seven categories they list as elements of a prototype information literacy curriculum: "Tool Literacy," "Resource Literacy," "Social-Structural Literacy," "Research Literacy," "Publishing Literacy," "Emerging Technology Literacy," and "Critical Literacy" (Shapiro and Hughes, 1996).

Their thoughtful analysis is an admirable step in pinning down the slippery definition of IL, as it goes a few steps beyond computer literacy and includes a historical, social, and philosophical contexts. Unfortunately, however, in spite of the title of their article ("Information Literacy as a Liberal Art"), they define many of their seven categories primarily in terms of electronic resources. For example, "Critical Literacy" is defined as "the ability to evaluate critically the intellectual, human and social strengths and weaknesses, potentials and limits, benefits and costs of information technology" (Shapiro and Hughes, 1996: online). They also argue that "'Resource Literacy,' . . . the ability to understand the form, format, location and access methods of information resources, especially daily expanding networked information resources . . . is practically identical with librarians' conceptions of information literacy . . . " (Shapiro and Hughes, 1996: online).

Information Literacy Instruction Encompasses Technology Literacy and More

Actually, librarians' conception of information literacy includes but also encompasses much more than simply "Resource Literacy." Shapiro and Hughes's 1996 definition ignores the fact that ILI from a librarian's standpoint involves helping people learn the basics of evaluating information resources and tools and identifying its source, purpose, accuracy, completeness and immediacy (Shapiro and Hughes, 1996). It also ignores the librarian's knowledge of a range of information resources and her or his ability to weigh their relative values and uses. There is much more to the evaluation or critical thinking aspect of IL than Shapiro and Hughes posit, and the librarian has a key role in helping learners understand its basics, particularly in a socially networked world that has become highly reliant on readily accessible online information.

How do librarians do this? When the Web was new, many were bedazzled by glitzy looking Web pages with fancy graphics. When Web sites added search capability to their own sites they attracted more users, but these sites were still one-sided as site designers were completely in charge of the content and structure of the site, as well as how searching could be conducted and how results were displayed. Web 2.0 offers many more possibilities but also a more complex world, with blogs, wikis, content management systems, Webinars, and sites that allow for tagging and user-generated ratings and comments. Who are the sponsors and authors of such sites, and what are their points of view? How current, accurate, and complete are they? Bloggers are hired to blog about products without indicating that they have been paid to do so (Honan, 2008). Others write political blogs, but can they be trusted (Meola, 2007)? Who are these bloggers, and who is watching them? Wikipedia is wildly popular and successful in terms of readership and participatory authorship, but it has generated much controversy over its seeming disdain for experts and a general public tendency to rely on it for accurate factual information. Wikipedia defenders trumpet near-equivalent error rate comparisons to standard reference tools like the *Encyclopaedia Britannica*, arguing correctly that even tried and true reference works contain errors, have particular points of view, and are not always complete or up to date (Giles, 2005; Encyclopaedia Britannica, 2006; Rosenzweig, 2006). However, they fail to point out that the text of most Wikipedia articles may be changed by anyone at a moment's notice so that comparisons of Wikipedia text to other publications are based on the Wikipedia text that existed at a particular minute and even second in time. But many people continue to trust Wikipedia articles and the "authority of anonymous strangers," as well as general mass opinion, while others are more interested in Wikipedia references (Ream and McCulley, 2007). Google reinforces this trust both by listing links to many Wikipedia articles in its results lists and by referring its users to Answers.com for word definitions, where, in turn, a number of definitions are taken verbatim from Wikipedia.

Some librarians have been trying to sort this out by offering Web 2.0 evaluation guides raising awareness of the need to be wary and maintain a questioning attitude toward all sorts of publications, regardless of the format (Cohen and Jacobson 2008; Grassian, 2008c; Maness, 2006). Others have discussed this issue on listservs and blogs and have recommended critical thinking approaches and rubrics (Blowers 2006b; Robertson, 2006; Washington State University. Center for Teaching, Learning & Technology, 2006; Beaman, 2008). Some have posted critical thinking exercises regarding Wikipedia articles and those in other wikis, like Conservapedia, a wiki-based encyclopedia with a conservative point of view (Rubick, 2007). Exercise examples include analyzing sources cited in articles (Suchy, 2007) and showing a controversial article's history page where edits can be viewed (Juettemeyer, 2007). Still others direct learners to determine the sponsor of a Web site by checking sites like DomainTools (accessed 2008) and Alexa (2008).

Badke suggests that librarians and other academics accept the fact that students will use Wikipedia. He offers a number of ideas for using Wikipedia to improve ILI, for instance, through group assignments to verify Wikipedia articles in other sources and then make corrections, certainly a useful approach. Unfortunately, he also assumes that many librarians are using Wikipedia and finding "much of what you [librarians] need there" (Badke, 2008: online). This is quite an assumption, as even if librarians' usage is high, this does not necessarily equate to high quality, completeness, or accuracy of Wikipedia articles. As Haynes (2008: online) puts it, "it still shakes me up to think that my students may read a completely different interpretation of [a] controversy in Wikipedia by the time I take them there 5 days from now, in a library instruction session." WikipediaVision may shed some light here. It offers a visual representation of Wikipedia edits and can serve as an aid to critical thinking and reflection about how Wikipedia and other wikis function. It is a Google Maps mashup of Wikipedia and a world map where the titles of Wikipedia articles that have just been edited pop up, in close to real time. Clicking on "diff" in the pop up displays the original and the edited portion of a Wikipedia article (Kozma, 2009).

Web 2.0 and Beyond

Are we keeping up with critical thinking about Web 2.0 and further developments? Virtual worlds like Second Life are becoming increasingly popular and offer simulated F2F synchronous (simultaneous, real-time) interactions that are much more satisfying to some people than many asynchronous (any time, any place, for a single individual) methods of communicating. Three-dimensional virtual worlds like Second Life also offer the opportunity to immerse oneself in a learning environment and the opportunity to build such environments as a teacher, as a researcher, and as a learner. Examples of such Second Life immersive learning environments include Virtual Hallucinations, Land of Lincoln, and Caledon, a nineteenth-century sim with a library. How accurate, authoritative, and complete are these environments? Critical thinking can be constructive rather than destructive. By thinking critically, you can offer advice and opinion on areas weak in authenticity as a means of helping people learn to question, with the goal of having an "eyes-open" approach to visual as well as textual objects and environments (Metros and Woolsey, 2006). Murdoch University's Second Life site, Steps to Research, already offers graphic and text representations of the research process in the form of a staircase with a series of rotating artistically designed balls floating above each step. Each ball represents another step in the typical information-researching process. When you click on a ball, you get a notecard describing details regarding that step, as depicted in the snapshot of this site on the CD-ROM that accompanies this book (Greenhill, accessed 2009). IL librarians in virtual worlds might also develop exercises that challenge their visitors and users to discover and identify objects and areas within those worlds that are authentic and others that need further work or are questionable regarding accuracy and completeness. In order to accomplish this, you can build on a rich trove of guides, rubrics, and exercises for evaluating Web sites, going back before the public introduction to the Web, and for critical thinking in general (Alexander and Tate, 1996; Beck, 1997, 2008; Facione, 1990; Facione and Facione, 1994; Grassian, 1995; Tillay, Nelson, and Hopgood, 2002; Grassian and Zwemer, 2008; Rio Salado College, 2008). For more on rubrics and assessment, see Chapter 11.

Exercises like these engage learners in specific tasks designed to help them discover evaluative criteria. Active learning techniques like these, both F2F and online, can be effective means of helping people learn to apply broad critical thinking criteria. In doing so, learners may change their internal mental models of information resources, as well as their information-seeking processes.

ACTIVE LEARNING

What and Why?

What is "active learning"? Allen (1995) points out that it is a concept that dates back to the Greek Socratic method, in which a teacher poses questions, students respond, and learning takes place through a back-and-forth student–teacher interchange of questions, responses, comments, and new ideas. In "The School and Social Progress" John Dewey (1915: 13) describes education as an interactive process, where "A spirit of free communication, of interchange of ideas, suggestions, results, both successes and failures of previous experiences, becomes the dominating note of the recitation." Dewey, one of the first to espouse educational progressivism, saw schools as democratic institutions that should help students learn through real-world, problem-solving experiences. Dewey's theories, and those of others, formed the basis for constructivist approaches to teaching and learning, based on real life (authentic) problems, and building upon or connecting to prior knowledge. They also form the basis for the practice of using active learning and guided or facilitated discovery in educational environments. For more on the psychology of learning, see Chapters 3 and 4.

For librarians, "active learning" is a phrase often used to describe participatory learning activities that take place in a synchronous F2F classroom setting or synchronous online courses, workshops, or Webinars. Learners participate in these online offerings through content management systems like Angel, Blackboard, Moodle, and WebCT or software like Wimba (2008) or even through virtual worlds like Second Life (accessed 2008). (See Chapter 15 for more on using technology to support pedagogy.) Some asynchronous instructional modes are also important forms of active learning instruction and can be used synchronously or asynchronously, remotely or in person, online or on paper. These include paper and online workbooks, online tutorials, Boolean identification exercises, topic narrowing/broadening worksheets, Web site evaluation forms, and plagiarism avoidance exercises. Even the act of filling out an online classroom assessment form asynchronously, adapted from Angelo and Cross' (1993) *Classroom Assessment Techniques,* can be a form of active learning through reflection. Other examples of active learning include hands-on instruction and participating in small- or large-group exercises in various synchronous instruction sessions, in person, or remotely.

Many definitions of active learning emphasize that, at its best, it engages learners, helps them discover conceptual models, and encourages them to learn by practicing various skills, especially learning how to learn (Fink, 1989; McKeachie, 1986, 1999; Svinicki and Schwartz, 1988). As Bruner (1966: 53) put it, "If information is to be used effectively, it must be translated into the learner's way of attempting to solve a problem. If such translatability is not present, then the information is simply useless. . . . Instruction is a provisional state that has as its object to make the learner or problem solver self-sufficient." Chickering and Gamson (1987: 5) take an important step further when they say, "Learning is not a spectator sport. Students do not learn much just by sitting in classes listening to teachers, memorizing prepackaged assignments, and spitting out answers. They must talk about what they are learning, write about it, relate it to past experiences, apply it to their daily lives. They must make what they learn part of themselves." For more on active learning, see Chapters 3, 4, and 12.

Indeed, the impact of learning often intensifies when learners can practice skills and get feedback either by following along with an instructor or by doing an exercise during or after instruction. At its most basic level, active learning simply involves having learners do something, write something, say something, play games, get up, move around, interact, and take part in learning, as well as in thinking about their own learning, rather than passively observing demonstrations or listening to facts, theories, and information about a topic or how to do something.

When, Where, and How?

In-class active learning exercises can occupy one or more portions of a class, an entire class session, or even stretch over more than one class session, but you do have to plan to include them or they may not occur (Warmkessel and Crothers, 1993). Active learning exercises can be designed for small groups, large groups, pairs, individuals, or a combination of any of these, for synchronous or asynchronous use, in-person, or remotely.

Instructor and Peer Questioning

ACRL, IS' *Designs for Active Learning* contains a wealth of active learning exercises geared primarily to undergraduates and meant to be used in a synchronous in-person classroom setting, but it is also adaptable for other audiences and settings (Gradowski, Snavely, and Dempsey, 1998). In "Structuring a Session with Questions," for example, students pair up and have three minutes to come up with three questions they would like answered regarding libraries and research. During this three-minute period, students tend to answer each others' basic questions. Then, the librarian writes his or her final questions on the board, groups them into categories, and asks attendees if they have answers to any of the final questions (Mestre, 1998). This exercise could be conducted as well asynchronously via a discussion board over a week's time. Then pairs of students could communicate with each other synchronously via chat or text message and post their questions on the discussion board. This combined synchronous (pairs communicating with each other via chat or text message) and asynchronous (posting questions on a discussion board for individual reaction) approach might encourage shyer learners to participate more than they would in an in-person group setting. It might also attract and hold the attention of more technologically sophisticated learners who may wrongly believe that, because they are good at using Google, Wikipedia, and Facebook applications, they are information literate.

Disciplinary Perspectives

Fink's (1989) *Process and Politics in Library Research* provides excellent in-class active learning exercises at the end of each chapter. For example, the class selects a topic, and students discuss how it might be approached from the perspective of different disciplines. Again, many of these exercises may be adapted for use with various kinds of technology.

Pause Procedure and Pairs to Squares

On a more traditional note, Bonwell recommends an "enhanced lecture," which intersperses active learning throughout a lecture. For example, he recommends the "pause procedure" where the instructor stops lecturing every 13 to 18 minutes and has students compare and review their notes with a partner (Bonwell, 1996). Walker (1998) calls this technique "bookends" and also describes another useful technique, "pairs to squares," a variation of "think–pair–share." The think–pair–share technique requires each student to consider a problem individually and make notes about it. Each then pairs up with another student to discuss and come to agreement on a solution to the problem. The pair then shares their solution with the entire group. "Pairs to squares" takes the discussion process a step further. Learners proceed as with think–pair–share, but, before reporting back, two pairs team up to form a "square" and again must discuss and come to agreement on a solution. Then each of those squares (two sets of pairs) reports back to the entire group.

Boolean Operators or Connectors

York County Community College's (2007) "Active Learning Techniques for Library Instruction" includes exercises such as "Boolean Burrito" and allows you to submit your own active learning exercises for consideration and possible editing. Short videos can be helpful in getting these kinds of concepts across to some students. Indiana University–South Bend (2007) has mounted a three-minute video on YouTube to do just that. "SOS for Information Literacy" (2006) reviews and provides access to lesson plans and training materials for K–12, higher education, continuing education, and professional development. Lesson plans include supporting materials, such as worksheets for active learning exercises. "Boolean Logic Is Yummy!," a lesson plan for seventh and eighth graders (Hanley, 2006), utilizes a candy sorting exercise.

Matching Exercises with Objectives

Tiberius and Silver (2001) provide additional highly useful active learning ideas that can be used during a workshop or class. They list these ideas according to the objectives you might want to address. These would include objectives such as "When practice with feedback is useful in achieving your objectives." For this example, you may want to try their "Helping Trios" technique to help learners get feedback while using an article index to identify useful articles on a topic. Divide the audience into groups of three. One person searches an article index database while a second person provides feedback. The third person observes and takes notes and may use a checklist. After finding one useful article, the observer discusses her or his observations with the other two learners. Learners switch roles until each person has had a chance to take on each of the three roles (Tiberius and Silver, 2001: 8).

Interactive Whiteboards

Schroeder (2007) describes using interactive whiteboards as a means of engaging each and every learner in an in-person session. These whiteboards are large touchscreen displays that also allow you to "write" on them with colored electronic ink and connect wirelessly to a keyboard and mouse. Learners are divided into groups, each with a different information-researching scenario and a set of questions to guide their investigation. Scenario questions may include whether or not the library owns a particular item (loosely described), additional topics related to that item, and where to find it. Groups have about ten minutes to find answers to these questions. Then each group uses the interactive whiteboard at the front of the room to teach the rest of the class as they show how they found the answers to these questions. Each learner in the group is required to have a speaking part (Schroeder, 2007).

Visiting and Revisiting

Bransford, Brophy, and Williams (2000) describe a learner-centered active learning exercise for courses in which they met with the same group of learners more than once over a period of time. Students experienced the same "event" when the course began and then at one or two intervals later in the course and analyzed the event each time. At three intervals during a term, the authors showed a 45-minute videotape and asked students to write down what they noticed and understood about it. As students learned more about the topic during the term, their analyses deepened and they became aware of their own learning. In an ILI setting, at the beginning of a term, you could have learners compare and contrast a print and a Web-based resource on a particular topic. Later in the term, you could ask them to reexamine both resources and critique their own earlier analyses, adding a new layer of observations. This could be a synchronous or an asynchronous exercise for individuals or groups.

"Inquiry Learning"

Jacobson and Xu (2002) describe a small group exercise utilized toward the end of a credit-bearing IL course. Students are given one of three articles to read in advance of class. Each article relates to some aspect of a social or ethical issue in information. During class, students are divided into three groups, corresponding to the articles they have read. In 15–20 minutes, groups identify the main theme of their article and do some additional research on the topic based on what they learned earlier in the course. Students may choose to use databases or Web search engines. Each group then has two to three minutes to report back to the class, with groups deciding who in their group will do the report (Jacobson and Xu, 2002). This active learning exercise fulfills the cognitive purpose of illustrating for the students what they have learned during the course and fulfills the affective purpose of instilling confidence.

Students have a framework provided by the readings and the exercise structure yet also have choices to make in doing research and developing and delivering a report on their findings to the class. A five-minute debriefing on the process would incorporate reflection, adding a metacognitive element (thinking about your own learning) and increasing the likelihood of deeper learning and retention. This exercise could be done partly or fully online, as well as in person, synchronously, or asynchronously. Readings could be linked or posted online, and students could form groups in Facebook or in a course management system in order to complete this exercise. In synchronous online courses, students could present their report to the entire class using voice or chat, followed by a few minutes for questions and then a reflective discussion. In asynchronous classes, reports could be posted on a discussion board, with the entire class asked to comment and reflect on the process with additional postings. This exercise is a microcosm of what Pappas (2000) describes as "inquiry learning," learning by questioning and investigating with others in a "learning community." Instructors guide learners' work, but learners are at the center of the process, directing their own learning.

Role-playing

Mudrock (2005) describes a role-playing game for a college history course that focused on the year 1918. Students choose from among fictitious characters provided by the instructor, along with their names, hometowns, and birthdays. Students roll dice to determine their characters' fates and spend the term researching the time period and possible fates. They invent life histories for their characters and in the end roll dice to determine whether or not their characters will live or die from war wounds or from influenza.

Learners can also take on roles in Second Life "historical sims" (virtual simulations of physical locations during a particular time period) by having their avatars (animated figures representing the learner) assume the identities of real or imaginary figures (Rymaszewski et al., 2007). In San Diego State University's Second Life Pioneers sim, students take on the roles of individuals from U.S. history (pilgrims or Chinese immigrants or others) by receiving folders that allow them to become those individuals by changing their avatar's appearance. Students then interact with one another based on their own Internet research on the role of their character at that time (San Diego State University, accessed 2008). This sim is based on a fifth-grade WebQuest called "Meet the Immigrants" (Roberson, 2004), illustrating the fact that active learning ILI can be adapted for use at different age and educational levels.

WebQuests

WebQuests like "Meet the Immigrants" provide younger students with preselected Web sites to visit in order to conduct their research. ILI for WebQuest creation could take place with teachers, alerting them to the criteria for selecting Web sites for their students, the need to have their students think critically about the Web sites they are assigned, and additional means of gathering information when researching a topic like immigrants.

Scavenger Hunts and Other K–12 Exercises

"SOS for Information Literacy" (2006) lessons include "Using an Encyclopedia Scavenger Hunt" (Dixon, 2006) for third and fourth graders. Valenza (2003a: 85–88) also offers a number of active learning exercises for middle school and high school students that could be completed in synchronous class sessions or asynchronously by students working on their own. These include separate exercises for high school and middle school students, "Comparing Subscription Services and Search Tools" and "Practice Ranking Sources."

Icebreakers

In synchronous in-person group settings, active learning exercises can also be used as icebreakers at the beginning of a class session, sprinkled throughout, or as a wrap-up at the end. You can even take activities designed for other purposes and use or adapt them for ILI. An ILI librarian participated in an introductory exercise about the island of Cephalonia during a trip to Greece. She and her colleagues then adapted this exercise so that it now serves as an ILI icebreaker called the "Cephalonian Method." This icebreaker combines preset questions on colored cards with matching PowerPoint slides enlivened with humorous questions and images as well as music. Students randomly receive colored cards with questions as they enter a room. Librarians ask students to stand and read "blue," "yellow," etc., questions one by one and display PowerPoint slides with answers that correspond to the questions. Students have reacted positively to this approach, and it has been used effectively even with very large classes of 150 to 300, although it does take some time to prepare (Morgan and Davies, 2004).

A simpler technique would be to distribute blank cards to learners as they enter a room and ask them to take a couple of minutes to write down any questions they may have. Then gather the cards and attempt to answer questions on the spot, or ask the group if they can answer the questions, filling in anything that is missing. This method requires no preparation and could replace a canned five- to ten-minute opening oration regarding library services. It also bubbles up questions that learners may feel shy about asking in front of an entire class.

Service Learning as Active Learning

Civic engagement and service learning take active learning to another level beyond the workshop and the online or in-person class. By entering into and participating in real-world environments, learners gain insight into the needs and aspirations of others. ILI librarians can play a large role in these endeavors by helping learners use research to deepen and contextualize their understanding of these real-world environments. For instance, Davis (2007: online) describes a biology assignment that requires students to research a biological topic and then write "a convincing and knowledgeable letter to a decision maker" regarding that issue. Librarians can help students find and evaluate research to use as evidence in such a letter. Abilock describes six approaches utilized by school librarians, including teaching third graders how to create simple bibliographies of the fairy tales, myths, legends, and other folk literature they had studied. The librarian who taught bibliography creation also worked with these students to create "fairy tale mock trials that she learned about on the American Bar Association Web site" (Abilock, 2006b: 14).

Assessment as Active Learning

Even assessment can be an active learning process. Angelo and Cross' (1993) "Minute Paper" is a good example of an active learning assessment exercise. At the beginning of the session, the instructor tells the group that at the end of the session they will need to write down their answers to two questions: "What was the main point of this session?" and "What is your main unanswered question?" Learners then pay careful attention throughout the session, trying to figure out what the main point is and also making note of their questions as the session proceeds. This exercise works best when you will see the same group of learners more than once so that you can respond to their unanswered questions at the next meeting. However, you can ask learners to do this one-minute paper orally at the end of a one-shot session as well. You can also respond to learners' questions by posting the questions and answers on a discussion board or a bulletin board or by e-mailing responses directly to the learners or to an instructor. You could also create a FAQ (list of Frequently Asked Questions) from these learner questions and post the FAQ on your Web site. As learners are gathering for an instructional session, you could ask them to read the FAQ. Then, during the first few minutes of a session, ask for volunteers to tell the group one useful piece of information they learned from the FAQ. This active learning exercise could be conducted in-person or remotely and would serve as an icebreaker or "sponge activity," drawing the learners' attention to the topic at hand. Online participants could respond via chat or voice if they use microphones, while in-person participants could simply call out answers.

To What Degree Should We Incorporate Active Learning Exercises?

Active learning exercises can be used with almost any size of group in-person, although very small groups of two to ten may respond better to individual, paired, or whole-group exercises. The same is true for synchronous online groups. How do you select among the many active learning techniques, and how many of these activities should you include in synchronous as opposed to asynchronous instruction? Your goals and objectives or expected learning outcomes (ELOs) should be your guide. If you have a good idea of what you want learners to know, it will be easier to decide what you want them to do in order to learn it (Bonwell and Sutherland, 1996). When there is limited learning time available, prioritize your goals and objectives or ELOs and consider whether or not you can identify or develop an exercise that would help people achieve more than one learning outcome at the same time. For more on developing goals, objectives, and ELOs, see Chapter 7.

For instance, using a "Flow of Information" exercise helps people think about how events are documented, the sequence of documentation, how to access documentation after the fact, and how to save time by using access tools appropriate for the type of information needed and the time period of an event. You can do this with a large group by drawing three columns on a board and asking how the audience first heard about a major newsworthy event. Radio, television, the Web, RSS feeds, or YouTube may be at the top of a list of types of sources that you can end with print encyclopedias and other reference materials. These sources go in the first column. Next, ask the audience how long it took from the occurrence of the event until it was reported in a particular medium. This information goes in the second column. Use the third column to identify access—how you would get to this information in a particular type of source at a later time, for example, from periodical indexes. Finally, ask the audience where in the flow of information they would start searching for information on a very recent event and explain that setting an event in a chronological context can save them time and result in much more focused search results. You may also want to refer them to the "Flow of Information" Web site for later review and refresher (Zwemer, 2000). You may need to invest more time to come up with exercises that would extend this learning by putting it in practice. With the "Flow of Information" exercise, you might ask learners to go directly to the Web site that illustrates that concept, take a few minutes to review it, and then use that Web site to respond to questions about finding information on specific historical or current topics.

If learning time is not an issue, with asynchronous instruction, for example, consider offering a number of different active learning approaches to help learners achieve objectives or ELOs. For instance, "Thinking Critically About World Wide Web Resources" (Grassian, 1995) offers a text-only list of criteria for evaluating Web-based materials. Learners could be asked to examine Web sites of their own choosing with these criteria in mind. You could also use November's (2008) "Information Literacy Resources," including his "Information Literacy Quiz" and answers and "Websites to Validate," or Grassian and Zwemer's (2008) "Hoax? Scholarly Research? Personal Opinion? You Decide!" exercise. The latter two provide preselected Web sites for comparison and evaluation and offer hints for figuring out correct answers.

Kyle (2008) and Olson (2008) describe how they have used Way's (accessed 2008) "Dihydrogen Monoxide in the Dairy Industry" bogus Web site to teach elementary school children about the importance of Web site evaluation. Schrock's (2008a) Web evaluation guides are useful for elementary school, middle school, and high school teachers, and for users at all levels, for such sites as virtual tours, blogs, and podcasts. Cohen and Jacobson (2008) offer useful evaluation tips for a wide variety of Web pages, blogs, wikis, and many other social networking sites, along with examples for each.

Gray and Madson (2007) reviewed 20 years of research into interactivity in teaching, drawing attention to Hake's (1998) study of 62 introductory physics courses taught to over 6,500 college physics students. Hake (1998: 64) concluded that the "48 courses which made substantial use of IE [interactive engagement] methods achieved an average gain of . . . almost two standard deviations . . . above that of the traditional courses." Their review led Gray and Madson (2007) to recommend ten ways to engage students, including maintaining eye contact, conducting daily quizzes, and using clickers or colored cards for polling. Some of their recommendations may not seem workable for classes, workshops, homework help for individuals, or other one-shot sessions in person or online. However, many may be adapted as needed or desired. Gray and Madson's (2007) last suggestion (no. 10) regards calling on one or another student to respond every two to three minutes. This technique has its pluses and minuses. Learners will be motivated to be prepared, as Gray and Madson point out, but they may also become quite anxious and fearful when put on the spot in front of the entire group. Of course, how you call on an individual can make a difference affectively. You could ask someone who has not responded if he or she has anything to add to a discussion. Another approach would be take volunteers who want to respond and then, after a while, ask if anyone who has not yet answered would like to respond. Generally, instead of forcing people into what may be an unwelcome limelight, just be positive, welcoming, and encouraging of all responses. Your attitude toward respondents, online or in person, synchronous or asynchronous, is critical to the success of your instruction and their learning. A helpful positive attitude is important in working with colleagues, too.

Turn Your Teaching into Learner-centered Active Learning

If you have been involved in ILI for a while, you probably have outlines, scripts, and other tried-and-true materials with which you are comfortable. You have an idea of what you are trying to accomplish and some means of interacting with your audience. If you are new to ILI, you may have gone through the preliminary planning process, written goals and objectives and ELOs, selected one or more modes of instruction, and even prepared outlines and scripts and other materials. Or you may have borrowed or adapted your instructional plans and materials from others.

At this point, you may be wondering if you can increase participation and improve learning outcomes by involving the learners more. If you have never been involved in ILI you are probably wondering how to involve learners in the first place. As we have mentioned, there are a number of active learning exercises you can investigate and adapt for your own environment. You could also take a teaching segment, or ELO, and turn it into an active learning exercise.

For example, instead of telling learners what the common features of databases are, you could have them complete exercises that require them to use two or three databases and then ask the learners themselves to describe the common features of these databases. This turns a teacher-centered approach into a learner-centered active learning approach.

See the following steps to turn this example into learner-centered active learning:

1. Write down your goals and objectives or ELOs—what you expect the learners to know and to be able to do following instruction.
   Example: ELO: Following instruction, learners will list three common features of databases (Barclay, 1995).
2. Identify or develop some practical, hands-on means of getting the learners to come up with these learning elements rather than supplying them yourself.
   Example: Have half of the groups look for articles on a topic in a general article index and then in Google Scholar; have the other half look for articles on the same topic in a specialized database like Gale's History Resource Center: U.S. or PubMed and then in Google Scholar in order to identify common features of these databases.
3. Use an exercise topic of interest to the learners.
   Example: In a predominantly Hispanic area, ask learners to work with one or two partners to find articles on Latino and Latina doctors.
4. Before they begin, tell the learners how much time they will have, how you will let them know when their time has run out (timer, flicking lights on and off, etc.), and how much time they will have to report back. At intervals, remind the learners of their remaining time.
5. When the time is up, ask groups to report back, with a time limit for each group to report.
6. Fill in any missing elements.
7. Check for understanding.

F2F: Look for body language, puzzled faces, yawns, or lack of participation.

Online: Look for participation or lack of it, and ask questions to check for understanding.

Both: Ask the audience what their questions are. Count seven to ten seconds silently, and, if there are no questions, ask if they are ready to move on.

This is one self-help approach to turning your own teaching into learner-centered active learning. Another approach would be to have the learners teach one another. Instead of having each group report back to the entire class, use a modified "jigsaw" approach. After all of the groups have looked at two databases and identified some common features, have one person from each group rotate to another group. That person can serve as an investigative reporter, sharing findings and identifying commonalities. Then have that person report back from each group.

If you want to help your colleagues incorporate more active learning into their instruction, you will need to work cooperatively with them in a trusting, nonjudgmental manner. The best way to build trust and effect change is to open your own instruction to observation and constructive criticism. Ask your colleagues to observe you teaching a live session and provide you with constructive criticism first. Give them observation forms and presentation checklists and ask them to describe what they liked and what they would teach differently.

This is an excellent way to begin a discussion on teaching techniques and how to incorporate new techniques into in-person and remote instruction, both synchronous and asynchronous. The next step, peer coaching, is an important way to help build momentum. Here colleagues observe one another and provide constructive criticism designed to support individuals and improve instructional techniques. Keep in mind, though, that individuals differ, as do teaching styles, and that change does not always happen quickly or all at once. Patience, goodwill, and trust are critical elements in supporting and effecting change of any kind (see Grassian and Kaplowitz, 2005, Chapter 3, "Embracing Cooperation and Change," and Chapter 4, "Fostering Growth in Yourself and Others").

In-person, Synchronous Active Learning

In synchronous, in-person group settings it is important to note that small group work may or may not appeal to all learners, as learning styles and preferences can differ dramatically in any given group. If you do decide to use active learning techniques like the ones described earlier, there are four important logistical techniques that can help ensure success for any size group but especially very large groups (40+).

Give Preliminary Instructions

If you want to divide a group up in order to complete an exercise, figure out in advance how you will divide them and explain this process clearly and simply or set up the room in advance (Silberman, 1996: 9–16). Be sure to give very careful, simple preliminary instructions about what is going to happen and why *before* the learners break into groups. Preliminary instructions to the entire audience might be as follows: "We are going to go through a topic selection exercise now that will take about ten to fifteen minutes. I'm going to ask you to count off from one to six, and then get into six small groups."

Break into Groups

Once everyone has counted off, tell them in which part of the room to meet the others in their groups. With very large groups it will be necessary to allot more time to get into small groups, get back to the large group, and report back. To save time, you could simply ask people to work with the five or ten people sitting near them. As for the size of small groups, a good rule of thumb is to aim for each small group to be composed of 10–20 percent of the large group. So, a large group of 100 could be divided into ten groups of ten, while a small group of 30 could have five groups of six. Sometimes fewer groups will be necessary because there are not enough flip charts or other equipment or because of a need to cut down on the time needed to report back. In terms of large group exercises in which the entire audience participates at the same time, an ideal number is around 30–40 to allow more of a chance that someone will come up with a response to any given question or discussion topic, but it is certainly possible to conduct engaging interactive exercises with groups as large as 200–300. You would just need to plan carefully, have exercise materials prepared in advance, time everything carefully, be sure that what you display can be seen and read quite clearly from the back of the room, and ensure that the entire group can hear individual audience members as they respond.

Give (and Display) Instructions Including Time Limits

Once everyone is divided into small groups or pairs, give the content instructions and ask them to look up at you when they are finished. Give groups an exact number of minutes for their group work and tell them how you will let them know that their time is up—by flipping the lights on and off, by using a timer, etc. Be sure to warn them a minute or two before their time is up, and when the time has expired ask if anyone needs another minute to finish up. It also helps to have instructions and questions on a handout, on an overhead, on a board, on a flip chart page, or on a PowerPoint slideshow for reference during the exercise in case anyone forgets or could not hear the instructions. The content portion of the instructions could be as follows:

> Each group has the same broad topic, "hunger." In the next five minutes, I'd like you to use any or all of four limiters to narrow this topic and come up with a topic sentence or argument—time frame, geographic region, person or group, and/or event or aspect. This timer will go off when your time is up, and then each group will need to report back to the entire class.

Call Groups Back Together

Call the groups back together by using whatever means were announced at the beginning of the exercise, and ask for volunteers to report back for each group, again, making sure to stick to the allotted time. As groups report back, other groups and individuals may experience an "aha" effect, as the same broad topic morphs into quite different, and more manageable, topic sentences or arguments when limiters are applied (UCLA College Library, 1997).

Asynchronous Active Learning

Simple active learning exercises like these can break up one-shot sessions or even repeated in-person group instruction where you do multiple or sequential sessions on different topics for the same group and make them more interesting by forming participatory "chunks." Of course, active learning and chunking are not necessarily restricted to classroom or other in-person group settings. Print library-skills workbooks, for example, were popular in the 1970s and 1980s and provided a prime and highly effective example of another approach to interactive learning. They utilized an asynchronous, learner-centered approach that involved discovery and practice in the use of reference sources by means of a set of self-directed, self-paced exercises usually arranged in systematic search strategy order. Workbooks were completed by individuals when they chose to do so, within a particular time frame. Learners would read instructions, find reference tools and the library catalog, and actually use them to answer a series of multiple-choice questions. Answers were corrected to provide feedback as quickly as possible so that learners could work on finding the correct answers for questions they had gotten wrong. Effective workbooks were carefully constructed and written using captivating, brief, and clear language for descriptions of types of reference sources, annotations of specific research tools, and exercises (Dudley, 1978; Phipps, 1980). People who prefer to work on their own at their own pace are especially fond of the workbook approach, although workbooks utilized as stand-alone instruction fell out of favor partly because some believed they were not relevant to specific immediate learning needs, too focused on mechanics of use, and lacking in the area of problem solving, critical thinking, and evaluation (Suprenant, 1981; Berge and Pryor, 1982).

During the late 1980s and the 1990s, one-shot sessions, synchronous, F2F group instruction took the place of a number of workbook programs, paralleling the lecture/classroom approach used in K–12 and higher education. Yet workbook-like approaches have come full circle now, as this approach is being used in the Web environment in the form of sets of interactive exercises and tutorials. Some are designed as a series of self-contained modules, with critical thinking, self-assessment, and immediate feedback at various points, for example, "Go for the Gold" (James Madison University, 2008a) and "Road to Research" (Grassian et al., 2008). At least one library has even turned back to print workbooks as a more cost-effective active-learning approach for a small institution with limited staff and funding (Trail, Gutierrez, and Lechner, 2006).

Self-reflective (metacognitive) assignments also involve active learning, as mentioned earlier in the discussion of problem-based learning and case-based learning. They require learners to think about their own learning, critical thinking, and problem-solving process (Blake, 2005). Georghiades' research suggests that even elementary school students can benefit from simple two- to six-minute exercises or "metacognitive instances" and retain more learning over time, up to an entire school year beyond the initial teaching time. These exercises include search logs, self-evaluations, annotated drawings, concept mapping, journal writing (keeping diaries) or reflective journaling, and classroom discussions generated by simple questions like, "How did you solve that problem?" In this research study, small group exercises were more effective than large group exercises (Georghiades, 2002: 25). Some teachers use "double-entry ledgers" for elementary school students. The journal can include drawings or diagrams, and the text can be on a separate page or in a second column (Manning and Manning, 1996). Reflecting on your own learning through these kinds of assignments can contribute to retention or "durability of learning" (Georghiades, 2004).

Reflective journals are sometimes called "I-Search papers" in which students describe their research process, including the information tools they consulted, their evaluation of these tools, as well as the problems and successes they encountered along the way (Mark and Jacobson, 1995; Blakey and Spence, 1990; Blake, 2005). This approach can be particularly useful if learners self-assess, as Silberman (1996: 171) suggests, using any of a number of active learning techniques. These techniques include having learners write about what they expect to get out of a class or session before instruction and then what they got out of it in the end. A more unusual technique asks learners to assign a percentage representing their return on investment of time and effort in achieving each of the class goals (Silberman, 1996: 172). Learners at many age and educational levels can also draw illustrations of what they have learned and then write brief explanations of their drawings or write multiple choice questions themselves about the concepts expressed in their drawings (Georghiades, 2004; Pillsbury, 2006). Drawing concept maps or creating them using software like Inspiration (2008) can help learners connect prior knowledge or learning with new knowledge and learning, as posited by constructivist theories of education (Royer and Royer, 2004).

Collaborative and Cooperative Learning Environments

In some cases, entire class sessions or even entire classes can be composed of a particular form of small group active learning called *collaborative learning*, an educational approach that has been popular for many years (Mallonee, 1981; Sheridan, 1990). Collaborative learning is really an extension of active learning. Its champions argue heatedly in favor of learning by doing and against the lecture method, which they almost invariably conceive of as a "tabula rasa" approach where the teacher "pours" information into the learner's empty head. In contrast, collaborative learners often work in groups of two to five with shared responsibility for gaining knowledge in rather open-ended manner. Groups can consist of learners, learners and teachers, colleagues, and/or other members of an institution. "Rather than having the teacher serve as a dispenser of facts and lower level cognitive information, constructivists believe that the teacher should serve as a facilitator who attempts to structure an environment in which the learner organizes meaning on a personal level; students and teachers should work in a collegial mode, often using small group procedures" (Cooper and Robinson, 1998: 386). So, with little or no instructor guidance, collaborative learning groups jointly investigate, discover, put together, and communicate the results of their information gathering and research, often posed as or based on real-life problems or issues, in keeping with constructivist theories. One method of doing this is to have groups collaborate in researching, constructing, and presenting concept maps to illustrate mental models (Gao et al., 2007). The key is that group members do not divide the work but, rather, share it as they work toward a common goal and come to agreement on the results (Brandon and Hollingshead, 1999; Case, Stevens, and Cooper, 2007).

Collaborative learning and cooperative learning are similar in many respects. Both involve group work and peer learning, but, as Resta and Laferriere (2007) point out, there are no standard definitions for either. Cooperative learning is usually quite structured group work, in contrast to collaborative learning. In cooperative learning, instructors usually provide written exercises and specific predefined roles for each participant, such as recorder, searcher, and someone who reports back for the group. The distinctions between collaborative learning and cooperative learning are similar to those between case-based learning and problem-based learning, popular active learning methods used in a variety of environments, from business schools, law schools, and medical schools to elementary schools.

Case-based Learning and Problem-based Learning

Both case-based learning (CBL) and problem-based learning (PBL) involve learners reading and thinking through stories or narratives describing fictional or real-life events or situations. Some use these terms interchangeably or call both *teaching cases* (Kim et al., 2006), or *inquiry learning* (Pappas, 2000); however, there are differences. CBL generally involves taking a given situation or event and its resolution, analyzing the decisions made to resolve it, researching the issues, and making recommendations regarding different directions and decisions that could have been made. In PBL, teams of learners work on an ill-structured problem situation that may cut across a variety of disciplinary or topic areas. The PBL problem is not resolved in the narrative and does not have a clear-cut solution. PBL team members work together on the problem, identifying the issues, conducting research, and coming up with recommendations for addressing the problem. Learners reflect on their process at the end and conduct self- and peer assessment (Savery, 2006; Barrows, 2006). Both CBL and PBL are learner-centered instructional methods designed to engage learners. However, the PBL instructor serves more as an expert guide and facilitator than the CBL instructor, as there is no single correct answer to PBL narratives, while there may be for CBL narratives. This illustrates the fact that the issue of instructor guidance or facilitation looms large in the debate over the value of constructivist teaching methods and learner-centered teaching (Mayer, 2004). See Chapter 12 for more on this topic.

How effective are these methods, and how can you apply them to ILI? Both CBL and PBL address John Dewey's call for education based on authentic real-world problem-solving, and both involve teamwork, collaborative or cooperative. Although both have been utilized in teaching for a number of years and their use is spreading, according to Savery (2006), there is insufficient research as of yet to determine whether these methods are superior to those of traditional instruction. A number of studies and reports indicate that these approaches can be engaging and effective, as long as they support and advance pedagogical goals and ensure that the process is learner centered, and that deep learning takes place, even in online modes (Ellis, Marcus, and Taylor, 2005; Savery, 2006, Gallucci, 2006).

A review of 100 studies of "case-based teaching" (including both CBL and PBL) identified two opposing views of key factors that impact the effectiveness of this instructional method: "a skilled discussion facilitator who unpacks the content" as opposed to "a well constructed case [that] affects the type and quality of inquiry learners generate, regardless of the facilitator's skills or expertise" (Kim et al., 2006: 867). This study identified five "core attributes" of effective cases, stating that they must be relevant, realistic, engaging, challenging, and instructional. Under "instructional," the authors include building on prior knowledge, assessment, feedback, and teaching aids, among other points (Kim et al., 2006). Other studies at the elementary school level and above support these findings in a blended instruction environment as well, where learning takes place partly F2F and partly online (Araz and Sungur, 2007; Lee, 2006; Warren, Dondlinger, and Barab, 2008).

In order to improve effectiveness, one study suggests providing examples of how learners have used case-based studies successfully in the past, as well as modeling how to go about the process of analyzing a case or problem, researching the issues, coming up with possible solutions, and reflecting on the process (Ellis, Marcus, and Taylor, 2005). Given the fact that it can be difficult for learners to alter their existing mental models, too, yet another study reported that having learners compare two cases and identify commonalities can lead to altered mental models and increased transfer of learning to new situations (Gentner, Loewenstein, and Thompson, 2003).

Another study, a meta-analysis of research into the effectiveness of case-based studies, surfaced three critical principles instructors need to keep in mind:

- Learners come to us with some incorrect preconceived notions that may be difficult to change.
- Competence in academic disciplines at many age and educational levels relies on knowing facts about those disciplines, organized in conceptual frameworks.
- Learner self-reflection regarding one's own learning process is essential. (Gallucci, 2006)

Awareness of these three principles may provide some insight into why some older research seemed to indicate that teams "usually do less well—not better—than the sum of their members' individual contributions" (Hackman, 1998: 246). Particularly in the sciences, collaborative learning approaches like PBL have not come naturally, as for many years emphasis was placed on lecture and individual mastery. Some scientists feared that when left completely to their own devices, collaborative learning groups might not be able to discover scientific principles and learn how to test theories in a scientifically valid manner. In some cases, learners might not be aware of dangerous circumstances or combinations of chemicals. The main argument against a constructivist collaborative learning approach, is, in fact, that "there is a body of knowledge that is fundamental or foundational and that such content is best presented in more traditional instructional formats, such as the lecture" (Cooper and Robinson, 1998: 386).

Putting It into Practice

However, the more recent studies cited earlier (published in the 2000s) strongly support posing real-life information researching and critical thinking problems to learners as a means of engaging them in learning and improving their IL skills. WebQuests in the K–12 environment generally use real-world issues or topics, as described earlier in this chapter. Examples from WebQuest.org (2007) include "Biographies of Native American Leaders" for third through fifth grades (Lipkind, 2008) and "Buried Treasure: A WebQuest in Optimization," for high school and college calculus students (Price, 2008). WebQuests may be more or less structured PBL exercises, depending on the educational level and the resources provided to student teams, preselected Web sites, and other materials. Library media teachers/school library media specialists can have an active role in collaborating with classroom teachers to develop WebQuest resources and help keep them up to date.

In academic libraries, one way to do this would be to gather students' research topics in advance and use some of them to pose short case study problems. In teaching topic narrowing or broadening, put a student's topic up on a slide. Then ask an F2F or online group to help that student identify keywords and related words in order to find more or less on the topic. In public libraries, ask users to register for workshops and list the topics that interest them. Then ask the attendees where they would look for information on those topics and which words they would use to search. In all sorts of information-researching environments, model the research process based on a learner's research topic and information need, with learners following along. Begin with identifying the information need (topic), moving through selecting an appropriate database to search and then discussing the mechanics of searching that database. You could even videotape yourself doing this and mount the video on YouTube. Or, ask learners to watch videos available through A.N.T.S. (2008), PRIMO (ALA. ACRL. IS, 2008e), or others or go through online tutorials regarding information researching (Grassian et al., 2008). Then have learners partner up or work in teams. Ask them to go through the same process based on their own or other real-life research needs or topics, with instruction to select two or more databases and compare them, in order to identify commonalities (UCLA Biomedical Library, 2007). Finally, have learners report back to the group F2F or post responses on a discussion board, blog, or wiki. These exercises can be adapted to a workshop in a public library, a special library, or a school library media center, as well.

In many groups, organizations, and businesses and at many educational levels, peer learning and problem solving based on real-life situations and issues now seems to have taken hold, although it may vary in its focus and structure, including the objectives, type of reinforcement, and assessment (Topping, 2005). For each type of library, collaboration between librarians and others can help increase the effectiveness of these instructional methods. Learning communities offer a useful example of how such collaboration can work.

Learning Communities and Librarian Collaboration

What is a "learning community," and what is its significance? DeMulder and Eby (1999: 893) say that learning communities "are interdisciplinary, collaborative, and participatory environments that foster the development of knowledge through multiple perspective." Others have described two types of "learning communities," apprenticeships in a discipline or profession (not limited to higher education) and school-based student/teacher learning communities that work on long-term collaborative and often multidisciplinary projects (Gordin et al., 1996). Pederson (2003: 2) describes learning communities as "a variety of ways to purposefully restructure the curriculum by co-enrolling students in two or more courses linked by a theme or question and including a pedagogy that allows more active learning and interaction between students." She describes a continuum of learning-community-type courses ranging from freshman interest groups, usually of two loosely linked courses, to "coordinated studies learning communities." The latter may occupy enrolled students full time in just this program, taught by a team of several faculty utilizing a variety of teaching/learning methodologies and focused around a unifying theme (Pederson, 2003: 7). As Jaffee (2007) points out, generally, studies of freshman learning communities (FLCs) indicate that they contribute to learning, retention, and academic success, but he also claims that they may have unintended negative consequences. On the plus side, Jaffee's (2007: 65) review of the literature indicates that there are four main positive effects of FLCs:

> First, students learn best when they are able to make substantive inter-disciplinary connections across their courses. . . . Second, learning is enhanced when students are able to interact and engage with their peers about the subject matter in their courses. . . . Third, students learn best when they are actively engaged. . . . Fourth, students tend to be more suc-

cessful when they are able to develop a meaningful academic relationship with faculty.

Beyond these positive effects, however, Jaffee (2007) points out a number of negative effects of this means of grouping students, primarily the "peer cohort" effect that can lead to dysfunctional us vs. them (students vs. faculty) problems. These problems can be forestalled or diminished, according to Jaffee, through the use of cooperative and collaborative learning techniques.

Librarians need to be aware of the benefits and potential difficulties that may face learning-community-type courses, as some include or appear in the form of "college survival" or "First Year Experience" courses for credit. These courses often include some IL or research skills, and librarians are important collaborators in planning curricula for these courses and in working to improve student engagement by integrating IL across the curriculum (Barefoot, 2006). Active learning and service learning contribute greatly to the level of student engagement at colleges and universities, as measured by the National Survey on Student Engagement (NSSE). Seven hundred seventy-four colleges and universities across the United States and Canada administered this survey in 2008, to 1.4 million undergraduates, a 27 percent increase in the number of participating institutions since the 2007 survey administration (NSSE, 2008). Hardesty's (2007) collection of essays on the first year of college provides much detail on NSSE and why and how librarians should be involved in First Year Experience courses. Authors focus on issues such as librarians' collaboration with teaching faculty and library anxiety. Many offer tips and examples of how to work effectively with First Year Experience students, courses, and instructors.

Learning communities like those described in the Hardesty (2007) collection can expose students to many different approaches to broad and far-ranging topics, such as human aging or interracial dynamics, from the perspective of several disciplines (University of California Commission on General Education, 2007). For librarians, they offer an opportunity to become part of a team of instructors, as they design curriculum and assignments and work together to provide balance and rigor in both, while at the same time allowing for open and frank discussion and readings related to these disciplines. For faculty coming from the perspectives and traditions of their disciplines, who are used to teaching autonomously, making all of this work among themselves as well as collaboratively with librarians is no mean feat. This is particularly true in relation to information researching, as subject experts in various fields are having a hard time just keeping up with new and evolving information resources in their own areas of expertise, much less opening their minds and curricula to other disciplines and ways of thinking and other forms of argument. More and more, faculty in higher education, at least, do seem to be turning to librarians as partners in the educational endeavor, particularly regarding information researching, generic critical thinking about information tools and materials, and the effort to avoid and combat plagiarism among students (Grassian and Kaplowitz, 2005, Chapter 3, "Embracing Cooperation and Change"; Mackey and Jacobson, 2008). As it turns out, librarians too are having a difficult time keeping up to date on information resources in many disciplines that seem to multiply and mutate daily. However, we are doing a better job of it than our users, so it is not surprising that they turn to us for help. In the foreseeable future it seems clear that a librarian's guidance will be essential in helping users at all educational levels learn to identify, locate, and evaluate research materials needed for multidisciplinary collaborative projects. For more on ILI in a variety of environments and on keeping up with technology, as well as online tools and resources, see Chapters 14, 15, and 16.

Online Learning and the Web

This debate may continue to rage and increase in temperature as the Web becomes easier to use for instruction. As we shall see in Chapter 15, the educational landscape is very different now than it was even five to ten years ago. Full courses are taught online, and other Web-based technologies like content management systems are becoming more effective instructional tools. The trend toward open source tools continues to grow, particularly with Google's massive influence, and social networking tools are leading to more and more group work. Some educators are writing books on how to convert courses to wholly online courses or blended courses, part online and part in person, as well as how to teach fully online or blended courses from the get-go (Ko and Rossen, 2004; Grassian et al., 2005).

Donovan (2006) offers a long list of active learning

activities and assignments that can be utilized or adapted for synchronous and asynchronous online courses. Examples include the following:

- Scavenger hunts created by learners in order to teach a topic to their classmates
- Virtual field trips and WebQuests with reports back to the class as a whole—oral or written
- Group games like "Half-life" in which groups respond to a question by posting a 32-word answer, then a 16-word answer, followed by an 8-word answer, and then a 4-word answer
- Learner-created quizzes and surveys

Many other popular Web-based resources can be utilized or adapted to suit ILI purposes and at the same time engage groups of learners or individuals through interactivity. For instance, Waelchli (2008) shared his lesson plan for fantasy football and ILI and mapped the lesson activities to the ACRL "Information Literacy Competency Standards" (ALA. ACRL, 2000). You can even use your own library's Web site to create a scavenger hunt (Moyer, 2007).

In fact, the Web's attraction lies partially in its interactivity, in the freedom it allows one to decide which way to go and what to do when. Clicking buttons with a mouse is both the same as and yet significantly different from using a television remote control device. Web users are not just picking a channel and then watching and listening passively. Deciding where to click, how many layers deep to go in a Web site, and which of many possible branches to take requires some thinking and decision making. The question is whether we can influence the decision-making process by helping users become more thoughtful about it, more selective in where they go and on what they click, more skeptical about the information they retrieve as well as the uses to which it is put, and more open to a continuous learning process throughout life.

FINAL REMARKS

Increasingly, both we and our learners are using Web-based and social networking tools and resources for teaching and learning. Regardless of the format or methodology, virtual or F2F, however, it does seem clear that people learn best by doing, by actively participating in their own learning. With all active learning exercises, online, in paper, or in other formats, including metacognitive assignments, you will need to think about and put effort into developing ELOs and designing engaging ways of having learners discover and practice the principles and concepts you want them to learn. Once you have developed these exercises, though, you will be able to utilize and tweak them for future uses. And, the more you develop these sorts of exercises for learners, the easier it will be for you to begin thinking in an active learning mode so that you can get in the habit of developing more exercises that engage your users. Exactly how to bring about enhanced learning by doing and by thinking about what you are doing (metacognition) may be an individual decision on the part of the ILI librarian or a joint decision between the ILI librarian and teaching faculty or other administrators. Nurturing collaborative relationships with others can help bring this goal to fruition.

EXERCISES

1. Design brief hands-on exercises that will help users learn the following:
   a. The mechanics of using their library catalog
   b. How to evaluate information tools
   c. How to evaluate individual retrievals
   d. How to distinguish among formats of information
2. Come up with an active learning (participatory) technique to teach people how to think critically about emerging IL-related online tools and resources.
3. Adapt a 50-minute exercise from *Designs for Active Learning* (Gradowski, Snavely, and Dempsey, 1998) to fit a 10-minute time period.
4. In your own words, respond to the following questions:
   a. Is there a body of knowledge that ILI librarians should pass along to learners? If so, should that knowledge be passed along via the lecture method or in some other way?
   b. Should we turn our synchronous instruction (in person or online) entirely into self-taught active learning tutorials or use these online tools as supplements to synchronous instruction, in person or virtual?
   c. How much guidance should the ILI librarian provide in synchronous and asynchronous instruction?

READ MORE ABOUT IT

ALA. ACRL. "Information Literacy" (September 16, 2008). Available: www.ala.org/ala/mgrps/divs/acrl/issues/infolit/infolit/index.cfm (accessed April 7, 2009).

Cohen, Laura and Trudi Jacobson. "Evaluating Web Content" (January 2008). Available: http://library.albany.edu/usered/eval/evalweb (accessed December 23, 2008).

Gradowski, Gail, Loanne Snavely, and Paula Dempsey, eds. 1998. *Designs for Active Learning*. Chicago: ALA.

Grassian, Esther. "Thinking Critically About Web 2.0 and Beyond" (2008). Available: http://www2.library.ucla.edu/librariesollege/11605_12008.cfm (accessed December 23, 2008).

Hall, Patrick. 2002. "Not All Sources Are Created Equal: Student Research, Source Equivalence, and the Net." *Internet Reference Services Quarterly* 7, no. 4: 13–21.

November, Alan. "Information Literacy Resources" (2008). Available: http://novemberlearning.com/index.php?option=com_content&task=category§ionid=5&id=27&Itemid=85 (accessed December 23, 2008).

Pederson, Sarah. 2003. *Learning Communities and the Academic Library.* National Learning Communities Project Monograph Series. Olympia, WA: The Evergreen State College, Washington Center for Improving the Quality of Undergraduate Education in cooperation with the American Association for Higher Education and the Association of College and Research Libraries.

Pithers, R.T. and Rebecca Soden. 2000. "Critical Thinking in Education: A Review." *Educational Research* 42, no. 3: 237–249.

Schrock, Kathy. "Critical Evaluation Surveys and Resources" (2008). Available: http://school.discoveryeducation.com/schrockguide/eval.html (accessed December 23, 2008).

Simmons, Michelle Holschuh. 2005. "Librarians as Disciplinary Discourse Mediators: Using Genre Theory to Move Toward Critical Information Literacy." *portal: Libraries and the Academy* 5, no. 3: 297–311.

Tapscott, Don and Anthony D. Williams. 2006. *Wikinomics: How Mass Collaboration Changes Everything*. London, England: Penguin Books.

Tiberius, Richard and Ivan Silver. "Guidelines for Conducting Workshops and Seminars That Actively Engage Participants" (2001). Available: www.aadprt.org/training/workshops/Guidelines_for_Conducting_Workshops_and_Seminars.pdf (accessed December 23, 2008).

Part III

Planning and Developing Information Literacy Instruction

Chapter 7

Planning for Information Literacy Instruction

Our plans miscarry because they have no aim. When a man does not know what harbor he is making for, no wind is the right wind.

—Seneca

WHY PLAN?

You would not set off on a trip without some idea of where you are going. You would not cook a meal without first thinking about the ingredients you wish to include. And you would not try to construct a building without a blueprint. So, why would you attempt to teach without a plan? Although it is reasonable to assume that no one sets foot into a classroom or develops a Web page, tutorial, or other type of online instructional experience without some idea of what they wish to accomplish, some of us may do our planning on the fly. With time such a precious commodity, we frequently take the easy road and rely on our knowledge and previous experiences, placing little effort on pre-instructional thinking. Even the newest of librarians may fall into the trap of thinking that they know the material so well that they do not have to develop extensive plans in advance.

Ironically, advance planning can be a time saver and an investment in the future. Although it may take some effort to plan for something you have never done before, the work you do now will make future planning and teaching much easier. Furthermore, given the fact that our contact with learners can be limited, it is important for us to determine how best to use the time we have. No matter how much time you have with your learners you need to make the most of it—whether it is face-to-face (F2F) or online instruction, synchronous or asynchronous. Planning makes teaching a purposeful and mindful act. It forces us to think about what we want our learners to take away with them from the experience and to consider thoughtfully what content to cover, how to cover it, and methods to determine what learners have gained from our instructional endeavors (Freilberg and Driscoll, 2005; Huba and Freed, 2000; Veldof, 2006).

Whether you are teaching a single F2F session, a full-term for-credit course, at the programmatic level, or at any point on this continuum, advance planning allows you to create instruction that is truly beneficial for your learners. Planning is equally important when working in the online environment. If you are creating asynchronous instructional materials that may be accessed whenever the learner needs it, contact time is no longer as much of an issue. However, you want to make sure that whatever you are designing will be worth the learners' effort and that it will accomplish whatever goals you have set out for the material. Synchronous online credit courses may offer more flexibility to both teacher and learner but share some of the contact constraint issues of a F2F format. Blended instruction formats that combine F2F with online instruction components have even more complicated planning issues, as the elements of instruction (regardless of delivery format) must all work together to support the whole enterprise.

Advance planning allows you to find out who

your learners are and to determine their information literacy (IL) needs. It enables you to decide where you want your learners to go; determine the skills, knowledge, and abilities they should acquire to meet their needs; and select the instructional opportunities you will provide for them. It answers the two fundamental questions related to instruction: "What do we want them to be able to do?" and "How will we know they are able do it?" Just as we advise learners to think about their information needs and determine how best to fulfill those needs before they begin their searches, we need to carefully and thoughtfully consider what we are trying to accomplish with our information literacy instruction (ILI) and how best to reach those goals.

Planning ILI can be done at both the macro (programmatic) and micro (individual classes or courses) levels. It occurs in all kinds of environments—academic, public, school, or special libraries and nonlibrary settings, including the workplace. Clearly macro and micro planning differ in both scope and audience, but the underlying process remains the same. It starts with gathering data about the target audience. ILI goals, objectives, and expected learning outcomes (ELOs) are then drawn from the data. Instructional methodologies, including ways to assess the attainment of ELOs, are developed next. Then comes the delivery of the instruction either F2F or virtually, followed by review and analysis of any assessment data that were collected during or after the instruction. Finally, revisions and modifications to the original instruction are made based on this analysis. Before we begin an in-depth discussion of these steps, let's take a look at how instruction typically gets initiated.

RECOGNIZING THE INFORMATION NEED

Where does the idea for instruction come from? What motivates us to begin the development process in the first place? In other words, what events in our environment trigger the idea that a new instructional endeavor is necessary? Something obviously drives us to feel there is a need and that instruction is the answer. The impetus to develop a new instructional endeavor can come from many places. In most types of libraries, the need materializes in three distinct ways.

- Reactive mode—Sometimes it comes from librarians' experiences answering questions or working directly with learners. Librarians detect a pattern of learners' needs and decide it would be more efficient to work with a group of them rather than with one at a time. User questions drive this type of instructional development.
- Interactive mode—In this mode someone requests the instruction. You receive a call, an e-mail, or a visit from someone who asks you to present some material, frequently in a classroom setting. The requester usually has an idea of what he or she would like you to teach and may collaborate with you on developing the instruction. In this case the requester is the driving force.
- Proactive mode—Here you do the driving. You and your staff do some preliminary research and identify areas where your patrons could benefit from instruction. Often the librarian must also pitch the idea to colleagues, administrators, and the audience for whom this instruction is intended. The important thing to remember about this mode is that it is neither a desperate attempt to deal with a preexisting situation (reactive) nor a response to an externally imposed request (interactive). The proactive approach comes from the librarian's professional judgment and often deals with broader IL issues. It is generally through the proactive mode that full-scale, sweeping IL programs are born.

THE PLANNING PROCESS

Regardless of how instruction gets initiated, or what your particular institutional environment might be, the steps for the instructional design planning process remain the same (Dick, Carey, and Carey, 2005; Elliott et al., 2000; Farmer, 2007; Grassian, Haras, and Pashaie, in press; Gratch-Lindauer, 2007; Huba and Freed, 2000; Jansen, 2003; O'Sullivan, 2002; Rockman, 2004b; Skoglund, 2003; Veldof, 2006; Walter, 2007; Weidenbenner, 2003; Wiggins, 1998):

- RECOGNIZE the learner's need.
- ANALYZE the present situation, including available resources.

- DEVELOP instructional goals, objectives, and ELOs.
- DESIGN appropriate instructional and assessment methods and materials.
- IMPLEMENT the instructional plan.
- ASSESS the ELOs—either during or after the instruction is delivered.
- REVIEW ASSESSMENT DATA, and REVISE as appropriate.

This chapter deals with the steps that precede the actual delivery of the instruction—recognizing the need, describing and analyzing the current situation, and developing goals, objectives, and ELOs. The link between ELOs and assessment will also be covered. Issues relating to selecting modes of instruction can be found in Chapter 8. For a more in-depth discussion of assessment techniques and methodology, see Chapter 11.

Obviously, the planning process can be time consuming, and in the reactive and interactive modes you may not be able to dwell on some of these preliminary steps. However, it is essential to the quality of your instruction that you pay attention to all of the steps regardless of who was the initiator.

Describe and Analyze the Current Situation—Needs Assessments

No matter what the plan's scope is, the process should begin with a Needs Assessment. This is the data-gathering step that enables the librarian to gain a clear and complete understanding of the targeted audience and the information needs of that population. To be complete, a Needs Assessment should consider the institution's culture, climate, and politics as well as the needs of the individual learners. This is your opportunity to identify yourself to those in your environment who share your interests in developing information literate individuals and who may wish to collaborate with you on these efforts. These early contacts may prove extremely useful as you develop your programs and courses down the road (Dick, Carey, and Carey, 2005; Freilberg and Driscoll, 2005; Grassian, Haras, and Pashaie, in press; Grassian and Kaplowitz, 2005; Hensley, 2007; MacDonald, 2008; Veldof, 2006).

If the goal is to develop a full-blown institution-wide program (macro planning), gathering population, institutional, and community data is crucial. It is also key at the micro level, because any ILI programs or courses you develop should resonate with the overall organization's mission, vision, and goals (Hensley, 2007; MacDonald, 2008; Peacock, 2007). At the micro level this means paying special attention to the information needs of the individual learners you are targeting. Let us say you are working with a specific campus department to develop ILI support for a discipline-based basic research methods course. In addition to looking at the ELOs for the department and the specific class, try to locate any discipline-specific standards and competencies. Check the appropriate national organizations and associations, especially those responsible for accrediting higher education programs (Lampert, 2003). All of this contributes to an understanding of learners' needs and helps align the ILI with the larger goals in the discipline as well as in your particular institution or community.

In the case of the reactive and interactive modes, the need has been identified for you. However, you should still try to gather additional information on the audience and the exact nature of the information need. In the reactive mode you may wish to talk directly to your users. In the case of the interactive mode the requester should be able to provide the necessary data.

A complete and thorough Needs Assessment lies at the heart of the proactive mode. No one is identifying information needs for you. You are actively going out there and looking for them. You set out to gather information about what is currently happening in instruction and compare that to what potential library users would like to have happen. You compile data about your users, your community, your current programs and materials, and your facility, staff, budget, etc. Use these data to evaluate your library's actual world against the ideal. This is the time to make sure the library is responding to real, rather than assumed, needs.

Needs Assessments do not have to be complex or complicated. Watching reference desk interactions or the behavior of users in the library can give you a good idea of what is needed. Talking informally to your colleagues or to library users can also help pinpoint problems that could be addressed through instruction. More formal approaches make use of surveys, interviews, focus group meetings, document analyses, usability studies, and so on (Freilberg and Driscoll, 2005; Loe and Elkins, 1990; Veldof, 2006) and are of special importance when planning at the programmatic level. Regardless of the approach you select, remember that your goal is to find out who your users are and what they need and want.

The more information you can acquire from your Needs Assessment the better able you will be to develop a clear and complete understanding of the characteristics of your target population (or TPOP) (Mager, 1997e). How formal or informal a Needs Assessment you undertake will depend on how much time you have to perform it and on the scope of the ILI for which you are planning. Your goal should be to gather as much information about your TPOP as time and resources permit. What are the groups' attributes in terms of age, educational background, cultural and ethnic groups, and language proficiencies (Freilberg and Driscoll, 2005; Loe and Elkins, 1990; Roberts and Blandy, 1989; Veldof, 2006)? You can contact government offices for demographics and other types of census-type data. Ask yourself, "Who would have these data in my institutional environment?" Meet with administrators, faculty, learners, community leaders, and members of local organizations and special interest groups to ask questions about population makeup and needs. In an academic setting try the registrar's office. Your local school board may be able to provide this information for a school library setting. City offices and library boards would be useful contact points for public library Needs Assessments. Personnel offices might be helpful in a special library setting.

You will also need to assess your potential learners' attitudes toward the library, previous experience in using libraries, ease of access, familiarity with searching for and accessing information, and preferred types of learning. This may require interviewing or surveying members of your target group or others in your community who have in-depth knowledge of the group in question. Keep in mind that most TPOPs will be composed of a mix of people, so make sure you gather all of the data you can in order to get a complete picture.

Study use patterns in your library. What time of day, what day of the week, and what time of the year is the library most heavily used in person? Check on remote use as well. When are library resources most often accessed remotely? Do use patterns fluctuate over the course of the day, week, or time of year for both F2F and remote use? For example, in a public library setting different age groups generally use the library at different times.

Talk directly with your users. Try to develop a procedure to assess both library users and nonusers. See if you can find out from nonusers why they are not using the library and what would entice them to use it—F2F or online. If time permits, go out into the community and talk to people on the street, or mail surveys to a representative sample of your population. Post interactive surveys on your library's Web site and any other sites that your users frequent within your institution, organization, or community.

If you use questionnaires or surveys, make sure they are clear, concise, and easy to return. Provide some kind of incentive for returning the surveys to increase your response rate (Grassian and Kaplowitz, 2005). You might even consider administering some kind of pretest to assess actual knowledge and skills. A pretest can help you determine what your learners already know and pinpoint what they still need to learn. Pretests can be paper based or interactive Web pages that include questions about the learners' knowledge of resources and/or strategies, a performance assessment in which you observe actual research behavior, or a product appraisal (examination of papers, projects, or bibliographies). Once instruction has taken place, posttests can be administered and compared to the pretests to help determine the success of your instructional endeavors. See Chapter 11 for more on how to develop these tools.

Make sure you are also gathering input from your library staff. Get their impressions of the user population. Do they see particular areas where users seem to have a lot of difficulty using the facility and its resources? Check with your library administrators to see if there are any upcoming technological changes on the horizon—such as a new library catalog, a new interface for an existing licensed database, or added or deleted databases. If so, you will need to think about how these changes will impact your user population. Keep an eye on what is happening overall in your institution regarding technology. Get to know your organization's computer center staff. They can keep you updated on the types of information and instructional technologies that are being supported in your community. For more on establishing relationships with others in your community, see the "Collaboration and Partnership" chapter in *Learning to Lead and Manage Information Literacy Instruction* (Grassian and Kaplowitz, 2005).

To be complete, your Needs Assessment must address institutional climate and politics. Any proposed instruction must fit in with the overall goals of your institution as well as those of your library. Review your institution's Mission Statement. Is IL included as part of the institution's mission? If so, how is IL defined? As we discussed in Chapter 1, IL can mean different things to different people. Interview key people in your organization to see what IL means to them. Finding out what your institution means by IL will help you tailor your initiatives to fit the goals of the larger organization. It will help you identify potential supporters and may even open lines of communication with and raise the consciousness of these key people. You may gain even more support for your proposals as a result of these interactions (Grassian and Kaplowitz, 2005). Looking at the larger institutional issues is especially important if you are trying to develop a larger scale program. The special considerations connected with planning at the programmatic level will be discussed at the end of this chapter.

Look at where the library fits into the overall organization. Who must be convinced of the merit of new instructional endeavors both within the library and in the broader organizational structure? Try to identify potential institutional partners and supporters. Media or computing centers can help with technology issues. Graphic designers and editors might help with handout and screen design. Research methods departments could help design surveys and so on. What does the library's Mission Statement say about instruction? What are the library's instructional goals? Who is the library mandated to serve? Are there stated user population priorities? Are there different goals for different groups, and, if so, how would that impact your instructional program (Grassian, 1993; Grassian and Kaplowitz, 2005)?

Now look at your identified needs as they relate to what you are currently doing. What instruction is currently in place, and how does it address (or fail to address) the needs identified by your assessment? Part of the planning process is to identify which of your current programs and materials should remain, be modified, or actually be replaced by something new. You may also come up with noninstructional solutions, such as better directional signs, screen design modifications, or reorganization of part or all of the collection to make it more accessible.

Finally, a Needs Assessment should look at what is possible. Be realistic. Do an honest assessment of your facility, space, staffing, and budget. A thorough Needs Assessment helps to determine both what you would like to do and what can actually be done given your present circumstances. Do you have the space, the people, and the resources to undertake a big, new initiative? Your ideal instructional program may not be practical at first. Start small, perhaps with a pilot project, and hope you can build on it. Nothing succeeds like success. If you are forced to make some compromises on your ideal, do not despair. Your success with a small segment or pilot will provide a strong foundation for the broader program. Prove yourself competent, creative, flexible, and capable of delivering what you promise, and your administrators may be willing to give you a chance to try something bigger (and more expensive) next time around. Keep in mind that research and grant support is often available to help both with the pilot project and with the larger initiative. Small successes can serve as evidence that larger endeavors are worth funding (Grassian and Kaplowitz, 2005; Veldof, 2006).

A thorough and complete Needs Assessment helps the ILI librarian gain insight into the IL needs of his or her community of learners. However, the reality is that there is not always enough time or resources to do a full-fledged Needs Assessment for each instructional endeavor you undertake. The scale of your Needs Assessment will depend upon size and scope of your intended instruction. If you are planning for a single class or workshop, it might be enough to just gather data from those directly involved (course instructor, classroom teacher, and potential participants). If your scope is a bit larger, say a full-term course, you may wish to involve members of the department that is sponsoring the course. In the case of a subject-specific IL class or course, you will also want to examine standards and competencies for the discipline itself. Planning for institution or communitywide programs will require a more complex and complete Needs Assessment. Keep in mind that any of the smaller Needs Assessments can provide valuable data, contacts, and information for the larger ones. ILI librarians might wish to conduct formal institution or communitywide Needs Assessments every two to five years in order to keep current with their populations. These periodic checks can be helpful in day-to-day planning as well. The data from these more formal Needs Assessments can serve as background for more focused planning.

Develop Instructional Goals, Objectives, and Expected Learning Outcomes

Your Needs Assessment identifies your population's IL needs and thus sets the stage for the development of goals and objectives. Taking the time to develop clear instructional goals, objectives, and ELOs helps you focus both your instructional and assessment efforts. The literature on this topic is large, frequently overwhelming, and often confusing. You may find it difficult to wrap your mind around the terminology, especially when it comes to the differences between objectives and ELOs and how these two concepts relate to goals. See Figure 7.1 for an overview of this topic.

Now let's look at these concepts in more detail. Goals represent the big picture. They describe your overall intent in broad, general strokes. Goals indicate what you would like to accomplish, set educational priorities, and are frequently stated as global abstractions. They act as the guidelines, blueprints, or road maps for your planning. Your goals must always be kept in mind as you select the specific objectives and ELOs for your instruction (Dewald, 1999a; Elliott et al., 2000; Freilberg and Driscoll, 2005; Grassian and Kaplowitz, forthcoming; Hensley, 2007; Huba and Freed, 2000; Linn and Gronlund, 2005; Macklin, 2008; Mager, 1997e; Sullivan, 2004; Veldof, 2006).

The definitions of objectives and ELOs often appear so similar that you might think that they are interchangeable. However, there is a subtle yet important distinction between the two. Objectives describe the end product (your desire or aim for learners). They explicate what the learner should be able to do following instruction. ELOs describe how learners will exhibit that they have attained the objective and usually include some kind of criteria for determining to what degree they have succeeded (Anderson and Krathwohl, 2001; Bloom, Madaus, and Hastings, 1981; Cruickshank, Jenkins, and Metcalf, 2003; Elliott et al., 2000; Freilberg and Driscoll, 2005; Kellough, Kellough, and Kim, 1999; Linn and Gronlund, 2005; Macklin, 2008; Mager, 1997e; Tyler, 1976).

Figure 7.1 A Brief Overview of Goals, Objectives, and ELOs

Goal: Overall intent of the instruction. Example: To teach how to critically evaluate Web sites.

Objectives: The behavior(s) learners will exhibit after instruction. Can include instructional methodology to be used. Example: After a 50-minute stand-alone instructional session that includes a mix of lecture, demonstrations, group exercises, and discussion instruction, learners will be able to determine the quality and appropriateness of Web sites for their research needs.

ELOs: The action(s) learners will perform to indicate they have attained the objective. Example: Learners will apply a list of criteria to Web sites found on a topic in order to rate the quality and appropriateness of these sites for their research needs.

In other words, objectives describe the behavior to be learned. ELOs deal with how the learner will show you that the behavior has been learned. The term objectives has been around for a long time and is certainly still in use. However, with increased emphasis for more accountability in our educational institutions, how and when learners exhibit the attainment of our objectives has come under scrutiny. Therefore, we must ensure that we do not use our objectives merely to plan our instruction, but that we also offer learners opportunities to exhibit ELOs during their learning experience and that we assess these opportunities to ensure learning has taken place (O'Hanlon, 2007).

Are ELOs just objectives dressed up in new language? The answer to this is a resounding no! Objectives are supposed to be written in terms of measurable, observable behaviors. ELOs are the behaviors you observe and measure to see if learners have achieved your expectations. ELOs also force us to consider what opportunities we include in our instruction that allow us to observe our learners in action, performing the ELOs described in our objectives. Basically, objectives ask us to address two fundamental issues regarding our interactions with our learners:

> What will they do?
> How will we know?

OBJECTIVES

Objectives, therefore, need to be written in terms of observable ELOs. Each objective may include more than one outcome, but an opportunity to observe learners exhibiting each outcome should be included in your instructional plan.

Both objectives and ELOs shift the focus from the teacher to the learner and emphasize the product rather than the process of teaching. By doing so they make instruction more meaningful and relevant by giving your learners a sense of how the instruction will enable them to lead a more successful and rewarding life (Bain, 2004; Battersby and Learning Outcomes Network, 1999; Driscoll and Wood, 2007; Freilberg and Driscoll, 2005; Hensley, 2007; Huba and Freed, 2000; Weimer, 2002; Wiggins, 1998).

Guidelines for Writing Goals and Objectives

Although most IL instructors agree in principle that good instruction starts with the writing of clear, concise, and meaningful goals, objectives, and ELOs, in practice these crucial steps may be skipped or not given the attention they deserve. We may rely on the ideas we have in our heads and perhaps on some informal notes, because we generally know what we want to teach and how we intend to teach it. But explicating these ideas not only helps us formulate our thoughts but also provides us with a way to communicate our intent to our learners. To those who have never done this work before in a structured manner, these preliminary steps may seem daunting indeed. However, with some practical guidelines and a little practice, you may find that following these steps becomes second nature. Taking the time to think about and write out your plans in this fashion helps you organize your thoughts and develop more meaningful and effective instruction. Conferring with people knowledgeable about the group to whom you will be offering instruction and/or those who requested the instruction can also help clarify your goals, objectives, and ELOs and ensure they are relevant and appropriate for your audience. A quick way to do this for interactive planning is to ask the person who is requesting instruction:

- What do you expect your learners to know and be able to do following instruction?
- What do you want your learners to get out of this instruction?

When writing your goals, objectives, and ELOs, always look at them from the learners' perspective. Remember that goals are broad, general statements that describe overall intent of the instruction. Goals frequently start with the word to and may not even be complete sentences. They can include global terms like *understand, know,* or *learn*. But how will learners be able to demonstrate their understanding, knowledge, or learning? Objectives operationalize how this intent will be accomplished. Objectives are usually written in complete sentences and describe the observable and measurable changes in learners' behavior that will result from instruction. ELOs are the learners' behaviors, skills, and attitudes that teachers will observe. We assess these observations to determine if learners have successfully attained the objectives set for the instruction. Furthermore, objectives and ELOs communicate your intent to your learners. They let learners know what is expected of them and where their efforts should be concentrated (Bain, 2004; Battersby and Learning Outcomes Network, 1999; Driscoll and Wood, 2007; Freilberg and Driscoll, 2005; Grassian and Kaplowitz, forthcoming; Hensley, 2007; Kellough, Kellough, and Kim, 1999; Mager, 1997e; Veldof, 2006).

If you have never done this type of writing before, you might wish to refer to some existing frameworks for doing so. One approach is called the ABCD formula (Armstrong and Savage, 1983; Cruickshank, Jenkins, and Metcalf, 2003; Elliott et al., 2000; Kellough, Kellough, and Kim, 1999). The first two components (audience and behavior) help you formulate your objective, while the second two (condition and degree) describe the ELOs and how you will measure them.

- Audience for whom the objectives are intended.
  Example: Senior citizens in a public library setting.
- Behavior that indicates learning.
  Example: To be able to locate call numbers for books held in the library.
- Conditions under which the behavior is to appear.
  Example: Given a list of authors' names, book titles, and topics, learners will be able to locate the call numbers for these items by searching the library catalog.
- Degree of competency that will be accepted.
  Example: At least 80 percent of the call numbers for items in the list will be identified correctly.

Another approach discusses objectives and ELOs in terms of tasks, conditions, and standards. Tasks are observable actions and should be included in your objectives. Conditions are the situations within which the tasks are carried out. They describe how the learner will demonstrate newly acquired behavior. These, therefore, are part of your ELOs. Standards are the criteria for successful performance of the ELOs. These three parts can also be referred to as *performance*, *condition*, and *criteria* (Freedman and Bantly, 1982; Mager, 1997e; Veldof, 2006). Here is the same example used in the ABCD format above but translated into the performance, condition, and criteria format:

- Task/performance: What someone will be able to do at the conclusion of instruction.
  Example: To be able to locate call numbers for books held in the library.
- Condition: The condition that will exist when the learner is demonstrating accomplishment of the objective.
  Example: Given a list of authors' names, book titles, and topics, learners will be able to locate the call numbers for these items by searching the library catalog.
- Standard or criterion: How to recognize that the performance is satisfactory.
  Example: At least 80 percent of the call numbers for items in the list will be identified correctly.

Goal analysis is another helpful method for determining where you want learners to be at the end of your instruction. It enables you to describe the performance that if exhibited would indicate you have achieved your goal and the learners have achieved the ELOs. As such, goal analysis can be extremely helpful in writing both objectives and ELOs. Ask yourself how you would identify someone who had attained your goal (Dick, Carey, and Carey, 2005; Mager, 1997a; Veldof, 2006). What would you take as evidence (in behavioral terms) that your goal had been achieved? How would you separate a group of people into two categories, those who had achieved the goal and those who had not? Identify people you know have reached the goal. What characteristics distinguish these people as having attained the goal? For example, an IL individual would be able to evaluate material found during his or her information search as to authenticity, authority, relevance, and timeliness.

Once you have generated a list of behaviors, you are ready to begin writing your objectives. Each objective statement should contain verbs that are specific and indicate definite, observable behaviors—that is, responses that can be seen and assessed. The following is an example of the type of verbs that can be found in many standard works on instructional design. Keep in mind that this is not a definitive list (Anderson and Krathwohl, 2001; Bloom, 1956; Bloom, Madaus, and Hastings, 1981; Driscoll and Wood, 2007; Huba and Freed, 2000; Linn and Gronlund, 2005; Mager, 1997c, 1997e).

- Build
- Classify
- Compare
- Construct
- Define
- Demonstrate
- Describe
- Distinguish
- Identify
- Name
- Order
- Recite
- Select
- Write

The specific behaviors are further clarified by listing some of the tasks learners are expected to perform to demonstrate achievement. These are the learners' ELOs. For example, learners can identify items by circling them, pointing to them, picking them up, touching them, etc. Returning to our distinction between objectives and ELOs, the verb *identify* would be part of the objective, but to circle the correct responses as a method of demonstrating "identifying" would be included as a measurable ELO. Remember to indicate any conditions under which the behavior would be performed and your criteria for measuring success.

Here is another example. Your objective is:

> Given a specific list of items, including Web sites, blogs, and journal, magazine, and newspaper articles, learners will be able to identify those that are scholarly in nature.

One learning outcome could be:

> Learners, having been provided with a list of items retrieved by searching a variety of resources, will be able to generate a list of those items that contain scholarly content. Instructors will evaluate items to determine the appropriateness of the selections.

The objective here is to be able to identify scholarly material. The conditions are that learners are given a list of items retrieved from a number of resources. In other words, they do not actually have to do the searches or retrieve the items. The ELO is that they successfully select (by creating a list) the ones that would be considered scholarly material. Note that a means of identifying appropriateness (the criterion for success) is also included in the above statement. While this statement may appear more convoluted and complex than you feel is necessary, it offers the advantages of both identifying how the learner will demonstrate competency and including a method for measuring that competency.

If keeping these two concepts distinct in your own mind makes it easier for you to develop your own goals, objectives, and ELOs, go ahead and do so. Or you may wish to combine objectives and ELOs in single statements. The idea is to work with what makes sense to you. In the end, your aim is to come up with a workable guideline for your instruction. Your plan must clearly articulate where you are trying to go and how you are trying to get there. It also must include some way to tell that you have reached your destination. Regardless of the terminology you use, a clear articulation of what you are trying to do will provide the means for proving that you did it.

Overt versus Covert Behaviors

Proponents of the above approach to goal, objectives, and ELOs writing say that if you want to teach something you should be able to describe performance (an observable action) that will indicate that the learner has succeeded in achieving the ELOs, thanks to your instruction. However, others critique the approach as being too behaviorist in its view of learning. Those adhering to a more cognitive/constructivist approach question whether performance-based ELOs can be used to demonstrate higher order cognitive thinking or more affective behaviors, which are more internal and thus difficult to define in these terms (Eble, 1988; Kellough, Kellough, and Kim, 1999). However, these nonobservable or covert aspects of learning can also be valid goals for instruction. How then do we write meaningful objectives and ELOs to deal with these internal or covert behavioral changes? Furthermore, how can we tell when our learners have obtained these objectives? In other words, how does the learner exhibit these ELOs?

These questions are the basis of the controversy. If we cannot find a way to ascertain that a learner has attained the objective, we have no way of knowing if our instruction has succeeded. One way around this quandary is to describe performance that would indicate attainment of the covert objective. In other words, because we cannot directly see the covert behavior, we need to find an overt behavior from which we can infer changes in the covert behavior. The area where this becomes most relevant is in the arena of affective objectives. We often wish to include changes in attitudes and feelings about information, our resources, our facilities, and even ourselves as information professionals in our goals and objectives. But we cannot see, hear, or touch these attitudes and feelings. We can, however, infer changes in an attitude toward something by how the person interacts with it. For example, a person who, as a result of our instruction, has gained a more positive attitude toward X, will be more inclined to approach or interact with X in the future. Conversely, a person who develops a negative attitude will try to avoid further contact with X. Using a concept mapping exercise to help learners express their library anxiety is another example of turning a covert behavior or feeling (anxiety) into a more overt and therefore measurable behavior. Analyzing the types of references included in a paper or project and how the content from those references has been analyzed, synthesized, evaluated, and used to support points in the paper is an example of how we can use overt behavior to determine the attainment of more covert higher order cognitive thinking abilities. For more on the psychology of learning, see Chapters 3 and 4. For more on mental models, concept mapping, and annotated drawing, see Chapter 5.

Using this rationale, we can include covert objectives in our plan as long as we can come up with an observable behavior (ELOs from which we can infer the attainment of the objective). Here is one final example of this process of converting covert to overt objectives. Let's say that one of our goals is for learners to access information in all formats. Therefore, we would like to address the problem of computer anxiety in our instruction. Our list of objectives would include something about learners acquiring a more positive attitude toward using computerized databases. After having participated in our instruction, learners' levels of computer anxiety will be reduced. Our objective, then, is a change in attitude. Because we cannot measure this directly, we must come up with an observable indicator of this change. What if we write our objective like this?

> Upon given the choice of using print material housed in the library versus resources accessible only via the library's computers, learners will select computer-accessible resources at least as often as they do print ones when researching their topics.

Now let's try the performance, conditions, criteria test again. Our performance is selecting print or computerized resources. Any number of ELOs could be developed that would enable us to see and measure that behavior. For example, we could offer learners equal access to these resources and observe the frequency of selecting one or the other format. Learners could point to their selections or make a written list of the ones they would use, or we could actually watch them as they made their selections and used the resources (all examples of observable ELOs). The conditions are that learners have a specific topic to research and must select resources from the ones to which we have given them access. The criterion is that learners select computer-based resources at least as often as they select print resources. Choosing computerized resources as often as print ones can be inferred as a decrease in computer anxiety. In other words, learners are now willing to approach computer resources as often (if not more so) than print ones.

Have we succeeded in writing an observable and measurable outcome for this covert behavior? The answer is yes. Although it may be a bit more difficult to develop ELOs for these types of objectives, they are well worth the effort. If we think something is worth teaching, then we must come up with a way for people to demonstrate they have learned it. Whether we decide to assess the behavior through an actual performance test, some sort of interview, a concept mapping exercise, an annotated drawing, or by means of a written survey or questionnaire are subjects for another chapter. But our objective has been written in such a way that we are able to measure the learning outcome in order to determine if our objective has been attained.

Reality Check

One more word on writing goals and objectives: While goals and objectives describe where you want to go with your instructional program and how you expect to get there, they must also be realistic, attainable, and appropriate. Your objectives must meet users' needs and should be consistent with the overall goals and objectives of your library and parent institution. Check to see if you have selected appropriate and rational objectives by looking at the following criteria (Linn and Gronlund, 2005; Mager, 1997e; Roberts and Blandy, 1989):

- Completeness: Do the objectives include everything learners need to know how to do in order to attain the instructional goal? If a person did all the things the objectives called for, would you be willing to accept that he or she had achieved your instructional goals? If not, what other additional objectives need to be added?
- Importance: Is the objective trivial? Look at the consequence of not achieving the performance. If there is no significant consequence, then the objective is trivial and should be cut.
- Appropriateness: Are the objectives consistent with the general goals of the institution and of your library?
- Soundness: Are the objectives consistent with current educational practices and principles of learning?
- Feasibility: Are the objectives realistic in terms of the abilities of the learners and the time, staff, facilities, and space available?

Your Needs Assessment data will prove invaluable in helping you determine the answers to these questions.

As with any skill, writing goals and objectives becomes easier with practice. Your first few attempts may leave something to be desired. But you can learn from doing. If you write your goals and objectives and then discover that at the conclusion of instruction there is no way of proving learners have attained them, you need to begin again. That is not to say that your instruction is a failure. It just means that you need to revise your objectives so that they include a means for your learners to demonstrate attainment of your goals in terms of observable, measurable ELOs. Remember that the reason for writing goals, objectives, and ELOs is to communicate your intent, describe desired performance, and provide a way to demonstrate success (Cruickshank, Jenkins, and Metcalf, 2003). If you include all these components in your game plan, you will have succeeded in writing meaningful goals and objectives.

TAXONOMIES AND STANDARDS

Writing appropriate goals, objectives, and ELOs requires that we can articulate where we are trying to go and how we are planning to get there. This in turn means that we have identified standard definitions or descriptions for the terms we are using. Educators frequently start with Benjamin Bloom's (1956) *Taxonomy of Educational Objectives*. An updated and revised version of this taxonomy was published by Anderson and Krathwohl in 2001. While some of the material in these works could be applied to ILI, it is better to refer to standards that have been developed specifically for our discipline (MacDonald, 2008). Both the AASL and the ACRL have developed such documents. The latest versions of these documents are available at the respective Web sites (ALA. ACRL, 2000; ALA. AASL, 2007b).

Both sets of standards were intended to provide a framework for determining whether or not a person is information literate. ACRL began its work in 2000 by building upon those developed for K–12 learners by the American Association of School Librarians (ALA. ACRL, 2000; ALA. AASL., 1998a), thus allowing for the development of a continuum of expectations for students of all levels. The ACRL standards include a definition of IL, a list of the characteristics or attributes that are viewed as the component parts of IL, and the behaviors if exhibited that identify a person as information literate. As such, they can provide guidelines as we develop our specific goals and objectives. The competencies are broken down into five standards, each with multiple performance indicators. Each performance indicator includes a list of measurable outcomes for assessing progress toward attainment of that particular IL standard. Although the language used in this document varies somewhat from that used in standard educational practice, the standards, performance indicators, and measurable outcomes can be used as the basis for writing ILI goals, objectives, and ELOs. If our aim is to produce information literate learners, then these standards help us determine how we can recognize someone who has become information literate. Although the ACRL standards are aimed at learners in the higher education setting, they represent generic IL competencies and can be modified to work in other environments as well. The 2001 IS "Objectives for Information Literacy Instruction" can be extremely useful as you develop your instruction's goals, objectives, and ELOs (ALA. ACRL. IS, 2001). The following is an example of how we could use these documents in our instructional planning.

Let's look at Standard One, which states that the IL student determines the extent of the information need. One performance indicator for this standard states that the information literate person can identify a variety of types and formats of potential sources for information. Clearly, this statement could be used as a learning objective. If we expand upon the measurable outcomes listed for this performance and include specific observable behaviors, as well as conditions and criteria for success, we would have identified how learners indicate they had successfully attained this objective.

One outcome for the performance indicator for Standard One is that the learner is able to differentiate between primary and secondary sources, recognizing how their use and importance vary with each discipline. If we include how this ability can be demonstrated, we would have a workable and measurable ELO. So, if we said that, when given a list of resources in a specific discipline, the learner could accurately separate them into two categories—primary and secondary resources—we have described a performance that can be both seen and measured. If accuracy is our criterion, we also need to include some method for determining correctness, such as comparison to an authoritative list in the field or to a list that we have come up with in advance based on our experience and professional judgment.

Here again we see the separation of objectives from ELOs. The objective is for learners to be able to determine the difference between primary and secondary sources. We determine if they reach this objective by creating an opportunity for the learner to demonstrate the behavior. The demonstration consists of having learners accurately sort material into primary or secondary categories. Our criterion for accuracy is to compare their results to what we have predetermined to be the correct result of this sort according to the standard definitions of primary and secondary resources in a given discipline.

The AASL and the ACRL standards are good starting points, but do not feel obligated to include every aspect of them in your own work. Documents like this are bound to undergo revision as people work with them. Wording may evolve, and the overall organization of the documents themselves may be modified as time goes on. However, these standards are excellent places to look for ideas about your own instructional goals and objectives. They have been designed to guide you. Modify them as needed, and make them work for you. To be most effective, the standards must be adapted to fit your particular institutional setting and the needs of your specific population. In other words, you must refine them until you can make them your own.

Standards have also been developed by individual institutions for specific disciplines and in other countries around the world. These can serve as additional resource material for you. Examples include the standards developed by the California State University system, the Anthropology and Sociology section of ACRL, and the Scottish IL Framework (ALA. ACRL. ANSS, 2007; California State University. Information Competence Assessment, 2002; National Framework, 2007).

TRIMMING THE FAT

There are lots of advantages to taking the time to articulate your goals, objectives, and ELOs. Doing so helps guide your planning; communicates your intent to your administrators, colleagues, and learners; and provides the means by which you can assess your successes. The process itself causes you to think seriously and deeply about what is worth teaching and how best to address your learners' needs (Driscoll and Wood, 2007; Freilberg and Driscoll, 2005; Mager, 1997a, 1997c, 1997e; Weimer, 2002). You may even discover that formal instruction may not be the answer at all. Maps, signs, changes in screen design, online tutorials, paper point-of-use guides, etc., may all be ways of solving your learners' problems. Improving systems and removing the barriers that make it difficult to use your facility and its resources may address many needs. However, if a more formal instructional approach does turn out to be the answer, written goals, objectives, and ELOs can prove invaluable in selecting what to include in your sessions, tutorials, or Web pages. Once you have decided upon your goals, objectives, and ELOs, you are ready to begin the development phase of the instructional planning process.

Look over your instructional plan and compare what you propose to include in your F2F or online presentations to your proposed objectives. Your objectives should be derived directly from the Needs Assessment. Teach only those things your target audience has identified as something they need or want to learn. Each objective should be addressed by the content of your instruction, and everything you include should support at least one of your objectives. Be ruthless. Cut out anything that is not essential for achieving your objectives. Use your objectives to critique the relevance of any active learning methods you were thinking of including. Activities that allow learners to practice behavior associated with desired objectives are particularly valuable and can be used to assess your ELOs (Bain, 2004; Battersby and Learning Outcomes Network, 1999; Driscoll and Wood, 2007; Huba and Freed, 2000; Veldof, 2006; Weimer, 2002).

FROM OUTCOMES TO ASSESSMENTS

Most instructional planning models list assessment, review, and revision as the final steps in the process. However, although the analysis of the data may not occur until after the instruction is implemented, it is important to consider how you will be assessing your objectives and ELOs at the point at which you develop them. This is where having well-thought-out and fully developed objectives and ELOs pays off. Your objectives identify the behaviors, skills, or attitudes you are expecting your learners to have at the conclusion of the instructional experience. Your ELOs describes the opportunities you will provide for your learners to demonstrate that they have attained those objectives. These opportunities, whether they consist of active learning exercises, hands-on practice, quizzes, term paper reviews, or annotated bibliographies, can all serve as assessment devices. Be sure that you have included some kind of assessment for each of your objectives and that each of your ELOs are measured in some fashion (Battersby and Learning Outcomes Network, 1999; Huba and Freed, 2000). Assessments can be formal or informal, but if you do not include ELO assessment, you have no way of knowing if your learners have successfully attained the goals and objectives you have set for the instruction. See Chapter 11 for more on assessment.

In many ways, writing goals, objectives, and ELOs is the hardest part of planning. Once you have completed this step, however, the rest of the process seems to fall into place. It is much easier for you to develop your instructional outline, determine what activities to include, and select appropriate assessment techniques after having given considerable thought to what you expect your learners to be able to do as a result of your instruction (Driscoll and Wood, 2007; Freilberg and Driscoll, 2005; Wiggins, 1998).

SPECIAL ISSUES AT THE PROGRAMMATIC LEVEL

Planning at the programmatic level follows the same basic steps as planning for an individual class, course, or workshop. However, programmatic planning, with its broader scope, involves some special issues and challenges. Remember in this case you are not focused on the target population, needs, and ELOs for a specific class or course. Program planners are aiming higher as they try to develop a plan that will result in an integrated, sequenced, and coordinated plan for a larger segment of the population (e.g., all senior citizens living in the community), students at a particular grade level (e.g., all students attending a particular middle school), those majoring in a specific discipline (e.g., all undergraduate students majoring in sociology), or at the broadest level, the entire institution and/or community. These more far-reaching plans must consider where IL is currently being taught, who is teaching it, and how (if?) all these individual pieces fit together to form a unified whole. Program planning, therefore, requires a great deal of coordination and outreach. In order to be successful, ILI programs must have buy in not only from those in the library but also from those in the larger institution or community as well. Program planners should keep an eye on any initiatives or reform movements in their environment that could have implications for or connections to ILI. They also need to go beyond the confines of their specific institution or community environment and examine any relevant IL discussions, documents, standards, etc., at the local, state, national, and even international levels. For more on issues related to individual environments, see Chapter 14.

The following is a review of the planning steps described earlier in this chapter with special emphasis on the special issues or concerns facing the ILI program planner.

- RECOGNIZE the user need. Programmatic planners must pay special attention to the needs of the entire institution or community. In general, the overall program need would be to have all members of the populations acquire the skills, knowledge, and abilities necessary to be information literate in that environment. Needs Assessments at the programmatic level tend to be more formal than those done for individual courses, classes, or workshops. They are broader in scope and are used to identify how IL is viewed in the particular environment under review. Care should be taken to identify important stakeholders and find out what (if any) opinion these stakeholders have about IL. It is also possible that IL may have to be defined and explained to them, as these stakeholders may not be as familiar with the term as you are. This is a crucial step, as it is likely that you will need the support of these stakeholders in order to implement an institution or communitywide ILI program plan.
- ANALYZE the present situation, including available resources. Having identified stakeholders and developed a shared view of the information literate individual with them, examine what types of ILI are already in place, who is involved in these individual endeavors, and what the ELOs are for component parts. It is possible that not all ILI efforts are based in the library. Examine what current and potential resources might be available to support the program. It is often possible to turn stakeholders into ILI program partners who can help provide needed resources and support.
- DEVELOP instructional goals, objectives, and ELOs. Programmatic goals are broader and even more general than specific course or class goals. You should use the definition of an information literate individual developed out of your talks with stakeholders to create the global goal as well as the objectives and ELOs for those who will complete the ILI program. Because you are working at the programmatic level, you will also have to consider who will have responsibility for offering various components of the program, where these elements will be offered, and to whom they will be presented within the targeted group/institution/community.
- DESIGN appropriate instructional and assessment methods and materials. Programmatic design issues relate to the types of instruction being offered. Will the program concentrate on F2F sessions, online sessions, or a combination of types? Will blended instruction that combines F2F with online components in the same ILI endeavor also be supported? How will the overall program be assessed? While individual elements of the program should include element-specific assessments, the success of the overall program needs to be assessed as

well. If the goal is to develop an information literate community, how will you assess that the members of the community are indeed information literate? Decisions about the ways that the program will be assessed need to be made during this design step.

- IMPLEMENT the instructional plan. Depending upon the size of your targeted group/institution/community and the scope of your program, it may not be possible to implement the entire ILI program plan all at once. Pilot projects are a good way to demonstrate the effectiveness of your overall plan and gain support for it. You may also need to stage your plan over several years. Developing a timeline for this staged implementation is vital to the success of the program, as it will help keep the implementation on track, offer milestones to celebrate, and help to demonstrate a long-term commitment to the program from all concerned.
- ASSESS the ELOs—either during or after the instruction is delivered. The types of assessments to be used will have already been selected and/or designed in the DESIGN step. Whoever is coordinating or overseeing the ILI program needs to make sure that assessment is, in fact, taking place at every appropriate level of the program. The assessment data that are being collected must be analyzed and evaluated in order to assess the overall effectiveness of the ILI program plan and that of its component parts. These assessments will identify successes as well as places that might benefit from improvements.

One more thing to consider about programmatic ILI planning is who will be coordinating this effort. Although those who work in the library frequently are the ones to initiate ILI program planning discussions, it is clear that the library cannot and should not try to create a program in a vacuum. Stakeholders should not only be involved in the preliminary discussions regarding what information literacy means in their institution/community, but they should also become partners in the entire endeavor. You may wish to form some kind of coordinating committee with representatives from a variety of stakeholders, or you might wish to keep the coordination within the library but set up an advisory group from your stakeholders groups that will work with the coordinators within the library. Whatever coordinating format you decide to use needs to be clearly described and agreed upon by all concerned. Furthermore, lines of authority should be established as well in order to ensure a smooth implementation process and to keep the program on track once it is in place.

We have provided a very brief overview and introduction to the issues involved in ILI program planning. See *Learning to Lead and Manage Information Literacy Instruction* (Grassian and Kaplowitz, 2005) and Mary C. MacDonald's (2008) chapter on program management in ACRL's *Information Literacy Instruction Handbook* for more in-depth discussions of this topic

FINAL REMARKS

By taking the time to perform a Needs Assessment and then writing appropriate, complete, important, sound, and feasible goals, objectives, and ELOs based on that assessment, you can develop an instructional plan that is both useful and effective. Furthermore, by placing your users' needs at the heart of your plans and communicating your intent to them, you are creating an instructional endeavor that demonstrates your care and concern. Your learners become participants, partners, and collaborators in the development process, and your instruction becomes more relevant to them. In a very real sense, the learners become part owners of the instruction. After all, you are including only what they have identified as important for them to learn. By word and deed you exhibit your respect for your learners and their abilities. A learner-centered planning approach such as this communicates your positive expectations. You have told them that by the end of the specific instruction (or the broader program) they will be able to do whatever you have set out to teach them. Your learners will complete the ILI experience or program with an enhanced belief in their own abilities and will be one step closer to becoming information literate individuals.

EXERCISES

1. Preparing for a Needs Assessment: Make a list of the information you might wish to gather for a Needs Assessment. Be sure to include questions about your population, library, and institution. Divide your paper into two columns, or create a two-column table using a word processing program. List your questions in the left-hand column. Now use the right-hand column to identify where in your institution you could find the answers to your questions. Look for relevant documents such as Mission Statements, program descriptions, and admissions requirements. Determine which offices or agencies collect the information you need. If possible, find out the name of the person who could actually supply the data.

   Match each question in the left-hand column with a potential source of information in the right-hand column. You now have a plan for going about collecting the data for your Needs Assessment. Even if you are not planning to undertake the task at this time it is a good idea to go through this preliminary planning stage. It will make it possible for you to start a Needs Assessment with very little advance notice. You might also wish to update the information once a year or so to make sure your contact people are still correct.

2. Writing goals, objectives, and ELOs: Think about something for which you would like to design a class. Alternatively, look at some already developed material such as a session you already are teaching, an online tutorial already in use, or a point-of-use guide that is already in place but for which there are no written goals, objectives, and ELOs at this time. Can you determine what the overall global intent of the instruction would be? That is, can you come up with a goal or goals for the instruction? Ask yourself, "What are the three most important goals of this instruction?"

   Once you have a goal (or goals), perform a goal analysis. Answer Mager's (1997a, 1997c, 1997e) question, "How will I know one when I see one?" Come up with a list of behaviors that if performed would convince you that your learners have attained the goal.

   Write an objective for each of the listed behaviors. Make sure to write them from the learner's perspective. Describe what your learners will be able to do (how they will perform) as a result of participating in your instruction.

   Determine what the ELOs (in observable, measurable terms) would be for each of the written objectives. Make sure you have described the performance, conditions, and criteria of success for each one. What will the learners do to convince you that they have attained each objective and thus have achieved the instructional goal?

   Finally, check your objectives and ELOs for completeness, appropriateness, importance, soundness, and feasibility. Use the data from your Needs Assessment to determine whether they meet these criteria.

Congratulations. You have now written goals, objectives, and ELOs for your instruction. Test them out in a real instructional situation and revise as needed.

READ MORE ABOUT IT

ALA. AASL. 1998. *Information Literacy Standards for Student Learning*. Chicago: ALA.

ALA. AASL. "Standards for the 21st-century Learner" (2007) Available: www.ala.org/ala/aasl/aaslproftools/learningstandards/AASL_LearningStandards.pdf (accessed December 22, 2008).

ALA. ACRL. "Information Literacy Competency Standards for Higher Education" (2000). Available: www.ala.org/ala/acrl/acrlstandards/informationliteracycompetency.htm (accessed April 20, 2009).

ALA. ACRL. Instruction Section. "Objectives for Information Literacy Instruction" (2001). Available: www.ala.org/ala/mgrps/divs/acrl/standards/objectivesinformation.cfm (accessed December 23, 2008).

Battersby, Mark and Learning Outcomes Network. 1999. "So What's a Learning Outcome Anyway?" Vancouver, BC: Centre for Curriculum, Transfer, and Technology. ERIC Document ED430611.

Driscoll, Amy and Swarrup Wood. 2007. *Developing Outcomes-based Assessment for Learner-centered Education*. Sterling, VA: Stylus.

Dick, Walter W., Lou Carey, and James O. Carey. 2005. *The Systematic Design of Instruction*, 6th ed. Boston: Pearson/Allyn & Bacon.

Elliott, Stephen N., Thomas R. Kratochwill, Joan Littlefield Cook, and John F. Travers. 2000. *Educational Psychology: Effective Teaching, Effective Learning*, 3rd ed. Boston: McGraw-Hill.

Himmel, Ethel and William J. Wilson. 1998. *Planning for Results: A Public Library Transformation Process: The Guidebook*. Chicago: ALA.

Kellough, Richard D, Noreen G. Kellough, and Eugene C.

Kim. 1999. *Secondary School Teaching: A Guide to Methods and Resources: Planning for Competence*. Upper Saddle River, NJ: Merrill.

Linn, Robert L. and Norma Gronlund. 2005. *Measurement and Assessment in Teaching*, 9th ed. Upper Saddle River, NJ: Prentice Hall.

Loe, Mary and Betsy Elkins. 1990. "Developing Programs in Library Use Instruction for Lifelong Learning: An Overview." In *The LIRT Library Instruction Handbook* (pp. 6–8), edited by May Brottman and Mary Loe. Englewood, CO: Libraries Unlimited.

MacDonald, Mary C. 2008. "Program Management." In *Information Literacy Instruction Handbook* (pp. 113–137), edited by Christopher N. Cox and Elizabeth Blakesley Lindsay. Chicago: ALA. ACRL.

Mager, Robert F. 1997. *Preparing Instructional Objectives: A Critical Tool in Development of Effective Instruction*, 3rd ed. Atlanta: Center for Effective Performance.

National Framework. "The Scottish Information Literacy Project." Glasgow Caledonian University (2007) Available: www.caledonian.ac.uk/ils/framework.html (accessed September 12, 2008).

Veldof, Jerilyn. 2006. *Creating the One-shot Library Workshop: A Step-by-Step Guide*. Chicago: ALA.

Chapter 8

The Instructional Menu

He ten times pines that pines beholding food. . . .
—William Shakespeare, *The Rape of Lucrece*

"What food these morsels be!"
—Heinz fresh cucumber pickles, 1938,
The New York Public Library Book of Twentieth Century Quotations

AT THE INSTRUCTIONAL CAFÉ

Our teaching and learning smorgasbord groans heavily with an array of choices—from simple signage to densely packed old-world-style lectures to workbooks, spa-like one-shot sessions and exercises, to full-length credit courses—in a continuum that includes evolving approaches such as social networking sites, virtual worlds, video- and image-sharing sites, blogs, wikis, text messaging, and more. Some eagerly gobble one after another new technology. Others find themselves starving amid this sea of plenty, gazing longingly at one after another teaching/learning confection, wondering which will delight and what the ingredients are for success. Which form of instruction is best or most suitable for which situation? What factors should one consider in selecting a mode of instruction, if, in fact, one has a choice? How many modes of instruction and what types should libraries offer? Which audience(s) should they serve, and which modes work best with which audience(s)? How do budget, staffing, technological know-how, equipment, software, access, and preparation time impact this decision? The list of questions goes on and on, and, given the many possible permutations of answers, instructional solutions may vary greatly from one environment or situation to another.

Sometimes we use a particular instructional format to teach because that is the method our library or information center has used for a long time. In some cases, administrators require you to teach using a particular format. Or, you may just feel comfortable teaching in a certain way, using materials you have already developed and just tweaking them, as needed. There may be many reasons why certain formats are favored, including perceptions or data regarding the learners themselves and the learning time they have available, as well as the time and other resources available for design, development, implementation, assessment, and revision of instructional programs and materials. Equipment, software, facilities, and expertise needed certainly play an important role as well. To top it off, administrative expectations and available resources can vary from one type of library to another and even within the same library with different learners, at different times of the day, week, or year.

In an ideal world we would each offer a mix of different instructional methodologies and formats, allowing our users to select the approach that best suits their learning style and current needs. In fact, many of us do offer a variety of instruction in library- and information-related resources, such as paper handouts, drop-in workshops, online instruction, links to Web-based instruction created by others, course-integrated or stand-alone face-to-face (F2F) group instruction, blogs, wikis, videos, and reference at an in-person desk, as well as through virtual means, including virtual worlds and mobile devices. Some of these forms of instruction, like signage, are so basic to libraries that it is easy to forget the instructional role they serve. However, most libraries do not have unlimited funds or staff time to develop and maintain all forms of instruction, and circumstances may dictate your making a choice among the ever-expanding multitude of instructional modes and formats.

Some instructional products, projects, programs, or sessions also have pre-established formats that administrators may require librarians to follow, or that an instructor prefers, or that the staff feel represents the best approach. Others may be more freeform where librarians volunteer or are assigned to deliver a product, project, program, or session but are free to determine modes and formats on their own or in consultation with colleagues as long as the goals and objectives of instruction or the expected learning outcomes (ELOs) are met. Even with a set format, though, often there are ways to enrich instructional efforts by using a variety of techniques and methodologies within a single program or by offering a larger variety of programs or one-time options—a cafeteria in a way, where the learners select modes and formats themselves to meet their own needs and preferred learning styles.

As an instructor, you can also choose to utilize many forms of instruction in different ways—passively, interactively, synchronously, asynchronously, F2F and remotely, online, as blended instruction, and in other ways. How you use these modes will depend upon a variety of factors, including the following:

- Age and educational level of the learners
- Size of audience
- Time available for design, development, and preparation of instruction
- Learning time available
- Space, equipment, supplies, and software for design, development, and preparation
- Facilities available for implementation or delivery of instruction (F2F, online, paper, electronic/electric)
- Learner access to equipment and software required for instruction
- Learner familiarity with equipment and software required for instruction
- Budget

In this chapter we identify categories of instructional modes and consider the factors you need to keep in mind when selecting a mode of instruction. Then we describe currently popular instructional modes, provide tips for effective use, and alternatives for each. For more help in making these important decisions, see Chapters 7 and 16.

WHICH FORM OF INSTRUCTION FOR WHICH SITUATION?

Synchronous or Asynchronous

In Chapter 2 we differentiated between "synchronous" and "asynchronous" instruction, providing broad definitions for both, with the intention of using these terms to refer to both remote and F2F instruction. Synchronous instruction takes place in real time. That is, the learners participate and interact with the instructor and/or one another at the same time, either F2F or remotely, often online, but also through teleconferences or other means. In academic libraries, most synchronous information literacy instruction (ILI) has taken the form of F2F group instruction for a set interval, a mirror image of the most common form of undergraduate instruction, the class lecture. Public libraries and school libraries also hold synchronous F2F group instruction sessions for their users in the form of workshops, class visits to the library or media center, and group homework help.

Synchronous ILI also includes formats such as one-shot stand-alone group sessions or workshops, credit information literacy (IL) courses, F2F guided tours, and guest lectures to classes. Fully course-integrated ILI includes librarian and instructor collaborative development of course curricula, materials, assignments, and, often, some mix of lectures and practical work conducted at the same time, such as synchronous hands-on exercises in an electronic classroom in the library. As technology has advanced, distance learning has become a viable alternative for many people. It has become possible to hold online courses where the learners and the instructor never or only rarely meet in person. Portions of some of these courses may be conducted synchronously, where all of the participants are working or meeting together online at the same time, for example, in a chat room, while others may be asynchronous, for example, when individuals discuss topics via an online discussion board.

Asynchronous instruction takes place anywhere at any time. It does not require simultaneous activity or the physical presence of instructor or learner(s). Examples of asynchronous instruction include paper materials, such as self-paced workbooks and point-of-use guides, as well as use of electronic/electric materials such as online tutorials and exercises or self-help kiosks. Examples also include videos, images, signage, exhibits, and other displays in physical libraries or online or even in virtual worlds. Librarians continue to develop and mount attractive and useful online versions of many types of asynchronous instruction in an effort to meet remote or distance learning instruction needs. Online courses may be conducted entirely asynchronously, too, often using the features of a course management system (CMS) or a learning management system (LMS), like a discussion board, a blog, or a wiki.

Some use the terms CMS and LMS interchangeably (Petherbridge and Chapman, 2007), while others draw distinctions between the two. According to Shankar (2007), CMSs, like Blackboard, Moodle, and Sakai, are generally used for academic courses, with a focus on the abilities to post course materials online and to provide forums for discussion, as well as "lock boxes" for assignment upload, announcements, learner assessment, and usage statistics. LMSs are used more for workplace training in a business setting or organization, including learner registration, class scheduling, fee processing, information transfer to human resources departments, and testing. As technology has advanced, however, and open source applications have appeared, these two types of systems have begun to look more similar, although migrating from one to another can be problematic (Petherbridge and Chapman, 2007; Schaeffer, 2008).

Distance education via fully online courses, too, has become increasingly popular and widespread. In some cases, librarians are teaching "hybrid" or "blended" instruction courses, some combination of online and F2F interactions, synchronous and asynchronous (Grassian et al., 2005; NCAT, 2005b). At some points during a hybrid course, the participants could chat online, possibly through a CMS/LMS or in a virtual world. At other times, the class would engage asynchronously, through a discussion board or by individuals using a tutorial or completing exercises.

In Chapters 15 and 16, we discuss a number of different social networking and distance education approaches, passive and teacher-centered and active and learner-centered. However, as we have seen in our discussion of learning theories and styles (Chapters 3 and 4), people prefer to learn in a number of different ways. To meet these needs, librarians are expanding both the variety and the forms of their instructional materials in many exciting ways, particularly as the continually evolving Web both invites and facilitates easy mounting and updating of instructional materials and interaction with learners, direct and indirect. Where should we put our time and energy? Should we focus strictly on online ILI, given the growing number of options for doing so? In what ways can and should we continue to help learners in person, as opposed to remotely?

Remote or Face-to-Face

"Remote" refers to instruction utilized asynchronously (any time, any place) by an individual *without* real-time contact with other individuals or utilized synchronously (in real time) *with* one or more other individuals but at a physical distance from them. This definition would include paper point-of-use guides or workbooks used independently at workstations in a physical library or from a distant location. It would also include online venues like discussion boards, blogs, and wikis used by one individual at a time, as well as fully online courses, social networking sites, virtual spaces occupied at the same time (synchronously) by a group of two or more, chat used simultaneously by groups, and e-mail, text messaging, and instant messaging.

"F2F" refers to instruction utilized synchronously (in real time) by one or more individuals, *with* real-time contact with one or more other individuals, in person. This would include guided tours, F2F group instruction sessions, flipcharts, blackboards, and whiteboards used in synchronous group instruction and reference questions that take place in person within the physical library. Both paper and online materials can be used F2F or remotely, synchronously or asynchronously. Which should you choose?

Paper, Online, or Other Technology

It is easy to get confused and to stereotype certain forms of instructional materials so that they seem to represent a single approach or fulfill just one need. When a particular approach is out of favor or appears to be out of date, it may seem quite simple to decide to dispense with it entirely in favor of another. Some libraries have decided to dispense with paper handouts, for instance, and instead have mounted informational and instructional materials on their Web sites. Paper materials, however, have multiple uses in many different settings—in group instruction or by individuals, F2F or online (Lombardo and Miree, 2003).

"Paper" instructional materials may take the form of single or multiple sheets of various sizes, shapes, and colors, such as signage, posters, and booklets. Paper materials may or may not have been designed and produced using some form of technology, such as word-processing or graphics software.

"Online" and "other technology" instructional materials require some sort of technology to use, including devices that simply require electricity in order to operate. CD-ROMs, DVDs, and overhead transparencies fall into this category, the latter because you need an overhead projector in order to use them. This category also includes all sorts of online materials, such as Web sites, social networking sites, virtual worlds, streaming videos, and podcasts.

As we examine a range of instructional modes, keep in mind that we are listing separately some formats that are currently popular for the sake of describing their value and use, but they are not necessarily mutually exclusive. You may want to utilize or repurpose more than one mode for a variety of instructional purposes and venues. For instance, you could use a point-of-use guide in a classroom setting as a learner's guide or outline for a synchronous session, or you may want to use videos embedded in asynchronous tutorials for a synchronous session, viewing them in whole or in part, in order to illustrate a point or start a discussion.

However, even though we live in a technology-focused world, you do need to be careful not to go overboard and get carried away with technology just because it is new, glitzy, or popular with others. You need to balance your use of technology by carefully considering the goals and whether or not use of any given technology will help the audience achieve ELOs. You should also consider the audience, the environment (including differing levels of access, hardware, and software), and how much time, effort, and money you have available to develop and maintain a particular type of technology. After you have looked over the instructional modes in this chapter and in Chapter 15, you may want to consult any of a number of excellent publications and Web sites that will help guide you in deciding which technologies to use for which sorts of instruction and how to use them.

SELECTING FROM THE MENU

As libraries recognize a variety of learning styles and preferences among their user populations, they may begin to take positive steps toward offering a wider range of instructional materials, sessions, and programs (see Chapters 3 and 4). This will allow learners to pick and choose among them to meet their current needs and preferred learning style. It is our responsibility to focus on pedagogical goals when selecting instructional modes that will appear on the user's menu. In doing so, we should reexamine all the forms of instruction we offer with costs and benefits in mind and not necessarily be tied to a single mode (Eadie, 1990; Zhang, Watson, and Banfield, 2007; Desai and Graves, 2008). On the other hand, we must be wary of automatically tossing out older forms of instruction such as paper and F2F modes in favor of exclusively online instruction. If we teach only via the Web, we run the risk of assuming that everyone knows how to use the Web, a mouse, or even a computer and has easy, free, and quick access. By default, this may lead us to teaching only the technologically fluent who are able to get online quickly and easily, while ignoring those who most need to learn, often at the lower end of the socioeconomic spectrum. As we discussed in Chapter 2, people in this position are disadvantaged. Although they may have Internet access through public libraries or other means, they do not use it much. As of December 2007, a majority of senior citizens (65 and older) and those with less than a high school education do not use the Internet and neither do 44 percent of non-Hispanic African Americans (Pew Internet & American Life Project, 2008a).

Having said that, the Web does present enormous advantages to ILI librarians as well as to learners. For ILI librarians, it turns the entire world into a wonderful, gigantic clearinghouse of materials for instruction and research, stimulating creativity and allowing us to pick and choose or link to or adapt a variety of ILI pages and sites, with permission of course ("SOS for Information Literacy," 2006; IFLA and UNESCO, accessed 2008; MERLOT, 2008; World Lecture Hall, 2008). Sharing, adapting, and cooperating can expand instructional horizons and stimulate creativity. For more on copyright, see Chapter 9.

This chapter lists and describes a number of different ILI methodologies, but the critical question for ILI librarians is still how to choose modes of instruction appropriate for particular circumstances or how to combine them for "hybrid" or "blended" teaching and learning. You might begin with some self-reflection. What is your teaching style? Do you like to lay out your instructional plan in detail or just have an outline and wing it on the spot? Do you like interacting with people on a personal level, or do you prefer to work behind the scenes? Would you rather work with groups or one on one with individuals? Do you prefer large or small group instruction? How comfortable do you feel about using technology in teaching? Which sorts of technology do you generally use, and are you open to experimenting with new technologies? Are you able to allow and encourage learners to delve into information-researching investigation on their own or with partners immediately? Or do you prefer to demonstrate first before learners can try it out on their own? Your answers to these questions and others like them may help determine the instructional role you would like to play and the sorts of teaching techniques or methodologies you would feel most comfortable using. Never taught anything? Oddly enough, your preferred learning style may be a good predictor of your preferred teaching style. However, sticking with just your own preferred teaching style means you will not be addressing a wide range of learning styles. So, open yourself up to trying and offering your learners a variety of instructional modes, if at all possible. For more on cognitive styles and on teaching techniques, see Chapters 3, 4, and 12.

Of course, as we have noted, you may not have a lot of choice, especially if you are assigned to work on a particular project. Assigned projects often come with predetermined instructional modes, whereas voluntary projects may allow for more freedom of choice. Even with assigned projects, though, you can make a case for experimenting with alternative instructional modes that may energize you by allowing you to try an approach that is new to you or to your institution or organization.

A number of other factors figure into the selection of instructional modes, especially audience and purpose (goals and objectives or ELOs to be achieved), cost and budget, time constraints, staff help available, equipment, software, facilities, materials, preparation time, and learner time available. You will also need to consider impact on other staff and programs, personal preferences (your own, as well as those of the administration, other instructional staff, learners, or faculty), and the perceived effectiveness of some modes or instructional tools over others. For newer online instructional tools like free Jing screencasting software (video capture of activity on a computer monitor, like database searching), look for evaluations, ratings, and comparisons in articles, blogs, and online communities, and post queries about their effective use in support of ILI pedagogy on listservs like ILI-L and InfoLit-L. For more on using technology to support pedagogy, see Chapter 15.

Once you have investigated a variety of instructional modes, you may be able to make some decisions on your own regarding ILI. When it comes to establishing a new program or revising an existing one, however, it is extremely important to include your colleagues in the process of selecting teaching modes, especially if they will be involved in the program in any way or if they will shoulder more responsibilities because of a revised or new program. This is true even if the plan is simply to propose a new or revised program to administrators. Remember, more than one person may be teaching group sessions and/or assisting with preparing or updating instructional materials. In other words, do not surprise your colleagues by keeping these kinds of discussions a secret. You will gain their respect and support if you engage them in the process, listen to them, and, in turn, respect their opinions and their right to provide input. To prepare for discussion of new or revised ILI, you will need to consider a number of factors.

KEY SELECTION FACTORS

What are the critical factors you should keep in mind when selecting a form of instruction, if indeed you have the luxury of choosing? As we explained in Chapter 7, you will need to begin by identifying needs and establishing or confirming instructional expectations (goals and ELOs), as well as the expected audience (type, skill levels, and size) and other key issues like staff, facilities, budget, and time constraints, both for preparation and delivery. ILI-L and InfoLit-L, both information literacy listservs, though with somewhat different missions, are excellent places to post queries about each of these factors to other instruction librarians if in-house advice is not available. Attending conferences and participating in online workshops and programs, as well as networking with others in instruction, can also be extremely helpful. Following are generic variables that you should take into account when choosing among instructional modes.

Audience/Learners (Type, Age or Educational Level, Skill Levels, and Size)

Who will the primary learners be, in which age group(s) or educational level(s) do they fall, and what is their level of IL expertise and computer literacy skills? How many learners do you need to teach at one time (synchronously)? Do space constraints limit the size of the audience, or is the size a given, for instance, enrollees in a particular class? Can the size be limited if demand is great? Can people learn just as well asynchronously as synchronously? Do they learn as well remotely as they do in person? For online instruction, the number of learners may not be a critical factor unless you expect to provide personal feedback to each, or grade assignments, or if a limited number of ports is available. However, you do need to determine who your primary audience is so that you can gear the level of instruction appropriately.

Computer literacy and IL skill levels may differ widely even within groups that are fairly homogeneous in terms of age and educational background, like college freshmen or senior citizens. Yet these are significant factors in ILI, particularly in a period of rapid technological advancement and increasingly widespread access to information resources of all kinds, both in information tools and in the data. You may be able to determine this to some extent through self-reporting Needs Assessments or through pretests, posttests, and other forms of assessment, like iSkills, that test for both (ETS, 2008). In Chapter 1 we delved into various definitions of *information literacy*, and in the Chapter 16 we discuss the differences between what computer trainers can do and what ILI librarians can do. We have also mentioned AASL's *Information Power* (ALA. AASL, 1998b), *Information Literacy Standards for Student Learning* (ALA. AASL, 1998a), and "Standards for the 21st-century Learner" (ALA. AASL, 2007b); ACRL's "Information Literacy Competency Standards for Higher Education" (ALA. ACRL, 2000); and the ACRL Instruction Section's "Objectives for Information Literacy Instruction for Academic Librarians" (ALA. ACRL. IS, 2001). These documents help us define what we mean by *information literacy* in measurable terms. They are excellent contributions to the ongoing dialogue on this topic and will help ILI librarians design and assess instruction. The "Objectives" can be particularly useful, as they provide many practical examples of specific ways to help learners achieve ELOs for each Standard and Performance Indicator in the ACRL Standards. You can adapt many of them to different types of libraries, age and educational levels, and circumstances. Examples include "Lists terms that may be useful for locating information on a topic," "Determines the period of time covered by a particular source," and "Explains the difference between the library catalog and a periodical index" (ALA, ACRL IS, 2001).

Purpose

What are your goals and objectives or ELOs? Which instructional modes will help your audience achieve the learning outcomes you have selected? Are particular modes better suited to achievement of one learning outcome as opposed to another? The answers to these questions will vary from one situation to another and one environment to another. Remember that you do not necessarily need to develop learning outcomes completely on your own. Depending on the audience level, you may be able to select from, mix, and match the standards mentioned previously in this chapter as you develop your own set of expected ILI learning outcomes. The set of standards and objectives or ELOs you choose may vary from one program to another, one session to another, or one audience to another, and they may change over time. Ideally, though, your institution or group should develop or identify its own set of IL competencies to meet the needs of your constituencies (see Chapter 1 and Grassian and Kaplowitz, 2005). Regardless of which standards and ELOs you use, you may want to check with other ILI librarians and experiment on your own, within your budget, of course.

Budget and Cost

Administrators ask lots of questions about proposals for new or revised instructional programs, including the all-important, "How much will it cost?" Prepare to answer by doing some advance research, using the following questions as a guide:

- Does your institution or group have a separate budget for instructional purposes?
- Who controls this budget, and how is it allocated?
- Is there anyone to consult with in-house for advice on weighing costs and benefits of various modes of instruction?
- How much money will be needed for the new program you would like to propose?
- Are administrators more amenable to a pilot project approach with lower initial costs before plunging headlong into a full-scale new or revised program?
- Are grant funds available in-house or externally to test out a new program or a revised program (see Grassian and Kaplowitz, 2005, Chapter 6, "Grant Writing and Grants")?
- Is it necessary to write a detailed formal proposal requesting approval and grant dollars for each aspect of a new or revised program, or does the institution generally provide support for both revisions and new instructional enterprises?
- Is advance administrative approval necessary in general even to apply for a grant, or do you have the leeway to do so on your own?
- If you are able to get grant funding to establish a new or revised program, will you be raising expectations for continuing the program after the grant funding has run out?
- If the program involves development of online materials, how will those materials be maintained and improved on an ongoing basis, who will do so, and at what cost in staff time and other resources?

Once you have scoped out the financial environment, including procedures and the approval hierarchy, you will need to estimate both direct and indirect costs. Direct costs include new or updated versions of software, hardware, outsourced design and development of materials or products, printing or photocopying, supplies, casual workers' time such as part-time student hours, materials, publicity, and marketing. Direct costs may also include room and equipment rental, refreshments for special workshops or programs, and replacements or substitutes for the time that librarians or other staff devote to instructional projects.

Indirect costs include the actual salaried staff time needed for design, development, implementation, evaluation, and revision for ongoing maintenance and improvement. These costs also include impact on other programs, departments, and staff within and outside the library, equipment wear and tear, and increased demand for services of all kinds. It is tempting to assume that there is no additional cost when salaried staff create or adapt instructional materials or offer additional forms of instruction. However, the time to do this must come from somewhere. Generally this means that other projects or responsibilities may take longer or may be dropped entirely unless individuals are replaced by other staff or by temporary hires. Administrators will want to know and probably have a say in how staff are prioritizing their work and what projects or responsibilities will be delayed or receive less attention due to focus on new or revised instructional programs.

We should also acknowledge and do our best to counteract "green" or environmental costs, although sometimes it is difficult to know which instructional format would be more cost-effective. Paper handouts use trees, ink, and electricity if you make photocopies or have them printed. Online materials must be accessed by using some sort of electronic device, which may require much more electricity than a photocopier. Teaching F2F requires learners to travel to a particular physical place, often requiring vehicle use and maintenance. Online instruction, again, requires electricity and use or ownership of devices that allow online access. We need to think about the environmental cost and the carbon footprints of our ILI activities and do our best to minimize our impact on the environment while fulfilling our ILI functions.

It is also important to acknowledge that tradeoffs often occur when it comes to budgetary matters. You may want to consider diplomatic negotiation by writing in-house proposals with goals that can be achieved by both a higher cost option and a lower cost one. For instance, you may want to create a quick paper point-of-use guide to identifying and evaluating materials through a newly licensed database, or a new interface, or a new integrated library system, etc. Or you may want to develop an online interactive tutorial or videos to help users learn the same things. However, online tutorials and videos may cost more in terms of initial outlay, especially if professional Web designers, programmers, actors, and others must be hired to work on the project or if expensive software is needed to develop them. On the other hand, if administrators decide to create videos or online tutorials in-house, they may need to purchase software and arrange training for staff to do so. It may then cost just staff time for the library to provide access to the site in contrast to the cost of reproducing paper products. A Web site or video could be created fairly quickly and cheaply, as well, without professional help, depending on the length and complexity, and then mounted on YouTube (2008). This approach may be more effective, easier to update, and reach more users than paper handouts, though keep in mind that it will not look as professional and you may need to take time from other duties in order to do it. Of course there are many other considerations to keep in mind, such as the cost of upgrading software as necessary, the need to update online materials regularly, and the need to maintain and update staff skills in design and use of various forms of software and hardware needed to maintain these materials. For more on using and keeping up to date with technology to support ILI, see Chapter 15.

Exactly what will it cost to develop, implement, and revise each of the many instructional formats or modes now available? This question cannot be answered here, for several reasons. First, it is difficult to project costs over time, particularly in light of the rapid pace of technological advances. We have also not addressed cost as a factor, because costs can vary depending on the staff time, effort, and level of complexity you choose to invest in a particular instructional mode. Basically, it costs money to design, develop, and implement any instructional mode, although sometimes these costs are indirect and therefore not obvious. Of course, cost and effectiveness do not necessarily go hand in hand, and there is no guarantee that a particular instructional mode will work well in a given situation, regardless of what it costs. Often sufficient staffing is an important key to success.

Staffing: Planning, Preparation, and Delivery

Is your library a single-person operation in terms of planning, preparing, and delivering instruction, or are others available to help? If one or more people can help, how much time can they put in, when, and will it be one-time help or on an as-needed basis? Keep in mind that clerical staff who work set schedules may not have the freedom to volunteer their help. In fact, negotiations with their supervisors or other administrators may be necessary, with focus on giving higher priority to IL efforts. If at all possible, it might be a good idea to request part-time temporary student help or to write a grant proposal to support some staff time, both clerical and professional, as the case may be (see Grassian and Kaplowitz, 2005, Chapter 6, "Grant Writing and Grants").

When new projects are added, what will staff push to the bottom of their lists of responsibilities or delegate to someone else? If you take on a large project, even if it is supported by grant funds, you may need to drop or cut back on some shared duties, like reference. This means that someone else will need to take up the slack, and somewhere down the road something will not get done. The best approach is to discuss the pros and cons of all of this with your immediate supervisor and your colleagues. A wise administrator would then work with you and your colleagues to examine everyone's responsibilities and guide and lead staff in prioritizing them. This can take time but will result in intentional review and prioritizing. As a result, decisions may be made to drop items off of the bottom of the list or find additional resources (especially staff) to help out on a temporary basis during the time you will be working on a special project. Reassigning existing staff can cause problems if people begin to feel like chess pieces, but it may be difficult, if not impossible, to recruit and train temporary staff, especially librarians, unless you are fortunate enough to have part-time librarians on your staff who would like to increase their hours.

You really do need to keep in mind the welfare of the institution and the library as a whole, as well as that of your colleagues, and be cautious about overcommitting yourself, your colleagues, or your library without additional support and without approval, no matter how exciting a project may seem to you. This can take time and hinder quick and nimble responses, particularly in large institutions or organizations with complex or lengthy approval processes. To alleviate this problem, you could propose a quick response IL team that has a budget and a charge to test new instructional modes and technologies in support of instructional goals. Administrative support is key, along with an expectation of some amount of failure on the road to success. You will learn from failures, perhaps even more than you do from successes, if you build in a mechanism for analyzing, assessing, and reporting on both. All of this takes time, of course.

Time Constraints: Preparation and Development

How much time is available for preparation? Is partial- or full-release time an option? Are there training manuals for existing programs or other efforts that can be adapted and utilized for this effort? It is a given that staff will need to spend time preparing and developing, as well as delivering, instruction, but how much time does or should one person or a group spend on each facet? Again, very importantly, what impact will this have on other staff and programs, and how should you weigh priorities?

It is difficult to estimate how much preparation and development time may be needed for a particular form of instruction, because people work differently and have different standards for acceptable products. In addition, some feel prepared to teach or to provide other instructional materials with minimal support, such as brief outlines of PowerPoint presentations, while others feel compelled to prepare everything in great detail. However, a good rule of thumb for preparing group sessions is to allow two hours of preparation time for each hour of F2F presentation time. When preparing interactive exercises for F2F group sessions, it may take many more hours per hour of learning time to develop goals and objectives for the exercise, come up with an interesting and usable format as well as examples, test the exercise with naive users, and revise it. If the exercise will be distributed on paper, you will need to allow extra time for printing or photocopying, stapling and collating, and then correcting. During the session, paper materials may be collated in a packet and distributed at the beginning of the session or handed out at key points. However, after the initial input of time and energy, you may be able to use that exercise many times and in many different situations. There are time factors and other tradeoffs to all of these approaches, and, in the end, administrators may need to decide how much staff time to devote to a particular project and which projects to "greenlight."

Time Constraints: Learning and Timing

How much of the learners' time is available for instruction? You may want to experiment with different lengths of synchronous, F2F group ILI sessions—15–20 minutes, 30 minutes, 50 minutes, 2 hours, as some have in years past (Engeldinger, 1988). At the very least, let instructors know how much time it usually takes to cover a particular concept or topic. You can do this by posting a list of instructional modules on your library Web site, with an estimated timeframe next to each (Benjes-Small and Brainard, 2006). Or you might just copy brief exercises and put them on handout racks or mount them on your Web site for self-teaching, with links to the answers. Because staff time may be limited, particularly if your user population is quite large, you may also want to consider cutting back on group instruction for basic ILI and offering online alternatives instead. When would it be best to provide instruction or instructional materials? The answer: primarily when learners need to know. In colleges and universities, most undergraduates work on research papers at predictable points in a term. They gain most from ILI and are most motivated to learn during these periods. On the other hand, library users in all types of environments will be motivated to learn a new library catalog when it is first introduced.

Facilities (Space, Equipment, and Software) for Development

What sort of technology is available for developing ILI materials and managing the ILI program? Examples include word-processing software, screen-capture and video-capture software, graphics programs, presentation software, Web browsers, scheduling software, database management software, CMSs, and spreadsheet programs for statistics. Are you able to make good use of "cloud computing," where the content of your materials resides on remote servers rather than on your own computer or on a server within your own institution? Examples include documents you create using Google Documents or PBwiki (2008) that are stored on a remote server rather than on your own computer's hard drive or even on your institution's or organization's server. Can you make good use of free or open source software, like Zoho (2008), a suite of free applications, or Moodle (accessed 2008), an open source CMS? Do you have access to a workstation and other equipment (e.g., a scanner) that may be used exclusively for development of instructional materials, or do you need to share equipment with others? Is a quiet space available for thinking, planning, designing, and developing materials? Where and how will you test your instructional materials for usability? We pose these questions here, as they should be considered along with other factors that enter into decision making regarding selection of ILI modes and materials. For more on usability testing, see Chapter 10.

Facilities for Delivery

What sort of space is available for ILI itself? If a classroom is available, is it in the library, and how is it equipped? What about high-speed Wi-Fi connectivity, outlets, phone lines, data lines, computers available for hands-on instruction, an instructor's workstation with a high-capacity graphics card, a data projector, speakers, an overhead projector, a large screen or large blank wall for projection, a monitor, VCR, DVD player or ability to play DVDs using the instructor's workstation, a slide/tape machine, and an Internet connection? Can you move the furniture around to accommodate different learning activities? Do these rooms and equipment serve other purposes? If so, do they need to be scheduled for use in advance? If not, should they be? What size groups can available classrooms accommodate? Do you have control over scheduling them, over the kinds of equipment and software they contain, and how they are configured? Or do you need to make an advance request to use a classroom outside the library? Who maintains equipment, upgrades software, and does troubleshooting?

If you must share facilities, or if you do not

have computer troubleshooting skills yourself, you will probably need to rely on computer technicians or other computer center staff for help. This goes without saying, of course, for any sort of online instruction, synchronous or asynchronous, as you may need to find the answers to many more and different sorts of questions. You may need to determine the type and speed of Internet connection you and the learners need to have for different purposes, as well as the graphics capability of your computer and those of your learners.

You may need to know if a CMS/LMS is available for you to use and, if so, which one it is, which version it is, and its capabilities. You should find out, too, whether or not your learners are familiar with the CMS you will be using. New versions of software, including Web browsers and productivity software, can cause problems for learners, particularly in online learning where computing capability and connectivity speed may vary greatly. Some applications may require high-capacity graphics cards. Others are available only for certain platforms, like Windows. If learners are using their own laptops or mobile devices, they may need Wi-Fi connectivity. Even if Wi-Fi is available, users may need to authenticate in order to connect, and those under 18 may be restricted to filtered access. So, you should make every effort to establish and maintain a good working relationship with computing center and other technical staff, regardless of your comfort level with evolving technology and whether or not you find yourself needing their help. We have a lot to learn from one another as we all aim to help our user populations (see also Grassian and Kaplowitz, 2005, Chapter 8, "Learning to Manage Technology").

Paper versus Online or Other Technology

Instruction can take many forms to accommodate different learning styles and situations. If possible, we should offer both F2F and online synchronous instruction for two or more individuals, as well as asynchronous instruction for individual use. Ideally, such instruction should utilize a combination of traditional, new, and emerging formats to meet learning preferences, as well as accessibility needs. Each library, institution, or organization needs to determine its fiscal, staffing, and time constraints, as well as its priorities in meeting its mission and goals. All of these factors play into decision making regarding which sorts of instructional formats you will be able to use for synchronous and asynchronous instruction.

What are the advantages and disadvantages of paper as opposed to online or other technology-based formats for instructional materials? Paper materials are portable, require no special equipment or software, are easily updateable, can vary in length from one sheet to one hundred or more pages, and can come in various sizes, shapes, and colors. In addition, paper materials are versatile. Groups may use them synchronously, or individuals may use them asynchronously for initial learning or for later reinforcement. They may be simple or complex in terms of both content and design. Depending on the design, learners may be able to skip around by looking through them quickly or by using an index to get to the sections that interest them. However, paper materials can be expensive to reproduce and can become outdated quickly. Most paper materials are designed in a linear fashion and take a single, simplified approach to instruction in order to save paper and to appeal to the lowest common skill levels. For more on designing instructional materials, see Chapter 9.

Many online materials are easily accessible and available, any time, any place. Although online materials may reach more people, it can take a lot more time, effort, money, and expertise to develop online materials than to develop paper materials. Online exercises, for instance may be one of the most important means of helping remote learners learn to use and think critically about technology. Depending on their complexity, however, online materials may or may not allow for quick and easy updating. Furthermore, if online instruction is created using a particular programming language, like PHP, you would need someone with PHP expertise to make changes to it.

The "green" factor may also play a part in your decision making. Paper consumes trees, ink, and electricity in order to print or copy. Yet, access to online materials is not completely green either, as it requires use of computers or mobile devices, both of which use electricity in one form or another and generate heat. Which should you choose? There are many factors to consider, including learner age and educational level, audience needs and learning preferences, the learning time available, the environmental impact, and staff time needed to design, develop, test, implement, assess, and revise each. The limitations of these parameters will help you determine the number and complexity of modes you can provide, as well as justify your choice. In the end you will need to weigh and balance all of these factors as you select instructional modes yourself or propose them to your administrators. Figure 8.1 provides an example of how to lay out these factors in table form. Figure 8.2 outlines a step-by-step approach to helping learners achieve the ELOs you may set under the circumstances outlined in the Figure 8.1.

The example offered in Figures 8.1 and 8.2 illustrates the fact that we can draw on a wealth of instructional materials and approaches and do not need to create all instructional materials from scratch each time we want to arrange for ILI. Sometimes it just may mean putting together your own grab-bag of useful instructional Web sites, videos, exercises, pathfinders, blogs, wikis, and other materials that you or others have created and possibly updating searching examples or replacing one or two tried and true materials with newer ones or those that meet specific ELOs more effectively. You can even draw on or adapt materials and approaches used in academic disciplines at instructional levels above or below that of your own learner population. If your learners are K–12 students, examine and consider adapting some of the instructional materials available through MERLOT (2008) or the World Lecture Hall (2008), sites that provide access to higher education instructional materials. If your learners are undergraduates, check instructional materials available through "SOS for Information Literacy" (2006) designed for 9–12 grade students or Kathy Schrock's (2008a, 2008b) guides for educators. Consider utilizing or building on tutorials you find through the A.N.T.S. (2008) site, PRIMO (ALA, ACRL, IS, 2008e), or IFLA and UNESCO's (accessed 2008) "InfoLit Global."

HYBRID OR BLENDED TEACHING AND LEARNING

What should you do if you would like to combine instructional modes and offer both in-person and remote or synchronous and asynchronous instruction to the same group? Again, ask yourself some important questions. What are your pedagogical goals? What do you want the learners to know and

Figure 8.1 Parameters for Selecting Instructional Modes with Sample Scenario

Parameters	Sample Scenario
Audience/learners (type, age or education level, skill levels, and size)	High school students; two English classes of 35 students each; novice IL skills; proficient information technology skills
Purpose	Basic IL: Help them learn how to evaluate the quality of Web pages
Staffing: planning, preparation, and delivery	One librarian; one clerical staff
Time constraints: preparation, and development	Two weeks
Time constraints: learning and timing	Thirty minutes learning time available for each of two class meetings, one during week 5 and one during week 8 of the semester
Facilities (space, equipment, and software) for development	Library office; one computer with a Web browser, word-processing software, graphics software, and built-in Webcam; headset; printer, copy machine
Facilities for delivery	School library and computer lab with 15 computers that have filtered Internet access and a Web browser

Figure 8.2 Sample Process for Figure 8.1 Scenario

Process

1. Administer brief diagnostic pretest for Needs Assessment to determine level of IL and computer skills.
2. Meet with the teacher to develop goals and expected learning outcomes (ELOs) for instruction and to come to agreement on content and supplementary materials.
3. Offer a face-to-face (F2F) synchronous group session to explain goals, ELOs, and the process, and to do a small group Web evaluation exercise.
4. Use the "Hoax? Scholarly Research? Personal Opinion? You Decide!" exercise, with learners partnering during the class (Grassian and Zwemer, 2008).
5. Assign Kathy Schrock's "Critical Evaluation of a Web Site: Secondary School Level" exercise as homework (Schrock, 2008a).
6. Offer a second F2F synchronous group session to debrief and to collect homework.
7. Administer a post-test.
8. Analyze the homework and the results of the post-test, comparing them to the pretest results.
9. Revise your goals, ELOs, and content accordingly, as needed.

be able to do following instruction? What kind of administrative support do you have? What sorts of equipment, software, staff time, and facilities do you have at your disposal? How much time do you have to design and prepare instruction? How will your learners get access to this instruction? How much learning time is available to them? Once you have answered these questions, you can consider what sorts of and how much technology to use in order to support your pedagogical goals. A range of types of blended instruction may meet the needs of a variety of learning styles, access, and interaction between you and the learners (Twigg, 2003; Grassian et al., 2005; Albrecht, 2006; Kraemer et al., 2007).

Some teach blended credit courses with just one or two F2F meetings or synchronous virtual meetings. Others may offer mostly F2F sessions, with occasional use of asynchronous discussion via discussion boards or online "drop boxes" for assignments (Grassian et al., 2005). The Teaching, Learning and Technology Group (TLT) offers additional interesting "Low Threshold Applications and Activities" that could be utilized in turning some F2F instruction into blended instruction to help you get started in this direction (TLT, 2008a). For more on a variety of technologies you can use to support your instructional goals, objectives, and ELOs, see Chapter 15.

PUTTING IT ALL TOGETHER

Many of the factors listed in the example in Figures 8.1 and 8.2 apply primarily to F2F group instruction, which represents only one form of instruction, albeit a popular one. Preparation and development time and many other factors may vary widely for other forms of instruction, depending partly on whether or not there are good models available that may be adapted for different circumstances. No matter how well designed, though, instruction can work only if it meets needs, helps users achieve ELOs, and is actually used. It follows that those who develop ILI and those who work with learners must know about what is available and its value and must gain administrative support before they decide whether to use it or not. Knowledge of the range of possibilities will then guide you in making many mode selection decisions, including whether or not to establish an organized, structured ILI program or to select instructional modes for a variety of situations as the need arises.

One way to publicize and promote your ILI offerings is to use a catchy hook to get learners' attention. You could offer an "Information Literacy Café

(ILC) & Cooking School," with three basic instructional modules:

1. For steady customers who dine at our café weekly:
   a. One- or two-unit adjunct courses (collaborative with faculty; interwoven with course goals and assignments)
   b. Term-long, stand-alone credit courses
2. For those who want to drop by for a quick meal, with or without a reservation, during open hours:
   a. In-person reference questions
   b. Research appointments
   c. Guided tours
3. For those who want "takeout":
   a. Phone, e-mail, text messaging, instant messaging, or other virtual reference questions
   b. Self-guided tours
   c. Virtual tours (including replicas of real-life libraries and institutions, mounted in virtual worlds)
   d. Point-of-use guides (paper and online)
   e. Paper exercises
   f. Online exercises (on a Web site, a blog, a wiki, or in virtual worlds)
   g. Workbooks (print or online)
   h. Slide shows mounted online
   i. Social networking sites and online communities (including special "groups" within sites like Facebook)
   j. Blogs
   k. Wikis
   l. Videos
   m. Online tutorials, interactive and passive

The Cooking School could be open to anyone interested: librarians, library media teachers, instructors, and so on, and could be available at different levels: sous chef, assistant chef, pastry chef, or head chef. The idea is that in the Cooking School, attendees would learn how to use various techniques to help learners achieve particular learning outcomes. If you want to attend this school and learn to cook for yourself, an important basic element would be deciding what it is you want to cook and then picking and choosing ingredients or whole recipes or menus that would give you what you want. The Cooking School would also help you learn to develop and make use of assessment instruments to gauge both customer satisfaction and the technical quality of various dishes (effectiveness of instructional approaches in terms of achievement of ELOs).

There are several difficulties with this approach, of course, including how to get across the notion that some "meals" and "dishes" need to be developed collaboratively and need to support the "party theme" (subject matter of instruction). Also, a number of instructional modes would require an enormous amount of initial work to develop and then ongoing staff for regular maintenance, assessment, and revision. Some modes would require additional staff for delivery of instruction as well, while others would not. All of this would require much initial and ongoing funding as well. However, this is an example of a structure that might work, especially if you think of it as analogous to a café where the menu and servers may change, the menu may be limited to just a few items, and there may be specials. The café and Cooking School continue to exist, though, with the goals of offering quality "food" and gently educating both customers and staff as to what actually constitutes quality and how best to achieve customer satisfaction (see Grassian and Kaplowitz, 2005, Chapter 7, "Marketing, Publicity, and Promotion").

INFORMATION LITERACY INSTRUCTION MODES AND MATERIALS

So, what are your instructional format/mode options? How do they work? How can we improve their effectiveness, and what are some alternative approaches? In this section, we describe currently popular forms of instruction in three categories: wayfinding, course related/research related, and stand-alone or supplementary aids, with more on social software and online communities in Chapter 15. Modes are arranged alphabetically within in each category, and these three categories are not mutually exclusive. For instance, some stand-alone or supplementary aids may be utilized for course-related/research-related instruction as well. For this reason, each mode below is identified as asynchronous (A) or synchronous (S) or both (A or S).

As you review these modes, consider trying something new to you. Propose a pilot project to your administrators and seek internal or external grant funding to support a trial (see Grassian and Kaplowitz, 2005, Chapter 6, "Grant Writing and Grants"). Figure 8.3 lists each of these modes along with its main uses and alternative modes.

Wayfinding

Signage (A)

Libraries use signage for many different purposes, including warning, direction, information, orientation, and instruction. Warning, directional, and informational signage appear most commonly in physical library locations, on paper posted in conspicuous public areas, and on Web sites as in the form of navigation buttons and icons. Some libraries are using digital signage for news, announcements, and other content (Villano, 2006). You can also create signs that show layouts and locations of different areas of a physical library, including call numbers and their topic areas, or post signs that illustrate flowcharts of the research process. Gliffy (2008) is free diagramming software that allows you to create floor plans and flowcharts so you can do just that.

Signs for a physical library can be hand lettered or created fairly quickly and cheaply with simple word-processing software and then photocopied or printed out on white or colored paper or one heavier paper stock. Professionally prepared signs cost more and take more time to prepare but may be more durable and attractive and serve as a better image for the library. Whether created in-house or professionally, signs may need to be updated frequently, resulting in additional cost, unless they are placed in slip-in frames so they can be replaced easily. If properly designed, however, they can serve as a welcoming, positive force, an aid in relieving library anxiety.

Tips for Effective Use

- Keep signs simple, clear, consistent, and brief.
- Use images, icons, or illustrations on signs to draw attention and get a message across.
- Signage that is phrased positively can be particularly effective. For example, instead of listing restrictions, such as "No Food or Drink," list what is allowable: "Drinks in Sealed Containers Only" (Kupersmith, 1984, 1987).
- Use signage at key points to avoid overwhelming users with too many signs.

Kiosks (A)

These touchscreen, stand-alone workstations are placed within a stand in the entrance to a library building. They may have a map of the building layout or provide quick answers to a list of frequently asked questions (FAQs).

Tips for Effective Use

- Before you decide to invest time and money in a kiosk, do a Needs Assessment of those who come to the physical library to find out if they would use it and what kinds of information they would like to get from it.
- Make sure screens are simple and that users need to go down only three levels at most to get to needed information.
- Remember to keep kiosk information up to date and provide help contact information.

Maps and Site Maps (A)

Many physical library users rely heavily on maps to locate library buildings and to locate service points and materials within a building. Research on museum handout maps indicates that visitors need and want simple "wayfinding" guides and are more satisfied with their visit if maps are available (Talbot et al., 1993). Free mapmaking software includes Google SketchUp (2008) for three-dimensional modeling for adults and for higher education. Google SketchUp for Education (2008) (educational license required) offers examples of how K–12 students are using it. Other free software programs

Figure 8.3 Instructional Modes and Their Uses and Alternatives

Instructional Categories and Modes*	Uses	Alternative Modes
Wayfinding		
Signage (A)	• Service point locations • Library layout • Self-help	• Kiosks • Maps • Tours
Kiosks (A)	• Service point locations • Library layout • Self-help	• Signage • Maps • Tours
Maps (A) and site maps (A)	• Building and service locations • Library layout • Web site layout • Self-help	• Kiosks • Signage • Tours
Tours: guided (S), self-guided (A), and virtual (A)	• Description and location of services • Brief ILI • Self-help	• Kiosks • Maps • Signage
Course related/research related		
Credit courses (A or S)	• Extended, in-depth study of information researching, the scholarly communication process, and various means of identifying, locating, evaluating, and using information effectively and ethically	• One-shot group sessions/ workshops • Online tutorials • Workbooks and exercises
One-shot group sessions/ workshops (S)	• Reach users when they have a need to know or a desire to learn • Can decrease library anxiety	• Credit courses • Online tutorials • Workbooks and exercises
Standalone or supplementary aids		
Blogs, wikis, and RSS feeds (A)	• Class assignments, including learner-created subject guides, easily updateable online tutorials, and a means of answering research-related questions	• Discussion boards/forums
Exhibits/displays (A)	• Visual presentation of ILI-related topics and services—virtually or in the physical library	• Signage
Flip charts/blackboards/ whiteboards (A or S)	• Spontaneous audience interaction to engage learners or illustrate points • Useful in F2F sessions when technology fails	• Overhead transparencies • Presentation slide shows
Online tutorials (A or S)	• Useful for remote users, 24/7, in order to provide basic ILI, along with immediate feedback • Portions can be used during synchronous instruction	• Credit courses • One-shot sessions/workshops • Videos and podcasts • Workbooks • Exercises

Figure 8.3 Instructional Modes and Their Uses and Alternatives *(Continued)*

Overhead transparencies (S)	• Introducing, outlining, and reviewing a synchronous F2F session • For spontaneous interaction with a group in synchronous F2F sessions	• Flip charts/blackboards/ whiteboards • Presentation slide shows
Pathfinders/subject guides (A)	• Search strategy guidance in researching a topic new to the user	• Online tutorials • Wikis
Point-of-use guides (A or S)	• Mechanics of using research tools for individuals or groups • Outline for ILI group sessions	• Online tutorials • Vendor-created help • Links to guides created by others • Web sites
Presentation slideshows (A or S)	• Introducing, outlining, and reviewing a synchronous session • Allows for quick demos of concepts like Boolean operators through the visual use of Venn diagrams • Can be mounted on a Web site for asynchronous use, with or without narration	• Flip charts/blackboards/ whiteboards • Overhead transparencies • Videos and podcasts
Reference and research consultations (A or S)	• One-on-one guidance and help with information researching, online or in person, to help meet ILI standards • Useful in person or remotely, in many different forms, including interactions at a reference desk, by appointment, by phone, or online (e-mail, chat, text messaging, instant messaging)	• One-shot group sessions/workshops • Online tutorials
Videos (A or S) and podcasts (A)	• Useful as tutorials and for tours, or to introduce library services, for individual or group viewing, in person or remotely • Can be useful in relieving library anxiety	• Presentation slide shows • Tours
Workbooks and exercises (A or S)	• Self-paced active learning, online or in paper, using researching tools and locating materials	• Online tutorials • Reference and research consultations • Videos and podcasts

*A, asynchronous; S, synchronous.

for mapping include MavericksPlan (2006) (PC only) and Envisioneer Express (accessed 2008) (PC only).

A single page can have a map on one side and additional important information on the other, including hours, phone numbers, important URLs, guidelines for library use, and information about how to get help. Printed maps provide a fairly low-cost visual aid. Online maps can become self-guided tours if there are links to descriptions and images of various areas of a building. Be careful not to cram too much onto a map, though, as you may be tempted to reduce the font in size to such a degree that users will not take the effort to read it through.

A "site map" provides an outline listing of all of a Web site's pages so you can see the categories and the hierarchy. In theory, this saves you time by providing quick and easy entry to a specific page or section of a Web site and a visual snapshot of the site's scope (Nielsen, 2008b). Site maps appeal more to learners who like to see the whole picture and then focus on specific segments and to those who know what sort of information they want to find but are not sure where the Web site designer has put it.

Tips for Effective Use

- Mount a library building map and a library layout map on your Web site, with links to relevant ILI.
- Annotate Flickr images of areas within a library, using the notes feature (Tompkins, 2007), or re-create a library building for orientation purposes within a virtual world like Second Life (Prange, 2007).
- If you have a map of the reference area, set it up so that clicking on the literary criticism area brings up a pathfinder or a Web page with tips and tutorials for identifying, locating, and evaluating literary criticism materials.
- Ask groups of learners to create models of your library's physical layout as a means of orienting them to locations of physical materials and thus alleviating library anxiety to some degree.
- Remember to update the site map each time there is a change to the library Web site.
- Include links to each and every page within your site on a site map but not to pages off site.
- Avoid jargon and obscure Web page titles so that your site map of those titles makes sense to users and leads them easily to ILI-related pages.

Tours: Guided (S), Self-guided (A), and Virtual (A)

General tours provide orientation to a building and a library's services. In some cases, ILI librarians may combine a physical tour with brief instruction in the use of reference tools. The goal is to serve as positive public relations for the library and to help users feel more comfortable and less anxious about using the library. Synchronous guided tours provide personal contact and allow visitors to ask questions. Research on museum tours in the mid-1980s indicated that guided (structured) tours resulted in significant increases in learning, while self-guided (unstructured) tours resulted in more positive attitudes (Stronck, 1983). A 2006 study of audio tour use at Carlsbad Caverns National Park indicated that this method "helped visitors integrate new understandings into an overall meaning" and that it offers much flexibility in terms of languages and age levels (Novey and Hall, 2006). As technology has advanced, museums have experimented with a variety of tour format alternatives, just as libraries have. These include use of self-paced "nomadic computing systems," where people walk around with a portable device, like a PDA, where they can both listen to audio and see images. A PDA or other mobile device, then, can serve as a kind of electronic guidebook that can be useful and effective for learning but can also be too distracting and complex in terms of hardware or overly scripted audio (Fleck et al., 2002; Woodruff et al., 2001). The challenge lies in how to increase both measures, cognitive and affective, for all types of tours and all sorts of environments, including libraries.

Some libraries provide self-guided tours on paper or on audiotape or CD-ROM, or as podcasts. Friendly prepackaged, self-guided tours can be useful substitutes when staff are unavailable or for remote users. Virtual tours can serve as a friendly and nonthreatening entree to more complex areas of a library's Web site, or for the layout of the physical library, and can even be designed in virtual worlds as replicas of physical buildings, inside and out. Users can meander here and there at their own pace, picking and choosing which areas they would like to visit and in which order. They can also stop to take more time to understand a particular point and return to a virtual tour at any time.

Tours can reduce the number of directional questions asked at a reference or information desk. However, they may reach relatively few users, and staff need to spend time planning and conducting F2F guided tours. It can be expensive to reproduce copies of paper self-guided tours or to purchase or replace worn out or damaged audio equipment. Like any tour, virtual tours may need to be updated frequently, too. Depending on its complexity, software to create virtual tours and staff time can be expensive, as well, and it can take staff time to check equipment in and out.

Tips for Effective Use

- For F2F guided tours, have a friendly, warm manner, match your walking speed to the tour participants', welcome questions, and be careful not to overwhelm people with too many facts and figures that could be conveyed in a paper handout or on a Web site.
- Offer tours to children, even if you are in a research library, if staff time permits (Young, 2007).
- Try following Marcus and Beck's (2003) lead and develop a self-paced treasure hunt tour, where learners go through the library figuring out clues in order to solve a mystery and then get a reward.
- For more traditional self-guided tours, have numbered stopping points and provide corresponding numbers on a paper handout or allow learners to select an audio segment by number.
- You can also create video or slide show tours and mount them on a Web site or upload them to YouTube (2008) or Slideshare (2008) and link to them from your library's Web site.
- Online maps and virtual tours may be linked to each other or to FAQs or even to the instructional areas of a Web site.
- In virtual worlds, you can create "tourbots" that can take your avatar to different locations within a virtual site and provide narrative descriptions along the way.

Course Related or Research Related

Credit Courses (A or S)

A credit course is usually a series of sessions with the same students, synchronous (in real time) or asynchronous (at any time, any place), F2F or remotely, for a term or a set period. IL credit courses may be standalone one- to four-unit courses, or institutions may offer a number of ILI credit courses if they consider IL a discipline in its own right (Badke, 2003; Owusu-Ansah, 2007). The World Lecture Hall (2008) lists and provides links to freely available syllabi and other materials for higher education courses taught worldwide on a wide variety of topics.

Credit courses allow you enough time to cover more material in depth, even in one-unit courses (Murray, 2008), and they can be quite effective (Wang, 2006). You can do diagnostic pretesting in order to develop curriculum targeting weak areas, to test for learning, and to reteach if necessary. You can also vary the pacing and structure of the course throughout a term, depending on the learners' skills, abilities, and interests. The first time you teach a credit course you will need to spend quite a bit of time developing goals and ELOs, preparing for sessions, developing assignments and active learning exercises, and grading. In the end, you may reach only small numbers of students each time you teach the course, although it will be easier to revise and update the course when you teach it again. Keep in mind that if your course is an elective, you may build it but students may not come unless you publicize and promote it widely and effectively, because some elective courses attract few learners. See Grassian and Kaplowitz (2005), Chapter 7, "Marketing, Publicity and Promotion," for more on this topic.

Courses taught entirely online can be a boon to those who have difficulty attending F2F class meetings. However, online courses must be constructed carefully to ensure a large amount of participation and interactivity as well as learner feedback. If you teach an online course, you will need to spend even more time laying out the course and online course materials, but you may be able to utilize the various features of a licensed or open source CMS (content/course management system)/LMS (learning management system) for your course materials and to interact with the students. These features may include various means of communicating with individual learners or groups of learners, such as discussion boards/forums, mounting the course syllabus and other items, and quizzing and grading options. Keep in mind that if you require use of a CMS/LMS or other online tools, you make some assumptions about the learners' computer literacy skill levels and their access to a computer with an Internet connection. See Chapter 17 for more on the debate over the value of technology use in education.

Tips for Effective Use

- Write down the goals and objectives or expected course learning outcomes, include them in the syllabus, and assess them (Angelo and Cross, 1993).
- Break the course into manageable chunks that can be delayed, moved around, or dropped as need be.
- Check on the learners' IL and technology skills and knowledge in advance and provide help as needed or desired.
- Build in a balance of lecture, demo, interaction, and learner-centered exercises, assignments, polling, and hands-on work (Williams and Zahed, 1996; Dods, 1997; Ko and Rossen, 2004; Conrad and Donaldson, 2004).
- Regardless of how much or how well you prepare, do not expect teaching and learning to be exactly the same each time. Learning and group dynamics can vary widely, and each class and person is a unique entity with different needs and interests, so flexibility is essential.
- For course-integrated instruction, ask the instructor if you can participate in the class discussion board to help answer information-research–related questions.
- If you are teaching a credit course yourself, require the students to post one or two messages to the class discussion board and also respond to one of their classmates' messages.

One-shot Group Sessions/Workshops (S)

One-shot instructional sessions or workshops may be simple or complex, may last for just a few minutes to a half or full day, and may or may not be related to other instruction such as academic courses. Often, the librarian meets with a specific group of learners just one time, in person or through some form of technology, such as the various features of a CMS/LMS or in virtual worlds. One-shot sessions require less preparation and presentation time than formal courses.

One-shot, course-integrated sessions can reach learners when they are most interested in instruction, when some sort of assignment or other extrinsic motivation guides them, a point at which they are most likely to retain learning. Some learners may be required to attend, however, and therefore may not be ready to learn or may find some information repetitive, and learners may retain just a few concepts over time from any sort of group instruction. Despite these drawbacks, personal interaction with a librarian can make the library and its resources seem friendlier and less anxiety provoking.

Voluntary workshops draw those most interested in the workshop topic, but they may attract few learners and require much staff time and other resources for preparation. Libraries tend to offer these sessions to meet instructional needs identified at a physical or virtual reference desk through users' requests or Needs Assessments. Some stand-alone workshops may be aimed solely at library or other staff, such as to introduce a new online catalog or database interface before it is released to the public. Staff workshops may be low cost or free in terms of direct cost if presented by other salaried staff within the same library or institution.

Tips for Effective Use

- Plan ahead by conducting a Needs Assessment and developing goals and ELOs.
- Incorporate active learning or collaborative learning to increase effectiveness, and adjust content to the time allotted (Gradowski, Snavely, and Dempsey, 1998; Grassian, 1993). See Chapter 6 for more on critical thinking and active learning.

Stand-alone and Supplementary Aids

Blogs, Wikis, and RSS Feeds (A)

Blogs are sites that allow you to submit postings (moderated or unmoderated), which appear in reverse chronological order. Some blogs allow you to post comments, while others do not. Once an item has been posted, it usually remains on a blog. Because there are so many thousands of blogs of potential interest, RSS feeds have become popular means of keeping up with blogs. You sign up for an RSS feed for a blog and then new postings are sent to an aggregator, a site where you can set up numerous RSS feeds for different blogs. You visit the aggregator site to see the updates rather than having to visit each and every blog. Wikis work quite differently. Wikis allow you to mount documents and allow editing of those documents. Some wikis are passworded and accessible only to those who know the password, while others are open.

Some libraries use blogs simply to post announcements. However, blogs and wikis can be used for many IL-related purposes, including learner-created or updated subject guides, easily updateable online tutorials, and a means of posting and answering research-related questions. RSS feeds allow options for users to sign up for updates to blogs and wikis fairly easily.

Tips for Effective Use

- Post research tool usage instructions as sample blog postings and examples of documents for editing on wikis.
- Update blogs regularly with "quality content" (Bell, S.J., 2007).
- Offer reference blogs where users can post queries and librarians can respond (Pomerantz, 2005; Farkas, 2007).
- Restrict class wikis and blogs to learners in those classes by passwording.
- Post answers to questions from classroom assessments completed at the end of a session, like the "one-minute paper" or "muddiest point" (Angelo and Cross, 1993; Farkas, 2007).
- Invite learners to post their notes from an instruction session or reflections on a blog or wiki and invite other learners to comment or edit (Harris, 2006).
- Incorporate into your ILI the why and how of using RSS feeds to keep up with blogs and wikis.
- Ask learners to create or edit wikis related to their research interests or needs as annotated pathfinders or subject guides.
- Use a wiki for an ILI tutorial, for quick updating (Lau-Bond and Jeremiah, 2008).

Exhibits/Displays (A)

Hand-lettered signs, glossy photos, professionally printed posters, blown-up sample Web sites, sample research papers—any or all of these (and others) can be put together to form an exhibit or display mounted in a physical library, on a Web site, or in virtual worlds. Exhibits and displays can be eye-catching and consciousness-raising, as well as instructional, by allowing you to get across important points briefly using visuals. Cunningham and Swanson (2006) created an ingenious and effective IL signage campaign for undergraduates by creating "portmanteaus," newly minted combined words and concepts, like "paperitis" and "researchology." Both exhibits and displays can take much time and effort to design, develop, mount, and keep up to date, though. In addition, professionally printed or prepared exhibit materials can be quite costly.

Tips for Effective Use

- Decide on a few simple objectives that meet critical user needs.
- Link to or make use of existing instructional material on your library's Web site or at other Web sites.
- Come up with an interesting hook that will get the attention of your learner community, like the steps of the information researching process for a term paper, along with icons for each of Kuhlthau's (1985) affective stages of the research process.
- Keep your focus on the basics or on a particular aspect of a topic, and distill words and ideas down to key phrases and images.
- Use popular pathfinders as guides to creating IL exhibits that are interesting and useful to your learners.

Flip Charts, Blackboards, and Whiteboards (A or S)

Flip charts are large pads of perforated paper placed on a floor or tabletop easel. Blackboards are made of slate, require the use of chalk, and are most often mounted on a wall. Whiteboards may be on a stand or easel or attached to a wall and require special marking pens. None require advance design, training, or electricity to use. Instructors can use them to engage learners and to illustrate or reinforce a point. They are useful particularly in F2F sessions for spontaneous audience interaction and feedback and as backups when technology fails.

Tips for Effective Use

- Write or print or draw large enough so that those in the back of the room can see it clearly.
- When writing on any of these with your back to a group, wait and speak to the group until after you have turned around to face them.
- Flip charts are particularly useful for brainstorming and small group exercises, as you can post them around a room. Sheets can also be saved for later review and further analysis by yourself or by the learners.
- You can partially prepare flip chart pages in advance, at least with questions or main points to be covered or reviewed.
- When working with a blackboard or whiteboard, ask the group if it is alright to erase what you have written once you are ready to move on to a new topic, concept, or activity.

Online Tutorials (A or S)

Tutorials may be passive or interactive general ILI guides, with the latter requiring input from the user and feedback from the system. Tutorials may also incorporate critical thinking and evaluation regarding a range of information resources, plagiarism, as well as guides to citation style, links to external resources or tools, and other topics.

Online tutorials are available 24/7 (24 hours a day/7 days a week) to anyone with an Internet connection. Basic online tutorials may even be combined with very brief F2F sessions and worksheets, to good effect. Tutorial maintenance can take time but may take less time in the long run than teaching numerous F2F one-shot sessions with a limited librarian staff, and online tutorials are at least as effective overall, according to some studies (Germain, Jacobson, and Kaczor, 2000; Nichols, Shaffer, and Shockey, 2003; Orme, 2004; Russell, 2008). Effectiveness may vary among individuals, depending on preferred learning styles; however, interactive tutorials do tend to engage learners and can provide immediate feedback. Users may be able to test out of specific areas of a tutorial or skip around in it, learning the bits and pieces that interest them or fill their current information need. Many useful tutorials listed on key ILI Web sites can stand on their own or may be used in conjunction with courses (ALA. LIRT, 2001; LOEX, 2007a; ALA. ACRL. IS, 2008b; A.N.T.S., 2008).

Tips for Effective Use

- Apply the same instructional principles to tutorials as to other forms of instruction.
  - o Establish ELOs and develop a plan for helping learners achieve them.
  - o Prepare and provide instruction.
  - o Evaluate and revise as necessary.
  - o Offer personal help and include active or collaborative learning (Dewald, 1999a, 1999b).
- Read up on multimedia instructional theory (Mayer, 2005a; Tempelman-Kluit, 2006; Kalyuga, 2007), as well as on the thinking, planning, development, evaluation, and revision process for online tutorials, and look at a variety of them before selecting this format to support your instructional goals (Caspers, 1998; Johnson and Sager, 1998; Nichols, Shaffer and Shockey, 2003; Orme, 2004; ALA. ACRL. IS, 2008b; A.N.T.S. Animated Tutorial Sharing Project, 2008).
- Consider developing or adapting brief Flash movies or other sorts of animation as tutorials, or embedded in tutorials, in order to engage learners, but be aware of the time commitment needed in order to do so (Markey et al., 2005; A.N.T.S. Animated Tutorial Sharing Project, 2008).

Overhead Transparencies (S)

Transparencies are 8 1/2" × 11" clear plastic sheets. You can write, draw, type, print out, or photocopy on them, in advance or during a session, to provide an outline of the session, illustrate a point, answer a question, or pose an active learning exercise. You do not need an Internet connection in order to use overheads. An overhead projector plugged into an electrical outlet enlarges whatever appears on the transparency and displays it by projecting the image onto a wall or a screen. Using an overhead projector for the first time can be daunting, as it may be difficult to know which way to turn the transparencies, how long to leave them on the projector, and what to do if you drop the entire stack and they get mixed up.

Tips for Effective Use

- Print out presentation slide shows on overheads as a backup in case the software is unavailable during a session.
- Put overheads in plastic sleeves and number them so that you can get them back in order quickly if you drop them.

Pathfinders/Subject Guides (A)

Pathfinders are brief, structured guides to identifying and locating (and sometimes evaluating) material on particular topics. These topics are often multidisciplinary or interdisciplinary, difficult to track down, of great interest to users who do not know how to begin researching that topic, or frequently used for research papers. Often, they are written in search strategy order and include key reference sources, as well as useful searching tips and subject headings or suggested search terms.

Most paper pathfinders are about one- to three-pages long; online versions may be longer. Paper versions may be prepared cheaply with word-processing software and photocopied, or they may be printed professionally at greater expense (Canfield, 1972; Stevens, Canfield, and Gardner, 1973; Thompson and Stevens, 1985).

It may take just a one-time investment of intensive staff time to create a pathfinder template and lay out the basics; however, the shifting nature of information resources can make pathfinder maintenance time consuming. Pathfinders can be useful instructional tools, though, especially if they follow other ILI (Staley, 2007), meet interests based on Needs Assessments or fulfill specific learning outcomes linked to courses, and are designed in collaboration with others. Creating a pathfinder can also be a good staff training project for a novice instruction librarian as an introduction to a more in-depth method of addressing research needs.

Tips for Effective Use

- Save time creating pathfinders and subject guides by developing or adapting templates or by linking to those created by others when permissible to do so (Wilson, 2005; Magi, 2003, 2007; Barnes and Riesterer, 2007; Internet Public Library: Pathfinders, accessed 2008).
- For-profit companies like LibGuides (2008), as well as open source applications like "Library a la Carte" (Oregon State University Libraries, accessed 2008), also offer templates for creating pathfinders and subject guides along with user-generated options, including the ability to rate, comment, and tag.
- Consider labeling and arranging pathfinder content in different ways, from the user's perspective, or perhaps directly incorporate Kuhlthau's Information Search Process steps (Kuhlthau, 1989; Staley, 2007).
- Add searching tips and techniques, in addition to recommended subject headings or key search words.
- Engage learners actively by asking them create their own annotated pathfinders, or ask them to tag and rate pathfinders that others have created and provide some reasons for doing so.
- Remember to include authorship, the date the guide was created, and contact information in order to encourage connection with learners (Brazzeal, 2006).

Point-of-use Guides (A or S)

Point-of-use guides provide simple, clear instructions to meet a learner's need to know how to use a particular tool, database, or system on the spot. In contrast to pathfinders or subject guides, point-of-use guides do not place a tool in context or provide a range of information sources available on a particular topic or in a discipline. Point-of-use guides can serve as substitutes for some one-on-one instruction at a busy reference desk and can be readily available when reference staff are not on duty.

Point-of-use guides are popular, given the enormous and confusing array of reference tools currently available in various formats (University of California. California Digital Library, 2008), because there is not enough time in a one-shot session to teach everything. Many librarians now try to teach basic transferable concepts during F2F group sessions and distribute point-of-use handouts for those who want additional details regarding the mechanics of using specific online researching tools.

Paper point-of-use guides are portable, suitable for note taking, and can be consulted while utilizing the resource for which they are providing instruction, assuming that learners have easy access to computers and printers and the technical expertise to utilize them (Freeman, 2008). Online versions can be printed out and consulted while a person is utilizing that resource, or versions can be laminated and posted in the physical library, near the resources to which they refer. Individuals can use point-of-use guides asynchronously or synchronously in hands-on group instruction sessions. A number of libraries mount point-of-use guides on their Web sites or link to guides and tutorials created by others. Some vendors' guides and tutorials may be useful too, while others could benefit from user feedback and IL librarian input.

Tips for Effective Use

- Create your own guides using free or low-cost screen-capture, graphics, and word-processing software (Picasa, 2008; SnagIt, 2008; Snapz-ProX, 2008) and mount them on your Web site as PDFs, or link to guides created by others.
- Print professionally at higher cost.
- Use a minimalist approach with error anticipation and prompts to try oneself (see Chapter 9).
- Use these guides as outlines for parts of hands-on sessions and give them to learners to take away for later use, for reinforcement (Turner, 1993).
- Put handouts on a table off to one side of a classroom or meeting room and allow learners to pick and choose from among them. As learners "shop" for handouts, you can see which are most and least popular, at least anecdotally, and focus on updating the most popular ones (Boyd, 2007).

Presentation Slide Shows (A or S)

When used appropriately, presentation software such as Microsoft PowerPoint (2008b) and Apple's Keynote (2008b) can be an effective supplementary instructional tool. Presentation slide shows are particularly useful for introducing and providing an outline, as well as a conceptual framework for a synchronous group session. They are also quite useful for reviewing main points. You can illustrate concepts like Boolean operators by using Venn diagrams, portrayed on a series of slides (see Figures 8.4 and 8.5), stopping to ask learners what they predict will be colored in to represent that particular operator (and, or, not). You can also put exercises on slides. When learners report back from small group work, you can type onto an additional slide as a way of keeping track of topics, issues, and important points for the entire group.

Some instructors and learners dislike presentation software. Criticism centers on some instructors' reading the text of a lecture from the slides, usually bulleted on each slide, and the use of templates to develop presentations. Others object to animated portions of slides and animated slide transitions, as they can seem distracting. Tufte (2003) also objects to the way that presentation software like PowerPoint encourages people to think in bullets, without regard to context and relationships, similar to infomercials. PowerPoint and other presentation software can be used effectively, however, particularly to encourage participatory learning in support of pedagogical goals. Maxwell (2007) describes his successful use of primary source material in presentation slide shows for history classes while at the same time decrying all of the criticisms mentioned above. According to Clark (2008), learners are in-

Figure 8.4 Venn Diagram Question: Boolean "and"

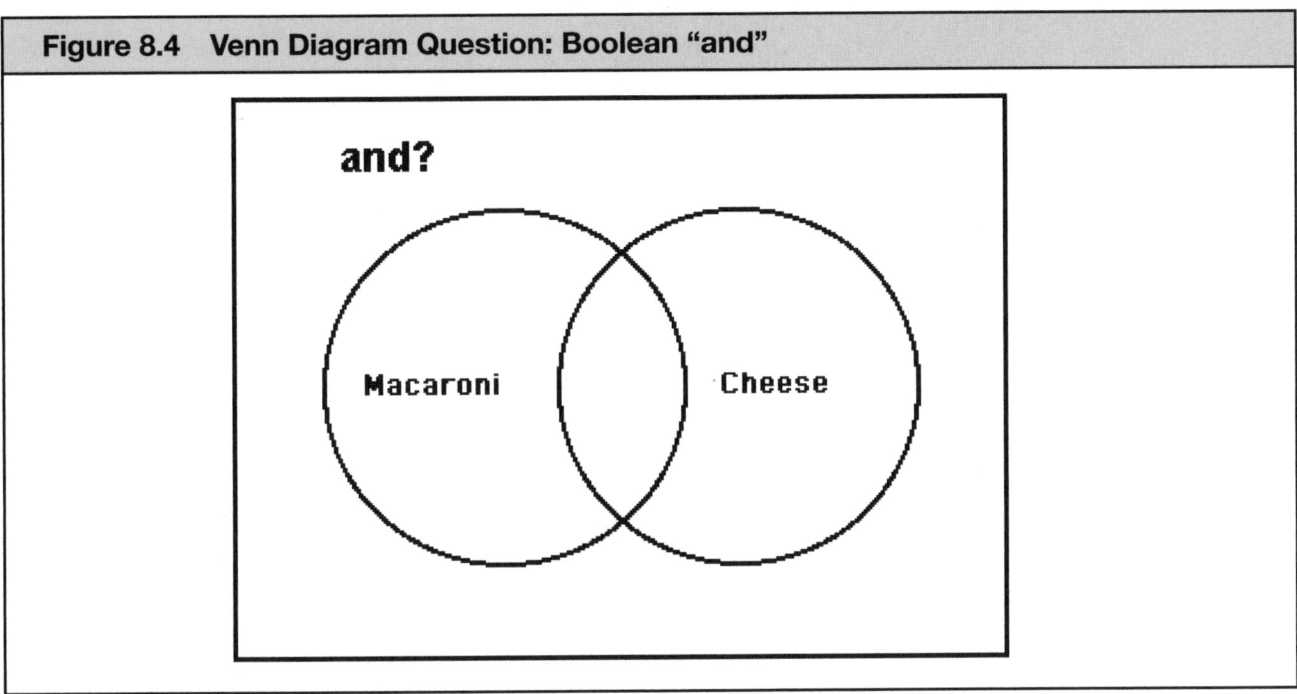

Figure 8.5 Venn Diagram Answer: Boolean "and"

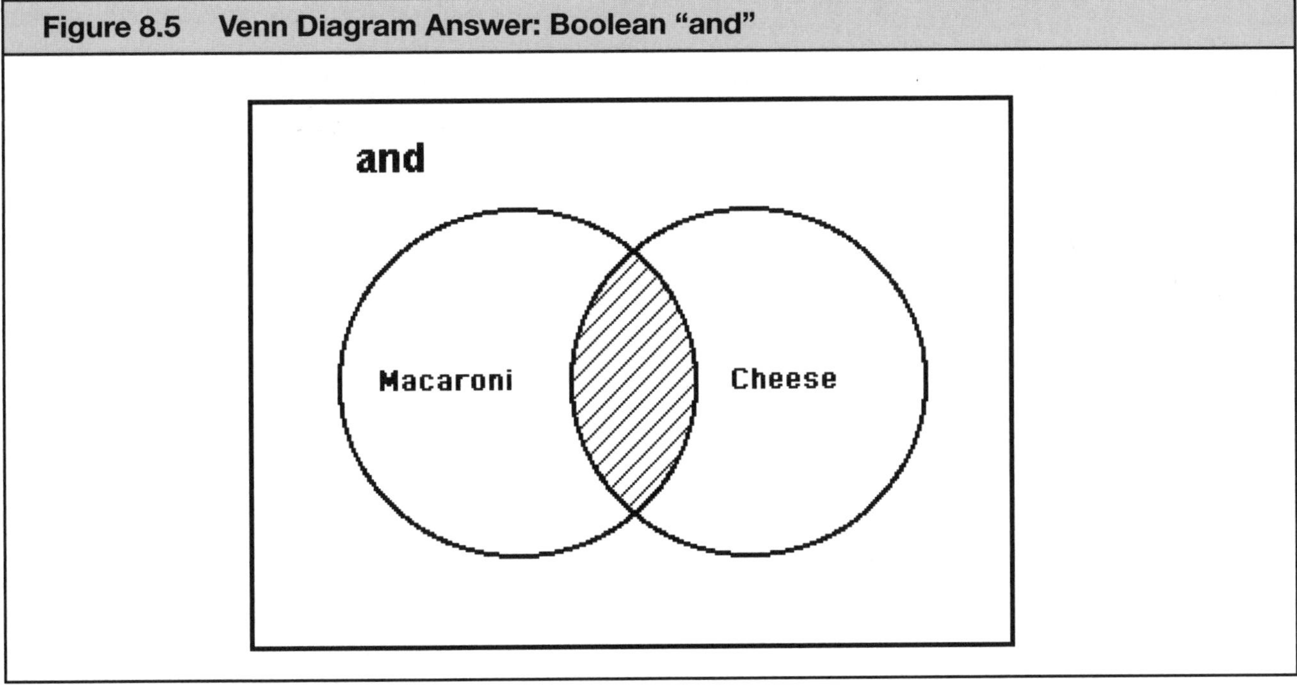

terested in presentation slide shows because they offer variety and novelty. Much depends on the instructor's ability to be spontaneous regarding its use and to make learners think and engage (Clark, 2008). Simplicity and judicious use are key to the effectiveness of presentation software. See Chapter 9 for more on design and Chapter 15 for more on using technology to support pedagogy.

Presentation software enables you to create simple, text-only slide shows or more complex ones that can include captured images, clip art, motion, animation, audio, and links within the slide show to Web sites, videos, and more. You can use slide shows in synchronous group sessions (F2F or remotely), or mounted on your library Web site for asynchronous use, or as part of a larger instructional package. You can print out slides on overhead transparencies or as handouts, and slides can be mounted with or without narration on a library Web site or on a Web site that serves a wider audience, like Slideshare (2008). Finally, development and use of slide shows with presentation software requires electricity, a computer, and a data projector. You may, instead, choose to print the slides out on overhead transparencies and use them with an overhead projector. Do not discount the alternatives, however, flip charts, blackboards, and whiteboards. These alternatives provide an option for "just in time" instruction and visual referral to different points made during the same session. They also tend to encourage more instructor gesturing, which can engage learners (Lanir, Booth, and Findlater, 2008).

Tips for Effective Use

- Speed up the software learning process by partnering with someone who is willing to coach you. Trade presentation software lessons from a computer trainer for information-researching lessons.
- Limit text on each slide to as few words as possible, ideally no more than four bullets, with no more than two words per bullet, and use images in place of words if possible.
- If you must use additional bullets and a few more words, use the "fade in" and "fade out" features to make each bullet point stand out from the other bullet points as you address it.
- Avoid reading text as is from the slides; instead, use brief text, clip art, images, or videos as a jumping off point to introduce and discuss a topic
- Limit the number of slides, movement, color, and other features to avoid overwhelming learners.
- To encourage spontaneity, insert an outline or table into the presentation itself, with each item linked to a different point in the slide show (Brier and Lebbin, in press).
- Turn off the projector or blank the screen when finished with the topic of a slide.
- Use the hidden "Notes" area under each slide for your own content.
- Print out and distribute handouts of slides or an outline so that learners do not have to take many notes.
- Mount the slide show on the library Web site or on the freely available Slideshare.net (2008) for later viewing and downloading,
- Record your voice during a presentation, save it as a digital file, and sync it with the slide show when you mount it on a Web site.

Reference and Research Consultations (A or S)

Reference and ILI both seek to empower users, and each complements the other (Burke, Germain, and Xu, 2005). At the reference desk, through an appointment, or by phone, mail, fax, and digital reference, including e-mail, chat, text messaging, and instant messaging, users can get answers to their questions. But reference interactions can be instructional as well. In fact, all of these reference venues help people become "self-directed learners" and meet ILI standards (Ellis, 2004). Learners who are willing to spend time working with reference librarians learn about the range of information sources that might answer their questions. Reference librarians also use questioning to prompt or coach users in how to evaluate and choose among these information sources for specific information needs and then how to use them effectively. In many environments, the reference librarian has, of necessity, turned into a teacher, a co-learner in investigating a research problem posed by a user, as well as an advisor and guide through the information morass (Pomerantz, 2005; Fields, 2006). Reference librarians continue to help users in traditional ways, but they are also using new technologies for reference services.

In-person, phone, and voice chat reference venues are synchronous. They occur in real time, with two or more individuals directly in contact with and interacting with each other during that time. In contrast, mail, fax, and e-mail reference venues are asynchronous. Individuals are in contact, but not directly and not in real time. Text messaging and instant messaging may be synchronous if both the sender and receiver happen to be online at the same time, but they can be asynchronous too. If the recipient is not online when a message arrives, it is stored for later retrieval.

Research consultations are extended, more in-depth versions of reference interactions. Users make appointments to meet privately with a librarian. Research appointments or consultations offer distinct advantages over drop-in reference (digital or F2F). You have an idea of the person's research interest so that you can prepare a list of potentially useful reference tools and approaches. During this concentrated one-on-one instructional session, you can help the questioner learn to select and use appropriate information sources and to evaluate their search results. While reference interactions and consultations may focus on specific topics, instruction that takes place in those arenas raises awareness of the value of IL and lays a foundation for more expanded ILI. Of course, if a user does not show up for a research appointment, your time investment may be wasted unless you can schedule another appointment or interact with her or him through some other means.

Tips for Effective Use

- Take an interactive, "neutral questioning" instructional approach to reference, where you guide the user through the information-seeking process while they explore a variety of information sources and choose an "answer path" (Dervin and Dewdney, 1986; Tyckoson, 2007).
    - After conducting an in-person reference interview, give the keyboard and mouse to the user to experiment and explore as you guide him or her.
    - During digital reference, pose questions that will help users think critically at all points during the process, beginning with defining their information need and ending with guidance on means of presenting or communicating information, as needed or requested by users.
- In synchronous online reference, use short, segmented responses to help the users know that you are continuing to respond and that they have not been cut off or ignored.
- Use analogies and examples in reference interactions just as you do in other instructional situations; for digital reference, do this as briefly as possible.
- Set up appointments for lengthy research questions encountered in person or online.
- Try to determine the learner's general IL and computer skills by incorporating a couple of questions into a research appointment form to be filled out in advance.
- Meet in a private area to diminish interruptions and to provide some confidentiality and a less intimidating and embarrassing environment.

Videos (A or S) and Podcasts (A)

Videos and podcasts can support many pedagogical goals. Both video and podcast content needs to be carefully defined and prepared in order to help viewers achieve ELOs and to avoid boring them. This can be quite a challenge, especially for video, given current expectations related to commercial films.

You can use videos in synchronous sessions or asynchronously in order to demonstrate selection and use of information-researching tools, as well as evaluation of materials retrieved through those tools. Videos can be useful for introducing library services. They can also guide learners through the process of identifying items online and then locating them on shelves in the physical library. Some ILI videos have a storyline that maps out or parallels someone struggling to find information or address common IL-related topics like plagiarism, and they may help alleviate library anxiety (Mizrachi, 2008a, 2008b). The University of Pennsylvania Libraries offers musical IL videos regarding services and IL (University of Pennsylvania, 2008).

Nonlibrary videos can be highly useful in drawing attention IL-related concepts. A fictional "future history" video like *EPIC 2015*, for instance, illustrates the issues of privacy and confidentiality by looking back at Google's fictional takeover of news outlets in the year 2015 (Sloan and Thompson, accessed 2008). You can mount your own videos on a Web site, or on YouTube (2008), and find many other videos useful for IL purposes there. The Library Information Literacy Online Network (LION, 2008) offers videos from the A.N.T.S. (ANimated Tutorial Sharing Project) collection (A.N.T.S., 2008). Another option is to embed videos within online tutorials (Grassian et al., 2008) or create "machinima" (videos) within virtual worlds for free. The Michigan Library Consortium (2007) mounted a machinima on YouTube regarding their services on their Second Life (SL) site in that three-dimensional virtual world. The machinima includes a rotating book floating in the air, along with instructions to click on it in order to contact a librarian if you have a question. The Xerox Corporation offers a machinima regarding its use of SL for corporate employees, with mention of exploring use of documents within SL (XeroxCorp, 2007).

A podcast is an audio file that can played on an MP3 player, like an iPod. You can record podcasts by using a computer with recording software, and a headset or microphone, or through other means, and then make them available online (Farkas, 2007). You can use podcasts for self-guided tours and descriptions of library services, as well as for brief ILI nuggets, although they must be engaging in order to attract and keep attention.

Tips for Effective Use

- Aim to create a three- to five-minute-long video both to keep an audience's attention and to minimize file size and time needed for streaming.
- Show a controversial video to illustrate a point about IL research or to start a discussion on how one might go about searching for information on a particular topic.
- Stop a video in midstream and engage the learners in questions about what will happen next and why.
- Use screencasting software to create videos with interactive quiz questions inserted at various points for asynchronous self-testing or for group responses during synchronous sessions.
- Ask learners to complete an ILI assignment, record some tips about it for other learners, and mount these podcasts on your library Web site, with permission.

Workbooks and Exercises (A or S)

Paper and online workbooks and exercises offer an important asynchronous "learning by doing" instructional mode for research. Workbooks usually consist of a series of brief explanations on the use of different reference tools followed by exercises requiring learners to use those tools in order to find answers. Exercises can be designed to teach the use of one or more tools (like ERIC), online systems (like Cambridge Scientific Abstracts), or concepts (like controlled vocabulary).

Workbooks often begin with a tour and are arranged in search strategy order. Dudley's *Library Skills Workbook* established a model for paper workbooks worldwide, some still in use (Dudley, 1978; Trail, Gutierrez, and Lechner, 2006). Some Web-based tutorials follow a similar model (Appalachian State University, 2007; James Madison University, 2008a; SUNY Buffalo, accessed December 31, 2008b). All offer users an opportunity for meaningful self-paced self-education, requiring hands-on experience with a wide variety of researching tools.

Workbooks and exercises can be tailored to any subject area (general or discipline specific), any age or grade level, and any environment. Although students tend to prefer an online to a print workbook, both are effective, but more so for those who use the library more frequently (Gutierrez and Wang, 2001). Both paper and online workbooks require much initial staff time to design, develop, and print or mount and more staff time to update and to correct or provide feedback. Paper workbooks and exercises do not require equipment or electricity to use and are easily portable, and learners may refer to them repeatedly, as needed. When instructors assign paper workbooks, learners may be able to buy them on a cost-recovery basis, or they could be mounted as PDFs so that learners can print them out. Following initial development, workbooks and exercises can reach many learners with a small investment of staff time.

Tips for Effective Use

- Determine goals and ELOs first.
- Request grant funding to develop a first workbook as a pilot project, with pretesting and posttesting, and be aware of the fact that it will take time and effort to develop a workbook as a measurably useful ILI product (Phipps, 1980; Grassian and Kaplowitz, 2005; Trail, Gutierrez, and Lechner, 2006).
- Build in personal interaction by doing an introductory synchronous session (Gutierrez and Wang, 2001) and by requiring learners to ask at least one question through some form of reference.
- Segment workbooks into independent parts so that learners can pick and choose which to complete and in which order.
- Use multiple choice questions.
- Integrate critical thinking throughout.
- Provide contact information for help.
- Stagger the due dates to help ILI staff manage a large workbook workload both in helping learners complete exercises and in correcting completed workbooks.
- Quickly correct exercises and workbooks for immediate feedback or allow for self-correction.

FINAL REMARKS

In this chapter we have discussed various categories of ILI modes, offered general advice on picking and choosing among them for your users, and suggested a structure for offering an array of learning options to meet various learning styles and access needs. We have also taken a close look at number of popular modes in the instructional menu. Instructional modes and venues for ILI continue to expand, and a growing number of librarians and other educators are testing uses of new technologies and modes in these new environments, including social networking sites like Facebook and virtual worlds. As these librarians do, we can only applaud their enthusiastic explorations and look forward to learning from their creativity, research, and critical thinking about how and when to use these new tools effectively in support of teaching and learning.

Which you choose in the end may come down to cost as well as to the current administrative culture, the risk-taking climate in your environment, and your ability to engage both your administrators and your colleagues in dialogue and experimentation. As you go through this process, you might consider asking learners to help construct at least part of the menu themselves so that you end up with a mixture of what you think learners should have and what they say they want. Openness to change is essential, as is flexibility and a spirit of objective scientific inquiry into effectiveness of instructional modes within a given environment, for a given audience, and under given circumstances.

EXERCISES

1. Identify a synchronous and an asynchronous instructional mode used in your environment (public, special, school, or academic library). Come up with a way to use the synchronous mode asynchronously and vice versa.
2. Find an instructional Web page that appeals to you and one that does not. Compare the two pages, and identify the characteristics that you like and dislike in each.
3. Come up with a way to build F2F interaction into the same instructional mode on paper and online.
4. Examine a paper point-of-use guide and an online tutorial for the same database or library catalog. Come up with two arguments for and two arguments against each form of instruction.
5. Examine the online help provided for a commonly used piece of software or a licensed database and compare it to the online help available for an online library catalog. Based on your comparison, come up with three ways you could improve each.
6. Compare and contrast a library-developed pathfinder on a specific topic with a Web site you find through Google on the same topic.
7. Visit a virtual world and identify a means of providing ILI within that world that would take advantage of its capabilities.

READ MORE ABOUT IT

ALA. ACRL. IS. "Objectives for Information Literacy Instruction: A Model Statement for Academic Librarians" (2001). Available: www.ala.org/ala/mgrps/divs/acrl/standards/objectivesinformation.cfm (accessed December 23, 2008).

———. "PRIMO: Peer Reviewed Instructional Materials

Online" (2008). Available: www.ala.org/ala/mgrps/divs/acrl/about/sections/is/iscommittees/webpages/primocommittee/primo/index.cfm (accessed April 27, 2009).

A.N.T.S. ANimated Tutorial Sharing Project. "About ANTS." COPPUL: The Council of Prairie and Pacific University Libraries (2008). Available: http://ants.wetpaint.com/?t=anon (accessed December 23, 2008).

Barnes, J. and L. Riesterer. "Pathfinder for Constructing Pathfinders" (November 2007). Available: http://home.wsd.wednet.edu/pathfinders/path.htm (accessed December 28, 2008).

Farkas, Meredith G. 2007. *Social Software in Libraries.* Medford, NJ: Information Today.

Grassian, Esther et al. "BICO Task Force: Final Report." UCLA Library, Information Literacy Program (September 30, 2005). Available: http://repositories.cdlib.org/uclalib/il/04 (accessed December 28, 2008).

IFLA and UNESCO. "InfoLit Global." Available: www.infolitglobal.info (accessed December 23, 2008).

Mayer, Richard E., ed. 2005. *The Cambridge Handbook of Multimedia Learning.* New York: Cambridge University Press.

MERLOT. "Multimedia Educational Resource for Learning and Online Teaching" (2008). Available: www.merlot.org/merlot/index.htm (accessed December 24, 2008).

"SOS for Information Literacy" (2006). Available: www.informationliteracy.org (accessed December 22, 2008).

Trail, Mary Ann, Carolyn Gutierrez, and David Lechner. 2006. "Reconsidering a Traditional Instruction Technique: Reassessing the Print Workbook." *Journal of Academic Librarianship* 32, no. 6: 632–640.

Chapter 9

Basic Copyright and Design Issues

Is't not enough to break into my garden,
And, like a thief, to come to rob my grounds,
Climbing my walls in spite of me the owner. . . .
—William Shakespeare, *King Henry VI, Part II*

GENERAL CONCERNS

Who owns graphics, design or structure, and text in media? Does it matter if the medium is print or technology based? What can you use freely when designing and developing your own instructional modes and materials? Is that wonderfully designed point-of-use guide or interactive tutorial you found available for the taking? Can you copy it wholesale and put your own institution's name and logo on it or just create your own instructions and link to it? What if you just copy parts of it and others like it and simply adapt or mix and match them to meet your own needs? How much can you use under "fair use" guidelines? Should you go for a linear or a modular approach? Synchronous or asynchronous? Remote or in person? Paper or electronic/electric? Interactive or passive? Detailed or succinct? What about mixed formats or multimedia? What sort of backup plans should you have in place?

Anyone planning or developing instructional modes and supplementary materials faces many copyright, design, and content questions. Fair use may or may not be permitted for some digital materials. Furthermore, well-intended but poorly designed instructional modes and materials can waste time, money, and effort or "die" through lack of use. They can also lower morale among staff and users and increase, rather than decrease, the number of repeat, basic questions at a reference desk, help line, or e-mail inbox.

COPYRIGHT, FAIR USE, AND INTELLECTUAL PROPERTY

Fair Use and the U.S. Digital Millennium Copyright Act

Any discussion of design in this technological era must begin with the issue of what is public domain material freely available for the taking, as opposed to privately owned items. Copyright ownership and fair use pertain to the ownership and degree of permissible usage of an original work. The purpose of U.S. copyright law is to provide creators of a work with exclusive rights to publish or sell their work, to prepare new works based on their own copyrighted work, and to perform or display their work publicly during their lives (and their estate for 50 years thereafter). The Copyright Act of 1976 includes an exception to copyright holders' exclusive rights, called *fair use*, and lists four ways to tell whether or not your use of a copyrighted item without permission is legally acceptable (*West's Encyclopedia of American Law*, 1998).

For information literacy instruction (ILI), the first factor, determination of educational as opposed to commercial use, was the most important part of the "test" in years past. The other three test elements involve the type of copyrighted item, how much of the entire item you were using, and whether the copyright holder would have lost income as a result of your use of her or his work. In practice, judges tried to balance these last three factors against the interests of the community, including scholars who wish to have access to copyrighted works for research, education, and personal interest (Nimmer, 2000; Stanford University, 2008).

How does this work in the technological world? The Digital Millennium Copyright Act (DMCA), enacted into law in the United States in October 1998, was supposed to provide clear copyright and intellectual property guidelines for technology-related issues like these. However, major questions about this law have emerged. These questions focus in particular on whether or not DMCA's digital rights management (DRM) is being used as intended—to protect copyright holders with antipiracy software or devices from potential copyright infringers. Instead, is DRM limiting consumers, libraries, and others from legitimate needs to preserve and repurpose material for educational and other uses (EFF, 2006; Moseng, 2007)? The Librarian of Congress is permitted to come up with exemptions to this law every three years, but this does not solve the problem. Even if usage exemptions are approved, tools to "unlock" protected digital materials are still illegal under the DMCA (Anderson, 2008; D'Andrade, 2008).

Some Internet enthusiasts, like John Barlow, one of the founders of the Electronic Frontier Foundation (EFF, accessed 2008), believe that copyright has been applied to the "containers" in which information has appeared, though information itself is free. Furthermore, he believes that anything put up on the Internet should be free to everyone (Barlow, 1993, 1996). Others believe that copyright laws established for paper materials should be strictly applied to the Web and to the Internet as a whole. Band (2007) reports that three cases decided in 2006 and 2007 cast a somewhat different light. In all three cases, the courts ruled that the defendants did not violate fair use, even when using entire works, as in all three cases their use was transformative. They used copyrighted or licensed material in a manner quite different from that originally intended. In one case, an artist used a portion of a photograph from an ad without permission, as a commentary on culture and fashion. In another case, the court ruled that people did not infringe copyright when they visited sites that illicitly displayed copyrighted images, even though their computers automatically kept a cached copy of those images, as the defendant (Google) transforms usage through the public benefit derived from its search engine function. Band (2007) goes on to say that these decisions sound a positive note for education and scholarship, as it may be possible to argue that some use of copyrighted materials for educational purposes is transformative if it represents a repurposing of the original. The third decision also relied on the concept of transformation as allowable use. Among its 2000 images, Dorling Kindersley's (DK) biography of the Grateful Dead contained images of seven posters owned by Bill Graham Archive (BGA). BGA sued because those images were used without permission. The court ruled in DK's favor because DK combined the images with text, a timeline, and other artwork (Band, 2007).

While this is hopeful, copyright ownership is still not clear-cut, particularly with regard to technology. Artists spend time and artistic effort designing clip art for Web sites. Some make their living by designing art and naturally do not want to give it all away for free. So, what constitutes fair use of art on the Web? Faculty spend time and intellectual energy designing Web sites, software, and virtual world sites for classes, some of which could be used for or viewed as research as well. To whom do these Web sites belong when faculty move to different institutions? This question becomes especially ticklish when the faculty member has come up with an idea for the content of these items but the actual design and implementation has been done by the staff of a campus computing network. Fossil Flash Cards was developed and mounted by the UCLA Social Sciences Computing Network, with content developed by Professor Rob Boyd in the Anthropology Department (Boyd, 1997a, 1997b). Who owns this product? The U.S. National Institutes of Health (NIH) has mandated open access to publications that result from NIH-funded investigations, and some Harvard University faculty have voted to allow more open use of their journal articles (Hahn, 2008). Does this foreshadow open access to other types of materials, like Fossil Flash Cards? And do similar circumstances surround creation of and access to ILI materials, including online tutorials? If so, will this access be "green" (self-archived for open access following publication in other more restrictive forms, as in digital repositories) or "born gold" (created from the get-go as open access items) (Adams, 2007; Harnad et al., 2004)?

The Technology, Education and Copyright Harmonization Act (TEACH Act), signed into U.S. law in 2002, was supposed to address copyright issues specifically related to accredited, nonprofit educational organizations' distance education (Technology, Education and Copyright Harmonization Act, 2002). However, it does not mention libraries, and it places a number of limits on use of materials for a course without obtaining prior permission. The Act provides protection only for materials that are part of "mediated instructional activities," that an instructor would use during a class period, and that are under the control or supervision of the instructor. Copyrighted materials obtained legally and utilized only for research outside of a class setting are not exempt, meaning that they may not be mounted for use by learners without prior permission from the copyright holder, in addition to other TEACH Act restrictions. However, one could argue that activities like one-shot sessions taught by librarians and the materials used for those sessions are exempt under this Act, as they are generally "mediated" by the instructor (Carter, 2007; Irwin, 2007).

ALA provides some guidance in understanding the various elements of the TEACH Act (Crews, accessed 2008), as does Hoon (2002), and Talab (2007) offers a useful Webliography of additional sources related to distance education and fair use. Stanford University's Copyright and Fair Use Center (Stanford University, 2008) provides useful links to copyright-related information, and the "Digital Copyright Slider" (Brewer and ALA OITP, 2007) provides guidance in judging whether or not a work published in the United States is still protected by copyright. How does all of this apply to ILI?

Implications for Information Literacy Instruction

In February 2000, the Pew Learning and Technology Program brought 14 higher education leaders together to discuss and analyze the knotty issue of intellectual property rights for online courses and course materials and to draw a clear distinction between these two categories. The symposium focused on online courses and course materials for credit-bearing courses taught by full-time faculty. Participants acknowledged that potential financial gain may be at the heart of the intellectual property debate in these areas. They concluded that a faculty member "who invents a better way to teach online or learn through technology might be deemed as having fulfilled his or her commitment to the institution. Beyond the fulfillment of teaching duties for the specific course in question, he or she should be free to market the unique creation to others and reap the rewards" (Twigg, 2000: online). They go on to recommend that "the default policy should be that the faculty member owns the course materials he or she has created," though institutions may want to establish "trigger mechanisms" in their basic policy that would enact a second policy, for example, if outside interests seek to commercialize course materials (Twigg, 2000: online).

How does this affect ILI? Questions still remain about intellectual property for which there is a growing, but not yet definitive body of litigation. In fact, there may never be a definitive body of litigation for digital or digitized materials, as the digital world keeps evolving quickly and is quite a different place from the print world. Yet we must do our best to respect the intellectual creations of others. For ILI purposes, court decisions allowing transformative use of original materials (Band, 2007) could mean a loosening of wariness in using digital images (screen captures, video screen captures, etc.) of licensed or copyrighted materials for ILI materials. Tushnet (2006) suggests, too, that libraries now exist in a peer-to-peer world, where iTunes and other digital copying capabilities erode the arguments for sharing a limited number of library-purchased items with a large number of users under the fair use doctrine. She makes several suggestions for positioning libraries as "good-faith" stakeholders in this environment, including adding value to their collections by helping users learn to sort and evaluate information (Tushnet, 2006). Who better to do this than ILI librarians?

In addition to helping people learn to think critically about information, instruction librarians have a long and admirable tradition of sharing their materials, their teaching methods, and even their course outlines and syllabi with others. However, sometimes they do not identify themselves on Web sites as content developers or Web site designers. Each of us should take credit for our creative work in all formats by including our names, dates of publication, and modifications on each item we develop, along with our supporting organization's or institution's name. We should also credit institutions and organizations for providing direct and indirect support as well, but keep in mind that institutions and organizations do not create materials—people do, and people deserve credit for their efforts.

No one, however, wants to waste time and effort duplicating work others have done. So, if you find something you want to utilize, and if you are not sure whether or not you need permission to use all or part of it, or even to link to it, protect yourself and your institution by requesting permission from the author or sponsor. If you receive permission, be sure to acknowledge the original source. If you do not receive permission, you would be well advised to look for something else, design it yourself, or pay someone else to design it for you. The Web is a giant clearinghouse, a wonderful treasure trove of ideas where we can share our own work and build upon the good work of others, but only if they permit us to do so.

Until the courts can sort out and balance conflicting interests, a high-minded approach is best. It would be a simple and generous gesture to continue the ILI tradition of sharing by indicating that permission is granted freely for noncommercial use of the instructional materials you are willing to share. Lessig's Creative Commons licensing hierarchy provides a clear method for easily doing so. It offers a variety of workable copyright approaches that protect some rights of authors/creators of works while at the same time providing usage allowances ranging from very limited to completely free usage, all with credit to the author/creator. The site also links to a means of turning a work into a completely public domain product, completely free of copyright (Creative Commons, 2008a, 2008b) U.S., Dutch, and Spanish court decisions are supporting the validity of open source (free) licenses like these in copyright infringement cases (Nas, 2006; *Jacobsen v. Katzer,* 2008). In order to create these "goods" in the first place, though, we need to look first at budget and administrative support, including hardware and software needed for design and development, and then at categories of instructional modes and materials. Finally, we need to consider general design issues, content, format, and general questions about software and equipment for design and development.

BUDGET, ADMINISTRATIVE, AND COLLEAGUE SUPPORT

Administrative Approval

As we pointed out in Chapter 8, cost is a critical factor in selecting an instructional mode. Design and development plans hinge on the direct and indirect costs your institution is willing to support, including hardware and software for design and development. So, you need to gain administrative approval before embarking on instructional projects. You should be prepared to defend your proposed design and development plans and to adjust them downward if necessary. It is important to keep in mind that instructional materials proposals that may seem wonderful, creative, and innovative are not always rewarded with approval and funding. There may be good or bad reasons for this rejection. Sometimes administrators may detect issues that have not been considered fully, such as staff time, equipment, software, or supplies needed for maintaining materials once they have been created, or the impact on staff time in other areas to compensate for the time you want to spend on this project. On the other hand, there may be more attractive competing projects for limited dollars, or political issues may interfere. Administrators often care about visible products that meet user needs, and they may be more amenable to smaller experimental pilot projects before committing to new large-scale programs. If you want their approval for any sort of project, you will need to address the issues of money and staff time, your own and that of others. The more money and staff time you need for a project, the more important it is to get administrators' explicit approval in advance and the more important it is to discuss your proposed projects in advance with your colleagues.

Software and Equipment for Design

Which basic software and equipment would be most helpful for creating instructional materials? The main considerations are the following:

1. What is already available for staff use?
2. What will the learners be using?
3. Which software and equipment would save time and help create more effective materials in a more efficient fashion?
4. Which would be essential or useful for pilot projects?
5. How much would additional software and equipment cost, and can they be put to multiple uses?
6. What sort of training would be needed in order to utilize both new software and equipment, and what sort of learning curve should we expect?
7. Who should constitute the instructional development team, and how should it be put together?
8. How can we keep up with new technology and at the same ensure access and effective use for those with legacy systems and software as well as those with devices for the disabled?

At the very least, ILI staff who design and develop instructional materials need to have the most up-to-date software and hardware the institution or organization can afford. At a minimum, you should have access to browsers currently in widespread use, like Firefox, word-processing software, a simple paint/graphics program, audio- and video-capture software, and inexpensive shareware screen-capture software like SnagIt (2008) for the PC or SnapzProX (2008) for the Mac. Some would argue that presentation software is essential as well. You may want to explore the growing number of open source software options (Sourceforge.net, 2008) and consider advice and help offered to "blended librarians," those who combine instructional design or instructional technology functions with traditional library and information-related responsibilities (Bell and Shank, 2008).

In any case, designers need to have some time to explore and learn to use new software or new versions of software they may have already used. They may need to take classes and attend conferences and workshops to keep up with new or revised software and techniques, in person and/or online. We can learn a lot from one another and from experimenting, but sometimes we need to turn to experts, so it is extremely important to remember that designers too have a learning curve and need training and support.

ILI material designers need up-to-date equipment as well. While they can use a laptop equipped with audio recording software to create podcasts, or a Webcam to create informal videos, at a minimum, designers should have the following:

- A PC or Mac with maximum RAM (Random Access Memory), hard drive capacity, and megahertz (processor speed)
- A high-capacity graphics card
- A CD-ROM/DVD read/write drive
- A number of USB ports
- A high-capacity Flash drive and an external hard drive to store large graphics, audio, and video files
- Wired and wireless connectivity
- A high-speed Internet connection
- A large monitor
- A sound card and headset
- A color printer
- Mobile devices on which to test ILI materials

Equipment becomes outdated very quickly, though, so it would be best to replace workstations and other equipment every two years and to consider purchasing newer devices even more frequently, for experimentation at the very least. Older equipment can be passed on to other less design-intensive staff, while the highest end equipment should be purchased for designers. In turn, designers can create voice and digital or video images of staff or other locations within a physical library. These can be wonderfully humanizing additions to a library's Web site.

Continuous heavy use of computer-related equipment comes with a physical, as well as a financial, price. An ILI designer needs to have an ergonomically well-designed space, including a supportive chair at the proper height, footrest, wrist rest, good lighting, properly operating optical mouse, and scheduled periods of working away from the computer where eyes and body can move and focus differently. Remote access, wireless connections, and laptops also make life easier for ILI designers.

However, good instructional material design does not just happen at random. It is easier for talented people to design quality instructional materials, but everyone needs humane support and quality tools with which to design and develop materials. Ideally, institutions need to support development of ILI materials by hiring specialists who can work with content providers. Often, these specialists are instructional technologists, skilled in using various technologies to support pedagogy. Some institutions are able to work with computing center or instructional development staff on projects that provide benefits beyond the library. Bartering IL training or advice for instructional design or technology help can be fruitful in many ways, both for work on individual projects and to raise consciousness about the value of librarians and IL.

This sounds straightforward, but be forewarned. It takes time, effort, and commitment on the part of the institution or organization, as well as individual ILI librarians, to work with "outside" experts. Instructional technologists are skilled in using and applying technology. You, the content expert, still have to know what you want the technology to accomplish in terms of expected learning outcomes. You should not expect an "outside" expert to intuit your intent regarding a project or means of implementing specific aspects of it. Have you selected a particular technology for your project? If so, what is it, and what do you expect it to do? If not, why not—what would you like to see in the end product, and are you open to technology recommendations from the "outside" expert? Is there a budget? If so, what is it, and who has control over it? Is there a time limit on designing, developing, testing, revising, implementing, assessing, and re-revising the project? Do you require regular reports and meetings with the technology expert in order to keep track of progress? Who will make the final decision regarding technology for the project? You will need to communicate all of this to the technology expert at some point. This can take time to do. It means that you cannot simply turn a project over to the technology expert. You need to be heavily involved to ensure that the project meets expectations and desires to the extent possible, given time and funding constraints as well as constraints imposed by the technology itself.

Sometimes an institution may be fortunate enough to hire an ILI librarian who already has instructional technology and instructional design skills and can undertake projects that require both IL and technology skills. If not, interested ILI librarians may wish to seek formal training in instructional design and technology and request institutional support to do so. Wise managers will support their staff in this way and will reap many short- and long-term benefits for the institution for doing so, even if individuals move on to other positions. Institutions and organizations also need to provide support for continuous training and release time to attend workshops and conferences and to network with others working on similar projects. Organizations also need to provide support and release time for other staff who may be impacted by new projects. Remember that working on these projects can take an ILI designer/developer away from the reference desk or other instruction, shifting that work to others who may already have heavy workloads.

Priorities

In order to propose a project or program, you will need to provide realistic estimates of planning, preparation, implementation, and maintenance time needed, as well as time constraints for learning and deadlines for designing and preparing instructional materials. Who is going to gather all of this? More often than not, it is the already burdened reference/instruction librarians who must gather the information, estimate the work involved, and then do the work of developing and implementing approved projects.

How can they fit this into their schedule when they are already responsible for an endless number of other duties, which may include reference, instruction, collection development, management duties of one kind or another, maintenance of blogs, wikis, and Web sites, training and supervising students and support staff, as well as various kinds of outreach, publicity, and public relations?

Given all of this, you must help administrators understand that staff at all levels have a finite amount of time, energy, and physical and emotional capacity, and that instructional projects usually take longer than estimated to complete. In fact, a good rule of thumb for creating or revising computer-based instructional products is to multiply your original time estimate by three. One way to draw attention to workload issues is to add a few sentences to each project proposal listing current priorities and suggesting reprioritizing to accommodate the new project or some partial release time or additional budgetary support for clerical or replacement professional staff through special funds. This is particularly important for time-intensive projects such as developing stand-alone or supplementary instructional materials, but it does not mean abandoning all other responsibilities. Rather, reprioritizing is a necessary means of temporary relief for the physical and emotional states of individuals and organizations and an important aid to successful attainment of goals.

Even if a project receives approval in concept but does not receive funding from the institution, all may not be lost. You might consider applying for grants, like instructional improvement grants, U.S. LSTA grants available to states, or partnerships with others—staff, community, government, or academic. In the end, partnership may reap more rewards, especially if materials are designed for use in sequenced instruction in various types of environments. Whether or not you partner with others, you need to keep some caveats in mind regarding willy-nilly, ad hoc, temporary professional replacements. Identifying, hiring, training, and supervising temporary replacements can be difficult and time-consuming for the remaining staff too. For all of these reasons, you should not go off and apply for grant funds on your own without full discussion and administrative approval or you risk wasting a lot of time and effort for nothing, and alienating administrators and your overburdened colleagues as well. See Grassian and Kaplowitz (2005), Chapter 3, "Embracing Cooperation and Change."

However, even sustained time and effort, as well as administrative and budgetary support, do not automatically ensure effective instructional materials. We need to adhere to some basic design principles for all formats of materials in order to help our learners achieve expected learning outcomes. Examining basic categories of instructional modes and materials and their design principles may help you select and design effective instructional modes and materials that suit your needs.

CATEGORIES OF INSTRUCTIONAL MODES AND MATERIALS

It is a truism to say that we live in a technological era. Nevertheless, it may be useful to categorize instructional materials on a continuum in terms of the level of technology needed to use them. At the low-tech end of the continuum are paper materials, including signs, maps, paper point-of-use guides, pathfinders, exercises, and workbooks. They may or may not be designed using some form of technology, but the product itself is meant to be used without hardware, software, or other electronic equipment.

Mid-continuum materials include overhead transparencies, audiotapes, videotapes, and presentation software used on a basic level. Most of these materials are designed using either specialized equipment or software and are meant to be used with electronic equipment, although overhead transparencies may even be handwritten or simply word-processed and printed out on transparencies or photocopied onto them.

At the high-tech end of the continuum are computer-based materials that include passive or interactive Web sites and multimedia and online versions of paper materials, as well as blogs, wikis, podcasts, videos, links to RSS feeds, chat, and other library social networking sites. High-tech materials are designed using computer hardware and software or other specialized equipment and are meant to operate by means of a computer or computer chip in some other piece of equipment, like an iPod, or equipment that can send or receive data streams, like cell phones and PDAs.

Some of these materials may be designed for synchronous (simultaneous) use either in person or remotely (e.g., overhead transparencies or PowerPoint slide shows used in in-person group instruction, Web seminars using live chat and other interactive features), and others may be designed for asynchronous (any time/any place) use. Examples include interactive Web-based tutorials, blogs, PowerPoint slide shows mounted on Web sites or course Web pages via a CMS (content/course management system)/LMS (learning management system) like Moodle or Sakai. In some cases you may want to mix and match two or more types of instructional materials, for example, handouts and a presentation slide show. On a practical level, though, what are the basics of actually designing print and electronic/electric forms of instruction?

GENERAL DESIGN PRINCIPLES

A number of basic design principles cut across all age and educational groups and are applicable to a variety of instructional materials and formats regardless of where they fall on a continuum of basic low-tech to complex high-tech materials. We have already discussed copyright, budget, and administrative support. Four other major issues remain:

- Audience
- Instructional needs (purpose)
- Content
- Format

Audience

The first and most important of these issues revolves around the audience and their needs. Who are the learners, what are their ages or educational levels and skill levels, and do they need any of the instructional materials described in the previous section? (See Chapter 7 for various means of determining need.) If the answer to the last question is "No," then continue on to the next chapter. If the answer is "Yes," then the next question is "Why?" In other words, what is the purpose of the material? To what uses will it be put? For instance, you may need to design and develop ILI for 6,000 undergraduates a year, and you may have selected expected learning outcomes, as well as modes of instruction and instructional materials. Now you need to decide how learners will make use of these modes and materials so that you can design them appropriately. You may want to design some as stand-alone items and others for support or reinforcement. The most cost-effective designs, of course, are multipurpose, such as paper point-of-use guides, which can be placed on handout racks for remote asynchronous use or utilized in synchronous in-person group instruction as step-by-step guides for hands-on segments. Presentation slide shows may be used during in-person synchronous instruction or may be mounted on a Web site for asynchronous remote use for review, reinforcement, or self-instruction.

Instructional Needs (Purpose)

Materials used strictly to support other forms of instruction will need to be designed differently from stand-alone materials. As accompaniments to other forms of instruction, support materials may address a particular instructional segment or may depend on an instructor's elaboration or explanation. Support materials can include simple printed instructions for in-person active learning exercises or very brief presentation slides to help introduce or sum up a lesson or group instruction session. On the other hand, effective stand-alone materials, those designed to be used without "intervention," must meet much tougher standards. When designing self-paced workbooks, self-guided tours, and interactive Web-based tutorials, you will need to anticipate various ways of thinking and learning and include more content, as there may be no one available to answer questions or explain complex concepts. The challenge of designing purposeful instructional material lies in balancing succinctness with clarity, as well as a means of engaging and maintaining the learner's interest.

How Much Content to Include

So often it seems that many of us fall into the trap of trying to include too much content in instruction. In many cases, we seem to do this no less with asynchronous than we have with synchronous instruction. In our sincere desire to help learners, we may try to introduce the library system and teach the mechanics of using the library catalog, as well as two or three licensed systems and databases, Boolean logic, and critical thinking skills—all in one 50-minute synchronous session or in an asynchronous linear online tutorial. How do you decide how much to include in a single instructional experience, and how can you keep the learner's attention so that she or he will complete it?

You might begin by determining the three most important things you want learners to take away from your instruction, for example:

- There are many different online systems, interfaces, gateways, databases, and Web search tools.
- There are similarities and differences among them, for example:
    - o You can search, display, and save (by e-mailing, printing, or downloading) in all of them (Barclay, 1995).
    - o Subject matter, types of items indexed or provided in full text, and time period covered may differ from one online resource to another.
- People have created all of the systems and in doing so have made conscious decisions (some of which may be politically motivated) about what to index, how to label materials, how you can search, how search results will appear, what time period will be covered, etc.

In planning instruction you may want to pick and choose even from the few items listed and try to incorporate some larger concepts, such as learning to question all sorts of assumptions regarding interface design, database coverage, sort, display and limit options, and thesaurus selection.

In addition, you can design many instructional modes and materials in modules or chunks, designed as self-contained independent instructional units. Some of these chunks can be quite short, like a one- to three-minute video or screencast. This approach will provide you and the learners options for picking and choosing the segments that meet specific needs at a particular moment. For each, you will still need to identify expected learning outcomes, address them succinctly and clearly, assess learning, review, and revise as needed. Following this process routinely with all instructional modes and materials will help you avoid making positive or negative assumptions about their continued viability and effectiveness.

Mechanics versus Concepts

Similarly, it is important to question other ILI assumptions. Can you handle the mechanics of using various information tools through asynchronous, interactive, modular tutorials or paper point-of-use guides or exercises, rather than synchronous, face-to-face group instruction? The "mechanics" could include using evaluative criteria in selecting a database for a particular topic, searching, focusing a search, evaluating items retrieved, saving items by downloading, e-mailing, or printing, or requesting them through interlibrary loan. What is it that can best be taught in person, face to face, or in other synchronous approaches, and to whom? What would be the best means of helping people learn generic basics like the differences between magazines and journals or between the "visible" (public, freely available) and "invisible" Web (the contents of many licensed databases)? Are issues of privacy, confidentiality, copyright, and intellectual property best learned through in-person discussion, though watching videos, through credit courses, or by reading and doing exercises on one's own? Is it sufficient to learn all of this well enough to function at an average skill level rather than to master them completely? Can we afford to offer a wide variety of the best means for all types of learners to reach complete mastery?

In addition to all of these questions, we must also consider learner age or academic level, as well as IL and computer literacy skill levels, when judging how much content to include in instructional materials. Generally, the younger the age group, the fewer concepts may be absorbed at one time or through a particular instructional "piece." Adult learners prefer practical learning, with real-world application as opposed to in-depth focus on theory and concepts. An outline of the most important points to get across can be extremely useful to adult learners. Examples and exercises should be geared to the interests of a particular audience. For all learners, we should strive to teach complex concepts in simple, basic terms using common language and real-life examples. (See Chapter 5 for a discussion of teaching conceptual frameworks and the use of analogies in instruction.)

Jargon, Computerphobia, and Accessibility

Jargon easily sidetracks learners. Distracted learners may stop dead mentally. They may not hear or absorb much that comes after a jargony word or expression they do not understand. Instead of concentrating on learning, they spend time trying to figure out what those words mean. The problem is that most people immersed in a topic or in a field tend to use thinking and speaking shortcuts ("jargon"). Sometimes we do not even realize that the terms we use quite frequently are mysterious jargon to a newcomer, for example, "search strategy," "online catalog," "stacks," "search terms," "subject headings," or "electronic resources." So, try to identify the jargon you use in instruction and then avoid using it unless it is essential for the concepts or skills learners will need. If you do use jargon, explain it in simple terms and check for understanding. Gear the material for the lowest common denominator, especially if a piece will operate by means of technology or involves learning any aspects of technology, and focus on the basics, what users need to know right away (Nahl, 1999).

We often take it for granted that all of our users know how to use a computer and a mouse. Yet research has shown that 25 percent or more of any given population (any age, male or female) can be computerphobic or can have low levels of computer skills, or none at all (Weil and Rosen, 1997; Thorpe and Brosnan, 2007). Our discussion of the digital divide in Chapter 2 indicated that large gaps in Internet use remain, even in the United States and particularly among senior citizens 65 and older and non-Hispanic African Americans (Pew Internet & American Life Project, 2008a, 2008b). One Web site reports that while almost three-quarters of the North American population use the Internet, just 5.3 percent of the African population and less than a quarter of the Latin American/Caribbean population do (Internet World Stats, 2008). Lack of use may or may not be due to technophobia. However, it does mean that you will need to consider how to find out what your target user population knows and how to help them address technophobia and lack of access, either with computer literacy help or alternate forms of ILI, or both. Remember to design for maximum accessibility as well, including alternate versions for the disabled, regardless of the medium. For more on accessible Web sites, see Chapter 9.

Keeping Learners' Attention

Attention, or "time on task," is a critical factor in successful instruction, particularly for asynchronous instruction. How do you keep the learners' attention and get them to finish an instructional experience? To get and keep the learners' attention, find out what they most need or want in the way of help and how they want to learn. Then, give it to them. Once you know what they want to know and how they want to learn, you may be able to get them to use your instructional materials and complete your lessons. At that point, you can test for learning outcomes. These learning outcomes need to be based on standards or benchmarks like AASL's and ACRL's information literacy standards, as we have discussed in previous chapters. However, none of this careful planning and extensive effort will help if your online instructional materials are unused or underused because of "Web fatigue" or rebellion against an impersonal electronic world. Do your learners simply want to know how to find a book by subject or how to get some articles at home at 2:00 a.m.? Are they looking for self-help with information researching? And how long will they stick with the library Web site in order to get answers to their question?

Compelling designs make people want to learn more and at the same time, provide content to meet their needs. Both can entice people to stick with a site. "The Librarian's Internet Index" offers substantial, carefully reviewed content. Its homepage lists categories and subcategories of Web sites in a traditional arrangement, with a link for more subtopics and a prominent search box (LII, 2008). What entices a user to click on a subject link, though? Google dominates search with its simple one-search-box design and its quick response. It invites quick and easy searching, and the sheer quantity of results for many searches give the impression that users are searching all the world's knowledge. Google surprises and delights users by playing with its name on its homepage, turning the letters into cartoons to represent holidays or important world events. Links to additional Google sites also entice with a single word to describe and link to each one, like Scholar, Finance, YouTube, Calendar, and Photos. Simple designs, minimal use of text, occasional use of engaging graphics, and the ability to navigate quickly and easily to one- to two-word category areas, like Books, Magazine Articles, Newspapers, Renew, Borrow, Learn, Evaluate—these are design lessons we should take from successful sites like Google (see Chapter 10 for more on this topic).

Are your instructional materials cluttered? Has your Web site "metastasized" over time, growing wildly, with too many pages, overabundant text, and too many levels through which users must click in order to get to what they really want or need (Duncan and Holliday, 2008)? How much interactivity do your instructional materials offer? Do you offer basic, midlevel, and advanced materials and other help? Are they serving their purpose well? How can you tell? Does usage tell it all?

The Minimalist Approach

Clutter can distract and repel learners. Beware of the urge to tell it all in endless conversations through your instructional material. Instead, reduce redundancy and apply minimalist design principles not only by trimming words but also by altering your approach. (See the CD-ROM that accompanies this book for an example of a modified minimalist approach to documentation.) Research has shown that learners who use minimalist documentation developed with four principles in mind, tend to complete tasks, recover from errors more quickly, and become more independent learners.

The four principles are action orientation, optimal use of text, support error recognition and recovery, and modularity. van der Meij and Lazonder (1993) and others have shown that learners prefer a problem-solving minimalist approach to instructional materials rather than more detailed materials that provide background and a very detailed step-by-step approach. When you use a minimalist approach to documentation, you use simple language, active commands, and questions rather than declarative statements, and you also provide error self-correction. A minimalist approach also presents prompts for learners to "get their hands dirty" as soon as possible by trying out procedures on their own rather than giving them lengthy step-by-step directions for many different uses or approaches.

The minimalist method is a constructivist or active learning approach that plunges the learner into a resource immediately, but it also includes techniques such as error-correction "life jackets" as guidance and "fading" in which successively fewer instructions are provided. Fading is a linear approach, however. It assumes that learners will begin at the beginning of a segment and proceed through the documentation, learning incrementally, with guidance, and experimenting on their own as they continue. In the modular world we live in, where learners tend to skip around and glean a concept here and a thought there, you might think that this approach is not appropriate. At least one study indicates quicker learning for those who use minimalist materials designed in this manner than for those who rely on more detailed conventional help (Carroll and van der Meij, 1996). In addition, the more independent learners become, the less anxious they are likely to be and the more willing to explore new resources. These are powerful advantages that may lead you to try at least a modified minimalist approach to all sorts of instructional materials, including those utilized in synchronous group instruction.

Learners also retain and transfer learning more effectively when they have some form of guidance, even in a discovery-type exercise (Mayer, 2004; de Jong, 2005). For ILI, this guidance can also take the form of structuring an exercise with a choice of examples to use, or a set of databases to search, or a series of questions to answer regarding their investigations. Modeling through "worked out examples" in advance of discovery can be effective for novices, though not necessarily for experienced users (Renkl, 2005). Again, this underscores the importance of knowing your audience through Needs Assessments.

For more on planning and assessment, see Chapters 7 and 11.

Humor

Design of instructional materials is serious business, as it can impact learning in significant, long-lasting ways. But how many of us are so caught up with the seriousness of our instructional tasks that we forget to inject some comic relief into our instruction? As Black and Forro (1999) point out, humor in the workplace can be an important antidote to stress and can improve both morale and productivity. A few well-placed jokes, even at our own expense, can also delight users. Humorous Web pages like "Librarian Avengers" (Olsen, 2007) and "The Lipstick Librarian" (Absher, 2004) can help change the image of the librarian. Humorous pictures or other visual communication in your handouts, presentation slide shows (face to face or remote), and on your Web pages can have a positive impact on recall as well (Ginman and Ungern-Sternberg, 2003). Cartoons or comic strips can break the ice at the beginning of a session or soothe tension when interspersed throughout a session. Many library-related cartoons are available on the Web now ("Library Cartoons," 2008) and can be quite useful in establishing rapport with and relaxing an audience.

Some instructors even plan to make humorous mistakes and ask a group to help problem solve as a means of learning through discovery. Others laugh at their own poor typing or spelling skills as they quite naturally make these common sorts of errors. In no case, however, should an instructor single out a learner or his or her attempt to do research as a subject for humor in any instructional setting (Sarkodie-Mensah, 1998). One joke at the expense of a learner can harm the person and derail even the most carefully planned instruction. Remember, to the learner you are a powerful person. You are responsible for earning the learners' trust by treating them with respect and dignity, regardless of their age, education, or skill level.

If you feel comfortable with humor, try using it in different formats, but test it out on friends and naive users before going to great lengths to incorporate it into instruction. As the famous satirist Stan Freberg put it, "Humor is such a fragile thing. . . . [It's] like a gun in the hands of a child. You have to know how to do it. Otherwise it can blow up on you" (Garfield, 1992: 52).

Format and Interactivity

As we have seen in this chapter and will learn more about in the next chapter, IL instructional material designers now have a great number of format choices to make regarding instruction modes and materials, ranging from high to low tech in a rainbow of colors, motion, sounds, and graphics. In addition, designers can build interactivity into many of these instructional options. What does "interactive" really mean in terms of instruction and instructional material? "Interaction is mutual action among the learner, the learning system, and the learning material" (Najjar, 1998: 314). What sorts of interaction can we build in and which instructional format(s) would be most effective to help our primary audience achieve expected learning outcomes? Interaction for ILI materials can include tutorials with Web-based quizzes that provide immediate self-checking and feedback as well as exercises or workbooks that users have to complete and for which they receive feedback in the form of comments or grades. Some interaction can occur, as well, without "graded" or "corrected" feedback. Just clicking buttons on a Web page can mean interaction of a sort, as the user makes cognitive choices about directions to take, further pages to view within a particular site, or links to external sites. What is the user learning, however?

There are many advantages to using Web pages for instruction, including the ability to provide updated information in a timely fashion, the ability to include interactivity for feedback and to maintain interest, and the ability to reach your learner audience at any time and in any place where they have an Internet connection. On a political note, using Web pages for instruction places us in the same position as teaching faculty, businesses, and other groups and individuals who are learning as they go and trying to make the best use of new technology to help and/or appeal to existing or new users. It also places IL and the ILI instructor in a logical and supportive position: We are able to relate to others in this world and draw attention to the need for IL skills at all levels. On the negative side, you need to remember that learners must have access to a workstation or other device with an Internet connection in order to view your pages. They must also know the basics of Web browser usage.

How can we focus our instructional efforts on user needs and design the most useful instructional modes and materials for our primary users? It all starts with the most important factor, the learner.

Learner Input in Meeting a Range of Needs

Donald Norman recommends using the Apple Corporation's approach to designing and developing highly user-friendly products by consulting users about products at every step of the way, from design through development and implementation, and even afterward ("Talking with Don Norman," 1999). Duncan and Holliday (2008) took this approach in redesigning their library's Web site. They started with users but also consulted library staff, weighing and balancing comments from both groups as they reconceptualized the architecture of the site. You could also routinize this process for ILI by establishing a working advisory board with representatives from user, staff, administrative, and other groups. This board could provide regular feedback on all sorts of ILI projects and plans, as well as suggest new ILI initiatives and aid in goal and priority setting for the entire organization. If an advisory board would not work in your environment, ad hoc focus groups, surveys, or questionnaires are other means for learners to participate in deciding which formats would be most useful to them for ILI (Greenbaum, 1998; Morgan, 1997; Quible, 1998).

Regardless of the form of learner participation, participants may need a jumpstart in terms of defining IL and coming up with ideas for ILI modes and materials. Examples of ILI materials from other locations can be helpful in this regard. Examine a number of different models of instructional materials, and pick out the most appealing elements or segments to share with the participants in order to get them started. In particular, look for models to emulate that have similar goals, regardless of the format. For instance, school library media specialists can offer all of us good lessons in how to design instruction for different learner levels. If the basics are simple enough for children, complexity can be added for older learners. Kathy Schrock's Web critical thinking "tests" or "exercises" are excellent examples of how this can work. Each test/exercise challenges students in an interesting, self-paced manner. Tests/exercises are designed for different levels, from primary to high school, and rise in complexity as grade levels increase. Most are available as Web pages, PDFs and Word documents, with some translated into Spanish (Schrock, 2008a). By providing all three formats, Schrock ensures that these tests/exercises can be used in a variety of circumstances.

In an ideal world with unlimited time, staff, and budget, we should provide a multiplicity of ILI formats to meet the needs and learning styles of most learners. Often, though, there is not enough time or money to develop and maintain a large number of different formats of instructional materials aimed at helping people learn the same things. At a minimum, you should try to meet the extremes of access to technology by providing a low-tech paper item and a corresponding high-tech version, keeping in mind the following features:

- Interest level
- Freshness
- Simplicity
- Content based
- Learner-centered structure

Continue involving users in the development process by testing materials on naive users. Listen carefully to their comments, revise accordingly, and test again for ease of use (Nielsen, accessed 2008). Remember to build in or separately design some means of testing learning outcomes, and ask the learners who used each format for user satisfaction feedback as well. For more on usability testing, see Chapter 9. See Chapter 11 for more on assessing instructional effectiveness.

FINAL REMARKS

Copyright, budget, and administrative and colleague support all impact instructional mode/material selection significantly. You will need to examine these issues within the context of your environment, the user groups you are addressing, and their particular needs. You need to do this before you can focus on specific instructional categories, decide on the balance of mechanics versus concepts, and how you will keep learners' attention, the format, and many other design questions. If you give serious consideration to each of the preliminary design issues discussed in this chapter, you will be well prepared to consider design and development of specific instructional modes and materials, addressed in the next chapter.

EXERCISES

1. Review your expected learning outcomes for basic IL. Determine where copyright, fair use, and intellectual property fit, or add an additional learning outcome. Come up with one example from an image-sharing site and one example from a video-sharing site that you would use to illustrate these concepts. Describe how you would use these examples for in-person instruction and for distance learning.
2. Take a one- or two-page paper point-of-use guide or online guide to using a database and determine its audience and purpose. Write a brief outline of the most important elements learners would need to know in order to use the resource. Highlight the most important elements provided in the guide. Were all of the elements in your outline included in the guide? Where would you place the missing elements? What would you delete from the guide in order to keep it the same length or make it shorter?
3. Take a wordy or technical help guide (online or in print) and modify it so that it has some minimalist features. Describe what you changed, how you changed it (or them), and why.

READ MORE ABOUT IT

Band, Jonathan. "Educational Fair Use Today." ARL (December 2007). Available: www.arl.org/bm~doc/educationalfairusetoday.pdf (accessed December 25, 2008).

Creative Commons. "Homepage" (2008). Available: http://creativecommons.org (accessed December 25, 2008).

Duncan, Jennifer and Wendy Holliday. 2008. "The Role of Information Architecture in Designing a Third-generation Library Web Site." *College & Research Libraries* 69, no. 4: 301–318.

Moseng, Christopher. 2007. "The Failures and Possible Redemption of the DMCA Anticircumvention Rulemaking Provision." *Journal of Technology Law & Policy* 12, no. 2: 333–374.

Nimmer, David. 2000. "A Riff on Fair Use in the Digital Millennium Copyright Act." *University of Pennsylvania Law Review* 148, no. 3: 673–742.

Pew Internet & American Life Project. "Demographics of Internet Users" (July 22, 2008). Available: www.pewinternet.org/trends/User_Demo_7.22.08.htm (accessed December 27, 2008).

Sarkodie-Mensah, Kwasi. 1998. "Using Humor for Effective Library Instruction Sessions." *Catholic Library World* 68, no. 4: 25–29.

Schrock, Kathy. "Critical Evaluation Surveys and Resources" (2008). Available: http://school.discoveryeducation.com/schrockguide/eval.html (accessed December 23, 2008).

Stanford University. "Copyright & Fair Use Center" (2008). Available: http://fairuse.stanford.edu (accessed December 25, 2008).

Tushnet, Rebecca. 2006. "My Library: Copyright and the Role of Institutions in a Peer-to-Peer World." *UCLA Law Review* 53, no. 4: 977–1029.

van der Meij, Hans and Ard W. Lazonder. 1993. "Assessment of the Minimalist Approach to Computer User Documentation." *Interacting with Computers* 5, no. 4: 355–370.

Chapter 10

Designing Instructional Modes and Materials

She comes in colors. . . .
—The Rolling Stones, "She's a Rainbow"

Teachers and librarians may not be trained in instructional or graphic design, yet often they must create a range of instructional materials and formats to support both in-person and remote learning for many ages and skill levels. Keep in mind that, as technologies evolve, we may need to add design principles for newer formats. Increasing use of mobile technologies means that Web sites and applications need to be offered in alternative forms. Although this means additional planning, design, and development, it does not necessarily mean that you should drop older formats because they may seem outdated. As we pointed out in Chapter 9, it is crucial to select modes of instruction and supplementary or stand-alone materials that best support your goals and objectives. Next, for each instructional piece, figure out what you want it to accomplish. Then write up the expected learning outcomes for each item—what the learners should know and be able to do after using the item. Each instructional item you create needs to support and further learning.

How many different kinds of instructional materials should you offer? This is a difficult question to answer, as it depends on a variety of factors, including resources such as staff and funding, as well as time available for planning, development, and field testing. Decisions about adding or dropping instructional formats should also be considered carefully and should be based on a Needs Assessments. Once you have selected modes and materials, though, how do you actually go about designing them? In Chapter 12, we focus primarily on designing and developing synchronous group instruction. This chapter covers designing and developing a number of other commonly used instructional modes and materials, as well as backup plans for inevitable glitches.

DESIGNING PRINT MATERIALS

What do you use to create print materials? Word-processing, screen-capture software, and graphics software come to mind immediately, but you can still use a typewriter or even paper and pencil to design print instructional materials like handouts, guides, maps, pathfinders, exercises, and workbooks. Print is comfortable, static, and predictable, as well as easily portable. Learners can put paper materials down next to them, make notes on them, paper-clip them, and highlight or circle important sections. Some learners still value print materials to such an extent that they print off page after page of material designed for online learning. They may do so for all the reasons mentioned here or simply because they prefer to see the whole picture before focusing on smaller elements. Even in the digital age, we must keep in mind that some still may not have easy online access or the technical expertise to be able to get to and save copies of online materials by printing, downloading or e-mailing (Freeman, 2008). Whatever the reason, it is still important to provide print materials for those who prefer them either as paper handouts copied and distributed by the library or mounted on Web sites in a format designed for printing. Paper point-of-use guides are also handy ways to reinforce learning in group sessions.

Well-designed print materials can help some people learn more quickly and easily (Merriman, 2006; Meyers and Nulty, 2008). Effective handouts are readable, legible, and meet intended learning outcomes. According to Allen (1993: 16), in designing handouts we need to make decisions in a variety of design categories, including size, shape, layout, font, and color. Parker (2006) suggests that we consider a number of design concepts when developing print materials, including relevance, proportion, consistency, and attention to detail. We also need to consider structure, which deals more with content than with the look and feel of a piece, as well as the time available for preparation.

Structure

Often, users learn more quickly if they know where to look for specific instructions on how to use or interact with a reference tool. Instructional materials with a consistent look and feel, and a consistent content structure, can be a big help. Check to see if your library has a preferred template for print materials, and, if not, consider designing one. If you do design a template, try to keep it as simple and uncluttered as possible. Templates often have a title at the top or bottom (header or footer) or even on the side. They usually include the library name and its logo or that of the parent institution. The occasional odd piece that uses off-center, unusual, or even bizarre combinations of color, graphic design, images, layouts, and wording may get more attention than a standard template but should be reserved for unusual or one-of-a-kind items, such as a search log (Wehmeyer, 1996; see also Figure 10.1 for an example). Even these sorts of pieces can include a small header with a logo, and all instructional materials should be dated, signed, or initialed by the author(s). Remember, libraries do not design materials. People do, and they should get credit for the items and content they create.

How structured and detailed should instructional materials be? Some have debated the advantages and disadvantages of linear, step-by-step instruction, particularly for online materials (Tennant, 1997; Milam, 2004). However, a logical linear structure can help learners orient themselves quickly and is essential for learning and utilizing various features of electronic resources. In some cases, you must use a linear approach in order to accomplish a particular task; there is no way around it. If you want to use a paper handout to help someone learn how to use an SFX link to get a copy of an online article, for instance, you will need to list a series of linear steps to accomplish this task. Learners could skip around even in a print handout if it goes on to describe how to use interlibrary loan to get copies of items that are not online or how to use the library catalog to find print copies. But for each operation, they will have a sequence of steps to follow. See "Find UCLA Library Books" (Grassian, 2006) for an example of a handout with linear instructions, mounted as a PDF.

White Space, Graphics, and Layout

"White space" speaks more to users than most words you write, so allow for plenty of it. Beware of some common pitfalls, though, including overly busy or dark backgrounds, headlines or titles that do not stand out from the text, and unnecessary use of graphics (Parker, 2006). As the well-known graphic artist Tufte (1983: 105) puts it, "Erase non-data ink" and "Erase redundant data ink." This means balancing the amount of content with the number of graphics and the number of pages permissible, both for print and online materials. Include appropriate graphics whenever feasible, but keep in mind that graphics can take up lots of space and the longer the print piece, the more costly and time-consuming it will be to reproduce. Too many graphics, or graphics that wink, blink, and move around on a screen, can clutter sites and distract learners in online instruction as well.

Graphics can be important, however, and can be more effective learning devices than text alone for recalling and recognizing items (Fletcher and Tobias, 2005). Often, though, they leave us in a quandary. How many should we include? How large? Should we use screen-capture software like SnagIt (2008) for the PC or SnapzProX (2008) or SnapNDrag (accessed 2008) for the Mac to "grab"

Figure 10.1 Sample Search Log

Name: ____

Topic: ____

Date	Information Source (Database name, Web page URL, etc.)	Search Words	Number of Results	Additional Subjects to Search

part of a window or screen or all of it? How do we indicate or maintain context if we take a small piece of a screen shot rather than an entire screen or window? As Najjar (1998: 313) puts it, and as the empirical research he cites indicates, "The information being presented in one medium needs to support, relate to, or extend the information presented in the other medium." Research also indicates that although graphics are important, we must be quite cautious about how we use them. Including just any graphics or a large number of graphics will not necessarily improve learning. According to Mayer, the dual-channel theory of multimedia learning contends that visual/pictorial and auditory/verbal processing take place in "channels" that are limited in capacity and involve a number of different cognitive processes. So we need to be wary of overloading one or both channels for multimedia. When trying to determine which and how many graphics to use, outline the main points. Then, note where graphics may be needed, and include both words and graphics only as necessary (Mayer, 2005a, 2005b, 2005c, 2005d; Sweller, 2005). "The illustrations must help explain information that is presented by the verbal medium . . . [as] supportive illustrations allow learners to build cognitive connections between the verbal and pictorial information" (Najjar, 1998: 313).

The theory of "dual encoding" may explain why this is so. This theory states that a person remembers a picture in two ways, as an image and also as a word or words, making for better recall of pictures than of words. According to Paivio (1973), the same effect occurs regarding recall of concrete as opposed to abstract words, which may also partially explain the power of concrete analogies used to explain abstract ideas. (See Chapter 5 for more on mental models.) According to Tufte (1983: 121), the best graphic representations of data "are *intriguing and curiosity-provoking*, drawing the viewer into the wonder of the data, sometimes by narrative power, sometimes by immense detail, and sometimes by elegant presentation of simple but interesting data." Tag clouds do this by displaying subject words listed one after the other, with more frequently used tags in larger font sizes, depending on their popularity. Wordle.net takes this a step further by allowing you to create tag clouds that are quite artistic and eye catching (Feinberg, 2008; Deitering, 2008).

In other words, use graphics sparingly and primarily to support the goals and objectives of the instructional piece. In addition, use the briefest and simplest context-setting language to describe where users should look for pieces of graphics—for example, "Scroll down and click on the box labeled 'go' halfway down the screen on the right-hand side." Remember, "Your writing does not need to be 'interesting'; it needs to be invisible" (Curtis, 1995: 55).

Finally, make sure your graphics add to understanding and are easily readable, especially if your audience will include adult learners. The basic rule of thumb is: If a user cannot see a graphic clearly and completely, do not include it. Share samples with learners who may utilize these materials. Increase the size of graphics if necessary, and consider eliminating some to hold down the number of pages or the size of a Web site. For print materials, this will help hold down reproduction costs and save trees. This is a delicate balancing act, though, because too few graphics may make a printed guide just as useless as too many. As Tufte (1983: 51) puts it so well, "Graphical excellence consists of complex ideas communicated with clarity, precision, and efficiency. Graphical excellence is that which gives to the viewer the greatest number of ideas in the shortest time with the least ink in the smallest place." So pick and choose your graphics carefully, use screen-capture software to take the most essential portions of screens or windows, and use graphics software to adjust them, both to fit the physical page constraints and to draw attention to specific points.

In general, your pedagogical goals and objectives, and your bare bones outline, should serve as guides for both content and graphics. You can improve usability as well if you share drafts with your colleagues (in your institution or remotely) and if you test drafts on naive users.

Typeface or Font

One of the glories of word processing and Web authoring is being able to choose among a large number of fonts, including picture fonts. In and of itself, a font can set a mood, suggest a content focus, tempt learners to read an item, or cause them to ignore it completely. Consider the following examples.

Verdana and Arial are rather modern looking sans serif fonts—that is, they lack the "little feet or appendages" (serifs) (Allen, 1993: 19). Some claim that serifs improve legibility in print materials, at least in smaller size fonts, as letters are more distinct from one another (Parker, 2006). Some people prefer these plainer san serif fonts, however, for larger font print and online instructional materials.

Palatino is a clean-looking serif font, a bit more modern and attractive than **Times New Roman**, the default font for Microsoft Word.

Comic sans mas is quite friendly and appealing for informal usage, even though it is a sans serif font.

Lucida Blackletter and HERCULANUM are too ornate or stylized for many instructional materials but might be eye-catching for titles or headers in course-integrated art or history materials.

♋♒●❍■⬧❑◆❖⌧🗁⌛🖰🗀🖎🖃🖹☺☹

Wingdings, shown above, is an example of a picture font that can be used for bullets or for illustration in place of clip art.

Try experimenting with different fonts, but be a bit cautious about mixing different fonts within the same document. Keep in mind, too, that words in italics are often ignored, and too much use of bold, underlining, shadow, and other special treatments like boxes and color can lessen their effect. If your audience includes adult learners, make sure the font size is easily readable by asking users to review samples and then making any necessary adjustments.

Color

Color can invoke psychological reactions and may even impact achievement. One empirical study found that participants who briefly viewed a red cover sheet prior to taking achievement tests performed worse than those who did not, and they even moved further away physically from the red test cover than those whose test covers were gray or green. Those who viewed the red cover sheet were unaware that this study focused on the impact of color on psychological functioning rather than on the tests themselves. This study was conducted in two countries and with two age groups, and repeated by altering other variables, with the same conclusion: "this undermining effect of red takes place outside of individuals' conscious awareness" (Elliot et al., 2007). Two authors of this study follow up by indicating that some effects of color are "biologically based and pancultural," while others may vary from one culture to another (Elliot and Maier, 2007).

Color is often used in advertising to entice people into buying particular products. The color yellow is an "attention getter," processed most quickly by the brain ("Supermarket Psych-out," 1999). Color can even affect perception of drug effects. One study found that "a blue sugar pill made medical students drowsier than a pink sugar pill" ("Why Blue M&M's Make You Drowsy," 1997). A study of problem-solving tasks showed that blue and white paper promoted better performance than red paper under low motivation conditions (Soldat, Sinclair, and Mark, 1997). Research on the impact of hue (tint), value or luminance (lightness or darkness), and saturation (deeply or lightly colored), indicated that "a modification of hue alone is not enough to trigger a change in attitude: levels of saturation must also be taken into account" (Lichtle, 2007: 55).

Because color does have an impact on learners, it can be an extremely useful tool for handouts, Web pages, and other online instructional materials. For asynchronous use in a physical setting, for instance when a library is open but the reference desk is not staffed, learners may look for and come to expect particular colors of paper point-of-use guides for specific services, resources, or systems. When a group has a large packet of handouts in a synchronous group session, you can get them to focus on a specific one by saying, "Now, let's take a look at the blue handout." Garish and neon-colored paper may make materials difficult to read, however, and it may be hard to read dark-colored handouts in dim light.

Essentially, then, color can attract a learner's attention and, when used appropriately, can enhance learning. Some good rules of thumb for color in instructional materials are the following:

- Use color sparingly and for a purpose.
- Avoid extremes, especially in paper and font colors.
- Always check for readability with naive users.
- Save the most easily readable color or the item with the most contrast for the most important handout in a packet.

Many of these same design criteria can be applied to a variety of instructional materials.

Preparation Time Available

Time constraints for preparing or updating instructional materials can impinge on creativity, clarity, and comprehensiveness. When you have very limited time in which to design and develop instructional materials, write up your goals and objectives for the piece and three to five things you want learners to know and be able to do as a result of using it. Make a quick list of all the points you would like to include and then cross off all but the most basic. You can also give copies of your list to two or three naive users and ask them to check off very quickly the three to five points they would most like to learn. Focus on explaining these functions clearly and concisely, with graphics inserted at the most critical junctions only. Try to weave critical thinking and evaluation into as many elements of the piece as possible.

DESIGNING AUDIO AND PODCASTS

In the 1970s, the most frequent use of audio for information literacy (IL) instruction took the form of self-guided audiocassette tours of the physical library. Some libraries are using podcasts and audio narration as part of presentation slide shows for in-person and virtual tours and descriptions of services, though they may also be used for public relations and fund-raising programs. Audio tours on CD-ROM or as podcasts can be quite handy, especially when few or no staff are available to give in-person tours and where individuals or small groups tend to wander in unexpectedly. Podcasts can be produced fairly quickly and cheaply and mounted on the library's Web site for use within the physical library or for downloading and remote use on MP3 players, away from a library building. To accommodate those who do not have MP3 players of their own, you might consider whether or not your library could afford to buy some and lend them to visitors who want to tour your library in person.

If you add audio to a presentation software slide show you can mount the entire show on a Web site. (See later discussion regarding presentation software for more on this topic.) Popular programs used for the latter purpose are PowerPoint (Microsoft, 2008b) and Keynote (Apple, 2008). Using audio on a Web site presents broader IL opportunities. You can add helpful tips or more detailed instruction to instructional Web sites, or even to library catalogs and other library Web pages, accommodating learners with audio-preference learning styles and the disabled, for instance, those with learning disabilities or reduced vision. In addition, audio options can be helpful to those for whom English is a second language, as they allow learners to replay audio privately.

In any case, effective audio materials require simple and to the point content, spoken by a narrator who pronounces words clearly and distinctly. For audio combined with visuals, narration needs to add value to what learners see on a screen rather than simply repeating or reading text on the screen, word for word. Professional narrators will raise costs and are not essential. Student or amateur actors or actresses may be willing to do narration for little or no fee, as long as they are given credit, or a library staff member may do the same. Again, be sure to give credit to the narrator, the content author, and to those who help with the production.

DESIGNING OVERHEAD TRANSPARENCIES AND PRESENTATION SLIDE SHOWS

Overhead Transparencies

There may be times when you cannot get an Internet connection for a synchronous in-person information literacy instruction (ILI) session. If you know this in advance, you can still lead an effective session by using an older lower tech format, overhead transparencies. You can write, draw, or print out onto overhead transparencies in black or in color. They are called *transparencies* because an overhead projector shines a light through them and projects a magnified image onto a screen, a wall, a sheet, or any other object in front of it. Currently, for $35–$50 you can buy a box of 100 blank overheads that you can write on or put through a printer or a photocopier.

The same principles apply to overheads as to print materials, with some added caveats. Be sure to make images and characters on overheads large enough so that those in the back of the room can read them clearly and easily. It is better not to use overheads at all if some of the audience will be frustrated because they cannot read the material—they will be thinking about your unreadable overheads during your entire session rather than the content.

Use as few bullets, words, and images as possible on a single overhead. If you write, print, or draw by hand on an overhead transparency, you need to use special pens, and your writing should be extremely legible. In many cases when you use overheads, lights will be dimmed, so learners will hear only your voice and see what is projected on the screen. They may or may not see your body language unless you turn off the overhead projector and turn on the lights. Thus, your voice and your overheads will have to speak for you. Remember that overhead transparencies are a static medium, but you can get some movement by uncovering some portions of an overhead image a bit at a time, by circling or drawing arrows on a transparency, by switching transparencies fairly quickly, and by turning the overhead projector off from time to time.

To spruce up a session, you can use overheads to pose questions, state premises for discussion, or provide instructions for an exercise. You can also copy comic strips, graphics, or clip art onto overheads, although you do need to be aware of copyright issues if you are using these items in a for-profit situation. See Chapter 8 for more on using overhead transparencies in instruction.

Presentation Slide Shows

Microsoft's PowerPoint, Apple's Keynote, and other presentation software applications can be extremely seductive instructional tools, sometimes too seductive, at least for instructors. You can choose from a large number of backgrounds and color schemes, insert clip art and other graphics, including screen captures, and even add all sorts of movement and sound effects to each slide. "Notes" pages are hidden from the audience but when printed out allow the presenter to match notes to particular slides. (See the Notes pages for the PowerPoint slide show on the CD-ROM accompanying this book for an example of how this can work.) You can also use presentation software to create a slide show and then print out the slides on overhead transparencies, or you can print out six- or nine-slide handouts for the audience (Gribas, Sykes, and Dorochoff, 1996).

The key words here, however, are *presentation* software and *presenter*. Although they are electronic, many people use presentation slide shows in a passive manner. Learners sit and watch as an instructor talks and shows slides, attempting to pour information into the tabula rasa of the learner's mind. As we saw in Chapter 5, though, learners really do not have empty minds. Often they have mental models of what we are trying to teach, sometimes incorrect models or other thoughts or motivations that may or may not have anything to do with our instruction.

To get their attention and to improve learning and retention, you should aim to make presentation software shows as interactive as possible, even if slides are created online and then printed out onto transparencies for use with an overhead projector. You could show a slide with two intersecting circles, called Venn diagrams, and ask the audience to predict which parts of the diagrams should be filled in to represent various Boolean operators. The next slide or overhead can then show the correct answer. Also, at various points, instead of just letting a bulleted point appear on the screen, ask the learners to guess what it will be. If you are using overheads created with presentation software and printed onto transparencies, you can uncover points one by one as you come to them or overlay transparencies with the correct answer. You can even add an outline of sections to cover with links to each section. Then you can engage the learners by asking them to vote on which section to start with and where to go next (Brier and Lebbin, in press).

Even if you increase interactivity, though, other pitfalls may confront you. Presentation software often unduly captivates instructors in many fields. Once you have learned how to use it, you will be sorely tempted to overuse it because it is fun, you can make words move, insert cute graphics and clip art, and you can have each slide "transition" to another slide by wiping right, uncovering left, cubing right, left, up, or down, and so on. You may also end up trying to dump too much information into the learner. The most common error is to convert to slides almost every word in your notes or every word you would speak. It is difficult and unnecessary for learners to sit in a room and read slides on a screen when you could just as easily have handed them a bunch of photocopies of your slides or mounted your slide show on Slideshare.net (2008) and told them to come see you if they had questions. You must work hard to resist this temptation. Keep words that represent key concepts only, bullet them, or get rid of bullets entirely and consider enlarging the font size. Use color to highlight important items, but check to see if colors will be clearly visible from the back of the room or via various Web browsers if mounted on a Web site. Use clip art and graphics in place of words whenever possible to illustrate points or for humor, but be careful to allow for white space on each slide. (See the PowerPoint slide show on the CD-ROM accompanying this book for an example. Presentation content appears in the Notes pages.) Instead of creating a slide that reads "Does anyone have any questions?" you might just have a slide with Microsoft Office clipart that looks like a cartoon figure of a man with his back to you, scratching his head. Or search for images with Creative Commons licenses in image-sharing sites like Flickr (Creative Commons, 2008a, 2008b; Flickr, 2008).

Dimming previous bulleted points can give the illusion of white space even on a crowded slide. (In Microsoft PowerPoint, this is called *custom animation*.) Movement attracts attention, so make use of transition options for slides and points on particular slides. Too much movement and highly detailed, cluttered, and deeply colored backgrounds can be quite distracting, however, so be judicious and choose colors carefully. Test out the entire slide show first by yourself and then with a colleague or a naive user. Above all, keep in mind that presentation software is just another tool, one that can turn learners off as easily as it turns presenters on. Use it sparingly (Pink, 2007).

DESIGNING VIDEOS AND VODCASTS

Formal or informal videos can capture attention and get points across quickly. In the 1960s, TV stations began using videotape widely. Artists began experimenting with it at that time too, though videotape had been available since the 1950s (Russell, 2007). Today, anyone with a Webcam mounted on a computer or a camcorder can create a digital video, and videos can be mounted on Web sites like iTunes for Macintosh, as MP4 files, or for Windows, as video for broadband, both available on demand, like podcasts (Feeley, 2006). Many mobile devices like cell phones also have digital video capability. You can use these devices at minimal or no cost to create informal videos. You can also create both formal and informal videos yourself by using screencasting software, or you can adapt an existing video, with permission, or even hire a professional to create a video for you, at a greater cost.

Videos may be embedded in course guides, tutorials, or instructional Web sites and may be designed for use on mobile devices as vodcasts. Once videos are available on a Web site, instructors can assign them prior to synchronous instruction or as part of asynchronous instruction. You could even rely on these videos as a partial substitute in the event of unexpected database connection difficulties during ILI sessions.

The most effective instructional videos are interesting, to the point, and short (three to ten minutes or less). *6 Ways to Ask a Reference Question* (Gould, 1977) is a classic "proto-ILI" video that uses gentle humor in six short minutes to illustrate the importance of asking detailed, explicit reference questions. The intent is to teach students to ask direct and complete questions at reference desks. In the process, though, it also teaches students that librarians are friendly and want to help, and it teaches librarians a variety of diplomatic means of interacting with users. This video is a kind of "proto-ILI" item because it was created toward the beginning of the modern-day ILI movement and had two specific goals related to reference questions in general: to encourage users to ask questions at a reference desk and to be forthcoming about their reference needs.

There are many other examples of videos either purposely designed for ILI or useful for ILI purposes. Some describe services, like the *Weigle Information Commons Music Video* (University of Pennsylvania, 2008). Others attempt to teach ILI concepts and practices directly. Examples of direct ILI include the Birmingham Public Library's (2008) *Placing a Hold . . . So Easy, but Can a Caveman Do It?* and the University of Auckland's (2008) *Boolean Operators*. You can also use other kinds of videos in order to help people learn IL concepts. These include *friendofdarwin's Darwin Poster* (2007), focusing on plagiarism, and *EPIC 2015* (Museum of Media History, 2007), covering many IL-related issues, including privacy, confidentiality, copyright, and fair use. With any video, you can stop it at one or more points, ask the learners to tell you what the underlying issues are, and hold a discussion on pros, cons, and concerns.

As we mentioned earlier in Chapter 9, videos sometimes include humor that is widely understood only at a particular point in time. In addition, videos with themes such as library detectives may be off-putting to more sophisticated audiences, especially adult learners, as they may seem too cutesy or condescending. On the other hand, eye-catching, 30-second to 5-minute spots broadcast in a dorm, on a public access cable channel, or on the Web via streaming video may grab a particular audience that otherwise would not be attracted to ILI. Mizrachi's LITE Bites, written, produced, and acted by UCLA students under her supervision, offer a case in point. They are short (2–5 minute), attractive, and appeal to UCLA undergraduates, who immediately recognize well-known and abiding themes represented by titles such as "The Librarian of Oz?" (Mizrachi, 2008a, 2008b) This type of peer-to-peer or learner-to-learner instruction can be quite effective and illustrates, too, the value of collaborating with groups outside the library (Mizrachi and Bedoya, 2007). (See Grassian and Kaplowitz, 2005, Chapter 3, "Embracing Cooperation and Change," for more on collaboration and partnership.)

Regardless of a video's level of sophistication,

remember to plan ahead, to help viewers achieve expected learning outcomes, and to avoid boring them. This can be quite a challenge, given current expectations for commercial films. As always, begin by identifying your goals and objectives or expected learning outcomes. Ask yourself what you expect the learner to know and be able to do after viewing the video. Keep in mind that attention spans are short, especially for instructional videos. Figure out the simplest, clearest, and shortest way to help learners achieve the expected learning outcomes. Search video-sharing sites, YouTube (2008), and blip.tv (2008) to see if anyone else has already created an ILI-related video that you can use to meet expected learning outcomes for your learner group. Library Information Literacy Online Network (LION, 2008) offers videos from the ANimated Tutorial Sharing Project collection (A.N.T.S., 2008) and code for embedding these A.N.T.S. videos in Web sites, including course Web pages. This is important, as Kazakoff-Lane (2008) points out, because it is often difficult to read the text present in ILI tutorial videos when viewing them through YouTube.

The following rundown of general steps may be useful when creating an ILI video:

- Identify goal(s) and objectives or expected learning outcomes.
- Storyboard and script the video.
- Consider doing the audio narration separately from the video.
- Rehearse and be prepared to have more than one "take."
- Edit as needed, including optional insertion of features like highlighting and audio narration, to engage learners.

Video Screen Captures (Screencasts)

If you decide to create a video of your own, or even adapt one, you may want to consider using free or low-cost screencasting software, like Jing (2008) (free), Camtasia Studio (2008), or Adobe Captivate (2008) to create and edit videos. In virtual worlds you can also create machinima (videos) for free. It can take time to learn the technical features of some screencasting software; however, there are a number of advantages to using this type of software. For instance, some screencasting software offers the option of inserting interactive quiz questions within the video so that learners can test themselves asynchronously, get immediate feedback, and then continue watching the video. You can also show the videos with interactive quiz questions during a synchronous session and ask for group responses.

Commercial screencasting software like Camtasia Studio and Captivate allow you to go through all of the steps of using a Web site, including searching databases, while capturing every window, cursor, point, and click. You can record an audio narration during or after creating a video screen capture, though you will probably find it much easier to do so afterward. You can also add "callouts," such as highlighting and bubbles or arrows with text, as well as captioning. Try to keep these types of movies to three minutes or less, particularly if you add features like callouts, both to maintain attention and to keep file size down for effective streaming, especially for dial-up connections.

Once you have created a video and added narration and other features, as desired, you will need to produce the video. You may have a variety of options to choose from, including the type of movie (Flash, MP3, RealVideo, etc.) to produce, whether or not you want the video to be "SCORM compliant"; SCORM compliancy allows the video to be placed within a CMS/LMS (course management system/learning management system) like WebCT, Moodle, or Sakai. You may also have the option of allowing learners to view and utilize viewing controls. The more control you turn over to learners, such as the ability to stop, start, and replay a movie at any point, the more you empower them. YouTube and other video-sharing sites recognize this value-added functionality and include viewing controls as a standard feature for videos mounted on their sites.

Professional Videos

If you decide to hire a professional to create a video for you, keep in mind that professional videos require costly preproduction, production, and postproduction time, money, and effort. Furthermore, when changes occur that impact video content, you may need to hire a professional to edit it or redo the video entirely. Actors and actresses speaking dialogue can account for much of the expense of professionally created videotapes, because dialogue often requires many "takes." Each take must be planned and set up in advance with proper lighting and equipment (both costly expenses), as well as accompanying personnel, whose wages must also be covered. One way around these particular expenses is to substitute as many "voice-overs" as possible for filmed dialogue, or just use music instead of narration. A voice-over is simply someone narrating off-camera while other items, people, scenery, or activities are being filmed. It is much easier and inexpensive to redo just the audio portion of a video than to keep reshooting people speaking their lines on camera. The fewer the takes, the less expensive the video.

COMPUTER-ASSISTED INSTRUCTION

Computer-assisted instruction (CAI) has a number of advantages over other formats. It can save staff time devoted to repetitive instruction by providing asynchronous instruction, available anywhere and at any time for initial use or review. Some CAI programs promise interactivity, color, movement, and the ability to utilize a simulation for parts or all of the material to be learned. However, creating simulations can be a quicksand approach to ILI if you want to develop such a program yourself, as it can draw you into a potentially enormous and costly project (Kaplowitz and Contini, 1998). If the authorware is fairly complex, it may mean additional expenditure and time for programmers and instructional designers to develop a fairly professional looking product and for librarians to review it for content. Meanwhile, interfaces may change dramatically in CAI as you are developing it. For staff training purposes, you may want to consider licensing CAI like Lynda.com (2008) rather than taking the time and trouble to try to develop and maintain CAI yourself. However, such licenses can be expensive and may or may not be available for all platforms (Mac, PC, etc.), and training can become outdated quickly. In addition, this format may not meet learning style preferences of all staff. For these reasons and more, many ILI instructors now rely on video and other formats that can be developed, edited, and utilized more quickly and easily than CAI.

DESIGNING WEB SITES AND WEB PAGES

Basic Design

After reviewing a number of instructional materials, online and in other formats, you may want to create some of your own. If you know how to use Web page authoring software like Adobe Dreamweaver (2008), you may want to start with a short, basic ILI-related Web site. Instructional Web sites can be just one page long or complex, with many different levels and categories of ILI-related help. You may even think that there are no IL-related Web pages on your library's Web site, and, indeed, they may not be labeled as such. However, the vast majority of library Web sites provide links to their library catalogs. Those catalogs usually provide some kind of online help or link to online help created by others, a form of ILI. How useful is that help to your users? This could be an area to investigate for additional or improved ILI help, particularly if your learner population has had trouble using your library catalog.

How will you know what sort of help your learner population needs and wants? Before creating instructional Web pages and Web sites, you need to determine the goals and expected learning outcomes for those pages through Needs Assessment, observation, and usability studies (Bell, 2008). In other words, you need to put in writing what you want learners to know and be able to do after using those Web pages or Web sites, just as you should do with any sort of instructional materials. It can take you some time to investigate and come to conclusions regarding needs, goals, and expected learning outcomes, particularly if you take into account the various ways that people learn and seek information (Westbrook, 2006). It will be worth your while to do this, however, as you may be surprised to discover that your learners have different levels of need. Some may not be computer literate and may need direct face-to-face help in figuring out what the Internet is, how to use a mouse, and how to move around on a Web page, as well as help on the Internet in general. Others may be quite experienced with a variety of technologies and interested in learning emerging technologies for information researching via the Web.

Once you have conducted and analyzed Needs Assessments for your learner populations, it will be easier to follow the first of four straightforward steps in actually creating Web pages and Web sites. Following these steps can also help you avoid the tendency to develop too large and complex a Web site that expands rapidly, wandering into areas of little use or interest to your learners (Duncan and Holliday, 2008). One Web designer even recommends cutting existing Web sites down by 80 percent and just keeping those elements that are absolutely essential and that support users' mental models (Hoekman, 2007).

1. Decide what you want to appear on a Web page, or Web site, keeping in mind the advantages of
    a. minimal text,
    b. "actionable content" (Nielsen, 2008a),
    c. clear and simple language that avoids jargon,
    d. easy navigation through as flat an architecture as possible, and
    e. graphics that enhance rather than clutter up and distract.
2. Outline and storyboard the site so you can see its architecture.
3. Write instructions (by using HTML tags or a Web authoring program like Dreamweaver or by creating a Microsoft Word document and saving it as a Web page) for what you want to appear on the page, how it should look, and how various parts of it should behave.
4. Save the page, view it with a Web browser, test it with users, and be sure to try out all of its features yourself, as if you were the user.

The two most challenging tasks may be steps 1 and 3, deciding what should appear on a Web page or Web site and writing instructions for it. You may not know how to accomplish either of these steps intuitively, but do not worry. Keep in mind that many creative people are developing Web-based instruction materials, so it may not be necessary to create everything from scratch. If there is an excellent and concise Web page or site that meets the needs of the primary learner group, regardless of the level or purpose for which it was originally designed, why not request permission to link to it? Just make sure to provide some kind of indication that this link will take the user off site. It would also be helpful to indicate how to return, or make the link open in a popup window. This is important, because, when links open in new windows, it is easy for users to get lost if they try to go back to a previous page by clicking on the Back button. Nothing happens when they do this, because the new page does not retain the search history from the original page.

In addition, there are many Web design books, articles (McDermott, 2007), Web pages, YouTube videos (barryrunner, 2007), and blogs (Scocco, 2007) you can consult and classes you can take to learn tips and tricks about Web site design (Hoekman, 2007; Nielsen, 2008b). The "HTML Links" (W3Schools, 2008) page offers links to many examples of basic tags and how they make text appear. This brief lesson may help you see that logic rather than magic is behind the Web page "curtain." But if you still do not want to learn how to use HTML to create Web pages, you may be able to build on the work of others rather than creating Web pages entirely from scratch. HTML, Hypertext Markup Language, is the basic programming language that uses "tags" like <table>, <form>, and <font>. These tags tell Web browsers like Firefox and Internet Explorer how to display Web pages, and which actions to take, based on particular prompts. You can identify elements of pages you like, view the page source, and then copy and paste it into your own page (with permission) or examine the source code to see how the page elements were designed (Snyder, 2008).

Macromedia's Dreamweaver can be a very handy and versatile Web authoring tool, as well. It allows you to view and work with both HTML code and "design" (the way the page will appear in a Web browser). Dreamweaver also allows you to FTP pages directly to a server to which you have access (transfer them remotely by using "file transfer protocol"). It then automatically "updates" (adjusts) links within those pages to match the server location where the files have been FTPed (Adobe Dreamweaver, 2008). It is important to update links within Web pages, as the links are like directions to a particular address on a street. Each URL tells your Web browser where to find a particular Web page within a hierarchical series of folders. This is the HTML code that tells a browser to go to the Web page "Top Twenty-five of LIRT's Top Twenty Instruction Articles" (ALA. LIRT, 2003):

```
<a href="http://www3.baylor.edu/LIRT/top25.htm">
Top Twenty-Five of LIRT's Top Twenty Instruction
Articles</a>
```

The **<a>** tag is an "anchor." It is followed by **href**, an equal sign, and the URL in quotes. This tells your browser to go to that Web address when you click on "Top Twenty-five of LIRT's Top Twenty Instruction Articles." The **</a>** is a tag indicating the end of this instruction to the browser. The URL itself indicates three levels. The first level (**www3.baylor.edu**) is the main site, in this case, Baylor University, which is hosting the LIRT Web site. The second level is a folder within the Baylor University site. That folder is a Web site indicated by: **LIRT/**. The last item is a Web page with the file name **top25.htm.** This hierarchy tells your Web browser to go to the Baylor University Web site, look for the LIRT folder, and, within the LIRT folder, look for the Web page with the title "top25.htm." W3Schools (2008) provides more information on HTML linking, along with examples.

A number of other commonly used tools also make it fairly easy to insert hyperlinks like this without having to remember or type in HTML tags. In Microsoft Word, and in Blogger, for instance, you can easily create links in documents and blog postings by using menu commands or icons to do so. Just highlight the characters or images you want to be linked to other Web sites, images, videos, etc. In Word go to the Insert menu, select "Hyperlink" and enter the URL to which you want to link. In Blogger, highlight whatever you want to be turned into a link, click on the icon for hyperlink, and insert a URL. The systems will then insert the appropriate HTML tags to create these links.

Enhancements like these and tools like Dreamweaver are making it easier and easier to create and update Web pages. If you or other library staff decide to create your own Web pages, though, you must be aware of some common pitfalls. First, it is very easy to get carried away and put too much material on a single Web page or even on an entire Web site. Be wary of simply putting on a Web page all of the words you would speak in an in-person instructional session. Pare down text and do some usability testing, revising iterative versions as you test with three naive learners at a time (Nielsen, 2000a, 2008b). Do learners finish reading everything on your pages? Are your pages engaging and easy to follow?

Second, it is quite simple to view the HTML code for a Web page and then copy and paste it into your own page. You can copy graphics quite easily as well, but for text, design, or graphics, you must be wary of using the intellectual property of others without their permission. Even small items you may think of as clip art, like Web page buttons, may be an artist's source of income. A Google search under "free clip art" or a Flickr search for images with a Creative Commons license will retrieve many sources of freely usable graphics and help you avoid this problem. There are also many Web page templates and other freely available Web items and tutorials you can use fairly easily. ("Open Source Web Design," 2008; A.N.T.S., 2008). For more on copyright, see Chapter 9.

You need to consider, too, how much time and effort you can afford to invest on your own to learn Web page/Web site creation skills. While it is not difficult to create a simple, basic Web page, if you want to include animation, video screen captures, and more complex graphics, you may need to learn how to use more software like Adobe Photoshop (2008), Camtasia Studio (2008), Adobe Flash (2008), or Picasa (2008). In addition, for a Web site, you will still need to plan, design, develop, and test the entire site on naive users. Given the time investment required for all of this, it might be more worthwhile for you to come up with the learning outcomes expected, an outline, a storyboard, and other content and then hire a professional who will consult with you and prepare the Web pages or

Web site for you. It takes time to work with an expert Web designer or instructional designer, as well, in order to accomplish what you intend, but you may end up with a more useful, sophisticated, and professional product.

Of course, there is no guarantee that anyone will actually use your Web pages, no matter who prepares them or how much time or money you spend creating them. Your pages will be competing for "eyeballs" (attention) with many hundreds of thousands, if not millions, of others. To get and keep users' attention, you or someone you hire will need to put some time and effort into ensuring its quality. You will need to maintain your Web pages, updating links that die or move, revising content as instructional tools change, learning new Web development skills, and always striving to simplify and standardize. It is a never-ending process and you may very well tire of doing it on your own, especially if you are responsible for maintaining a number of pages. If you decide you need help with Web site maintenance or revision, keep in mind that students of many ages are "digital natives," those who have grown up with computers. They may be a wonderful source for technical aid in developing online ILI programs, including Web pages.

Instructional Web Page Design Principles

In a number of respects, guidelines for instructional Web site design are very similar to those for print materials. For starters, if "content is clearly king" for Web sites, in terms of both accuracy and completeness, then *need* is surely "emperor" (Stover and Zink, 1996). Do the primary learners need the site and why? What are the expected learning outcomes for the site and for each page? Storyboarding and brief outlines for each page and site maps diagramming site layout and structure can be very helpful in this regard (Fryer, 2001). You can do this quickly and easily by using free sites like WriteMaps (2008) or Jumpchart (2008). These sites allow you to create a hierarchy of Web pages for a site and move pages around simply by dragging and dropping. Like print materials, once the need for and content of a Web page have been identified and described in writing, important decisions remain, especially concerning layout, font, color, and other design considerations specific to the Web (McDermott, 2007).

Layout and Typeface

Web sites cry out for a consistent look and feel, for buttons and navigation bars that appear in the same place on each page within a site, for similarly styled graphics (cartoon-like, photographs, drawings, and so on), and for consistent use of fonts and colors. The principle of consistency applies to homepage layout too. Even if learners are computer literate and have used Web sites, many will look for a site search box when encountering unfamiliar sites (Nielsen, 2008b). Some mistake a library catalog search box on a library homepage for a site search box. Then, too, even if they intend to use the library's catalog, searching it by keyword may provide so many results that the user is overwhelmed and lost. This can happen because many people do not know how to limit their searches to controlled vocabulary subject headings, to specific types of materials, or to publication dates. Faceted browsing with many categories off to one side or tabbed results can also overwhelm someone used to simple Google searching. Added to this confusion is the fact that users do not understand that the library's catalog does not list periodical articles.

So, think carefully about what to put on your library's homepage. Consider it the equivalent of a store's main window, advertising its goods. Ideally, you would want to make the most important sections of your "store" visible and easy to use. After all, this is not just the realm of systems designers. As ILI librarians, many of us have direct and indirect experience with interfaces that help or confuse learners, including the library homepage and the library catalog, and can provide useful Web site design advice. The clearer and easier it is to use a system, the easier our jobs will be in helping learners grasp basic underlying frameworks and concepts, as well as mechanics of use.

If you agree with this rationale, consider the following approaches, some of which are controversial. Some may argue that basic library catalog searches could benefit in a number of ways from a single Google-like search box, as long as there is an Advanced Search available with additional options.

These could include options familiar to many users. In addition to subject headings, each library catalog record could have a link labeled "More like this," as well as options for user-generated tags, ratings, and comments. Individual records could link to maps showing shelf locations in a physical library. A link could also appear in each catalog record to a mash-up of Google Maps and Open WorldCat, making it much easier for anyone using your library catalog to locate a print copy of an item. If you add links to Google Books, or Amazon's "Search Inside This Book," learners may be able to get to all or part of a book online.

On the other hand, we do need to be wary of looking too much like Google so as to be indistinguishable from it. In designing search interfaces, we could take a page from some of the standardization that seems to be occurring with many databases. Some licensed databases and catalogs already offer three sets of search boxes, with a choice of "and," "or," and "not" vertically between each of the three layers. This could certainly improve the transferability of learning from the library catalog to commonly used databases and, with some publicity and branding, could illustrate distinctive benefits to searching library catalogs and licensed databases as opposed to general Web search tools or even Google Scholar.

We could also learn from businesses' Web experiences. In 2000, Jakob Nielsen recommended improving usability by standardizing and simplifying, for example, by using a shopping cart icon and concept for personalized selection (Nielsen, 2000b). This suggestion is still valid. When you search a library catalog or an online article database, instead of saying you are saving a "list" of items, just call it a "shopping cart." Instead of buying what's in your shopping cart, you can save copies of items by downloading them to a USB drive, printing, or e-mailing them.

Keep in mind that if we confuse people, if we do not ask them what they look for on library Web sites, if we design our Web sites for ourselves or to meet some artistic ideal, we will see fewer and fewer "eyeballs" (people visiting our sites). On the other hand, we do need to be wary of drawing conclusions strictly on the basis of usage statistics. Are people going to your library's homepage, catalog, or ILI site for short periods and then leaving? This may or may not mean that they are abandoning your site out of frustration but simply that they have found an answer or are leaving it for some other reason. We should not be surprised by the fact that some learners spend short periods of time on Web sites. Bouncing around from one site to another is simply the way some among the younger generation use the Web (British Library and JSIC, 2008). This is a particularly vexing problem these days, given the common perception that Google searches the entire universe of knowledge.

Color

Color choice is extremely important for Web sites, especially in backgrounds and for links and graphics. The "Web Designer's Color Reference Poster" (VisiBone, 2008) can be quite helpful with color selection, as it graphically illustrates 216 different colors supported by most Web browsers. Dark or heavily patterned backgrounds can be distracting and annoying to the point where users will avoid them if at all possible. Red lettering should be used sparingly on Web pages, and combinations of link colors and backgrounds should be checked for readability thoroughly on a variety of platforms and browsers before finalizing. Colorblindness may make it difficult for some to use Web pages as intended, as well. For instance, if you use red to emphasize one type of item and green to emphasize another, some people may not see the difference. McDermott (2007) offers a number of links to useful sites that will help you understand color theory and select harmonious colors for Web pages.

Differing browser displays add to the complexity of designing Web pages. No matter how hard you work at designing pages that have graphics of just the right size and color, in just the right position, and the most readable fonts for your page, learners may use browsers that display colors, graphics, fonts, tables, and other items differently from the way you intended or, in some cases, not at all. Older versions of browsers may not be able to display tables or frames. The images on your page may display when you use Firefox but not when you use Internet Explorer, Safari, or other browsers.

So, be sure to check your Web pages/Web sites in a variety of browsers to see how they display and then work on making improvements.

Usability and Accessibility

Now you know what goes on behind the Web pages that you see. It takes time and skill to create effective instructional Web sites. But even if you put much time and effort into designing and developing your ILI Web site, can you be sure that people will visit and learn from it? There are no guarantees of visits or of effective use. You will be competing with professional Web site designers and programmers developing hundreds of thousands of pages and sites, trying to get people's attention. And some of those people may not have all of the skills and abilities required to make effective use of your site. Some may have learning disabilities, may be colorblind, or have reduced vision or hearing, or they may not understand the idiom of a particular language. For these reasons and more, you need to be aware of important Web site accessibility issues to meet the U.S. Americans with Disabilities Act (ADA) requirements and the accessibility policies and requirements in other countries (W3C, 2006a). Web browsers utilized by those who are vision impaired cannot read tables or frames properly and may have problems reading some PDF documents. Turro (2008) describes these potential problems and includes some highly useful "checklists of checkpoints" for PDF document accessibility.

To help meet accessibility policies and standards, avoid frames and provide additional non-tables or text-only versions of Web pages, as well as alternative text for graphics. Alternate versions will also allow easier access by those with low-end hardware and software. Links labeled simply "Click here" do not provide useful information for the vision-impaired person using a reader, so make it a habit to use key words or phrases as links instead. Both abled and disabled learners also appreciate an easy way to enlarge text size on the screen, sometimes indicated by the following just above the page content: **AA**. Some screencasting software also allows you to create videos with captions, as an aid to those with hearing and learning disabilities. The Web Accessibility Initiative's (WAI) Web site is a treasure trove of links, including news, technology tools to check for accessibility, descriptions of how to change text and color in various browsers, and means of becoming involved in this area (W3C, 2006a, 2006b, 2008). ALA's Association of Specialized and Cooperative Library Agencies (ASCLA) also offers a highly useful accessibility toolkit related to electronic resources, "Think Accessible Before You Buy" (ALA. ASCLA, 2008).

What is the answer? Should you just put up your Web page as it is and then see if anyone uses it or has problems with it? In 2000, Nielsen described this as the mud-throwing approach, "throw it at the wall and see if it sticks!" (Nielsen, 2000c). As he pointed out, this is a tactic that may very well backfire, as anyone who even happens upon your poorly designed site and tries it may be so turned off they will not come back to it even if you make major improvements later (Cunningham, 1999; Nielsen, 2000a). Nielsen's advice is even more important today than it was in 2000. This is especially true given the explosion of all kinds of online information and a lack of patience with sites that make it difficult to find information quickly and easily.

Will throwing money at your Web site help? Maybe, but remember that the most important design factors for Web sites are usability and accessibility, so make sure that you have thought about and tested your Web site before mounting it publicly. Checking for accessibility using sites such as those listed on the W3C (2008) Web site and doing usability studies with your primary learner group(s) are essential, because you will find out what your users value and which areas you need to fix to improve ease of use (Nielsen, 1999a; ALA. LITA. Human/Machine Interface Interest Group, 2005). If you want design ideas, you might try Nielsen's (1999b) commonsense advice and look at the sites that get visited most often. What are they doing right? Can you identify any common design elements or approaches? For example, how many times does a user have to click on links before she gets to desired content? How does the site provide help? How successful are these sites in achieving their goals? For instructional sites you will need to test for learning outcomes as well if you want to determine the effectiveness of your site.

Many of these design considerations are similar to those for printed materials. Unlike print, however, the Web offers many advantages, but also some sand traps. For those with Internet access, most Web sites are available whenever and wherever there is a Net connection. Time and place are of little or no consequence for asynchronous Web use. This is a significant advantage for instruction, as, theoretically at least, users can get help when they most need it. The question remains as to whether the kind of help they can get is best suited for their needs.

Online Courses, Workshops, and Conferences

Are online courses worthy alternatives to in-person instruction? They are certainly growing in popularity. Many institutions and organizations offer synchronous or asynchronous online courses for credit, or as workshops or seminars, at various educational levels. About 700,000 K–12 students engaged in online courses in 2005–2006 ("Online Learning Booms as More States Expand and Plan Initiatives," 2007). The Sloan Consortium reports that in Fall 2006 close to 3.5 million students were taking an online course (Allen and Seaman, 2007). Some conferences, one-shot classes, and workshops are also completely online affairs offered synchronously through Webinars or in virtual worlds, with no face-to-face aspects at all (New Media Consortium, 2008). Others may be available as "mixed reality" events, offered simultaneously in virtual worlds and in real life; some offered in face-to-face settings may be replicated at a later time in a virtual environment. Workshops and Webinars may be offered through other commercial software systems, like Learning Times (accessed 2008), in real life or in virtual worlds like Second Life (accessed 2008).

Often, online credit courses are offered through CMS/ LMS, like WebCT (Blackboard, 2008), Sakai (2008), and Moodle (accessed 2008). CMS/LMS systems began as collections of various pieces of software, like a discussion board, a "homepage" where an instructor could place links to a syllabus, announcements, assignments, chat, and more. WebCT, one of the most widely used CMSs, was developed at about the same time as its competitor, Blackboard; then they merged in 2006 (Quick Takes, 2006). However, institutions were paying a lot of money to license these systems, and, at the same time, Linux (2008), wikis, and the open source movement were taking off. As a result, a number of institutions banded together to develop Sakai and Moodle. These open source CMS frameworks for various types of applications offer exciting possibilities for everyone involved in teaching, training, and learning, as we shall see in Chapters 15 and 16. (See Grassian and Kaplowitz, 2005, Chapter 3, "Embracing Cooperation and Change," for more on collaboration and partnership, and Chapter 8, "Learning to Manage Technology," for more on instructional partnerships and other details regarding technology management.)

Fully online courses offer many benefits, including access for distant learners who may be fully employed or, literally, may be too distant to benefit from such courses otherwise. Learners also appreciate the convenience of online instruction and the ability to move along at their own pace (Tallent-Runnels et al., 2006). However, learners who take online courses can feel lost or left out, particularly when taking asynchronous courses, as there may be little sense of community and connectedness with other learners or with the instructor. Drawbacks include "distance," lack of personal interaction and belonging. Is there a middle way? Some research indicates that blended or hybrid instruction is more popular and effective than either fully online or fully in-person instruction and that students learn more in well-designed online courses (Twigg, 2003; Tallent-Runnels et al., 2006). Can and should you turn your in-person courses into blended courses? If so, why and how? (Chickering and Gamson, 1987; Grassian et al., 2005; TLT Group, 2008a). From 1999 to 2003, Pew funded research into blended instruction by offering Requests for Proposals for academic instructors in colleges and universities to convert their in-person courses to blended courses (NCAT, 2005b). Twigg (2003) describes the five types of blended instruction courses that resulted, ranging from simple tacked-on uses of technology to complete course and assignment transformation.

In order to take an online course, you need to have access to a computer with an Internet connection. However, access and connectivity, in and of

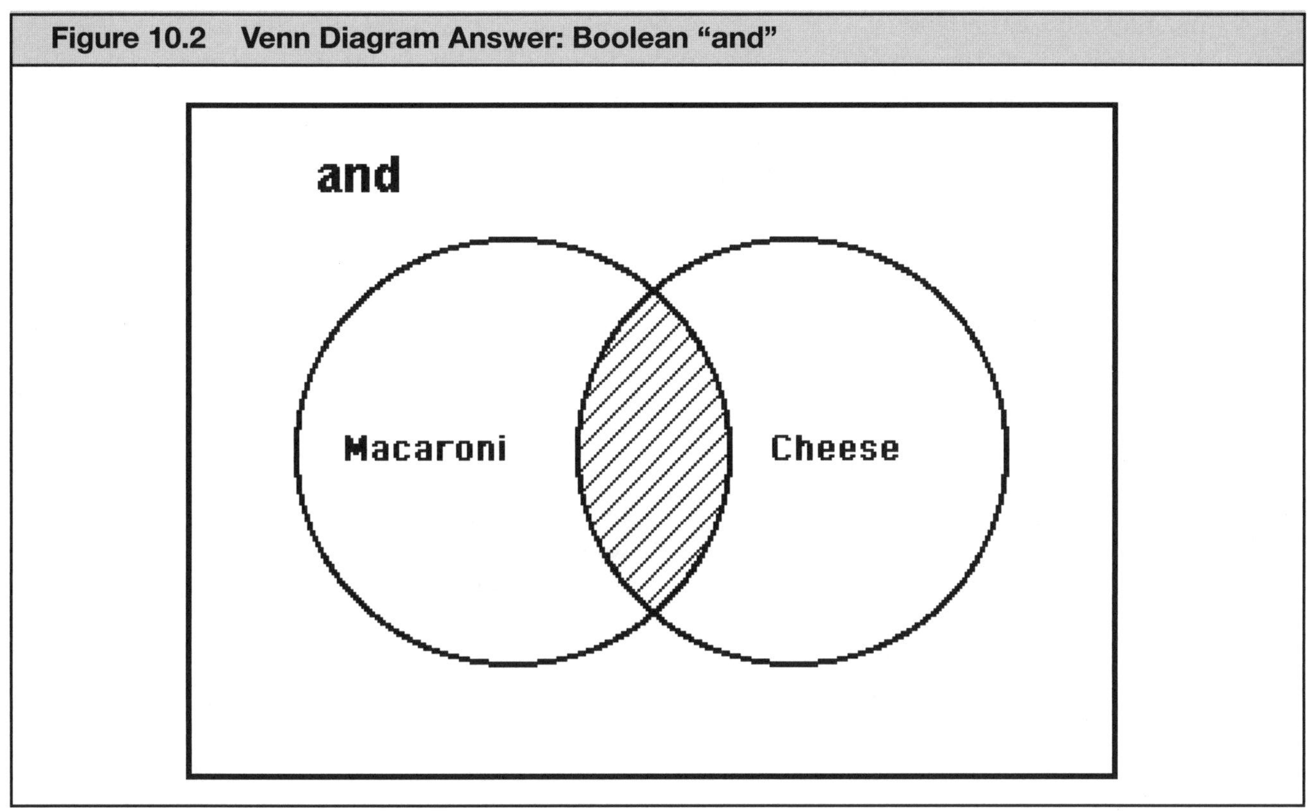

Figure 10.2 Venn Diagram Answer: Boolean "and"

themselves, do not always equate to access to a particular site or even to specific information on a site. The disabled and those with older hardware and software or low-end dial-up connections may not be able to utilize the snazziest and newest features, such as video streaming, and graphics-intensive materials. Be wary of frames and tables, because some users may not have hardware or software capable of displaying these features or may be visually handicapped and rely on a reader for content. If you use more advanced features, be sure to provide text-only alternative pages as well. Also, remember to use "alternative text" for any graphics included on a Web site, again for the benefit of the visually impaired. The example in Figure 10.2 is an image of a Venn diagram illustrating the Boolean operator "and." The HTML code for this image includes the following to describe an image that Web page readers utilized by those who are visually impaired can read: alt="Venn diagram and".

```
<img src="/library/modules/Find/Connector-
sAND.jpg" alt="Venn diagrams and" width="376"
height="228"><br>and</b>
```

This will certainly mean more time in the planning and development stages, but it is essential to provide these easily accessible alternatives to high-tech Web sites both for equal access at the lower end and for adherence to U.S. ADA regulations and policies regarding the disabled in other countries.

Even if they can navigate to your Web pages, visitors to a site can feel lost in "verbiage" (Duncan and Holliday, 2008). Given the fact that there is little or no cost to providing lengthy, wordy materials on the Web, there is a great temptation simply to transcribe the contents of an oral presentation or lecture to a Web site. As a result, some Web site content providers fall into the trap of using overly wordy expositions or lengthy conversational-style discourse when simple instructive language would do. A good way to avoid this problem is to pretend that each Web page is a print handout with very limited space, and sparingly use only those words essential for basic understanding.

If your Web site consists of multiple pages, carefully examine every sentence and every word on each Web page, keeping in mind the goal of each page. Try to delete as many words as possible and still maintain the integrity or core of the Web page, using graphics or icons in place of words if possible. Break long pages up into smaller chunks or provide a table of contents at the top or side of the Web page, and also provide an easy way to get back to the table of contents once you are deep into the page. If Web pages are broken into smaller chunks, though, try to provide content that is no more than three easily navigable steps or clicks away.

Visitors may get annoyed and frustrated when images load slowly and may abandon a site rather than wait to see the images. If text is located well below a large image, visitors may not even realize that scrolling down will provide them with some information while they are waiting for images to appear. One solution is to define the height and width of the image, using HTML tags. The browser then recognizes the size of the image, sets aside space for it, and continues to bring in the rest of the page without waiting for the entire image to download first. Another solution is to place brief text above or next to images and to try to keep image size down.

Some Web site visitors may enter a site at a level below the homepage, which would be like receiving only the middle page of a multipaged paper handout. The visitor is once again lost, wondering where this page came from, what its purpose is, and how to get to the starting point. When the Web was fairly new, Tennant (1997) recommended that we avoid this problem by abolishing "linear thinking" because we really cannot know how a visitor may arrive at or use our site. He said that it is important to design all pages so that each can be used or understood independently of the remainder of the site.

While avoiding linear thinking remains a worthy goal, linearity still has its place on the Web. This is particularly true for instructional Web sites where the goal is to help users learn the mechanics of using a system or database, as mentioned in regard to paper handouts. However, you do need to be wary of creating lengthy, linear exercises that require the user to continue answering a specific series of questions in order to progress through each segment of an exercise in order. Users may feel lost and helpless, or lose patience, and may end up abandoning the exercise completely rather than go through every part of it. Whatever the goal of the site, it is important to allow users the option of skipping around within a site in order to self-select for their individual learning needs. Learning modules offer a compromise solution and resemble the concept of in-person group instruction modules. Learning use of a new library catalog may be broken down into basic and advanced searching modules, as well as other modules on saving and e-mailing results. Again, following the rule of three can be helpful here. Try to have no more than three linear steps in an exercise before allowing the user to proceed to whichever segment of the exercise she or he would like to try next.

How much content should you include? What is the maximum number of instructional "chunks" for effective learning? How many separate pages should one have on a single site, and how much content is too much for a single page? Nielsen's (2008a) research indicates that often users read Web sites quickly by scanning through them and, at most, read 28 percent of the words on a Web page during a typical visit. Determining a happy balance in terms of text, numbers of pages, modules, graphics, and other features can be difficult, just as it may be difficult to determine balance in all sorts of instruction. Again, this is where user input, examples of effective and well-designed instructional Web sites, as well as some publications on Web site design created especially for libraries can be extremely helpful (Dewald, 1999; McDermott, 2007; Breeding, 2008).

What about online interactive materials? Effective online exercises and tutorials, at the very least, should meet the standards we impose on these materials in other media. They need to fulfill important purposes in an interesting or even captivating way. The learners need to have a good chance of succeeding if they try the exercise or tutorial out, and they need to get as much immediate feedback as possible. Ideally, both groups and individuals would be able to use online materials, and the materials would be available in different forms, depending on the audience size, experience level, age, or other characteristics.

Graphics design, backgrounds, fonts, images and other artwork, as well as layout, present additional dilemmas for Web site designers, regarding copyright and intellectual property, as well as design. Chapter 9 offers some basic copyright guidance for ILI, and general Web site design publications can be helpful, those published both in print and on the Internet (Hoekman, 2007; Nielsen, 2000a, accessed 2008). Tufte's five basic data graphics principles can be applied quite usefully to the Web as well. We have already mentioned two of them—"Erase nondata ink" (eliminate irrelevant or needlessly elaborate information) and "Erase redundant data ink" (eliminate repetitive information). The remaining three are (Tufte, 1983: 105):

- Above all else show the data.
- Maximize the data/ink ratio.
- Revise and edit.

"Above all else show the data" translates into identifying the key points you wish to get across and highlighting them unmistakably. "Maximize the data/ink ratio" is a call for simplicity and clarity. The BUBL Information Service's homepage for example, looks simple and clean (BUBL LINK, 2007). "Revise and edit" seems self-evident, and yet there is so much we would like our users to know, so much help we would like to provide them. With few space and size restrictions, we may use overly elaborate words, too many words, too many repetitive instructions or descriptions, too small a font size, too many graphics, too many frames, too many glitzy features like blinking or rotating images, and so on.

Personalized and Customized Web Sites and Portals

How can we, much less our users, sort through all of this? Some suggest that personally customized instructional Web sites or specialized portals geared to specific groups of users would allow each to pick and choose the kinds of help she or he wants to use or revisit (Liu, 2008). Personalized Web sites like MySpace and Facebook are popular, but they do have drawbacks, some of which may not be immediately obvious. For one, learners would have to take the time to sort through and then pick and choose among the kinds of help we have to offer. It may be some time, in fact, before these sites have a variety of options, from "stripped down" minimalist help to the equivalent of an entire course, or something in between.

In another vein, one study indicated that instructor use of a Facebook account may make her or him seem more approachable, especially to shy learners who would otherwise feel uncomfortable asking questions. The study authors warn instructors to be consistent, however, in terms of their personal portrayal on Facebook and their behaviors and attitudes in teaching, as learners may judge instructors' credibility based on self-disclosure through this popular social networking site. In turn, this can lead to a positive or negative affective reaction among learners (Mazer, Murphy, and Simonds, 2007). Other personalized sites like portals also offer benefits as well as drawbacks.

Portals geared to particular groups sound useful on the surface, but portal designers may make a lot of assumptions about the interests, skills, and abilities of those characterized as special portal audiences. Undergraduates span a huge range, for instance, from the first-time freshman who needs to learn about the library catalog, reserves, and library locations for materials, to seniors working on honors theses or serving as paid researchers for faculty members. When we steer learners to portals, supposedly designed just for their cohort, we deny them the opportunity to view and explore the entire range of research tools available and then select for themselves.

In 2000, a study indicated that librarians tend to be highly enthusiastic about personalized library Web sites, while users generally are not. However, the same study found that both learners and librarians make good use of class Web pages created by ILI librarians to meet the needs of particular courses, especially in colleges and universities (Ghaphery and Ream, 2000). Interestingly, a 2007 study regarding personalized and customizable portals for undergraduates came to the same conclusions regarding student attitudes (Mellinger and Nichols, 2007). A compromise approach might be to identify research tools that may be of interest for particular purposes and educational levels, use icons to identify those tools, and allow learners to sort, resort, and tag items or even to create these sorts of subject guides themselves, perhaps as a group project. Learners greatly appreciate the time-saving shortcuts, including recommended databases, tutorials, and links to reference materials like citation style guides. ILI librarians appreciate having a template where they can fill in all of these items easily, without having to learn and use HTML.

It seems logical, then, to capitalize on the features of this approach that most interest learners: focused pages created by librarians for particular groups at specific times. These pages need not be limited to higher education. In spring or summer each year, public libraries might want to develop Web pages for parents considering schools in which to enroll their children or online courses for home schooling that go beyond a list of links or links with descriptions. Online homework help pages might be easier for public library librarians to create and maintain if they have templates they can use for this purpose.

ILI librarians might consider developing a page with links to articles regarding points to consider when selecting a school or an online course and links to AASL's IL standards (ALA. AASL, 1998a, 2007b). High school library media centers might do the same for colleges and universities, with a link, instead, to the "Information Literacy Competency Standards for Higher Education" on the ACRL Web site (ALA. ACRL, 2000). Academic libraries, public libraries, and high school library media centers might link to consumer health information suitable for their user populations, like MedlinePlus (U.S. National Library of Medicine and National Institutes of Health, 2008), highlighting the need for caution in relying on Web-based health sites, and linking to Web evaluation criteria. Special libraries might consider offering workbook-type ILI tutorials during new employee orientations, and academic libraries could do the same for new faculty and Teaching Assistant orientations, as well as for new students. All sorts of libraries might consider reaching out to potential students, parents, and employees at critical times of the year with information, helpful links, and recommended, evaluated information sources suited to specific needs of that population group, including a variety of career-related links. Pages like this could include links to a variety of materials, including podcasts and videos—that is, multimedia instruction and help.

LibGuides (2008), a commercial software program, offers a popular fee-based approach to creating specialized Web pages like these. Free open source alternatives, where programming code is available freely for review and adaptation, are also available or in development, including "SubjectsPlus" (Ithaca College Library, accessed 2008), and "Library a la Carte" (Oregon State University Libraries, accessed 2008). As these types of guides become more robust, librarians are sharing their completed templates with others. Interesting LibGuides examples include those created at Loyola Marymount University (Hoffner and Slater, 2007), the Burlington County (NJ) Library System (accessed 2008) (a public library), the NASA Glenn Science and Engineering Library (accessed 2008) (a special library), and the Northfield Mount Herman (MA) School Library (accessed 2008). "SubjectsPlus" examples include Elmira College's (2008) Gannett-Tripp Library, the CUNY Graduate Center's (2008) Mina Rees Library, and the University of Victoria Libraries (2008). "Library a la Carte" offers templates for subject guides and course guides, with a number of Oregon State University Libraries (2004a, 2004b) examples of both. Usability studies can help libraries trying to decide which of these alternatives would work best for their learners within the context of the cost and the time commitment needed to create and maintain them.

SOCIAL SOFTWARE

As with any type of technology, before plunging into designing and using social software, you need to decide why you would want to use it, ideally based on a Needs Assessments of your user population(s) and staff. In Chapter 15, we discuss various types of social software, including their pros and cons, and how you may want to use them yourself or offer them to your learners. Farkas (2007) provides informative detailed descriptions and library uses for many types of social software, including blogs, RSS feeds, wikis, online communities, social bookmarking, podcasts, and screencasts.

Many of these social software tools and resources are available via the Internet. This means that you should consider many of the principles described earlier for designing Web pages when designing social software tools—layout and typeface, color, usability, and accessibility. In the following sections, we describe some additional design considerations specific to a few examples of currently popular social software tools.

Blogs and RSS Feeds

In a sense, blogs consist of ongoing conversations arranged in reverse chronological order. In order to maintain interest in your blog, you should update it regularly with brief postings that focus on meeting the needs of your intended audience (Bell, 2007). Rather than simply copying and pasting information from listserv messages or Web sites, consider how you would add value to your blog postings. Pose a question or point out a particularly relevant aspect of the information you are posting, and provide live links directly to other sites for additional information.

Thanks to simple interfaces now available for blogs, you can compose blog posts fairly quickly and easily without needing to know HTML. You can embed links in your blog posts, as well. Once you have composed a blog post or comment, it would be wise to preview it for typographical or other errors before posting to the blog. You may add postings to a blog at a later time to update, correct, or clarify previous posts, but you cannot alter previous blog postings.

If you set up a blog yourself, you will be the administrator or manager of that blog. This means that you will be able to select various settings for your blog, including who can post to it, who can comment, and whether or not it is a public blog. Keep in mind, too, that if your blog is public, searches in Google and other search engines may retrieve your postings.

Most blogs provide an icon you can click on in order to sign up for an RSS feed. This means that rather than going to visit a number of blogs to check for new postings or comments, any messages posted to those blogs will appear in a syndication service or aggregator Web site, like Google Reader (2008), Bloglines (2008), or NetNewsWire (2008). You can also subscribe to blogs through the aggregator you use, even if the blogs you are interested in do not have an RSS feed icon.

Wikis

Unlike blogs, wikis provide opportunities for people to collaborate remotely on individual documents. This means that you can post a document and invite others to make changes to it or post new documents, which can also be changed. This is one way to avoid e-mailing numerous versions of a document back and forth between two or more people. You can set up a passworded wiki or a public wiki, using free wiki software.

Regardless of which wiki software you choose to use, check to be sure that it will retain a history of editing changes so that you can revert to an earlier version if need be (Farkas, 2007). Wikipedia (accessed 2008), for instance, allows anyone to edit most of its pages, and you can see what those changes have been over time by clicking on the History tab for any given page. The "Wiki Choice Wizard" (WikiMatrix, accessed 2008) can help you select from among over a hundred free and licensed wikis, based on the features you would like. The WYSIWYG (What You See Is What You Get) editing feature, for instance, allows you to apply formatting to a document and see that formatting as it will appear when the document is printed. If you use a wiki that does not have a WYSIWYG feature, you may need to reformat documents for the final version by using a word processing application.

DESIGNING MULTIMEDIA

A mix of instructional formats is often interesting and appealing to learners used to sound bites, videos, videogames, motion, and "performances." Learners can take control of their own learning if they are able to pick and choose from a variety of instructional materials and approaches. We can offer separate paper, online, or other audiovisual instruction from which learners can pick. Multimedia instruction, on the other hand, can offer a mix of paper and electronic materials within a single instructional framework, such as a synchronous Webinar, or a synchronous or asynchronous course that links to podcasts, videos, interactive or printable exercises, PDF handouts, blogs, discussion boards, and online communities. Interactivity, in itself, can take many forms and is not new, as the late Douglas Adams (1999: online) reminds us:

> "[I]nteractivity" is one of those neologisms . . . the reason we suddenly need such a word is that during this century we have for the first time been dominated by *non*-interactive forms of entertainment: cinema, radio, recorded music and television. Before they came along *all* entertainment was interactive: theatre, music, sport—the performers and audience were there together, and even a respectfully silent audience exerted a powerful shaping presence on the unfolding of whatever drama they were there for. We didn't need a special word for interactivity in the same way that we don't (yet) need a special word for people with only one head.

Moreno and Mayer (2007: 311) identify five different types of interactivity: "dialoguing, controlling, manipulating, searching, and navigating." They also identify five important multimedia instructional design principles: "guided activity, reflection, feedback, pacing, and pretraining" (Moreno and Mayer, 2007: 315). Some of these principles are covered in Chapters 5 and 6. It bears repeating, however, that attention to all of these principles can help improve the effectiveness of many types of instruction. If you are creating an instructional video, for instance, be sure to allow learners to start and stop it at any point, to control the speed, and to start again from the beginning or at any point.

It can take a lot of time, money, and energy to develop many types of interactive multimedia instructional materials. As we have seen in Chapters 5 and 6, interactivity can help learners construct knowledge in the form of mental models, but, as Moreno and Mayer (2007) also point out, we cannot assume that interactivity and multimedia instruction guarantee learning and understanding, particularly as learners may become overwhelmed by the content, the number of choices, and the variety of interactivity offered. We need to pay attention to research findings and multimedia design principles like these as we define expected learning outcomes and plan and develop instruction that incorporates multimedia and interactivity (Mayer, 2005c, 2005d). Then we need to test and assess for achievement of those learning outcomes in order to evaluate the usefulness of these materials.

How many different kinds and formats of instructional materials should you use to meet the same pedagogical goals for the same audience? For in-person synchronous group instruction, you may want to use a presentation slide show to display an outline of the session, illustrate a couple of points, and, at the end of the session, do a review. In between, you might lecture a bit and do a demonstration with the learners following along on workstations. Then you might have them do a paper exercise, show a short video clip or streaming video, and set up small or large group exercises. Some freely available movies are quite dramatic and can set the stage for discussion. *EPIC 2015* is a nine-minute movie about Google joining with Amazon.com and together "eating up" other news media and using personal information about individuals to offer only individually customized news portals (Sloan and Thompson, accessed 2008). Watching this movie in person or remotely can lead to some very intense and important discussion on critical IL-related issues, including privacy, confidentiality, and intellectual property. As previously mentioned in this chapter, you can spark this kind of discussion by stopping the video at critical junctures and asking learners to tell you what sorts of controversy a particular point illustrates and their views on that issue.

All of this requires careful planning, timing, and pacing to avoid losing learners with a scattershot approach, however. This is especially important for sessions that are scheduled for specific lengths of time, often a single 50-minute to 2-hour guest session. Remote instruction, too, may work best with a mixed or blended approach. There are many ways to offer blended or hybrid instruction, which can include a range of various combinations of online and in-person instruction. Even before online instruction was available, though, in the early 1960s, Patricia Knapp (1966) held preliminary and then debriefing sessions for learners, in-person, before and after they completed exercises on their own (remotely). Mimi Dudley (1978) also built in-person reference desk interaction into her workbook program throughout the 1970s, also completed by individuals on their own (remotely). Successful online courses utilize a variety of approaches, including chat, exercises, discussion boards, and group and individual assignments, some taking place in virtual worlds like Second Life (accessed 2008). Even traditional in-person lecture-type courses for large numbers of students may include discussion board interaction and group chats, as well as guest lecturers who may appear live in person or via chat.

ILI Web site designers may also want to offer text or voice chat for synchronous online classes or text messaging or instant messaging for reference questions. These services allow you to send messages in real time to and from computers, cell phones, and virtual worlds like Second Life (accessed 2008). If the recipient is online at the time and has signed up for one of these services, these brief messages then pop up on the recipient's screen in a small window. The recipient can then respond, in essence having a synchronous—at the same time—live "conversation" with the original sender but without waiting for a response. In other words, both sender and recipient can send messages to each other close to simultaneously, in real time. Meebo (2008) is an example of a popular free instant messaging service that allows you to sign in to any of a number of accounts via the Web, including AOL Instant Messenger (AIM, accessed 2008) and Google Talk (2008). This may or may not work out for instruction in every case, because for instructional purposes the sender would have to understand that there may not be an instant response. However, chat, instant messaging, text messaging, and other services, such as Twitter (2008), Facebook (2008), and Second Life (accessed 2008), present an evolving set of options that we should experiment with for ILI.

With all of these modes, you may also want to provide printed point-of-use guides and search logs so that learners can pick and choose the forms of instruction that appeal to them most. Sometimes, though, we may have to simply give learners as much of a variety of materials as we have the time, staff, and money to develop well, in the hope that one or more may appeal and sink in.

BACKUP PLANS AND PROCESS

"If anything can go wrong, it will" (Murphy's Law) most definitely applies to instructional materials. Handouts become outdated; presentation software ceases to function or will not open at critical junctures; Web servers go down; interfaces change at a moment's notice or with no notice at all; and network connections fail. These are just facts of life in the technological age. Instead of panicking when they happen, you may as well expect them and have some contingency plans, especially if you have just one chance to teach or help someone learn.

Salvaging Outdated Materials

You may be able to reuse portions of outdated handouts, presentation slide shows, and other ILI materials even if there have been drastic changes in what you are trying to teach. In some cases, you might just need to make a few updates, checking examples and interfaces. Perhaps you can still use a handout or some of the slides in a presentation slide show to teach users how to mail Web pages even if you suddenly have to use a new version of a Web browser. Like encyclopedias, not all portions of software are automatically changed with each upgrade or new version. At the very least, you might be able to use that handout or slide show to structure your session or to help users learn how to approach a piece of software or an online information researching tool. When using a handout, you can draw their attention to the fact that the handout begins with the top of the window and works its way down from there. Then learners might begin exploring a new piece of software in the same fashion, by pulling down each menu and exploring the options listed, and continue by experimenting with buttons and other icons. Or you might point out that the handout has some specific goals in mind, for example, to help you learn the basics of searching, displaying, and saving information retrieved from a database.

Preparing for Nonfunctioning Presentation Software

It is always a good idea to prepare a "speaker's outline" handout listing the main points you are planning to cover in a presentation slide show. The outline helps learners see the structure of the session and eliminates the need to take extensive notes. When the software fails, the outline can serve as a reminder of what you were planning to cover, and parts of it could be used without the software. You might have some in-class exercises ready to go in case of a software failure and then ask the group which they would like to try out. Remember that you do not need to have a live connection to the Internet to use Microsoft PowerPoint or some other presentation software packages. In fact, you can download a presentation to a disk and take with you a separate free copy of the Microsoft PowerPoint Reader software that allows you to view and display PowerPoint slide shows even if you do not have Microsoft Office software or if your Office software is not functioning properly. If you create a presentation using a free Web-based application like Zoho (2008), you can use it anywhere you have an Internet connection, as the site will store your presentation on its own servers ("cloud computing"). For more on using technology to support pedagogy, see Chapter 15.

What to Do When the Web Server Is Down

Offline browser software like "WebWhacker" (2008) allow you to download and save copies of Web pages with their associated images and view them even when you are not connected to the Internet. So, when the Web server goes down in the middle of a session, you can switch over to a "canned" set of pages. You may also be able to alternate between these pages and a presentation software show (for text-based information using clip art and other features, such as slide transitions) just as though you had a live connection. Video screen captures utilizing software like Camtasia Studio (2008), Adobe Captivate (2008), or Jing (2008) can also be a lifesaver if you lose an Internet connection or if you must teach in a location where you cannot get a live connection. As mentioned earlier, capturing and producing videos allows users to see every step and click as you demonstrate database searching. Quiz questions embedded in the movie can be used as a large group exercise.

On the other hand, if you have a connection but cannot get to a particular site, check to see if Google has a "cached" copy of the page you want to show. Or, just type a URL into the Internet Archive's (accessed 2008) "Wayback Machine" search box and get links to all versions of the page. YouTube (2008), PRIMO (ALA. ACRL. IS, 2008e), and A.N.T.S. (2008) also offer video options. Someone else may have already created a video that would work well as an alternative to a live demo or hands-on session. Connection problems also offer a good opportunity to point out to learners that they should allow enough time to complete their assignments, as these kinds of failures can happen to anyone at any time.

Preparing for Unexpected Changes in Web Interface or Content

At some point you may face one of the most interesting and challenging "teaching emergencies"—unexpected changes to a familiar, tried and true Web site. What do you do when all of a sudden it does not look or act as it has in the past? You will need to practice diplomacy and nimble footwork, and have a good sense of humor about it. Depending on the extent of the changes, you may be able to recoup and continue instruction by quickly scanning menus and buttons to locate the most critical functions you were planning to teach. Tell the learners that you are surprised and ask them to help, but spend as little time as possible fumbling around while a large group watches. Patience is thin when the instructor does not seem to be in charge.

You may be able to turn this situation into an important teachable moment, though, as it will give you the opportunity to remind learners to print copies of important and useful Web pages, as they may change or disappear at any moment. Printouts will provide them with URLs and Web page titles and document what the learner saw when doing Web-based research. If all else fails, have some active learning activities or exercises with you and use them if necessary or simply skip over this portion of the session and go on to something else after explaining to the learners that sometimes that is just the way it works with the Web. You must be patient and flexible and allow lots of extra time for connection, distraction, and unexpected pitfalls.

What to Do When the Network Connection Fails

Failed network connections can make us all realize how much we have come to depend on computers for teaching and learning. It is important to note, though, that teaching and learning can go on and pedagogical goals can be met without computers. When network connections are down, you can teach with overheads or a whiteboard and paper handouts. This does not mean you have to draw complete copies of Web pages on the board, but you can pose questions to a group, for example, asking which commands they would type or which buttons they would click in order to do a keyword search. You might pose a couple of command options and ask what each would retrieve. Or you might just draw some Venn diagrams on a board and teach Boolean operators, go through a small group topic selection exercise, mind-map topic words, etc.

No matter what the computer glitch happens to be, or how many of them there are, just try to keep cool, maintain a sense of humor, and connect with the learners any way you can. They will feel a lot better about their own computer glitches if they see you handle these almost inevitable problems with aplomb.

FINAL REMARKS

This chapter has focused on the practical aspects of designing print and electronic/electric instructional materials that you have presumably selected based on your pedagogical goals and objectives or expected learning outcomes. Some of these design guidelines may be familiar to you, while others may be new. In fact, many may seem straightforward and oversimplified. It is often the case, though, that the clearest, most simply designed materials can take enormous time and effort to develop. When they are completed and ready for use, learners and teachers alike may take them for granted or may consider them simplistic or too elementary, yet they can make an enormous difference in ensuring that significant learning takes place. After all, is that not our ultimate goal?

EXERCISES

1. Locate an instructional Web site that is not interactive. Come up with one simple and inexpensive way to make it interactive. What mechanisms could be utilized for feedback to the learners?
2. Identify a paper handout that has an online equivalent. In what ways are they the same? What is lost or gained by each format?
3. Compare your institution's library catalog help function to that of a Web search tool of your choice. Which features are most essential for each? Which features need improvement, and how would you improve them?
4. Compare three instructional Web sites. Are there features that make them easier to use? Are there features that interfere with use and learning? Do they suggest a standardized approach in terms of help, navigation, icons, layout, learning options (text, video, podcast, etc.)?
5. Compare and contrast an IL video and an IL Web site that have the same or similar goals and objectives.
6. Analyze accessibility (usage capabilities for the disabled) for an interactive and a passive instructional Web site. How could they be improved?

READ MORE ABOUT IT

Farkas, Meredith G. 2007. *Social Software in Libraries.* Medford, NJ: Information Today.

Grassian, Esther et al. BICO "Task Force: Final Report." UCLA Library. Information Literacy Program (September 30, 2005). Available: http://repositories.cdlib.org/uclalib/il/04 (accessed December 28, 2008).

Mayer, Richard E. 2005. *The Cambridge Handbook of Multimedia Learning.* New York: Cambridge University Press.

McDermott, I.E. 2007. "Escaping Ugly: Graphic Design Aids for Untrained Librarians." *Searcher* 15, no. 5: 12–16.

Moreno, Roxana and Richard Mayer. 2007. "Interactive Multimodal Learning Environments. Special Issue on Interactive Learning Environments: Contemporary Issues and Trends." *Educational Psychology Review* 19, no. 3: 309–326.

NCAT. "Program in Course Redesign" (2005). Available: www.thencat.org/PCR.htm (accessed December 27, 2008).

Nielsen, Jakob. "Jakob Nielsen's Website." Available: www.useit.com (accessed December 24, 2008).

Parker, Roger C. 2006. *Looking Good in Print.* Scottsdale, AZ: Paraglyph Press.

Pink, Daniel H. 2007. "Pecha Kucha: Get to the PowerPoint in 20 Slides Then Sit the Hell Down." *Wired* 15, no. 9 (August 21, 2007). Available: www.wired.com/techbiz/media/magazine/15-09/st_pechakucha (accessed December 26, 2008).

Tufte, Edward R. 1983. *The Visual Display of Quantitative Information*. Cheshire, CT: Graphics Press.

W3C. "Policies Relating to Web Accessibility" (August 25, 2006). Available: www.w3.org/WAI/Policy (accessed September 20, 2008).

———. "Evaluating Web Sites for Accessibility: Overview" (2008). Available: www.w3.org/WAI/eval/Overview.html (accessed December 27, 2008).

Chapter 11

Assessment: Improving Learning; Improving Teaching

Self-knowledge and self-improvement are very difficult for most people. It usually needs great courage and long struggle.

—Abraham Maslow

WHY ASSESS?

Why bother with assessment? Quite simply, we do so to improve both learning and teaching. We assess, review, and revise because we want to find out and document whether or not our instruction has been effective and which methodologies, technologies, and materials work best in particular environments and for specific learners. We also assess in order to provide evidence of the need for and value of the time, energy, and funding expended to support information literacy instruction (ILI). If we are truly dedicated to empowering our learners, we need to assess the impact of our efforts. Have our learners attained our proposed learning outcomes and, if so, how well? Learning can happen without assessment, but you and others will not know for sure if it did unless that learning is assessed. Furthermore, without feedback on their accomplishments, our learners cannot really know if they have learned anything. And we have no idea if our efforts have had any effect. Learners and teachers alike need to know that learning has taken place. Assessment can document this for all of us.

But we do not have to think about assessment until after instruction has occurred—right? Wrong! Although completing your Needs Assessment; identifying instructional goals, teaching objectives, and learning outcomes to address your learners' needs; and selecting the most appropriate methodology to deliver this instruction gets you well on your way in your instructional planning process, you are not quite ready to move on. While logic seems to dictate that you should now proceed to designing your instruction and subsequently delivering it to your learners, there are a few more things to consider before you do so. How will you know people have learned what you set out to teach? How will you discover if the methodologies you selected are effective? How will you demonstrate that effectiveness to the stakeholders in your environment? This is where assessment comes in.

Effective teachers engaged in face-to-face (F2F) teaching often assess, evaluate, and revise the success of their instruction as they go. They watch for signs of boredom and confusion while they are teaching and, if possible, make on-the-spot adjustments to address any problems. Online instructional endeavors that include some kind of feedback mechanism for users to comment on their interactions with the product provide teachers with information that can be used to revise the online material. But as valuable as all of this instructional fine-tuning is, it is not sufficient to address the question of how effective our instruction might be. In order to really know what and how much people are learning, we need to assess the intended learning outcomes.

As discussed in Chapter 7, the time to plan your assessments is in the early stages of instructional development—right after you have developed your expected learning outcomes (ELOs); that is, what you expect learners to know and be able to do following instruction. Although the actual assessment may occur during or after the instruction itself, deciding how you will be conducting your assessments needs to be one of the preliminary steps in your instructional development planning process. Regardless of the motivations for your assessment, you need to select your assessment methodology sooner rather than later. Unfortunately, many ILI librarians view assessment as an afterthought. However, the methods you use for assessment can not only provide the data you might need to improve your ILI, but help you design the instruction itself as well as illustrate to your administrators that your have built in a means of judging and documenting effectiveness. Furthermore, your assessments can provide valuable feedback to your learners and thus become an integral part of the learning process.

There is a direct, almost reciprocal, relationship between learning outcomes and assessment. Assessment looks objectively at what was or was not learned. Deciding how best to assess learning as we are deciding on ELOs makes both endeavors more effective and meaningful. Formulating your assessment ideas immediately after developing your learning outcomes ensures you are assessing each outcome in some way. Furthermore, some of the methods you decide to use may end up driving the way you teach. For example, well-designed and appropriately placed instructional activities and exercises can serve a dual purpose. They give learners some important practice time and also serve as a way for the instructor to assess learning—while it is happening. For more on this idea see the section on classroom assessment techniques (CATs) (Angelo and Cross, 1993) later in this chapter as well as material on teaching, critical thinking, and active learning in Chapter 6.

When assessment is built into the planning process from the beginning, it allows us to determine how well our learners have attained our ELOs (Loe and Elkins, 1990; Shonrock, 1996). The importance of writing clear, concise, and meaningful goals, objectives, and outcomes cannot be overemphasized. Thinking about how to gather evidence that our learners have attained what we intended them to learn, in parallel with developing learning outcomes for your instruction, will not only force you to write more precise outcomes but also help you make decisions about what methods and techniques to use during the assessment phase. You will know what type of data you need to collect in order to answer your assessment questions, and you will have identified the criteria for success that you will need to use when you are evaluating these data (Wiggins, 1996). Determining assessment methodologies at this point in the development process will help ensure that you will be collecting the most appropriate data and will be analyzing them in the best possible fashion for your purposes.

We can also use assessments to help highlight areas where our efforts could be improved for the future. Developing instruction is an iterative process. We plan. We develop. We deliver. We assess and evaluate the results of the assessment. We revise, deliver the revised material, and assess and evaluate again. Perfection is always just out of our reach, but continually striving for perfection contributes to keeping our instruction fresh and our interest in teaching piqued.

Improving teaching and improving learning are both excellent reasons to assess our efforts, but they are not the only driving forces behind assessment. Recent trends in education have contributed to a renewed interest in assessment among information literacy (IL) instructors. In an era of financial retrenchment, institutions everywhere are taking hard, long looks at where the money is going. The expense of ILI programs must be justified to the parent organization, or these programs may no longer be supported (American Association for Higher Education, 1992; Avery, 2003; Bober, Poulin, and Vileno, 1995; California School Library Association, 1997; Dolphin, 1990; Gibson, 1992). Assessment lends credibility not only to the program but also to the library, especially if the programs can be shown to support institutional, organizational, or governmental goals and mandates such as IL and lifelong learning.

Financial pressures are not the only external motivators for assessment. Accreditation organizations, government agencies, employers, parents, and learners themselves are all questioning the effectiveness of educational practices (Budd, 2007; Colborn and Cordell, 1998; Driscoll and Wood, 2007; Gelmon, 1997; Gratch-Lindauer, 2007; Huba and Freed, 2000; Spellings, 2006; Thomas, 2004). The common cry is "Are our learners learning?" Educational institutions are being pressured to measure ELOs and to reexamine their assessment methodologies. Counting how many sessions were offered and how many people attended each one are no longer sufficient measures to justify an educational program or institution (Cameron, 2004). The emphasis on outcomes has caused institutions, programs, and individual instructors to look at both their teaching and their assessment methods and to frame both in terms of ELOs rather than institutional, programmatic, or teaching objectives. For more on developing ELOs and using them in your teaching, see Chapters 7 and 12.

The political context of assessment should not be taken lightly. Keep in mind that administrators will be using the results to make decisions about the fate of your programs. Furthermore, IL instructors should never lose sight of assessment's program improvement goal (Loe and Elkins, 1990). While positive assessment results can be used to promote the value of the program and increase its support base, even negative results can be helpful. If an assessment indicates that the program or class is falling short of expectations, this information can be used to pinpoint problem areas where improvements could lead to a better, stronger program in the future (Corcoran and Langlois 1990). Your assessment results can then be used as an appeal to administration to gain that support.

As already mentioned, increased interest in the process of learning has also contributed to the growing emphasis on assessment. Teachers and even governments everywhere are concerned with learning in the larger sense. They want to know if learners not only can recall facts and bits of knowledge but also if they can apply that knowledge in real-world situations (Wiggins, 1996, 1998). The goal here is not accountability to some outside agency; it is to find out how and what people are learning in order to improve the experience (Cross, 1998; Gilchrist, 1997; Huba and Freed, 2000; Shavelson and Huang, 2003) and to provide learners with helpful and supportive feedback that can actually enhance learning. Sharing the assessment results with the learners closes this feedback loop and creates an opportunity to discuss ways to improve the learner's experience (Angelo and Cross, 1993; Driscoll and Wood, 2007; Wiggins, 1997). Assessment used in this fashion becomes integral to the learning process and not just a goal in itself (Battersby and Learning Outcomes Network, 1999; Nicol and Macfarland-Dick, 2006). For more on accountability demands, see Chapter 14.

Assessment can also help us improve our instructional programs and sessions. It may highlight areas of instruction that are not contributing to the learning outcomes as well as we had expected and thus can be used as the basis for revisions in methods, techniques, and materials (Huba and Freed, 2000). We can use the results of our assessments as a diagnostic device that points out the direction we need to go with our ILI and may even suggest new ways of doing things (Cameron, 2004). Assessments can be used to provide information on the effectiveness or efficiency of new or existing programs, compare the outcomes of two or more methods for teaching the same content, and identify areas in which staff needs training. Although assessments such as these are often intended to provide internal feedback to ILI instructors or coordinators, the data collected can also be used to promote ILI programs to people outside of the library. Results can be communicated to administrators as a means of bolstering budget requests and providing data that could expand political support for your programs (Kellough, Kellough, and Kim, 1999; Linn and Gronlund, 2005; Loe and Elkins, 1990; Svinicki and Schwartz, 1988; Westbrook, 1993). They can also be a way to document how the library and its instructional programs contribute to the goals and mission of the parent organization. Sharing assessment results with appropriate stakeholders helps to garner support for ILI especially if it can be shown how the assessment was used to improve and enhance the program (Gratch-Lindauer, 2007; Maki, 2004).

The presence of a strong institutional mission statement provides an invaluable starting point for the assessment process. When questions about educational mission and values are skipped over, assessment may become an exercise in measuring what is easy rather than what is meaningful (American Association for Higher Education, 1992; Banta et al., 1996). Worthwhile assessment can take place only when there is a clear sense of what matters in the library and to the parent institution as well. In order for assessment to lead to improvements, it must reflect on what is valued in that environment regardless of whether that environment is a school, a university, a business, or a community. The process of transforming the broader group's mission into specific goals for our library as well as for our IL programs and instructional efforts allows us to link our assessments to improvement and to collect useful data that inform our parent organization or broader community about the impact of our instructional endeavors (Gelmon, 1997; Huba and Freed, 2000; Maki, 2002; Rockman, 2002). For more on ILI mission statements, see Chapter 2. Sample ILI mission statements are also included on the CD-ROM that accompanies this book.

So, we assess for a multiplicity of reasons. We do it to find out what learners know and can do, to monitor effectiveness for accountability purposes, to identify and improve instructional practices, and to ensure that our efforts match our stated goals, outcomes, and standards (ALA. ACRL, 2003a; Gratch-Lindauer, 2007). Whether we are assessing the effectiveness of our individual courses, sessions, or overall program, our goal remains the same—to make sure that our learners are attaining the ELOs with the hope that these outcomes will empower them throughout their lives.

LEVELS OF ASSESSMENT

The first step in your assessment planning is deciding on your assessment goal or goals. In other words, what are you trying to find out about your learners? You need to decide this in order to determine the methodology you will use for your assessment. Different types of assessments tell us different things about our learners. Kirkpatrick refers to these variations as the four levels of assessment: reaction, learning, behavioral, or results assessments (Kirkpatrick, 1998; Veldof, 2006). Each level answers a specific question about learning, and our decisions about assessment methodology are dependent upon which of these questions we are trying to answer (Grassian and Kaplowitz, forthcoming). If your assessment is intended to answer more than one of these questions, you will probably need to use a combination of methodologies to accomplish your goals.

- **Assessment Goal: Did they like it?**
  Level One: Reaction
  Reaction assessments measure what learners think of the session. They generally take the form of surveys or questionnaires and often use Likert scales methodology. Although they are often referred to as "happiness scales," they nonetheless provide some valid data. If learners dislike the learning environment and/or the presenter, they will be less engaged in the process. Factors that contribute to "unhappiness" need to be examined and revised (Grassian and Kaplowitz, forthcoming).
- **Assessment Goal: Did they get it?**
  Level Two: Learning
  Learning assessments can occur either during or after instruction has taken place and usually require learners to perform in some fashion. Teachers offer learners opportunities to demonstrate their grasp of the concepts, often through the use of exercises or activities. The teacher presents the learner with a problem or question and asks the learner to apply what has been learned. Alternatively, the learner can be presented with some kind of instrument that tests comprehension. Although a step above the "happiness scales," these still do not measure how the learner will react when presented with a situation in real life (Grassian and Kaplowitz, forthcoming).
- **Assessment Goal: Can they do it?**
  Level Three: Behavioral
  Level three assessments can be used to assess the process used to perform, the product that results from the performance, or both. Behavioral assessments include so-called "authentic assessments" in which learners are asked to apply what they have learned in real-life situations. Level three assessments are intended to examine whether the learner's method of solving the problem has

changed as a result of the instruction. If you compare papers, projects, or other assignments before and after instruction, you are engaged in behavioral assessment (Grassian and Kaplowitz, forthcoming; Veldof, 2006).

- **Assessment Goal: Does it matter?**
  Level Four: Results
  This is one of the more difficult levels to accomplish in ILI because it measures the effect of the instruction on the learner's life. Level four assessments can examine whether instruction leads to better retention rates or higher grades in college or if K–12 students get accepted at better schools and/or do better when they get there. Did learners who participated in our ILI endeavors seem to get higher paying jobs? In the corporate world, did our ILI endeavors contribute to the company's productivity, sales figures, or market share? Obviously we cannot answer these questions alone. Level four assessments require librarians to collaborate with people and groups outside of the library. Results assessments tend to be done infrequently or not at all, because they can be complicated and costly to accomplish. Unfortunately, this means that there is little evidence to support our belief that an information literate person will be more likely to succeed in life. This is a ripe area for future research efforts to provide librarians, our institutions, and our communities with even more evidence of the necessity of ILI sessions, courses, materials, and programs, synchronous or asynchronous, F2F, remote, or online (Grassian and Kaplowitz, forthcoming; Veldof, 2006).

DESIGNING YOUR ASSESSMENT

As you review these levels to determine where your assessment goal or goals fall, it is often useful to ask yourself the following questions. The answers to these questions will help you to decide what types of assessments can provide you with the information and data you are looking for.

1. **Who wants to know?** Are you assessing for internal feedback purposes or because of externally imposed pressures? Determining this will help you decide how formal or informal your data gathering needs to be. Asking yourself why you are doing the assessment and to whom (or even if) the results need to be reported will help you select your assessment methods and data collection techniques. Learner-centered assessments that provide feedback to improve learning are very different from accountability assessments that are often undertaken to justify the existence of a class, course, or program (Gratch-Lindauer, 2007; Sonntag and Meulemans, 2003; Wiggins, 1996).
2. **What questions are you trying to answer?** That is, what is the aim of your assessment? ILI assessments generally look at one or more of the following issues. Data from these types of assessment can provide feedback to learners and/or teachers. They can also be used to report effectiveness to administrators and can be included in accountability reports.
   a. Have the participants learned the intended content; that is, have they attained the ELOs?
   b. Have program objectives and outcomes been attained?
   c. Have participants improved their research skills?
   d. Were the instructional methods and materials effective?
   e. If the assessment is comparing different instructional methodologies and/or materials, which of these methods or materials were more effective?
   f. Have participants' attitudes toward information, libraries, and librarians been modified?
3. **What kind of data do you need?** Descriptive data may be sufficient for informal assessments intended to provide feedback to learners and/or teachers. These can be in the form of self-reports from the learners themselves or observations of their performance during and following the instructional experience. For more formal research studies (i.e., comparing instructional methodologies, assessing long-term effectiveness of your instruction) or for justifying your ILI programs, courses, or classes to your supervisors, administrators, or beyond, you may need

to collect numerical data that can be statistically manipulated. Keep in mind that qualitative data (descriptive) can be turned into numerical data through content analysis and well-developed rubrics (descriptions of what the learner is expected to do that include the criteria by which performance is judged and the range of quality for that performance). A detailed discussion of rubrics can be found later in this chapter.

4. **What are the ELOs for your instruction?** The question to ask at this point is not "What are we trying to teach?" but "What do we want learners to be able to do after they have completed the instruction?" (Alverno College Faculty, 1979; Gilchrist, 1997; Iannuzzi, 1999). Remember that the data you collect will indicate how well your learners attained these outcomes.
5. **How will your learners exhibit what they have learned?** In other words, what opportunities will you provide during or after instruction for your learners to demonstrate what they did or did not gain from the instructional experience (Maki, 2002)? This is when you will gather data about what has actually been learned and can take a number of forms that will be discussed later in this chapter. When planning to develop some kind of formal instrument tools (surveys, questionnaires, forced-choice tests), you should include a period for field testing the instrument. Find a group of learners who are similar to those you will be assessing, have them try out your instrument, and then ask them for comments on it. This will help you to uncover any areas of confusion and other potential pitfalls with your instrument and will improve your assessment efforts. If you have adequate funding, from either your institution or a research grant, it may be useful to enlist the assistance of test construction and design experts if you wish to use these types of instrument tools. Talking to experts in educational assessment may also be useful if you are developing assessments using open-ended questions, interviews, performance, or product assessment. These experts can provide advice not only about how to develop these assessments but also about the best way to both score and analyze the resulting data. (For more on the research process and grant writing, see Chapter 5, "Adding to the Knowledge Base Through Research," and Chapter 6, "Grant Writing and Grants," in *Learning to Lead and Manage Information Literacy Instruction* by Grassian and Kaplowitz, 2005.)
6. **What will you do with the data collected?** It is during this stage that you determine how well the outcomes have been met. Depending upon why you undertook the assessment in the first place, you can use the results as a means to provide feedback to your learners, justify your instruction to others, or improve and revise your own program, teaching techniques, and methods.
7. **Is this a formal assessment that requires the preparation of a report describing your findings?** If you are doing an accountability type of assessment, data should be summarized and analyzed for inclusion in a formal report. Use these reports as a way of sharing instructional objectives, trends, and accomplishments with everyone who needs to be kept informed, that is, administrators, instructors, the public, and other governmental, community, and user groups. State the implications of the data clearly. If the results indicate that some of your efforts need improvement, use this as an opportunity to explain what you have learned and, more important, how you will apply that learning to the improvement of your instructional endeavors (Loe and Elkins, 1990; Shonrock, 1996). These reports should aim to produce evidence that relevant parties (internal or external) will find credible, suggestive, and—above all—applicable to decisions that need to be made. The challenge is not collecting the data; it is using the data to effect change (American Association for Higher Education, 1992; Banta et al., 1996; Gelmon, 1997; Maki, 2002, 2004).

Practical Considerations

In addition to determining your assessment level and deciding which of the seven questions you are trying to answer with your assessment, you need to stop and do a reality check regarding resources available for your project. Here are a few things you should take into account:

- How much time you have available for your assessment
- Who on your staff will be involved
- The costs involved and how you will cover those costs
- What, if any, assessment expertise is available to you
- Who the stakeholders are to whom you will be reporting the results

Furthermore, IL instructors have to deal with other constraints peculiar to our association with the people who attend our classes or courses or who use our online material. With the exception of full-term "for-credit" IL courses, we generally have little or no authority over our learners, have limited contact time with them, may never get the opportunity to see how they might perform in real life, and often do not get the chance to examine the products of their learning. So, many ILI assessments occur and are incorporated into the instruction itself.

You can also extend your contact time by asking learners to complete some type of assessment at a later date. These can be distributed in print or be made available online. If your learners have a required assignment, this post-instructional assessment could be turned in or submitted online along with the course assignment. In the case of classes for the general public, you could ask for e-mail addresses so that you could follow up later. Or you could have participants fill out a form indicating what they will do with what they have learned and put it in a self-addressed, stamped envelope. You could then mail these envelopes back to the participants three to six months later, along with a survey form or a URL for an online survey to see if they have retained or utilized what they learned from the instruction. This approach can be used in any kind of library environment. The advantage of such an approach is that the learners would have had the opportunity to apply what was presented in the ILI to their own problems, projects, and/or assignments and would therefore have a better idea of whether or not the instruction seemed to help them in the research process. Asking people to describe what they learned about the research process and/or about themselves as researchers can supply you with valuable information, and it also encourages learners to think about the process and self-assess the experience (Gilchrist, 1997). See Chapters 3, 4, and 5 for more on mental models and metacognition.

In the K–12 and higher education environments, you could also collaborate with classroom teachers to create an IL assessment that measures how learners apply their knowledge to real-world tasks. Examples include paper, projects, portfolios, problem-based exercises, and product reviews. Your role would be to examine the types and appropriateness of references selected, the effectiveness of the search strategy, the appropriateness of research tools used, and whether or not learners applied critical thinking criteria in selecting items. It could extend to analyzing how the references were used in the assignment itself, although some might argue that this enters into the realm of subject expert, that is, the domain of the course instructor. Depending on the level of collaboration, these reviews could even become part of the grades for the assignment.

Assessing learning outcomes and the success of your instructional efforts should not be restricted to F2F instructional situations. With more and more instructional materials, classes, and courses being provided online and with the increased use of course management systems (CSMs) as a teaching mechanism, especially in higher education, it is important to include these online, synchronous, and asynchronous instruction venues into your assessment plans. Fortunately, many types of assessment can be adapted to an online environment. Learner satisfaction questionnaires or surveys, as well as tests that measure learners' progress, can be distributed via e-mail or interactive Web forms. Many CSMs actually come with built-in assessment modules for the instructor's convenience, such as quizzes, surveys, and other types of feedback forms (Bradford et al., 2006–2007; Dewald, 1999a, 1999b; Dewald et al., 2000; Papastergiou, 2006). Furthermore, learners are frequently required to post their assignments on the course Web site. The ILI instructor should request access to the site so that he or she would be able to monitor (and participate) in course discussions as appropriate and offer informal or formal (graded) feedback on assignments. See Chapters 15 and 16 for more on assessing your online instructional offerings. Whatever your mode of delivery, including assessment should be a fundamental part of your instructional planning process.

Learner-centered Assessment

Although examining the effectiveness of our ILI methods and techniques and reporting our successes to the appropriate authorities are both strong motivations for assessment, we generally do not undertake these types of elaborate and complex assessment projects on a regular basis. We might review our programs annually or every few years. And often we are called upon to do accountability type assessments when the library or its parent organization is under some kind of review or accreditation. However, we should endeavor to assess our ELOs each and every time we teach. This learner-centered assessment provides both instructors and learners with valuable information—information that we both can use to improve the process. Providing feedback to our learners during the instruction itself can help them reflect upon their own learning and enhance their understanding. Incorporating some type of hands-on active learning exercises in our F2F sessions offers the opportunities for learners both to practice what they are learning and to the chance to see how well they are doing. As we guide and offer feedback to them during these experiences, we are helping them to self-assess their progress and to make improvements (Angelo and Cross, 1993; Huba and Freed, 2000; Weimer, 2002). As we observe our learners "in action," so to speak, we can also reflect upon our own teaching methods and pinpoint where we may need to make changes. For more on incorporating active learning exercises into your instruction, see Chapter 6.

We can use techniques like the one-minute paper or the muddiest point (Angelo and Cross, 1993) during or at the end of a session to encourage learners to reflect upon the learning experience. Their responses to questions such as "What were the most important things you learned today?" or "What is still confusing to you about what we covered today?" can tell you a lot about how the session went. Leaving time to discuss their responses also provides for additional teaching and learning moments. If time is short, you can ask for e-mail addresses and respond to the learners after the class is over. If you have the luxury of meeting with your learners more than once, you can start each subsequent session with a review of what was covered in the previous session based on the comments from these types of assessments. You can also assign projects that are completed in stages, offering constructive feedback after each stage is completed—again with the goal of learner improvement rather than evaluative grading. Authentic assessment techniques provide excellent learner-centered experiences and are discussed at length later in this chapter.

Learner-centered assessment does not have to be restricted to F2F instruction. Online tutorials or other Web-based instruction can also provide for practice exercises and quizzes. Depending upon your situation and the sophistication of your product, you may or may not be in a position to collect the results of these exercises and quizzes. However, you can (and should) build in some kind feedback for the learners—so they can monitor and reflect upon their own progress with the material.

The efficacy of learner-centered assessment is supported by the various learning theories discussed in Chapter 3. The behaviorists would applaud its use, as it relies heavily on immediate feedback and reinforcement. Furthermore, staged assignments are excellent examples of learning through successive approximations and mastery of steps. The cognitive/constructivists would appreciate the opportunities offered to the learner to work at problems on their own and find their own answers to them. And, of course, the humanists would be pleased with the self-efficacy, reflection, and self-improvement goals of the process. Overall, these techniques, which we can easily incorporate in all of our teaching, give us a lot of bang for our buck. We can, of course, use them as a way to monitor the effectiveness of our instructional efforts. In addition, we can use them to teach, not just to measure our learners' progress (Bain, 2004; Liles, 2007; Wiggins, 1997, 1998) as our learners are given the opportunity to explore, practice, receive feedback, and then improve their skills and knowledge. Ultimately learner-centered assessment helps our learners become more self-confident about their IL skills and abilities and helps us as IL instructors become more certain that our efforts are successful and that learners are attaining the intended learning outcomes.

METHODOLOGICAL ISSUES: TIMING AND DATA FORMAT

Now that we have examined the reasons for assessment and have discussed some of the fundamental issues involved in assessment planning, we are ready to turn to the specifics of designing an assessment methodology. One of the first decisions you must make regarding your assessment methodology is whether you are interested in summative or formative assessment. This will determine the timing of your assessment.

Summative assessment, regardless of the assessment level or tool used, always occurs after the instruction has taken place. Data from summative assessments are generally used for accountability purposes. However, these data can be either quantitative (numerical) or qualitative (descriptive) in form. What makes the assessment summative is its placement after instruction and its purpose—justifying the class, course, or program (Cruickshank, Jenkins, and Metcalf, 2003).

Formative assessment, on the other hand, can occur at any point during instruction. Its main purpose is feedback—either to the learner or to the teacher or to both. Formative assessment is used to improve the learning experience, to help learners reflect upon what they have learned, and, if necessary, to modify their methods and try again (Bransford et al., 1999b; Hunt and Pellegrino, 2002). Teachers can use the information gathered from formative assessment to make changes to their instruction. Because formative assessments occur during the actual instructional experience, teachers can review, reiterate, and restate material that may not have been grasped quite as well as they would have liked. They can also gather this information and use it as a way to improve the instruction for the future. Just as with summative assessment, any of the various assessment tools to be discussed later in this chapter can be used for formative assessment. It is the placement of the assessment during learning itself and its use as a feedback mechanism for improvement that makes it formative.

Next, we must decide what type of data we wish to collect. Because we can use any kind of assessment tool that we feel is appropriate to our needs for either formative or summative assessment, it also stands to reason that the data we collect from them can be in either words (qualitative) or numbers (quantitative). Furthermore, qualitative (word-based) data can be turned into numeric data through response analysis and the use of well-constructed rubrics. Rubrics are especially helpful when using the type of authentic assessment techniques that are quickly gathering favor at all levels of education. Accountability agencies want to know not only how well individuals learned but also if they are prepared to function effectively in the real world. Authentic assessments, which are based in reality, directly address these questions. Scoring rubrics can turn authentic assessment data into the type of numerical report that is so appealing to administrators, government agencies, and accreditation organizations. Developing rubrics is discussed later in this chapter.

Finally, a word needs to be said about the ever-popular pre- and posttest design. The important word here is *design*. Although most typically associated with forced-choice types of tests (multiple choice, matching, true/false, fill-ins), any type of assessment tool can function in a pre- and posttest design. Data collected can be in the form of words or numbers. What makes it a pre- and posttest design is that learners are assessed prior to and then again after the instructional intervention. Asking learners to write a short essay on how they would approach research on a specific topic before we start instruction and then repeating the question after they have completed our class still qualifies as a pre- and posttest design even though the data we collect are in the form of words.

It is important to note that the decision to use quantitative or qualitative data does not reflect on the rigor of the assessment. Both types of data can be collected, counted, analyzed, and interpreted. They can both be used in pre- and posttest experimental designs in which data collected prior to instruction are compared to those collected after the instruction has taken place. A change in these data can be used to decide if the instruction had any effect. Furthermore, both quantitative and qualitative data can be collected from learners who have had instruction (the experimental group) and compared to a similar group composed of learners who did not receive the instruction under review (the control group). Quantitative versus qualitative issues refers only to the type of data (numerical vs. descriptive) that are being collected, not to the assessment design used to collect those data.

SELECTING YOUR ASSESSMENT TOOL

Once you have decided on the timing of your assessment and the type of data you wish to collect, the next step is to select the most appropriate tool to answer your assessment questions. In order to make this selection you need to have a thorough understanding of the strengths and weaknesses of the various assessment tools available to you so that you can design your assessment in a way that will best fulfill your intended purpose. In other words, you need to know enough about the various tools so that you can determine what type of information will be provided by each and how that information can be tabulated and presented.

Keep in mind when you are making your selections that the distinction between qualitative and quantitative techniques refers to the format in which data are collected—it does not refer to how that data are analyzed and presented in your final report. As already discussed, while quantitative data are obviously easier to manipulate statistically, qualitative data can be organized in such a way as to allow for their statistical manipulation as well. For example, essay examinations and term papers, which have long been used to assess learner success, seem on the surface to be qualitative in nature. In most cases, however, a numerical score or grade is assigned to the essay according to some preselected rubric and criteria. These grades can be used in quantitative statistical data analysis. Therefore, the seemingly qualitative nature of these techniques can be deceptive. Rubrics can be developed for assessing the quality of annotations included in a bibliography as another way to turn qualitative (descriptive) material into quantitative (numerical) data.

The more descriptive data that are usually collected from such qualitative methods as interviews, open-ended questions, or focus group transcripts can also be organized in such a way as to result in numerical data. Descriptions can be grouped into like categories, and the number of people responding in each category then can be manipulated and compared. For example, at the completion of your instruction, you could ask learners to describe (in writing) how they would go about gathering information on a specific topic. Their responses could be analyzed for use of similar resources and/or strategies and then grouped into like categories. The number of learners who used the same resource or strategy could then be calculated and reported as quantitative data.

So, do not dismiss the use of qualitative data collection methods just because you need to report your assessment findings in terms of numbers and statistics. Such statistical analysis is possible whether you have used quantitative (numerical) or qualitative (descriptive) methods of data collection. What you do with that data after they are collected is up to you and will depend in large part upon whether those for whom this assessment was undertaken require narrative or numerical results or a combination of both. Furthermore, qualitative data allow you to collect learners' impressions in their own words. Quoting actual learners in your report can have a powerful impact on the reader.

When making your selections, keep in mind that each type of assessment tool is neither good nor bad in its own right. The problem arises when an inappropriate tool is used to answer a particular assessment question (Dick, Carey, and Carey, 2005; Marzano et al., 1988). For example, many ILI instructors make use of the so-called happiness scales at the end of their instruction. These usually take the form of surveys that ask the learners to rank how much they liked the instruction and/or the instructor as well as whether or not they felt they learned something useful that they would use in their subsequent information-gathering research. While these scales provide valuable information about the affective effect of the instruction (Level One: Did they like it?), the scales should not be used as an indicator of whether or not they got it

(Level Two) or they can do it (Level Three) or that the learning mattered (Level Four) in Kirkpatrick's (1998) scheme.

Comprehensive assessments such as those that deal with more than one of Kirkpatrick's (1998) levels frequently require a variety of procedures. Mixed data collection and triangulation (the use of both qualitative and quantitative methods) is increasingly the norm in this case (Frick, 1990; Morse and Field, 1995). Using a variety of assessment tools enhances the chances that you will collect the type of data that will answer your assessment questions. In triangulation, a combination of methods is used to explore a single situation, including product and performance assessment along with skills and attitudes. The strengths and weaknesses of individual methods are balanced to produce a more complete picture of the situation (Banta et al., 1996; Colborn and Cordell, 1998; Morse and Field, 1995; Westbrook, 1997). In an ILI situation, you could combine the use of CATs during instruction itself, with a happiness scale at the end of instruction, and follow up with faculty feedback on a paper or project that learners completed by gathering information using the resources and strategies covered in your instruction—thus gathering data on Levels One, Two, and Three.

Assessment Parameters

Assessment tools should be selected because of their relevance to the learning outcomes or performances to be measured and to the questions you are trying to answer. Selection is also dependent upon knowing the limitations of each tool, the type of information that will be provided by each, and how well a tool can answer the questions under review. The tool must also provide information in the form that will meet the needs of the identified audience (ALA. ACRL, 2003; Avery, 2003; Gratch-Lindauer, 2003, 2007; Linn and Gronlund, 2005; Woods, 1990).

Assessment tools vary along several parameters. They can be formal or informal. They can result in numerical data (quantitative assessment) or descriptive information (qualitative assessment) as described earlier. They can differ in how closely they simulate real work experiences (relevance) and in how much the test administrator can regulate the testing and/or the scoring situation (control). Assessments can take place during the development process (formative assessment) or once the instruction is implemented and in place (summative assessment). They can rely on recognition (picking out the correct answer from a given number of choices) or on recall (when learners must supply the answer to the question from memory). Scoring can be either norm-referenced, in which student scores are compared to one another, or criterion-referenced, in which scores are measured against some standard or criterion. Furthermore, different tools can vary as to their reliability, validity, and usability. The table presented in Figure 11.1, "Talk the Talk: The Language of Assessment," includes brief descriptions of each of these parameters and can serve as background as you consider the various tools available to you. The information used to create this table was drawn from a variety of sources (Adams, 1993; Bloom, Madaus, and Hastings, 1981; Carspecken and Apple, 1992; Cruickshank, Jenkins, and Metcalf, 2003; Dick, Carey, and Carey, 2005; Dolphin, 1990; Driscoll and Wood, 2007; Elliott et al., 2000; Frick, 1990; Huba and Freed, 2000; Hunt and Pellegrino, 2002; Knight, 2006; Linn and Gronlund, 2005; Mager, 1997d; Maki, 2002; Marzano, Pickering, and McTighe, 1993; Montgomery, 2002; Patton, 1980; Scriven, 1973; Shonrock, 1996; Stripling, 2007; Tancheva, Andrews, and Steinhart, 2007; Veldof, 2006; Wergin, 1988; Wiggins, 1998).

Types of Assessment Tools

Although there are a number of different types of assessment tools, we can actually group them into categories.

- Forced-choice assessments include multiple choice tests, matching, true/false, and fill-ins. The defining characteristic is that there is only one right answer, and the test designer determines the answer in advance.
- Surveys and questionnaires generally offer a range of options and tend to be used to gather demographic, opinion, and attitude information.

Figure 11.1 Talk the Talk: The Language of Assessment

What Is It Called?	What Does It Means?
Formal	Assessments that are undertaken for accountability purposes—for example, for programmatic reviews or institutional accreditation.
Informal	Assessments that are done for internal purposes to monitor and improve learning and teaching.
Formative	Assessments that provide feedback during instruction itself or during the developmental stages of a new program or product. They include the on-the-spot corrections that instructors make while teaching. They frequently rely on informal assessment techniques, such as observing verbal or nonverbal behavior during in-class exercises or activities. Feedback can be offered to learners during instruction itself to enhance the experience and to improve learning.
Summative	Assessments that are administered once the instruction is complete to measure the degree to which learning outcomes have been attained. Results are used to determine if some standard or educational mandate has been met—either for the learner (i.e., grades) or for the instruction itself. They tend to use more formal assessment protocols. Programmatic assessments are frequently summarized for accountability reporting and try to answer the question "Should the instruction in its present form continue?"
Direct	Learners are asked to demonstrate what they know or can do with their knowledge. Direct assessments are often associated with the concept of authentic assessment and can take the form of projects, papers, exhibitions, case studies, performances, etc.
Indirect	Self-reports such as surveys or questionnaires that ask respondents to share their perceptions about what they know or can do with their knowledge.
Quantitative	Quantitative techniques provide data in numerical form. They deal with questions of how much or how many.
Qualitative	Qualitative methods collect more descriptive data in the form of words rather than numbers. They typically take the form of journals, interviews, observations, open-ended questions, self-reports, and analysis of written material. Qualitative assessment permits (and may even encourage) responses not anticipated by the evaluator. Note: Qualitative data can be turned into numerical data through the use of scoring rubrics.
Control	Control assessment methods are concerned with ensuring comparability between students. Assessments that rate high on control rely on objective techniques and are designed to be identical from student to student. The goal here is to minimize the possibility of extraneous influences. Assessment situations are kept as uniform as possible when control is the uppermost concern. Therefore, all learners would be assessed in the same place, at the same time, and on the same questions or problems.
Relevance	Relevance deals with how well the skills being tested relate to the performance of the task in a real-life situation. Assessments that are high in relevance tend to include some kind of simulation or performance assessment. The assessment situation should approximate the real-life behavior as much as possible. Watching learners actually perform database searches or examining their database search logs could be used for this type of assessment. While both control and relevance are desirable criteria for an assessment, they tend to be difficult to combine in a single task. Tests high in control tend to be low in relevance and vice versa.
Reliability	Reliability refers to consistency. The same student taking the same test at different times should obtain the same or similar scores.

(continued)

Figure 11.1 Talk the Talk: The Language of Assessment (*Continued*)

Validity	Validity refers to meaningfulness. Does the assessment method measure what it is intended to measure? For example, does the assessment tool accurately measure if a student can pick an appropriate database for a particular topic?
Usability	Usability deals with practicality. It refers to the ease or difficulty of designing, administering, and evaluating the results of the selected assessment. A technique that is high in both reliability and validity may still be worthless if the cost (in time, effort, and money) makes it impractical to use.
Norm-referenced	Participants' results are compared to each other, and the relative position of each student is given a score as a result of this comparison. Often called "evaluating on a curve," it is not always a good measure of instructional or learner success. The students who rate the best in this method will get a high score regardless of whether or not they learned anything.
Criterion-referenced	Judgments are made based on a comparison of a measurement to an objective standard. Criterion-referenced evaluations are appropriate when we want to know whether an expectation, outcome, or criterion has been achieved. We are not interested in whether one person scores higher than another but rather in who has and has not attained the learning outcomes originally set for the instructional endeavor.
Authentic assessment	Authentic assessments measure how students apply their knowledge to real-world tasks. Authentic tasks can take the form of papers, projects, problem-based exercises, portfolios, etc. and allow learners to solve the types of problems professionals face in the field.
Rubrics	Rubrics are descriptive measurements for defining what the learner is expected to be able to do. They include criteria by which performance is judged as well as the range of quality for that performance.

- Open-ended assessments (short answer or essays) allow more latitude in response, but there still is some right answer being sought.
- Interviews and focus groups allow for discussion of process as well as skills. Though the questions are structured in advance, there is no right or wrong response. Skilled facilitators encourage respondents to express themselves freely on the topic under discussion.
- CATs generally take the form of exercises, worksheets, and other classroom activities interspersed within the instruction itself. CATs support learning by providing practice opportunities as well as feedback to both learner and teacher on to how well the learners are performing.
- Authentic assessments are based in reality and explore both process and product. Learners are presented with a real-life, important question or problem to solve. Although some direction and constraints may be given for how the learners will present their solutions, authentic assessments allow learners the most latitude regarding the methods they use to get to that solution.

As you can see from the table in Figure 11.2, these six tool types vary with regard to the control and relevance parameters described earlier, with forced-choice being highest in control and lowest in relevance, while authentic assessments fall at the other end of the continuum—lowest in control and highest in relevance. The more latitude the learner has in performing the task and providing a solution, the less control the assessor has over the assessment process.

Your selection of an assessment technique should take this continuum into account. If you

Figure 11.2 The Control–Relevance Continuum

	Forced-Choice	Surveys/ Question-naires	Open-Ended	Inter-views/ Focus Groups	Classroom Assessment Techniques	Authentic Assess-ment
Control	High	High	High	Moderate	Moderate	Low

are looking for ease of administration and scoring, instruments that are high in control are the right ones for you. However, you must take into consideration that tools high in control tend to be low in relevance. That is, they do not measure skills, knowledge, or performance in real-life situations (Battersby and Learning Outcomes Network, 1999). Forced-choice and open-ended questions provide data on what respondents think is the right answer (Marzano, Pickering, and McTighe, 1993). Surveys and questionnaires provide information on how respondents feel about instruction but are not intended to measure learning (Barclay, 1993; Colborn and Cordell, 1998). Because items on surveys and questionnaires do not have right or wrong answers, they cannot provide information on the attainment of skills, abilities, and/or knowledge. Although skills tests are often referred to as *surveys* or *questionnaires,* any instrument that consists of items with right or wrong answers really fall into the forced-choice category described earlier.

Interviews and focus groups allow respondents more latitude in their responses, but data are still in the form of descriptions rather than actual performance (Glitz, 1998). Learners are just describing what they think they would do in a given situation. So, again, interviews and focus groups do not measure actual performance. Although CATs often give learners the opportunity to exhibit what they have learned, they are exhibiting learning in the controlled and somewhat artificial environment of the classroom (Sonntag and Meulemans, 2003). Authentic assessments ask the learner to demonstrate what they know or can do in real-life situations. They are often referred to as *direct assessments*, whereas those in which learners select what they think is the right answer or share their perceptions, feelings, or attitudes about the learning are viewed as *indirect assessments* (Huba and Freed, 2000; Rockman, 2003a; Thomas, 2004). For more about each of these assessment types, see "Assessment Tools: Pros and Cons" on the accompanying CD-ROM.

THE MOVEMENT TOWARD AUTHENTIC ASSESSMENT

As we have already discussed, current trends in education have called into question the way learning has typically been assessed. Educators and government officials want to know that learning outcomes have been successfully attained and also if learners can apply what they know beyond the classroom. They want to go beyond recall and recognition types of tests, which assess the acquisition of isolated facts and bits of information. Recognition and recall tests, typically assessed by the high-control forced-choice methodology, can test what learners remember about the content covered during instruction, but they do not adequately test for learners' abilities to apply that content appropriately to solve real-world problems. Therefore, they do not provide information on the application and transfer of learning beyond the specific instruction.

Although high-control assessments are still in widespread use, often in the form of standardized forced-choice tests, interest in more authentic assessment techniques seems to be on the rise. High-control assessments measure discrete and isolated bits of knowledge and so have been criticized as not being representative of real behavior (Avery, 2003; Callison, 1998; Knight, 2006; Montgomery, 2002; Rockman, 2002). As such they may not provide a clear indication of learning. People who score well on these types of tests may only be showing that they are good at test taking. High scores do not necessarily mean that learners can actually apply what they learned in a real-world situation (Courts and McInerney, 1993; Halpern and Hakel, 2003). So, while learners may be able to select the correct search strategy for a particular topic from a list of possible strategies, when faced with researching their own topic they are unable to formulate an appropriate strategy.

Authentic assessment methods seem particularly suited to the assessment of higher order processes such as problem solving and critical thinking. They also directly measure transfer of learning, as learners must take what they know and apply it in a new situation. Because they are anchored in the kind of work that people really do, authentic assessments provide a better picture of how people will behave and perhaps even innovate in the real world (Driscoll and Wood, 2007; Wiggins, 1998).

Authentic assessment is supported by the cognitive/constructivist approach to learning, which suggests that assessment should move away from the passive responses to a more active construction of meaning. Authentic assessment challenges learners to demonstrate, in a meaningful way, what they have learned and what they are able to do with that newly acquired knowledge (Liles, 2007; Montgomery, 2002; Pappas, 2007; Rockman, 2003a; Wiggins, 1996). Humanists would also applaud the use of authentic assessment because it exemplifies self-directed learning and promotes self-efficacy for the learner.

Authentic assessment also addresses the learning styles issue. Because people learn in a variety of ways, it seems only logical that assessment techniques should offer some flexibility in how that learning is exhibited. Forced-choice and other high-control methods, with their emphasis on numbers, norm-referenced scoring, and competition, require that learners all perform in one standard, uniform manner. With their "only one right answer" philosophy, they reinforce the teacher-centric approach to learning that requires rote memorization and exact repetition of what has been presented. For more on the psychology of learning and learning styles, see Chapters 3 and 4.

Authentic approaches, on the other hand, reinforce learner-centered teaching approaches through the use of ill-structured problems. As opposed to questions that have only one right answer, these ill-structured problems allow for multiple solutions and a variety of solution paths. They have fewer parameters and contain uncertainty about which concepts, rules, and principles are necessary for the solution of the problem (Jonassen, 1997; Wiggins, 1996). Authentic assessment approaches, therefore, acknowledge diversity of styles, backgrounds, and behavior in the classroom. If assessment ignores the "voice of the other," then it is forcing learners to follow one style of learning and performance and ignores deeply embedded cultural practices of many of the test takers (Belenky et al., 1986; Courts and McInerney, 1993; Huba and Freed, 2000; Irvine, 2003; Thomas, 2004). Again, this may not be a true measure of achievement. If there is no overall "best" way to teach everyone, what does a single assessment score mean? Poor results may result from a mismatch between the learner's style and the teaching mode and/or the assessment technique and therefore may not be a true indication of the learner's accomplishments (Kaplowitz, 1995). For example, Western educational methods have been known to emphasize competition (as in norm-based assessment). However, many other cultures emphasize cooperation and collaboration over competition, and learners from those cultures are uncomfortable when their results are judged against those of their fellow learners. See Chapter 14 for more about diversity issues in ILI.

A Word About Rubrics

We cannot leave the discussion of authentic assessment without addressing the topic of rubrics. The products used in authentic assessment (papers, exhibits, portfolios, performances, etc.) require special handling in order to be graded consistently and fairly. Like real-life tasks, authentic assignments do not have one correct answer. There can be many ways to approach the problem and successfully complete the task, so they must be assessed based on well-defined criteria or standards (Cruickshank, Jenkins, and Metcalf, 2003; Marzano, Pickering, and McTighe, 1993; Neeley, 2006). Authentic assessment techniques can also provide extensive information and feedback to the learner on his or her progress toward reaching some professional or real-life standard of performance. This is especially true if the rubrics are shared with the learner in advance. Well-developed rubrics allow for consistency in grading and can support the learning process by taking the mystery out of what is expected of the learner doing the assignment (Cruickshank, Jenkins, and Metcalf, 2003; Driscoll and Wood, 2007; Huba and Freed, 2000; Marzano, Pickering, and McTighe, 1993; Montgomery, 2002; TLT Group, accessed 2008; Wiggins, 1998).

Rubrics are descriptive, not judgmental. They are intended to measure the learners' results, responses, or products against some criteria or standard of performance. Rubrics consist of performance criteria, indicators for each of these criteria, and proficiency levels for these indicators. Learners' work is assessed according to how well it matched the criteria listed in the rubric. Proficiency levels are often described in terms such as basic, proficient, or advanced—with advanced meaning that the product approaches professional standards for the work (Callison, 1998; Cruickshank, Jenkins, and Metcalf, 2003). Rubrics can also be laid out on a numerical scale, providing points for each of the proficiency levels, which can then be used to justify a specific grade level. Although much of the literature on rubrics is directed at the classroom teacher, librarians are beginning to adapt this work for ILI (Knight, 2006; Veldof, 2006).

Developing rubrics for your ILI assignments may seem like a daunting task. But you do not have to start from scratch. The ACRL "Information Literacy Competency Standards for Higher Education" (ALA. ACRL, 2000) is a good place to begin, as is the California School Library Association's (1997) IL handbook. Web sites such as RubiStar (4Teachers.org, 2008) can also be helpful as you develop your ILI rubrics. Although intended for classroom teachers, RubiStar allows you to use an interactive tool to develop rubrics for your specific situation. See "Read More About It" at the end of this chapter for more resources on developing rubrics.

ASSESSING INFORMATION LITERACY INSTRUCTION

Do ILI librarians regularly engage in assessment? There is both good news and bad news in this area. The good news is that the number of conference presentations, Web sites, and publications devoted to the topic has been steadily increasing. The bad news is that much of the material on ILI assessment still seems to be related to Level One (Did they like us?) or at best Level Two (Did they get it?) data. Assessment efforts at Levels Three (Can they do it?) or Four (Does it matter?) are still in short supply. While useful, these Level One and Two assessments do not provide a full picture of the effectiveness of ILI.

There is still also a tendency among ILI instructors to rely on attitudinal measures to determine the overall success of a program (Bober, Poulin, and Vileno, 1995; Colborn and Cordell, 1998; Ragains, 1997; Wong, Chan, and Chu, 2006). We ask participants if they liked the program and us and/or if they think they learned anything useful. Rarely, however, do we delve any deeper into the question of whether or not they had actually learned anything. Even when we are testing skills, we tend to rely on forced-choice recognition and recall-type tests rather than assessing actual behavior. Up to a few years ago, furthermore, there has been almost no research on the impact of ILI on education or subsequent employment.

This situation seems to be improving. A 2007 literature review by one of the authors of this book indicates an increased interest in assessment issues and a more rigorous approach to research on the topic. Many ILI books contain chapters on the topic, with some books dedicated in their entirety to it (see "Read More About It" at the end of this chapter for some of these titles). Librarians, primarily at academic libraries, have taken the issue to heart and are exploring how to determine if our learners are learning and, even more important, what our learners can do with this knowledge. Librarians are using both formative and summative assessment methodologies. On the more formative side, a whole body of literature exists on the use of CATs and other forms of active learning exercises that not only provide practice opportunities for the learners but also offer feedback to both learners and instructors alike. These more informal methodologies help learners to improve learning as it happens and also offers the ILI instructor insight into what parts of the instruction might need to be modified, updated, or revised. See Chapter 6 for more on active learning and Chapter 12 for ways of incorporating CATs and active learning into your teaching.

In the summative arena, librarians are using pre- and posttest designs, assessing the long-term impact of their instruction, examining the effectiveness of both credit and noncredit courses and classes, and trying their hands at authentic assessment using portfolios, research journal analysis, as well as bibliography and paper reviews, often in collaboration with classroom faculty. They are even beginning to look at ways to assess online instruction and to examine their IL programs overall (Burkhardt, 2007; Carter, 2000; Colborn and Cordell, 1998; Emmett and Emde, 2007; Emmons and Martin, 2002; Kivel, 2003; Knight, 2003; McCarthy and Heald, 2003; Mezick, 2007; Moore et al., 2002; O'Hanlon, 2007; Pinto, Fernandez-Ramos, and Doucet, 2008; Rabine and Cardwell, 2000; Riddle and Hartman, 2000; Scales and Lindsay, 2005; Sharma, 2006; Stevens and Campbell, 2006; Tancheva, Andrews, and Steinhart, 2007; Wong, Chan, and Chu, 2006). Many of these papers include the assessment instrument used for the study.

Unfortunately, many of these studies tend to offer only preliminary, though suggestive, data due to implementation constraints or design issues, which are frequently problems in ILI assessment studies. We often do not have access to the number of subjects needed to collect data for a statistical analysis. Because grades on our assessments usually do not count toward course grades, our subjects may not take the assessment seriously. Furthermore, it seems unethical for us to create a control group by offering instruction to some but not to all of our learners. Finally, pre- and posttest designs have some built-in problems. First, the act of taking the pretest may sensitize the learner to the important parts of the instruction, thus skewing the results. Furthermore, statistical analysis must be very precise to obtain significant differences between pre- and posttest scores. For example, matched-paired analyses (where the individual learner's pre- and posttest scores are compared) are more likely to show differences than group mean score comparisons (Fry and Kaplowitz, 1988; Kaplowitz, 1986; Rabine and Cardwell, 2000; Riddle and Hartman, 2000).

ILI librarians should take heart that assessment can and is being done. However, they should be careful about how they use the results of these studies to justify the worth of ILI. While studies like the ones indicated earlier are providing useful information about improving programs, course, and classes, and have some interesting data on the long-term effects of ILI, more work needs to be done in this area. Stronger data need to be collected. More rigorous studies that result in statistically significant differences need to be conducted, and better, more authentic instruments need to be developed.

The instruments used in the studies cited earlier could act as a starting point for your assessment projects. Although these instruments may not be directly transferable to your particular environment, they can serve as models and guidelines for developing instruments more directly suitable for your institution and specific assessment needs.

Toward Standardized Information Literacy Instruction Assessment Instruments

Developing your own assessment instrument can take time, money, and expertise that may not be readily available to you. The strong need for ILI assessment, however, has prompted several groups to begin developing large-scale, standardized IL assessment tools. Some examples are the Bay Area Community Colleges Information Competency Assessment, Educational Testing Services' iSkills instrument, James Mason University's Library Skills Test, Project SAILS, and St. Olaf's Research Practices Survey (Bay Area Community Colleges, 2004; Cameron, 2004; ETS, 2004; Gratch-Lindauer, 2007; Gratch-Lindauer and Brown, 2004; James Madison University, 2008b; Kent State University, 2008; Rockman, 2004e; Rockman and Smith, 2005; Sharma, 2006; Somerville et al., 2007; St. Olaf College, 2008), and more may be on the horizon. Tests such as these use a variety of formats, including real-life scenarios that provide a more authentic assessment experience. Issues with these tests include cost, accessibility for those with disabilities, and the ability of test producers to keep up with swiftly changing information research tools and versions of software. iSkills, for example, tests for both IL and information technology abilities in scenario-based performance tests, an interesting yet highly challenging endeavor (Brasley, 2006).

Educators and librarians alike are looking toward these tools as a possible way to have IL assessment become a standard part of our educational system. These tools are intended as both diagnostic and competency measures and can be used to assess IL skills at various educational levels. Results of these tests could be used as input measures (what our learners know and are able to do) before they enter our schools and programs, as an indicator of progress toward a major, as a graduation competency, and quite possibly to test the long-term impact of ILI.

FINAL REMARKS

The shift toward process over product in education and the current emphasis on lifelong learning skills and information literacy have promoted a reexamination of how to measure educational competencies. The relative merits of qualitative versus quantitative modes of assessment, as well as issues of control versus relevance, are becoming more critical than ever. ILI professionals must become even more versatile and flexible in the way they design their assessments. They must be willing to embrace the notion that different types of assessments are valid under different circumstances. They must be knowledgeable about the strengths and weaknesses of each type of assessment tool. They must move toward testing for learning. And they must be willing to mix and match approaches so that their assessment results in the greatest amount of usable information possible.

Our learners can also gain from the assessment process. As we ask them to reflect on the instruction, what they have learned, and how that information has been useful to them, learners begin to explore the learning process itself, thus engaging in metacognitive thinking. They consider how they interacted with the information being presented and think about how they might do this more effectively in the future. A well-designed assessment not only provides useful information for the instructor, but it actually benefits the learner and helps to reinforce the material that was taught. Research has indicated that people who become aware of themselves as learners—that is, those who are self-reflective and analytic about their own learning process—become better learners. They move from being "surface learners" who merely reproduce information provided by others to "deep learners" who not only understand the information but also apply it appropriately in a variety of settings (Corno and Mandinach, 1983; Cross, 1998; Huba and Freed, 2000; Wiggins, 1998). As a result, thoughtfully designed assessments can enhance the learners' abilities to become lifelong learners. Assessment, therefore, contributes to the overall goals of ILI. It enhances the learners' experiences by allowing them to examine how they learn and to develop more efficient and effective IL strategies and skills.

EXERCISE

Step 1. Select the ILI learning outcomes that you wish to assess.

Step 2. Assume that you are assessing in order to provide feedback to the learner on his or her progress toward these learning outcomes. What sort of assessment(s) would you design to provide that information? Why did you choose to assess learning in that way?

Step 3. Now assume that you want to provide feedback to the instructor or developer about the effectiveness of the instruction. What if any changes or additions would you make to the assessments chosen in Step 2 and why?

Step 4. Next consider a situation in which you are being asked to justify your ILI program, courses, or classes to the appropriate people in your parent organization. How would you modify the assessment to produce the appropriate results and why?

Step 5. Compare the methods used in Steps 2, 3, and 4. What are the advantages and disadvantages of each?

READ MORE ABOUT IT

For Further Information About Educational and ILI Assessment

Bloom, Benjamin Samuel, George F. Madaus, and J. Thomas Hastings. 1981. *Evaluation to Improve Learning.* New York: McGraw-Hill.

Cameron, Lynn. 2004. "Assessing Information Literacy." In *Integrating Information Literacy Into the Higher Education Curriculum* (pp. 207–236), edited by Ilene Rockman. San Francisco: Jossey-Bass.

Elliott, Stephen N., Thomas R. Kratochwill, Joan Littlefield, and John F. Travers. 2000. *Educational Psychology: Effecting Teaching, Effective Learning,* 3rd ed. Madison, WI: Brown and Benchmark.

Gratch-Lindauer, Bonnie. 2007. "The Role of Assessment." In *Proven Strategies for Building an Information Literacy Program* (pp. 257–277), edited by Susan Curzon and Lynn Lampert. New York: Neal-Schuman.

Shonrock, Diana, ed. 1996. *Evaluating Library Instruction: Sample Questions, Forms, and Strategies for Practical Use.* Chicago: ALA. LIRT.

For Further Information About Classroom Assessment Techniques (CATs)

Angelo, Thomas A. and K. Patricia Cross. 1993. *Classroom Assessment Techniques: A Handbook for College Teachers,* 2nd ed. The Jossey-Bass Higher Education and Adult Education Series. San Francisco: Jossey-Bass.

Cross, K. Patricia. 1998. "Classroom Research: Implementing the Scholarship of Teaching." *New Directions for Teaching and Learning* 75: 5–12.

For Further Information About Authentic Assessment and Rubrics

4Teachers.org. RubiStar (2008). Available: http://rubistar.4teachers.org/index.php (accessed October 28, 2008).

Callison, Daniel. 1998. "Authentic Assessment." *School Library Media Activities Monthly* 14, no. 5: 42–43.

Huba, Mary E. and Jann E. Freed. 2000. *Learner-centered Assessment on College Campuses.* Boston: Allyn & Bacon.

Knight, Lorrie A. 2006. "Using Rubrics to Assess Information Literacy." *Reference Services Review* 34, no. 1: 43–55.

Montgomery, Kathleen. 2002. "Authentic Tasks and Rubrics: Going Beyond Traditional Assessments in College Teaching." *College Teaching* 50, no. 1: 34–39.

Neeley, Teresa Y., ed. (2006). *Information Literacy Assessment: Standards-based Tools and Assignments.* Chicago: ALA.

Oakleaf, Megan. 2007. "Using Rubrics to Collect Evidence for Decision-making: What Do Librarians Need to Learn?" *Evidence-based Library and Information Practice* 2, no. 3: 27–42.

Pappas, Marjorie. 1998. "Designing Authentic Learning." *School Library Media Activities Monthly* 14: 29–31, 42.

TLT Group. "Rubrics." Available: www.tltgroup.org/resources/Flashlight/Rubrics.htm (accessed September 12, 2008).

Wiggins, Grant. 1998. *Educational Assessment: Designing Assessments to Inform and Improve Student Performance.* San Francisco: Jossey-Bass.

Part IV

Delivering Information Literacy Instruction

Chapter 12

Learner-centered Teaching: Listen, Engage, Inspire

Education is not filling a bucket, but lighting a fire.
—William Butler Yeats

WHAT MAKES A GOOD TEACHER?

Why are some teachers more effective than others? Are good teachers born or made? How do we forge connections with our learners? How do we put the learner in the center of our teaching? For many of us, getting up in front of a group or having to create any kind of online instruction is a frightening and intimidating idea. Often we have little training or experience in teaching and/or instructional design. Yet we are told that instruction is a primary part of our job responsibility. We are expected to stand in front of a room full of people, capture their attention, engage their interest, and communicate appropriate information or to develop some online form of instruction using synchronous (real-time) or asynchronous (any time, any place) modes of delivery. Unfortunately, instruction on how to do either face-to-face (F2F) or online instruction effectively is not a regular part of the curricula for most graduate programs in library and information science. Instruction may be included as part of courses such as reference services, but few programs offer an entire course dedicated to the topic. Those that do include such courses generally classify them as electives rather than as part of the core curriculum for the degree (Julien, 2005).

Although few of us have been teachers prior to entering librarianship or have had any special preparation for our teaching role, all of us have been students. So we all have had experience with the good, bad, and maybe even ugly aspects of teaching. If we take the time to think about what was most effective for us as learners and, furthermore, what turned us off in a learning situation, we can begin to generate a list of characteristics of effective teaching. High on our lists are probably knowledge and enthusiasm for the subject material and a genuine concern for the learners. Effective teachers tend to be positive people. They are encouraging, supportive, and hold high expectations for learners' success (Bain, 2004; Barnes-Whyte, 2008; Cruickshank, Jenkins, and Metcalf, 2003; Freilberg and Driscoll, 2005; Irvine, 2003; Palmer, 1998). Whether they are working in F2F or online environments, effective teachers pay attention to individual differences and try to connect with their learners. Effective teachers exhibit these traits through the manner in which they interact and communicate with their learners, in the ways they offer feedback both during and after instruction via the use of relevant examples, and by varying the teaching methods they use. Furthermore, they try to help learners to bridge the gap between theory and practice by offering opportunities to apply the newly acquired knowledge to actual experiences (Bain, 2004; Freilberg and Driscoll, 2005).

Can we learn to be effective teachers? Of course we can. Many fine books have been written on the subject. F2F and online workshops and courses are available both from our own professional organizations and from those dedicated to improving teaching in general. And of course some library programs do offer courses, not only to their own students but also to nonstudents via extension classes—some of which can be accessed remotely. To become effective, however, takes a commitment to change, a willingness to experiment, and the courage to face and, hopefully, conquer some personal fears—including fear of failure. Furthermore, we need to accept that we will never reach perfection. Effective teachers are self-reflective (Bain, 2004; Brookfield, 1995; Cruickshank, Jenkins, and Metcalf, 2003; Weimer, 2002). They review their presentations for what worked and what did not go quite right, and they use that information to improve their instructional skills. Whether teaching synchronously or asynchronously, teachers are forever destined to be works in progress, as are the content and methods of their instruction. But in many ways that is what makes being a teacher fun, exciting, and eternally challenging.

Effective teachers listen to their learners and understand and are respectful of their learners' needs. These teachers use this knowledge to engage their learners and to inspire them to become lifelong learners. Whether they are working toward F2F, blended instruction (part online and part F2F), or a completely online mode of delivery, good teachers create a learning environment that contains relevant and useful content. They select the most appropriate modes of delivery in order to capture their learners' attention and involve learners in the learning process. Finally, effective teachers model their passion for the information so that learners are motivated and inspired to learn both during and after participating in the instruction.

As you read this chapter, keep in mind that effective teaching practices and principles can and should be applied whether you are sharing the same physical space as your learners (F2F delivery mode) or you are working with learners remotely via online modes of delivery. To help reinforce this idea we have included examples of how effective teaching principles relate to both F2F and online forms of instruction (synchronous and asynchronous). You have only to look at the PRIMO (ALA. ACRL. IS, 2008e) or A.N.T.S. (2008) Web sites to see how much online information literacy instruction (ILI) has already been developed. For more examples of how to apply effective teaching principles in your instruction, see Chapters 4 and 6. For additional help using technology to teach, see Chapters 15 and 16.

Learner-centered Teaching and the Effective Teacher

How does the information literacy (IL) instructor develop the characteristics of the effective teacher described—especially if he or she has not had any formal teacher training? What techniques, methodologies, and teaching practices support effective teaching? The learner-centered teaching (LCT) philosophy of instruction offers us a framework in which to examine and reflect upon our teaching practices. When applied to both the ways in which we deliver our instruction and the techniques, methods, and materials we use to support it, the LCT approach can help us increase our effectiveness and enhance the learning experience for our learners.

LCT is often described as moving from the transmission or banking approach, in which teachers just deposit information into the tabula rasa (empty vessel) brains of their learners, to the facilitation or shared responsibility mode in which learners take a larger role in the process (Bligh, 2000; Keyser, 2000). With an LCT approach, teachers offer support and direction, but learners do the actual work of learning. Also referred to as moving from the "sage on the stage" to the "guide on the side" (King, 1993), this approach is a way of inviting the learners into the experience and allows you to both listen and respond to their needs as learning progress. LCT lets learners work with and create or construct their own understanding of the material being presented (Huba and Freed, 2000; Liles, 2007). As you will see in later sections of this chapter, many learners seem to find LCT approaches both engaging and inspiring. Furthermore, LCT has been found to be more effective at achieving higher cognitive objectives, such as analysis, synthesis, and evaluation, than more passive learning situations and contributes to the development of lifelong learning skills, attitudes, and behaviors. LCT encourages deep understanding rather than surface (or, as one author has called it, "bulimic") learning in which learners only hold on to material long enough to "spew" it back on examinations or assignments. Learners are not just passively absorbing facts and information. Instead, they are encouraged to restructure their thinking by connecting new knowledge to that which is already known. In short, learners are encouraged to go beyond merely reproducing or regurgitating information. They are challenged to become critical thinkers and problem solvers who produce, create, and construct knowledge (Bain, 2004; Biggs, 1999a, 1999b; Bligh, 2000; Gagnon and Collay, 2001; Hansen and Stephens, 2000; Johnson, Johnson, and Smith, 2007; Jonassen, 2000; King, 1993; Ramsden, 1988; Ridgeway, 1989; Weimer, 2002, 2003).

Interestingly enough, LCT has its roots in all three major psychological learning theories. Behaviorists applaud the more "doing" aspects of the methodology as well as the immediate feedback and reinforcement opportunities available as teachers see and respond to learning as it happens in synchronous situations or build self-correcting mechanisms into quizzes and exercises as well as ways to interact with their learners remotely (via e-mail, for example) in asynchronous modes of teaching. Cognitive/constructivists approve of the fact that learners are interacting with the subject matter, building their own mental models, and organizing material in ways that make sense to them so that information can be retrieved more readily when it is needed in the future. Humanists like the idea that learners are given more opportunities to work on issues and problems that have meaning to them. Learner input is valued and rewarded, further reinforcing the LCT notion of learning as a shared responsibility. Humanist teachers are empathic and supportive of their learners' fears and anxieties and so appreciate that LCT allows learners more freedom in deciding how they will interact with the material. Humanist teachers believe in the capabilities of their learners to succeed and indicate this belief in words, gestures, and deeds. Humanists commend the self-efficacy aspect of LCT as learners see that they are accomplishing something of value and are practicing how to apply important and useful skills, knowledge, and abilities. Furthermore, these teachers support LCT principles by being accessible and real and by sharing their passion for the material with their learners (Rogers and Freiberg, 1994). For more on learning theory, see Chapter 3.

Fundamental to LCT is learner involvement, so it might seem that LCT is just another name for active learning. However, while active learning experiences play an important part in LCT, they do not represent the whole approach. LCT rests on three principles—**C**ollaboration, **P**articipation, and **R**esponsibility. Learners are invited to collaborate with us as teachers in a variety of ways. They are often asked to take part in the organization of instruction, for example, by ranking topics of interest and/or the order in which topics might be covered. Learners frequently are given options regarding how they wish to interact with the material during instruction itself (in groups or individually, for example), and the ways in which their learning will be assessed (i.e., by selecting from a menu of possible assignments, exercises, activities, or projects). These teacher–learner collaborations all help to create an environment in which learners have more of a say in their own learning. Collaboration and participation does not end there. Learners are often given the chance to interact through collaborative projects, peer-to-peer teaching, and multiway discussions between teacher and learners and/or among learners themselves. LCT's emphasis on collaboration and active participation results in learners who are taking responsibility not only for their own learning but also for that of their colleagues (Weimer, 2002).

Overall LCT is more a way of thinking about teaching than a specific methodology for it. The LCT mind-set permeates every facet of instruction—from planning to delivery to assessment—with the goal of giving the learners more of a role in the process. However, adopting an LCT approach does not mean abdicating your role as teacher. While learners in this type of environment are invited to become active participants in their own learning and are given the opportunity to make some of the decisions about how they want to engage with the material to be learned, the teacher is always monitoring and guiding their progress. He or she makes decisions about how much and when to put control in the hands of the learner. Furthermore, he or she must make sure that learners are given appropriate resources and information (through readings, teacher-lead demonstrations, lectures, discussions, etc.) so that they are able to tackle the problems, exercises, and activities that play such a large role in LCT. In short, learners are not allowed to just run amok with the material. LCT requires careful design, coordination, guidance, and direction from the teacher so that expected learning outcomes (ELOs) are met during the experience.

Good teaching requires that we listen to our learners and both engage and inspire them. LCT offers many ways to accomplish these laudable teaching goals whether we are sharing the same physical space or are working with learners remotely in an online format. Let us now turn to how an LCT approach can help us reach these goals by encouraging us to pay attention to our learners and their needs as we create appropriate, engaging, and inspiring instructional experiences for them.

LISTEN TO YOUR LEARNERS

Listening to your learners is vital to your effectiveness as a teacher—especially when using an LCT approach. This might strike you as strange, because as instructors we are the ones who know the information to be shared with our learners. But unless you have a thorough understanding of your learners and their needs, you cannot effectively reach and teach them. That is why planning for instruction starts with a Needs Assessment, as we have discussed in other chapters in this book. What better way to find out who your learners are and identify how best to support them via our instructional endeavors (Vella, 2000)? You can demonstrate that you really heard them by creating goals, objectives, and ELOs that are based on their Needs Assessment and so are customized specifically for them. Finding out as much as you can about your learners in advance helps to ensure that your instruction is relevant to and appropriate for them. For more on the Needs Assessment process, see Chapter 7.

Listening does not end with your Needs Assessment. The most effective teachers are those who find a way to listen to their learners during the instructional experience or as close to it as possible in time. If you are working in a F2F setting, always be aware of the atmosphere in the room. Jacob Kounin (1970) called this "with-it-ness." Watch your learners' body language and facial expressions. Are they engaged or bored? Are they listening attentively, or are they restless and disinterested? Use these cues to gauge your effectiveness (Bligh, 2000; Freilberg and Driscoll, 2005; Vella, 2000). If your learners start to lose interest, maybe you are dwelling too long on a particular point. Move on. You may have reached the "too much of a good thing" point of your instruction (Elliott et al., 2000; Mager, 1997b). Change the pace. Introduce something new. Change activities. If your learners seem confused, repeat or restate your point or add a few more examples. If they are excited and enthusiastic, build on that energy. Take a moment to congratulate yourself on doing a good job of getting them involved and engaged and try to keep that engagement going.

Clearly this "temperature taking" becomes harder when working in an online setting. However, if you are working synchronously with your learners and are engaging them in some kind of chat or other conversational exchange such as a discussion board or blog, you may be able to monitor this factor through the tone and content of the messages and questions you are receiving. You could also poll your learners at various points during the session to see what topics might be of the most interest to them, if they are ready to move on to a new topic, and if they have opinions about concepts you might be discussing—thus inviting them to be more active participants in the process. In addition, you could survey learners prior to your instruction to gather some of this information and then present these results at appropriate points during the session. Examine the features of the technology you will be using to deliver your instruction. What options are available for you to communicate with your learners? Look for ways learners can communicate with one another as well. For example, does the technology allow for break-out sessions in which subsets of learners can have private conversations? If it does, you can use this feature to replicate small group, collaborative activities that are common in F2F instruction. Can the learners use headsets in a synchronous online session or voice chat in a virtual world to communicate with you (the instructor) or other learners? If so, much of the advice provided earlier for F2F sessions can be applied to online instruction as well. Be imaginative. Think outside of the box. Even though you are not all in the same room, at the same time, with some creative thinking you can still craft opportunities for you to listen to your learners and for them to listen to each other.

If you are using an asynchronous delivery mode, invite questions and comments via e-mail, social networking sites, or other technologically supported communication modes. Be sure to reply to those who contact you as soon as you can—especially if they seem confused about the content of the instruction in which they have participated. You can analyze this learner provided feedback to assess how well your material is being understood and then make adjustments as needed. These changes will benefit future learners who use this material and show that you are not a person who develops instruction, puts it out there, and then forgets about it. Even in this asynchronous format, you are making an attempt to listen to your learners.

Listening to your learners invites them into the process. It means that you are engaging them in a dialogue—rather than just spewing information at them—and demonstrates that you believe in the "inclusive" rather than the "transmission" mode of teaching. LCT asks learners to participate in their own learning, to work collaboratively with you and their fellow learners, and to take responsibility for their own and for co-learners accomplishments. As such it shifts the balance of power from teacher to learner (Bain, 2004; Felder and Brent, 1996; Freilberg and Driscoll, 2005; Ridgeway, 1989; Weimer, 2002). Learners are not viewed as passive receptacles into which our collective wisdom is poured. Learning under these circumstances is a shared responsibility, and learners are as accountable as we are for the outcome. Viewing our learners as partners communicates our respect for them and our belief in their ability to learn. When learners are given ownership in the process, they are more likely to buy into the ideas being presented (Bain, 2004; Chickering and Gamson, 1987; Cook, Kunkel, and Weaver, 1995; Frederick, 1981, 1986; Lorenzen, 2001a; Weimer, 2002, 2003). Furthermore, LCT allows people to put the material into a meaningful context and to make the information part of their personal worldview. Motivation increases, and more attention is paid to the material. Retention improves as learners grasp the importance of the material and see how they can apply that material to their own lives (Bain, 2004; Jonassen, 2000; Ridgeway, 1989; Vella, 2000; Weimer, 2003).

ENGAGE YOUR LEARNERS

From Teacher-centered to Learner-centered Teaching

The cornerstone of LCT is that learners are active participants. Furthermore, active participants tend to be engaged learners. How you structure your instruction plays a large part in creating an LCT environment. What you do communicates your attitude toward the learners as much as what you say, illustrate, or demonstrate. You have a range of format options at your disposal: lecture, modeling, discussion, questioning, guided practice, independent practice, collaborative/group activities, and reflection. In general, these formats fall on a continuum from teacher centered (direct learning) to learner centered (indirect) (Bain, 2004; Biggs, 1999a, 1999b; Bligh, 2000; Costa and Kallick, 2000; Cruickshank, Jenkins, and Metcalf, 2003; Elliott et al., 2000; Freilberg and Driscoll, 2005; King, 1993; Svinicki and Schwartz, 1988). The direct "sage on the stage" lecture format has long been the model for teaching, especially in the higher education arena. Defenders of this format insist that it is the only way to present large amounts of information in brief periods of time. While this may be true from the presenter's point of view, it is questionable whether learners gain anything by being bombarded with this type of information overload especially for extended periods of time (Bligh, 2000; Clark and Taylor, 1994; Cruickshank, Jenkins, and Metcalf, 2003; Freilberg and Driscoll, 2005; Veldof, 2006). A major advantage of the direct format, however, is that it offers the teacher the opportunity to summarize, synthesize, and pull together information from a variety of sources. It also models the intellectual process involved in this sort of analysis. The direct approach should be used judiciously, however, as its effectiveness begins to dwindle after 10 to 15 minutes in part because of its lack of learner involvement (Biggs, 1999a; Bligh, 2000; Cruickshank, Jenkins, and Metcalf, 2003; Eble, 1988; Frederick, 1986; Freilberg and Driscoll, 2005; Jacobson, 2008; Jacobson and Xu, 2002; Kroenke, 1984; Rockman, 2003a).

A good way to make sure your learners are not losing interest, and to avoid them being overwhelmed by information overload, is to use a variety of formats (both teacher centered and learner centered) in your instruction (Bain, 2004; Bligh, 2000; Bransford et al., 1999b; Cruickshank, Jenkins, and Metcalf, 2003; Frederick, 1986; Freilberg and Driscoll, 2005). There are several advantages to this mix of direct and indirect techniques. For one thing, it helps deal with the variety of learning styles that will be represented by your learners. For some, listening to you talk F2F or online in a Webinar/Webcast, a podcast, or a video will be just fine, especially if you have an entertaining and engaging delivery style. Others may need to see and/or actively interact with the material in order to absorb what you are trying to teach. Mixing formats also seems to keep attention and motivation high. Furthermore, it ensures that a variety of voices are heard. Indirect teaching techniques, in which learners are actively participating rather than just passively listening, show learners that you care about what they think and feel. It allows them to relate to the material in a personal way, and it addresses issues of learning styles and cultural diversity by letting everyone put the information into a context that is individually meaningful. See Chapters 3 and 4 for additional information about learning styles and Chapter 13 for a discussion of ILI for diverse populations.

Offering a variety of learning opportunities also helps deal with the information overload issue. According to George Miller's (1956) classic article, learning does not happen until new material is transferred from short-term to long-term memory storage. Too much information overloads the learners' ability to make this transfer. Therefore, newly presented information is not absorbed because the learner is still trying to move the previous information into long-term memory. Imagine that you are trying to pour water into a glass that is already full. You cannot add anything to the glass until some of the content is moved to another receptacle. Changing formats breaks up instruction so that learners have time to absorb material. Learner-centered activities are especially effective as they offer the learners a chance to practice what they have learned as well as the time for that learning to transfer into long-term memory storage. Furthermore, getting to apply what has been learned further solidifies the material in the learners' memory (Clark and Taylor, 1994; Denman, 2005; Mayer and Moreno, 2003; Veldof, 2006).

LCT activities offer learners opportunities to think critically about information and encourage them to reflect on their own learning, thus engaging in metacognition. This in turn results in a greater degree of transfer of learning and ultimately encourages a lifelong learning mind-set. If people are to become information literate, they must be able to incorporate IL strategies, values, and concepts into their own mental models. According to Piaget and Inhelder (1969), people can become uncomfortable when presented with new information. If information cannot be assimilated easily into their understanding of the world, people may even reject it. However, if people are allowed to interact with the material, they can construct a modified mental model that accommodates the new experience (Allen, 1995; Bain, 2004; Bransford et al., 1999b; Jonassen, 2000; King, 1993; Liles, 2007; Meyers and Jones, 1993; Nelson, 1994; Weimer, 2002).

To facilitate this accommodation, learners must analyze, evaluate, and synthesize the new material themselves. As they interact with the material, learners move from thinking in absolutes (the idea that there must be right and wrong answers if only the teacher would just tell them the "truth") to the idea of multiplicity (Perry, 1981) whereby they can view the world from multiple perspectives, question the material, consider their options, and make decisions based on a critical examination of the material (Bigge and Shermis, 1999; Bransford et al., 1999b; Elliott et al., 2000; McKeachie, 1994, 1999; Nelson, 1994). Knowledge is constructed, not merely absorbed. These learners question authority—including that of the teacher. They are flexible, adaptable, and open to new ideas, and they are better prepared to deal with an uncertain, complex, diverse, and often confusing world. For more on the psychology of learning, see Chapters 3 and 4. For additional information on library anxiety, mental models, and conceptual frameworks, see Chapter 5.

Incorporating indirect, learner-centered activities into your instruction encourages this final stage of thinking (Allen, 1995; Bain, 2004; Conrad and Donaldson, 2004; Cruickshank, Jenkins, and Metcalf, 2003; Eble, 1988; Elliott et al., 2000; Gradowski, Snavely, and Dempsey, 1998; Weimer, 2002). It allows the learner to experience, reflect, construct, and understand the IL material for himself or herself. The new information is now a part of the learner's own mental model. Because the learner has organized the IL material in some meaningful fashion and has stored it in a personally relevant and logical way, there is a greater likelihood that it will be retrievable in the future. For more on how to incorporate active learning and critical thinking elements into your teaching, see Chapter 6.

Learners seem to find LCT activities motivating and fun, especially if they have some control over the topics they are discussing and the resources they will be using or if they are working on real-world authentic examples. Finally, these activities give the teacher an opportunity to assess learning during the instruction itself (Angelo and Cross, 1993). Learners get to practice and, you get to watch them do so. For more on assessment, see Chapter 11.

Mix and Match

The lecture–demonstration approach to synchronous (F2F or online) ILI is still widely used. It has the advantage of being able to present a large amount of material in a small amount of time. Instructors can also model IL skills and strategies for the learners. While lecture–demonstration can be a valid approach to some degree, interspersing some of the following more learner-centered and/or indirect approaches may increase the effectiveness of your instructional efforts, whether you are working in a synchronous or asynchronous mode, F2F or online.

When working in an online environment, it is especially easy to fall into the habit of just delivering information because you are not sharing the same physical space with your learners. You cannot see them, and they cannot see you. This is particularly true in the asynchronous mode, as learners are interacting with the material at their convenience—at any time. If you put on your LCT thinking cap, however, you can look for ways to move away from the "delivery-only" mode of teaching. Much will depend on the technology you will be using to deliver the instruction. Make sure you explore your options as you develop your online material. Look for ways to break up your material into manageable chunks to avoid overload. Incorporate activities that will engage your learners and help them practice and apply the material. Many F2F activities can be adapted for online instruction, although the asynchronous mode offers more challenges. Including quizzes, exercises, self-tests, reflective journals, educational minigames; varying the presentation form, and giving the learners ways to contact you and other learners with questions or comments are all ways to "mix and match," for both synchronous and asynchronous instruction, and will help to keep your learners engaged. As you read the options we present, try to think about how they could be used in all instructional settings—F2F or online, synchronous or asynchronous. Some suggestions for adapting these techniques to a variety of settings are included to get you started. However, as instructional technology advances even more options will undoubtedly be developed to help expand the ways in which you can interact with your learners both F2F and online.

Questioning

In the questioning approach, the instructor asks specific and focused questions in order to get the learners to think about topics and come to some conclusions for themselves. Questions, especially unexpected ones, stimulate curiosity about and interest in the material (Bain, 2004; Bligh, 2000). You might present your questions to the group F2F or through a discussion board posting. For synchronous instruction, allow for a few minutes of quiet thinking, or let learners mull over the question in pairs or small groups. For asynchronous instruction, give the learners a day or two to respond or up to a week, depending upon the total learner time available for instruction. Giving the learners time to consider the question before they have to answer increases the likelihood that they will respond to your questions. For example, ask learners "How trustworthy is the information found on Wikipedia or in a more traditional reference source like *Encyclopaedia Britannica*?" If you are trying to teach how to identify parts of a citation, ask the learners what types of information would they need to find a specific journal article. As they reply with answers like "journal name," "article author," and so on, they will be building the citation for themselves and will be more likely to remember the information. You can repeat the same exercise for a book, a book chapter, and a Web site.

In synchronous online settings, you might pose questions at intervals and use interactive chat or polling technology to gather your learners' responses. In asynchronous settings, build in short quizzes or exercises that replicate this questioning method. If possible, include ways for learners to check their answers to mimic a live question and answer interaction. For example, if you are using presentation software such as PowerPoint, you can insert slides that indicate if the learners' selection from a choice of options is correct or not. You can even set it up so that if the response is incorrect, the learner is allowed to try again. Another approach would be to ask learners to contribute to a wiki asynchronously, where they both develop a list of criteria for evaluating traditional and emerging online tools and resources and provide their own examples.

Discussion

The discussion technique is similar to questioning in that you present something for the learners' consideration. However, topics here tend to be more complex and even controversial. A question, a quote, or even a video clip can trigger discussions. Good discussions focus on important questions and stimulate learners to think about key ideas. They encourage intellectual curiosity and give learners a chance to construct their own understanding of the material (Bain, 2004; Cruickshank, Jenkins, and Metcalf, 2003; Frederick, 1981; Freilberg and Driscoll, 2005; Johnson and Cooper, 2007). For example, show a TV or film clip of someone searching for information. Then have the group critique the approach used. This can lead to a lively discussion of different ways to look for information. For synchronous online instruction settings you can use text chat or voice by headsets or have learners call in or e-mail their reactions to the material. Or you could make use of polling technology in which learners could indicate whether or not they agree with the material just presented or are neutral about it. If space can be provided for comments, that would be even better. You can also meet with learners in a virtual world for synchronous avatar-to-avatar discussions using text or voice chat.

Lively discussions can also be generated in online asynchronous teaching environments through the use of discussion boards, wikis, blogs, or social networking technology such as Facebook (2008), where you can establish groups and post messages on the "Wall," or VoiceThread (2008), where you can annotate a video with your own audio, video, or text comments. Whether you are interacting with your learners F2F or online, remember that your role is to moderate, not to dominate, the discussion. Monitor and guide the discussion, but do not overwhelm it with your own opinions. It is often a good idea for instructors to hold off expressing their own ideas until after all the learners have expressed theirs.

Guided Practice

The guided practice approach is commonly used with the lecture–demonstration teaching approach. Here learners are invited to follow along as you demonstrate some resource or technique. While this does have the benefit of getting the learners more actively involved in the material, it is not as learner-centered as other techniques. However, it can be a good way to help novice learners feel less anxious and more comfortable about trying out an online tool. It combines hands-on practice with modeling and is extremely valuable when the task being demonstrated is very complex with multiple steps. However, because people follow along at different speeds, you might wish to also supply a point-of-use guide to help everyone stay on track and for them to take away for future reference

(Cruickshank, Jenkins, and Metcalf, 2003; Freilberg and Driscoll, 2005). Frequent checks with learners can also help a lot, for example, asking, "Are you with me?" and "Are you ready to move on?"

In a synchronous online setting, guided practice might require giving the learners a break during which they try to simulate what you just demonstrated—perhaps in a separate window. Learners could be invited to comment on the experience via chat, e-mail, instant messaging, telephone, or whatever communication mechanism is available to you through the technology being used. Asynchronous online tutorials often use this approach as well. A technique, strategy, or approach is described and demonstrated—followed by a "try it yourself" segment.

Individual Practice

The individual practice method is also often used following a demonstration of some kind and/or in the lecture–demonstration approach. It is a bit more learner-centered than guided practice, as learners can be given more options about the topics, resources, or even approaches they wish to use during the practice period. Individual learners or groups of learners get the chance to apply what was just presented and to organize the material in a way that makes sense to them. Following an individual practice period with a discussion, that allows learners to talk about how they approached their work, to share their successes, and to point out any problems they may have encountered, adds to the effectiveness of this approach (Cruickshank, Jenkins, and Metcalf, 2003; Freilberg and Driscoll, 2005). As opposed to guided practice, learners in individual practice are encouraged to apply what they have learned to something new rather than simply to replicate or follow along with what the instructor is doing.

Collaborative/Group Work

Collaborative/group work is a very popular methodology in learner-centered teaching circles, because it offers both cognitive and social learning experiences. Working in groups, learners can be assigned to solve some relevant, authentic, real-world problems. They can compare ideas and work out solutions together, thus helping them see the value of diversity of thinking. These activities also allow for practice in higher level cognitive processes such as analysis, synthesis, and evaluation (Bligh, 2000; Burkhardt, Macdonald, and Rathemacher, 2003; Hensley, 2007; Jacobson, 2008; Jacobson and Mark, 1995; Jacobson and Xu, 2002; Johnson, Johnson, and Smith, 2007; Jonassen, 1997, 2000; Lorenzen, 2001a; Lowyck and Poysa, 2001; Ridgeway, 1989; Weimer, 2002, 2003).

As discussed earlier with regard to listening, opportunities for collaborative work can be built into your online synchronous instruction via features provided by the technology you are using (i.e., chat, polling, breakout rooms, etc.). Learners can discuss topics via "private chat" between pairs of learners or in breakout rooms that accommodate small group interaction. The results of these discussions can then be reported back to the entire group via chat or whatever communication technology is available to you. Promoting collaboration in the asynchronous setting may be a bit more challenging. If you are using a course management system to support your instruction, you can have learners interact via discussion boards or collaborate on, review, and critique assignments posted to the site or on a wiki. Obviously in the case of online tutorials, instructional Web sites, podcasts or vodcasts that individuals view or listen to individually at their own convenience, collaboration during the experience is not possible. However, you could build in links to a blog where learners could post comments about the instruction and how they applied what they learned from it. Learners could then compare their experiences with those of other learners. Instructors should monitor the blog and offer feedback as appropriate to further show you are listening to your learners. Use of these tools would, of course, depend upon the interest level and motivation of the individual learners, unless they are required to do so.

Reflection

Asking learners to spend some time reflecting on what they have learned and how they learned it contributes to the creation of lifelong learning skills (Bransford et al., 1999b; Costa and Kallick, 2000;

Jacobson, 2008). Allowing a few minutes at the end of a F2F session for this exercise is also a great way to have the learners summarize the material themselves, and it is probably far more interesting than having you do so. You can also use these reflections as a way to gauge the effectiveness of your instruction. Ask learners to tell you, either verbally or in writing, "What stuck?" as well as what still seems confusing to them. In an online synchronous setting, learners would respond to these questions via chat or whatever communication technology is available to you. Classroom assessment techniques such as the one-minute paper, the muddiest point, or 3-2-1 cards are some examples of ways to encourage reflection (Angelo and Cross, 1993; UCLA College Library, 2004) and can be adapted to either the synchronous or asynchronous online environment.

You can also build in reflection opportunities in your asynchronous instruction. Encourage learners to reflect upon the instruction and to consider what they have learned from it. Learners could be invited to e-mail these reflections to you if they wish to do so—especially if they still have questions about the material. Offering to respond to these e-mails turns the asynchronous experience into one in which you as the instructor become a real, flesh and blood person who has a genuine interest in helping them.

Can You Do It?

Many teachers are reluctant to include indirect methods like these in their synchronous instruction. They equate using indirect techniques with loss of control over the learning situation. While admittedly there is some risk involved in using these techniques, careful planning and preparation can minimize the dangers and enhance the experience for teacher and learner alike. For indirect-learning activities to be effective, the teacher must maintain even more control or guidance over the situation than in the direct approach. Although learners are given the freedom to interact with one another and the material, the teacher sets the stage, determines the rules, monitors, facilitates, and generally keeps things moving in the appropriate direction. Learners must be kept on task, and it is the teacher's job to make sure that this is happening. The teacher must also set up the activity so that everyone gets a chance to participate. Finally, the teacher puts closure on the activity by making sure that either he or she or the learners spend some time summarizing and synthesizing what has gone on in the instruction. This is true whether you are working in the F2F or an online setting (Bain, 2004; Clark and Feldon, 2005; Cruickshank, Jenkins, and Metcalf, 2003; Eble, 1988; Elliott et al., 2000; Jacobson, 2008; Jacobson and Xu, 2002; Macklin, 2008; Mayer, 2002, 2004). If you are working in an asynchronous setting, do some testing ahead of time to make sure the directions for the activities are clear and understandable and that the activity can be completed in a reasonable timeframe. Ask your colleagues to try out the material. Testing it out on a sample set of learners from the population you expect to use the material is an even better approach and would give you some valuable feedback for improving the material and keeping it fresh and relevant. See Chapter 6 for more about active learning and ILI.

No matter how much advance thought we put into an activity's design, indirect learning, by its very nature, is to some extent unpredictable. Each time we use an activity in our teaching may be a bit different from the last. This unpredictability actually adds to the technique's appeal. When faced with the prospect of repeating our instructional efforts over and over again, it is hard not to become stale and lose interest in our task. In a less-structured indirect learning setting, the material remains fresh. Each group, whether we are working with them F2F or in an online setting, brings its unique insights to the activity, and each event has its own individual character.

INSPIRE YOUR LEARNERS

Whatever methods and activities you decide to include in your instruction, remember that one of our goals is to motivate and inspire our learners and send them away feeling better about the material and their abilities to interact with it. Can you motivate and inspire your learners merely by modeling your personal passion? To a certain extent, the answer is "Yes." Passion is contagious, and your learners will pick up on the excitement you are communicating (Bligh, 2000; Freilberg and Driscoll, 2005; Jacobson and Xu, 2002; Oswald and Turnage, 2000). Your own passion, however, may not be enough. The relevance of the material is so obvious to you that you may forget that it is not quite that clear to your learners. It is up to you to explicate how what you are teaching relates to them both in the short run and over the long haul. In many ILI situations, we have little in the way of external rewards to offer, so we must pay special attention to demonstrating the relevance of our information. We want to encourage our learners to continue to explore the material on their own and without the need for external rewards to spur them on. In short, we want to move them from being motivated solely by extrinsic or tangible rewards to a state in which they are intrinsically motivated, one where learning becomes its own reward. One way to do this is to use examples to which the learners can relate. This is another area where background work pays off. The more you know about your learners and their information needs, the better you can relate your material to what is important to them. Giving people some freedom in choosing topics for their activities helps them make this connection for themselves. Using LCT approaches that give learners a chance to interact with the material in a meaningful way also helps them discover how the information fits into their own lives (Bain, 2004; Biggs, 1999a; Eble, 1988; Elliott et al., 2000; Jacobson, 2008; Vella, 2000; Weimer, 2002). Once you have done this, your learners will become more self-sufficient and will have taken a step closer to being people who have learned how to learn.

A fundamental principle of IL is that it enables people to be lifelong learners. To encourage this, we must not only teach them about resources and the skills and strategies to select among and use them but we must also help them to become comfortable and confident about the information seeking process (Sullivan, 2004). Many of the characteristics of LCT help to create a learning environment in which learners can develop these more affective IL traits. LCT views learners as shareholders in the instructional process. Your role in this type of environment is to show by words and actions that every voice has value and that it is safe for everyone to express his or her views, opinions, and ideas—regardless of whether those discussions are occurring F2F or online. Allowing learners to discuss their thoughts in small groups or with a partner prior to an all-inclusive full group discussion emphasizes the openness and nonjudgmental nature of your teaching. Furthermore, the ways in which you moderate live or online discussions and/or reply to messages from your learners can all contribute to these feelings of comfort and confidence. It can also help to instill an atmosphere of trust and safety, and it promotes a shared responsibility for learning. By asking learners to join in, and by really listening to what they have to say, you create the sense that the instruction belongs to everyone (Bain, 2004; Freilberg and Driscoll, 2005; Johnson, Johnson, and Smith, 2007; Ridgeway, 1989; Vella, 2000; Weimer, 2002).

LCT not only involves the learners in the process but also encourages them to try things out and think for themselves. Learners want to participate because the activities we have chosen for them are meaningful and important. In other words, the learner can clearly see the value of completing the activity. Furthermore, the atmosphere of shared responsibility and trust that we have created communicates our belief that learners can succeed at the tasks presented to them. Giving people the chance to interact and succeed with new material can greatly enhance their feelings of self-efficacy—a belief in their own abilities—that can carry over to new situations beyond the ILI itself (Biggs, 1999a; Jacobson and Xu, 2002). LCT also encourages learners to reflect on the material under discussion and on what they have learned. Being self-reflective is crucial to becoming a lifelong learner. We do not truly know if we learned anything unless we reflect upon the experience. The very nature of LCT, with its emphasis on group problem-solving, discussion, and feedback, invites this self-reflection and hopefully instills a self-monitoring and self-directed attitude toward learning that lasts throughout the learners' lifetime (Bransford et al., 1999b; Costa and Kallick, 2000; Freilberg and Driscoll, 2005; Weimer, 2002).

Motivating and inspiring our learners begins with us. We should be role models of enthusiasm for our material. We must exhibit care and concern for our learners—and we must help them make the connection between what we are doing in our instruction and what they will need to be doing throughout their lives. Your enthusiasm for the subject (as demonstrated by the way you interact with the material—verbally and/or in writing), coupled with the learners' own improved attitudes toward the material, should increase their willingness to approach the material in the future. Furthermore, it should promote an eagerness in your learners to keep learning about the material long after the instructional experience is over.

PRACTICAL CONSIDERATIONS: TIPS FOR TEACHING

Teaching as Performance

The principles of listening, engaging, and inspiring your learners apply to both F2F and online modes of teaching, although each mode has its unique and special characteristics. Although the following performance tips, strategies, and techniques seem most applicable to a F2F teaching situation, keep in mind that online instruction formats (streaming video, podcasts, Webinars, etc.) all include elements of performance as well. Stage fright affects those working with a live audience as well as those being filmed or recorded. Voice quality and pacing are issues when you are doing narrations and voice-overs for both synchronous online instruction (like Webinars) and asynchronous modes (as in tutorials, presentation slide shows, or podcasts). Considering eye contact, immediacy factors, gestures, and voice quality can turn a fairly boring "talking head" Webcast into a more engaging and dynamic one. Even teaching in virtual worlds like Second Life involves a particular kind of performance as you work through the gestures and movements of your avatar. Examples of both F2F and online forms of teaching will be included in the following material whenever possible. For more on using technology to support pedagogy, see Chapter 15.

In your preinstruction planning, you have thought long and hard about how to listen to, engage, and inspire your learners. You have settled on the content to include and have selected the methods and modes to use in your instruction. So, you are good to go. Or are you? The best material in the world is worthless unless you can present it in a dynamic, enthusiastic, and effective manner. Teaching is performing, and, as such, teachers are a lot like actors. Getting psyched to teach (especially in the synchronous mode) is not an easy task. It is a widespread and commonly held belief that people rank public speaking as their number one fear—higher even than death. So it is no surprise that even experienced teachers will tell you they still get the jitters before having to "perform." They may love the act of teaching when they are actually doing it, but they still dread it as they wait "to go on." Sound crazy? Well, most performers will say that they feel the same way. In the *Confident Performer,* David Roland (1997) interviews athletes, musicians, film and theater actors, and other performers who all agree that if you are not nervous you should not be performing. Being nervous is part of caring about doing a good job. Whether you are working in front of a live audience, teaching to the camera, narrating a slide presentation, or recording comments to accompany asynchronous material (podcasts, vodcasts, or videos, for example) being nervous is all part of the performance package.

Dealing with Stage Fright

Being too nervous, of course, can interfere with your teaching effectiveness. At that point, panic sets in and you may be unable to think, speak, or move. You may make mistakes or rush through the material, leaving important points out. But being totally relaxed could be detrimental as well. You may not be alert and may appear disinterested in the material. If it seems as though you do not care, why should your learners? Accept the fact that you may be nervous, and make it work for you by discovering your personal level of optimal arousal state (Bligh, 2000). One way to do this is to learn more about the physiological aspects of anxiety.

What happens when you are feeling threatened? Your heart beats faster, your mouth gets dry, you may shiver or sweat, and your breathing may become shallow. These are all normal reactions to stress, and they signal your body's readiness for dealing with it. Now think about what happens when you are excited about some challenge. The symptoms are the same. So, what does that mean in terms of dealing with anxiety? If you can view these physiological signals in a positive way, as the body preparing you to meet a challenge rather than urging you to run from a threat, you will have a much more positive attitude about the upcoming experience. There is nothing wrong with some honest sweat or palpitations as you get ready for your instructional endeavor. Just view these bodily changes as symptoms of your concern and commitment to doing a good job. It means you are excited about the upcoming experience and are ready to do your best (Roland, 1997). The following are some simple ways to get to that optimal level of arousal as you prepare yourself to walk into that roomful of people, gear yourself up to facing the camera, or get ready to record your narration.

- **Personal tension points**—If your anxiety gets to the point where it interferes with your performance, there are ways to keep it under control. Learn some relaxation techniques, and use them just before you begin your instruction. Do whatever works for you. Some people feel tension in their necks. Others feel it in their shoulders or their backs. Concentrate on relaxing your personal tension points. Books on acting, sports psychology, yoga, and meditation can all offer suggestions. Some basic stretching techniques include rotating your neck, raising and lowering your shoulders, and shaking your arms and hands. Do not forget to warm up your voice by humming or subvocalizing. See the CD-ROM that accompanies this book for a two-minute yoga routine that you can use as a warm-up before teaching. You can also use it as a stretch break for your learners during multi-hour sessions.
- **Breathing**—Pay special attention to your breathing. Yoga breathing exercises can be very helpful. For example, to learn to take deep breaths, place one hand on your chest and the other on your abdomen while breathing. Which one moves? The healthiest, deepest breathing is from the abdomen. Chest breathing is shallower, quicker, reduces your oxygen intake, and can increase feelings of anxiety. When you are feeling anxious, consciously monitor your breathing and focus on abdomen rather than chest breathing. Slow down your breathing rate by increasing the length of your inhales and exhales. Doing so will result in a decrease in anxiety-related physiological symptoms and will calm you down. Another breathing/meditation technique is to take ten breaths, counting one as you inhale, two as you exhale. Continue until you reach ten. Repeat the sequence two more times. By the end of the third sequence, you should find yourself calmer and less anxious about the task ahead.
- **Rehearse**—Know your stuff. Practice your material thoroughly in advance by speaking it out loud and timing it so that your instruction is smooth and unflustered. Prioritize the most important points. For synchronous instruction that must fit into a specific timeframe, be prepared to toss out some portion of your planned instruction if need be in order to stick within the allotted learning time. Test your demos and examples to make sure they work the way in which you intend them and that they illustrate the points you are trying to model. Try out the directions for any activities you plan to include. If possible, ask a colleague (or, better yet, someone from the instruction's target group) to test out the activities with you. This both helps to see if the directions are understandable and gives you a better idea of how long an activity might take. Rehearsal helps reduce performance anxiety. It alerts you to where you may run into trouble before it happens for real. Try to identify potential logistical problems. If you are preparing for F2F instruction, go to the space ahead of time so that you are familiar with the layout and any equipment you will be using. You might have to modify some of your activities depending upon the physical arrangement of the room. If you are preparing for a podcast, vodcast, or Webcast, see if you can get some practice with the layout of the physical and virtual space in which you will be Webcasting, filming, and/or recording. Try doing some trial runs to make sure your delivery is smooth and engaging. Watch and/or listen to the "rehearsals" to see if any adjustments need to be made. Pay special attention to timing, especially if there is any restriction on the timeframe for your instruction. Even in an asynchronous setting that

offers the possibility of unlimited time, keep in mind that there can be too much of a good thing. You do not want to overwhelm your learners, so set a time limit for yourself for your asynchronous material, and stick to it. Even if learners can stop and start the asynchronous material, you still want to make sure that you are holding their interest so that they are motivated to return.

- **Practice positive self-talk before the session**—You are the expert on this material. You have tried out your material ahead of time, familiarized yourself with the teaching, filming, or recording space, and know what you want to teach. Tell yourself that you will give it your best and that you are good at what you do. Pump yourself up just like athletes do before competing. Visualize doing an excellent job, and expect to succeed.
- **Focus on the content you are trying to present**—Once you start your instruction, try to concentrate on the points you are trying to make and on what the learners need to know. Remember to include comprehension checks to make sure you are succeeding. If you get caught up in getting your ideas across, you will become less self-conscious and nervous.
- **Deal rationally with mistakes**—Everyone makes mistakes. Do not let mistakes throw you. You probably will notice them much more than your learners will. Acknowledge and correct your errors, and the learners will empathize. There is actually a benefit to making mistakes. If you can make mistakes, it is okay for your learners to do so and still expect to succeed at the task. Put your mistakes in perspective. Do not dwell on them. Take pride in what went well. View your successes and your mistakes as learning opportunities. Concentrate on emphasizing what went well and improving what did not. Your goal is to learn from the experience in order to do better the next time. Remember that mistakes can occur in all instructional formats—F2F and online. They may be especially obvious in online asynchronous instruction, particularly if you are communicating to your learners in writing via e-mail, discussion boards, and the like. Follow up with your correction as soon as the error comes to light. Of course, for many types of asynchronous instruction, you may be able to correct your mistakes before you learners even see the material.
- **Be prepared for anything**—Another way to alleviate anxiety is to be prepared for any contingency, especially when you are working in the F2F mode. Keep in mind that all the advance planning in the world will not help if the projector light bulb blows out, the extension cord is too short, your network or broadcast system goes down, microphones or cameras fail, or any number of random acts of chaos occurs that can plague a teacher. When teaching F2F, create a kit that you take with you whenever you teach (Smith, 1991). This kit can include such standard items as tape, push pins, chalk, markers (regular and erasable), clips, scissors, flashlights, and so on. Include whatever you can think will help you deal with unforeseen circumstances, and then continue to add to it as you experience other "surprises." For example, some people include a couple of nightlights in their kits. You can use these to create ambient illumination if you have to dim the lights for part of your presentation. Paper towels are good to include in case of spills. You might want to have cough drops in your bag or carry a water bottle to help with dry mouth. Manila file folders make great emergency charts. Swizzle sticks can be used as pointers in a pinch. Post-it pads can be used for sorting ideas into categories during learning activities. File cards of all sizes are also useful. Learners can use small or mid-sized ones to record questions or comments for discussion. Larger ones can be folded in half and used as name cards placed in front of each learner. A few pages of self-sticking flip chart paper, rolled into a compact cylinder are also a useful part of your kit. They can be used for learners to post their ideas following small group exercises and can serve as your "board" if there is none in the space in which you are teaching.

If you are working in an asynchronous online mode and something goes wrong, see if you can arrange to do it again at a later time. If you are "going live," try to maintain your composure and sense of humor and hope that your technical support will be able to make things right as quickly as possible. In extreme cases, you might have to reschedule the event. Your participants will probably be very understanding, as they might have experienced similar problems on other occasions. Try not to blame yourself for technical problems. As much as we try to anticipate them in advance, we cannot always do so. And do not let the possibility of technical glitches prevent you from trying to take your teaching into the online world. For more help with dealing with problems when teaching with technology, see Chapter 15.

Whichever methods you use to deal with stage fright, remember that getting yourself up for the task of teaching is crucial. Try to set aside a few minutes before you have to teach so you can prepare yourself psychologically for the task ahead. Use this time in ways that can calm your nerves, as well as get you motivated and energized. Breathing exercises, meditation techniques, positive self-talk, stretching, and humming are all useful ways to use this time. Come up with a routine you like and make time for it. Doing so will make you more relaxed and primed to teach. Your enjoyment and that of your learners will be increased because you are in the right frame of mind to "go on."

Stage Presence

Now you are fairly calm, or at least you know how to make your anxiety work for you. What else goes into getting ready to teach? You need to know how to use your instrument to put the material across. The instrument in question is not a piece of technology, such as your projector, microphone, or computer. It is your voice and body. Verbal and nonverbal cues can make or break your instruction. You need to know how to use your voice and your body as emphasis and as a means of motivating your learners (Jacobson and Xu, 2002; Lowman, 1995).

- **Make yourself comfortable**—You may read a lot of advice about the type of clothes to wear and how to move, gesture, talk, and behave in front of a group. Pay attention to what makes sense to you. Work on what you can do to improve your presentation, but do not make yourself crazy. Do what feels right. If you like bright, cheerful colors, wear them. If flashy jewelry makes you feel confident, go for it. If you tend to make wild gestures to emphasize a point, do it (as long as you do not poke anyone's eye out in the process). If you are working in an online setting, you still want to make sure that you are relaxed and comfortable. So feel free to be yourself—whether you are actually facing a camera or just providing narration to go with an online instructional endeavor.
- **Adopt an easy conversational tone**—Prepare your session for the ear rather than the eye. Listen to yourself as you practice. Do you sound like you are chatting to a friend or lecturing to a group of strangers? You have a better chance of connecting to the group if you talk with them rather than at them. Again this is true regardless of the delivery mode—F2F, online, synchronous or asynchronous.
- **Use your voice for emphasis**— Highlight important points by changing the speed at which you are talking, pausing after a point, and/or adjusting your inflection (up or down). If something is important, repeat it. Many presenters actually give a verbal cue such as "This next point is crucial" or "You really need to remember this next point" (Bligh, 2000; Stewart, 1993). Tell people that if you were going to remember anything at all about the session, this is it! Using your voice as a way to emphasize and highlight material is even more important when you are narrating and/or speaking in online settings than it is in F2F ones. Because you are not interacting physically with your learners, your voice may be the only thing you have to get your points across.
- **Articulate clearly**—No Professor Mumbles allowed! If you expect to be speaking to your learners, either F2F or in some kind of online format, make sure you can speak clearly and in an understandable manner. Practice volume and pitch control, and learn to project. Lower pitches seem to go further. If you are having trouble being heard, try lowering your pitch. In F2F situations always make sure you can be heard in all parts of the room. As you begin, ask people in the

back of the room if they can hear you. Even if they say yes, ask them to give you a cue if your voice fades at some point—perhaps by raising their hands. If you are doing a live broadcast that includes real-time chat, you can also ask people to let you know if they can hear you. In any kind of broadcast or filming situation in which you have a sound crew, work with them to ensure good audio quality, or record the material and then listen to how you sound. Make sure you test out any asynchronous material with others before you release it publicly for clarity and voice quality.

- **Vary your pitch**—A voice that exhibits a range of pitch is much more interesting to listen to than a monotone. Think about using your voice as a musical instrument. While you probably do not want to try singing your material, you do want to keep the sound interesting. Shifts in pitch can work to hold your listeners' attention. Pitch shifts can also be used as emphasis and to mark changes from one topic to the next. This is equally true if you are in the same room with your learners or are speaking to them in an online mode.
- **Speak at a comfortable speed**—Do not speak so quickly that learners are unable to keep up with you or so slow that it sounds like you are playing a recording at the wrong speed. Stop every so often to allow note takers to catch up. Again this is equally true for online as well as F2F instructional endeavors.
- **Try moving around a bit to add variety to the presentation**—If you are illustrating varying viewpoints on a subject in a F2F situation, try changing your position when you switch sides. Or change your physical location to indicate that you are moving to a new topic or are changing activities. You may also be able to use gestures or other types of body language to convey these messages. In F2F situations move closer to the group during interactive question and answer periods or discussion segments or lean toward the person who is speaking to convey interest in what he or she has to say. Obviously it will be easier to do all this in a F2F situation. If you are filming your instruction, you could have the camera zoom in on your face for question and answer exchanges. Also make sure you are looking directly at the camera to give the impression you are talking with your learners. In all cases, use appropriate and meaningful gestures to emphasize your points.
- **Maintain eye contact with the group**—Never, ever speak entirely to your notes or talk with your back turned to the group. If you are writing on the board or on flipcharts, or pointing to material being projected on a screen in a F2F setting, make sure you turn toward the group before you begin to speak. This takes some practice, but it is crucial not only to be heard but also to maintain your connection with the group. In a standard auditorium-type classroom, think of the room as organized into two zones—the U, which includes the side and back rows, and the T, which covers the front and center rows. Make sure you are looking and speaking to those seated in the U area as well as the easier to see T section (Biggs, 1999a). While it may seem strange to talk about eye contact in an online setting, remember that when you look directly at the camera it will appear that you are making eye contact with your learners.
- **Do not read verbatim from your notes**—Use your notes to keep yourself on track. If you were just going to read to the group, they could have stayed home and read your notes themselves. So do not read word for word from either your written notes or your presentation slides. Remember that you are there to add value to what they could learn on their own. Your job is to summarize, synthesize, emphasize through examples, and make sure they understand the material. Develop your own cue card technique. Some people use oversized (5" by 8") cards with just a few important cue words on them. Others outline the whole session (usually in very large point font) and then highlight the key phrases. Or, if you are utilizing a presentation slide show, use the Notes section of each slide to insert what you are going to cover. These Notes will not appear when you display the slides, but you can print them out so they appear under a smaller image of each slide. Whatever you do, make sure your notes are easy to follow and that you can find what you need when you need it. If you are recording voice-overs (background narrations) for asynchronous delivery,

you may be tempted to write out your remarks ahead of time and just read them. If you use this approach, make sure you rehearse the material ahead of time so that you sound as natural and conversational as possible while you are reading. Again, do not simply read what appears on the screen, whether it is a presentation slide show, a screencast (video capture of activity that is displayed on a computer monitor), or a video.

- **Be positive, upbeat, and enthusiastic**—Discussions of master teaching frequently include references to how teacher's attitudes affect learning. You need to care about what you are teaching and to show that you care. Even if you have to teach something that may not really excite you—such as the latest incarnation of your institution's library catalog—see if you can find something to be enthusiastic about the material. If you are not passionate about what you are doing, it will show. Learners will pick up on your attitude. If you are not interested in what you are saying or showing, why on earth should they be?
- **Create a warm, supporting, and encouraging learning environment**—Welcome questions and comments. Frame your responses positively, and thank people for their questions and comments. In the F2F setting, be sure to look at people when they speak. Respond to their comments with smiles and nods. In synchronous settings (F2F or online), make sure your comments are respectful and encouraging. Do not be judgmental or critical of what anyone thinks or says. If you are responding to questions or comments in an asynchronous setting, thank the learner for the question. Make sure the tone of your written responses also reflects this concern for your learners. Treat your learners with dignity and respect. Do not lecture to or talk down to them. Engage them in the exploration and discovery of new ideas. Make learning a shared responsibility.

For more hints on these topics see Bain (2004), Conrad and Donaldson (2004), Cruickshank, Jenkins, and Metcalf (2003), Eble (1988), Elliott et al. (2000), Freilberg and Driscoll (2005), Kroenke (1984), Lowman (1995), Mager (1997b, 1997c); McKeachie (1986, 1994), Palmer (1998), Smith (1991), and Veldof (2006).

Lesson Planning: General Considerations

Your instructional goals and objectives help you determine and prioritize what to include in your instruction—whether you are meeting your learners F2F or will be interacting with them via some kind of technology. After you have identified what your learners need to know, do, or feel at the end of your instruction, ask yourself the following questions (Bain, 2004; Biggs, 1999b; Cruickshank, Jenkins, and Metcalf, 2003; Vella, 2000; Weimer, 2002, 2003; Wiggins, 1998):

- Which examples, experiences, or activities should you include that will enable your learners to achieve your ELOs?
- How can you make your session relevant to your learners?
- How can you exhibit listening skills as you involve your learners in the learning experience?
- How can you engage and inspire your learners?

Like any good book, well-constructed instruction has a definite beginning, middle, and end, all of which require planning and preliminary effort. Everyone has his or her own idiosyncratic method of developing a session. But here are some things to consider. Remember that the following points can be applied to both F2F and online forms of teaching.

Get Their Attention

Although some librarians may teach full-credit courses, more often than not they meet with learners only once or twice, at best, and for limited periods of time. In addition, they are often guests on someone else's turf. Or they may be "meeting" with their learners (synchronously or asynchronously) via some type of technology. Regardless of the setting, what you do in the first five minutes of instruction will determine how effective your instruction will be. Most people will pay attention for at least the first few minutes, so use this time to capture everyone's attention and build rapport.

Holding on to their attention for the long haul can be a bit more problematic (Lowman, 1995; Oswald and Turnage, 2000; Rockman, 2003a).

What can you do in those first five minutes to ensure instructional success? If you were able to conduct a Needs Assessment and/or a pretest in advance, you already have a lot of information about your learners and what they need to know. If not, you can build in some questions during that first five minutes that will help give you some clues as to their skill levels and experience. In an online environment you can conduct interactive chat or use polling technology to gather some of this information fairly quickly. Capture their attention by showing them the relevance of what you are about to cover. In other words, use those first five minutes to find out more about them and to let them know what they will gain from the instruction. However you choose to use those initial minutes, keep in mind that this opening segment is crucial to your overall success. For an asynchronous setting, starting the material with information that lets learners know how this instructional material will benefit them is a good way to capture their attention. Asking for their reactions via a wiki or a blog is also a way to gain (and keep) learners' attention.

In F2F settings, it is a good idea to get learners engaged as soon as they walk in the door. Make sure you get to the room before they do, and chat with them as they come in. Plan an activity for people to do as soon as they enter the room. Often called sponge, hook, or "gotcha" activities, these "soak" people up as they arrive and immediately make them part of the learning process (Freilberg and Driscoll, 2005; Hunter, 1985; Liles, 2007; Rockman, 2003a). You can give out small file cards and ask learners to write some questions they may have about the topic, or have them use the cards to describe a previous experience (good or bad) they have had searching for information. Place a thought-provoking quote or question on the board and ask people to describe their reactions to it (Bain, 2004). You could give a brief quiz to help people see what they do (and do not) already know about the subject. This activity also functions as a quick Needs Assessment (Keyser, 2000). Have a list of topics on the board or on a slide, and ask learners to vote on what interests them. Tell them you will use the list to structure your instruction.

Or try this experiment for a F2F or a synchronous online environment. Outline your presentation as usual, but hold off referring to your outline until you respond to the learners' questions as described in the preceding paragraph. You may be surprised about how much of your material gets covered as you address these questions. Once the question and answer session is over, you can then return to your outline and fill in what might have been missed. This more interactive approach goes a long way to really engaging your learners in the process. Furthermore, because each instruction ends up being a bit unique, the sessions can be a bit more fun and interesting to the instructor as well.

These more dynamic approaches to teaching can go a long way to staving off the dreaded teacher burnout syndrome and can help you maintain your enthusiasm for teaching. Using a sponge activity puts you in control from the very start of the session. It sets the tone and lets people know that you are interested in what they think. Furthermore, you can gain a lot of useful information about the group, their background, and previous experiences. Again these techniques can be used in both F2F situations as described earlier or in online settings through the use of chat, wikis, blogs, discussion boards, etc.

However, make sure your activity is relevant and connected to your instructional objectives. If it is viewed as busywork, you will lose rather than gain respect and credibility (Lorenzen 2001a). Use your sponge activity to engage your learners and to build rapport. From a stranger talking at them, you become a person who is listening to and engaging in a dialogue with them. Dealing with your learners' responses in a warm, friendly, nonthreatening, and accepting manner creates an atmosphere that is conducive to learning and involves everyone in the process.

Have a Big Finish

Just as you win or lose your learners in the first five minutes of teaching, you can undermine the entire instruction by the way you end it. Make sure you plan an upbeat and appropriate finish and that you leave the proper amount of time for it. In F2F instruction, give your learners five minutes at the end of the session to tell their neighbor what they think was the thrust of the session and how they plan to apply what they learned. Then ask for some comments from these pairs. Or use the last few minutes to ask the whole group "What stuck?" as a way to get learners to summarize and reflect upon the most important points and then briefly fill in with important points you want them to take away. Or you could use this time to check on the learners' achievement of ELOs, perhaps by posing questions to the group. You may need to leave a bit more time for this type of activity in a synchronous online setting, as participants may be working through interactive chat or polling technology to provide this feedback to you and to the rest of the group. In either F2F or online settings, make sure you invite learners to contact you later if they have additional questions or need further help. For asynchronous instruction, you may wish to build in some kind of summary of the material as well as invite learners to contact you if they have additional comments or questions. At the top or the end of each instructional item, including materials like an exercise, provide an e-mail or an instant messaging address or a Facebook account for questions and comments. Regardless of the setting and delivery mode, end the instruction the same way you began it—by listening to the learners and responding to them. Trying to cover a few more points as the clock runs down on your instruction, or just dwindling off into nothingness when you run out of things to say, can defeat all the good you may have done during the instruction (Biggs, 1999a; Cruickshank, Jenkins, and Metcalf, 2003; Lowman, 1995).

What Goes Between

You have an attention-getting opening and a smash finish. What goes in the middle? Here is where you have to make some tough decisions. Return to your goals, objectives, and ELOs. Are you being realistic about how much you can accomplish or that learners can grasp in the time allotted? A good teacher emphasizes the important material, deletes the unimportant, and can tell the difference between the two (Veldof, 2006). The overriding rule should always be "less is more" (Ramsden, 1988). It is far better to cover two or three important items in a clear, thorough, and memorable fashion than to attempt to quickly cram a dozen items into the instruction with the hope that people will remember some of it. They will not retain that material, and you will have set them up for failure. The topic will seem overwhelming, and your learners will get the impression that it is impossible for them to learn it. This is definitely not what we want to have happen in our instruction. We want our learners to become engaged and have them leave feeling inspired, confident, and competent in their abilities to use what you presented. Here are some tips to help you as you are thinking about what to include in the body of your instruction.

- **Consider how much time has been allotted for the instruction carefully**—Do not try to pack too much into your given timeframe. Use handouts, Web sites, and other supplementary material to expand your F2F "contact" time. Supplemental material can also be provided to learners, either before or after, online instruction. For live (F2F or online) instruction, try developing only enough content to fill about two-thirds of the allotted time. This leaves room for questions, unexpected learner-generated topics, technical difficulties, late arrivals, and other acts of God and nature. Although asynchronous online instruction may not seem to have these time restrictions, consider how long you will be able to hold a learners interest in this format and plan accordingly.
- **Have something extra up your sleeve**—Most learners in the F2F situation will be happy to leave early if you run out of material before the time is up. But if that really bothers you, try developing a tiered approach to your outline. Prepare three levels of material. The first contains the crucial material they have to know. Next comes the "it would be nice if I could get it in" stuff. The third level contains the bonus information that they really do not need to know but might be of some interest to them (Veldof, 2006).

  Highlight your notes, using three different colors, to indicate the three levels. Put timing notes on the edge of your outline to indicate when you need to move on to the next segment.

Keep a clock or watch handy so you can stay on track. Add or skip over material depending on how well you are sticking to your plan. If you have a bit more time for a given section, add some of your level two or level three material. If not, just cover the level one material and move on. You can always return to the level two and/or three material at the end of your session, if time permits, or offer it via handouts or accompanying material mounted on the Web. This approach is also useful if you are working in a live, online environment. If you are using an asynchronous online delivery mode, you can include all three levels in discrete and separate sections and then let the learner decide if he or she wants to go beyond the basics.

- **Think like a novice**—To determine what goes into each of the three levels, think back to when you were first learning the material. What did you need to know to get started? If it is hard for you to remember what it was like to learn something for the first time, ask for comments on your material from a novice or a colleague. Use this feedback to identify the main points that must be presented or the learner will be unable to function. Next think about what you wanted to know once the basics were conquered? This will be the material for your second layer. Finally, which extra (bells and whistles) features/skills/strategies did you pick up after you had developed some expertise? These can be added as your third level and usually include special tips and techniques that make sense only after you have had some experience with the material. If you do not get to this material (and you might not be able to), it will not stop your learners from functioning successfully.

Lesson Planning: Specific Segments

Whatever you decide to include as your content, here are some segments that could be part of your lesson plan (Bain, 2004; Cruickshank, Jenkins, and Metcalf, 2003; Elliott et al., 2000; Freilberg and Driscoll, 2005; Hunter, 1985; Jacobson and Xu, 2002; Liles, 2007):

- **Introduction**—Introductions follow the sponge activity, set the stage, and put the instruction in context for the group. Appeal to the "what's in it for me" factor during your introduction. Be as succinct as possible. Remember, you are just giving hints about what is to come. Use the introduction to present the conceptual framework for the session and to provide the group with whatever facts or background material they may need to understand the material that will be covered. Some teachers like to share the ELOs for the instruction with their learners during this segment of instruction. Your introduction is especially important in asynchronous settings, because you are not available to answer questions or clear up confusion in real time.
- **Active learning experiences**—Distribute these throughout your session. They can be used to break up the more formal presentation or demonstration segments of your session or as a means for self-discovery. Each activity should be a method for illustrating and reinforcing important points and concepts. Use your session objectives as a guide to determining the usefulness of an activity. Will the activity help the learners demonstrate they have reached the instructional objectives? If the answer to the question is "Yes," then use it; if not, delete it. Such an activity might be fun, but in the end it is only busy work and can detract from the overall effectiveness of the session (Allen, 1995; Conrad and Donaldson, 2004; Freilberg and Driscoll, 2005; Johnson and Cooper, 2007; Keyser, 2000; Lorenzen, 2001a; Ridgeway, 1989). For more on active learning, see Chapter 6.
- **Checks for understanding**—You should end each segment with some kind of comprehension check. Never allow your learners to go on to the next segment until you are sure that they are ready to do so. You can ask specific content-related questions or invite learners to summarize what has just been covered. Or you could query learners directly if they are ready to move on. In a synchronous online environment, see if there is any kind of voting or polling mechanism (clicking on thumbs up or down, for example) that can be used to gather this information. If you decide to go with "temperature-taking" questions, make sure you use the kind that cannot be answered

by "Yes" or "No." Instead of asking, "Do you have any questions?" ask, "What questions do you now have about what we just did?" Remember that you can (and should) include such comprehension checks in your online instructional endeavors as well as in your F2F ones. In the case of asynchronous online instruction, it is helpful to provide a means for learners to determine if their answers are correct. This can be done by having self-correcting mechanisms built into the comprehension check or by having these checks e-mailed to the librarian for feedback.

Asking for learner input should not be a pro forma exercise. Whenever you ask for learners' responses, whether in the F2F or synchronous online setting, make sure you give them enough time to actually respond. Most people are uncomfortable with silence, and teachers are no exception. Hold firm and wait for them to respond, or your learners will think you are not really interested in what they have to say. Show them you mean it by waiting for the reply. If you find yourself jumping in too soon to fill the silence, force yourself to count very slowly to yourself from one to ten. If you still get no reply, try rephrasing the question and then count to ten again. You will be surprised at how often people will respond when given an appropriate amount of time. In an online environment you might try asking for responses to your questions via online chat or polling technology. You may have to allow for a bit more response time as people have to type out their comments. It can also be helpful to ask a colleague to monitor these responses and summarize them for you and the online group. Once you hear or read a response, provide some feedback and summary to show that, once again, you have listened to your learners.

Try It All Out

There is one last thing to do before you are ready to "go on." Follow the theatrical model and do a dry run and time it, if possible with a trusted friend watching and providing constructive feedback. Are you being realistic about what you plan to include? Will it fit? If you start to feel rushed, look for places to cut. Rehearsals help you smooth out the rough spots and alert you to where you may run into trouble with a segment or an activity. Be especially cautious when including learner activities, because they frequently take longer than you think they will. It helps to specify a timeframe for activities and to let learners know what that time is before you turn them loose. For instance, you can say "I'd like you to take two minutes to write down (or submit via chat in an online environment) any questions you may have about information researching." In F2F settings, if learners need to move around to form groups for an activity, be sure to factor in the time it will take to do so. Remember, it generally takes some time to get everyone out of the groups and back to their seats as well. Develop some attention-getting signal that will get their eyes back on you. For example, flick the lights on and off or use a timer that makes a loud and obvious noise. In the case of synchronous online instruction, you might show an image of a countdown clock to help keep the participants on track. Of course, you could also make announcements at intervals to let people know how much time is left for the exercise.

Planning an effective instructional session takes practice, and, no matter how hard you try, you may not get it right every time (especially if you are new to using LCT approaches)—no one does. Learn from your experiences. If you run into problems, try to do some postsession analysis to see what went wrong. Even more important, see if you can figure out what you could do next time to make it better.

Classroom Management

If you have done your homework, prepared an engaging and relevant session, and honed your performance/presentation skills, you should have little trouble keeping the class motivated and on track. If you are fortunate enough to be in a situation where people are attending your sessions because they want to, half the battle is won already. Sometimes, however, learners, especially in the school and academic environments, are required to attend a "library session." The relationship between the session and their regular course work may seem unclear to them, and they might view themselves as unwilling "victims." Even in the public library setting, where attendance is generally voluntary, participants may be unclear about what will be included in the instruction or how it will really relate to them. Regardless of the environment in which you work, it will be up to you to win your learners over by using the various methods already discussed in this chapter. In most cases you will succeed. But what do you do about learners who not only remain unconvinced about the worth of the instruction but also actually expend some energy to disrupt it?

This can be especially problematic when we are doing a guest appearance in someone else's class as is common in school and academic environments. It is hard for us to assert ourselves when we know we have no real power over the group. We cannot flunk them for interfering with our session, and we often find it hard to ask them to leave the room. As much as we try to establish a relationship with our learners, it may still be a very tentative one. So, what are we to do? If we are fortunate to have good rapport with the person who has requested the instruction, we can ask him or her for assistance at this point. An even better approach is to ask in advance how he or she would like you to handle disruptions. Try including management questions into your preinstruction information-gathering discussions and pointing out that it is crucial for the instructor to be present during the session in order to give you this type of support as well as to indicate the value of the ILI. This is true in the school and academic setting as well as in public libraries that are offering instruction to specific classes in their neighborhood schools.

In addition to asking for help from the classroom teacher, here are a few other things you can try. First of all, remember that most of the group is probably interested in the material or at least sympathetic to you. The loudmouth is generally the exception, not the rule. Do not judge your effectiveness by one or two unruly people. If someone is being really loud or disruptive, stop talking. You probably cannot compete anyway, so do not even try. Suddenly the disrupter is the only voice in the room. This could be sufficiently embarrassing to cause him or her to shut up. Walking toward the disrupter can also be effective. If you feel comfortable about confronting the person, ask him or her if he or she has a question that you could address. Finally, you can tell the person that if he or she is not interested in what is going on, perhaps he or she should leave, and let the rest of the class proceed with the instruction. You can also forestall this type of behavior to begin with by first acknowledging that some of those attending the session may already know some of what is going to be covered and that you hope to add some tips and tricks that will help save them time and maybe even money. Remember that learners can also try to disrupt or dominate the "chat" area in a synchronous online setting or be less than totally cooperative if you are incorporating any group work and/or discussions into your instruction. Setting ground rules in advance may help. However, you may have to step in verbally or via "chat" (perhaps privately to the offending person) to remind him or her of those ground rules.

This may not be the most comfortable of situations, but, if you have set the right tone from the beginning of the session, most of the group will be on your side and will support your action. They are probably just as annoyed at the disrupter as you are and will admire you for taking a stand. This is just another example of how you take what you are doing seriously and care about getting the information across to your learners. Do not worry too much about this sort of thing. It rarely happens, especially if you have created a positive learning environment from the start. The most effective classroom management techniques are those that prevent problems from happening in the first place (Cruickshank, Jenkins, and Metcalf, 2003; Elliott et al., 2000; Freilberg and Driscoll, 2005; Laslett and Smith, 1984; McKeachie, 1994, 1999). Create a positive learning environment. Mix formats so that everyone remains involved. Stress the relevance of the material to your learners. Display your interest and enthusiasm, and you will head off most problems before they begin.

PLAYING TO OUR STRENGTHS

People who are drawn to public service in our libraries seem to be naturals for the task of teaching. They genuinely want to help people, have strong interpersonal skills, are excellent communicators, and show interest in and respect for a diverse clientele. All of these traits serve as a sound foundation for teaching. However, many institutions require that all librarians participate in live, F2F group instruction whether they are motivated to do so or not. Unfortunately, reluctant teachers may not be the most effective ones—especially in a F2F setting. It is hard for such a person to motivate learners or engage their interest. It is vitally important that those who are recruited into a teaching role be given training and support in order to develop the skills necessary for all types of teaching (Hansen and Stephens, 2000; Julien, 2005; Liles 2007; Sonntag, 2007).

Today's instructional technology provides a variety of opportunities for people to teach in an online setting. Although everyone may be asked to be part of the teaching community, not everyone need be the person who is center stage. There are many places where such librarians can contribute to the instructional mandate of an institution without ever having to be the person in the spotlight. They may be able to develop and teach fully online classes or create interactive Web-based tutorials or other online instructional material. The F2F teacher will also appreciate assistance in the development of handouts, slides, and other visual presentations, as well as any course-related Web pages. All of these activities contribute to the ILI effort and in many ways make life easier for the F2F teacher who can then concentrate on getting the content together for the session. The teacher may also need volunteers to try out proposed activities, to attend rehearsals, and to give honest and constructive feedback. Having rovers during hands-on exercises is also useful. Working in teams and playing to the strengths of each member of the team can in the end improve the overall instructional program. For more on how to provide instructional support through technology, see Chapter 15.

Playing to our strengths is also relevant when assigning people to the various types of instruction that we do or when asking for volunteers for particular instructional endeavors. In the name of equity we sometimes try to develop instructional sessions as a group. The goal is to come to consensus about the session—especially in regard to the ELOs—so that the instruction is acceptable to all those who will teach it. The end product, however, may not be instruction that fits all but rather one that fits none. While it is important to agree on the goals, objectives, and ELOs for a given instruction that will be taught by a variety of people, the methods used to present that material should be left to each individual instructor. A useful technique is for one person to take the lead in developing a particular instructional endeavor, including the outline and possible examples, and then offer it to his or her colleagues for discussion and comment. These conversations can enrich the instruction and provide for sharing of different approaches. Then each instructor is free to customize the instruction—within certain set parameters and according to the agreed upon ELOs—so that it suits his or her individual style. Material that will be delivered online (synchronously or asynchronously) can be developed in much the same manner.

Another consideration is preferred teaching style. Because people vary in their comfort levels regarding direct versus indirect methods, perhaps we should consider these variations when we ask people to contribute our instructional efforts. Even those who are comfortable in the actual F2F teaching role may differ in how they like to teach. While some people seem to enjoy the free and open atmosphere of the question and answer, active-learning, indirect format, others prefer a more structured, direct approach. One solution for synchronous instruction (F2F or online) is to use a team teaching approach in which different types of teaching styles can be used for different segments of the session. Varying who is leading the instruction also can help to hold learners' interest.

Another advantage of team teaching is that it exposes us to other styles. Trying new techniques can be scary. But they can also be energizing and may breathe new life into our work. Watching someone else take the risk may very well be the first step toward our taking the risk ourselves. Keep in mind that not everyone is comfortable having his or her teaching observed. So make sure you talk to anyone you wish to observe in advance to make sure they are willing to have you watching them teach. You could also see if you can form a peer teaching partnership with a colleague in which each of you takes turns watching the other teach and providing feedback on that teaching. For more on this topic, see the "Fostering Growth in Yourself and Others" chapter in *Learning to Lead and Manage Information Literacy Instruction* (Grassian and Kaplowitz, 2005).

However you participate in your library's ILI efforts, find your own voice, and be true to your inner teacher (Palmer, 1998). Not everyone is equally comfortable being center stage, but we can all contribute to the process—each according to his or her particular strengths, interests, and abilities.

FINAL REMARKS

How can we make sure we listen to, engage, and inspire our learners while we teach? First of all, a good match between who you are, what you teach, and how you teach is crucial. Your comfort with the task at hand communicates itself to your learners. If you are well prepared, care about what you are teaching, believe in the methods you have selected, and developed a personal style that really suits you, you cannot help but create an environment conducive to learning.

Show your commitment to your craft by continuing to challenge yourself. Look for ways to incorporate new ideas and techniques into your instruction. Expand your horizons by reading literature not only in ILI but also in that of education and psychology as well. Attend workshops and classes on teaching and performing. Develop a critical eye whenever you view any presentation or participate in F2F or online instruction or training of any kind—synchronous or asynchronous. What did you like about it that you might be able to use? If a technique appeals to you, try it out in your own endeavors. You can also learn something from techniques that do not appeal to you. Identify what did not work for you. If you did not like the technique, ask yourself why you did not like it. Even more importantly, ask yourself if there is some way you can modify the technique so you would want to use it. You may find that with a little tweaking a less than appealing technique might also turn into something useful for your teaching repertoire.

Make sure you reflect upon all of your teaching experiences both as they are happening and once they are completed. Congratulate yourself on what went well, and consider how to improve what might have been less effective. Never be completely satisfied with anything you do. Make sure you revisit your asynchronous material at given intervals to see if they are still meeting your ELO goals and revise them as needed. Check with learners (through surveys and/or F2F interactions) to see which portions of your asynchronous instruction were useful to them and which were not. Changing and improving your efforts will keep your interest high and that of your learners as well. Accept that you will never, ever "get there" in your teaching. There is no destination. There is only the never-ending journey (Bain, 2004; Fink, 2003; Ridgeway, 1989; Weimer, 2002).

Avoid complacency at all costs. Nothing is worse than a teacher who has not changed his or her approach over time. No one can continue to listen, engage, and inspire if they, themselves, are thoroughly bored with the material being presented and the modes used to present it. Shake yourself up from time to time. Change is good. Change is exciting. Change keeps your passion high. And change shows that you are willing to take risks in order to continue to grow as an effective teacher.

Teaching can be fun. It can be exhilarating to be in front of a group and see them gain new insight and understanding. It can be exciting to try out new instructional technology to expand our reach. Seeing our learners acquire new information and skills, a more positive attitude toward information gathering, and an eagerness to learn more is extremely rewarding. Our contact with learners is often limited. We have very little time to really get to know them during our sessions. By modeling our enthusiasm for the subject, by allowing learners to interact with the material and experience success with it, and by showing we respect their thoughts, opinions, and capabilities, we can create a positive learning environment. In the end we will win them over with our sincere and heartfelt passion for what we are doing. Learners complete the instructional experience feeling better about both the material we have included and their own abilities to apply what they have learned to their own lives.

EXERCISES

Exercise One

1. Think about the most effective teachers that you have ever had. What made them effective teachers? Make a list of the characteristics that made them effective teachers.
2. Now think about some less than effective teachers you have had. What made them ineffective? Make a list of the characteristics that interfered with their effectiveness.
3. Group the characteristics from your lists into categories. Use these categories to identify your particular strengths and weaknesses. Be honest with yourself. Capitalize on your strengths as you plan your instructional endeavors. Try working on correcting any weaknesses that seem to be interfering with your effectiveness as a teacher.

Exercise Two

1. Identify your favorite methods for F2F or synchronous online teaching and those you do not particularly like.
2. Develop an instructional piece that is *not* in your preferred style. Plan this piece for only a limited portion of a bigger session. Try to adjust the piece for your own comfort level.
3. You do not have to use this small instructional piece right away. Look for an opportunity where you are willing to try it out. Just thinking about using a non-preferred style may help you get used to the idea.
4. Once you do try the piece, analyze the results. How did it work? How did it make you feel? Can you adjust it to not only make the piece more effective but also to increase your comfort level with it?
5. Keep working at it until it becomes your own. This is a good method for expanding your instructional bag of tricks.
6. Repeat this exercise for asynchronous instruction.

READ MORE ABOUT IT

Bain, Ken. 2004. *What the Best College Teachers Do.* Cambridge, MA: Harvard University Press.

Bligh, Donald A. 2000. *What's the Use of Lectures?* San Francisco: Jossey-Bass.

Cruickshank, Donald R., Deborah Bainer Jenkins, and Kim K. Metcalf. 2003. *The Act of Teaching*, 3rd ed. New York: McGraw-Hill.

Eble, Kenneth Eugene. 1988. *The Craft of Teaching: A Guide to Mastering the Professor's Art*, 2nd ed. The Jossey-Bass Higher and Adult Education Series. San Francisco: Jossey-Bass.

Elliott, Stephen N., Thomas R. Kratochwill, Joan Littlefield Cook, and John F. Travers. 2000. *Educational Psychology: Effective Teaching, Effective Learning*, 3rd ed. Boston: McGraw-Hill.

Freilberg, H. Jerome and Amy Driscoll. 2005. *Universal Teaching Strategies.* Boston: Allyn & Bacon.

McKeachie, Wilbert J. 1994. *Teaching Tips: A Guidebook for the Beginning College Teacher*, 9th ed. San Francisco: New Lexington Press.

———. 1999. *Teaching Tips: Strategies, Research and Theory for College and University,* 10th ed. Boston: Houghton-Mifflin.

Mager, Robert F. 1997. *Making Instruction Work, or, Skillbloomers: A Step-by-Step Guide to Designing and Developing Instruction That Works*, 2nd, completely rev. ed. Atlanta: Center for Effective Performance.

Palmer, Parker. 1998. *The Courage to Teach: Exploring the Inner Landscape of a Teacher's Life.* San Francisco: Jossey-Bass.

Roland, David. 1997. *The Confident Performer.* Sydney: Currency Press.

Smith, Terry. 1991. *Making Successful Presentations: A Self-teaching Guide*, 2nd ed. New York: Wiley.

Veldof, Jerilyn. 2006. *Creating the One-shot Library Workshop: A Step-by-Step Guide.* Chicago: ALA.

Vella, Jane. 2000. *Learning to Listen. Learning to Teach*, 2nd ed. San Francisco: Jossey-Bass.

Weimer, Mary Ellen. 2002. *Learner-centered Teaching: Five Key Changes to Practice.* San Francisco: Jossey-Bass.

———. 2003. "Focus on Learning. Transform Teaching." *Change* 35, no. 5: 49–54.

Chapter 13

Teaching in a Diverse World: Knowledge, Respect, and Inclusion

Many do not know that we are here in this world to live in harmony.

—BUDDHA

REACHING AND TEACHING DIVERSE POPULATIONS

Who are your learners? This is one of the most fundamental of all questions when you are developing information literacy instruction (ILI). How you answer this question can have a profound impact on the ways in which you interact with your learners. Each person who walks through your classroom door, visits your Web site, uses your print or online tutorials and guides, or approaches you at the reference desk is a unique individual. At the same time, everyone belongs to and identifies with a variety of different groups. Groups tend to have their own set of affective, behavioral, and cognitive attributes. Each of us, learner and teacher alike, is influenced by the cultures and groups to which we belong (Rosinki and Abbott, 2006). How closely we identify with a particular group and are committed to that group's belief or value system affects our behaviors, habits, emotions, and ways of thinking. These cultural and group-based thoughts, feelings, and behaviors can and do influence how each of us approaches the educational process in general and ILI in particular. The purpose of this chapter is to help the information literacy (IL) instructor develop an increased sensitivity to these diversity issues. To do so requires an understanding of the parameters that can be used to describe how cultures and groups can differ. These parameters include the following:

- Context factors
- Social interaction
- Separate versus connected learning
- Rewards and punishment
- Communication styles
- Immediacy factors

These parameters will be described at length later in this chapter. Keep in mind that we will be discussing the parameters themselves rather than associating them with any specific culture or group to avoid any unintentional impression of stereotyping those entities.

Today's global economy demands that we all are able to successfully interact with a wide variety of people. We must be conscious of how the norms of groups to which we belong influence our own behavior, and we must try to gain insight into the norms, values, and ways of behaving typical of other groups and cultures. In a globally interconnected world, we cannot afford to remain isolationist and ignorant of other ways of being (Banks, 2007; Banks et al., 2005). With this goal in mind, educators at all levels of schooling are reexamining their curricula and ways of teaching to take a more multicultural education approach. Those of us who teach IL should also be asking ourselves how to address these issues in our instructional endeavors. ILI can be seen as a way to enhance global citizenship by helping people develop competencies that allow them to gain a better understanding of their world, the role that each of their choices and actions has in shaping that world, and the political, cultural, social, and ideological contexts of the information they find (Norgaard, 2003; Stevens and Campbell, 2006).

Taken broadly, a multicultural education approach includes issues related to gender, race/ethnicity, sexual orientation, socioeconomic status, religion, age, language, geographic origins, and ability/exceptionality (disabled or gifted) (Banks and Banks, 2007; Elhoweris, Parameswaran, and Alsheikh, 2004). Multicultural education helps individuals learn more about the various types of people with whom they interact. It is an unfortunate fact of life that the less we know about various groups and cultures, the more we are inclined to make up. Multicultural education promotes knowledge of people, places, events, and issues beyond one's own perspective and does not privilege any one group or culture over any other. Furthermore, multicultural approaches help people develop positive attitudes toward individuals from all kinds of groups. It calls for the valuing of non-Western cultures and histories and for an acceptance of all cultural views of knowledge by making the histories, customs, and traditions of all learners visible and appreciated. It is intended to be inclusive by fostering an appreciation and respect for all. With its goals of showing people that a particular group's ways of seeing the world is only one of many possible ways and helping individuals to view the world from multiple perspectives, multicultural educational practices have much in common with the types of critical thinking librarians and educators alike wish to instill in their learners (Abilock, 2006a; Banks, 2007; Banks et al., 2005; Cooper and Slavin, 2001; Elhoweris, Parameswaran, and Alsheikh, 2004; Elmborg, 2006; Ford and Harris, 1999; Gaitan, 2006; Grant and Sleeter, 2007; Salili and Hoosain, 2001). ILI can contribute to a multicultural education approach by helping our learners to take a broad, diverse, global view and to think critically about how information affects teaching, learning, research, politics, government, and daily life around the world. For more on critical thinking, see Chapter 6.

Educational practices generally reinforce the values and beliefs of what is considered to be the "dominant" culture in any society and to accept interpretations of knowledge by this culture as true. The result is the marginalization of cultural viewpoints and values of other groups in the community (Banks, 2007; Cruickshank, Jenkins, and Metcalf, 2003; Elhoweris, Parameswaran, and Alsheikh, 2004; Elmborg, 2006; Pawley, 2003; Salili and Hoosain, 2001). Historically, public schools were originally designed with a homogenous group of children in mind—those with a common culture and shared values, morals, ambitions, and parental expectations. Deviations from these norms were not encouraged. Success in school was dependent upon adapting to these norms and adopting them as the "accepted way to behave." As far back as John Dewey's work in the early twentieth century, school was viewed as the place for people to assimilate the norms of the dominant culture. Once assimilated, these norms would help them to succeed in that culture (Dewey, 1916; Elmborg, 2006; Ford and Harris, 1999). However, at a time when ease of travel and new communication technologies allow us to interact with people from all over the world to a greater degree than ever before, awareness of and attention to diversity issues are on the rise. As a result, the idea of any culture or group being dominant over the rest is being is called into question. Increases in so-called minority populations in the United States seems to indicate we will soon be a country with a "majority of none"—that is, one in which no group has a demographic majority (Halualani et al., 2004; Salili and Hoosain, 2001).

Many ILI models also seem to be grounded in Western social and intellectual structures. Care must be taken to develop instructional methodologies that are inclusive and honor the traditions and learning styles of all our learners (Dorner and Gorman, 2006; Gaitan, 2006; Williams, 2007). We must also keep in mind issues associated with the "digital divide." Although ownership and access to technology has increased in all segments of the population, inequities still exist. Lower socioeconomic groups and certain minorities still lag behind their more affluent neighbors, as do people who live in inner cities and rural areas (Christian, Blumenthal, and Patterson, 2000; Downing, 2000; Huang and Russell, 2006). This digital divide extends to all sections of society worldwide, especially in developing countries where the technological explosion has barely touched many of the more marginalized populations (Neelameghan and Chester, 2006). Taking a more instructionally diverse approach can offset the problems that many of our learners face as they try to adapt to a way of teaching and learning that is unfamiliar and often uncomfortable for them. Using a variety of strategies, ILI instructors can help all learners profit by their experiences (Kapitzke, 2003; Sanchez, 2000). For more on library anxiety, see Chapter 5. For more on the digital divide and technophobia issues, see Chapter 15.

To be truly multicultural teachers means acknowledging our own personal and cultural values, beliefs, and assumptions about our learners. We all have been shaped by our own cultural upbringings. This sometimes results in a disconnect (or "situative" cognition) between our own cultural values and those of our learners (Cooper and Slavin, 2001; Garner, 2008; Rosinki and Abbott, 2006; Whitfield, Klug, and Whitney, 2007). To avoid exhibiting "situative" cognition, we must explore the different "ways of knowing" that are represented by our learners. In some respects this is similar to the concept of learning styles discussed in Chapter 3. The mix of learners that we encounter in our ILI endeavors suggests that no one teaching style will fit all (Dunn, 2000). We must have a clear understanding of our own preferences, and we must develop an understanding, appreciation, and acceptance of those of our learners. The rest of this chapter will describe the ways in which groups can vary and will explore methods that should help you learn about the groups and cultures that make up your community of learners.

KNOW YOUR LEARNERS

Obviously knowing your own personal and cultural makeup and preferences is only one of the first steps toward becoming a multicultural instructor. You must also try to discover the makeup and backgrounds of the people involved in your ILI. If properly done, a Needs Assessment (see Chapter 7) will identify the various groups and special populations that comprise your intended audience. This assessment process can sensitize you to the needs of those who are different from you (in language, cultural, gender, age, ethnic or geographical background, physical or mental abilities, and so on). Finding out more about the characteristics of these groups can help you identify ways to make the instructional experience a welcoming one for all concerned. Contacting appropriate offices or agencies in your institution or community who deal with diverse groups is key to this process. Clearly you may not have the time to do a complete Needs Assessment for every one of your instructional endeavors—especially the one-shot types of teaching. However, many IL instructors conduct periodic Needs Assessments in order to gather these data, which can be referred to when planning a specific instructional endeavor. Having these data on hand is an effective way to prepare for any teaching situation. Furthermore, it is always helpful to hold some advance discussions with those connected to the group to whom you will be offering instruction. These preliminary conversations, with those who are requesting the instruction and/or members of the group to be instructed, can help to inform you about your learners and any cultural, ethnic, or group-membership-related issues to which you need to be alert.

Once you have identified the various groups, spend some time learning more about them. Pay special attention to differences that may have been identified in the way people view libraries and librarians in their cultures, child-rearing practices that can influence interpersonal interactions, and attitudes toward education. The more you know about a group, the more barriers to cultural compatibility you can eliminate when designing your instruction (Banks, 2007; Gilton, 1994; Moeckel and Presnell, 1995). Finally, engage in a little bit of self-reflection. Ask yourself how you feel about members of the groups with which you will be interacting. Do you have any prejudices toward the various groups or associate any stereotypes with them? Are you unfamiliar with some of the groups? Do you need to find out more about their cultures? Examine their beliefs and values for possible conflicts with your own (Elliott et al., 2000). Again, gathering information about those to whom you will be offering instruction is critical. In addition to your Needs Assessment data and your conversations with appropriate contact people, educating yourself about cultural norms and preferences, through reading, courses, or classes, can also be worthwhile. In general, identify points of potential conflict in advance and work to correct them. In some cases this will require you to modify some of your teaching approaches.

Knowledge, Not Stereotypes

While it is important to learn as much about the characteristics of all the groups and cultures that comprise your learner population as you can, you must use caution about how you apply that information. Literature certainly exists that describes the characteristics found most often in different groups. Researchers in gender and ethnic studies, cross-cultural psychology, and sociology have contributed to our overall understanding of this issue. However, it is important to understand that these studies are discussing characteristics associated with an entire group. They are not meant to describe the characteristics of any particular member of that group. Keep in mind that these studies are talking about what is referred to as the *modal personality* of the group. "Modal" in this context is a statistical term referring to anything that occurs most frequently in a given group. Therefore, the term *modal personality* merely refers to traits that occur most often in a sample of the population. It does not imply that everyone in that group exhibits those traits (Shade, Kelly, and Oberg, 1997).

To better understand this concept, let's think about the range of hair colors that could exist in a specific gathering of people. Brown, black, red, blond, silver, and gray hair could be present. However, depending upon the group, one color would appear more often than others. So this color (for the case of this discussion, let's select brown) will be the modal color. Although it appears more often than any of the others, this does not mean that people with black, red, blond, silver, or gray are not represented in the group. Describing a characteristic as modal does not imply that everyone in the group exhibits that characteristic.

By seeking to identify distinctive characteristics and orientations that define a given group and trying to put cultures and groups into finite boxes, we can run the risk of practicing sophisticated stereotyping or neostereotyping (Erickson, 2007; Osland and Bird, 2000; Rosinki and Abbott, 2006; Tayeb, 2001). Because the descriptions are based on research, we feel they are representative pictures of the group or culture under consideration and so can be trusted as valid. However we must view these data carefully and critically—being especially alert to any indications of researcher bias. A great deal of diversity can and does exist within each group and culture. Variations and differences within a group may be as great as or even greater than differences between groups. Members of a given group do not all behave identically nor do they all identify with their group and its norms to the same extent (Banks, 2007; Dunn, 2000; Grant and Sleeter, 2007; Irvine, 2003). Groups can even deviate from the identified "modal" characteristic under certain circumstances. For example, a culture that prizes individuality and self-reliance may also be one in which charitable giving and voluntarism is also looked upon with favor (Tayeb, 2001). Furthermore, because people tend to belong to several groups and have varying levels of commitment to these groups, it is difficult to predict how a specific individual might think, feel, or behave in any given situation. Too heavy a reliance on this research may result in teachers' developing predetermined ideas and expectations about their learners. Trying to teach to a "group norm" ignores the variabilities that can exist within any group we are trying to reach through our instructional endeavors (Banks, 1993, 2007; Banks and Banks, 1993, 2007; Dunn, 2000; Elhoweris, Parameswaran, and Alsheikh, 2004; Elliott et al., 2000; Grant and Sleeter, 1993; Grant and Sleeter, 2007; Osland and Bird, 2000; Sanchez, 2000).

While we must take all these cautions into account when thinking about our learners, the researchers in this field have offered us some very useful ways to think about cultural and group differences. They have identified a variety of ways in which groups and cultures can differ. An understanding of these characteristics or parameters can give us insight into our learners and helps us to develop a variety of instructional methodologies that reaches everyone we are teaching. The following section will describe these various parameters but will not report on the findings that tie any of them to particular groups or cultures. If you decide to follow up on any of the group-specific research, remember to apply the results judiciously and always keep in mind that individuals within a group may or may not represent the group norm.

VIVA LA DIFFÉRENCE: CULTURAL AND GROUP PARAMETERS

Groups can vary in many ways. Rather than discuss these variations group by group, we will look at the characteristics themselves. In order to avoid the perpetuation of any cultural or group stereotypes, no individual group will be associated with any specific characteristic. Given the possible variations that can exist among members of any group or culture, it is better to acquire an understanding of the characteristics themselves rather than look at those that might be associated with different groups. As in the case of learning styles discussed in Chapter 3, there are many different characteristics that can be used to describe cultural and group differences (Dorner and Gorman, 2006; Dunn, 2000; Ford and Harris, 1999; Hofstede, 1986, 2000; Kabagarama, 1997; Lage, Platt, and Treglia, 2000; Sanchez, 2000; Thomas, 2004). So, how does this research help the ILI instructor? Fortunately for us, these parameters seem to fall into categories that can be more easily addressed as we plan our teaching. These categories were listed at the beginning of this chapter. As a reminder, they are: context factors, social interaction, separate versus connected learning, rewards and punishment, and communication styles.

Context Factors

Let's begin by looking at context factors. Generally, cultures are considered high or low context. The culture that has traditionally been reflected in the K–20 educational systems in the United States tends to represent the low context approach. Low context groups are very open to outsiders. Members of these groups view time in a linear fashion in which things happen sequentially rather than simultaneously. Low context cultures value competition over cooperation and promote self-sufficiency and independence rather than interdependency. In the low context approach, the emphasis is on questioning and challenging authority (Banks, 1993, 2007; Dorner and Gorman, 2006; Dunn, 2000; Ford and Harris, 1999; Hall, 1966, 1976; Moeckel and Presnell, 1995; Roberts and Blandy, 1989; Sanchez, 2000). There is also a strong tendency toward individualism and independent work. Group formation is based on task, shared interests, or friendships rather than group affiliation. Open discussion and differences of opinion, even conflict, are valued. Education in individualist societies focuses on learning how to deal with the new, unknown, and unforeseen situations. They emphasize learning how to learn, because in this view learning never ends (Dorner and Gorman, 2006; Hofstede, 1986, 2000).

In high context approaches, asking questions or seeking help can be frowned on as a sign of weakness (Dunn, 2000; Kabagarama, 1997; Keefer, 1993; Shade, Kelly, and Oberg, 1997). High context societies are collectivist in nature. The success of the whole is viewed as more important than individual success (Chatto, 2000; Hofstede, 2000). People from collectivist/high context societies prefer to form groups based on common background. Being asked to participate in small group exercises or work on joint assignments with a variety of different people may be uncomfortable for individuals from high context societies.

Saving face and maintaining harmony are extremely important in a collectivist/high context society. Learners from these societies may be more reflective in their approach and prefer to think things over before answering a direct question. The fear of losing face often makes it difficult for them to speak up in classroom situations or even on Web-based discussion boards where their comments are on view to all. Collectivist societies stress adaptation to the skills and virtues necessary to be an accepted group member. Emphasis is placed on tradition and learning how to do things in a way that conforms to societal norms (Dorner and Gorman, 2006; Hofstede, 1986, 2000; Sanchez, 2000).

High context groups are characterized by greater interdependency among group members. They tend to be less accepting of outsiders than low context ones. Language involves subtlety in discussion in which vocal inflection, gestures, and the association of words in a sentence can influence meaning. Members of high context groups also have the ability to deal with polychronic time (many things happening at the same time). Cooperation is a highly valued trait in these cultures. Learning is a process of imitation and rote memory in high context cultures. The teacher is viewed as an authority figure whose statements are absorbed without question. For groups in which authority is unquestioned and cooperation is valued, copying from either an expert or from a fellow student is not considered wrong. The high context individual is rewarded for exact replication of authoritative material. The teacher, through his or her vast store of experience, is expected to be able to identify the source without further information. Citing the authority is unnecessary. In addition, because working together is encouraged, copying from a fellow learner is considered a cooperative act without the negative connotations attached to it in a low context environment. So, even the ideas of plagiarism and cheating are not universal concepts (Liu, 1993; Natowitz, 1995).

Furthermore, there is a difference in how high and low context societies view ambiguity and uncertainty. In a high context society, with its respect for authority, there is a tendency toward looking for the one right answer and a presumption that the instructor is the one who will decide what that one answer might be. In the low context society, there is more of a tolerance for ambiguity and a belief in the idea that there can be many correct answers. Originality of thought is praised in low context groups (Dorner and Gorman, 2006; Hofstede, 1986, 2000).

Many minority or nondominant cultures in the United States exhibit characteristics of high context groups. Problems can therefore arise when high context learners encounter an instructional experience that stresses low context characteristics. For example, learners with high context backgrounds refrain from asking questions during instruction for a number of reasons. First, because learning is dependent on absorbing authoritative material, asking questions might display their "shameful" ignorance. Furthermore, they do not wish to appear to be questioning the authority of the instructor. When asked if they understand presented material, high context individuals may politely nod and say yes rather than ask for clarification. Learners with English as a second language may also be self-conscious about speaking up in class and displaying their linguistic errors. An instructional situation that emphasizes learner participation, discussion, and debate can be very uncomfortable to the high context learner. Engaging such learners in active learning experiences and group discussions can be quite challenging (Dorner and Gorman, 2006; Elliott et al., 2000; Ford and Harris, 1999; Gilton, 1994; Grossman, 1990; Moeckel and Presnell, 1995; Natowitz, 1995; Sanchez, 2000).

Growing up in a high or low context environment also influences how people perceive and process information. The high context individual tends toward a holistic worldview, while the low context individual is more a serial thinker. In other words, the high context person wishes to understand the big picture before trying to absorb specific details, while the low context person wants to start with specific examples and build up to the more global view. If you try to teach holistic learners individual skills without first presenting the context, they may become confused. Conversely, starting with the big picture may bore the low context learner, who wants to acquire the skills to use specific tools and finds discussion of the overall system irrelevant (Lin, 1994). High context individuals may also be more field dependent in their learning style. The field-dependent individual tends to pay attention to the whole pattern instead of the individual objects that make up the pattern and concentrates on relationships between concepts rather than individual bits of information. They learn best when material is directly relevant to their own experience (Dembo, 1988a; Sanchez, 2000). Advance Organizers can be very helpful to the high context individual. They provide a framework for the high context, field-dependent learner to follow and highlight the important aspects that will be covered. Low context people, on the other hand, tend toward field independence in their learning style. Field-independent learners prefer to focus on individual objects. They process information sequentially and try to impose their own structure on the material (Dembo, 1988a; Dunn and Griggs, 2000). Low context learners appreciate the chance to try things out for themselves. Hands-on practice is very appealing to this type of learner. See Chapter 3 for more information on these learning style concepts.

Social Interaction

The degree to which social interaction influences behavior also varies from group to group. People from high context cultures that emphasize interdependency tend to be viewed as people specialists. They are taught to be empathic with people and social dimensions and to pay less attention to impersonal or inanimate cues. These people specialists attend to facial expressions and social situation nuances and frequently use the interpersonal dimensions of a situation to determine decisions rather than depending solely on the content being presented. Classroom environment and teacher–learner interactions are critical to successful instruction with these learners. Cooperative or group experiences, peer coaching, and curriculum material with social applications and meaning are particularly successful techniques for them (Chatto, 2000; Dorner and Gorman, 2006; Ford and Harris, 1999; Sanchez, 2000; Shade and New, 1993; Thomas, 2004).

Real-world examples are crucial to this type of learner. Showing how the Web can be searched to find information about global warming and its implication for society should capture their attention. People specialists need to see that what they are learning matters to themselves, the people in their lives, and society in general. Low context cultures that favor independence and individuality pay less attention to these interpersonal and social components of learning. They are more inclined to search for topics of personal relevance rather than something with more broad-based societal implications. Learners from these cultures might be engaged by asking them to search the Web for information about a particular vitamin or herbal supplement that they themselves are considering taking. Or they can look up the ingredients in a nutritional bar or drink to see what they can find out about these ingredients and their actual benefits or lack there of.

Separate versus Connected Learning

Related to social interaction is the concept of separate versus connected learning (Clinchy, 1994; Dorner and Gorman, 2006; Ford and Harris, 1999). The heart of separate learning is detachment. Separate learners hold themselves aloof from the object being analyzed. They are impersonal and objective in their analysis and follow explicit rules and procedures to ensure unbiased judgments. Personal feelings are discounted. The primary mode of discourse is the rational argument. Separate learners look for what is wrong in whatever they are examining. They tend to take a position that is contrary to that which they are examining regardless of whether or not they agree with that position. On the other hand, connected learners look at ideas and try to make sense out of them. Connected learners try to figure out how each position might be correct. They are not dispassionate, unbiased thinkers. Rather, they bias themselves in favor of getting inside all the opinions and views. Connected learners put aside their own views and try to see the logic behind every approach. They may not in the end agree with the position, but while they are examining it they empathize with it and try to think and feel like the person who created it. Although emotion is not outlawed, as it is in separate learning, reason is also present. Personal experience is drawn upon as a means of understanding what produced the idea under examination. The goal is to develop a nonjudgmental, noncritical approach that accepts all points of view as equally valid. While the separate thinker takes nothing at face value, the connected learner takes everything at face value. These connected learners do not try to evaluate the perspective under review. They try to understand it. Connected learners do not ask whether a viewpoint is right or wrong. They try to determine what it means.

Separate learners favor a more critical approach. While connected learners are looking for consensus, separate learners are trying to discover the best answer. Connected learners enjoy group discussions in which all views are valued. The separate learner prefers debate and other competitive situations in which the goal is to determine which viewpoint is the most correct. Instructors who fail to appreciate and encourage both modes of learning can disenfranchise what might be large segments of their learner population. Obviously no one mode of learning will appeal to both types, but allowing for some collaborative learning experiences as well as more competitive ones can widen the appeal of any instructional session, and gives both types the opportunity to learn in a way most suited to their individual styles.

Before we move on we should look at the relationship between the three parameters just discussed. One way to look at these parameters is to view context as what influences the ways people think (cognition), social interaction as how people behave with other people (behavior), and separate versus connected as to what degree people deal with and honor feelings (affect).

The context parameter, with its emphasis on thinking and cognition, looks at the ways in which people think about the information itself and the source of that information. Do they question it and/or its source (low context), or do they accept the information based on authority of the source (high context)? Context deals with the independence from or reliance upon the group. The low context person prefers to work alone and forms his or her own conclusions without reference to the group or any authority figure. The high context individual, on the other hand, is more concerned about the group's ideas and opinions and relies heavily on those in authority when problem solving and making decisions.

Social interaction looks at behavior—specifically how much or how little people wish to interact with other people. The social interaction parameter comes at this individual versus group idea from a different angle. This parameter looks at how much or how little people relate to and interact with other people. It is closely related to the context parameter, as high context individuals tend to be more people oriented than those from low context backgrounds and therefore are more inclined to interact with other people than their low context counterparts. But the social interaction parameter deals with how much or how little those interactions influence their behavior.

Separate versus connected learning deals with affect—describing the degree to which emotions, feelings, and empathy affect behavior. The separate versus connected parameter is concerned with the more affective or feelings side of life. Separate learners distance themselves from the problems and tasks at hand. They do not let their personal feelings or the feelings of others affect their behavior. Connected learners, on the other hand, are highly attuned to feelings (both their own and others) and try to take them into account as they work. It is important to keep these distinctions in mind as you examine these parameters.

Rewards and Punishments

The nature of reward (and punishment) can also vary from group to group. For example, some children are raised in an environment with lots of attention and frequent rewards. Progress toward a final product is encouraged through this attention and reward system. Public praise, awards for excellence, and competition/winning are highly prized. In other environments children are encouraged to work more independently and unsupervised until the job is done. They are more comfortable working in private and do not expect rewards until they are finished (Dorner and Gorman, 2006; Hofstede, 1986, 2000).

The more interdependent, collectivist, socially oriented groups tend to view isolation and loss of attention as punishment. Loss of privilege or autonomy may be experienced as punishment in more individually oriented groups where independence and self-sufficiency is valued. Teachers who engage in active questioning with the goal of getting the learner to the correct answer can therefore be viewed as either very helpful or quite intrusive, depending upon the learner's upbringing and background (Dorner and Gorman, 2006; Elliott et al., 2000; Ford and Harris, 1999; Grossman, 1990). Singling people out in class and asking for responses to individual questions appeals to those learners who enjoy this type of competitive challenge and the opportunity for frequent rewards. However, for those who prefer a more reflective approach in which they are allowed time to think through a problem on their own, this targeted attention is disconcerting, often anxiety provoking, and can even be counterproductive to learning.

Communication Styles

The most obvious differences between groups lie in the area of communication style. Message transmission is accomplished through the verbal and nonverbal codes used in a particular group as well as a set of rules or guidelines about the appropriate application of those codes (Heath, 1996; Irvine, 2003; Shade and New, 1993). These codes and rules are acquired during the socialization process. Children not only learn the vocabulary and grammar necessary to communicate. They are also oriented toward what types of information are important to transmit and receive, how to listen, methods for getting attention, appropriate vocal quality and level, and how to interpret nonverbal cues (Grassian and Kaplowitz, 2005; Heath, 1996; Irvine, 2003; Lewis, 2000).

Communication style differences can create serious problems in and out of the classroom. Those who share the same style are better able to interpret each other's spoken and unspoken messages. They can make fairly accurate predictions about behavior based on that message. When people who do not share the same communication style attempt to interact, they are unable to correctly interpret the cues. Since they cannot count on their interpretations, they frequently fail to understand the meaning behind the message. This uncertainty is uncomfortable and leads to anxiety. In an attempt to reduce anxiety, people may fall back on stereotypes to make their predictions or try to use their own stylistic rules to interpret the conversational cues. The net result can be communication misunderstanding, misinterpretations, and false predictions (Ford and Harris, 1999; Gross, 1997; Kabagarama, 1997; Thomas, 2004).

There are many contributing factors to a communication style. First, there is the concept of personal space or comfortable conversational distance. Imagine someone whose acceptable space is one foot from the speaker trying to communicate with someone who is only comfortable with a three-foot separation, and you can see how this factor can be problematic. Eye contact is another consideration. Many groups favor direct eye contact. However, others view this direct eye contact as rude, overly assertive, and intrusive. Then there is rhythm of speech and length of speaking turns. This variation is usually reflected in number and length of pauses. One person, thinking the other has completed a response, may interrupt what to the other was only a pause for thought. In addition, some people need to verbalize their thoughts. What appears to be intentional, disruptive outbursts during the communication process (or in the classroom setting) may only be the person verbalizing that he or she has gotten the concept or perceived a relationship. Furthermore, physical gestures and facial expressions are not universal. What may be acceptable to one group may turn out to be offensive to another. Whether and how people touch each other during communication is yet another parameter. So, words may acquire shades of meanings dependent upon these possible variations in intonation, facial expression, and body language (Elliott et al., 2000; Grassian and Kaplowitz, 2005; Irvine, 2003; Jenkins and Bainer, 1994; Johnson, 1997; Kabagarama, 1997; Lewis, 2000; Longstreet, 1978; Moeckel and Presnell, 1995; Shade and New, 1993).

Expressiveness of verbal delivery can also vary. Theatricality of presentation, amount of emotion exhibited, response rate, and energy levels all contribute to this dimension. On the one hand is the informal, animated, percussive, and active style. On the other hand is the more formal, detached, literal, and legalistic mode, with a range of possibilities in between (Seton and Ellis, 1996; Shade and New, 1993).

Immediacy Factors

Studies on what many researchers refer to as immediacy factors in face-to-face (F2F) instruction indicate a relationship between these factors and teacher effectiveness. Immediacy cues include the use of vocal expressiveness, eye contact, gestures, relaxed body position, directing body position toward the learner, smiling, movement, and proximity, as well as soliciting learner views and using personal examples during instruction. The results of these studies can be extrapolated to online teaching situations as well, because the effectiveness of a presenter in a video or teleconference presentation can also be affected by these immediacy factors. Certainly the difficulty of maintaining some of these factors such as eye contact or proximity must be taken into account when the teacher and the learner are not sharing the same physical space. The immediate back and forth between teacher and learner can also suffer. Although learners may be able to ask questions via chat, instant messaging, or video or phone conferencing, these questions are not always answered immediately after they are asked. Frequently specific times are set aside to deal with these questions. So a lag can result between the time that the question was asked and then subsequently responded to. To counter this problem, teachers often refer to the questioner by name and summarize the topic of the query when they are about to answer a specific question. The lag between when a learner poses a question on asynchronous discussion boards or via e-mail and when the instructor responds to that question could also be viewed as relevant to immediacy factors. Teachers working in an asynchronous environment should try to respond to comments, questions, and issues as quickly as possible. Learners soon lose interest in the discussion and faith in the teacher if their postings are not dealt with in a timely fashion. The most effective teachers respond to all messages within 24 hours or less.

A further factor to consider is that members of different groups react differently to these immediacy cues. Certain immediacy cues may be positively viewed by members of one group and negatively by members of another. For example, groups with more formal interpersonal and communication styles might find particular expressions of immediacy such as the sharing of personal stories or instructors who stand close to their learners uncomfortable or distasteful. Because groups vary in their reaction to immediacy cues, it stands to reason that the effectiveness of these cues will also vary (Sanders and Wiseman, 1994).

Avoiding Cultural Clash

A general understanding about how groups can vary is only part of the equation. When people from different cultures meet, their different filters or worldviews can conflict, leading to uncertainty, confusion, and anxiety. Neither completely understands the rules by which the other is behaving and so can misunderstand the meaning behind that behavior. This can potentially lead to further misunderstanding and the possibility that each will wish to avoid such interactions in the future (*Culturgrams*, 2008; Kabagarama, 1997).

School culture is usually carefully defined to reflect the socialization process of the cultural majority in any society. Any deviation from this defined norm may be viewed as either a disciplinary problem or evidence of lack of ability (Dorner and Gorman, 2006; Sanchez, 2000; Shade, Kelly, and Oberg, 1997). However, the classroom is really made up of members of this cultural majority or macro culture and those who belong to a variety of micro cultures (Banks, 1993, 2007; Banks et al., 2005; Grant and Sleeter, 1993; Grant and Sleeter, 2007). Clashes between micro and macro cultural rules and norms can result in a disproportionate number of micro culture learners being labeled as behavior problems or as learning deficient (Cruickshank, Jenkins, and Metcalf, 2003; Hilliard, 1992; Irvine, 2003; Shade, Kelly, and Oberg, 1997). Cultural compatibility between the school environment and the learner's home culture can therefore have a great deal of influence on individual achievement. Children from micro cultures that emphasize different ways of thinking, feeling, interacting, and behaving from that of the macro or dominant culture often find it difficult to work in a classroom climate that is counter to their accustomed ways of behaving. This cultural discontinuity between macro and micro cultures can cause miscommunication between teacher and learner and can even result in learners experiencing feelings of hostility, alienation, and diminished self-esteem (Elhoweris, Parameswaran, and Alsheikh, 2004; Elmborg, 2006; Erickson, 2007; Ford and Harris, 1999; Hofstede, 2000; Irvine, 2003; Pawley, 2003; Salili and Hoosain, 2001). For example, learners coming from cultures in which it is frowned upon to look authority figures in the eye and to avoid the appearance of questioning authority might be viewed as paying less attention to the instruction than those who come from backgrounds in which looking people in the eye is a sign of respect. Changing our perspective from one in which learners who are not compatible are viewed as deficient to one where these differences are appreciated and incorporated into teaching can enrich the experience for all concerned (Ball, 2000; Banks et al., 2005; Cooper and Slavin, 2001; Cruickshank, Jenkins, and Metcalf, 2003; Elliott et al., 2000; Ford and Harris, 1999; Gaitan, 2006; Natowitz, 1995; Shade, Kelly, and Oberg, 1997).

Because most of our institutions and schools are organized in keeping with the macro culture's rules and norms, helping members of specific micro cultures benefit from our ILI also depends on knowing something about their special needs. So let us take a look at some of these groups. Keep in mind that the general parameter variations discussed in this chapter can be applied to the following situations, but each of the groups discussed also has some identifiable group-related characteristics.

SPECIFIC GROUP ISSUES

Adult (Re-entry) Learners

Adult (re-entry) learners are usually people returning to school after having been in the workforce and/or raised a family. On the whole, they have a very strong need to succeed and may feel at a disadvantage when comparing themselves to their younger classmates. This combination can lead to very high levels of anxiety especially when it comes to the use of computers and other newer forms of instructional technology (Given, 2000; Grabowski, 1980; Gust, 2006; Holmes, 2000; Juznic et al., 2006; Lenn, 2000). In addition to possible lack of experience with computers and technology, these learners may also suffer some physical restrictions. For example, arthritic conditions can make "mousing" difficult. Many of these learners appreciate a slower pace of instruction (Christian, Blumenthal, and Patterson, 2000). However, remember that these older learners will vary greatly as to their educational background and familiarity with and acceptance of technology. Many of these learners are highly educated and have embraced technology with an enthusiasm that rivals their younger colleagues. So be careful not to appear condescending to your older learners. Ask them how they feel about libraries and technology to get a better picture of their strengths, skill levels, and concerns. For more on library anxiety, see Chapter 5. For more on technophobia, see Chapter 15.

Studies on the characteristics of the adult learner indicate a different approach to learning from that of the child or adolescent. As a result, a different teaching paradigm has been proposed, called *andragogy*, to differentiate it from the standard pedagogy used with younger learners (Knowles, 1980; 1996). To Knowles (1980, 1996), the typical adult learner is one who is motivated to learn when faced with a particular need or interest. The adult, re-entry learner's orientation is typically life or work related. Adult learners are interested in practical application, not theoretical issues. In other words, learning is problem centered rather than subject centered. Adult, re-entry learners are motivated to learn only when they think the subject will have real meaning or relevance for their lives. They tend to prefer active participation rather than passive reception and are self-directed in their approach to learning. However, keep in mind that people from different backgrounds, cultures, and ethnicities may vary in their acceptance of and comfort with active learning techniques.

The "less is more" principle is especially appropriate for this group. Try to avoid bombarding these learners with large amounts of material. It is better to present them with small, manageable amounts of information that they can learn well than to overwhelm them with lots of information that may result in increasing their anxiety about the library and its resources. Research indicates that adult, re-entry learners prefer being taken through progressive steps, starting with the essentials and ending with the "nice to know" but not essential material (Curry, 2000; Gold, 2005; Holmes, 2000; Ingram, 2000; Lenn, 2000). Adult, re-entry learners also appreciate paper handouts and guides that can both be used during a F2F session and taken away to refer to later (Gust, 2006). Adding PDF versions of your paper handouts to your library's Web site that your learners can print as needed is also a boon to this group of learners.

Adult, re-entry learners can be expected to take a more active role in deciding what is relevant or useful to them. The extent of their participation will therefore be shaped more by their own circumstances and perceptions than by passive acceptance of what is being presented to them. Adult, re-entry learners tend to have relevant life experiences that can be drawn upon and are more motivated than younger learners (Gold, 2005). Learner-centered, problem-based approaches work best with this group, as does the use of relevant examples such as consumer health topics or life/fun-type Web sites that feature movie reviews, government or legal information, maps and weather sites, and so on (Gust, 2006). Adult, re-entry learners tend to be pragmatic, practical, and extremely goal oriented. They expect to be taught skills that have direct application in their lives. If you are working in an academic setting, make sure you include examples to which this group of learners can relate. You can even ask these learners to supply their own examples in order to increase the relevancy factor.

A major consideration when dealing with the adult, re-entry learner is that for these learners participation in the educational process is often voluntary. Adult, re-entry learners also bring vast amounts of life experience and highly developed life skills to the instructional setting and expect these to be acknowledged. Adult, re-entry learners benefit from an atmosphere of mutual respect, in which all participants are viewed as both learners and potential teachers. No one member is regarded as having a monopoly on insight. Adopting the interactive, self-directed, and collaborative style of teaching that appeals to the adult, re-entry learner requires the instructor to abandon the more authoritative "keeper of the keys" model of teaching. Knowledge is no longer dispensed in carefully measured doses by the "sage on the stage." Instead, the instructor becomes the "guide on the side," facilitating the exploration and discovery of knowledge (King, 1993). Reaching the adult, re-entry learner requires an atmosphere of mutuality and shared responsibility. The adult, re-entry learner will ask questions, demand clarification, and will not settle for imperfect understanding. Dissension and criticism are regarded as inevitable and desirable elements of the learning process (Brookfield, 1994; Curry, 2000; Gold, 2005; Gust, 2006; Ingram, 2000; Roberts and Blandy, 1989; Sheridan, 1986).

The adult, re-entry learner has more clearly defined ideas about what is useful in an educational setting than younger learners, who may not as yet have settled on their ultimate goals. Because their time is limited adult, re-entry learners want to learn very practical, efficient methods of gathering information and creating specific end products. With their wider life experiences and the fact that they may be juggling multiple roles, adult, re-entry learners tend to select more personally relevant research topics. These topics are frequently interdisciplinary and thus more difficult and complex to research (Gold, 2005; Howard, 1983; Roberts and Blandy, 1989). Finally, adult, re-entry learners often travel long distances to get to classes and may wish to use facilities closer to their home or workplace to do their research. Therefore, ILI may need to be a bit more generic for this group to prepare them for work in a variety of library environments, public as well as all levels of academic. It may also focus on what can be accomplished remotely through the use of electronic resources. Appropriately designed, self-paced, online tutorials that can be accessed remotely and at time of need are greatly appreciated by this busy group of learners (Christian, Blumenthal, and Patterson, 2000; Gold, 2005) as are online courses, which do not require that the learner physically come to a teaching facility.

Gender Issues

Although males and females can be members of a variety of different groups and thus exhibit characteristics associated with those groups, research has identified some specific gender-related traits or tendencies. On the whole, studies seem to indicate that females are more connected learners and males more separate learners (see earlier discussion) (Belenky et al., 1986; Clinchy, 1994; Hickson and Baltimore, 1996). However, although these results indicate the characteristic is gender related, it is not gender exclusive. Again, this is an example of being able to predict group characteristics but not individual behavior. While it is more likely that females in general prefer the connected approach, some may in fact be separate learners. The same holds true for males, some of who may be connected learners even though the majority of males are more likely to be separate learners. A traditional educational system that emphasizes the abstract, teacher-centered mode of teaching can favor the separate learner. Therefore, connected learners are often forced to adapt their style to that of the school's in order to succeed. However, the movement toward more learner-centered teaching with its emphasis on collaboration, authentic practice, and hands-on experience should appeal to the connected learner and make him or her feel more at home and comfortable in the learning environment (Philbin et al., 1995).

The question also arises as to whether these gender differences are innate or acquired. It turns out that gender identity (the perception of one's masculinity or femininity) may be a better predictor of an individual's behavior than is his or her actual gender. If this is the case, then socialization, cultural, and environmental pressures may be responsible for the differences between men and women noted earlier (Cruickshank, Jenkins, and Metcalf, 2003; Severiens and Ten Dam, 1997; Weiner, 1995).

Immigrants, First Generation, and ESL Learners

The United States is a nation built on immigration, and our communities and schools reflect this rich ethnic mix. According to census data available for the first few years of the twenty-first century, the United States is experiencing the largest influx of immigrants since the late nineteenth and early twentieth centuries (U.S. Census Bureau, 2007). These immigrants and their children must adjust to an educational (and library) culture that may be very different from what they are accustomed to. Furthermore, they are trying to learn in a language other than their own. Many of these learners speak their native language at home and in their communities but must switch to English for their educational experiences (Fisher, Durrance, and Hinton, 2004; Freilberg and Driscoll, 2005; Irvine, 2003; Li, 1998; Scitikus and Varghese, 2007). So, they are trying to adjust to United States culture and converse in a second language (English) all the while endeavoring to study their academic subjects—a very challenging task indeed.

Many immigrants and first generation learners come from lower socioeconomic backgrounds and view educational accomplishments as a way to better themselves and their families (Bui, 2002; Lee, 2001; Tyckoson, 2000). In addition to cultural and language differences, first generation learners may not have had the same level of access to and training in the use of computers and online resources (Kamhi-Stein and Stein, 1998). While it is important to avoid library jargon when teaching any of our learners, it is of the utmost importance with English as a second language (ESL) learners, who not only are unfamiliar with the terminology but also lack the context in which to place it. Gestures, graphic illustrations, handouts, rephrasing, speaking clearly and slowly, and restating ideas in different ways are all methods that can help these learners (Conteh-Morgan, 2002; Kamhi-Stein and Stein, 1998; Scitikus and Varghese, 2007).

Remember that these learners may feel anxious about their English language skills. Try to make them feel welcome and do your best to show that you are not making value judgments about their "less than perfect" language abilities. Hands-on practice is a useful technique with this group. You can get immediate feedback on how much your learners have gotten out of your session so far. Asking learners to perform what was taught is a quick way to judge how well they learned the task and is especially useful when language difficulties may be an issue (Conteh-Morgan, 2002). Keep in mind that there may be experts in your community that can offer you insight and suggestions about how best to interact with immigrants, first generation, and ESL learners. Learners from other countries who have been in the United States a bit longer may also be called upon to help ease the way for these "newer to the United States" learners. Some of the hints in the next section about working with international students may also be applicable to this group.

International Students

People from countries outside the United States, especially those for whom English is a second language, face many difficulties when attempting to study in this country whether it is formally through enrollment in schools, colleges, or universities or informally through self-education for personal, political, or work needs. Library jargon such as "stacks," "checked out," "on reserve," and "circulation desk" can present particular difficulties and should always be defined when used in instructional situations. Even those learners coming to the United States from other English-speaking countries could experience problems. They may not understand the cultural nuances provided by both verbal and nonverbal cues that affect the meaning of words as spoken in this country. Furthermore, the informality of interpersonal interactions both in and out of the instructional setting may be very different from their experiences at home. The tendency toward active participation and interactive discussion and the emphasis on independent research, all of which are so much a part of the Western educational process, may be quite disconcerting to someone with a very different background and upbringing.

Studies indicate that learners for whom English is not their native language experience high levels of library anxiety. This may be due not only to language difficulties but also to cultural differences as well. The ways libraries are organized and how information is accessed also have cultural variations. Depending upon their cultural background, international students may also have difficulty with many characteristics of Western-type libraries. These can include left to right arrangements, alphabetical arrangements used in call numbering systems, asking a woman for help, returning materials on time, doing things for themselves, questioning authority in the form of either the instructor or the written text, and learning outside of the classroom. In many countries, library resources are scarce and books are considered precious commodities whose use is strictly regulated. The concepts of open stacks, traditional research tools, centralized catalogs, classification systems, and Western-style reference service may all be unfamiliar to varying degrees. Self-service often does not exist in many developing countries. As a result, even doing their own photocopying may be a totally new experience to some international students. In some cultures, wealthy students are used to buying whatever sort of information they need rather than sharing material placed in reference or reserve collections for all students to use. Furthermore, these students are frequently those who have excelled in their home countries and may even hold advanced degrees there. As they struggle to make sense not only of the content material but also of the language in which it is being taught and the social and cultural context that surrounds it, they may feel insecure and anxious. Finally, they may find it difficult adjusting to what seems like a loss of status. After all, they have moved from being a respected professional at home to a somewhat lowly student in an environment quite unlike their own (Ball and Mahony, 1987; Baron and Strout-Dapaz, 2001; Chatto, 2000; Chau, 2002–2003; DiMartino and Zoe, 2000; Hurley, Hegarty, and Bolger, 2006; Jiao, Onwuegbuzie, and Lichtenstein, 1996; MacDonald and Sarkodie-Mensah, 1988; Onwuegbuzie, 1998; Roberts and Blandy, 1989; Sarkodie-Mensah, 2000; Seton and Ellis, 1996).

Many international students are reluctant to approach the reference desk with their questions. This may be because of insecurities about their communication skills or because of the lack of attention paid to reference service in their home countries. In many cultures the library is primarily a place to study. Students who are accustomed to learning by passively listening to lectures and reading and absorbing textbook material may find the idea of using the library for independent, creative research a strange one indeed. Furthermore, depending upon whether they are from a high or low context environment (see earlier discussion) the concepts of copying another's work may have very different meanings. What constitutes cheating and plagiarism is culturally defined and so can vary from country to country (Ball and Mahony, 1987; Baron and Strout-Dapaz, 2001; Chatto, 2000; Chau, 2002–2003; Gilton, 1994; Hurley, Hegarty, and Bolger, 2006; Liu, 1993; Moeckel and Presnell, 1995; Natowitz, 1995; Seton and Ellis, 1996).

All of these factors come into play when planning your ILI. Although these learners may be quite familiar with the lecture format, this may not be the best approach for them when they are studying in countries other than their own. For one thing, they are trying to listen and absorb information in a "foreign" language and cannot always keep up with the pace of the presentation (Conteh-Morgan, 2002; Hurley, Hegarty, and Bolger, 2006; Kamhi-Stein and Stein, 1998; Ladd and Ruby, 1999). The more learner-centered, active learning approach can actually be beneficial to these students, as it offers them an opportunity to work at their own pace and to interact with the material rather than just listen to descriptions about it. However, language and cultural differences may still be a problem. Class progress may be slow. Information needs to be delivered in small chunks, and frequent checks for comprehension can help you make sure you have not left any of your learners behind (Baron and Strout-Dapaz, 2001; Hurley, Hegarty, and Bolger, 2006). Differences in communication styles can also result in some serious miscommunication. Nodding and smiling is a form of respect in some cultures, but the Western teacher could view it as a signal of understanding and move on with the session (Chatto, 2000). Providing handouts or Web-based help guides in multiple languages can go a long way to help these learners become more familiar with our libraries and the resources they provide (Chau, 2002–2003). Online tutorials, which are available at any time for repeat viewing, can be useful for international learners, especially if the tutorial includes captions or translations into other languages.

Contact organizations, agencies, or institutional departments that assist international students in your environment and ask for suggestions about how to modify your ILI to assist these learners. These groups may be able to provide people who can translate your print and online material, act as peer tutors and translators in your classrooms, and serve as tour guides during orientations. If you have the time, resources, and staffing, you might consider providing special workshops and orientations geared toward the special needs of the international students. And try to include dictionaries that translate English to other languages dictionaries, as well as other reference material in your reference collection. The goal here is to make these students feel welcome and supported both in your library and in your ILI sessions (Baron and Strout-Dapaz, 2001; DiMartino and Zoe, 2000; Sarkodie-Mensah, 2000; Scitikus and Varghese, 2007).

People with Disabilities

Disabilities can be physical and/or mental. The Americans with Disabilities Act (ADA) of 1990 raised awareness of the needs of people with disabilities in our communities, schools, and libraries (Norlin, 1992; U.S. Department of Justice, accessed 2008) and put into place requirements that we accommodate these disabilities. Educators have responded to all of this by slowly shifting from the idea of providing separate learning experiences (independent special education classes) to one of integration and participation (mainstreaming) as much as possible (Heward, Bicard, and Cavanaugh, 2007). This increases the likelihood that teachers and librarians will have a range of "differently abled" learners in their classes. Public libraries, too, have a mandate to serve everyone in their communities and therefore must make accommodations for a wide variety of people—some with special needs. Facilities and equipment within the library itself—including the teaching facility—must take into account the needs of all its users. Some libraries take this a step further by offering services for "shut-ins."

The physically disabled can often be helped by the removal of physical barriers. Special devices for the visually or hearing impaired can be employed to help them make use of library materials. Workstations can be set at levels that accommodate those in wheelchairs. Computers can be equipped with software that reads Web pages to the visually impaired user. Following ADA compliant protocols when we develop our Web pages and online help guides is also key. People with learning disabilities can present a special challenge, because their disability may not be obvious. Research indicates that these learners respond better to auditory and visual stimuli than to print media, so using a mix of formats in your ILI should help to reach these learners (Murray, 2001; Norlin, 1992). For more on design issues see Chapter 10.

A combination of commonsense, sensitivity, courtesy, and good teaching practices goes a long way to make people with disabilities feel welcome in our libraries and our classrooms. For example, facing the class when you speak, speaking clearly and at a moderate rate of speed, and checking for comprehension are examples of good teaching techniques that will be helpful to all of your learners, but these techniques are crucial if you have hearing-impaired people in the group. If given enough notice, you might also request that a signer be assigned to the classroom for the hearing impaired. Reading aloud the material written on the board and repeating important points will help the visually impaired learners in your group (Murray, 2001; Roberts and Blandy, 1989) as will enlarging whatever is displayed on a screen at the front of the room when working in a synchronous F2F instruction.

Using a mix of mediums in your ILI is good practice for just about every kind of learner, but it is especially important when teaching those with disabilities. Use verbal as well as written explanations followed by hands-on practice. This approach will ensure you reach everyone, regardless of learning styles or disabilities (Applin, 1999). The key is sensitivity. Be aware of where your learners might need help, identify the barriers that make it difficult for your physically or mentally challenged learners to acquire the IL skills they need, and modify your instruction accordingly. Work with groups and specialists that assist people with disabilities in your organization and community. Special education teachers can be useful resources as well (Murray, 2001).

SOLUTIONS

Our schools, communities, and libraries are made up of a rich mix of diverse individuals. How can we accommodate them all in our ILI? One solution is to develop specialized instruction directed at a particular group. Teaching to a homogeneous population offers the advantage of addressing the group's specific needs. However, targeting special groups (international students, older adults, or people with disabilities, for example) must be done carefully and diplomatically. The members of a particular group may not wish to be identified as needing special attention. They may feel they are being labeled as less competent than the general population. Part of your Needs Assessment should be to contact agencies and offices that deal with special groups. In doing so, try to determine how members of each group wish to receive instruction. Would they be interested in targeted instruction, or would they prefer to be incorporated into the general group?

Opportunities to actually teach to a targeted, homogenous group may be rare, but the likelihood that the learners you encounter in any ILI situation will be representatives of a variety of groups is high indeed. So, how do you cope? First, know the composition of your overall population, and educate yourself on the various characteristics of as many members of this population as possible (Kabagarama, 1997). Next, be alert to the various needs of all your learners. Finally, vary your teaching techniques and delivery modes in order to maximize the possibility of reaching everyone you are trying to teach. No matter how you categorize group differences, varying your methods and mixing approaches increases the likelihood that you will reach everyone regardless of their background, culture, gender, language, age, communication mode, or learning styles. Add large doses of sensitivity, courtesy, and mutual respect and use clear and jargon-free language and you have the formula for teaching in a diverse environment. The rules, as always, are as follows:

- **Knowledge**—Know your audience.
- **Respect**—Relate in a positive and respectful manner to your audience.
- **Inclusion**—Help your audience put the information into a context that makes sense to them.

A review of the suggestions made for teaching to each of the groups highlighted indicates some common themes. Moving from the more teacher-centric lecture mode to one that is more learner centric seems to be a good approach when dealing with diverse populations. This more inclusive approach invites all learners to participate in the process (Grant and Sleeter, 2007; Weimer, 2003). Demonstrate or model what you are trying to teach. Observational learning is reinforced in many communities and cultures. By showing rather than telling, you can overcome both behavioral and communication barriers that make it difficult for learners from a variety of backgrounds to process the information. Keep in mind that your learners do not all share the same frame of reference for the material you are teaching—they have the added problem of trying to fit the information into a context that makes sense to them (Banks et al., 2005; DiMartino and Zoe, 2000; Erickson, 2007; Irvine, 2003; Scitikus and Varghese, 2007). You can help them by starting with some kind of conceptual framework or mental model (see Chapters 3 and 5). This method also appeals to global thinkers, who prefer to see the big picture before being presented with the individual pieces.

Although many learners come to our instruction with very little experience with active or collaborative learning methods, these very techniques can be applied to great advantage in a multicultural, diverse setting. By encouraging learners to interact with one another, many cultural and language barriers can be overcome. Concepts can be discussed in the context of each learner's traditional values of heritage, history, custom, and language (Cooper and Slavin, 2001; Ford and Harris, 1999; Johnson, 1997; Scitikus and Varghese, 2007). Group work provides the opportunity for many different ideas to be expressed. Learners who may be reluctant to speak up in the larger forum may be willing to do so in the smaller, more intimate situation that small group work provides. Collaborative methods also provide opportunities for learners to take a more responsible role for their own education. It improves interpersonal skills, helps develop critical thinking, and encourages the recognition, acceptance, and value of diverse opinions (Freilberg and Driscoll, 2005; Hanson, 1995; Weimer, 2002). See discussions of active and collaborative learning in Chapter 6.

Because the idea of active participation is unfamiliar to many, instructors must make opportunities for everyone to contribute and respect those who wish to participate on a minimal level or not at all. Learners may opt out of discussions because of past unpleasant experiences in the academic setting, because they lack confidence in their language skills, or because they are reflective types who need to think about a topic for longer than is allowed in a quick-paced, interactive discussion. Some of your learners may come from high context backgrounds where debate and questioning is frowned upon, or they may be connected learners who empathize with everyone's point of view and so are uncomfortable questioning other people's opinions for fear of hurting their feelings. Setting up a variety of situations that encourage different types of participation will help to deal with these issues. In other words, invite them all to the dance by giving everyone a chance to perform each in his or her own way. Some of your learners will be more willing to dance than others. Try to be sensitive to their feelings. For example, while it might seem like a good idea to call on people to increase participation, this technique can be quite disquieting to some of your learners. Instead, try giving your learners options about how and when to respond. One nice approach in F2F teaching is to let your more vocal learners speak up first and then ask if anyone who has not as yet spoken would like to add something. This takes the pressure off your quieter learners and makes them feel less threatened and more willing to contribute. See Chapters 6 and 13 for more on indirect and active learning techniques.

Giving learners the opportunity to practice what is being taught is also valuable when dealing with a diverse population. It allows learners to test out what they think they understand from your demonstration, lecture, Web-based material, or other forms of instruction. What receives nods of understanding when described may prove more perplexing and difficult when put into practice (AT&T Knowledge Network, 2008a; Hanson, 1995; Huba and Freed, 2000; Freilberg and Driscoll, 2005; Frogg, 2007; MacDonald and Sarkodie-Mensah, 1988). Hands-on practice, therefore, can serve as a comprehension check for both F2F and online synchronous instructional situations. It also allows the instructor to offer immediate feedback, answer specific questions, and address individual concerns that learners may not have been willing to bring up to the full group for fear of appearing stupid. Web-based tutorials can also provide opportunities for practice. Be sure to build in mechanisms for feedback such as e-mailing quizzes to the instructor for review or self-correcting exercises that provide the learner with information about the appropriateness of his or her responses.

Appealing to a variety of sensory modes is also good practice, especially in a diverse environment. Handouts, guided exercises, and print and Web-based teaching aids are especially important. Many learners may find it difficult to follow the spoken lesson because language barriers, learning styles, or communication differences. However, they may be able to follow along in print, on a Web page, or through a PowerPoint or other presentation software program. Remember to use the chalk or whiteboard, or even a flip chart, to emphasize important points. Combine verbal instructions with visual cues and hands-on experiences to accommodate auditory, visual, and kinesthetic learners (Jiao, Onwuegbuzie, and Lichtenstein, 1996). Finally, prepare glossaries of library terminology. Remember that learners vary in their experience with and exposure to the types of services and procedures you will be discussing. If you have a large international student population, look for glossaries in both English and several native languages. One such glossary, ACRL's Instruction Section's Instruction for Diverse Populations "Multilingual Glossary," may be of assistance (ALA. ACRL. IS, 2008d). Try to avoid the use of jargon, little known words, ambiguous statements, abbreviations, and acronyms. If you must use them, make sure you define the terms and refer learners to glossaries. Repeat or paraphrase important points to emphasize their significance. Learners may be too shy or embarrassed to ask for clarification. Above all, avoid using ethnic or culturally tinged words, phrases, or gestures that might be offensive to some or all of your learners (*Culturgrams*, 2008; DiMartino and Zoe, 2000; Downing and Diaz, 1993; Liu, 1993; MacDonald and Sarkodie-Mensah, 1988; Scitikus and Varghese, 2007).

Provide a friendly and welcoming environment. Indicate by words and deeds that you recognize and value the diversity represented in your population. Developing a climate that acknowledges, accepts, understands, and accommodates various interpersonal and communication styles is crucial, especially for those learners who have felt disenfranchised in the past. Rather than forcing the learner to choose between his or her own cultural style and that of the majority or macro culture represented by the educational system, the culturally responsive teacher allows learners to build bridges between both worlds (Freilberg and Driscoll, 2005; Irvine, 2003; Scitikus and Varghese, 2007; Shade, Kelly, and Oberg, 1997; Shade and New, 1993). Remember that learners work best and are more highly motivated when the curriculum reflects their own culture, experiences, and perspective. Reflect on how you felt in situations where you were viewed as an "outsider." Empathize with learners who do not find themselves reflected in textbooks, instructional material, or even the library's collections. Work at making your material relevant to everyone. Be inclusive, not exclusive, in your illustrative choices and examples (AT&T Knowledge Network, 2008a; DiMartino and Zoe, 2000; Downing and Diaz 1993; Freilberg and Driscoll 2005; Garner 2008; Irvine 2003; Kabagarama 1997; Salili and Hoosain, 2001; Scitikus and Varghese, 2007). Whenever you have a choice, use examples that reflect diversity rather than homogeneity.

Teaching to different cultures and different learning styles requires a shift in how instruction is organized. It depends upon the use of more interactive, learner-centered, problem-solving, self-directed forms of teaching. Cooperative or collaborative learning experiences are especially successful in reaching a variety of learners. Problem- or case-based instruction in which learners can bring their own perspectives and experiences into play as they deal with some real-life issue is also a good approach when working with diverse populations. Keep the variations in cultural and group characteristics in mind when you develop your instruction. For example, although high context learners are community or group-oriented in general, they are often reluctant to express opinions that seem to counter those of the group or anyone in authority. Therefore, they may not feel comfortable during brainstorming, debate, and the open discussions that characterize collaborative, group work. However, they may be very good at keeping track of the different ideas being presented and may even be helpful in categorizing and grouping ideas that seem related or similar—thereby helping the group toward the selection of a final solution. Group or collaborative work is also a problem for the separate learner who prefers to work on his or her own. However, their objective and detached approach to problem solving can be helpful in getting a variety of ideas on the table. Their connected counterparts, on the other hand, will shine during the consensus building aspects of those activities with their respectful attitude toward all points of view. As you introduce the various activities you have in mind, make sure you show all your learners how the characteristics and values of their different backgrounds and cultures can contribute to the successful completion of the task. Each type of learner should be invited to contribute in his or her own way. Urge your learners to celebrate the richness that diversity brings to any situation and promote their understanding and acceptance of these differences. Encourage your learners to see how the very things that make us different contribute to better, more complete solutions to any problem under consideration.

Our communities, educational institutions, and day-to-day lives have been enriched by the influx of diverse populations. As we move toward a society where no single group represents a majority, the cultures and learning styles of all groups must be recognized and acknowledged. It is interesting to note that as more and more adult learners, women, and people from "micro cultures" enter our school systems, educators at all levels have responded by incorporating approaches that are more closely aligned to the norms, values, and behaviors of these groups. The rise of methods such as cooperative/collaborative teaching, learner-centered teaching, and authentic assessment seems to reflect the influence of these learners on the educational enterprise and has profoundly affected what is now considered best practices in teaching.

FINAL REMARKS

The principles of good instruction should apply to everyone we teach, and the more we understand about our learners and their diverse cultures, values, and backgrounds, the more sensitive we can be to their needs. While you should be familiar with the demographics of your institution, it is important to avoid making assumptions based on easy group stereotypes. Do not make judgments based on age, physical appearance, speech, or behavior. Both teacher and learner bring certain expectations about diverse groups to the classroom. The resulting interactions affect the classroom atmosphere. As a teacher who is aware of his or her own cultural preferences, you must be sensitive your own expectations and attitudes. Such self-analysis will help you develop more respectful interactions that will result in a better learning environment for everyone.

Remember that your attitude toward your learners has enormous influence on the effectiveness of your instruction. If you have formed expectations about your learners based on physical, cultural, gender, age, or socioeconomic factors, you will consciously or unconsciously communicate them to your learners. Learners will quickly grasp the message, react to it accordingly, and behave according to your example and expectations. The impact of these reciprocal interactions is clear and easy to observe. You expect certain behavior from the learner. The learner interprets your spoken and unspoken message and responds accordingly. You have set up a self-fulfilling feedback loop where learners perform only as well as you think they will. But you can make this situation work for you. Develop a teaching style that communicates a positive attitude about everyone's abilities. Expect the best from everyone. Let them know that is what you expect, and you will find that is what you will receive. It is up to the teacher to establish a climate in which everyone feels welcome, all learners are viewed as competent, and all ways of thinking are accepted (Ball, 2000; Freilberg and Driscoll, 2005; Frogg, 2007; Garner, 2008; Shade, Kelly, and Oberg, 1997). Many principles associated with the humanist theories of learning are applicable here. See Chapter 3 for more on the humanist approach to teaching.

Our classrooms can serve as laboratories where people from different backgrounds, cultures, and experiences can interact and broaden their perspectives. Raising your own consciousness about all types of diversity, including your own, will help you create instructional sessions that are more meaningful and effective for all of your learners. Encourage your institution to offer staff development opportunities so that you and your colleagues can enhance your understanding about all members of your population. The more we know about people, the easier it is for us to respond appropriately. The keys are knowledge, respect, and inclusion. Becoming knowledgeable about your population will alert you to the needs of all your learners. It will help you create an atmosphere of mutual respect and inclusion where diversity is not only recognized but also celebrated and valued. To do so will enrich the learning experience for teacher and learner alike and better prepare us all to live in our wonderfully multicultural and varied world.

EXERCISES

Working with homogeneous groups:

1. Make a list of all the groups that are represented in your population.
2. Write down all that you know about each group.
3. Now write down information that you need to find out.
4. Research the groups to check the accuracy of what you know and to fill in the gaps in your knowledge.
5. Pretend that you were preparing instruction for each of the groups listed. Assume that the group would be homogeneous (made up of members of only one group). What three things would you include in your instructional plan to make it especially appropriate for each of the groups you have identified? Make a separate list for each group.

Working with heterogeneous groups:

1. Now assume that you are preparing instruction for a group made up of representatives of all of the groups listed in the first exercise.
2. Review your responses to the fifth step. Can you combine the methods identified for each group into an instructional design that accommodates the needs of all these different groups?
3. List three methods, techniques, or strategies that you would employ to ensure the effectiveness for instruction for this type of heterogeneous group.

READ MORE ABOUT IT

AT&T Knowledge Network. "21st Century Literacies: Multicultural Literacy" (2008). Available: www.kn.pacbell.com/wired/21stcent/cultural.html (accessed December 31, 2008).

Banks, James A. and Cherry A. McGee Banks. 2007. *Multicultural Education: Issues and Perspectives*, 6th ed. Hoboken, NJ: Wiley.

Gaitan, Concha Delgago. 2006. *Building Culturally Responsive Classrooms*. Thousand Oaks, CA: Corwin Press.

Jacobson, Trudi E. and Helene C. Williams, Eds. 2000. *Teaching the New Library to Today's Users: Reaching International, Minority, Senior Citizens, Gay/Lesbian, First Generation, At-risk, Graduate and Returning Students, and Distance Learners*. New York: Neal-Schuman.

Kabagarama, Daisy. 1997. *Breaking the Ice: A Guide to Understanding People From Other Cultures*, 2nd ed. Boston: Allyn & Bacon.

Shade, Barbara J., Cynthia Kelly, and Mary Oberg. 1997. *Creating Culturally Responsive Classrooms*, 1st ed. Washington, DC: American Psychological Association.

Chapter 14

Delivering Information Literacy Instruction in Various Environments

No man is an island, entire of himself; every man is a piece of the continent.

—John Donne

INFORMATION LITERACY INSTRUCTION—IT TAKES A WORLDWIDE VILLAGE

One of the most fundamental aspects of information literacy (IL) is the desire to promote lifelong learning (ALA. Presidential Committee on Information Literacy, 1989, 1998). To accomplish this laudable goal, libraries at all levels and in all environments must participate in information literacy instruction (ILI). Although instruction in some form has long been incorporated into the mission of most academic and school libraries in the past, it has played a much smaller part in public and special libraries. However, advances in information technology and the proliferation of information in both print and electronic formats have created an even more pressing need to develop an information literate society. Furthermore, attention to IL has grown worldwide as organizations and people everywhere acknowledge that in order for people and nations to remain competitive in an information-dependent global economy, and to participate knowledgably in democratic societies, they must hone their IL skills.

A series of reports ranging back to the late 1980s have addressed this issue and have urged governments everywhere to view IL as a serious concern. Examples of these documents include the ALA's Presidential Committee's IL reports (ALA. Presidential Committee on Information Literacy, 1989, 1998), *Information Power* (ALA. AASL. AECT, 1988, 1998), the *Secretary's Commission on Achieving Necessary Skills* (Thompson and Henley, 2000; U.S. Department of Labor. Secretary's Commission on Achieving Necessary Skills, 2000), *America 2000* (U.S. Department of Education, 1991), *Greater Expectations: A New Vision for Learning as a Nation Goes to College* (American Association of Colleges and Universities, 2002), the IFLA and UNESCO *Manifestos* on both public and school libraries (IFLA and UNESCO, 1994, 2006), "The Prague Declaration" (Thompson, 2003; U.S. NCLIS and NFIL, 2003), the Spellings Commission's report (Budd, 2007; Spellings, 2006), and *Tough Choices or Tough Times* from the National Center on Education and the Economy (2007). These reports call for the restructuring of the educational system globally, with the goal of producing a population equipped for the information age (Doyle and ERIC Clearinghouse on Information & Technology, 1994; Spitzer et al., 1998). Furthermore, these reports all support the idea that lifelong learning, critical thinking and problem solving skills, and the ability to use a variety of information technologies are key survival skills in today's society. Implicit in all of this is the idea that it is more valuable to know how to find and utilize useful information effectively than merely to memorize and store specific facts that will quickly become out of date (Gibson, 2008).

Further evidence to support this worldwide interest is the development of Web pages by both IFLA and UNESCO (IFLA, 2007, 2008; UNESCO,

2008b) dedicated to the support and promotion of IL. Representatives of both IFLA and UNESCO also attended the 21st Century Information Summit (Information Literacy Summit, 2006; Perraut, 2006) held in Washington, DC, along with representatives from various U.S. businesses, schools, universities, and accreditation and governmental agencies, with the goal of promoting IL at all levels of education and in all parts of the world. This summit, jointly sponsored by the National Forum on IL, the National Education Association, the Educational Testing Service (ETS), the Committee for Economic Development, and the Committee for a Competitive Workforce (an affiliate of the U.S. Chambers of Commerce) called for the development of national standards for IL and for the integration of IL into K–12 as well as postsecondary education. Finally, the proposed Strengthening Kids Interest in Learning and Libraries (SKILLS) Act, which has bipartisan support in both the U.S. House of Representatives and the Senate, will, if passed, mandate that every public school district have at least one highly qualified school library media specialist in each public school. The sponsors of this act intend it to provide the additional federal support and incentives needed to strengthen school libraries and thus improve the American educational system ("SKILLS Act Gives High Marks to School Librarians," 2007).

Clearly, IL is a hot topic everywhere, and librarians at all levels are beginning to realize that if lifelong learning is truly our goal, then we must join forces with our colleagues in all types of libraries to make this happen. The unifying thread running through all of these initiatives, reports, and discussions is the need for an information literate populace. The goal of creating an information literate populace impacts libraries in all types of environments and serves as the impetus for various types of libraries to work more closely together to provide a framework in which IL permeates all aspects of life. The goal is to develop a continuum and a connection between all libraries.

ILI has a long and rich tradition in both academic and school libraries, but IL cannot remain the sole responsibility of the K–12 and/or the higher education environments. The needs of businesses and industries and of local communities and the general population have created a place for the inclusion of both public and special libraries in the mix. From the community to schools to colleges and on to the workplace, people are expected to be able to access, use, understand, and apply information. The shared aim is to foster people who are ready to enter the workforce as competent, ethical, and productive users of information and technology (Ark, 2000; Barbour, Gavin, and Canfield, 2004; Maehl, 2003; Rockman, 2004a; Rockman, 2004b; Warlick, 2004). All four environments (public, school, academic, and special) must work together in a coordinated and synergistic manner and in collaboration with one another and with others beyond libraries if the ultimate goal of an information literate populace is to be realized. And libraries in all environments have embraced this idea (Burger, 2008). Although awareness of IL is still more prominent in the school and academic worlds, interest in the topic is on the rise in both public and special libraries. Furthermore, partnerships and collaborations among libraries in different environments are also growing in number with the creation of sequenced and coordinated IL efforts as the desired outcome.

Advances in information technology and the delivery of information are also contributing to this synergy. In a world where a growing number of libraries truly have no walls, and libraries emphasize access over ownership, the concept of "library as place" loses its meaning. Resources that were previously available only in the library are now accessible in the user's home, office, and even in Internet cafés attached to coffee shops and restaurants, not to mention through mobile devices. Users can now find information remotely, and that material can be delivered (albeit sometimes for a fee) directly to their "doorsteps" or to their mobile devices. Most library users consider document delivery, either in print or electronically, a standard service.

A further consideration for remote users is licensing agreements that limit use of certain resources to specific user groups. For example, a remote user may be able to visit a particular library's Web page but will be blocked from using certain resources because of license agreements that restrict use to people with authorized IP addresses only. Remote users are understandably confused and frustrated when searchers can freely use a library's online catalog and certain publicly accessible databases, such as the National Library of Medicine's PubMed® system, but are asked for a password when trying to search other proprietary databases. The needs of these remote users should be examined in all types of libraries.

Although libraries will continue to be defined by the ways in which they relate to their parent organizations, their clientele will develop more and more mixed loyalties. People may go to the most conveniently located library rather than the one to which they have some sort of institutional association. They may visit many different libraries via those libraries' Web pages, or they may make use of the specialized content from unique collections that are accessible through the Internet. If individuals no longer limit themselves to using one specific library or collection, then all our libraries must work together to provide the type of ILI that is necessary to make use of information however and wherever it is found.

THE ENVIRONMENTS—WHAT ARE THEY?

Although this brave new technological world has somewhat blurred the distinctions between types of library, library environments are still typically categorized into four distinct groups—public, school, academic, and special. Each has a unique relationship to the organization, institution, or community in which it exists. While people of all ages may indeed use the public library, and community members may consult the resources found in academic libraries, each type of library considers certain users its primary clientele. Who these users are and what constitutes their specific types of information needs help to shape the type of ILI that is developed for each environment.

Even though the environment in which each type of library operates has a strong influence on how, when, and where instruction takes place, many of the principles discussed in other chapters certainly still apply. Information professionals need to be familiar with their environmental climate and culture, and with the characteristics and needs of their users, in order to design appropriate and effective instruction. Needs Assessments remain a key component of the planning process. Clear, appropriate goals and expected learning outcomes (ELOs) must be written as part of the process of preparing for instruction of any kind. Modes, formats, and methods of instruction must be selected, and instructional efforts should be assessed for effectiveness. See Chapters 7, 8, and 11 for more on these topics.

The success of your programs also depends on making the right connections in your environment, finding the appropriate partners in your institution, and promoting the value of your programs to your community at large. Find out who needs to be convinced and get them involved. Continue to keep them informed about your successes and any need for new programs that might have been identified as you go along. You may have to start small and build on your successes. Use your assessment data to gain support. Show how the library is a key element in the environment's goals and mission. Who the key players are will differ in each environment, and thus methods of contact, promotion, and communication will also vary. But the principles remain the same. Know your population (both your users and the movers and shakers in your environment), target your programs accordingly, and promote the reasons for your decisions with the people who can help you make it happen. *Learning to Lead and Manage Information Literacy Instruction* also by the authors of this book has more information on topics such as marketing, collaboration, and organizational culture that might be useful in your outreach and collaboration efforts (Grassian and Kaplowitz, 2005).

Although a library is a library is a library, each type of library has its own unique qualities. The relationship between the library and its parent organization affects the way in which instruction is undertaken in that library. Let us take a look at each of the environments, one by one, in order to discover the special characteristics of each. We will describe the primary users for each type of library, the role each library plays in its community or organization, IL challenges for each environment, and close with a discussion of current IL practice in the various types of libraries. In keeping with our notion that each type of library plays a role in lifelong learning, we will start with the public library, whose users run the gamut from very young children to senior citizens and all ages in between. We will move on to the school library, followed by the academic environment. The special library, with its role as serving the needs of the workforce, will be covered last.

USER CHARACTERISTICS, ISSUES, AND INFORMATION LITERACY INSTRUCTION EFFORTS

The public library's main function is to serve its community's recreational and self-educational needs as well as the needs of school-age children in the area. The school and academic library share the educational goals of their parent institutions and contribute to the instructional and research needs of their students, faculty/teachers, and staff. The special library's job is to support an organization or business' employees in the production of their jobs and to contribute to the overall success of that organization or business.

The Public Library

Public libraries, with their varied and diverse user groups, have traditionally tended toward individualized instruction and teach-yourself or self-help types of instruction. Instruction is frequently one on one and often occurs via an interaction at the reference desk or through some other form of remote reference such as live chat. Workshops or classes targeted toward particular user groups such as older adults are also a feature of the public library environment. Because the local public library may be many people's only means of computer access, these libraries have taken on a major responsibility for providing instruction in computer use to their constituents. Public libraries also rely heavily on signs, handouts, point-of-use instruction, their Web sites, and online tutorials that people can use whenever the need arises.

Who Are the Users?

Public libraries with their historical tradition of being the "People's University" epitomizes the library profession's dedication to lifelong learning (Jackson, 1995; Petruzzi and Burns, 2006; Walter, 2007). Anyone and everyone from the community it serves is welcome in the public library and may use the library's Web site. Some libraries extend remote access to anyone who requests a library card (sometimes for a fee) whether or not they live in that library's community area. And the resources and services provided support users at every stage of life. Offering preschool story hours, school-age reading clubs, homework centers, young adult services, career skills training, and special services for senior citizens, public libraries are dedicated to helping their users succeed throughout life. For many, the public library is the only place individuals can go to enrich their own lives and enhance their skills. People who are not affiliated with a college or university, those whose workplaces do not offer the training they need to improve their careers, individuals who are changing jobs or returning to work, children and teens whose school libraries are inadequate to support their research projects, and senior citizens who are intimidated by the new technologies that surround them all count on the public library as a nonthreatening, welcoming, and supportive environment where they can learn what they need in order to live a successful life (Jehlik, 2004; Juznic et al., 2006; Kelly and Hibner, 2005; Skoglund, 2003; Walter, 2007).

The public library is a reflection of the community it serves. The users in a public library can represent a diverse mix of ages, cultures, ethnic groups, educational and socioeconomic levels, lifestyles, and languages. Information needs tend to be specific and are often unique to the particular individual requesting help. In addition, use of the library can be intermittent and random. The diversity of user needs coupled with a lack of consistent contact has resulted in public libraries tending to adopt a more informal and ad hoc approach to instruction (Jehlik, 2004; Juznic et al., 2006; Skoglund, 2003; Walter, 2007; Woods, 1990).

The public library's mission and its role in the community depend upon the needs of those who live in that community. As communities differ, so do the roles, missions, and activities of the libraries within those communities. In order for a library to best meet its public's current and future needs, a thorough Needs Assessment must be undertaken. For the public library, a crucial part of the Needs

Assessment stage of the planning process is a Community Needs Analysis (Dempsey, 2004; Himmel and Wilson, 1998; Hovius, 2006; IFLA and UNESCO, 1994; Jackson, 1995; Jehlik, 2004; Nelson, 2001; Skoglund, 2003; Walter, 2007; Woods, 1990).

All Needs Assessments start with an examination of the library's target population. See Chapter 7 for details on how to design a Needs Assessment. However, because the public library tends to serve a more diverse population than other types of libraries, it is extremely important to gather data about the composition of the library's community and how its various subpopulations might vary as to age, sex, family life cycle (singles, young-marrieds, retirees), income, occupation, educational levels, race/ethnicity, cultures, languages spoken, etc. This is where the Community Needs Analysis comes in. The data for this analysis can be found in census reports, the city planner's office, the zoning office, and other government agencies. In addition, it is important to find out who does and does not use the library and why. For what purposes do people use the library? What barriers keep others from using the library? Are there geographical or physical obstacles to use? Do some members of the community feel that they are not welcome in the library? Interviews with users, community leaders, and representatives from community organizations; focus groups; and surveys of both users and nonusers can provide this information.

The Community Needs Analysis should also assess transportation. Do people use public transportation or own their own cars? How difficult is it to get to the library? Look at travel time, parking, traffic patterns, and public transportation routes and schedules. The community's transportation office as well as its city planning office should have these data. Scheduling face-to-face (F2F) instruction may depend on these travel considerations. If a large proportion of your population has transportation difficulties, issues of distance or remote education may need to be considered. Usage patterns should also be examined. Scheduling synchronous F2F or online instruction should correlate with periods of heaviest use by likely participants.

The businesses, stores, and organizations (cultural, educational, and recreational) that are located in the community also help to define it. Check on what types of businesses or industrial organizations are located in your community. Where do people shop? Are there daily, weekly, or seasonal patterns to their shopping behavior? What types of organizations are located in your community? Can you identify times of the year when these organizations are most active? Newspapers, community directories, telephone books, and the Chamber of Commerce should be able to provide this information. Use this information to enhance your marketing and outreach efforts and to help identify potential community partners.

What Are the Issues?

The increasing need for everyone to have access to and effectively use all types of technology have provided the public library with an obvious niche in the ILI arena. Where else can those on the wrong side of the digital divide go to gain free access to computers? Furthermore, public libraries have dedicated themselves to helping their users gain the computer skills needed to effectively access information on these computers. Teaching everything from basic computer use and "mousing" techniques to word processing and spreadsheet programs, as well as how to use library-provided resources and find trustworthy information via the Web, the public library offers a variety of ways for people to improve their lot in life (Huang and Russell, 2006; Juznic et al., 2006; Walter, 2007). Needless to say, the range and mix of users can be quite a challenge for the public library. ILI programs and classes are often directed toward a particular type of user, such as senior citizens with little or no computer expertise or school-age children who do not have access to adequate resources and/or services in their own school library. Some public libraries are even luring patrons into the library by offering classes that help them "keep up" with technology, instructing them in the use of e-mail, cell phones, and even iPods (Kelly and Hibner, 2005). For more on issues related to the digital divide, see Chapters 2, 15, and 16.

K–12 students are also turning to their local public libraries as budget cuts slash away at school libraries. With fewer and fewer schools having the funds to employ qualified school librarians and the money to support the school library's collection, these students must rely on the public library and its staff not only to provide the resources they need (both print and electronic) but also to teach them how to use those resources effectively and ethically. It is becoming more and more common for public libraries to offer IL classes for K–12 students. These classes, sometimes developed in collaboration with the neighborhood schools, are dedicated to providing students with the IL skills and strategies they need to support their educational efforts and to help them become lifelong learners. Public, as well as school libraries, also must deal with filtering issues as they design instructional endeavors and choose instructional examples. Although intended as a protection for K–12 students, filtering may result in blocking useful as well as potentially dangerous sites. For example, IL instructors may have difficulty helping high school students learn how to find information on breast cancer if school or public library filtering programs block the word "breast."

Funding is, of course, also an issue for public libraries, especially with the increasing pressure for them to provide computer access as well as classroom and meeting spaces for their users. The Community Needs Analysis can be used to determine the needs of the various groups that make up a library's user population. The analysis may identify more groups and possible programs than can be handled by your library. Remember that part of your Needs Assessment is to determine what your library is currently doing and to rationally examine its facilities, staff, and budget constraints that might impact future programs. List all the possibilities, and then prioritize them. You may be faced with some hard decisions as you select which groups and programs to concentrate on. If you have more than one primary user group with a variety of needs, where will you focus your efforts first? Community politics and your library's long- and short-term goals will affect your selection of which programs to implement. Your goal is to make the most positive, productive impact possible on your community based on the library's available resources (Walter, 2007; Woods, 1990).

Fortunately the business world is beginning to recognize the need for an information and technology literate populace, and large corporations are working with public (and school) libraries to help provide financial support for this effort. Furthermore, enterprising libraries are starting to incorporate commercial entities into their spaces as yet another way to raise necessary funds, which could be funneled toward computers and instructional needs. Coffeehouses, cafés, and other types of businesses are popping up in many public libraries, and there is a growing movement toward the renting out of library space for after-hours community events (Dempsey, 2004).

Public librarians need to be proactively identifying potential partners and actively developing these important relationships. Use your Needs Assessment to identify potential interinstitutional partners. Local agencies, businesses, and even schools and higher education institutions may be interested in forming alliances to provide resources and services to members of the community. Local businesses may be willing to provide financial support for equipment or supplies in exchange for a display in the library acknowledging their contributions (and thus creating positive public relations for the business itself). Schools with limited resources and local companies with no library of their own may wish to use the public library as their instructional setting. Academic libraries might provide information about when it is appropriate to refer public library users to a nearby academic institution and some information about the type of services and resources that would be available to these community users. Make sure you determine how the responsibility for delivering these joint efforts will be shared. Where will instruction actually take place? Who will pay for materials? Does the proposed joint effort fit into the overall goals of the library's IL plan? Finally, how does working with the outside agency impact the programs and services for those who are more regular users of the library (Brey-Casiano, 2006; Bundy, 2002; Hovius, 2006; Mediavilla, 2001; Petruzzi and Burns, 2006; Shaffer, 2006; Woods,1990)?

Public librarians must serve as advocates both for the acquisition of equipment and software to support instructional efforts and for the development of appropriate ILI programs in their libraries (Brey-Casiano, 2006; Walter, 2007). A promising sign is the inclusion of ILI as one of the service responses in *New Planning for Results* published by the ALA. This document, which has been implemented in public libraries across the country, offers support and advice to librarians who wish to develop ILI programs in their library (Himmel and Wilson, 1998; Jehlik, 2004; Nelson, 2001).

Interinstitutional cooperation and collaborative efforts with government agencies, community groups, and the private sector can pay off in many ways. Libraries that actively form alliances with other organizations learn even more about the information needs of their community. Teachers and schools are the natural allies of the public library in promoting the concept of information as a useful commodity. Businesses and industries are taking a steadily increasing role in workforce development. Employers are beginning to perceive the importance of having information literate employees, thus opening a wedge for the enterprising public librarian. Connecting with social service agencies also opens the door for libraries to respond more directly to societal needs. Overall, partnerships and alliances such as these are a way to work effectively in the community, overcome institutional isolation, and promote the value of information and the library's role in making that information available to all (Jackson, 1995). These alliances also create positive public relations for the library and may even pay off financially. The more friends the library has in the community, the more likely it will be seen as a valuable asset that deserves fiscal support.

Another challenge for ILI in the public library is that many of the librarians lack teaching experience. Part of the transformational process that public libraries must undertake is to help these librarians develop themselves professionally in order to take on this different type of teaching role. If public libraries are to take their place in providing lifelong IL skills to their users, librarians must move beyond just providing answers at the reference desk. The reference interaction itself can be transformed into a teaching opportunity when reference librarians incorporate the "talk aloud" technique into their exchanges with their F2F users and through their written messages during live reference chat exchanges. By describing what they are doing and even sharing a view of their computer screens with them, the reference interaction can become a "teachable moment" (Walter, 2007).

Finally, there is the challenge of attracting users to classes offered by the library. Public library users tend to be self-directed and self-motivated, so it is up to the library to market their classes and other instructional efforts (F2F or online) with an eye to showing how the instruction can help users in their daily lives and in their educational, career, and recreational endeavors. Offering classes and instructional support materials in the variety of languages that are spoken in a community, as identified in your ongoing Needs Assessments, is also a good way to appeal to those users who do not speak English or for whom English is a second language.

What Are They Doing?

Formal instruction programs are developed in the academic and school library settings because of the way the library relates to the educational process. Group needs are identified and instruction can be implemented within the framework of the academic or school enterprise. The parallel for this sort of sustained instructional contact does not generally exist in the public library where populations are diverse, and it is difficult to identify a commonality of backgrounds among users. Instructional needs in such an environment are amorphous and constantly shifting. The focus in the public library is on the independent, individual library user and his or her unique needs (Jackson, 1995). Public libraries' instruction often relies on methods that support self-directed learning. Signs, print materials, and point-of-use instruction are all heavily used in the public library setting (LILi, 2008; Woods, 1990). However, other forms of ILI are increasingly appearing in public libraries.

One interesting trend is the development of "homework help" centers as a sort of specialized reference/instruction service. These centers offer informal, one-on-one help, much like a reference desk, but are dedicated to helping K–12 students in the community complete their research papers and projects (Mediavilla, 2001; Rua, 2008; Shaffer, 2006; Walter, 2007). Online homework help is also being offered in some locations, for example, in New York City (New York Public Library, Brooklyn Public Library, and Queens Library, 2005). Some libraries expand this effort by offering in-library workshops dedicated to teaching K–12 students how to use the library's Web-based resources. Other librarians offer off-site instruction to students in their own schools (Jehlik, 2004; Tosa and Long, 2003).

More and more public libraries are offering F2F group instruction in computer use and Internet searching (Kelly and Hibner, 2005; Walter, 2007). While it may be hard to find much published literature on these endeavors, a glance at most public libraries' Web pages will confirm that classes are being taught. A quick Google search on "public library classes" yields an extensive list of classes taught at libraries such as the Milwaukee Public Library (accessed 2008), New York Public Library (accessed 2008), Omaha Public Library (accessed 2008), Santa Monica Public Library (accessed 2008), and the Seattle Public Library (accessed 2008). Libraries like the Omaha Public Library offer both F2F and online classes. Although public libraries may not use the term *ILI*, their workshops serve a vital function for their users—they provide a safe place for these people to build the foundational computer and IL skills needed in today's world.

Public libraries are also offering Web-based tutorials geared to the public library audience. Obviously these are intended for users who either are already comfortable using computers or who have taken the library's basic computer classes. These tutorials may be "home-grown" or based on open source tutorials such as TILT. But they all serve as ways to expand the library's ILI reach, allowing users to learn at their own pace and providing them with help whenever and wherever they need it. With remote access to library resources becoming more and more the rule, it is only natural that public libraries would also try to offer remote asynchronous ILI opportunities as well (Heintzelman et al., 2007; Huang and Russell, 2006; Jehlik, 2004; Tosa and Long, 2003).

The IL vision embraced by the American Library Association in 1989 challenges libraries to make a difference in people's lives and calls upon librarians to contribute to the betterment of society by creating a population of independent seekers of truth (ALA. Presidential Committee on Information Literacy, 1989, 1998). Public libraries have historically seen themselves as committed to the needs of both their particular community and society at large. It is only natural and right that the public library has become the primary setting for its constituents to come together and develop the skills necessary to become IL individuals. In doing so public libraries have identified their special niche in the ILI universe and have identified themselves as the place to go when people need to gain the computer and IL skills (through formal classes, Web site support, and reference exchanges) necessary in today's world.

The School Library

School librarians, often referred to as school library media specialists (SLMS), tend to work in conjunction with classroom teachers and administrators who are also part of the school libraries' user base. In some cases, library media teachers (LMT), who are certified as teachers but may not have a library degree, staff a school's library. Regardless of who the school "librarians" might be, all of them face the challenge of working with teachers who use and refer students to Google and/or Wikipedia rather than to "library recommended" sources. In order to help both teachers and students see the merit of going beyond these freely available resources, ILI should support the curriculum and be integrated within it. The aim of instruction in the school library is to provide the student with skills that eventually will result in his or her ability to be independent information users. Teaching tends to be to groups and is meant to promote self-reliance and the acquisition of transferable skills. The differences between school and academic library settings center on age level and on the magnitude of the enterprise. In general, the school librarian is dealing with a narrower range of subject material, a smaller body of research resources, and fewer users than the academic librarian. Furthermore, there is generally only one SLMS or LMT per school—even in high schools with large student populations. K–12 school librarians also must be concerned with issues of developmental readiness and appropriate levels of both materials and instruction. School librarians should try to keep apprised of current pedagogical practices, changes in technology, educational reform movements, budget issues, and the general political climate of their school districts and beyond, which could impact the schools and their libraries. This can be a challenge as many school libraries are "one-person" shows, making it difficult for the SLMS or LMT to get away for professional development opportunities. To do so might mean shutting down the library.

Who Are the Users?

Whereas the public library's user group is quite broad, the school library's clientele seems on the surface to be much more focused. Each school library serves the students, faculty, and administrators in their school. However, although the needs of these users will be determined by the school's curriculum, the population itself could be as varied as in any public library, with a wide range of languages, cultures, and other diversities and abilities being represented in the student body (Kleinman, 2000).

As in all environments, the more the librarian knows about the students who make up the school's population, the better. Performing regular Needs Assessments (see Chapter 7) should be part of the school library's routine. A special aspect of Needs Assessments in the school environment, however, is the curriculum analysis. An examination of curriculum guides, course syllabi, classroom textbooks and other instructional materials, and grade-related standards and requirements can help pinpoint where information skills might help students attain instructional objectives. A careful study of course descriptions, syllabi, and/or grade requirements can indicate the type of information skills that students need to successfully complete their academic program. The information skills demanded by the academic curriculum represent the actual information needs of the students. Take a look at standard tests, review some representative written assignments, and, of course, talk to the teachers (Corcoran and Langlois, 1990; Farmer, 2007). Use any and all opportunities to learn about the material being taught and the methods in which it is being presented. See if you can develop a file of assignments and a calendar of units being covered by the different grades in your school. Encourage teachers to send you copies of all assignments in advance. Use this information to create coordinated displays and exhibits in the library, to develop appropriate library experiences for the students, and to use as a starting point for discussions with teachers that will result in a closer integration of the library into the classroom teaching process.

Your Needs Assessment should look at the computer skills of both students and teachers and should also examine how much access students have to computers in the school and at home. Furthermore, a visit to public and academic libraries in the vicinity of the school is also in order. Find out what computer access is available and if there are any restrictions on access and use—especially for K–12 students with regard to filtering software. This visit is also a good opportunity to start developing a relationship with public and academic librarians that could lead to collaborations and ILI partnerships in the future. Finding out what is available to your students in terms of access and instruction beyond the school grounds can help you decide what sort of ILI support you need to develop.

Although the current crop of K–12 students has grown up in a digital world, the librarian cannot assume uniform familiarity and comfort with technology among the school's student population. The digital divide can exist within the school and even within individual classes, so finding out what your students know and do not know about technology is a vital part of your Needs Assessment. Pay special attention to the types of technology they use. Although many students may be comfortable with text messaging and using their cell phones, they may not be as familiar with the types of technology that would assist them in their information searches. They may think they are extremely technologically savvy, but in fact they are not as sophisticated as they would like to believe. Do not forget to survey the teachers and administrators. You may find a range of technology skill levels among them as well.

What Are the Issues?

Educational systems are under close scrutiny all over the world, and the K–12 environment is no exception. Faculty members in institutions of higher education are bemoaning the fact that entering freshmen are ill prepared for the rigors of college and university studies. Employers are dissatisfied with the skill level of their new hires, and parents are wondering what is being taught in their children's schools to cause such a situation (Harris, 2003). Suggested remedies include the shift toward more authentic, resource-based instruction. Ironically this movement, which relies heavily on a well-stocked and well-staffed school library, comes at a time when school libraries are severely underfunded. The SKILLS act, if passed, is meant to remedy this situation by mandating that every public school district has at least one highly qualified school library media specialist in each public school ("SKILLS Act Gives High Marks to School Librarians," 2007). Paying for such an initiative may prove to be a real challenge for schools everywhere, especially if funding to support it is not incorporated in the legislation.

The evolution of the school library's role from the 1950s to the present can be characterized in four stages. In the early and mid-1950s, the concentration was on collections. The 1960s saw the library program used to promote the usefulness of the collections. A major emphasis on instruction developed in the 1970s and 1980s. Today's focus is on integrating instruction into the curriculum and emphasizing the teaching process rather than the use of individual tools (Stripling, 1996). Key to this approach is close collaboration between classroom teachers and school librarians. ILI is most effective when it is seamlessly integrated into the curriculum and aligns with the papers and projects assigned to the students by their teachers (Farmer, 2002, 2007; Harris, 2003; Lance, 2002; Lance and Loertscher, 2003; Valenza, 2003b).

Several process-oriented methods for presenting ILI in the school environment were developed in the 1980s and 1990s, and many are still very much in use. These include the Big Six Skills Approach (Eisenberg and Berkowitz, 1990), the Information Search Process (Kuhlthau, 1985, 1989, 1991), Pathways to Knowledge (Pappas, 1998; Pappas and Tepe, 1997), Virginia Rankin's (1988) metacognition approach, and the Research Process Model (Stripling and Pitts, 1988). All of these methods are based on the psychological learning theory known as *constructivism*. This theory emphasizes personal knowledge construction and a more holistic approach that integrates content and process skills. The movement toward a more integrated, process approach to ILI closely mirrors current school reform initiatives that emphasize thinking and inquiry skills and the fostering of communities of learners. Both educational reform movements and the process-oriented ILI approach challenge students to assume responsibility for their own learning in today's global society where information and knowledge are the key elements for success (Harada and Tepe, 1998; Harris, 2003; Stripling, 1996).

Constructivist models promote active participation in the learning process, and problem-based, authentic interaction with materials is used to support that learning. The result is learning experiences in which learners create meaning and understanding for themselves rather than just copy and memorize facts (Pappas, 2007; Snavely, 2004; Thomas, 2004; Weidenbenner, 2003). Resource-based teaching techniques are a good fit with this model. In this approach, learners spend time prior to engaging in library research determining what understandings, experiences, and knowledge they already possess. It is only after they have identified what they know, and even more importantly what additional information they need to find out, that they begin to use library resources for their research. Both teacher and librarian work together to provide learners with opportunities to expand and extend their baseline understanding and then to construct new knowledge (Hainer, 1998; Oatman, 2006; Paige, 1996; Rankin, 1988). When material is turned into language they can understand, students as young as third graders can be taught how to evaluate Web sites. Asking them to think about who, what, when, where, and why Web sites were developed is a good way to instill critical thinking attitudes into these young learners (Franklin, 2006). For other examples of how teachers and school librarians at all grade levels are applying constructivist approaches to Web-based instruction, see "WebQuest" (Dodge, 2000a) and *Kathy Schrock's Guide for Educators* (Schrock, 2008b). WebQuests make use of Web resources to promote an inquiry-oriented learning experience. They focus on using information rather than just locating it, are intended to promote the analysis, synthesis, and evaluation of information, and as such support the goals of IL in the school environment. Kathy Schrock's Web site offers a range of worksheets and exercises that can be used to encourage critical thinking and engage the learners.

Position papers and standards published by state and national organizations interested in the quality of school libraries emphasize a new image for the school librarian. The librarian's role is described as having shifted from passive "keeper of information" to key participant in the learning process (ALA. AASL, 2007b; ALA. AASL and AECT, 1988, 1998; Association for Teacher-Librarianship in Canada and Canadian Library Association, 1998; California School Library Association. Standards Taskforce, 2004; CMLEA, 1994; IFLA and UNESCO, 2006; Kentucky Department of Education, 1995; Utah State Office of Education, 1996). Today's school librarians are perceived as agents for change in the restructuring of the educational process. Their role is to provide a variety of resources as the basis for experiential or authentic learning, share with teachers the process by which students acquire needed information skills, and encourage students' pursuit of individual interests (Doyle and ERIC Clearinghouse on Information & Technology, 1994; Farmer, 1999, 2002, 2007; Spitzer et al., 1998). Furthermore, recent research studies on the impact of school libraries support the idea that the exposure to a strong school library staffed with a professional librarian enhances students' educational experiences and academic achievements ("School Libraries Work!," accessed 2008; Huang and Russell, 2006; Lance, 2002; Lance and Loertscher, 2003; Lance, Rodney, and Hamilton-Pennell, 2005; Logan, 2008; Small, Snyder, and Parker, 2008; Todd and Kuhlthau, 2004).

Creating dynamic, integrated ILI in the school environment can be a major undertaking. Faced with limited space, staff, and funding, K–12 school librarians must be creative and flexible in their approaches. Because resource-based instruction is more student centered, the library may need to expand its hours and provide for more open access to the facility. However, budgetary constraints as well as union issues must be taken into consideration. Self-help materials, such as pathfinders, point-of-use guides, self-guided tours, multimedia, and Web-based tutorials, will allow for more individualized instruction at the point of need. Consider the importance of a good signage system as well. This indirect teaching method can go a long way toward easing the day-to-day workload on you and your staff (Corcoran and Langlois, 1990). Although supplementing your staff by the use of parent or community volunteers may be an appealing idea, think about the time and effort necessary to train and supervise these aides before adopting this approach.

Adding services, extending hours, and enhancing instructional methods and materials can all have financial implications and may impinge on union contracts. Here is where outreach and communication with your community is extremely important. Contact community libraries to discuss how your students can make use of these facilities during hours your library is not available. Appeal to your principal, district supervisor or coordinator, the parent–teacher association, local businesses, the school board, the city council, and other interested community groups for assistance. Show how ILI can enhance the educational experience. Make sure that you have thoroughly assessed the effectiveness of any programs you currently have in place (Corcoran and Langlois, 1990; Farmer, 2007; Stripling, 2007). Use positive outcomes to promote the value of ILI and as a means of gaining support, including support through grants. Assessment data can also be used to highlight what equipment and resources might be needed to enhance the program and can provide highly useful quantitative support for grant proposals. See Chapter 11 for help with this assessment process. For more on grant writing, see Chapter 6 in *Learning to Lead and Manage Information Literacy Instruction* (Grassian and Kaplowitz, 2005).

Librarians working in K–12 environments occupy a unique position in their schools. With a more holistic view of the entire curriculum, these librarians can promote interdisciplinary collaboration and a spirit of cooperation among both teachers and students. They can connect process with content, teacher with resources, and students with information both within the library and in the world at large (Stripling, 1996), especially through the Internet. The development of IL in the school-age child depends upon school librarians at all grade levels taking a proactive and dynamic place in their individual schools, their communities, and the educational process as a whole.

What Are They Doing?

Despite challenges and real financial hardships, school librarians are finding creative ways to bring ILI opportunities to their students. They are taking advantage of grant opportunities to augment their budgets, especially in the area of information technology. Just like their counterparts in public libraries, school librarians are looking for ways to partner with the business and corporate community to bring richer and more diverse resources (both print and electronic) into the library. And they are creating collaborations with both public and academic libraries to expand the resources available to their students (Weidenbenner, 2003). See "Breaking Down the Silos" later in this chapter for more details about collaboration.

The school librarian is often the person who can be counted on to help train everyone in the school community on "new happenings" in technology, and the school library is the logical place for members of the community to be introduced to them. The school librarian can also be the intermediary for teachers when it comes to new technology. The school library is frequently the first place where technology is successfully installed and used. It may also serve as the primary access point for this technology. If the school district has adopted a computer literacy requirement, the school librarian can perform a tremendous service by demonstrating how computers can be used to support curricula objectives. The library can host special workshops and in-service training opportunities so that teachers can enhance their skills and become familiar with how to use these new resources. Take advantage of these opportunities to demonstrate how new resources can be incorporated effectively into classroom instruction. For example, teachers and students alike would be delighted to find out about the ALA/AASL KidsConnect Web page where students can get help organizing their research, find material on specific topics, and even submit their own questions to be answered online (ALA. AASL, 2007a). The school librarian can also serve as instructional technology consultant to both teachers and students, helping everyone in the school create their own Web pages, PowerPoint presentations, wikis, blogs, and whatever else the future has to offer (Farmer, 2007; Geck, 2006). However, school librarians should be careful not to overextend themselves by trying to take on more than their limited resources (both materials and staffing) can support.

Combining computer literacy instruction with ILI increases student involvement and motivation. Incorporating computer skills into ILI provides a meaningful framework for the student that teaches these computer skills not for their own sake but as an integral part of the entire educational process. It also enhances the role of school librarians by placing them center stage as vital and indispensable instructors who can help ensure that all students master the skills they need to thrive in a technologically based and information-rich world (Johnson and Eisenberg, 1996).

The school library is pivotal for the creation of an information literate populace. Working hand and hand with both public and academic librarians, the school librarian can ensure that IL is not only incorporated into all levels of education but also sequenced properly so that students IL skills build and become more sophisticated as they, themselves, mature and move on to higher education or the workplace. Sequencing within school systems is always an admirable goal. However, in today's mobile society people move around quite a bit, so students will not all be entering a grade level with the same background. Therefore, continued testing needs to be done at each and every grade to ensure appropriate ILI is being offered.

The Academic Library

ILI in its many forms and under a variety of names has a long history in the academic library setting. The current emphasis on lifelong learning serves only to strengthen this instructional function. Colleges and universities concerned with the quality of education on their campuses and how effectively they are preparing students for lifelong learning are being encouraged to foster new approaches to teaching. More and more emphasis is being placed on independent research and self-directed learning. Faculty are being encouraged to reexamine their teaching role and to move from the teacher as lecturer to the teacher as facilitator model (Breivik and Gee, 1989). This learner-centered learning movement invites students to go beyond their textbook and reserved readings in their search for information. It is intended to mimic the real world and to prepare students for the future by teaching them how to gather, evaluate, and utilize resources on their own (Dalsgaard and Godsk, 2007; Jonassen, 1997; Macklin, 2008; Moran, 1990; Rockman, 2004a; Rockman, 2004b; Rockman, 2004c). A similar trend has been identified in the school (K–12) setting with its movement toward resource-based learning. With students at all levels being encouraged to pursue their own independent research, the implication for both school and academic libraries is obvious. The academic library shares much in common with the school library. Both support the educational mission of their parent institutions and need to work within the framework of the classroom curriculum and the institution as a whole. Librarians in both environments must form strong partnerships with classroom instructors and their administrators. In a way, the school library environment can be viewed as a microcosm of the larger and more complex academic library environment where the targeted user population includes faculty and staff as well as students. Granted, there is the obvious difference in the age of the user and the scope and diversity of programs being supported. However, just as in the school library, many forms of ILI in the academic setting work best when they are integrated into the overall curriculum. Strong partnerships between faculty/instructors and the librarians are crucial for this type of ILI to succeed. An awareness of new technological initiatives and educational reform movements provides academic librarians with opportunities to be proactive in offering ILI support related to these changes.

Concerns about the quality of higher education have been voiced for many years. Starting with a *Nation at Risk* and continuing through to the more current *Spellings Commission Report*, the preparation students receive at both colleges and universities has been called into question (Bennett, Miranda 2007; National Commission on Excellence in Education, 1983; Spellings, 2006). Pressure from accreditation groups, government agencies, employers, and the public at large has also contributed to a call for higher education reform with the goal of preparing our students to be competitive in a global society (Barbour, Gavin, and Canfield, 2004; Rockman, 2002; Rockman, 2004c). With colleges and universities turning their attention to issues such as critical thinking, lifelong learning, transferable skills, and ELOs, there has never been a better time for academic librarians to step up and show how IL can support all of these noble goals.

Who Are the Users?

The academic librarian deals with a wide range of adult learners from those fresh out of high school to those older adults who are returning to school after long absences. Faculty and staff are also among the academic library's user groups. However, the primary focus of the academic library's ILI program tends to be the student population.

Although there are some variations within the academic environment (two-year and community colleges, four-year colleges, and universities offering both undergraduate and graduate/professional programs), all libraries share the same goal, which is to educate their users for the information age. ILI should equip students, faculty, and staff to successfully meet their information needs for work and leisure and provide them with lifelong learning skills. The emphasis of ILI in an academic library is on teaching the process of research. As in the school library, the goal is for students to learn how to apply what they have been taught and to replicate the process in a variety of different circumstances with little or no further assistance from the librarian (Curzon, 2004; Eisenberg, 2007; Ready et al., 1990; Rockman, 2004c).

Needs Assessments in the academic library should focus on student, faculty, and staff characteristics. The institution's definition of *user* is key. This definition is expanded or limited by the institution's mission statement, sources of funding, and community mandates. Is the institution directed by state mandate to serve community citizens as well as the campus community? How restrictive are licensing agreements for electronic resources? In a private institution, are students or faculty from surrounding local public institutions welcomed or barred? In either case, what is the status of K–12 students who wish to use the college or university library? Are visiting scholars and outside researchers welcome, or must they have a letter of introduction from administration on their home campus? What is the status of extension students, distance education enrollees, private sector partners, and friends and patrons courted by the development office? Are members of the public allowed to use the facility (Wilson, 1992) and licensed material? The answers to these types of questions will help you define who your users actually are. Contact appropriate campus offices to acquire the documentation that can help you develop a true picture of the mix of users your library is mandated to serve.

Assessing what, if any, computer and IL skills your learners already have when they enter your institution is also a critical element in your Needs Assessment. This may require doing research on the general characteristics of particular age groups who comprise your student population (millenniums, gen-next, re-entry students, etc.) and working with librarians and faculty in your "feeder" high schools, four-year institutions, and community colleges as well (Howe and Strauss, 2000; Tompkins, 2003; Warren, 2006; Wilson, 2001). Standardized IL assessment instruments (such as Project Sails or ETS's iSkills) being developed by various organizations, institutions, and corporate entities can be of use to gather this kind of information. If your "feeder" schools have these data, you can get a good picture of your incoming students. If this information is not available to you, you could use these instruments or those of your own design to assess the computer and IL skills of your new students yourself. See Chapter 11 for more about these IL assessment instruments.

The academic community can also be quite diverse in its makeup. Are your students primarily residential or commuters? What is the ratio of full-time to part-time students and faculty (Paglia and Donahue, 2003)? Be sure your Needs Assessment addresses issues of culture, ethnicity, gender, age, disabilities, languages, and computer literacy. This is of particular importance in the community-college environment where students can represent a wide gamut of academic skills and age levels, as well as a variety of educational goals and experience. Students may have aspirations of transferring to a four-year school or may be taking only a few courses to upgrade their job skills. Community-college students may be pursuing a technical certificate or just attending classes for intellectual stimulation. Designing instruction for this very diverse group can be extremely challenging (Miller, 1999; Ready et al., 1990; Warren, 2006). See Chapter 13 for a discussion of ILI for diverse populations and Chapter 7 for more suggestions about Needs Assessments.

Determining the makeup of your population is only the first step. You also need to do an environmental scan that looks at the curriculum, types of special research, professional or interdisciplinary programs, levels of enrollment in different departments, and so on. Course catalogs and campus Web pages can be very useful in performing this scan. Students, faculty, and administrators should be approached in person, in focus groups, or through surveys to gather information about their perceived needs and attitudes toward using the library and information, as well as recommendations for where they feel ILI might best fit into the curriculum (Grassian and Kaplowitz, 2005; Ready et al., 1990). Integrating ILI instruction into course requirements increases its relevance and its effectiveness (Bodi, 2002; Hutchins, Fister, and MacPherson, 2000; Rockman, 2004b; Van Cleave, 2007).

Developing good relationships with the teaching faculty in your institution improves the likelihood that this connection can be made. Administrators can also provide information about campus initiatives that might affect ILI. Their knowledge of available financial resources could also prove useful as can their willingness to provide other types of resources for your program. Administrators can put you in contact with appropriate departments, agencies, and offices on your campus that might be interested in partnering with the library. Having the backing of the campus administration can go a long way to promoting the library as a key player on campus. Developing mutually supportive collaborations among administrators, faculty, librarians and information technologists will turn IL into a core competency for the campus community. The workshops sponsored by the Council of Independent Colleges and the National Institute of Technology and Liberal Education are good examples of what can happen when these collaborations are encouraged and nurtured. These workshops, which took place from 2004 to 2006, brought together chief academic officers, library directors, faculty, and information technologists to discuss IL issues and to develop strategies to transform campus cultures into ones in which IL is valued and supported (Bennett, Scott 2007).

What Are the Issues?

Although the need for integrating IL into the academic curriculum is widely accepted among librarians, convincing faculty, staff, and administrators of this fact can prove very challenging. Students often feel that their "Googling" skills make them expert searchers. Although faculty disagree with this assessment and support the idea of IL in principle, they seem happy to leave its instruction to librarians in separate and independent classes (McGuiness, 2006). Academic faculty members do not always understand the skills and knowledge that librarians possess, creating a sort of cultural clash between the teaching faculty and the IL instructors (Badke, 2005; Hardesty, 1995, 1999). The term *information literacy* is often misunderstood. Many faculty find the ACRL Competency Standards hard to comprehend and do not know how to connect them to their own instructional efforts. Even those who agree that IL proficiencies are important are unsure how, when, and where students should acquire them (Gullikson, 2006). Faculty members frequently seem unwilling to give up class time for IL efforts. They prefer to leave the design, implementation, and delivery of IL instruction in the hands of librarians in the form of stand-alone workshops and courses. Even when they agree to "guest" appearances by librarians, they do not always make it clear to their students how the ILI session relates to the course. Faculty/instructors may not participate in these so-called one-shot sessions and in extreme cases do not attend the session at all (Paglia and Donahue, 2003). If this is the case, it can send a message to students that IL is an add-on rather than an integral part of their educational experience. Librarians must counter all of this with proactive outreach and marketing efforts to show the connection between ILI and the educational mission of the institution. Fortunately an increased awareness of the importance of IL is improving this state of affairs, with more and more faculty/instructors collaborating fully with librarians on ILI and its integration into the curriculum. A growing number of instructors and faculty are embracing IL as a means of combating widespread reliance on Google and Wikipedia by their students and students' increased tendency to plagiarize from print and Web-based sources (Curzon and Lampert, 2007; Rockman, 2004a).

Fortunately librarians can turn to research studies and reports that can support their ILI efforts. For example, a 2006 Educational Testing Service report indicates that although students may have technological know-how, when it comes to entertainment, they do not have the necessary information seeking and evaluation skills necessary for academic success (Katz, 2007). The University of California Berkeley has assessed the IL competencies of its students for several years. The surveys compare students' self-assessments to IL skills test results. The conclusion of these studies is that students underestimate their abilities when it comes to accessing information and conducting library research (Maughan, 2001). Furthermore, research into student information-seeking behavior indicates that most go to the Internet first and in most cases use general search engines such as Google when they get there (Maybee, 2006; Thompson, 2003). Finally, recent research indicates that a strong academic library contributes to student retention (Mezick, 2007).

Librarians can also use the outcomes-based, accountability climate as further indication for the necessity of curriculum-integrated IL. All six accreditation agencies for higher education include IL or IL-like language in their standards for colleges and university accreditation (ALA. ACRL, 2006a; Bennett, Miranda 2007; Gelmon, 1997; Middle States Commission on Higher Education, 2006; National Council for the Accreditation of Teacher Education, 2002; New England Association of Schools and Colleges—Commission on Institutions of Higher Education, 2001; North Central Association of Colleges and Schools, accessed 2007; North West Commission on Colleges and Universities, accessed 2007; Saunders, 2007; Southern Association of Colleges and Schools, accessed 2007). Furthermore, many professional associations have incorporated IL skills into their standards for competency in the discipline (American Chemical Society, 2002; American Psychological Association. Board of Educational Affairs. Task Force on Undergraduate Major Competencies, 2001; Lampert, 2005; Murray, 2002; National Council for the Accreditation of Teacher Education, 2002).

Check the mission statements and strategic plans for higher education in your state and region and on your own campus. Look for appropriate language that supports IL concepts, and use these ideas to tie IL to these broader endeavors (Kalin and Snavely, 2001). Check to see if your institution is exploring IL competency standards for their academic programs. Show how the ACRL Competency Standards for Higher Education relate to both accreditation standards and the campus' missions and plans (McDaniel, 2007; Sonntag, 2007; Warren, 2006).

Making your case for ILI and getting it integrated into the curriculum, however, are two different matters. Librarians rarely have the same kind of access to students as the faculty do and so must work with and through regular classroom faculty in order to get ILI integrated appropriately (Bodi, 2002; Curzon, 2004; Lindstrom and Shonrock, 2006; Rockman, 2004b; Sanburn, 2005; Sonntag, 2007). These librarian–faculty partnerships offer the best opportunity for the success of ILI. Working together, faculty and librarians can develop the type of instruction and assignments that clearly illustrate how IL skills support the academic enterprise and lead to lifelong learning (Scales, Matthews, and Johnson, 2005; Stoffle, 1998).

The growing emphasis on learner-centered teaching in K–12 as well as in higher education offers both a challenge and an opportunity to ILI librarians. On the one hand, the more active-learning, authentic, problem-based, and resource-intensive approach relies heavily on the use of resource material. Students have an even greater need to develop their searching, critical thinking, and evaluative abilities in this type of learning environment, and ILI clearly supports this development (Snavely, 2004). On the other hand, this more constructivist approach to teaching requires librarians to change their pedagogical methodology—moving from sage on the stage, teacher-centric lecturers to guide on the side, learner-centric facilitators. Academic librarians and their school librarian counterparts must dedicate themselves to learning how to successfully teach in this new educational climate (Barbour, Gavin, and Canfield, 2004; Scales, Matthews, and Johnson, 2005). Partnering with instructional designers and technologists or developing those skills yourself will help you create effective ILI opportunities for your learners (Bell and Shank, 2004; Boisselle et al., 2004). For more on active learning, constructivist approaches, and learner-centered teaching, see Chapters 3, 4, 6, and 12.

Changes in information technology have impacted the library and as a result have changed the face of instruction in the academic library setting. Students no longer have to go to the library to do their research or acquire much of their material. By removing the physical barriers separating the classroom and the library, the library can be integrated into every classroom, dormitory room, and faculty office. However, if the student is not coming to the library, new ways of delivering ILI to these remote users must also be developed (Breivik and Gee, 1989, 2006; Campbell, 2006; Moran, 1990). New information technologies can deliver information directly to the user, but this information remains inaccessible if the user cannot utilize the technology or systems effectively, even if they are readily available. It is up to librarians to participate in the creation of simple, easy-to-understand interfaces that help remove these technological and intellectual barriers to locating and accessing information. For more on ILI and technology, see Chapters 15 and 16.

Pay special attention to any information technology initiatives that might provide partnership openings for the library. Librarians have typically been in the forefront when it comes to learning about new information technologies and how to think critically about them. So we can help others in the campus community "get up to speed" on technology and the effective, ethical, and critical use of it. Web 2.0 and beyond has transformed the way people interact, study, and work. The development of information commons in many academic libraries is just one example of how libraries are responding to these changes (Albanese, 2004) and may provide new ILI opportunities.

The timing and the scheduling of ILI can also be challenging and complex. Which is more effective—stand-alone, independent ILI courses or course-integrated "guest" appearances in academic classrooms? How do we provide students with basic IL skills as well as those associated with their major discipline? How do we provide for appropriately sequenced IL throughout a student's higher education experiences while avoiding unnecessary redundancy? How do asynchronous forms like online tutorials compare with synchronous forms of instruction? How do we balance all of this by leveraging limited staff and librarian time as we work with large user populations and the complexity of doing well-reasoned, effective, and ethical information research. A discussion of these issues and some of the ways that various academic librarians have responded to them are covered in the following "What Are They Doing?" section.

What Are They Doing?

Academic librarians offer stand-alone IL courses, course-integrated sessions, general orientation sessions, drop-in workshops, point-of-use guides, pathfinders, exercises, and Web-based tutorials. They review syllabi to identify where ILI might be most appropriate, participate in course discussion boards, join learning communities, and develop course-specific Web pages (Grassian, 2004b; Lippincott, 2002). They also develop "train the trainer" programs or boot camps during which librarians introduce teaching assistants to ILI concepts and demonstrate ways to teach it to their own students (Millet and Samson, 2003). Much can be said about each of these methodologies. ILI programs can be composed of many different elements. The incorporation of any of these techniques will depend upon your institutional culture and the resources available within your library. For further descriptions of these modes and the pros and cons of using each of them, see Chapter 8. Below are some specific issues regarding using a few of these methods in an academic setting.

General library orientation sessions are frequently a part of freshman or transfer student orientation programs. New students are given a tour of the library and told a bit about services and resources. There is little or no attempt to provide in-depth ILI, as contact time is brief and students are not quite ready to absorb more than a general impression of the library. However, these sessions can be an important part of the overall ILI program as they help to reduce library anxiety and offer an overview of what the library has to offer, serving as a nice foundation for the more in-depth ILI students hopefully will be exposed to later in their academic careers.

So-called drop-in workshops, those sponsored by and held in the library, offer the advantage of letting students decide when they want to learn the material. Because these workshops do not take up class time, faculty often are in favor of this approach and may even promote or assign attendance at these workshops. Despite this kind of support, drop-in workshops may have low attendance and so offer a poor return for the librarian and staff efforts needed to prepare for and teach these sessions. Drop-in workshops seem to be more successful at the beginning of the academic year when students are most anxious to learn about the library. However, because students do not as yet know how they will be applying what they learn, there is some question as to how much they remember when they actually have library resource-based assignments. On the plus side, drop-in workshops, like general orientation sessions, can help students feel more comfortable in the library, reducing library anxiety. At the same time they serve as a way to introduce library resources and services in much the same way that general orientation sessions do.

Stand-alone credit courses (F2F or online) offer continuity and extended contact time with the students. They provide the opportunity to present IL concepts and strategies in depth and allow the students to apply what they are learning (Webber and Johnston, 2000). Furthermore, because these are credit-bearing courses, students are motivated to do well since they are working for a grade. Plus, having the library offer credit-bearing courses lends legitimacy to the library's educational role and reinforces the importance of ILI within the campus community (Owusu-Ansah 2007). However, on the negative side, students may not relate what they learned from these independent courses to the rest of their studies. In addition, there are usually too few librarians on a campus to offer more than just a handful of these courses. Therefore, stand-alone ILI courses tend to reach only a small portion of the student body. In addition, the reasons students elect to take stand-alone F2F or online courses can vary widely. Some students see IL as a necessary skill, while others need one or two more credits and think this would be an easy way to get it. It is not unusual to find juniors and seniors opting for these courses in order to round out their breadth requirements or to pile on some additional credits.

Offering these ILI courses online broadens geographic reach, as students can "attend" classes from any location. Keep in mind, however, that using an online mode of delivery does not necessarily increase the number of students who can attend a particular class/course, as there is a limit to how many students an individual IL instructor can handle at one time. Teaching in a virtual environment can make heavy demands on anyone teaching in this environment, as they must monitor the activity on the course site, participate in discussions and other online activities, provide prompt feedback on assignments, and respond in a timely fashion to messages from individual students (Diaz and Cartnal, 1999; El Mansour and Munpinga, 2007; Papastergiou, 2006; Rovai and Jordan, 2004; Yi, 2005).

Embedding IL credit courses within discipline departments, and developing them in collaboration with the faculty within those departments, can counter the disconnect often experienced by students in stand-alone-type ILI courses. Because these courses are taught with an eye toward what students in a major need to know about how information is organized, disseminated, and accessed in that particular discipline, they are often seen as more relevant than stand-alone ILI courses. Linking the ILI material to research papers or other course assignments also increases its relevance for the students. However, the magnitude of an enterprise that would embed ILI into every major is daunting indeed. To fully implement such a program would require a re-deployment of resources and personnel within the library. Pilot projects in a few selected departments might be a good way to begin. Success on the smaller scale could help to build support for the larger endeavor (Badke, 2005; Mizrachi, 2004). However, if the larger project becomes a reality, it may create a situation in which the bulk of your resources are dedicated to these upper division ILI endeavors. You may need to rethink how you handle your lower division, more basic or introductory ILI—perhaps using more asynchronous online delivery modes for this group.

At the other end of the spectrum are the course-integrated ILI sessions, the most effective of which are developed in close collaboration with faculty. These offer the advantage of being tied directly to the curriculum and, if timed properly, can offer direct aid to students right when they need it (Norgaard, 2004). However, these are generally in the form of "one-shot" guest appearances. Because faculty are understandably reluctant to give up a lot of class time, these sessions offer only limited contact with the students. IL is a highly complex and complicated concept, and librarians are hard pressed to decide which aspects to include in the 50- to 90-minute segments usually allotted to them. Furthermore, there is strong pressure from both the faculty and the students to teach only what is needed in order to complete upcoming assignments. As a consequence, universal IL concepts and strategies are often sacrificed to make room for demonstrating the catalog and relevant databases

(Orme, 2004; Webber and Johnston, 2000). So, although these guest "one shots" have a built-in relevancy aspect, they are too brief to offer more than a glimpse into the overall IL picture that is needed to create lifelong learners (Swanson, 2004; Veldof, 2006).

Furthermore, there is the issue of redundancy. Clearly some redundancy can be useful, as it reinforces concepts from different perspectives and gives students additional opportunities to practice what they are learning. Because the "one-shot" sessions tend to be negotiated with individual faculty members, students can end up being presented with the same material in a number of courses and become frustrated, bored, and completely turned off by these "library" lessons. At the other extreme, students could manage to miss the entire experience if none of their teachers decides to include a "library session." Identifying key courses that all students are required to take at some point in their academic career is one approach academic librarians are taking. Incorporating ILI into general education courses is another widely used technique (Rockman, 2004c; Sharma, 2006). Writing courses are especially good ones for the incorporation of basic IL skills. Research methods classes in specific disciplines are good targets for more advanced ILI (Paglia and Donahue, 2003). Ideally, these basic and advanced sessions would be linked in such a way that the advanced sessions build upon the basic ones. The ultimate goal would be to offer an integrated, sequenced ILI program that builds on what came before in K–12 and public libraries. As students move on to institutions of higher education, they would be offered ILI starting when they are freshmen and progressing through core courses to discipline-specific and advanced ILI in every major and at all levels, from undergraduate through graduate, thus preparing students for their place in the workforce and in society in general (Hutchins, Fister, and MacPherson, 2000; Knapp, 1956; LILi, 2008; Rockman, 2004a; Sonntag, 2007).

Remote access further complicates the ILI mission. Accustomed to F2F interactions, librarians must now anticipate needs and respond to and help those they cannot see. Librarians have responded to this challenge by developing systems and implementing services tailored to the needs of these remote users. Web-based tutorials are a wonderful way for the librarian to expand their reach (Orme, 2004). They can be used in conjunction with F2F instruction or as an alternative to it. However, they can be complicated and time-consuming to develop. If you do not have the resources, expertise, and budget to design your own, there are many ILI tutorials, Web sites, podcasts, and other technologically supported alternatives available for adaptation for your local needs. Check ACRL's "IS Innovation in Instruction Awards" (ALA. ACRL. IS, 2007a) and "PRIMO: Peer-Reviewed Instructional Materials Online" (ALA. ACRL. IS, 2008e) sites, ALA's Library Instruction Round Table's Library Instruction Tutorials (ALA. LIRT, 2001), the Animated Tutorial Sharing Project (A.N.T.S.,2008), and the LOEX Clearinghouse for Library Instruction's Instruction "Links" page (LOEX, 2008) for more examples of this sort of Web-based ILI.

Academic librarians are also getting out of the library themselves and partnering with various groups and organizations on campus to reach out to and interact with students on their home grounds. Collaborations with admissions officers, athletic departments, student services divisions, offices for students with disabilities, transfer students organizations, international and minority students organizations, teaching English as a Second Language departments, writing programs, instructional technology and design units, ROTC, and new student orientation groups are just some of the ways IL librarians are actively working to "be where their learners are" and expand their ILI reach (Boisselle et al., 2004; Cummings, 2007; Kraemer, Keyse, and Lombardo, 2003; O'English and McCord, 2006; Tag, 2004; Tipton and Bender, 2006).

The development of a successful ILI program requires that teaching faculty and instruction librarians engage in frequent contact and view each other as partners in the educational enterprise. This is especially critical when trying to develop a sequenced and integrated ILI program. Faculty and librarians alike would agree that all students need grounding in general, globally applicable IL skills and strategies. However, once they declare their majors, students need to be introduced to the specialized ways that research is done in their discipline. The types of information needed and the strategies used to find that information vary greatly in the arts and humanities, the social sciences, and the physical sciences. To be successful, students need to learn those specialized approaches. Collaborating with discipline faculty about course content, requirements, and assignments helps librarians incorporate the most appropriate resources and strategies into their ILI (Bodi, 2002). Many libraries are promoting this type of collaboration by assigning library liaison or subject-specialist librarians to academic departments to encourage in-depth and long-lasting faculty–librarian relationships (Lampert, 2005; Lindstrom and Shonrock, 2006; Sharma, 2006; Sonntag, 2007). The development of discipline-based IL standards strengthens this connection, particularly if they have been developed jointly with faculty in those disciplines—for example, the "Information Literacy Standards for Anthropology and Sociology" (ALA. ACRL. ANSS, 2008).

Collaborative relationships are also encouraged when librarians invite faculty to take part in collection development and discussions of scholarly communication, copyright, and intellectual property issues. The relationships benefit from frequent updating of the faculty about resources available and frank discussions about those resources the faculty feel are lacking (Stoffle, 1998; Stoffle, Guskin, and Boisse, 1984). If funding is an issue, these discussions can help the library prioritize purchases or may even result in departments offering to help fund a resource they feel is of particular interest. If good relations are consistently cultivated, collaboration has a better chance of occurring. Good friends tend to work together better than do total strangers (Kotter, 1999). Successful teacher–librarian collaboration results in more appropriate ILI that truly supports the educational objectives of the institution. The final result is improved student products and an enhanced learning experience for everyone: student, teacher, and librarian.

Establishing credibility for you and the library instruction program takes visibility and rapport with the teaching faculty. Advanced degrees in subject disciplines promote collegiality with the teaching faculty. Make any membership and involvement in professional associations known. Find out about individual faculty's research interests and contact them when relevant material or resources are added to the library. Help them keep up to date by alerting them to the online current awareness resources such as the database alert services. Inform them about the library's interlibrary loan and document delivery services and licenses for online resources, journals, and books. Participate in campus committees and governance, university wide clubs and organizations, and any other groups where you can keep in contact with both faculty and administrators. Promote the library at every opportunity, and be alert for ways to connect the library to existing or new campus initiatives. Key players are the faculty senate and the faculty senate committees (Curzon, 2004; Young and Harmony, 1999). Examine committee charges and campus initiatives to see if IL outcomes are being incorporated. Are IL outcomes being assessed, and, if so, how and where (Iannuzzi, 1998; McDaniel, 2007)? As always, make sure that any new ILI initiative has the support of your library colleagues and can be supported by current staffing, space, and budgetary constraints. Linking ILI efforts to the institutional mission and demonstrating how it supports the entire educational enterprise not only helps our users; it also helps to enhance the image of the library and the librarian as key players in that enterprise and solidifies your role on campus (ALA. ACRL, 2003b).

The Special Library

Special libraries as a group represent the most eclectic type of libraries. In some regards the special library can be defined as any library that is not a public, school, or academic one. They can be found in corporate, museum, medical, legal, government, religious, cultural, nonprofit, and private research facility settings (Jansen, 2003). What they tend to have in common is a service rather than a teaching orientation. The mission of the special library is to support the function of its parent organization. Special libraries, regardless of where they are located, are dedicated to helping employees "get the job done," and library services are dedicated to improving employee efficiency and productivity.

Special libraries, therefore, do not include libraries associated with law or medical schools, which have more in common with academic libraries than they do with special libraries.

Another way to look at this is that special libraries are found in environments that are results and/or profit rather than education driven. Librarians in a special library setting, therefore, tend to emphasize service over teaching. *Efficiency* is the watchword here. Much like the public library, individual information needs frequently are unique, so instruction often tends toward the individual rather than the group setting. Furthermore, because of the growth of intranets and other electronic communication technologies, the special librarian often communicates with an invisible clientele that rarely, if ever, enters the library F2F. Online tutorials in the use of many of the library's resources can also be mounted on the company's intranet, providing ILI wherever and whenever the employee needs it.

Who Are the Users?

Everyone in the parent organization is a potential user of the special library. The information needs of these users are focused on the work that needs to be accomplished. User characteristics are often associated with the type of work that is going on (e.g., engineering, museum curating, fund-raising, pharmaceutical research).

When completing a Needs Assessment in this environment, the librarian should pay attention to the importance of each group within the organization. Consider the political aspects as well, such as which groups provide financial or influential support for the library. Finally, primary or heavy users may already be very knowledgeable, but at the same time services and instruction for them may take priority because of their relation to the library (Birch, Bergman, and Arrington, 1990). Make sure your Needs Assessment is used to identify potential allies in the company or organization. Marketing departments can help with the design of materials. Computer centers may assist in the delivery of instructional material via e-mail, the company's intranet systems, or other computer-based technology. Human resources departments and training and development units may have suggestions for the best approaches to instruction in your environment.

What Are the Issues?

Because the existence of the library is so closely related to its perceived value to the overall organization, it is imperative that the special librarian develops an in-depth knowledge of the organizational structure and politics, especially where the library fits into the overall hierarchy. Make sure you identify the information needs of your organization and determine if you are meeting those needs. Special librarians must position themselves and their library so that those making budget decisions recognize the library's contributions to the effectiveness of the organization (Adams, 1995; Strife, 1995). Special librarians should alert management to reports discussing the importance of IL in the workplace, such as the Spellings Report (Budd, 2007; Spellings, 2006) and the report from the Information Literacy 2006 Summit (Perraut, 2006) discussed elsewhere in this chapter. They should emphasize how having information literate workers will help give the parent organization a competitive edge in a knowledge-based, global economy and show how the library helps improve productivity and is an integral and vital part of the organization (Abell and Oxbrow, 2001; Office of Economic Co-operation and Development, 1996; O'Sullivan, 2002; Rockman, 2002).

Although the term *information literacy* is not widely used or well understood in the corporate environment, "knowledge management" (capturing, sharing, using, and creating knowledge to add value to the organization) is an accepted concept and has much in common with the characteristics of IL. Furthermore, a good deal of the information in this environment tends to be in the form of internally produced documents that are shared formally or informally with co-workers often in digital format via e-mail or open access formats rather than in traditional publication systems. These documents may never be added to the library. Yet this material still needs to be collected, organized, indexed, and effectively presented, all skills of the special librarian. So, in addition to teaching workers how to locate, access, and evaluate publicly available information, special librarians can help workers manage their own personal knowledge collections (Kirton and Barham, 2005).

What Are They Doing?

Special librarians offer the range of ILI from one-on-one consultation to large and small group instruction in what is often promoted as "information discovery" (retrieval, search techniques, and source selection) and "information management" (organization and sharing). They tend to make heavy use of the company's intranet to offer classes, distribute self-help guides, and alert their users to new resources available in the library. E-mail alerts and the use of the companies' online newsletters are both common practices. Instructional methodology relies heavily on techniques favored by adult learners, emphasizing discussion and practical and relevant exercises (Cibbareli,1998; Kirton and Barham, 2005). Furthermore, because many settings rely heavily on team-based projects, a heavy emphasis is placed on collaborative learning experiences (Lloyd, 2006).

Although most special library users have had some previous library experience, each special library collection is unique and geared directly to the needs of the larger institution. Therefore, while some general IL skills may carry over (i.e., the abilities to distinguish between primary and secondary sources and to critically evaluate information), much will be new. Users need to be introduced to the unique and sometimes idiosyncratic organization methods in the field as well as to a wide variety of specialized and often highly complex resources (Jansen, 2003). In many ways the special library is the place where new workers can become further socialized into the methodologies of the field, as well as the culture of the institution, organization, or corporation of which they are a part (Lloyd, 2006).

Justifying an ILI program in a special library, where users frequently expect the librarian to provide answers, can be more difficult than in other settings where ILI is seen as an extension of the educational process. However, as employees learn to access library resources previously unknown to them, or are alerted to updates and changes to those they have used in the past, their job performance will improve. Employees will be able to use their time more efficiently and find better information to support their work. Special libraries can educate the organization's employees to make more and better use of the library's resources. Employees will then be able to formulate, on their own, more effective information searches. They will be more aware of and kept up to date on what information is available, and they will know how to access it most thoroughly, systematically, and easily. Employee interactions with the library staff will be enhanced as employees will be able to determine when to do research themselves and when it is more efficient to turn it over to an information professional (Birch, Bergman, and Arrington, 1990; Jansen, 2003; Kirton and Barham, 2005; Lampert, 2003).

Because productivity is so important in this environment, employees may be reluctant to take time away from their primary job responsibilities to attend special presentations in the library. Technology can help. Even in a small company, your users may access the library and its resources only remotely and may prefer to do their research during hours the library is not open. Developing electronically accessible user aides, especially Web-based ones, and designing remote instruction methods not only will be valuable for the user but also will keep the library and its services visible and at the heart of the organization. Using instructional technology approaches will also enhance the image of the library as a cutting-edge facility that provides support and access to information in the most appropriate format and at the exact moment when people need it. Helping to promote the value of information in the workplace, acting as an intermediary for accessing that information, and being a facilitator who helps employees maintain their IL skills will support the national mandate toward creating an IL population.

BREAKING DOWN THE SILOS: COLLABORATIONS, PARTNERSHIPS, AND SEQUENCING

One of the most promising trends to develop in recent years is the growing number of partnerships and collaborations forming among libraries from different environments. High school librarians are working with academic librarians to ensure that entering freshman have the basic IL skills needed to succeed in the higher education arena. Academic libraries are opening their doors to high school students, offering a variety of services including tours, ILI, and access to some of the academic library's licensed databases and other online material (Burhanna, 2006; Calderhead, 1999; Gresham and Van Tassel, 2000; Jackson and Hansen, 2006, in press; Lonsdale and Armstrong, 2006; Mitchell and Brasley, 2001; Nichols, 1999; Pearson and McNeil, 2002). Librarians in the State University of California system are working with their counterparts in the California Community Colleges system to ensure that students transferring from the two-year community college experience to the four-year college or university setting are armed with the basic IL skills they need to succeed in their new educational setting (Klingberg, 2005).

School librarians are working with librarians in neighboring public libraries to ensure that their students have access to the resources (print and electronic) needed to complete their homework assignments. They are also collaborating to develop homework centers in the public library that provide IL assistance to individual students. Public librarians are offering classes either at their local schools or onsite in the library geared to helping students attain IL skills needed at each grade level. School and public librarians are visiting each other's libraries in order to become more familiar with the resources and services offered. Schools are sending homework alerts to their local public libraries to help the staff there prepare for possible onslaughts of students (Harris, 2003; Huang and Russell, 2006).

Public libraries are also reaching out to their communities and looking for partnership opportunities. Some public libraries are creating reading literacy centers in collaboration with local schools and members of the community (Petruzzi and Burns, 2006). The Omaha Public Library's Community Training Center is sponsored by a consortium of business, education, and government entities (Jehlik, 2004). The Hamilton Ontario Canada Public Library has a long-standing history of partnerships with local colleges and universities, the Hamilton school district, local businesses, clubs, and newspapers, as well as with the city government, to promote and support library services and resources (Hovius, 2006).

The Lifelong Information Literacy (LILi) project in California is bringing together librarians from all types of environments to examine how and where IL is being taught and to identify overlaps and/or possible gaps that need addressing sequentially at all levels (Grassian, Haras, and Pashaie, in press; LILi, 2008). Librarians in Australia did a similar study in 2002. The study results showed that librarians in school and public libraries share a sense of common purpose. Interactions between librarians in different types of libraries are on the increase. Although this is taken as a good sign, the study's author suggests more could be done on the local, state, and national levels to break down professional insularity and promote mutual support of and advocacy for one another's issues (Bundy, 2002). The necessity for cross-library cooperation led AASL and ACRL to jointly develop the Blueprint for Collaboration Web site, which is dedicated to promoting collaborative efforts (ALA. AASL/ACRL. Task Force on the Educational Role of Libraries, 2004). The site includes recommendations and strategies for collaboration, a list of collaborative efforts already in place, and links to grant opportunities to support these efforts.

The impetus for all of these efforts comes from two directions: economic and political. Budget cuts have adversely affected libraries of all kinds. Library staff must engage in creative and innovative thinking in order to continue to provide quality services, including ILI—not the least of which is pooling resources and staff efforts across libraries. However, there is even more behind this idea. With IL coming to be recognized all over the world as a lifelong survival skill, where and when people acquire these skills become increasingly more important. Thus the idea of sequencing (ILI that is cumulative, building throughout students' educational experiences and then on into their careers) has gained momentum. In order to make this idea a reality, libraries at all levels must proactively exchange ideas and work at building a coordinated ILI effort. These efforts take time to develop and grow and money to finance, so they are not widespread as yet. However, they are increasing in number and are a good indication that all librarians are supporting the idea that they must break out of their silos and reach out to their colleagues in order to help create the information literate society that is so very important in today's information-dependent world.

FINAL REMARKS

The many national and international reports referred to at the start of this chapter all support the idea that IL is a critical life skill in today's global and competitive society. If people of all ages and in every walk of life are to develop and maintain IL skills, then every library bears the responsibility for providing ILI. Teaching becomes the obligation not only of the school and academic libraries that have traditionally seen it as part of their role but also of public and special libraries as well. Whenever and wherever a lifelong learner turns to his or her library—at work, at school, or in the community—the means of further developing his or her IL skills should be available. Every librarian in every library plays a part in this endeavor.

Partnerships and collaborations between a library and appropriate members of the population are crucial to the success of ILI in every environment. But partnerships can also cut across library lines. School and academic libraries should work together to ensure that IL skills are both appropriate at each grade level and form a continuum that builds as children move through the educational process. Public and school libraries form a natural alliance in providing ILI to the children of their communities and can link to academic libraries through their high schools. Special libraries can work closely with academic and public libraries to make sure potential employees are developing IL skills appropriate to the workplace. As already discussed, many of these types of partnerships are on the rise.

Developing effective ILI in any library requires effort, knowledge, and a firm understanding of where the library fits within its environment. However, changes in the delivery of information, in the national and international mandates for lifelong learning and for the development of an informed citizenry, and in the educational reform movement that emphasizes independent, self-directed learning have created a situation where no single type of library can afford to operate in isolation. Skyrocketing costs of both print and electronic materials are encouraging libraries of all types to develop consortia for the provision of information to all of their constituents. Public, school, academic, and special libraries are beginning to see the benefits of acting together in many arenas.

Where people go for their information is also changing. At one time people went to a particular physical place when they had an information need. They looked for and visited the nearest, appropriate library facility. With information now being packaged in a variety of ways and being accessible from almost anywhere, however, knowing which library actually "owns" the information becomes confusing to our users. The lines are blurring, and users find it harder and harder to tell which library is theirs or where the information is coming from. The successful development of an IL population depends on creating alliances among libraries, developing collaborations between libraries and appropriate interest groups in their respective environments, and using a proactive approach that champions the cause of IL at every opportunity. Librarians must act as IL advocates in their communities and schools, on their campuses, and in their organizations. If we value the goals of the IL movement, it is up to us to promote those goals and make IL a reality for all.

EXERCISES

1. Identify three organizations, agencies, or community groups within your environment that you feel would be useful partners for your ILI program. How would this alliance benefit your ILI program? Develop an action plan to establish an alliance with each of those groups.
2. Identify three administrators, managers, or community leaders whose support you need to implement an ILI program in your environment. Develop an action plan for contacting these people.
3. Create an ILI advocacy packet that can be used to promote the value of ILI in your environment. Include references to national and local mandates for IL, as well as concrete evidence about the success of current IL endeavors in your library.

4. Think about how a sequential plan could link public, school, academic, and special libraries in your community in a joint IL effort. Identify the IL aspects that would be the responsibility of each type of library. Consider how each type of library contributes to the overall aims of IL and how each aspect relates to and builds on other aspects.

READ MORE ABOUT IT

Brey-Casiano, Carol. 2007. "From Literate to Information Literate Communities Through *Advocacy." Public Library Quarterly* 25, no. 1/2: 181–190.

Brottman, Mary and Mary Loe, eds. 1990. *The LIRT Instruction Handbook.* Englewood, CO: Libraries Unlimited.

Curzon, Susan and Lynn Lampert, eds. 2007. *Proven Strategies for Building an Information Literacy Program.* New York: Neal-Schuman.

Jehlik, Theresa. 2004. "Information Literacy in the Public Library." *Nebraska Library Association Quarterly* 35, no. 4: 7–13.

Kirton, Jennifer and Lynn Barham. 2005. "Information Literacy in the Workplace." *Australian Library Journal* 54, no. 4: 365–376.

Rockman, Ilene, ed. 2004. *Integrating Information Literacy Into the Higher Education Curriculum.* San Francisco: Jossey-Bass.

Thomas, Nancy Pickering. 2004. *Information Literacy and Information Skills: Applying Research to Practice in the School Library Media Center.* Westport, CT: Libraries Unlimited.

Chapter 15

Using Technology to Support Pedagogy

We need to remember that the measure of a civilization is not the tools it owns but the use it makes of them.

—EDITORS, *NEW YORK TIMES*, JANUARY 3, 1999, 4: 8

GIVE US THIS DAY OUR DAILY TECHNOLOGY?

The shirt on your back may soon be your favorite mobile device, generating electricity when you move (Macey, 2007) or finding you a Wi-Fi hotspot! (Lawson, 2007). Soon one side of a stick-on, paper-thin lamp may light up your room while the other side absorbs solar energy (Fallon, 2008). Polaroid is developing a one-button Zink Pocket Printer the size of a deck of cards that will connect to a camera phone, such as the iPhone (White, 2007). A bionic contact lens can now display a driving route or a virtual world or measure your cholesterol level and transmit that information to a computer (Staedter, 2008).

Are you thrilled? Do you welcome these advances? Or do you worry that technology is advancing too quickly, perhaps altering and taking over our lives? Technology is such an integral and yet subliminal part of lives today that we hardly seem to notice it even if it is brand new or beeps, blinks, buzzes, rings, rotates images at us, or even speaks to us. At one extreme, some of us are preoccupied with computers to the point of addiction, while others go to great lengths to avoid them; worse yet, some have little or no access at all. Those on the "dark side" of the digital divide are particularly concerned about the pace and scope of technology. Yet most of us drive cars and use cell phones, microwave ovens, clock radios, and watches, often not realizing that many of these items contain computer chips that keep time, regulate temperature, set off a variety of alarms, and generally keep these products running smoothly.

We have become comfortable with many forms of impersonal technology, both obvious and subtle, but we are in a semipermanent transitional state when it comes to using technology for instruction. This is partly because we are worried about being bypassed by popular new technologies like Google and social software of all kinds (Farkas, 2007). These technologies offer quick, easy, and seemingly comprehensive access to the worlds' knowledge. Want to meet and greet "Friends"? Try Facebook (2008). Want to make business connections? Check out LinkedIn (2008). Twitter (2008) your activities to your "followers" in 140-character "microblogs," a series of short diary-like, dated postings. Search or review lists or collections of blogs, such as "Technorati" (accessed 2008), "Internet Public Library: Blogs" (2008), "School Libraries—Blogging Libraries" (2008), "Academic Libraries—Blogging Libraries" (2008), and "Special Libraries—Blogging Libraries" (2008), for topics that interest you as well as examples of blogs created by others. Check information literacy blogs, such as "Information Literacy Weblog" (Webber and Boon, accessed 2008) and "Information Literacy Land of Confusion" (Lorenzen, 2008), and consider creating your own using free blog software like Google Blogger

(2008) or WordPress (accessed 2008). Watch videos on YouTube (2008), both serious and for entertainment. Find or upload images of all kinds on Flickr (2008) or Google Image Search (2008). Set up a free wiki so you and others can collaborate on documents remotely by using Wetpaint (2008) or PBwiki (2008). Try using a wiki or a blog to post an outline of an ILI session. Send learners the URL and invite them to post questions and comments before, during, and after an ILI session.

We are trying to jump on new technologies as fast as our users do, or faster. We are constantly adopting and adapting new technologies for instruction, sometimes without careful consideration of why we would want to use them for ILI and how they may or may not enhance teaching and learning. So, let us examine the use of technology in teaching and learning, focus on some currently popular technologies, and consider some means of keeping up and experimenting with new technologies as they appear.

QUESTIONS ABOUT TECHNOLOGY USE IN INSTRUCTION

It is important to note that your definition of and comfort with various forms of technology often depend upon your level of exposure to and experience with each. What constitutes technology use in an instructional setting, though? What sorts of technology can and should we use, if any, and for what purposes? Does technology hinder or help learning? How much technology is too much? What can be done to help ILI librarians and other library staff feel comfortable using the technology of their choice and exploring the use of new technologies as they are developed? And how do we handle the issue of lack of human contact so often associated with technology use?

What Is It?

Most people would call computers, data projectors, Web sites, Web browsers, mobile devices, podcasts, presentation software, videos, instant messaging (IM), and text messaging "technology," but what about blackboards, whiteboards, flip charts, overhead transparencies, overhead projectors, slide/tapes, and videotapes? The *Oxford English Dictionary* (1989) defines "technology" broadly, as "the scientific study of the practical or industrial arts." Today, most people think of technology as what the same venerable dictionary calls "high-technology," referring to "a firm, industry, etc., that produces or utilizes highly advanced and specialized technology, or to the products of such a firm."

Yet, in the nineteenth century, chalk, slate (chalkboard), books, and even pictures were innovative instructional technologies. Film, a major technological innovation, was first used in a classroom in 1910. Radio and television use in the classroom came next, beginning respectively in 1923 and 1939. When each of these technological innovations was introduced, it promised "individualized instruction, relief of the tedium of repetitive activities, and presentation of content beyond what was available to a classroom teacher" (Cuban, 1986: 4). In the twentieth century, instructional innovators eagerly used radio, television, film, whiteboards, presentation software, and more. In the early twenty-first century, teaching and training innovators are trying out rapidly developing social software, streaming technology, virtual worlds, personal audience response systems using clickers, laptops, or other handheld devices for polling in face-to-face (F2F) synchronous group sessions (Burnett and Collins, 2007; Collins, 2007; Martyn, 2007), and mobile devices for teaching and learning, any place, any time.

Online learning is on the rise, too, although it is often mistakenly equated with "distance education" and sometimes with "e-learning." *Online learning* refers to any sort of learning that takes place primarily through the Internet. *Distance education*, on the other hand, began in the nineteenth century with "correspondence courses," and it most often refers to courses offered through an institution for credit or certification, today—largely offered online (Fritsch, 2001; Naidu, 2005). *e-Learning* is sometimes equated with distance education, but most use it primarily to refer to instructional materials offered through some electronic means, including online (Zemsky and Massy, 2004).

It is interesting to note that from 1995 to 1998 the number of distance education programs offered in the United States rose by 72 percent (Carnevale,

2000). Distance learning continues to expand in higher education. In Fall 2006, close to 3.5 million students took one or more online courses, almost 20 percent of all U.S. higher education students (Allen and Seaman, 2007). Sloan Consortium reports like Allen and Seaman's (2007) define online courses as those where "80 percent of the course is delivered online" as opposed to "blended/hybrid" instruction that combine online and F2F instruction, with 30 to 79 percent of the content online. Definitions can be fuzzy regarding the distinction between online courses and blended instruction, however, as some would say that "blended instruction" courses include all online courses, or courses that are partly online and partly F2F (NCAT, 2005b; Grassian et al., 2005). For instance, some high school students may take online AP courses and meet F2F with the instructor just once or twice during the term. During F2F classes, other students may simply spend some time working on Web-Quests, guided exercises using the Web (Dodge, 2000b; AT&T, 2008b).

In the United Kingdom, distance learning for higher education has been a reality since 1971. In 1997–1998, the largest U.K. university was the Open University (OU), enrolling 21 percent of all part-time higher education students in the country. In 2008, OU enrolled 150,000 undergraduate students (70 percent of whom work full time) and over 30,000 graduate students. OU offers over 600 undergraduate courses in 14 subject areas, plus postgraduate study in a wide variety of disciplines (Open University, accessed 2008a).

How individualized are these courses, and what proportion of their assignments and other activities are self-paced? Those who teach courses completely online recommend that instructors send students off regularly to complete brief, self-paced exercises or activities (Ko and Rossen, 2004). Do these recommendations include use of print materials in a physical library or licensed databases and other licensed materials? It is difficult to know. OU provides a handy online "Information Literacy Toolkit" for its instructors (Open University, accessed 2008b), as well as a variety of online help materials, including tutorials for graduate and undergraduate students, as well as a self-rating tool and a course called Beyond Google (Baker, 2008). Does the OU faculty make use of this Toolkit, and do the students get the kind of help they need, when they need it? How, in fact, can we best meet the needs of remote, as well as in-person, learners, including those with low-end access, equipment, or software? Can technology help or hinder?

According to one researcher, history tells us that most technologies (with the exception of chalk, slate, books, and pictures) fail as widely used teaching tools (Cuban, 1986). The reasons given for this failure sound remarkably familiar to reasons given today for lack of widespread implementation of current technology in educational settings of all kinds, including libraries (Cuban, 1986: 18):

- Teachers' lack of skills in using equipment . . .
- Cost of . . . equipment, and upkeep . . .
- Inaccessibility of equipment when it is needed . . .
- Finding and fitting the right . . . [tool] to the class

Another researcher supports this claim by stating that numerous studies have concluded that there is no significant difference in learning, no matter what sort of technology you use in instruction—radio, television, video, Web—or if you use no technology at all (Russell, 1999, 2008).

What does work? Bernard et al. (2004) conducted a meta-analysis of empirical studies of distance education. They concluded that pedagogical excellence and "strategic use of interactivity" are key to effective distance education, specifically, "'deep interaction' among learners . . . promoted through effective communication," as well as engaging learning materials and tasks (Bernard et al., 2004: 413). Other researchers have found that computers and software, too, may fail to change instructional practice if they are not accompanied by professional development efforts to help instructors consider how such technology can help their learners better achieve pedagogical goals and learn practical means of helping them do so. According to another study, elementary school teachers selected software that matched their own teaching preferences, with the vast majority (85 percent) selecting skill-based software as opposed to learner-centered, inquiry-based software. They conclude that just providing computers and software to schools does not in itself lead to changes in instructional practice (Niederhauser and Stoddart, 2001).

What Good Is It?

So, what good is technology? As we pointed out in Chapter 5, computers have aggravated stress levels among library users. Although we are now used to change, library staff also suffer from technostress. How many library catalogs has your library had over the past three to five years? How many new databases and interfaces have you had to learn and then teach in that same period? Updated or "enhanced" database interfaces, new library catalogs, more, more and more online resources, not to mention updated versions of software, new hardware—all of this constant change, almost daily, is now the norm. As people juggle an ever-growing number and variety of tasks and responsibilities, many of which involve technology use, they may feel more and more anxious and stressed. They may also feel continuous pressure to learn new technology and new versions of technology the minute they are released, both in order to teach it and in order to use it to support other forms of instruction, such as text messaging for reference or adaptation of online instruction for use with mobile devices.

Likewise, new technologies for teaching, or new technological approaches to teaching, seem to pop up almost daily. Yet we are at different skill levels on the technology continuum, and we have differing ideas about which technology to use in teaching, as well as their effectiveness. Even tasks that appear simple on the surface benefit from technique tips and practice, like learning how to write on a board or flip chart while maintaining the learners' attention, creating and using a blog or wiki for instruction, developing instructional videos, or using other forms of technology. It is natural for us to be fearful and stressed about what we do not understand or, at the other extreme, to be carried away with glitzy new technology and use it simply because it looks attractive. These good-looking "shows," however, may be ineffective or little used by learners if they do not support or enhance pedagogical goals.

In this chapter we shall see that many kinds of technology can be useful in helping people achieve learning outcomes, as long as we take the time to define goals, objectives, and expected learning outcomes (ELOs) first and if we spend some time planning, developing, and field testing before implementing, as well as evaluating and revising afterwards. For those on the hesitant end of the spectrum, we shall try to dispel your fears by demystifying a representative sample of technology and technological approaches that may be useful in instruction. Our focus throughout will be on the judicious use of technology to support ILI goals.

Advantages and Disadvantages of Technology Use in Instruction

Some of the controversy over whether or not to use technology in instruction seems to have died down. Instead, a number of publications seem more and more focused on the effective use of technology to support pedagogy and on how to move beyond minimal technology use in order to do so. Publications regarding technological transformation of higher education seem to indicate a growing recognition of the need to move ahead to help faculty make better and more expanded use of technology to support and enhance pedagogy (NCAT, 2005a, 2005b; McLoughlin, Wang and Beasley, 2008). Mackey and Jacobson's (2008) *Using Technology to Teach Information Literacy* also offers a number of excellent examples of collaborative efforts by librarians and others to use new technologies to enhance curricula and help students achieve ELOs. These include assignment of a holistic service learning/information literacy project (Mackey and McLaughlin, 2008), creation of World War II virtual posters and a virtual library (Clobridge and Del Testa, 2008), and taking and reporting on virtual field trips (Briggs and Skidmore, 2008). These admirable projects came about through collaboration between librarians and faculty as well as technologists and offer lessons gained both through success and through failure.

As information resources and tools increasingly move online or are "born digital" (exist only in online form), public libraries worldwide are moving to raise awareness of the need for IL and training staff in ILI (Brey-Casiano, 2007; Julien and Hoffman, 2008). A study of the PuLLS (Public Libraries in the Learning Society) project reported on lifelong learning programs in six European countries, under the auspices of the EU Grundtvig program. While most of the participating libraries offered computer skills classes, several included elements of lifelong learning. The study authors point out that by offering courses that include elements of IL, public libraries are moving away from simply providing information to helping users learn to learn themselves. In other words, "Libraries are moving away from passive modes of information provision towards actively seeking to engage and engage with their users—and crucially, attract new ones" (Eve, de Groot, and Schmidt, 2007: 404). Public libraries in the United States also offer workshops for their adult users and homework help for younger learners. The South Carolina State Library posted on Flickr images of learners in its May 2007 Flickr class (Rogers, 2007). The Princeton Public Library (2008) in New Jersey offers a "Wikipedia vs. Encyclopedia Britannica" class, among many others.

Despite growing interest in IL and technology, some still question technology use in instruction and wonder how much of a benefit computer technology offers (Bell, M.A., 2007; Bartlett, 2007). Technology critics like David Noble have insisted that technology use in instruction is not inevitable if we object publicly to its use. Noble characterized distance education as impersonal, business-like "digital diploma mills" and believed quite strongly that it endangered the highly personal, interactive, and dynamic nature of teaching and learning in higher education. He fought desperately to beat off what he saw as Big-Brother-esque use of technologies such as e-mail and online course builders like WebCT and Blackboard.com (Noble, 1998a, 1998b, 1998c).

Course management systems (CMSs) like the merged Blackboard/WebCT, as well as open source CMSs/LMSs (learning management systems), have come a long way since the late 1990s and early 2000s when Noble and others raised these objections. However, they do allow instructors to track students' use of the CMS to such an extent that some consider it to be a serious invasion of privacy. The growing popularity of sites like YouTube and iTunes U (Apple, 2008a), counter those like Noble who saw technology use in education as a tool for financial gain and administrative control over personal intellectual property created by faculty. Faculty may still consider syllabi to be their intellectual property, but a growing number are sharing instructional materials with students through podcasts, vodcasts (video podcasts), presentation slide shows mounted on course Web sites, and more. They are moving ahead with more interactive, learner-centered instruction, some in person, some blended, and some completely online. In 2002, MIT posted instructional materials for all of its courses, starting an "OpenCourseWare" movement, but does not provide a means for learners to interact directly with the instructors of those courses if the learners have questions or wish to make a comment. In addition, there is no synchronous (simultaneous, in real time, with two or more individuals) learner-to-learner interaction through this site (MIT, 2008). This approach, in itself, illustrates the value that one prestigious university places on learner–instructor and learner–learner interaction, as opposed to instructional material. It negates arguments of those like Noble who worry that, in higher education at least, institutions may try to gain ownership of course syllabi mounted on Web sites, may videotape or otherwise record courses, dispense with expensive faculty, and instead just use these materials for courses.

In October 1999, *The Chronicle of Higher Education* reported that the state of Kentucky had contracted with the University of Nebraska's for-profit company, Class.com, to provide courses for a completely online high school in Kentucky (Carr, 1999). Distance education for high schools has grown and spread widely since that time. A U.S. study estimated that 40,000 to 50,000 students were enrolled in online courses in 2001, while in 2005–2006, enrollment was estimated at 700,000 (Picciano and Seaman, 2007: 17). The same study found that in 2005–2006 students were taking online or blended courses in almost two-thirds of the 366 school districts reporting from across the country. This includes 12 percent of K–5 students, 20 percent of students in grades 6–8, and 67 percent of students in grades 9–12. About 57 percent of the 366 districts used an independent vendor to provide online or blended courses. The most important reasons given for offering online courses included the fact that these courses were not available at the school, that they met special student needs, and that they were Advanced Placement or college-level courses (Picciano and Seaman, 2007).

Is this a trend that will impact education globally at all levels? Commercial distance education providers are increasingly interested in the sizable K–12 population. In 2007, two large vendors, Kaplan and Apollo, bought companies that manage online high schools (Damast, 2007). Gen X, millenials, Gen Y, each new cohort that comes along seems to be more and more technologically oriented, more native to and immersed in technology of all kinds, and interacting more with the technology than the previous cohort. e-Learning of all kinds, whether formal for-credit distance education or informal, synchronous and asynchronous learning (any time, any place, involving a single individual), is evolving into a natural part of the environment. Younger cohorts turn to YouTube, Facebook, Twitter, blogs, virtual worlds, and Wikipedia for community and for information and learning.

It is true, however, as Nardi and O'Day (1999: 42) put it, that "Every technology change needs critical friends to watch what happens, think about it, and provide useful feedback." But why should ILI librarians care about all of this? These trends in the educational realm have major implications for libraries, for librarians, and for ILI. The number and variety of both fee and free online information tools and resources continues to expand dramatically. Will educational administrators, businesspeople, and the general community continue to see a need for libraries and librarians if they are under the impression that all information is freely available on the Internet?

In the school environment, one has to wonder what sort of personal interactions students in an online high school can have with their teachers, with librarians (if they have any), and with other students. Who owns online course materials created by teaching faculty and IL instructors? Are there benefits to using technology for instruction of all kinds, including ILI, that outweigh the negatives? How can we best use technology to support IL teaching and learning?

Like faculty and others who develop instructional curriculum and materials, ILI librarians need to be aware of concerns about quality and intellectual property issues related to the use of technology in instruction. As Bransford, Brophy, and Williams (2000: 67) put it, we need to consider "*what* students need to learn, *how* they learn, and *what counts as evidence* for their learning." Have we identified learning outcomes, selected a variety of learning modes, and developed a means of measuring learning? Have learners used technology at appropriate points to get an overview, test ideas, review, and self-assess (Castellan, 1993)? Have we, in fact, considered whether or not technological tools can help us improve the effectiveness of our instructional handouts, syllabi, Web sites, and other materials and programs and improve ELOs?

As we have seen, some researchers see no added value to teaching with technology (Cuban, 1986; Ruth, 1997; Russell, 1999, 2008). Their admonitions are valuable counterarguments to those who make technology use the center of their instructional effort, rather than being guided by pedagogical goals. However, only briefly do they acknowledge that computers and the Internet have opened many doors to learning (Pallis, 1997). Despite its drawbacks, technology use in instruction can serve varied teaching and learning styles both in person and remotely. Some forms of technology offer learners new and more flexible ways to learn and interact. This is particularly important for those who do not have easily accessible or reasonably priced, quality in-person equivalents. Distance education courses now span the globe. The European Distance and e-Learning Network offers conferences and publications, including the *European Journal of Open, Distance, and E-Learning* (EDEN, accessed 2008). As mentioned earlier, the British Open University, strictly an online institution, offers distance education courses in many parts of the world to those who live in remote areas or cannot afford the time or money to attend traditional educational institutions. For low income people or those in rural areas, school library media centers and public libraries may in fact provide the only access to computers and the Internet. A recent Pew Internet & American Life (2008a) survey revealed that just 53 percent of U.S. households with an annual income below $30,000 use the Internet at all, as do 63 percent of those in rural areas of the United States.

However, distance education (formal coursework) requires the ability to read, and even basic reading literacy is not universal, particularly in developing countries. Neither is access to the equipment, connectivity, and bandwidth currently needed for distance education. As Baggaley (2008) reports, too, some developing countries seem to be rejecting Internet-based e-learning in favor of interactive texting via mobile devices. This problem may ease in the future as distance education and e-learning move to mobile devices and as those devices become more powerful, with increased capability to handle large audio files, images, and video in addition to text (Baggaley, 2008). This will mean empowering more people, including those who are not fully reading literate, especially as the cost of these mobile devices goes down and availability increases.

Whether you are using technology for ILI in a wealthy urban area or in an isolated disadvantaged area, you need to remember that technology is no more than a tool (Ruth, 1997). Technological tools rise and fall ever more rapidly as new tools enter the marketplace and supplant older ones. In-depth, effective teaching and learning, of necessity, involves interchange between learner and teacher in order to meet pedagogical goals. The use of technology can and should support these pedagogical goals and the teaching–learning interchange. Some have moved to "blended instruction" in order to address this concern. In 1999, a Pew-funded study reported on a wide range of blended instruction approaches in higher education and identified five different categories of blended instruction on a continuum, beginning with "Supplemental," continuing with "Replacement," and then "Emporium," followed by "Fully Online," and ending with "Buffet." The "Supplemental" and "Replacement" categories are fairly self-evident, with online activities tacked on in the former and some in-person activities replaced by online activities in the latter. "Emporium" represents more of a structural alteration by eliminating in-class meetings and substituting learner work in a learning resource center with personalized faculty and teaching assistant help. "Fully Online" courses may be synchronous or asynchronous and are moderated by an instructor, with no in-person meetings. The "Buffet" approach is the most radical, as it turns over to the learner responsibility for developing her or his own learning plan for mastering the content to be covered, with options for many different instructional formats (NCAT, 2005b; Twigg, 2003; Grassian et al., 2005).

Be aware, however, that effective teaching and learning requires more than just mounting instructional materials and moving to a completely learner-driven discovery approach. Some guidance, structure, and interaction with instructors and other learners make for more robust, engaging, and lasting learning (Mayer, 2004; Baggaley, 2008). MIT's (2008) OpenCourseWare initiative, described earlier in this chapter, underscores this point. Even more interesting is the fact that in at least one country, Pakistan, MIT's instructional materials have been downloaded on CD-ROM and distributed widely to universities (Baggaley, 2008), where learners may, indeed, interact with instructors and with one another. The challenge lies in determining the most effective balance of these ingredients for your learner population, given their needs and technological circumstances.

LEARNING AND TRYING OUT TECHNOLOGY FOR INSTRUCTION

In Chapter 8, we described a number of different instructional modes, including some technology-based modes that you might want to try out. Presentation software like Microsoft's (2008b) PowerPoint, Apple's (2008) Keynote, and Zoho's (2008) Show, are good examples of new technology that seems dauntingly complex. Those who use these applications (software programs) seem to create and alter slide shows with ease, making slides fade in and out, and making bulleted points fly onto slides. Colors, clip art, and captured images on slides appear as if by magic. Yet presentation software can help get users' attention, quickly reinforce important points, and even help you organize a synchronous group instruction session. You know it can be useful, but how can you learn the basics of new technology like this quickly?

You may be surprised to find that you know more than you think you do about technology. You can also apply what you already know in order to learn the basics of new technologies more easily. You might begin using software new to you by trying to identify familiar elements from other technologies you have already used. If you have used a word-processing program like Microsoft's Word, then you already have many skills that you can apply to a number of other applications. Many PC and Mac applications come with menus that have standard labels, like "File" and "Help." The choices listed under these menu labels vary, but often there are some commonalities like "Save" and "Print." It is important to note, however, that Microsoft made radical changes in its menu labels for Word 2007 (PC), and where it placed commands, after decades of offering a standard set of menus. To offset confusion caused by these changes, Microsoft offers a Flash guide that illustrates graphically how to find many commands in Word 2007 that are equivalent to those same commands in Word 2003.

Many applications also come with "wizards," quick, step-by-step guides to help you get started using the program by creating a simple document or file. You can also search the online Help for individual applications or view the contents. Some online Help includes video as well as text and screen captures. The PowerPoint slide show on the CD-ROM that accompanies this book is a somewhat complex example, which includes much content in the Notes view, beneath the slides. The Notes do not display for the audience but can be handy for an instructor. You can enter an outline, bulleted points, questions you want to pose to the learners, or even a complete script for each slide in the Notes area below the slide. Then you can print out your slide show in the Notes format and use that set of printouts (one page per slide) to guide yourself as you go through the slide show.

If you want to learn how to use a presentation slide show in synchronous instruction, start with just two or three slides, an outline for the introduction, a graphic or a question for discussion on a second slide, and a review slide for the conclusion. You can still put points to remember and examples on any number of Notes pages and just use those for yourself. You can also insert a list of your slides and link them so that you can move around in your slide show in a nonlinear fashion based on learner needs and interests (Finkelstein, 2008). You will need to learn how to open the slide show, how to interact with the learners as you use the software, and how to move forward and backward between slides while you are conducting an instruction session. The next step is to practice incorporating the new technology you learn into a class session, especially if you can get a colleague or a naive user to provide some constructive criticism. At this point you may feel ready to try using this technology. Keep in mind that you can try it out with learners in an electronic classroom or remotely through distance education. Remember, too, that you can ask for patience and understanding by explaining directly to the learners that this technology is new to you.

This is one way to get started trying out a technology that is new to you. Some people prefer to learn new technology by following basic instructions on their own or by reading a guide or even by trying out all of the options and printing out all the help screens. Others may only want to learn bits and pieces of technology as the need arises. Still others prefer to take a class or find it easier to learn the software from someone who is familiar with the technology and is willing to serve as a mentor. Which approach is best? The answer is, whichever is best for you. If you are overwhelmed by new technology and need to take it one step at a time, then try using a brief guide and focus on mastering just one element of it at a time. If you learn best by watching a demonstration and listening to a linear presentation, and possibly trying out technology at intervals, then take a class or get some one-on-one help from someone who remembers what it is like to be a novice user of this technology.

You can even use some online tools to learn about others for yourself or for your learners. Check YouTube (2008), TeacherTube (2008), A.N.T.S. (2008) tutorials on LION (2008), or Slideshare (2008) for videos and presentation slide shows on IL-related topics. TeacherTube (2008) even allows you to refine your search by focusing on a number of useful educational and work-related categories, including "College and University," "High School," "Middle School," "Elementary," "Career and Technology," and "Professional Development." Remember, you can also consult with colleagues within and outside your library, take synchronous (real-time) classes or training online, or use free asynchronous (any time, any place) ILI materials you may find through a general Web search tool like Google (2008). Simple, freely available CommonCraft (2007) videos like *RSS in Plain English* and *Social Bookmarking in Plain English* can be helpful to you and your learners regarding the basics of many online tools.

Regardless of how you prefer to learn, it takes time to learn anything new, and learning to make effective use of technology can take quite a lot of time. In deciding whether or not to use a particular type of technology in teaching/learning situations, you will need to weigh two factors. First, consider whether or not using the technology will actually improve the learning experience and the ELOs. Second, figure out in advance approximately how much of your own time you are able and willing to expend on learning how to make effective use of this particular technology.

Just as we need to set goals and objectives or ELOs for our audience, we also need to set goals and objectives or ELOs for our own learning. In teaching synchronously, in person, or remotely, we must work within specified timeframes. We must decide on the most important points we want people to learn and, similarly, on what the technology ELOs should be for ourselves. Which technologies should we learn? A good rule of thumb is to invest your time in the simplest form of technology that would help improve learning outcomes for your audience. You can get some ideas for how to do this by looking over the "'Seven Principles: Collection of Ideas for Teaching and Learning with Technology" (TLT Group, 2008b), based on the Chickering and Ehrman (1996) article "Implementing the Seven Principles: Technology as Lever." These low-threshold applications (LTAs) and activities include "Ideas for Supporting Student–Student Cooperation," such as "Learning Contracts with Individuals and Groups." If you are in an environment with more than one staff member, you may be able to share the burden of keeping up with and trying out new technologies by divvying up responsibility for becoming the "expert" in different technologies. If possible, you might consider team teaching with your colleagues, with each of you using the technology with which you feel most expert or most comfortable. Computer classrooms can be good settings for this sort of team teaching, because they often have a variety of technologies in one physical location.

COMPUTER CLASSROOMS

When online library catalogs were new and other electronic resources were few, librarians often did in-house and end-user training by lecturing and by drawing or writing on blackboards and whiteboards. Demonstrations in classrooms or meeting rooms came next. At first some libraries used screen prints that were turned into overhead transparencies, then progressed to using data monitors, and then data projectors.

As computer and data projector prices declined and technology improved, many libraries began to establish computer classrooms or labs where learners could try out online resources themselves during a class session. ILI librarians were then faced with the dilemma of figuring out how best to help learners achieve increasingly complex learning outcomes for a mushrooming number of electronic resources. Faced with the 50-minute (one-shot) dilemma, ILI librarians like Barclay (1995) attempted to distill the essence of electronic resources for teaching purposes. Many leaned more heavily on print point-of-use guides for the myriad databases and systems that could not be covered in detail in one brief synchronous F2F group session. This is particularly problematic, because it takes longer to teach a hands-on session than a demo. Learners tend to wander off on their own if the session proceeds too slowly for them, or they may not be able to keep up if it proceeds too quickly. In other words, it can be quite a bit more difficult to find and teach to the middle level of any given group when you are teaching a hands-on, F2F group session, especially to learners whom you will encounter as a group only once. One way to help determine the mid-level is to do a quick oral pretest.

Ask learners to rate themselves on a scale of 1 to 5, from someone who has never used a computer, a mouse, or the Internet to a computer user who is skilled with a variety of software and one or more platforms (Macintosh, PC, etc.) and has excellent mouse and Web skills. Then ask experienced learners to sit next to and partner up with those less experienced. For more on teaching online tools and resources, see Chapter 16.

If you are teaching a F2F session in a room with computers, you may also want to control the learning environment, because learners do tend to wander off and explore on their own, do e-mail, chat, text message, or IM, even during what you may consider to be the most relevant portions of a session. If you decide to go this route, you might want to use classroom control software like NetSupport School (2008). This type of software allows you to control all of the learners' screens. You can display the instructor's screen and disable the keyboards, or you may "grab" a learner's screen and display it for the group to see. Classroom control software can come to the rescue if the projection system fails or if you are teaching in a very large room with 40 or more computers, where you may not be able to walk around to see what is on all the learners' screens. This type of software can be useful, too, if you want to get the learners' attention from time to time by displaying a particular screen. There are pitfalls to this approach, however. Learners may become quite frustrated because they have computers in front of them but are not allowed to use them. You may also unintentionally embarrass a learner by using what is on her or his screen as an example for all to see. So, difficult as it may seem, depending on the learners' age and educational level, you should try to balance your desire for control of the learning environment with a more learner-centered approach where learners have the option of following along during a session, just watching, working with a partner, or simply wandering on their own.

Whether teaching online or F2F, try breaking your session into 10- to 15-minute chunks, and include some partnering or small group exercises, like one or two of the exercises from *Designs for Active Learning* (Gradowski, Snavely, and Dempsey, 1998) or *Engaging the Online Learner* (Conrad and Donaldson, 2004). Alternate between using or showing online resources and interacting personally with the learners. Ask questions, praise learners for responding, and encourage learner questions. Walk around and draw or write on a board F2F. Show some presentation slides (online or F2F). Consider asking learners to use clickers (personal audience response systems) or try online polling in F2F or online sessions. Try holding a discussion using text chat in a virtual world, even if you and the learners are in the same computer classroom during a synchronous session.

This is a long list of things to try, and, if you try them all at once, you and the learners may end up feeling scattered. So, you may want to start with just one or two of these suggestions. Map out and rehearse your session in advance based on the ELOs you selected. It is very easy to get sidetracked by technology that is new to you, as well as by a myriad of points regarding the mechanics of using one or another database or system. Try to balance concepts and mechanics equally, if possible, seamlessly weaving them together, and include critical thinking wherever possible. If your goal is to help people learn how to identify and locate useful books, you might outline your group session with approximate times indicated for each segment, as in the sample class outline on the CD-ROM that accompanies this book.

When learners can follow along or watch, as they choose, the learning environment changes and the computer classroom can become a less threatening place. In sum, we can help people improve learning outcomes for F2F synchronous group instruction by using a hands-on computer classroom if we are organized, keep on track, and maintain a positive, friendly, and helping environment, just as we should in synchronous and asynchronous online teaching/learning environments. Whenever possible, try to build some online self-paced, individualized learner participation into instructional materials, as well. In this way you will help meet the needs of a growing number of remote learners, both those enrolled in distance education and those who conduct information researching remotely, even for F2F courses, workshops, or homework needs.

EXAMPLES OF POPULAR TECHNOLOGIES TO TRY

New technologies can be exciting or off-putting depending on your learning preference. Some enjoy jumping in and testing out any new technology or even "mashup," a Web application that combines two or more other applications (TechTerms.com, 2008a; "Mashup Awards," 2008), while others prefer to wait to see which technologies enter the mainstream before investing time and energy in learning them. Figure 15.1 describes a number of technologies you may wish to try, along with examples of how you can use each in ILI. These technologies are popular currently but may grow, evolve, mature, and fade away as some other newer technology comes along that attracts attention or fills a niche at a particular time. This is particularly true as the open source movement becomes more widespread. Open source advocates often lobby software producers to allow programmers to improve and adapt software and gear it to a variety of learners and environments of their choice. For instance, the University of Minnesota (2006) developed the "Assignment Calculator" to help undergraduates who need some structure in the process of developing, researching, and writing a paper. The university then generously made the programming for this tool available to anyone interested in utilizing or adapting it for their needs as long as credit is given for the source of the programming.

Open source alternatives to commercial products like LibGuides are attractive as well, because they are freely available. For instance, "Library a la Carte" (Oregon State University Libraries, accessed 2008) is a tool that allows you to create Web pages similar to LibGuides, with interactive elements, such as chat and RSS, in an attractive format. In general, open source software does not require you to design a tool from scratch or hire a programmer to develop it from the ground up. Instead, you may be able to get some much less complex and costly programming help from an intern or a student on a one-time or infrequent basis. This approach may enable you to do some quick fixes in order to adapt that tool for your own environment and learners, although you will still need to provide supervision and guidance. Open source developers contribute to and correct programming on an ongoing basis. Because programmers anywhere may work to improve open source software, you may also benefit from their contributions and collaborative efforts, as updates are posted for anyone to use (Tapscott and Williams, 2006).

Some open source software does not offer all of the bells and whistles of commercial software, but may serve the main purposes and allow you to use limited funds for other essentials. You may find, too, that open source software allows you to experiment with the use of a type of tool in order to see how effective it is for your learner population, without spending a lot of money to license a commercial product and without spending a lot of time converting materials for use only with that particular product. Easy to use commercial software like LibGuides may also tempt you to get carried away with too much text and too many features that simply overwhelm the learner. You also need to keep in mind that technology is evolving so quickly now that it simply may not be cost-effective to spend a lot of time and money selecting among, negotiating, licensing, and using specific commercial software. Using commercial software, too, may mean that you will need to use its set structure and cope with inevitable bugs or develop workarounds without any recourse to fixing or adapting software yourself or collaboratively with others.

What are some other examples of emerging online tools and resources that could be utilized for IL purposes? In *Social Software in Libraries*, Farkas (2007) describes a number of new and emerging tools and how libraries can use these tools. These include blogs, wikis, online communities, social bookmarking, online reference tools, podcasting, screencasting, and even gaming. She describes social bookmarking as a "recommendation system," where you indicate your preferences for items, as do others, and where you can "tag" items with descriptive words. Then whoever uses this system can see ratings based on preferences as well as tags. At the University of Pennsylvania, users can add tags to the Catalog, using PennTags, and then create bibliographies (Farkas, 2007). As some of Farkas' examples indicate, some of these tools are either merging into one another or feeding into one an-

Figure 15.1 Examples of Technologies to Try

Applications/ Hardware: Examples	Description	Information Literacy Usage Tips
Audience response systems	Software and hardware (clickers, laptops, PDAs) are combined for face-to-face (F2F) synchronous group instruction, especially for large groups.	• Insert a few questions during a session, ideally those that will prompt learner-to-learner discussion or lead down a path chosen by the learners (Collins, 2007).
Blogs	Free blog creation sites like Google-owned Blogger allow you to create and customize public or private blogs where you can post a series of dated messages, similar to entries in a diary, and where others can comment on those messages or post messages of their own.	• Accept and post reference questions on a library blog (Farkas, 2007) or post homework help tips. • Create an information-researching tips blog and call it something that will attract the attention of your learner group—e.g., "Secret Searching Tips & Tricks!" • Allow and encourage learners to help one another by posting their own searching tips and queries. (See Chapter 6, "Active Learning.")
CMSs/LMSs	Content or course management systems/ learning management systems (CMSs/ LMSs) provide a variety of class functions, including the ability to post syllabi, outlines, readings, links to Web sites and videos, as well as discussion boards, group discussion areas, rosters, and grading. Some CMS/LMS software is open source, such as Moodle and Sakai, while others are commercial, such as Blackboard and Angel.	• Request guest access to discussion boards so that you can answer research-related questions and post useful IL-related tips. • Create subject guides for courses or research areas using open source or commercial software and ask that instructors put links to those guides on the top CMS/LMS page.
del.icio.us	On this social bookmarking site, you log in, "register" sites of interest to you, tag them with words that are meaningful to you, and share them with others.	• Ask learners to compare the most popular items on a topic in del.icio.us with those they find through Google Scholar and through a licensed database. • Alternatively, ask learners to compare and contrast tags for a particular topic to subject headings and write an essay on the pros and cons of using each, with examples of both.
Extensions	Extensions are downloadable tools or small programs that "extend" the capabilities of your Web browser. Examples include toolbars, plugins, bookmarklets, and widgets. They provide quick and easy access to Web sites, applications, and functions by means of icons on a desktop, on the "dashboard" (Macintosh), or the Yahoo! "Widget Engine." Or, they may appear as a panel of icons next to or under the toolbar at the top of a browser window ("Web Browser Extensions," 2008).	• If your library does not have a downloadable extension for its catalog search, lobby for one. • If approved, link to it from the library homepage and subject guides, and use it in publicity and promotion. • Download a countdown widget for the instructor's computer in a computer classroom and project it to time exercises. • Get the MeeboMe (2008) widget and try it out for reference instant messaging.

(continued)

Figure 15.1	Examples of Technologies to Try (*Continued*)	
Facebook	Facebook is primarily a social networking and interaction tool where people connect with friends and acquaintances, exchange information, and generally communicate personal and professional information.	• Interest groups like "First Year Experiences Librarians" and "Second Life Link," libraries, and even database vendors like JSTOR are posting applications for this tool, including catalog and database searching. • Keep in mind that any personal information you post would be available to those you "Friend" (Mazer, Murphy and Simonds, 2007). If you feel comfortable with this, ask learners to contact you via Facebook for research or homework help. If you do not, consider setting up a Facebook group for this purpose for your library or area of interest.
Flickr	Flickr is a free photo- and video-sharing site with options to add up to 75 tags and a Creative Commons (CC) license to each photo or video.	• Search for images with CC licenses for "Attribution-NonCommercial-ShareAlike use (Creative Commons, 2008b). • Alternatively, check the Library of Congress' Flickr site for useful images. Use images to illustrate presentation slide shows, handouts, Web sites, and blogs (U.S. Library of Congress, accessed 2008).
iTunes U	iTunes U offers many lectures, podcasts, videos, audiobooks, virtual tours, student presentations, and other materials mounted by colleges and universities, as well as by K–12 schools and other organizations or institutions.	• Hold a student contest to create a virtual tour of your library or a podcast, or create them yourself and mount them on iTunes U. • Link to your library's iTunes U materials on your library's home page and on subject guides you create. • Link to other useful iTunes U items in your subject guides.
Mashups	Mashups are programs that draw upon two or more applications to produce new information or services.	• Use mashups to illustrate IL concepts. WikipediaVision combines Google Maps with Wikipedia edits, offering a visual representation of how common it is to edit Wikipedia pages worldwide (Kozma, 2008). • Check "Mashup Awards" (2008) regularly for other mashups that may help illustrate IL concepts in an engaging manner.
Podcasts, Screencasts, Presentation Slide Shows, Slidecasts, and Vodcasts	Audio-only (podcasts), video (screencasts, vodcasts), presentation slide shows with narration (slidecasts), or without, can be mounted on Web sites and used in synchronous and asynchronous instruction.	• Describe services or teach ILI concepts and mechanics of use through any of these tools or have teams of learners create them for other learners. • Alternatively, ask learners to compare and contrast two different formats of ILI, identify the expected learning outcomes for each, and reflect on how well they were achieved. • Mount learners' content on a Web site, with their permission.

(*continued*)

Figure 15.1	Examples of Technologies to Try (*Continued*)	
RSS	Often said to stand for "Really Simple Syndication" ("RSS Syndication," accessed 2009), RSS offers a way to subscribe to sites, such as blogs, so that you are notified when there are changes or new postings rather than having to go to each and every site in order to check for the latest posts. RSS aggregators allow you to get to all of your RSS feeds at one site or through one feed.	• Ask learners to sign up for feeds for two blogs that represent opposing points of view. • Ask them to identify a common topic, and compare its treatment in each blog, as well as in an online subject encyclopedia, licensed or free. • The comparison should include a list of three or more criteria to keep in mind when reviewing material from each type of online resource.
Screencasting	Screencasts are created by capturing video of whatever appears on a computer monitor, such as a database search. Some screencasting software is free, like Jing, while others are commercial, for instance, Camtasia Studio and Captivate.	• Create two- to three-minute online video tutorials to teach selecting, using, and evaluating databases. • Pose interactive quiz questions within the videos.
Twitter	Twitter is a quick, real-time communication tool, a kind of microblogging application with a limited 140-character text box.	• For credit courses or workshops, ask learners to Tweet their quick feedback throughout a session. • Alternatively, at the end of a session, have learners respond to the one-minute paper. • In a large F2F or online group, try the Pause Procedure at 10- to 15-minute intervals by asking learners to Tweet to a partner what they think was the main point of the session up to that time. Have them continue to Tweet for another few minutes to come to agreement on the main point just covered and to share a few with the group as a whole (Angelo and Cross, 1993).
Virtual Worlds	Interactive massively multiplayer online role-playing games (MMORG) and multiuser virtual worlds (MUVE) have grown rapidly in popularity since 2003 when the three-dimensional virtual world of Second Life was launched. For educational purposes, virtual worlds can combine games and the ability to create and manipulate representations of yourself in order to interact synchronously with others who are right next to you physically or thousands of miles away. In 1998, one of the authors of this book predicted the use of avatars for reference and development of libraries in virtual worlds, a prediction that came true in Second Life (SL) eight years later (Grassian, 1998; Alliance Virtual Library, accessed 2008; Educause Learning Initiative, 2008b).	• Have learners meet in an immersive learning environment in Second Life, like Renaissance Island, Land of Lincoln, or Caledon (a 19th century sim). • Ask them to pair up or work in teams to look critically at an aspect of the sim, conduct research on the historical accuracy of the representation, and write a paper on it, with an annotated bibliography. • Alternatively, ask them to construct an SL object that would help other learners identify, locate, and critically evaluate virtual world objects utilizing criteria they develop themselves.

(*continued*)

Figure 15.1 Examples of Technologies to Try (*Continued*)

WebQuests	WebQuests are structured group research projects that use preselected Web sites and a research topic (Dodge, 2000a, 2000b), similar to case-based learning.	• Look for WebQuests in a topic area that will interest your learners at their educational or age level (WebQuest.org, 2007). • Check links and adapt the WebQuests as needed.
Wikis	Free wiki sites like PBwiki allow you to set up passworded or open sites where you can share and annotate documents with others, remotely. They keep track of document changes in their history areas. Wikipedia is the most well-known and popular, mostly open wiki, allowing anyone to edit most articles.	• Set up a free wiki site and password it for a group of learners (WikiMatrix, accessed 2008). • Ask the learners to create an annotated pathfinder on a topic of their choice with categorized information resources. • Alternatively, ask small groups of learners to pick a broad topic, focus on an aspect of their choice and then create an informational wiki on that topic for other learners. • Experiment with various means of helping learners discover the benefits and limitations of Wikipedia.
YouTube	YouTube is a free Google-owned video-sharing site with options to search for videos and to upload your own videos and add tags to them. You can add comments or annotations to videos you find and view there. You may also set up playlists or channels and share them with others.	• Make use of three kinds of videos in synchronous or asynchronous ILI: 1. Descriptions of library and information services ("Weigle Information Commons Music Video," 2008; Mizrachi, 2008) 2. Directed help with information researching, such as tutorials regarding use of specific databases and critical thinking ("Boolean Operators," 2007) 3. Non-IL videos that illustrate IL concepts (Museum of Media History, 2007)

other. She describes "moblogging," for instance, as "blogging from mobile devices" (Farkas, 2007: 95). You can also search some traditional online IL-related tools through Facebook, as mentioned earlier, or even while in virtual worlds like Second Life. You can view YouTube and other videos through Facebook and link to them through a CMS/LMS or embed links in an online tutorial or research guide.

Whether you are looking at commercial or open source technology, however, some basic means of figuring them out may be helpful. Determine what the software's purpose is by checking the Web site's About page. Look through the online Help. Try out its features, and look for new developments or beta features. Google has been exploring and acquiring many different sorts of applications for some time, so keep an eye on Google applications. The Google homepage "More" menu lists some of the most popular Google applications, but "Even More" at the bottom of the "More" menu will lead you to a long list of them, plus search tips for special searches, mobile applications, and much more.

Zoho (2008), a Google competitor, also offers many free applications, including e-mail, word processing, a spreadsheet, a wiki, chat, presentation slide show, desktop sharing, and Web conferencing. Many Zoho applications are also available through Facebook (see later), and you can log in to Zoho with your Google or Yahoo! account rather than creating a separate account just for Zoho. This illustrates the increasingly interrelated nature of social software and those who use it. How long will

Google, Zoho, or any of the software mentioned earlier last? No one can tell, but it does seem as though something new pops up daily that builds on what came before it or puts a creative new twist on it.

PUTTING IT ALL TOGETHER

If you are new to ILI, all of this may seem daunting, if not overwhelming. After all, in addition to determining instructional needs and setting goals, objectives, or ELOs, coming up with content (including illustrative examples), writing an outline or script that incorporates active learning, preparing supplementary materials like handouts and/or a presentation slide show, and rehearsing and timing your session, you need to figure out how to handle both the instructor's and learners' computers and other equipment, when and how to meld it all together smoothly, all the while keeping learners interested, motivated, and on task. This is not only a mouthful to say, but also requires an incredibly complex set of skills, all of which need to be blended together for a smooth, effective, and efficient session.

Take heart! You can learn to do this by working with other ILI librarians to find out how to use the equipment and then by observing other ILI librarians teaching live sessions by taking notes on the techniques and wording you liked, by practicing with them in rehearsals, by thinking about how you would do it differently, by keyboarding for a class, and even by team teaching (LaGuardia et al., 1996; Kipnis and Childs, 2004). Ask for or make up your own simple checklist for using technology to teach and for how to set up a computer classroom before a session based on whatever sort of equipment training or other instructions you receive regarding the computer classroom. See Figure 15.2 for an example of this sort of checklist.

Be sure to allow plenty of time to set up the equipment, check your handouts, and review your session script, outline, and/or presentation software slide show before the session begins—set aside, generally, about an hour to prep before a class session. Figure 15.3 provides an example of a computer classroom teaching preparation checklist.

The computer classroom, of course, represents an effective means of helping users in a synchronous, F2F group instruction environment. Remote instruction, particularly in the forms of online learning, distance education, and e-learning, offers many other benefits and challenges.

DISTANCE EDUCATION AND INFORMATION LITERACY INSTRUCTION PRINCIPLES FOR SUCCESS

Poverty, isolation, disabilities, and physical distance from educational institutions—thankfully, these too commonplace barriers to achieving one's potential are melting away as technology access broadens and as distance education takes hold at many levels. Synchronous and asynchronous distance education for academic credit suits learners who are unable to

Figure 15.2 Using Technology to Teach: Self-checklist

- Do you really need to use technology to teach or to help learners achieve expected learning outcomes?
- If so, what is the minimum amount of technology you can use that will allow you to achieve your pedagogical goals and at the same time offer a variety of options to meet differing learning styles?
- Is the technology you want to use readily available?
- How much time do you have available to learn technology that is new to you?
- Have you used it before? Do you need training or a refresher?
- Are you aware of and prepared for possible glitches?
- Have you tested the equipment in advance? Do you know how to turn it on and off and to logon and logoff?
- Which platform will you be using—Mac or PC? Are you familiar with both?
- Have you tested the software and tried out examples in advance but close to the time when you will be teaching?
- What kinds of troubleshooting/trouble call mechanisms do you have in place?

Figure 15.3 Sample Computer Classroom Preparation Checklist

- Turn on the data projector.
- Switch the media cabinet display to VHS or some other medium by pressing button 2, 3, or 4 to the right of the data projector ON button. (This will blank the screen so it does not display what appears on the instructor's monitor.)
- Lower the electronic screen.
- Turn on the monitor on the instructor's computer, logon to the network, and open the Web browser you are going to use for the session.
- Boot up each of the 20 computers for learners, but do not log on—learners will log on using their own logon IDs and passwords.
- Go back to the instructor's computer:
  - Go over your script or outline.
  - Test out each site and example you plan to use and make any necessary changes.
  - Test out your presentation slide show if you plan to use one.
  - Decide and test out how you will point to items on the electronic screen (mouse, pointer pen, laser pointer, your hand).
- If you want to distribute handouts at the beginning of the session, have them in packets and place them on chairs in the room.
- If you want to distribute handouts at intervals during the session, make sure you have enough of them, stacked in the order in which you want to distribute them, and in handy reach.
- Test out the lighting.
- Write your name and e-mail address or phone number on the board, or have this information on the first slide in your slide show or on the outline for the session, or distribute copies of your business card.
- During the session, while displaying a presentation slide show, press the B key to blank the screen completely when focusing on discussion rather than on the slide displayed.
- When the session is over, if the room will not be used for the rest of the day, go back through each step, picking up leftover handouts, turning off lights, logging off computers, etc.

attend traditional in-person classes at a physical location, scheduled at regular intervals during a term. Some learners may need to work full time when a particular class is offered, or they may not be able to get to the physical location at all or on a regular basis. They may even be in a different part of the country or the world where there are scant opportunities for education.

What does learning at a distance mean, though, when geographic boundaries have eroded and learners can be at a "distance" a mere building away or anywhere in the world? Day and night, too, are losing meaning as companies, organizations, and educational institutions, including libraries, furiously scramble to offer 24/7 (24 hours a day/7 days a week) services. For academic libraries and some school libraries, it means blurring distinctions between those who take courses on a physical campus and those who enroll in online or blended distance education courses for credit (ALA. ACRL. Distance Learning Section, 2008a, 2008b). Online learning and e-learning at any level, however, can also include static and interactive Web pages, discussion boards, chat, blogs, wikis, IM, videos, slide shows, and podcasts. It can also include online distance education courses that incorporate all of these modes and more, some through services like iTunes U (Apple, 2008a) and others through virtual worlds, such as Second Life, with much moving rapidly to mobile devices like cell phones, iPods, and iPhones.

For many of these instructional approaches, ILI librarians in many parts of the world have been using Web-based exercises, tutorials, online courses, videos, and many other methods and formats to help their users and staff achieve both narrow and broad IL learning outcomes remotely, primarily online. Libraries also offer help for distance learners taking academic courses. The University of South Florida (2008) offers an information-packed Web page simply called "Distance Learners." Many libraries of all types also offer live chat or e-mail reference for those who need help or have questions they cannot answer by searching the library's Web site.

What underlies successful distance education efforts? How are they distinct from general online help and online homework help, as well as other programs that merely utilize technology? The ALA, ACRL Distance Learning Section (2008b) published revised and helpful "Standards for Distance Learning Library Services" that define distance education from an academic library perspective. The standards cover topics such as access, management, finances, personnel, resources, services, and documentation. They focus on library resources and services for distance education or extended campus programs, although they include "courses attended in-person" as well as online. The ACRL guidelines strongly emphasize the importance of lifelong learning, to be instilled through "general bibliographic and information literacy instruction . . . [which] must be provided to all distance learning students" (ALA. ACRL. Distance Learning Section, 2008b: online). They state further that, at a minimum, librarian administrators of these programs should "provide a facilitating environment in support of teaching and learning, and in the acquisition of lifelong learning skills" (ALA. ACRL. Distance Learning Section, 2008b: online). They should develop a mission, goals and objectives for the program, needs and outcomes assessment, collections and services, and work "collaboratively with teaching faculty in distance-delivered programs to integrate information literacy into courses and programs in order to foster lifelong learning skills" (ALA. ACRL. Distance Learning Section, 2008b: online). They also state that originating institutions should have on hand 18 types of documentation to prove that they are meeting these guidelines. Interestingly, print and/or user guides and other library instructional materials are first on their list.

The North American Council on Online Learning (NACOL, 2007) published "National Standards of Quality for Online Courses" in 2007 for K–12, composed of six useful self-checklists for institutions covering the topics of course content, instructional design, student assessment, use of technology, course evaluation and management, and "21st Century Skills." It may be useful to examine these guidelines and those produced in other countries, as well, to see how they frame IL-related topics and where they appear . NACOL's Category II, "Interactions," for example, emphasizes that it is through interaction with an instructor and others that people learn. This is true both for in-person and for distance education. In a distance education environment, the ILI librarian could offer to monitor the class discussion board for information-research issues and could be available via e-mail for individual consultation. The ILI librarian could work with the instructor to devise a series of interactive Web-based exercises or a workbook that distance education learners could complete asynchronously. But who is our audience, and what is their level of expertise and experience with technology? What are their age and skill levels? What do they already know about the topics you want to cover and about related areas?

Audience and Purpose

As we have mentioned in previous chapters, audience is one of the most critical factors we need to consider in developing and providing ILI in any format. This is particularly true for distance education or other forms of online learning and e-learning materials, as our potential learner base has grown to include anyone who has an Internet connection anywhere in the world. For online learning and e-learning materials, in particular, we must define and actively target our primary learner groups, gearing ILI to their needs first. In public libraries, for example, primary learner groups include all levels of society, all age groups, and all educational levels within particular geographical regions. Academic, school, and special libraries each have smaller bites of the user pie, often defined in their mission statements, sometimes reflecting aspects of their institutional mission statements that relate to ILI but may not use the words "information literacy." You can find some sample IL-related mission statements on the CD-ROM that accompanies this book. For more on IL in different environments, see Chapter 14.

Are Online Learning, Distance Education, and e-Learning Best?

Physical distance of any kind becomes almost irrelevant once you have defined targeted user groups. Academic libraries, for instance, will want to provide ILI to undergraduates in dorm rooms at 2:00 a.m., as well as to their own faculty doing research while on sabbatical in other parts of the world. It is easy to keep campus or local community populations in mind when planning ILI, even if they are in dorm rooms or at home, because they have a physical connection to the institution when they attend classes or come to a library building for materials.

It is more difficult to think about online learners' information research needs when they are essentially invisible unless they make themselves visible through technology such as e-mail, IM, or text messaging, through social software, or in virtual worlds. How are these people getting their research materials? Can they get some research materials for free through library subscriptions? Do they know about SFX links and proxy server settings that allow them to get to these materials? Are they using Web search tools like Yahoo! and Google to identify and locate materials? Are they using sites like Google Scholar without setting it up for authentication, or are they going directly to magazine and journal Web sites and paying for articles and other items they could get for free through a library catalog or licensed databases? Who is helping them sort through the information muddle? How can we address all sorts of online IL learning needs? Many of the sample technologies we have already discussed could be utilized for this purpose, but what sorts of distance education techniques should you use?

TECHNIQUES

Academic libraries have developed Web-based online courses and tutorials, as well as Web pages targeted specifically at distance education learners (SUNY Buffalo, accessed 2008b); the business community and the U.S. government have focused on Web-based training, including simulations; schools have developed WebQuests for K–12 students; and public libraries have led in developing digital collaboration for reference. WebQuests, in particular, can be adapted to a variety of environments. They provide a structured approach to using the Web to support instruction (Dodge, 2000b). Instructors select topics and Web sites for students to use, develop a research focus, and assign members of student teams to investigate various aspects of a topic, such as the art and environment of the Navajo (Dodge, 2000b). Then teams meet together to meld what they have found into a completed project. WebQuests make learning fun, interesting, and relevant, and as a result learners may be more motivated to complete instruction and to retain learning.

Educational games also attract interest and can hold learners' attention (Blum and Yocom, 1996; Childers, 1996; Doolittle, 1995; DeLorenzo, 1999; Prensky, 2001, 2007; Smith, 2007). How can you use games and virtual worlds for ILI? "Ancient Spaces" offers an example. University of British Columbia students who were gamers started this open source multiproject effort to reconstruct ancient Mediterranean and other sites in a 3D virtual environment, currently utilizing the open source Croquet software. Undergraduates can use pieces from a set of building parts, "professionally developed 3D 'primitives'," to assemble reconstructions. Students must defend their reconstruction, based on data from archaeological sites as well as interpretations of that data, and may be asked to build multiple sites based on varying interpretations of that data ("Ancient Spaces," 2006; University of British Columbia, 2007). Rather than relying on instructor-provided research studies, ILI intervention could help the "Ancient Spaces" students learn how to identify, locate, and evaluate the studies for themselves. This would provide a solid ILI foundation, enabling students to research and prepare literature reviews for their more advanced research in the future.

Although "Ancient Spaces" is not a game, working with it is similar in some respects to designing and using educational games. Learners investigate and build reconstructions using virtual objects, in a 3D immersive learning virtual environment. Prensky (2008) suggests strongly that student-created games are the most effective for student learning, both short, casual "minigames" that take less than an hour to play and "complex games" that can take the place of an entire course. The latter would be similar to commercial games and can take up to 60 hours to play, have multiple levels, and require multiple skills. Because complex games are extremely time- and cost-intensive, Prensky (2008) suggests that, instead, instructors ask teams of students to build minigames that will teach small units of a curriculum. These minigames can be shared with others, rated by students and instructors, and then maintained through an iterative process or replaced by more effective minigames. Developing games like these could be a way to show the instructor that you understand the material enough to be able to teach it to others. According to Prensky (2008), students may even end up learning more from creating games than from playing them, and contests for the best or most effective games may entice reluctant learners to participate, as well.

How does this apply to ILI? If you teach a term-long IL course you may want to ask students to create minigames for discrete IL-related concepts, such as the use of Boolean operators or evaluative criteria for blogs. Younger learners could create crossword puzzles or mazes using the free "Puzzlemaker" (Discovery Education, 2008). If your students give you permission to mount and adapt those games, you could follow Prensky's (2008) lead by asking other groups of learners to build on the original minigames created or mash them up with one or more other games or applications to create something entirely new. Or you may want to challenge learners to develop somewhat more complex approaches like the "Save the Village" game, created completely remotely by high school students from three countries for their award-winning ThinkQuest Web site, "Volcanoes Online" (accessed 2008). Teaching others helps you learn. Creating games to teach others can make that learning fun and more effective (Prensky, 2008).

There are many other alternatives to developing entire complex online games yourself, though. Some simple, as well as more complex, games can be incorporated into ILI, particularly online formats. You can use the free "eGames Generator" (accessed 2008) to create any of nine different types of games, including "Name It!," "Arrange It!," and "Order It!" Descriptions of each type of game include "Instructional Value," with tables describing learning objectives and providing examples. The idea is to challenge learners to test their "Information Literacy IQ," solve an IL puzzle, or find answers to interesting questions.

You can also consider participating in virtual reality worlds that can be altered by the participants. Examples of these massively multiplayer online role-playing games (MMORPGs) include Second Life (2008), NeverWinter Nights, (2008), and Everquest (accessed 2008). Some of these MMORPGs offer free basic accounts, while others are fee based. Plunge in and try it. Look for librarian involvement, and offer to volunteer some time in reference or in other areas depending on your skills, your interest, and the time you have available to learn new technologies. The Alliance Library System's Information Island opened in Second Life in early 2006 with the Alliance Virtual Library (accessed 2008). Now there are about 130 libraries in this 3D virtual world, including public, special, and academic libraries. A few libraries are experimenting with IL-related displays and games within Second Life, including the Murdoch University Library, Western Australia's beautifully designed "Steps to Research" (Bell and Trueman, 2008; Grassian and Trueman, 2007; Grassian, Trueman, and Clemson, 2007; Greenhill, accessed 2009). Some school library media teachers and public library librarians are also involved in Teen Second Life. Adults 18 and over must get a separate avatar and undergo a background check in order to participate in Teen Second Life.

Tutorials, WebQuests, and games can be highly useful in ILI and address preferences for both learner-to-learner and learner-to-interface instructional modes, although remember that some people prefer learner-to-instructor modes. Each of these approaches should be selected and designed to support your pedagogical goals of course, and you will need to consider all of the mode selection factors mentioned in Chapter 8, as well as copyright, intellectual property, and privacy issues. Access is a critical issue, particularly with online educational games, especially MMORPGs, as they often require high capacity for graphics and lots of RAM. You will also need to consider whether or not there will be free and easily accessible technology sophisticated enough to handle whatever ILI you devise, and available to the target audience in your environment—academic, school, public, or special library/information center. This includes consideration of filtering in public and school libraries for under-18-year-olds that may restrict their access to certain sites for research and examples.

How effective is distance education? Are learners achieving ELOs? Are they meeting the standards or goals you have set? Evaluation and assessment of learning will help answer these questions. Schrock (2008a) has created excellent Web site evaluation tools for grade levels ranging from primary through high school. These forms could be assigned as homework and used to assess learning following a group instruction session . You may also want to adapt these or other forms for adult learners, with the authors' permission, of course.

More Web-based ILI tutorials seem to appear almost daily, many of which are listed on the LOEX (2007a) Web site, in the PRIMO database (ALA. ACRL. IS, 2008e), and on the A.N.T.S. (2008) Web site. These tutorials may address different audiences and have different purposes, but the primary question is whether or not their primary audience is achieving the learning outcomes expected of them after they have completed the tutorial. Online quizzes and tests may help, if you can get the learners to your site and if they complete the instruction. At this point, there are more questions than answers regarding the effectiveness of ILI online learning on the cutting edge of new technologies. New technologies are often in an uncertain state, but they offer great opportunity for small-scale experimentation. You may be pleasantly surprised at the results of such experiments or you may be disappointed, but in any case you will surely learn a lot and will be better prepared for the next experiment.

USING TECHNOLOGY TO PREPARE FOR BOTH LOW-TECH AND HIGH-TECH ENVIRONMENTS

How do you prepare when you are unsure of whether or not you will be using technology at the higher end of the instructional technology continuum? If you are organized and have a variety of backup plans and materials, people will learn whether or not you have one or more computers up and connected to the Net. Be prepared to pose questions to the learners, go through interactive exercises that help people learn concepts, and provide paper handouts for mechanics. If all equipment fails, you may still have a speaker's outline, point-of-use guides for the library catalog, and one or more licensed databases, as well as a blackboard, whiteboard, or flip chart. Even without equipment, you can begin by asking learners to write questions on blank cards and then use their questions to frame and conduct the session. You can still do small and large group exercises on topic selection, on the flow of information, on Boolean operators, and on the differences between magazines and journals, including critical thinking about what you can expect to get from each. Even without looking at Web sites, blogs, or popular social networking tools like Facebook, you can ask learners what they generally use these tools for and how they weigh their value. With or without use of technology, you can get the learners to work in small groups to come up with evaluation checklists or ways to rate and rank these types of resources themselves for the benefit of others.

You can also use word-processing software to prepare a session outline, and you can use presentation software to prepare overhead transparencies. You can send follow-up information or answer questions later though an online discussion board or by e-mail. Many kinds of technology can be useful in instruction in a range of environments and circumstances, indirectly as well as directly, but it is possible to lose learners with too much technology.

HOW MUCH TECHNOLOGY IS TOO MUCH?

Are in-person groups of learners falling asleep? Are their eyes glazed over? Do they seem dazed and overwhelmed or turned off? Are they having trouble following along in a hands-on environment or grasping basic concepts in a demonstration or other synchronous learning environment? Stop. Ask questions to check for comprehension. Above all, listen carefully and respectfully to the learners' answers (or lack of them). Always blame the machines and the software for difficulties rather than the learners (Agre, 1996). Turn off the display, slow down, simplify, and offer friendly words of encouragement and support. Proceed with machines and other electronic/electric equipment in person only when learners indicate they are ready to do so. Drop back to simpler electronic/electric modes if synchronous online participation drops off.

Is your wonderful new interactive Web-based tutorial unused or underused? Are learners starting it, but not finishing? Are instructors and learners alike ignoring your blog, your chat reference, or your Web-based exercises, hints, tips, and forms? Usage statistics can provide some indication of the success of your Web site, although testing for learning outcomes is the real indicator of success. If usage is low and learning outcomes are not satisfactory, usability testing with naive users and subsequent revisions may help. Most of all, we should not be discouraged by underuse of our electronic products and services. It takes time for new forms of instruction to take hold, and we may have to do some marketing to bring them to the attention of those who need them. (For more on this topic, see Grassian and Kaplowitz, 2005, Chapter 7, "Marketing, Publicity, and Promotion.")

SYNCHRONICITY AND ASYNCHRONICITY, REDUX

There is still much demand for synchronous ILI, both F2F and online. However, the development of asynchronous online instruction presents a singular opportunity for ILI to meld with academic curricula at all levels, from kindergarten through higher education, and to provide support and lifelong learning opportunities for learners in all sorts of environments. This is a very exciting opportunity for ILI librarians, as it opens the door to many creative approaches to ILI that will be able to reach many more people at many different levels. Scarcity of staff time has long been a mitigating factor in offering in-person, synchronous ILI and has in effect forced us to focus on our primary users largely to the exclusion of others. Synchronous and asynchronous online learning allow us to reach out to a larger variety of user groups by offering various forms of ILI in learner-centered approaches. For example, academic libraries could create ILI self-tests designed for high school students who would like to prepare in advance for their freshman year in college. These self-tests could help students identify weak areas and also link to instruction designed to strengthen skills or knowledge, such as critical thinking about Web pages. High school librarians can link to college-level help to give their students an advance boost for college preparation. Public libraries may want to work with school libraries in developing materials for K–12 as well.

THE CRUX OF LEARNING AND TEACHING

With or without technology, however, most people would probably agree that "Effective teaching is that which leads to engaged and intelligent learning" (Koppi, Lublin, and Chaloupka, 1997: 245). In other words, the core of effective teaching and learning is interaction between learner and teacher. Interaction among learners can support and enhance interaction between learner and teacher. Both types of interaction can take place synchronously in F2F group instruction or remotely in group sessions, and they can also take place asynchronously, any time, any place, one person at a time (Chickering and Ehrmann, 1996; TLT Group, 2008b.).

It seems fairly obvious that teacher and learners can interact synchronously in F2F group instruction. The instructor can ask questions, answer questions, query learners who have puzzled looks, set up active learning exercises for large and small groups, get learners to lead discussions, organize debates, use think–pair–share and other creative problem-solving techniques, and even use active learning assessment techniques to review and stimulate learning (Angelo and Cross, 1993; Gradowski, Snavely, and Dempsey, 1998). Instructors can use many of these same techniques in synchronous remote instruction, such as chat, but the instructor has to work harder to engage learners, and there are more caveats. There is no body language to observe (except in virtual worlds), so verbal and text cues are very important, as is participation. It can help to ask questions and to chunk learning into manageable bites, interspersed with exercises or activities like polling. Polling can be quite effective, especially if the instructor knows the content well, interprets results on the spot, and asks for confirmation from the audience via a "show of hands" online.

But how, you may ask, can instructor and learners interact asynchronously? They can interact remotely through discussion boards or listservs where an entire group or a subset can respond to issues and questions. They can also interact privately via e-mail or text messaging or through blogs or wikis. Instructors can post messages that take controversial stands on issues of interest to the group, encourage debate and discussion, and draw attention to key points, as well as to strengths and weaknesses of arguments. To stimulate discussion, you could also post links to controversial Web sites and streaming videos, like *EPIC 2015* (Museum of Media History, 2007), which posits a massively Google-dominated world. Learners can interact asynchronously as well with interactive Web-based materials and with printed materials. They can do Web-based exercises and receive feedback on their answers. They can send e-mail or text-message reference questions and receive answers that help them learn how to learn. In print, they can complete worksheets, turn them in, and receive corrections and comments.

It is difficult, if not impossible, however, to predict which form of interaction between learner and teacher would work best for a particular individual with a given information or learning need at any given time or place. From the learner's standpoint, the best approach for one situation may not be best for another, and the same is true for the teacher. Ideally, the instructor should provide several different alternative means of interacting with learners and respond flexibly to whichever method the learners use. Of course, little of this will simply happen on its own. You must plan ahead in order to select, install, test, and adapt (if necessary and if possible) interaction methods you can utilize in online learning. Successful teaching with technology (synchronous or asynchronous) may very well hinge on the well-organized, timely, capable, and supportive work of librarians and others who serve as technology managers (Conrad and Donaldson, 2004; see also Grassian and Kaplowitz, 2005, Chapter 8, "Learning to Manage Technology").

KEEPING UP

In *Learning to Lead and Manage Information Literacy Instruction* (Grassian and Kaplowitz, 2005, Chapter 8, "Learning to Manage Technology"),we suggest that technology managers take the lead in learning and sharing information about new technology developments by tracking listservs and blogs, by reading a variety of publications, and by keeping in touch with other tech-savvy colleagues. We also suggest that any librarian can get in the habit of watching for or seeking out technology-related news and information.

All of this is still true. You can educate yourself continually regarding new and developing technology through a variety of media within and beyond the profession of librarianship. Some people do this instinctively and eagerly, as new technologies are developed, becoming intentional or "accidental library technologists" who fall into technology expertise by chance or circumstance (Kern, 2006), while others prefer to wait until a technology has taken hold before learning to use it. Both approaches may work, although ideally each institution, organization, or environment would be better served by having at least one person who stays on top of new technologies and shares what she or he learns with other staff. The sharing process can enthuse and invigorate people but only if it is supportive, encouraging, and noncondescending. Try e-mailing some quick tips to colleagues every once in a while or provide a reference to a new and easy to understand publication. Within librarianship, even general publications such as *Library Journal* and *American Libraries* offer useful tips, columns, and articles related to technology that can be applied to IL ("Techlistmania," 2008; "Technology News," 2008; Janes, 2008; Farkas, 2008).

Intentional staff training offers another approach to keeping up with technology. The Public Library of Charlotte & Mecklenburg County developed "Learning 2.0," "a discovery learning program designed to encourage staff to explore new technologies and reward them for doing 23 Things" (Blowers, 2006a: online; Notess, 2006). The "23 Things" include small exercises related to learning about blogs and trying blogging, tagging (adding your own topic words to describe an item), folksonomies (collections of tags created by users), and even self-reflection on what you have learned. Staff who complete all 23 items within a given time period get prizes of various kinds. This approach provides a robust combination of structure and learner-centered choice in terms of which areas to investigate first and which exercises to complete, as well as when to complete them. Each weekly segment includes a short podcast explaining the exercise and providing some guidance. Interesting and fun activities and exercises complement work-related exercises. Week 8, "Online Applications & Tools," includes an exercise in exploring Web 2.0 award winning Web sites (SEOmoz, 2008). Each weekly segment includes a self-reflective exercise, and the entire nine-week program ends with a self-reflection assignment about the program as a whole (Blowers, 2006a). Another option would be to license a product that teaches use of many different types of software, such as Lynda.com (2008), a large set of commercially produced videos.

As the concept of "information literacy" has caught hold worldwide, there are now additional publications, organizations, and institutions beyond librarianship that can help you learn about new technologies and help your colleagues, as well. The annual "Horizon Report," published each January by the New Media Consortium and Educause, identifies technology trends in the making and classifies them in terms of "time-to-adoption," anywhere from one year or less to four to five years. The January 2008 edition identified "Grassroots Video" as one year or less to adoption and "Collective Intelligence" and "Social Operating Systems" as four to five years to adoption. The report includes "Relevance for Teaching, Learning, and Creative Expression," as well as examples for each technology trend (Johnson, Levine and Smith, 2008). Some of this may be developing faster than even the annual "Horizon Report" can keep up with, though. "Grassroots Video" via YouTube is already extremely popular and widely used for education, self-education, and, of course, personal interest.

Educause provides access to highly useful materials on its ELI Resources site, including its series called "7 Things You Should Know About..." a growing number of new technologies. Each is clearly and simply laid out and can help you see both how the technology works and why and how it may be useful in supporting pedagogy (Educause Learning Initiative, 2008a, 2008b, 2008c). Farkas' (2007, Chapter 15) "Keeping Up: A Primer," her column in *American Libraries* (Farkas, 2008), and even Gizmodo can be quite useful and interesting, as can the *Chronicle of Higher Education*'s "Information Technology" section, *Wired*, and even the weekly Business section of the *New York Times*. CommonCraft (2007) and YouTube (2008) videos offer visual and auditory help with understanding and keeping up with new technologies.

The Gartner Group (2008) offers licensed access to reports on "Hype Cycles." In 2008, Gartner listed these reports for 27 different categories of technology, including "Social Software" and "Consumer Mobile Applications." Each "Hype Cycle" is an annotated graph showing highs and lows in five stages: "Technology Trigger," "Peak of Inflated Expectations," "Trough of Disillusionment," "Slope of Enlightenment," and "Plateau of Productivity." Each item on the graph is also labeled in terms of how many years it will take until that particular technology becomes mainstream. According to the 2008 "Social Software" "Hype Cycle," for instance, "Public Virtual Worlds," "Immersive Learning Environments," and "Folksonomies/Tagging" are all headed down to the "Trough of Disillusionment." The first two are two to five years to mainstream adoption, while the last is less than two years away from mainstream adoption. Blogs, on the other hand, are headed up the "Slope of Enlightenment" from the "Trough of Disillusionment" and are on their way to the "Plateau of Productivity" (Gartner Group, 2008). One has to wonder how the Gartner Group comes up with these determinations and how accurate and meaningful they are. Generally, we should be aware of these forecasting tools but look at them critically and thoughtfully, always asking who has developed them, on what basis, for which audience, and for what purpose.

The list of publications and blogs to check for new technology developments can seem endless. Keeping up with technology can be a full-time job, but do not let it overwhelm you. You may never know about or be an expert at every kind of technology or even a huge number of technologies. But, if you can, try to develop a fearless attitude and just jump in and try technologies as you encounter them. Once you see that you can learn how to use new technologies, try teaching some of them to others, always with a noncondescending manner and with an understanding of how a newbie to that technology must feel and think. You may discover that you will want to seek out and explore more new technologies, always considering at the back of your mind how they may be able to help support your teaching and your learners' learning regardless of their age or educational level. Be brave and intrepid—you have nothing to lose but a little time—and we will all have so much to gain from your efforts.

FINAL REMARKS

Does technology hinder or help? Is there a significant difference in learning when we utilize technology in teaching? Do people learn more, better, or differently when we use technology in instruction? What levels and percentages of use, as well as types of technology, are best, for which situations? What sort of technology can and should we use in person and remotely in order to support our ILI goals? How have ILI librarians adjusted to a constant barrage of new and altered technologies? Quite well for the most part. Many participate actively in selection and feedback regarding new and enhanced software and hardware and eagerly help their colleagues learn how to use new technologies. More often than not, we have come to accept the fact that nothing is perfect and that we are able to help people learn to evaluate and make effective, efficient use of the "information arsenal" available to us.

In this chapter we have attempted to help you along in your search for answers to important technology-related questions, answers that will vary according to your institution's or organization's current needs and circumstances. Most important, we need to keep asking questions and keep developing and adjusting our questions and our answers as often as necessary in our exciting, sometimes overwhelming, and certainly ever-changing world.

EXERCISES

1. Use Figure 15.1, "Examples of Technologies to Try," as a model for a new table of emerging technologies that you may want to consider for ILI. With one or two partners, fill in the first column with the names of these technologies and add a brief description in the second column. Then, fill in the third column, "IL Usage Tips," with two or three ideas for each technology. Keep this table up to date by adding new technologies as they appear.
2. In which of these situations would you want to use technology to teach? What would be the advantages and disadvantages for each?
   a. F2F group instruction
   b. Individual instruction
   c. Distance/remote instruction
3. Which sorts of technology would you use for a group of 15? Which sorts of technology would you use for a group of 50? What would work best for formal distance education? What about informal asynchronous instruction for individuals?
4. Sample situation: You have 50 minutes to teach a group of learners how to think critically about social software, such as blogs, wikis, and virtual world simulations.
   a. Which technology or technologies would you want to use to engage a group of distance learners?
   b. What sorts of technology would you use to engage a group of F2F learners?
5. Pick a mashup or a virtual world simulation that would be useful for ILI. List two or three ELOs and describe how and why you would use it in ILI.

READ MORE ABOUT IT

Agre, Philip. "How to Help Someone Use a Computer" (1996). Available: http://polaris.gseis.ucla.edu/pagre/how-to-help.html (accessed December 28, 2008).

ALA. ACRL. Distance Learning Section. "Distance Learning Section" (January 16, 2008). Available: http://caspian.switchinc.org/~distlearn (accessed December 27, 2008).

Allen, I. Elaine and Jeff Seaman. "Online Nation: Five Years of Growth in Online Learning." Newburyport, MA: The Sloan Consortium (October 2007). Available: www.sloan-c.org/publications/survey/pdf/online_nation.pdf (accessed December 27, 2008).

Bernard, Robert M. et al. 2004. "How Does Distance Education Compare with Classroom Instruction? A Meta-analysis of the Empirical Literature." *Review of Educational Research* 74, no. 3: 379–439.

Chickering, Arthur W. and Stephen C. Ehrmann. 1996. "Implementing the Seven Principles: Technology as Lever" (October 1996). Available: www.tltgroup.org/programs/seven.html (accessed December 27, 2008).

Conrad, Rita-Marie and J. Ana Donaldson. 2004. *Engaging the Online Learner*. San Francisco: Jossey-Bass.

Dodge, Bernie. "A WebQuest About WebQuests" (September 10, 2000). Available: http://edweb.sdsu.edu/WebQuest/webquestwebquest-es.html (accessed December 27, 2008).

Educause Learning Initiative. "7 Things You Should Know About . . ." (2008). Available: www.educause.edu/ELI7Things/7495?bhcp=1&time=1225774460 (accessed December 28, 2008).

Farkas, Meredith G. 2007. *Social Software in Libraries*. Medford, NJ: Information Today.

Grassian, Esther et al. "BICO Task Force: Final Report." UCLA Library, Information Literacy Program (September 30, 2005). Available: http://repositories.cdlib.org/uclalib/il/04 (accessed December 28, 2008).

Mackey, Thomas P. and Trudi E. Jacobson. 2008. *Using Technology to Teach Information Literacy*. New York: Neal-Schuman.

NCAT. "Program in Course Redesign" (2005). Available: www.thencat.org/PCR.htm (accessed December 27, 2008).

Schrock, Kathy. "Critical Evaluation Surveys and Resources" (2008). Available: http://school.discoveryeducation.com/schrockguide/eval.html (accessed December 23, 2008).

TLT Group. "Seven Principles: Collection of Ideas for Teaching and Learning with Technology" (September 27, 2008). Available: www.tltgroup.org/seven/Library_TOC.htm (accessed December 27, 2008).

Webber, Sheila and Stuart Boon. "Information Literacy Weblog." Available: http://information-literacy.blogspot.com (accessed December 22, 2008).

Chapter 16

Teaching Online Tools and Resources

> *We no longer think of chairs as technology, we just think of them as chairs. But there was a time when we hadn't worked out how many legs chairs should have, how tall they should be, and they would often 'crash' when we tried to use them.*
>
> —Douglas Adams, 1999

TECHNOLOGY IMMERSION?

Technology surrounds many of us. We are so immersed in it that we hardly notice it any more except when it fails. Emergency crews of all sorts train for disasters with intercoms and cell phones. But when Hurricane Katrina hit New Orleans in 2005, emergency communications failed completely, with the exception of ham radio operators, leaving people lost, not knowing what to do or where to go (AARL, 2006). What sorts of information literacy (IL)–related technologies are people using? How does this impact information literacy instruction (ILI) in terms of learning effective, ethical use of online tools and resources?

In 2005, Educause's "Educating the Net Generation" described a cohort always connected to others through technology, speaking, listening, watching, texting and downloading using cell phones, iPods, digital cameras, and other technologies (Oblinger and Oblinger, 2005). Also in 2005, Dede described "mediated immersion" through learner participation in virtual environments and augmented reality as complements to "The standard 'world to desktop' interface . . ." (Dede, 2005: online). A year later, Tapscott and Williams (2006) described a global move to mass collaboration in a wiki-type economy, with many working on small chunks of problems posed as challenges.

Hinton took us a big step further in 2007, into the developing and expanding world of "Communities of Practice," describing the *Encyclopaedia Britannica* as an example of "instruction" handed down by experts, in contrast to Wikipedia, an example of "conversation." For Hinton and others, social networks, particularly voluntary "community of practice" subsets, represent conversations that focus on the conversation, and conversants learn how to improve the content of their discussion through interaction. These organic conversations, when "cultivated" (nourished and encouraged), often lead to practical innovation even within hierarchical structures (Hinton, 2007). We are now beginning to see dynamic and expanding uses of social networking on the Web, as we are told that Gen Y'ers are plugged in, multitask continually using many types of technology, and care most about what their friends think, as opposed to "experts" (Perez, 2008).

Also in 2007, two anthropologists at the University of Rochester published the results of a research study they conducted on the "Net Generation" of undergraduates at that institution. Their research question was, "What do students *really* do when they write their research papers?" (Foster and Gibbons, 2007: 1). They asked students for library design ideas and came up with five top findings. Students want flexibility, comfort, technology and tools, staff support, and resources, including traditional library materials. They also asked students to keep diaries of their activities and discovered eight common functions, including the fact that students do concentrated work between 10:00 p.m. and 1:00 a.m., study and use technology in many locations, but often do not carry laptops around with them. Despite their heavy reliance on technology, some in this cohort still preferred to print out articles and even their own papers in order to absorb and proofread them.

It is interesting to note that Foster and Gibbons (2007: 67), too, make much of Millennials' ability to multitask, claiming that these students think they can learn while doing other things, like listening to music: "This is such an important part of their lives that they may even think differently from previous generations." They acknowledge the fact that, although these students may be technologically sophisticated, they may not be skilled in communication and particularly may have short attention spans and poorer listening skills (Foster and Gibbons, 2007: 70). In addition, these students rely heavily on their parents for advice and guidance. Foster and Gibbons (2007) conclude that libraries need to continue to offer public computers for student use, should draw clear distinctions between computer labs and libraries, and should describe the librarian's role to students.

Even in regard to this cohort, however, some of the authors' conclusions and data are questionable. For instance, multitasking in itself is not new. College students of previous generations multitasked too, although in different ways, including reading, writing, and typing on typewriters while listening to music and enduring, or even welcoming, other distractions. Sadly, the authors also cite Wilder, assuming that his 2003 description of the average academic librarian is still correct. Finally, the authors claim that students like personal interaction, yet also state that "The student model of service is self-service" (Foster and Gibbons, 2007: 75), and, as mentioned earlier, they often turn to their parents for help. Despite these drawbacks to the study, there are lessons here for many types of libraries, including the importance of reaching out to parents, particularly for ILI. If we expand parents' ILI skills through school, academic, and public library ILI, we can leverage our limited librarian staff and add another important means of reaching this learner population.

A later study, by the British Library and JISC (2008: 9), reports that the "Researcher of the Future" looks for information in a very different way: "horizontal[ly], bouncing, checking and viewing in nature." The report goes on to say that children who comprise the "Google Generation" spend a lot of time speedily finding their way around the Web and not much time evaluating the information they find. According to the report, part of the problem is that young people do not have accurate mental models of what the Internet is, especially the variety of information providers, and have difficulty developing and adapting effective searches. The report concludes that libraries should work toward more integration with commercial search engines, design simpler and more visible Web sites, and use Amazon.com's successful search guidance as a model.

Again, there are valuable lessons to be learned here for ILI, and these are mostly admirable goals. However, the report also posits Google Scholar (2008) as a threat to libraries. It is true that we do not know the scope of Google Scholar's coverage. While this is a serious shortcoming, however, one can argue that Google Scholar's very existence is actually an asset to libraries for several reasons.

First, Google clearly distinguishes Google Scholar from general Google searching. This means that learners who use Google Scholar will already have the idea that doing a general Google search does not search all of the world's publications and Web sites. In itself, this concept can alter mental models, as it lays the foundation for introducing other databases, free and licensed. Second, it can also lead to related explanations of how to access scholarly materials through Google Scholar or other databases using authentication with a link resolver that allows users to get directly to copies of online materials if their library subscribes to them.

Finally, Google clearly reveres the concept of "scholarship," as it has set aside a special search for scholarly literature. Interestingly, this reverence for scholarship is in direct contrast to studies like those mentioned previously in this chapter that point out younger generations' reliance on mass opinion and the opinions of friends and parents rather than on experts' views and opinions.

Generation Y, the "Millennials," is a cohort born around 1977 through 2003 (Shaw, 2008). In 2002, Manuel reported that the over 70 million American Gen Y'ers want customized experiences, are easily bored, and prefer peer learning. A 2007 Pew Internet & American Life report provides some surprising data about this cohort, however. According to this report (Estabrook, Witt, and Raine, 2007: online), Gen Y'ers are "the most likely to use libraries for problem-solving information and in general patronage for any purpose" and 40 percent of Gen Y'ers indicated they would use libraries in the future if they had problems, as opposed to just 20 percent of those over 30. This last point, and Google's reverence for scholarship, both underscore the importance of avoiding generalizations and stereotyping of entire user populations based simply on their age.

These studies focus on particular age groups. Others have also studied and documented current and emerging education and technology trends among the general population. The January 2008 "Horizon Report" identifies seven "metatrends" that have appeared broadly over a five-year period (New Media Consortium and Educause, 2008: online):

- Communication between humans and machines
- Collective sharing and generation of knowledge
- Games as pedagogical platforms
- Connecting people through the network
- Computing in three dimensions
- Shifting content production to users
- Evolution of a ubiquitous platform

These metatrends illustrate and expand upon the Oblingers' 2005 observations and Hinton's 2007 premises. Many of us are living in the midst of a world that is very different from the pre-Web era. Online learning and the "Stay-at-Home Worker" microtrend (Penn and Zalesne, 2007) also are quickly becoming commonplace at many age and educational levels, thanks to increased access to computers and high-speed connectivity. Many of our users are whizzes at using Web search tools like Google, as well as cell phones and other devices. But are they information literate? What is the cost to society of their information illiteracy?

All of these studies help us understand and grapple with the technology-rich aspects of the world in which we live and their impacts on mindsets, teaching, and learning. The data and the trends they describe are fascinating but are not entirely surprising to many of us in ILI when we think about the concept of "technology" and its history in relation to teaching and learning, as described in Chapter 15. The hypnotic nature of technology can lead us to focus too heavily on technology-based online tools and resources as the source of all information and the answer to all ILI problems, regardless of the environment, the user population, their needs, their interests, their technology competencies, and their access to online tools and resources. We must resist the natural tendency to generalize results of studies that focus on specific cohorts, those born during particular time periods. Most libraries of all types have more than one learner population. In addition, some among our potential learner groups may be cut off from online tools and resources through poverty, ignorance, or both. (See Chapter 2 for a discussion of the digital divide.) Furthermore, in addition to those we normally think of as our user groups, we need to remember that librarian colleagues and other staff also comprise learner groups. They need to keep abreast of all sorts of online tools and resources, as well, in order to help people learn in employee training, during reference interactions, in group instruction sessions, and through design and development of instructional and training materials of all kinds. They just have to do this faster and on a larger scale than our typical user groups. ILI librarians face many challenges in this regard, on many levels, and for many different learner groups. The following series of questions may help focus attention on the areas we need to address regarding teaching online tools and resources.

First, what are we referring to when we talk about teaching IL-related online tools and resources? How can we learn for ourselves and then introduce our learners to IL-related online tools and resources, those utilized to seek or provide information? Finally, how can we help them learn to identify and make effective use of these tools and resources for their information needs?

ONLINE TOOLS AND RESOURCES AND INFORMATION LITERACY INSTRUCTION

Information seeking and provision occurs at all ages and educational levels. Libraries and information centers are all about identifying, gathering, collecting, and providing tools to access information. Some look for published materials, while others want unpublished items, in many formats, common and easily recognizable, as well as new and unusual. Books, newspaper, magazine, and journal articles are commonplace and familiar. Many libraries provide access to these materials online through their catalogs and free or licensed databases of articles. Reference tools, like encyclopedias, are also migrating online, with some published only online ("born digital").

When reference and research tools as well as other published materials were first available in computerized form, however, even just as text, both library staff and users were taken aback. Computers were a new phenomenon in libraries. They seemed scary and impersonal and consisted of "emerging technologies," beginning with CD-ROMs and later the Internet. First staff and then users had to learn what CD-ROMs were and how they worked. Then the Internet broadened the scope of online tools and resources enormously. When the Web came along, it pulled the rug out from under what had become familiar, "traditional" online tools and resources. We all needed to learn what the Web was and how it worked in order to make use of online tools and resources available through it. Now, the Web is familiar, and Web sites seem like "traditional" technology. As people got comfortable with the Web, new online tools and resources emerged, and this cycle continues.

In each case, when they emerged, new technologies seemed scary, confusing, and overwhelming to a number of people, including library staff. They were new and different. It was hard to know what purposes they might have. Sometimes they worked, and sometimes they did not. Features available in one did not appear in another that was supposed to do something similar. Interfaces differed widely and changed frequently. Some popped up and generated a lot of excitement and then disappeared. Others were absorbed into traditional online tools and resources, evolved, or combined with other emerging online tools and resources to create something even newer. How do we cope with all of these continuous changes ourselves and help our learners as well?

TEACHING "TRADITIONAL" VERSUS EMERGING TECHNOLOGIES

What kinds of traditional and emerging online tools and resources should librarians learn and teach? Which of these are available in or accessible through libraries? How can we hope to learn, feel comfortable with, and then teach an ever-vaster universe of "mutating" tools and resources, especially given our already overfull plates?

To some of us, teaching online tools and resources means teaching what many now consider more traditional information-researching technologies, such as the library catalog, licensed and free online databases, and online reference tools. Others focus on emerging technologies for ILI, such as social software, visual Web browsers (Kartoo, accessed 2008; Search-Cube, 2008; SearchMe, 2008; Viewzi, 2008), immersive learning environments through virtual worlds (Second Life, accessed 2008), and other technologies yet to be invented.

The list of emerging technologies, some of which we now label "Web 2.0," changes rapidly, though. Some become "traditional," more mainstream, while others may morph or meld into even newer online tools or resources, or even disappear altogether.

What is "Web 2.0"? Beginning around 2004, the label "Web 2.0" took hold to describe a more interactive, as opposed to passive, Web. In 2005, O'Reilly described seven different characteristics of this new approach:

1. The Web as Platform
2. Harnessing Collective Intelligence
3. Data is the Next Intel Inside
4. End of the Software Release Cycle
5. Lightweight Programming Models

6. Software Above the Level of a Single Device
7. Rich User Experiences

According to Peterson-Lugo (2006), Web 2.0 centers around interaction and participation and is "people-centric." Many "traditional" online tools and resources have evolved to include interactivity and participation by those on the connected side of the digital divide. There are many interactive online ILI tutorials with exercises and multiple-choice questions that individuals can utilize online. Some screencasting software, such as Camtasia Studio, allows you to insert interactive quiz questions within a video. Discussion boards embedded in course management systems like Moodle and Blackboard allow learners to post queries, responses, or comments for others in a group to see or comment upon themselves. Blogs, sequential online journals, also allow others to post comments. Wikis provide an online space where you can post documents, and others can edit them remotely.

What about the next step, Web 3.0, sometimes called the "Semantic Web"? In 2006, Markoff envisioned Web 3.0 as a kind of expert system where you could enter a question like the following and get an answer directly from the system: "I'm looking for a warm place to vacation and I have a budget of $3,000. Oh, and I have an 11-year-old child." A year later, Spalding offered a number of examples of Web 3.0 types of applications, including "StumbleUpon (2008)," with an expert system where you fill in a profile, and the system finds Web sites based on your profile, continually learning from your votes which sorts of sites you prefer. Spalding (2007) predicted much more of a focus on "People Search" in addition to automated software agents and expert systems.

A year later, Kiss (2008: online) wrote, "If web 2.0 could be summarized as interaction, web 3.0 must be about recommendation and personalisation." She goes on to explain that Web 3.0 focuses on improved technology that can make automated and personal recommendations based on data mining of collective actions and information. Kiss cites "Last.fm" (2008) as an example, a site that offers live streaming of music, along with discussion and community. It uses "scrobbling," an automated means of figuring out which music is most popular, simply by adding up the number of times people listen to each song on the site, and then the system recommends music to individuals based on this data analysis (Kiss, 2008). The *New York Times* reported on another example of a Web 3.0 development. SRI International has developed automated personal assistant software called "CALO," for "cognitive assistant that learns and organizes." The software acts like an efficient secretary, for business and entertainment, including scheduling and even filtering your e-mail for you (Markoff, 2008: online). This illustrates that Web 3.0 technology is entering the popular realm.

For the most part, ILI librarians have embraced online tools and resources, sooner or later. Some are eager to explore and utilize emerging online tools and resources for ILI, while others are content to wait and teach them after they become more mainstream and traditional. With both emerging and traditional online tools and resources, effective ILI involves helping users of all ages do the following:

- Gain access to and navigate a dizzying array of online tools, resources, and interfaces
- Distinguish among "visible" and "invisible" Web sites
- Think critically about all forms of information
- Use information effectively and ethically

It also requires ILI librarians to reach out to those who lack access to or are frightened and intimidated by the technologies they must use in or through libraries. This huge task keeps growing, too, as databases and interfaces proliferate. It becomes all the more difficult when some wrongly blame the victim—libraries and librarians—for the proliferation of databases and their many diverse and confusing interfaces (Wilder, 2005; Grassian, 2005).

In Chapter 5 we discussed library anxiety and its relationship to technophobia on the part of both learners and library staff. Demystifying technology of all sorts, including IL-related online tools and resources, can go a long way toward helping both you and the learners feel less anxious and stressed regarding technology. By removing or diminishing library anxiety and technophobia, you may feel more comfortable trying out technologies in order to support and improve your ILI goals. And learners will be more likely to use online tools and resources that are new to them.

In this chapter, we discuss methods for learning and teaching both traditional and emerging online tools and resources related to ILI in order to demystify them and to lower frustration and anxiety levels about them. We will provide examples and explanations throughout to help guide you through today's online tools and resources and give you some means of approaching tomorrow's.

History, Practice, and User Needs

In considering what sort of approach to take, begin by surveying the landscape. What sorts of ILI have librarians in your own institution or organization already prepared and utilized regarding IL-related online tools and resources? How do they prepare themselves and help their colleagues learn and then teach these tools and resources? What do other librarians use elsewhere? What do you, your colleagues, and your learners need and want to know? Ask other library staff to fill you in on your library's and your institution's ILI history and mission statements (see samples on the CD-ROM that accompanies this book) and to steer you to sample materials. Next, review some ILI literature and check ILI Web sites and instructional material at other libraries.

Then, try to find out exactly what your users do and do not know about ILI-related online tools and resources with which you are familiar and also what their knowledge and skills are regarding the technologies (hardware and software) required in order to utilize them. As emphasized in other chapters of this book, this means that you will need to take the preliminary steps necessary in designing all kinds of instructional programs: identify the audience and conduct one or more Needs Assessments. Then, based on the results of the Needs Assessments, write goals and objectives and expected learning outcomes (ELOs)—what you expect learners to know and be able to do following instruction. The goals, objectives, and ELOs, together, should incorporate critical thinking, assessment of learning, program evaluation, and a plan for ongoing revision based on assessment and evaluation results. For more on planning for ILI, see Chapter 7.

A fairly quick and nonthreatening way to do this is by means of self-assessments or checklists, although questions must be phrased carefully so that they focus on specifics. Examples include questions like the following:

- How would you rate your skills in using chat, on a scale of 1 (no chat skills) to 5 (very skilled at chat)?
- How skilled are you at distinguishing among types of Web sites, such as governmental, educational, or commercial, on a scale of 1 (no skills) to 5 (highly skilled)?

A self-assessment, of course, reflects only the user's own opinion of her or his skill levels. A pretest that asks users to demonstrate skills will reveal the actual mastery level of those skills. Whichever it is to be, it will be much easier to customize instruction to user needs and interests if the assessment instrument is distributed in advance and the results are used as input in deciding on instructional gaps and then determining goals and objectives or ELOs. Which online tools and resources should you learn and then teach? How can you do so in order to help your learners achieve ELOs for effective, ethical use of IL-related online tools and resources?

Teaching "Traditional" Information Literacy Instruction–related Online Tools and Resources

As mentioned earlier, ILI librarians often teach use of "traditional" online tools and resources, currently composed largely of library catalogs, free and licensed databases, and reference tools such as encyclopedias and dictionaries. Most libraries offer free access to their library catalogs in the physical library and remotely. Many libraries of all types also license databases for use by a defined user population within the physical library. A large number of these libraries also provide their cardholders with remote access to licensed databases. Can these users select databases appropriate to their information needs? Are they able to determine on their own how to use multiple interfaces? Do they know how to get to materials in a variety of formats, like PDF files, videos, and podcasts? What sorts of help do these libraries provide for remote users? Can users easily find and utilize the help provided remotely? It is important to keep in mind that just mounting databases or reference tools online does not automatically make them easy to use or understand. Likewise, users will not automatically benefit simply from having access to an increasing number of online tools and resources, in person or remotely. They may not even know why they should use library resources at all as opposed to using a general search engine, such as Google.

Starting with Yourself and Your Colleagues

You need to be proactive in learning IL-related online tools and resources for yourself so that you can teach them to others. Consider the following ideas and approaches for doing so.

Begin by listing the tools and resources you want to teach—those that will meet the learners' information needs and interests as identified in the Needs Assessment. Explore the universe of other free and licensed online tools and resources that might be useful for these purposes. Keep an eye on notices of new interfaces and emerging online tools and resources.

Check with colleagues in person and through listservs. Try to find a buddy, another librarian or computer trainer, and see if you can exchange knowledge and experience with online tools and resources on a regular basis. Ask more knowledgeable librarians to share what they know and their approaches, through one-on-one mentoring or by doing presentations for you and other staff

Be open to new online tools and resources. Make time to try them out, even if it is just one new online tool or resources each week. Share what you learn by reaching out to your colleagues. Ask them to teach you about online tools and resources too. Be on the lookout for other learning opportunities, workshops, programs, Webinars (interactive, Web-based seminars or sessions), and classes, face-to-face or asynchronous. Ask colleagues to recommend effective presenters.

Once you have settled the types of IL-related online tools and resources you want to teach, ask questions about them. If you are unfamiliar with them, try to answer the following:

- What is the scope and purpose of each?
- What are their basic and advanced features?
- What are the advantages and disadvantages of using basic features as opposed to advanced?
- What do you think might trip up your learners?
- What are some key points that will help your learners decide for themselves which of these tools and resources would be most useful for a particular information need?
- What are some good examples you can use with each?

If you have already used these tools and resources, try answering somewhat different questions:

- Has the scope or purpose changed in any way?
- Does the tool function in the way it did before?
- Have any features been added, deleted, or changed since you used them last?
- Are search fields defined in the same way?
- Can you identify features that are common to more than one tool?
- What has tripped up learners in the past that may continue to trip them up?
- Which points have helped learners in selecting the most useful tools and resources for their information needs?
- Which types of examples have worked well, and which have not?

JSTOR is a case in point here. It is a highly popular journal article database, fairly easy to use, and seems to include all journal articles in all disciplines. Many users are surprised to find out that it does not include the latest five to seven years of most of their journals, and it does not include all of the important journals in all disciplines. If users know about Google Scholar, they may be just as surprised to find out that it does not include all scholarly materials either.

Clearly, whether they are in the library or getting to library materials remotely, many users may need clear and simple help in selecting appropriate IL-related online tools and resources, including free as well as licensed databases. Can they simply rely on help from the vendors themselves?

Vendor Help

In general, vendors have improved their database online help features, adding some image captures of portions of screens along with related instructions in the mechanics of using the tool. Learners may also absorb some ILI lessons indirectly from vendor-provided help features. PubMed's online Help serves as an example. Learners may derive useful evaluative criteria regarding types of publications and research methodologies from the PubMed Quick Start "How do I search PubMed?" Here PubMed offers a brief segment on identifying and expanding upon key terms to search for a given topic. While this PubMed feature is useful, vendor-produced online help features are not always effective, as they are often overly lengthy and text heavy.

In addition, some online help may open in another window, forcing users to flip back and forth between windows in order to compare their own displays with the online help, if they know how to do that. Worse yet, some help comes only in the form of online videos, disadvantaging those with older (legacy) equipment and software and having limited or no ability to pause a video or replay a portion in order to hone in on a specific problem. Learners may find it difficult to apply what they learn about one database or system to others, too, especially when the same search labels, such as "Keyword," search some fields in one database and other fields in another. All of this makes effective use of a myriad of interfaces all the more taxing and stressful, even if the learner ends up selecting the most useful databases for a specific information need.

Vendor-provided help also does not delve directly into the value of their tool(s) in contrast to other sources of information. This is where you, the ILI librarian, can provide tremendous added value. Your contribution as an ILI librarian builds upon and expands beyond knowledge of the mechanics of use to cover critical ILI concepts. You know about and have probably used many different information-researching tools both in print and online formats. You know their scope, or you know which questions to ask regarding scope and where to look for answers. You can also compare the scope, structures, and interfaces of online tools with other related researching tools in a variety of formats. Let us explore some approaches to doing this effectively.

A Baseline Learning Approach

After Needs Assessment results are in and you have surveyed existing instructional materials regarding teaching technology, you may want to consider a baseline teaching/learning approach for your primary learner group(s). This approach focuses mainly on teaching the basics of the most highly used information-research–related tools available in the physical library and remotely in order to help people achieve particular competencies. As mentioned in other chapters, we need to remember that some segments of our user populations are not computer literate or may have very low computer literacy skills. Some may have skills only in using cell phones or other common household technologies. If learners are not computer literate, you may need to teach computer, Internet, and Web browser basics first. After learners have mastered these skills, they can move on to learning IL-related online tools and resources, beginning with those that are common and "traditional," including the library catalog, free and licensed databases, and online reference tools.

Once you have checked for basic mastery of computer and Web skills, you can address other learner needs and interests identified in your Needs Assessments. If your aim is to help people learn how to identify, locate, and evaluate books, for instance, you will need to teach the mechanics of getting to and using the library catalog, as well as critical thinking about what the library catalog contains and how to evaluate its search results. One way to do this is to compare the same search in Google and in the library's catalog, including the search limit options available in both, although Google's search limits appear only in the Advanced Search. Although it is limited to "Did you mean . . . ," Google's "fuzzy logic" can be an advantage over most library catalogs. Learners value suggestions like this for additional search terms, as they may find it difficult to come up with alternative search words for a given topic. Some suggest that learners would much appreciate suggestions for additional "see also" subjects to search from controlled vocabularies. These could be provided with library catalog results or through links to subject guides developed for courses (Mellinger and Nichols, 2006).

The Barclay Approach

Barclay (1995) primarily takes a "mechanics" approach to IL technology instruction. He recommends teaching users that there are standard features of many databases. You can search, display, and save, as well as get help online. This is an extremely useful basic introduction to any sort of instruction in the use of IL-related online tools and resources. It can help users make sense of an amorphous collection of these items and understand that there are similar concepts underlying many of them. It can also help the ILI librarian to make sense of these resources and tools by categorizing them as "full featured," that is, having all or most of a series of features, including "luxury" items as opposed to the "stripped down" variety with just the basics.

For instance, the "PsycINFO" (Cambridge Scientific Abstracts) interface is full featured. There are 55 different search fields ("anywhere," "keyword," "descriptors," "e-mail address," "number of references," etc.) in a range of time periods, and there are seven other limit categories, each with its own menu, including any of 16 different methodologies, such as "empirical studies" and "literature reviews."

On the other hand, Wilson's "Readers' Guide Retrospective" interface is fairly simple and basic, with fewer limit options. There are 14 search fields ("keyword," "subject," "personal author," "title," "historical subject," etc.), and just three categories of limits ("date," "document type," and "physical description"), though again, each limit category has a menu of choices. Yet both of these databases have certain common features. They both allow searching, they both allow the user to display and e-mail results, and the search interface, displays, and search history all look very much the same. In a brief instruction session or in a reference interaction, it is fairly simple to explain the common features of databases such as these and to focus attention on their differences instead—topic coverage, types of materials indexed, date coverage, limits available, and so on.

Each of these concepts or features has to do with how a database functions and what it is designed to do. It is tempting to take this "functional" road and offer simple, brief explanations of basic features and mechanics, which may in fact be all the learner can or needs to absorb in a short period of time. Brief as learning time may be, however, the librarian can and should insert critical thinking elements throughout, focusing on what is important to the learners. You might appeal to undergraduates, for instance, by emphasizing that they will save time and end up with better research papers if they learn and apply critical thinking criteria as they proceed through the research process.

In addition, PsycINFO and other databases, including Web of Science and Google Scholar, offer features popular with faculty, researchers, and graduate students and useful to undergraduates as well—links to the bibliographies for many items retrieved, as well as links to "cited by . . ." "Cited by . . ." are items published at a later date that list in their bibliographies the item you have retrieved. This means that viewing an article's references provides you with a look back in time at the evidence an author used to support her or his arguments in a publication. When you use the "cited by . . ." references, you are looking forward in time at other publications that later used this item as evidence to support their own arguments. This is one way to help learners grasp the flow of information and the process of scholarly communication, although you must impress upon them several points, including the fact that newer materials are cited less frequently and that the quantity of "cited by's" is not equivalent to the quality of a publication.

For free and licensed databases, Barclay's standard database features (searching, viewing results, saving results, and getting help online) may apply to many different information-research-related tools. In teaching the mechanics of use of an online database, you could also focus on how to get to the advanced search, which buttons to click in order to select an additional database for searching, what to enter for a keyword search, how to e-mail results, and how to view your search history, as well as how to request an item through interlibrary loan.

Specific usage options may vary greatly, however, from one database or system to another. You may use full Boolean searching in some, while others may only allow use of "and." In addition to searching for materials, displaying results, and getting some sort of help online, some go further and allow you to limit searches, sort results, establish personal profiles, save lists beyond the current session, e-mail individual items or lists, and connect or link to other databases or Web sites, including online periodicals. Truncation is available in some but not in others, and, unfortunately, truncation symbols still vary from one system to another. Limits differ widely in type and number, as do subject headings or descriptors. Of course, the more standardization and the more generic the concepts we can define, the easier it will be for people to learn, as they will be able to transfer what they know about using one tool to another. For instance, increasingly, we are seeing sets of several search boxes in advanced database searching, with drop-down menus of search fields and Boolean operators between each box, as well as a range of search limits that appears below the search boxes. Save, e-mail, download, and export options increasingly include a choice of citation styles. Many databases also include the complete text of items indexed or link resolvers, allowing learners to locate online or print copies of items they have retrieved in searching that database.

For better or worse, though, link resolvers are blurring the distinction somewhat between Google Scholar and licensed databases, as they may allow you to go directly to an online copy of an article, bypassing those databases and the library catalog completely. This is a great benefit to learners, but the learner then may not know that the material is online because the library subscribes to it. In our efforts to make it quicker and easier for people to get the material they want, sometimes we shortchange ourselves and miss opportunities to make it clear to learners that some of the materials they find online are not free to everyone. This is true for Google Scholar, too, in spite of the fact that you need to set its preferences for your institution in order to see link resolvers and get directly to many articles online. In general, we need to do a better job of publicizing and promoting the library's role in making these materials available and brand them prominently. (See Grassian and Kaplowitz, 2005, Chapter 7, "Marketing, Publicity, and Promotion," for more on branding.)

Given all of this, there is no question that users still need to know the mechanics of using a variety of different interfaces or they will be unable to use the many online information resources we have so generously made available to them. Web instructional designers, with all good intent, often make some basic assumptions about users' skills and knowledge, however, including easy access to the latest Web browser software, up-to-date hardware with high-capacity graphics, and facility with using a mouse. As we acknowledged in Chapter 5 in our discussion of library anxiety, discomfort with or fear of using hardware and software can stop a person in her or his tracks and block out any additional information you may wish her or him to learn, including database content, structure, and critical thinking about online resources. However, in today's world, technology competency, especially computer literacy, is a prerequisite to gaining information literacy competency, and this is where the computer trainer can be of great help.

Partnership with a computer trainer can mean that users get a solid foundation in basic mechanics of computer use and will then be prepared to move on to IL competency taught by a librarian. Three-way collaboration with technical staff, instructors, and librarians can be even more powerful (Mackey and Jacobson, 2008).

Computer trainers can teach many of the mechanics of use of free and licensed databases as well as other sorts of technologies. They can also draw users' attention to some of the more obvious similarities and differences among different types of technologies. However, the librarian's instructional role is quite distinct from that of the computer trainer in some ways. Your unique contribution lies in identifying and learning about online tools and resources that relate to IL and then teaching learners which of them to use, for which purpose, how to think critically about these tools and resources, and how to use them effectively and ethically. You can do this by helping learners get in the habit of posing critical thinking questions.

In relation to databases, for instance, you may want to pose provocative questions, such as:

- Who created a particular online index, and how did they decide which journals or other publications to index?
- How did they decide which words to use as subjects, descriptors, or "library tags"?
- Why does the number of "cited by . . ." items differ in Google Scholar and in licensed databases?

The idea is that information tools do not simply appear out of thin air. People make decisions about which items are indexed, topics and time period covered, limits available, structure, means of access and use, how information will be labeled, displayed and laid out in an information tool, how it will be retrieved and saved or exported, etc. Whether intended or not, these are political decisions that impact how information seekers search for information and what sorts of information they can find readily. Figures 16.1 and 16.2 are examples of exercises you can use to help people learn these points. Figure 16.1, a "high-tech" approach, requires learners to use a wiki with live links to databases and Web sites, while Figure 16.2 offers a "low-tech" approach, utilizing paper notecards. For more on critical thinking, see Chapter 5.

Transitioning to Emerging Technologies

Critical thinking about online tools and resources includes identifying their commonalities, as well as their differences, as discussed earlier in this chapter. For many learners, beginning with commonalities helps both in understanding underlying concepts and in mastering mechanics of use. This is true especially if you can use a familiar tool or action and compare it to a new tool or action (see Chapter 6 for more on mental models and conceptual change).

This can be a challenge, however, as emerging online tools and resources can be quite different from traditional IL-related online tools and resources both in intent and in functionality. New and expanding uses for hardware, like mobile devices, for instance, present additional challenges and opportunities, especially because they are becoming ubiquitous (Corbeil and Valdes-Corbeil, 2007). Many applications are being developed or adapted to run on and send messages to mobile devices. For instance, you can text citations from some library catalogs to a mobile device (Reinhardt, 2008). You can go to a physical library looking for books on a shelf, and check a library catalog while standing at bookshelves, by using a Web browser on your mobile device. You can get the library catalog homepage by going directly to that URL or by going through a social networking site, such as Facebook. Other traditional IL-related online tools and resources, too, are transitioning to social networking approaches, moving to adapt to altered expectations and ways to get to and utilize information. Federated and faceted searching methods are examples of this evolution.

Federated and Faceted Searching

Full federated searching (across a library's many databases, systems, and other online materials) and faceted searching (single results list with options to view results by type of material, by date, by topic, and more) allow you to identify items in areas you may not have thought of searching. When a vendor like Cambridge Scientific Abstracts (CSA) provides access to many different databases, users can cross-search CSA databases simultaneously, conducting "federated searching" within a system.

Both federated and faceted search interfaces are intended to save time and lessen confusion over which information tool to use and how to use a variety of individual interfaces for each of many different databases. They may be helpful to some; however, both federated and faceted searching can be problematic as well. On the positive side, federated searching can save users' time and may retrieve interesting and useful results they did not anticipate. This kind of cross-searching also supports and enhances multidisciplinary and interdisciplinary approaches to topics. Faceted searching may offer additional help to some, as it provides a variety of means of focusing search results by broad category or specific topic, type of material, date

Figure 16.1 Small Group Exercise Using a Wiki

1. Prepare three to five wiki documents with links to a variety of sources on each, such as the following:
   a. Licensed database
   b. Library catalog
   c. Blog
   d. Google Scholar
   e. Flickr
   f. Freely available commercial Web site
   g. Freely available government Web site
2. Divide the audience or class into small groups, and assign one of the wiki pages to each group.
3. Ask the groups to take ten minutes to do the following:
   a. Look at all of the sites on their wiki page.
   b. Figure out what each tool does, and describe it on the wiki in a few words.
   c. Label each with a category. (Learners are free to use any categorization they like.)
   d. List the most important features to look for when evaluating an item that fits into these categories.
4. Ask groups to report back and then discuss your own descriptions, categories, and critical thinking criteria, which can include the following:
   a. Sample descriptions:
      i. PsycINFO database
         Lists articles with abstracts
      ii. UCLA Library Catalog: UCLA Libraries & Collections
         Lists library books and subscriptions to periodicals
      iii. Academic Search Complete database
         Lists magazine and journal articles with abstracts and many articles fully online
      iv. "Mr. William Shakespeare and the Internet" (see Gray, 2009)
         Provides links to full text of works and much other Shakespeare-related information
      v. Flickr
         Allows you to tag and share images with others
   b. Sample general categories (see Figure 16.2 for sample subcategories):
      i. Software
      ii. Web sites
      iii. Social software (for various purposes)
      iv. Formats
      v. Intent
      vi. Audience
   c. Critical thinking criteria—For each, the prime evaluative criteria are the following:
      i. Topics covered
      ii. Types of materials indexed, listed, or provided in full
      iii. Dates of coverage
      iv. Authority or expertise

Figure 16.2 Small Group Exercise Using Notecards

1. Divide the audience or class into small groups. Provide each group with 3 × 5 notecards, each of which has an information tool written on it with a few words of description, for example:
   a. PsycINFO database
      Lists articles with abstracts
   b. UCLA Library Catalog: UCLA Libraries & Collections
      Lists library books and subscriptions to periodicals
   c. Academic Search Complete database
      Lists magazine and journal articles with abstracts and many articles fully online
   d. "Mr. William Shakespeare and the Internet" (see Gray, 2009)
      Provides links to full text of works and much other Shakespeare-related information
   e. Flickr
      Allows you to share images with others
2. Give the groups three minutes to sort their cards into categories and label each category. Categories can include the following:
   a. Article indexes
   b. Web sites
   c. Web search tools
   d. Full-text works
   e. Library catalog
3. Ask the groups to take ten minutes to do the following:
   a. Look at all of the sites on their cards.
   b. Figure out what each tool does, and write a brief description of it.
   c. Label each with a category. (Learners are free to use any categorization they like.)
   d. List the most important features to look for when evaluating an item that fits into these categories.
4. Ask the groups to report back, and then discuss your own descriptions, categories, and critical thinking criteria, which can include the following:
   a. Categories:
      i. Software
      ii. Web sites
      iii. Social software (for various purposes)
      iv. Formats
      v. Intent
      vi. Audience
   b. Critical thinking criteria:
   - Topics covered
   - Types of materials indexed, listed, or provided in full
   - Dates of coverage
   - Authority or expertise

range, author, and more. Valuable as these features may be, they still may not address a major concern regarding federated searching. Users may not be aware of the scope of a federated search, and there may be too many choices offered in faceted searching, displayed in a confusing, complicated-looking list rather than in tabbed format.

Additional disadvantages include difficulty in understanding that individual databases may utilize different controlled vocabularies, may cover different time periods, and may offer different types of search limits. Federated searching can be slower than using a general search engine like Google, too, and its use may involve many additional steps before you can actually retrieve the text of an item (Wrubel and Schmidt, 2007). Results may not include full citations, and search history may be lacking, in addition to other drawbacks (Williams, 2005). Learners often confront an intermingled list of results, with many choices for sorting and subdividing, too many for some, who may give up entirely (see Chapter 6 for more on thinking critically about federated searching).

Beyond the Baseline . . . Teaching Emerging Online Tools and Resources

From the previous discussion, we can see that our users need help in selecting and making effective use of a variety of information-researching tools. As researching tools and libraries move from their own silos and into newer technologies, such as social networking sites, the technological landscape is becoming increasingly complex and confusing to many, librarians and learners alike. We see traditional online tools and resources like library catalogs juxtaposed with or accessed through rapidly developing technologies, including social networking tools. We still need to provide help in learning effective, ethical use of these traditional online tools. Now we may need to add a layer by helping our learners get to these IL-related tools through social networking interfaces.

More often than not, social networking sites emphasize the "social." Users register and provide some kind of personal information in the form of a profile. Each profile may include photos of the registered user and lists and photos of others who have signed up for the same site (Boyd and Ellison, 2007). Some of these sites, such as Facebook, offer many different uses and applications, such as messaging, community building through groups, games, and surveys. Increasingly, these sites are opening themselves up to cross-usage but with traditional and other emerging tools and resources. For instance, in addition to library catalogs, you can access some licensed databases like JSTOR when logged into Facebook. Of course, your institution must have a licensing agreement with JSTOR, and you will have to be authenticated in order to use it. This means you may need to provide some kind of identification that will prove to the system that you are a member of the licensed community, such as a library card number or an ID and password. In some cases, you may first need to set up your Web browser so that it directs your database usage request to your institution's or organization's proxy server, a computer that will send you a request for authentication before allowing you to make use of that licensed database.

In LinkedIn (2008), a business-oriented social networking site, those in your network can view the presentation slide shows you have uploaded to Slideshare (2008). Other social networking sites include social bookmarking tools like del.icio.us and image-sharing tools like Flickr (2008), where you can view and learn about Web sites, images, and other materials valued by other users. In many social networking sites like these, you can tag items with words that have meaning to you. Some sites are set up to display "tag clouds," which indicate visually which are the most popular tags, often by displaying them in a larger font size than other tags. Collections of tags are called "folksonomies," user-created subject taxonomies (Gordon-Murnane, 2006). For more details about technologies like these, see Figure 15.1 in Chapter 15.

What are the implications for ILI? Should we focus our ILI efforts on popular social networking sites? If so, are we invading largely personal social arenas and leaving behind other learners who do not use these kinds of sites? How do our learners do information research, and what sorts of trends do we see in relation to evolving technology?

If your learners are familiar with them, you can

use tags and folksonomies to explain the concept of controlled vocabularies. The "Library of Congress' photostream" on Flickr includes "No known copyright restrictions" under each of its photos (U.S. Library of Congress, 2008). You can use this phrase to start a discussion about copyright and intellectual property. You can also use "pedias" created with wikis, like Conservapedia (accessed 2008) and Uncyclopedia (2008) in order to help people learn about the importance of identifying the purpose and point of view of a site. VoiceThread (2008), a multimedia site, offers other ILI possibilities. Take an IL-related slide show, image, or video, upload it, and invite learners to identify IL concepts or provide critical comments on it in text, audio, or video.

Some online tools can even help you learn different teaching techniques, or you may find instructional materials others have created that would work well for one of your own learner groups. For yourself, consider the elementary school level video *Power Teaching Critical Thinking AMAZING STUDENT ENGAGEMENT!* mounted on TeacherTube (2008). In this video, the teacher describes four levels of critical thinking and asks the students to teach these levels to each other in small chunks (CBiffle, 2008). Or, consider the presentation slide show and Word document outline, both mounted on Slideshare.net, "Wikipedia, YouTube & Information Literacy" (Grassian, 2008d, 2008e). Here you can find examples of how to use these tools and others for ILI, including "WikipediaVision" (Kozma, 2008). See Figure 15.1 in Chapter 15 for more ideas on using emerging technologies for ILI.

These new tools are exciting and fascinating. However, ILI librarians need to do more than just stand by and watch as technology unfolds. We need to be active participants in experimenting with and advising on how to improve new technologies for our own use and that of our users and learners.

FINAL REMARKS

We face a societal continuum of use of emerging versus more traditional online tools and resources. More technologically skilled users may still need to learn how to identify, locate, evaluate, and make effective and ethical use of information tools and resources for a particular need, perhaps more so through the use of technologies. Less technologically skilled users may need more help, first in the basics of using even more traditional technologies like online catalogs and then with use of these technologies within social networking tools or on mobile devices.

ILI librarians cannot do it all alone, as the world of information resources continues to expand geometrically. Partnering with computer trainers, instructors, and colleagues is practically essential these days, but just wishing for an ideal partnership will not make it happen. We need to be proactive and take the first step toward open and generous sharing of our materials and our expertise, at all levels and in all sorts of environments (school libraries, special libraries and information centers, organizations, businesses, government libraries, academic libraries, public libraries, etc.) (Mackey and Jacobson, 2008; see also Grassian and Kaplowitz, 2005, Chapter 3, "Embracing Cooperation and Change").

As our world relies more and more on computers, the Web, and connectivity, many more individuals and institutions within and beyond libraries worldwide are recognizing the need for an information literate populace. Partnering with others can help us help our learners achieve this goal.

EXERCISES

1. Find an IL-related online tool or resource that is new to you. Label it as "traditional" or "emerging," and write a paragraph justifying your classification. Learn this online tool or resource yourself. Then develop an outline for teaching your colleagues how to teach it.
2. Interview a computer trainer and an ILI librarian about their method(s) of teaching the use of new online tools and the learning outcomes they expect. Compare and contrast their approaches and ELOs.
3. Deconstruct and critique the following exercise for users by:
   a. Identifying the ELOs
   b. Identifying the instructional methodologies
   c. Describing how their use can support the pedagogy

   End with your prediction of the effectiveness of this exercise in achieving the ELOs.

Individual User/Large Group Exercise

People use the Internet in a variety of ways, some of which are questionable, if not controversial. In the February 2008 issue of *Wired*, Mathew Honan reported that he and other bloggers sometimes get paid to write favorably about topics. In one case, a librarian paid him $10 through a site called PayPerPost (2008) to discuss on his blog "how librarians 'can help you make sense of a confusing world where information providers have all sorts of differing agendas'" (Honan, 2008: online). He did not have a problem with this. Bring to class an example of Internet use that illustrates a controversial or questionable use of the Internet. Be prepared to share your example and discuss it with the class.

READ MORE ABOUT IT

Barclay, Donald A. 1995. "Teaching the Standard Features of Electronic Databases." In *Teaching Electronic Information Literacy: A How-To-Do-It Manual* (pp. 57–75), edited by Donald A. Barclay. New York: Neal-Schuman.

Boyd, Danah M. and Nicole B. Ellison. 2008. "Social Network Sites: Definition, History, and Scholarship." *Computer-mediated Communication* 13, no. 1: 210–230. Available: www3.interscience.wiley.com/cgi-bin/fulltext/117979376/PDFSTART (accessed December 27, 2008).

British Library and JSIC. 2008. "Information Behaviour of the Researcher of the Future" (January 11, 2008). Available: www.twine.com/_b/download/1y8bplft-4x/b0bsl79jx59rwtw7lr978psshbdk7tsxlb1w4wlpmfhprmt/1y8bplft-4x/b0bsl79jx59rwtw7lr978psshbdk7-tsxlb1w4wlpmfhprmt/gg_final_keynote_11012008.pdf (accessed December 22, 2008).

Corbeil, Joseph Rene and Maria Elena Valdes-Corbeil. 2007. "Are You Ready for Mobile Learning?" *Educause Quarterly* 30, no. 2: 51–58.

Gordon-Murnane, Laura. 2006. "Social Bookmarking, Folksonomies, and Web 2.0 Tools." *Searcher* 14, no. 6: 26–38.

Grassian, Esther. "Wikipedia, YouTube, IL 9 20 08" (September 20, 2008). Available: www.slideshare.net/estherg/wikipedia-you-tube-il-9-20-08-presentation (accessed November 23, 2008).

———. "Wikipedia, YouTube & Information Literacy" (September 9, 2008). Available: www.slideshare.net/estherg/wikipedia-youtube-information-literacy-presentation (accessed November 23, 2008).

Mackey, Thomas P. and Trudi E. Jacobson. 2008. *Using Technology to Teach Information Literacy*. New York: Neal-Schuman.

Mellinger, Margaret and Jane Nichols. "Subject Search Disconnect: Or, How Do Our Users Want to Search for Subject Information." *Oregon Library Association Conference*. Salem, Oregon, April 12, 2006. Available: http://hdl.handle.net/1957/1642 (accessed December 27, 2008).

Tapscott, Don and Anthony D. Williams. 2006. *Wikinomics: How Mass Collaboration Changes Everything*. London, England: Penguin Books.

Part V

The Future of Information Literacy Instruction

Chapter 17

Visions of the Future: Two Perspectives

ESTHER S. GRASSIAN'S PERSPECTIVE

Have we solved the riddle of effective information literacy instruction (ILI) for you? I think not. Riddles are perplexing. Some are unsolvable, while others require time for concentrated thought, consultation, collaborative effort, and experimentation. Instead of solutions, we have tried to provide you with tools and techniques to help you think about and solve a variety of ILI riddles for yourself, within your own environment and circumstances. In the 2001 edition of this book, I proposed three principles to guide you in solving the riddle of effective ILI: patience and respect for the past, judicious use of technology as a tool, and joy in empowering all learners. As you use the tools and techniques we describe in this book, and as you discover or invent others, I hope you keep these abiding principles in mind.

Patience and Respect for the Past

In this impatient world it may seem incongruous to suggest slowing down a bit, waiting, building relationships within and beyond your own library, collaborating with others, and letting people think about, discuss, and debate new ideas. If you slow down, will opportunities pass you by? Technology does not stand still while you consider positives, negatives, and costs, and past experiences cannot mean anything now in a world where technology permeates or impacts almost everything we say, do, or encounter. Or can they? How can you respect and learn from the past, while moving forward?

As you look into and experiment with new approaches to instruction, take the time to investigate and document what worked well in the past rather than discarding everything and starting completely afresh. What can you learn from your colleagues in your own institution or elsewhere? Have they tried pre- and post-testing? How about online or face-to-face (F2F) interactivity? Have they developed or adapted exercises, workbooks, tutorials, or videos? Have they experimented with learner-centered instruction? Have you observed their instructional techniques, examined their instructional materials, talked to them, and listened carefully to what they have to say about the benefits and drawbacks of their approaches to teaching and learning? What can you learn from your colleagues within and beyond your library, and how can you work with them in moving forward rather than operating within your own silo?

You may know a lot about present capabilities, but your patient and respectful queries can uncover invaluable treasures that may be reused or reformulated to fit new uses. Did your library run a successful print workbook program? Can you develop an online tutorial with interactive exercises and videos that helps learners achieve the same expected learning outcomes (ELOs)? Can you get some feedback from learners on how to experiment with turning a F2F credit course or a workshop into blended instruction, part online and part in person? Which of your learner populations would prefer to learn from printed materials as opposed to videos, live chat at a time of need, or Web sites, such as research guides?

Document what you learn, old and new, and share with your colleagues. Help them learn about uses, benefits, and drawbacks of new technologies. Look into adapting Blowers' (2006a) Learning 2.0 "23 things" approach to staff training. Publicly honor your staff's achievements, small and large. Ask for their advice and invite them to join you in experimenting with new approaches to supporting pedagogical goals, perhaps through an ILI team designed to experiment with new technologies for this purpose. Be prepared to fail, to acknowledge your failure, and to learn from it as you continue to experiment, revise, and reach out to others. Openness, sharing, and respectfully bringing your colleagues along with a smile and a warm, encouraging, helpful attitude can go a long way toward success with ILI endeavors of all kinds.

Judicious Use of Technology as a Tool

Many of us continue to be caught up in an endless cycle of new and upgraded technology. Some worry about being replaced by e-reference and e-learning commercial enterprises if we do not jump on each new form of technology as it comes along. Some are hooked on change, constantly seeking the next new technological high. This new world is enticing and so bedazzling that it is difficult to look away and think about our purpose. Why are we using technology to teach? What pedagogical goals does it support? Which forms of technology would best meet our needs? Would it be better in some cases simply to interact on a personal basis, face to face? Or can we interact just as effectively in a pseudo-F2F way through virtual worlds or other synchronous methods, such as live chat? Must we continue to fight a reference vs. instruction battle? Instead, can we simply consider all of public service on a continuum, from signage to tours, to reference in all of its formats, through F2F group instruction, individual research consultations, asynchronous online tutorials, social networking communities, and more?

New technology may be able to help us improve all of our instructional efforts along the entire continuum, as long as we keep our pedagogical goals and the learners' ELOs at the forefront. What do your learners already know, and what do they need to know? What do you expect them to gain from ILI of any sort? How will you tell that they have achieved those ELOs? How will you adjust your ILI in order to help your learners do a better job of achieving ELOs the next time, or how will you adjust those ELOs in order to make them more realistic? For example, does it seem as though learners remember only that there is an ILI Web page for their class and nothing else from your one-shot group sessions? You can use technology to see if your impression is correct. Ask faculty/teachers to put a link to a pre- and posttest on the class Web page. Before the session, ask learners to take the pretest. A month after your instructional session, ask learners to take the posttest. Compare the results to the pretest and you will have your answer. Remember that synchronous one-shot group instruction is just one of many viable instructional formats. It may work well in some instances and not in others, or it may just be an approach your library cannot afford to continue, with limited staff and budget and large numbers of learners.

Just remember that you are in control of technology and of the instructional formats you choose. You can do your best to make it all work for you and for your learners. As long as you focus on your destination, the learning outcomes you expect to see and their retention, you will maintain power over your technological tools and can apply them to support your pedagogical goals.

Joy in Empowering All Learners

ILI is also supposed to empower learners so that they have control over information tools and know how to learn on their own. It is easier to do this when learners have widespread high-speed access to the Internet as more and more information tools appear online daily. But how do we help the Internet have-nots and the newbies? We need to make Internet access a part of everyone's life and then help our user populations progress further so that they learn to think critically about online tools and the items they create, identify, or retrieve through those tools. Basically, we need to help them learn to question information they receive or retrieve on their own in order to help them become fully functioning members of a democratic society.

Can you make this happen? Yes! ILI librarians like you, from all sorts of environments, have worked to develop standards and objectives that define information literacy (IL) in measurable terms. As we mentioned in Chapter 2, accrediting agencies in the United States now include reference to ILI-related concepts in accreditation standards for schools and colleges. Worldwide, we see IL rising in consciousness, with governments of various countries, as well as UNESCO, joining IFLA and other groups to train IL trainers. InfoLit Global, SOS for Information Literacy, and other databases now collect and make available free lessons and other teaching/learning materials. You can draw on these databases and on the collective advice and wisdom of others through listservs, publications, conferences, workshops, and social networking communities of those interested in IL and instruction in general. Your contributions to these databases and groups can also help others, as we share our experiences and build on those of others (Tapscott and Williams, 2006).

In 2001, I speculated that one day the SAT and GRE would measure IL competencies. Now there are several standardized tests that do just that, including iSkills, developed by the Education Testing Services, the very company that offers the SAT and GRE tests. Currently, none of the IL standardized tests is required for college admission or for employment, although one can only hope that in this complex and data-driven world IL competency will be a requirement at some point and will be tested in some fashion. How else will learners prepare themselves for jobs that do not yet exist? They will need to learn how to solve problems, how to think critically, and how to learn how to learn for themselves and on their own. While some may think they already do this by experimenting with new technologies, do they know which sorts of questions to ask regarding authority, accuracy, currency, and completeness? Where will they learn these skills and how? Challenge the learners to work with you in helping them and other learners achieve core ELOs that can be applied to all sorts of new situations and technologies.

It is our role and our privilege to work toward these goals, to bring information power to everyone through IL, especially underrepresented minority groups and the impoverished, those whom the Consumer Federation of America labeled the "Disconnected, Disadvantaged, and Disenfranchised" (Cooper, 2000).

The Solution?

After reading this book, I hope you see that there is no one solution and that there may not be one instructional program that will meet all of your learners' needs. You, your colleagues, faculty/teachers, your learners, and your administrators alone can answer questions such as: "How can we adapt these lessons to our environment?" "What can we learn from past experiences?" "What are the newest questions?" "How can we continue to create new opportunities for learning and teaching in our swiftly evolving technological world?" and "How can we best support, assess, revise, and improve what we do?"

In the end, ILI is still what you make of it. You will need to decide for yourself when continuous change becomes change for its own sake, how you will judge the effectiveness of instruction, which instructional modes will best suit your environment and circumstances, whether or not to create a single program or a multipronged one that can flex with shifting needs and circumstances, and when to let go of a mode that is no longer effective. You can create collegial coalitions by building on the past, by working in the present, and by looking to the future. You have the power to transform and empower your learners through ILI, and I am confident that you will.

JOAN R. KAPLOWITZ'S PERSPECTIVE

When the first edition of this book came out in 2001, I looked into my crystal ball and predicted that "The more things change, the more they will remain the same." I envisioned that new and unexpected technologies would continue to transform our lives. I expected that people would become even more overwhelmed by the vast amounts of information available to them and that they would continue to need information professionals to help them navigate this complex and often confusing landscape. All of this has come to pass, but some new issues have also materialized.

Power, Politics, and Information Literacy Instruction

This first one is not so much a new idea but more a reframing of a continuing problem—that of the image of the information professional. Will ILI instructors be seen as relevant in this rapidly changing world? We can be, but only if we dedicate ourselves to keeping up with the issues. I believe to fully leverage the current interest in ILI, librarians must re-examine their views of information in the modern world. Technological and cultural forces have caused a shift in the organization and classification of knowledge from a hierarchical, classified scheme to one that is more fluid and flexible and is rooted in personal or personalized meaning (Pawley, 2003; Shapiro and Hughes, 2001; Williams, 2007). In order to promote IL to our users, we need to understand how they behave in this nonlinear world—how they are making decisions as they follow the links they are uncovering. We must help them make more informed decisions about the pathways they follow and about the information they are finding regardless of format (Bates, 1989; Bodi, 2002; Swanson, 2004). And we need to help them to understand not only what information is available but also how it is created and where it is stored (Swanson, 2004). The concepts of text, knowledge, and authority are now in question as people become empowered to be active participants and contributors to the information culture (Kapitzke, 2001; Pawley, 2003; Reed and Stravreva, 2006).

Even more importantly, we must teach our learners that information does not exist in a vacuum. It is the product of the social, cultural, and historical environments in which it resides—an environment that is constantly changing (Swanson, 2004). What is "true" today may not be viewed as such tomorrow. Moreover, what is "true" is often defined by the dominant culture and is disseminated through the educational process. Diverse voices may be overlooked or ignored in favor of more established "truths." Education is in many ways a political act. Even John Dewey (1916) in his classic work *Democracy and Education* said one of the main functions of school was assimilation—teaching children how to behave in our society. But who defines that behavior? And who defines what is "acceptable" information and knowledge? Higher education serves as the means to acculturate students into a discipline and the ways that information is organized within that discipline. Freire (2002) called this the banking model in which educators and researchers deposit into the knowledge bank and students make withdrawals from it. This banking model conflicts with the more learner-centered, critical thinking approaches currently favored in higher education and ignores the reality that people are now both creators and consumers of information (Elmborg, 2004). The nature of the Internet with its blogs, wikis, and social networking encourages people to interact with information, not just absorb it (Shapiro and Hughes, 2001; Tapscott and Williams, 2006; Weinberger, 2007).

Librarians over the years have tended to concentrate on the "access" and "locate" aspects of the search process in part because access and location tools resided with us in the physical library or were connected to us via the online library environment. However, as these tools continue to grow in number, complexity, and diversity, even librarians (especially those in very large libraries) may have trouble remembering all of the tools they have access to and the many nuances of using these tools. Librarians also have taken on the task of helping learners understand the issues surrounding intellectual property and plagiarism, again because these issues seem so closely aligned with our expertise. Will ILI librarians continue to teach our learners how to locate and search for information and how to use it ethically once they find it? Of course they will. But while it is certainly important for people to understand the differences between types of materials and resources and how to use them efficiently and ethically, we must also encourage our learners to look at the nature of information itself and begin to ask themselves critical questions about its creation. Who created that information? And perhaps even more important, what motivated them to create it? We need to help learners realize that context is every bit as important as content when evaluating the worth of any information they uncover—regardless of whether it is a book, journal article, Web site, wiki, blog, or some new format yet to come. We need to expand our instructional goals for ILI to include discussions about how information is created and disseminated and how through discourse and social cognition that information turns into what society views as knowledge (Kapitzke, 2001, 2003; Pawley, 2003; Reed and Stravreva, 2006; Swanson, 2004). Although thinking critically about information has always been part of what librarians taught, it is even more important in a world where information is viewed as a commodity and when understanding the creation, use, political implications, and influential nature of information is crucial to function in a global economy.

Our Information Is Out There—Information Literacy Instruction and Privacy Issues

As I predicted in the first edition of this book, technology has continued to evolve and to become an even more pervasive aspect of just about everyone's life. We not only search for information on the Internet, we keep in touch with our friends and family via e-mail and social networking sites. We shop, renew our library books, keep track of our appointments, and pay our bills online. Our hand-held devices allow us to talk and text to others, listen to music, and watch videos. They can connect us to the Internet and provide us with driving directions should we lose our way. Web sites that we frequent send us "suggestions" about items that may be of interest to us based on previous activity on that site. If we buy our prescription drugs online, we may get e-mails reminding us when we need to renew. Want to know what is the hottest, latest thing? You can check Google Trends (2008) to find out what keywords are most being searched on a daily basis—some of them even broken down by geographical regions. How wonderful and convenient it all is. But is there a hidden price? How much and what kind of personal information is being stored about each and every one of us? And who has access to this information? Although we assume that the sites we use are "secure," we cannot be sure that this is really so. If the information is out there, someone who is really motivated to find it can probably do so.

And if that were not scary enough, look around you as you travel through your daily life. Security cameras are everywhere—at traffic lights, ATM machines, in public garages and parking lots, and in many buildings. And let us not forget that the wonderful GPS devices that we have in our cars and in our cell phones have the capability to pinpoint our location as we use them. Are our everyday movements being tracked through these devices? Probably not, but the potential does exist. If information is being collected, there is always the possibility that it can be accessed and used.

In addition, let's not forget how great it is to be able to connect to the Internet just about anywhere these days through wireless Internet connections. The downside? Others may be able to monitor what we are looking at as we surf the Web via these wireless connections. Think this is all the stuff of science fiction or TV crime shows? Not so. All of this is possible today. And as technology continues to evolve and we become even more reliant on it, the possibility for real invasions of privacy will also increase. So, what does this all have to do with ILI? It seems to me that we need to let our learners know about the risks as well as the conveniences of information technologies—so that they can make intelligent, informed decisions about how much personal information they are willing to "put out there" for the sake of expediency. While I am not advocating giving up all these wonderful things, I believe we have a responsibility as information professionals to share what we know about the potential risks and hazards of using them.

Where Do We Go from Here?

How often are you asked if you think there is a future for librarianship? After all, everything is online and easily accessible. Why would anyone need an intermediary to function in this wonderful world? The answer to that question, of course, is that as long as people continue to access information, they will need to turn to us—the information experts—to help them find their way in a complex and information-rich landscape. We will show them how to discover the characteristics of the information they find—who created it; why it was created; how the manner in which information is stored, disseminated, and shared can affect its nature; and the ways in which information can be used politically and personally to influence our lives and society as a whole. Furthermore, we will alert them to methods that can be used to protect themselves against the misuse of their own personal information. In order to maintain our roles as advocates and teachers, we must keep ourselves apprised of changes—technological and societal—that would impact IL and make sure that we pass this knowledge on to our learners. Will librarians become obsolete in the brave new technologically dependent world to come? I think not! We will remain the ones who invite our learners into that world and teach them to function effectively, efficiently, and ethically in their pursuit of the information they need.

Bibliography

4Teachers.org. RubiStar (2008). Available: http://rubistar.4teachers.org/index.php (accessed October 28, 2008).

AARL. "Ham Radio Operators 'True Heroes,' Rep Mike Ross, WD5DVR, Says in 'Salute'" (February 9, 2006). Available: www.arrl.org/news/stories/2006/02/09/100/?nc=1 (accessed December 27, 2008).

Abell, Angela and Nigel Oxbrow. 2001. *Competing with Knowledge: The Information Professional in the Knowledge Management Age*. London: Library Association Publishing.

Abilock, Debbie. 2006a. "Educating Students for Cross-cultural Proficiency." *Knowledge Quest* 35, no. 2: 10–13.

———. 2006b. "So Close and So Small: Six Promising Approaches to Civic Education, Equity, and Social Justice." *Knowledge Quest* 34, no. 5: 9–16.

Absher, Linda. "The Lipstick Librarian" (2004). Available: www.lipsticklibrarian.com (accessed December 25, 2008).

"Academic Libraries—Blogging Libraries" (December 27, 2008). Available: www.blogwithoutalibrary.net/links/index.php?title=Academic_libraries (accessed December 28, 2008).

Ackerman, Edith. 1996. "Perspective Taking and Object Construction: Two Keys to Learning." In *Constructionism in Practice: Designing, Thinking and Learning in a Digital World* (pp. 25–35), edited by Yasmin B. Kafai and Mitchell Resnick. Mahwah, NJ: Erlbaum.

Adams, Andrew A. 2007. "Copyright and Research: An Archivangelist's Perspective." *SCRIPTed 285* 4, no. 3. Available: www.law.ed.ac.uk/ahrc/script-ed/vol4-3/adams.asp (accessed December 25, 2008).

Adams, Douglas. "How to Stop Worrying and Learn to Love the Internet" (August 29, 1999). Available: www.douglasadams.com/dna/19990901-00-a.html (accessed December 27, 2008).

Adams, Mignon. 1993. "Evaluation." In *Sourcebook for Bibliographic Instruction* (pp. 45–57), edited by Katherine Branch. Chicago: ALA.

———. 1995. "Library Instruction in Special Libraries: Present and Future." In *Information for a New Age: Redefining the Librarian* (pp. 79–87), edited by LIRT Fifteenth Anniversary Task Force. Englewood, CO: Libraries Unlimited.

Adobe Captivate. "Adobe Captivate 4" (2008). Available: www.adobe.com/products/captivate (accessed December 25, 2008).

Adobe Dreamweaver. "Adobe Dreamweaver CS4" (2008). Available: www.adobe.com/products/dreamweaver (accessed December 26, 2008).

Adobe Flash. "Adobe Flash CS4 Professional" (2008). Available: www.adobe.com/products/flash (accessed December 26, 2008).

Adobe Photoshop. "Compare CS4 Photoshop Editions" (2008). Available: www.adobe.com/products/photoshop/family (accessed December 26, 2008).

Agre, Philip. "How to Help Someone Use a Computer" (1996). Available: http://polaris.gseis.ucla.edu/pagre/how-to-help.html (accessed December 28, 2008).

AIM. "Dashboard." Available: http://dashboard.aim.com/aim (accessed December 27, 2008).

ALA. AASL. 1998a. *Information Literacy Standards for Student Learning*. Chicago: ALA.

———. 1998b. *Information Power: Building Partnerships for Learning*. Chicago: ALA.

———. "INFOLIT (Information Literacy Discussion List)" (2006). Available: www.ala.org/ala/aasl/aaslproftools/aasledisclist/INFOLIT.cfm (accessed September 12, 2008).

———. "KidsConnect" (2007a). Available: www.ala.org/aaslTemplate.cfm?Section=k12students&Template=/ContentManagement/ContentDisplay.cfm&ContentID=21725 (accessed February 20, 2008).

———. "Standards for the 21st-century Learner" (2007b). Available: www.ala.org/ala/aasl/aaslproftools/learningstandards/AASL_LearningStandards.pdf (accessed December 22, 2008).

ALA. AASL/ACRL. Task Force on the Educational Role of Libraries. "Blueprint for Collaboration" (2004). Available: www.ala.org/ala/acrlpubs/whitepapers/acrlaasl/blueprints.htm (accessed February 2, 2008).

ALA. AASL. AECT. 1988. *Information Power: Guidelines for School Library Media Programs*. Chicago: ALA.

ALA. AASL. AECT. 1998. *Information Power: Building Partnerships for Learning*. Chicago: American Library Association.

ALA. ACRL. "Information Literacy Competency Standards for Higher Education" (2000). Available: www.ala.org/ala/acrl/acrlstandards/informationliteracycompetency.htm (accessed April 20, 2009).

———. "Assessment Issues" (2003a) Available: www.ala.org/ala/mgrps/divs/acrl/issues/infolit/resources/assess/issues.cfm (accessed April 27, 2009).

———. "Characteristics of Programs of Information Literacy that Illustrate Best Practices: A Guideline" (June 2003b). Available: www.ala.org/ala/mgrps/divs/acrl/standards/characteristics.cfm (accessed December 28, 2008).

———. "Information Literacy: Accreditation" (2006a). Available: www.ala.org/ala/mgrps/divs/acrl/issues/infolit/standards/accred/accreditation.cfm (accessed April 27, 2009).

———. "Institutional Strategies: Best Practices" (September 29, 2006b). Available: www.ala.org/ala/mgrps/divs/acrl/about/sections/is/iscommittees/webpages/bestpracticesa/bestpracticesproject.cfm (accessed April 27, 2009).

———. "Standards for Proficiencies for Instruction Librarians and Coordinators" (June 24, 2007). Available: www.ala.org/ala/mgrps/divs/acrl/standards/profstandards.cfm (accessed April 27, 2009).

———. "ACRL Standards & Guidelines" (2008a). Available: www.ala.org/ala/mgrps/divs/acrl/standards/index.cfm (accessed April 27, 2009).

———. "Information Literacy" (September 16, 2008b). Available: www.ala.org/ala/mgrps/divs/acrl/issues/infolit/index.cfm (accessed April 27, 2009).

———. "Information Literacy Around the Globe" (2008c). Available: www.ala.org/ala/mgrps/divs/acrl/issues/infolit/resources/global/globalil.cfm (accessed April 27, 2009).

ALA. ACRL. ANSS. "Information Literacy Standards for Anthropology and Sociology" (2008). Available: www.ala.org/ala/mgrps/divs/acrl/standards/anthro_soc_standards.cfm (accessed December 22, 2008).

ALA. ACRL. BIS. 1983. *Evaluating Bibliographic Instruction: A Handbook*. Chicago: ALA, ACRL, BIS.

———. 1991. *Read This First: An Owner's Guide to the New Model Statement of Objectives of Academic Bibliographic Instruction*, edited by Carolyn Dusenbury et al. Chicago: ALA, ACRL, BIS..

———. 1993a. *Learning to Teach*. Chicago: ALA.

———. 1993b. *Sourcebook for Bibliographic Instruction*. Chicago: ALA.

ALA. ACRL. CARL. SCIL. "Southern California Instruction Libraries" (December 18, 2008). Available: http://carl-acrl.org/ig/scil (accessed December 22, 2008).

ALA. ACRL. Distance Learning Section. "Distance Learning Section" (January 16, 2008a). Available: http://caspian.switchinc.org/~distlearn (accessed December 27, 2008).

———. "Standards for Distance Learning Library Services" (July 1, 2008b). Available: www.ala.org/ala/mgrps/divs/acrl/standards/guidelinesdistancelearning.cfm (accessed December 27, 2008).

ALA. ACRL. Institute for Information Literacy. "Immersion Program" (2008). Available: www.ala.org/ala/mgrps/divs/acrl/issues/infolit/professactivity/iil/welcome.cfm (accessed December 22, 2008).

ALA. ACRL. IS. "Objectives for Information Literacy Instruction: A Model Statement for Academic Librarians" (2001). Available: www.ala.org/ala/mgrps/divs/acrl/standards/objectivesinformation.cfm (accessed December 23, 2008).

———. "Research Agenda for Library Instruction and Information Literacy" (2002). Available: www.ala.org/ala/mgrps/divs/acrl/about/sections/is/publicationsacrl/researchagendalibrary.cfm (accessed December 22, 2008).

———. "Instruction Section Innovation Award" (2007a). Available: www.ala.org/ala/mgrps/divs/acrl/awards/innovationaward.cfm (accessed April 27, 2009).

______. Library School Outreach Task Force. 2007b. "Draft Library School Outreach Toolkit: Ideas and Examples." Unpublished.

———. "Analysis of Instructional Environments: Regional Accrediting Agencies" (November 5, 2008a). Available: www.ala.org/ala/mgrps/divs/acrl/about/sections/is/publicationsacrl/instructionalenvironments.cfm (accessed April 27, 2009).

———. "Information Literacy in the Disciplines" (2008b). Available: www.ala.org/ala/mgrps/divs/acrl/about/sections/is/projectsacrl/infolitdisciplines/ (accessed April 27, 2009).

———. "Instruction Section" (2008c). Available: www.ala.org/ala/mgrps/divs/acrl/about/sections/is/homepage.cfm (accessed December 22, 2008).

———. "Multilingual Glossary" (2008d). Available: www.ala.org/ala/mgrps/divs/acrl/about/sections/is/publicationsacrl/multilingual.cfm (accessed April 27, 2009).

———. "PRIMO: Peer Reviewed Instructional Materials Online" (2008e). Available: www.ala.org/ala/mgrps/divs/acrl/about/sections/is/iscommittees/webpages/primocommittee/primo/index.cfm (accessed April 27, 2009).

———. Professional Education Committee. "Library Instruction Courses in ALA-accredited Schools" (November 5, 2008f). Available: www.ala.org/ala/mgrps/divs/acrl/about/sections/is/iscommittees/webpages/educationa/libraryschools.cfm (accessed December 22, 2008).

______. Information Literacy Best Practices Committee. (April 21, 2009). Available: www.ala.org/ala/mgrps/divs/acrl/about/sections/is/iscommittees/webpages/bestpracticesa/index.cfm (accessed April 21, 2009).

ALA. ACRL. NELIG. "New England Library Instruction Group" (2008). Available: www.acrlnec.org/sigs/nelig (accessed December 22, 2008).

ALA. ACRL. STS. "Information Literacy Standards for Science and Engineering/Technology" (2009). Available: www.ala.org/ala/mgrps/divs/acrl/standards/infolitscitech.cfm (accessed April 21, 2009).

ALA. ASCLA. "Think Accessible Before You Buy: Questions to Ask to Ensure That the Electronic Resources Your Library Plans to Purchase Are Accessible" (October 13, 2008). Available: www.ala.org/ala/mgrps/divs/ascla/asclaprotools/thinkaccessible/default.cfm (accessed December 27, 2008).

ALA. LIRT. "Library Instruction Tutorials" (2001). Available: www3.baylor.edu/LIRT/lirtproj.html (accessed December 24, 2008).

———. "Top Twenty-five of LIRT's Top Twenty Instruction Articles" (2003). Available: http://www3.baylor.edu/LIRT/top25.htm (accessed December 26, 2008).

———. "Library Instruction Round Table" (2008a). Available: www3.baylor.edu/LIRT (accessed December 22, 2008).

———. 2008b. "LIRT Top 20." *Library Instruction Round Table News* 29, no. 4: 5–8. Available: http://www3.baylor.edu/LIRT/lirtnews/2008/jun08.pdf (accessed December 28, 2008).

ALA. LIRT. Fifteenth Anniversary Task Force. 1995. *Information for a New Age: Redefining the Librarian*. Englewood, CO: Libraries Unlimited.

ALA. LITA. Human/Machine Interface Interest Group. "Usability Testing Resources" (September 7, 2005). Available: www.vancouver.wsu.edu/fac/campbell/hmiig/usabres2.htm (accessed December 27, 2008).

ALA. Presidential Committee on Information Literacy. "Final Report." (January 10, 1989). Available: www.ala.org/ala/mgrps/divs/acrl/publications/whitepapers/presidential.cfm (accessed April 22, 2009).

———. "A Progress Report on Information Literacy: An Update on the ALA Presidential Committee on Information Literacy: Final Report" (March 1998). Available: www.ala.org/ala/mgrps/divs/acrl/publications/whitepapers/progressreport.cfm (accessed December 23, 2008).

Albanese, Andrew Richard. 2004. "Campus Library 2.0." *Library Journal* 129, no. 7: 30–33.

Albrecht, Bob. 2006. "Enriching Student Experience Through Blended Learning." *Educause Center for Applied Research. ECAR Research Bulletin* 2006, no. 12. Available: www.educause.edu/ir/library/pdf/ERB0612.pdf (accessed December 24, 2008).

Alexa. "The Web Information Company" (2008). Available: www.alexa.com (accessed December 23, 2008).

Alexander, Carter. 1939. "Criteria for Evaluating Instruction in the Use of Library Materials." *Elementary School Journal* 40, no. 4: 269–276.

Alexander, Jan and Marsha Tate. "Evaluate Web Pages" (1996). Available: http://www3.widener.edu/Academics/Libraries/Wolfgram_Memorial_Library/Evaluate_Web_Pages/659/ (accessed December 23, 2008).

Allen, Eileen E. 1995. "Active Learning and Teaching: Improving Postsecondary Library Instruction." *Reference Librarian* no. 51/52: 89–103.

Allen, I. Elaine and Jeff Seaman. "Online Nation: Five Years of Growth in Online Learning." Newburyport, MA: The Sloan Consortium (October 2007). Available: www.sloan-c.org/publications/survey/pdf/online_nation.pdf (accessed December 27, 2008).

Allen, Susan M. 1993. "Designing Library Handouts: Principles and Procedures." *Research Strategies* 11, no. 1: 14–23.

Alliance Virtual Library. "Info Island." East Peoria, IL: Alliance Library System. Available: http://slurl.com/secondlife/Info%20Island/114/237/33 (accessed May 24, 2009).

Alverno College Faculty. 1979. *Assessment at Alverno College*. Milwaukee, WI: Alverno College.

American Association of Colleges and Universities. "Greater Expectations: A New Vision for Learning as a Nation Goes to College" (2002). Available: www.greaterexpectations.org (accessed September 8, 2008).

American Association for Higher Education. 1992. *Principles for Good Practice for Assessing Student Learning*. Washington, DC: AAHE.

American Chemical Society. "Chemical Information Retrieval" (2002). Available: portal.acs.org/portal/fileFetch/C/CTP_005584/pdf/CTP_005584.pdf (accessed December 22, 2008).

American Psychological Association. 2000. "Mental Models." In *Encyclopedia of Psychology*, vol. 5. New York: Oxford University Press.

American Psychological Association. Board of Educational Affairs. Task Force on Undergraduate Major Competencies. "Undergraduate Psychology Major Learning Goals and Outcomes" (2001). Available: www.apa.org/ed/pcue/taskforcereport.pdf (accessed December 22, 2008).

Amsel, Abram. 1989. *Behaviorism, Neobehaviorism and Cognitivism in Learning Theory: Historical and Contemporary Perspectives*. Hillsdale, NJ: Erlbaum.

"Ancient Spaces." Educause Learning Initiative (June 2006). Available: http://net.educause.edu/ir/library/pdf/ELI5012.pdf (accessed December 28, 2008).

Anderson, Lorin W. and David R. Krathwohl. 2001. *A Taxonomy of Learning, Teaching and Assessing: A Revision of Bloom's Educational Objectives*. Boston: Allyn & Bacon.

Anderson, Nate. "Library of Congress: DRM a Serious Obstacle to Archiving." ars technica (July 16, 2008). Available: http://arstechnica.com/news.ars/post/20080716-library-of-congress-drm-a-serious-obstacle-to-archiving.html (accessed December 25, 2008).

Angelo, Thomas A. and K. Patricia Cross. 1993. *Classroom Assessment Techniques: A Handbook for College Teachers*, 2nd ed. The Jossey-Bass Higher and Adult Education Series. San Francisco: Jossey-Bass Publishers.

Antell, Karen. 2004. "Why Do College Students Use Public Libraries? A Phenomenological Study." *Reference & User Services Quarterly* 43, no. 3: 227–236.

Antell, Karen and Jie Huang. 2008. "Subject Searching Success: Transaction Logs, Patron Perceptions, and Implications for Library Instruction." *Reference & User Services Quarterly* 48, no. 1: 68–76.

A.N.T.S. ANimated Tutorial Sharing Project. "About ANTS." COPPUL: The Council of Prairie and Pacific University Libraries (2008). Available: http://ants.wetpaint.com/?t=anon (accessed December 23, 2008).

Appalachian State University. "Library Research Tutorial" (September 17, 2007). Available: www.library.appstate.edu/tutorial (accessed April 27, 2008).

Apple. "iTunes U" (2008a). Available: www.apple.com/education/itunesu_mobilelearning/itunesu.html (accessed December 27, 2008).

Apple. "Keynote" (2008b). Available: www.apple.com/iwork/keynote (accessed December 25, 2008).

Applin, Mary Beth. 1999. "Instruction Services for Students with Disabilities." *Journal of Academic Librarianship* 25: 139–141.

Araz, Gulsum and Semra Sungur. 2007. "Effectiveness of Problem-based Learning on Academic Performance in Genetics." *International Union of Biochemistry and Molecular Biology* 35, no. 6: 448–451.

Areglado, Ronald J., R.C. Bradley, and Pamela S. Lane. 1996. *Learning for Life: Creating Classrooms for Self-directed Learning*. Thousand Oaks, CA: Corwin Press.

Ark, Connie E. 2000. "A Comparison of Information Literacy Goals, Skills and Standards for Student Learning." *Ohio Media Spectrum* 51 no. 4: 11–15.

Armstrong, David G. and Tom V. Savage. 1983. *Secondary Education: An Introduction*. New York: Macmillan.

Arp, Lori. 1990. "Information Literacy or Bibliographic Instruction: Semantics or Philosophy." *RQ* 30, no. 1: 46–49.

———. 1993. "An Introduction to Learning Theory." In *Sourcebook for Bibliographic Instruction* (pp. 5–15), edited by Catherine Branch. Chicago: ALA.

Associated Colleges of the South. "ACS Information Fluency Working Definition" (2003). Available: www.colleges.org/techcenter/if/if_definition.html (accessed December 22, 2008).

Association for Teacher-Librarianship in Canada and Canadian Library Association. 1998. "Competencies for Teacher-librarians in the 21st Century." *Teacher Librarian* 26: 22–25.

AT&T Knowledge Network. "21st Century Literacies: Multicultural Literacy" (2008a). Available: www.kn.pacbell.com/wired/21stcent/cultural.html (accessed December 31, 2008).

———. "WebQuest Overview" (2008b). Available: www.kn.att.com/wired/webquests.html (accessed December 31, 2008).

Ausubel, David P. 1960. "The Use of Advance Organizers in the Learning and Retention of Meaningful Verbal Material." *Journal of Educational Psychology* 51: 267–272.

———. 1977. "The Facilitation of Meaningful Verbal Meaning in the Classroom." *Educational Psychologist* 12: 162–178.

Ausubel, David P., Joseph D. Novak, and Helen Hanesion. 1978. *Educational Psychology: A Cognitive View*, 2nd ed. New York: Holt, Rinehart and Winston.

Ausubel, David P. and Floyd G. Robinson. 1969. *School Learning: An Introduction to Educational Psychology*. New York: Hold, Rinehart and Winston.

AVERT. "History of AIDS up to 1986" (November 28, 2008). Available: www.avert.org/his81_86.htm (accessed December 23, 2008).

Avery, Elizabeth Fuseler. 2003. "Assessing Information Literacy Instruction." In *Assessing Student Learning Outcomes for Information Literacy Instruction* (pp. 1–5), edited by Elizabeth Fuseler Avery. Chicago: ALA.

Aydelott, Kathrine C. "IL Analogies." Personal e-mail (June 24, 2008).

Badke, William B. 2003. "All We Need Is a Fast Horse: Riding Info Lit Into the Academy." In *Musings, Meanderings and Monsters, Too: Essays on Academic Librarianship* (pp. 75–88), edited by Martin Raish. Lanham, MD: Scarecrow Press.

———. 2005. "Can't Get No Respect: Helping Faculty to Understand the Educational Power of Information Literacy." *Reference Librarian* 89/90: 63–80.

———. "What to Do with Wikipedia" (March/April 2008). Available: www.infotoday.com/online/mar08/Badke.shtml (accessed December 23, 2008).

Baggaley, Jon. 2008. "Where Did Distance Education Go Wrong?" *Distance Education* 29, no. 1: 39–51.

Bain, Ken. 2004. *What the Best College Teachers Do*. Cambridge, MA: Harvard University Press.

Baker, Kirsty Louise. "Information Skills." Open University (November 24, 2008). Available: http://library.open.ac.uk/help/stuskill/index.cfm (accessed December 27, 2008).

Baker, Pam and Renee R. Curry. 2004. "Integrating Information Competence Into an Interdisciplinary Major." In *Integrating Information Literacy Into the Higher Education Curriculum* (pp. 93–132), edited by Ilene Rockman and Associates. San Francisco: Wiley & Sons.

Ball, Arnetha F. 2000. "Empowering Pedagogies That Enhance the Learning of Multicultural Students." *Teachers College Record* 102, no. 6: 1006–1034.

Ball, Mary Alice and Molly Mahoney. 1987. "Foreign Students,

Libraries and Culture." *College & Research Libraries* 48, no. 2: 160–166.

Band, Jonathan. "Educational Fair Use Today." ARL (December 2007). Available: www.arl.org/bm~doc/educationalfairusetoday.pdf (accessed December 25, 2008).

Bandura, Albert. 1977a. "Self-efficacy Toward a Unifying Theory of Behavioral Change." *Psychological Review* 84, no. 2: 191–215.

———. 1977b. *Social Learning Theory*. Englewood Cliffs, NJ: Prentice-Hall.

———. 1982. Self-efficacy Mechanism in Human Agency. *American Psychologist* 37: 122–147.

———. 1986. *Social Foundations of Thought and Action: A Social Cognitive Theory*. Englewood Cliffs, NJ: Prentice Hall.

Banks, James A. 1993. "Multicultural Education: Characteristics and Goals." In *Multicultural Education: Issues and Perspectives,* 2nd ed. (pp. 3–28), edited by James A. Banks and Cherry A.M. Banks. Boston: Allyn & Bacon.

———. 2007. "Multicultural Education: Characteristics and Goals." In *Multicultural Education: Issues and Perspectives,* 6th ed. (pp. 3–30), edited by James A. Banks and Cherry A. M. Banks. Hoboken, NJ: Wiley.

Banks, James A. and Cherry A. McGee Banks, eds. 1993. *Multicultural Education: Issues and Perspectives*, 2nd ed. Boston: Allyn & Bacon.

———, eds. 2007. *Multicultural Education: Issues and Perspectives*, 6th ed. Hoboken, NJ: Wiley.

Banks, James A. et al. "Democracy and Diversity: Principles and Concepts for Educating Citizens in a Global World" (2005). Available: http://depts.washington.edu/centerme/demdiv.htm (accessed March 10, 2008).

Banta, Trudy W., Jon P. Lund, Karen E. Black, and Frances W. Oblander. 1996. *Assessment in Practice: Putting Principles to Work in College Campuses*. San Francisco: Jossey-Bass.

Barbe, Walter Burke and Michael N. Milone. 1982. "Teaching Through Modality Strengths: Look Before You Leap." In *Student Learning Styles and Brain Behavior* (pp. 54–57), edited by National Association of Secondary School Principals. Reston, VA: NASSP.

Barbe, Walter Burke and Raymond H. Swassing. 1988. *Teaching Through Modality Strengths: Concepts and Practices*. Columbus, OH: Zaner-Bloser.

Barbour, Wendell, Christy Gavin, and Joan Canfield. 2004. *Integrating Information Literacy Into the Academic Curriculum*. Boulder, CO: Educause Center for Applied Research.

Barclay, Donald. 1993. "Evaluating Library Instruction: Doing the Best You Can with What You Have." *RQ* 33, no. 2: 195–203.

Barclay, Donald A. 1995. "Teaching the Standard Features of Electronic Databases." In *Teaching Electronic Information Literacy: A How-To-Do-It Manual* (pp. 57–75), edited by Donald A. Barclay. New York: Neal-Schuman.

Barefoot, Betsy. 2006. "Bridging the Chasm: First-year Students and the Library." *Chronicle of Higher Education* 52, no. 20: 16.

Barlow, John Perry. "The Economy of Idea: Selling Wine Without Bottles on the Global Net" (December 13–14, 1993). Available: www.eff.org/~barlow/EconomyOfIdeas.html (accessed December 25, 2008).

———. "A Declaration of the Independence of Cyberspace" (February 8, 1996). Available: www.eff.org/~barlow/Declaration-Final.html (accessed December 25, 2008).

Barnes, J. and L. Riesterer. "Pathfinder for Constructing Pathfinders" (November 2007). Available: http://home.wsd.wednet.edu/pathfinders/path.htm (accessed December 28, 2008).

Barnes-Whyte, Susan. 2008. "Finding Ourselves as Teachers." In *Information Literacy Instruction Handbook* (pp. 50–56), edited by Christopher N. Cox and Elizabeth Blakesley Lindsay. Chicago: ALA, ACRL.

Baron, Sara and Alexia Strout-Dapaz. 2001. "Communicating with and Empowering International Students with a Library Skills Set." *Reference Services Review* 29, no. 4: 314–326.

Barr, Robert B. and John Tagg. 1995. "From Teaching to Learning—A New Paradigm for Undergraduate Education." *Change* 27, no. 6: 13–25.

Barrows, Howard. "Problem Based Learning Initiative: Generic Problem-based Learning Essentials" (April 3, 2006). Available: www.pbli.org/pbl/generic_pbl.htm (accessed December 24, 2008).

barryrunner. "C.R.A.P.—Basic Layout and Design Principles for Webpages" (November 29, 2007). Available: www.youtube.com/watch?v=mF_mWi6r-9I (accessed December 26, 2008).

Bartlett, Thomas. 2007. "Out with the New, In with the Old." *Chronicle of Higher Education* 54, no. 17: A1–A10.

Bates, Marcia J. 1979. "Information Search Tactics." *Journal of the American Society for Information Science* 30: 205–14.

———. 1989. "The Design of Browsing and Berrypicking Techniques for the Online Search." *Online Reviews* 13, no. 5: 407–424.

Battersby, Mark and Learning Outcomes Network. 1999. "So What's a Learning Outcome Anyway?" Vancouver, BC: Centre for Curriculum, Transfer, and Technology. ERIC Document ED430611.

Bay Area Community Colleges. "Bay Area Community Colleges Information Competency Assessment" (2004). Available: www.topsy.org/ICAP/ICAProject.html (accessed January 14, 2008).

Beall, Jeffrey. 2007. "Search Fatigue." *American Libraries* 38, no. 3: 46–50.

Beaman, Diane C. "Evaluating a Web Site for Research Rubric" (February 4, 2008). Available: www.nhema.net/rubric.pdf (accessed December 23, 2008).

Beaubien, Anne K., Sharon A. Hogan, and Mary W. George.

1982. *Learning the Library: Concepts and Methods for Effective Bibliographic Instruction.* New York: Bowker.

Bechtel, Joan. 1986. "Conversation, a New Paradigm for Librarianship." *College & Research Libraries* 47 no. 3: 219–224.

Beck, Susan E. "The Good, the Bad, & the Ugly, or Why It's a Good Idea to Evaluate Web Resources" (1997). Available: http://lib.nmsu.edu/instruction/eval.html (accessed December 23, 2008).

———. "Evaluation Criteria" (December 28, 2008). Available: http://lib.nmsu.edu/instruction/evalcrit.html (accessed December 28, 2008).

Bedord, Jean. 2007. "Distance Education." *Searcher* 15, no. 9: 18–22.

Belenky, Mary Field et al. 1986. *Women's Ways of Knowing.* New York: Basic Books.

Bell, Lori and Rhonda B. Trueman. 2008. *Virtual Worlds Real Libraries.* Medford, NJ: Information Today.

Bell, Mary Ann. 2007. "Should We All Be Technophiles?" *MultiMedia & Internet@Schools* 14, no. 1: 34–36.

Bell, Steven J. 2007. "Library Blogs: The New Technology Bandwagon." In *Using Interactive Technologies in Libraries* (pp. 59–80), edited by Kathlene Hanson and H. F. Cervone. New York: Neal-Schuman.

———. 2008. "Design Thinking." *American Libraries* 39, nos. 1 & 2: 44–49.

Bell, Steven J. and John Shank. 2004. "The Blended Librarian: A Blueprint for Redefining the Teaching and Learning Role of Academic Librarians." *College & Research Libraries News* 65, no. 7. Available: www.ala.org/ala/mgrps/divs/acrl/publications/crlnews/2004/jul/blendedlibrarian.cfm (accessed March 24, 2009).

———. "The Blended Librarian Portal" (December 17, 2008). Available: http://blendedlibrarian.org (accessed December 25, 2008).

Benjes-Small, Candice and Blair Brainard. 2006. "And Today We'll Be Serving . . . An Instruction a la Carte Menu." *College & Research Libraries News* 67, no. 2: 80–82, 96.

Bennett, Miranda. 2007. "Charting the Same Future?" *College & Research Libraries News* 68, no. 6: 370–372.

Bennett, Scott. 2007. "Campus Cultures Fostering Information Literacy." *portal: Libraries and the Academy* 7, no. 2: 147–167.

Berge, Patricia A. and Judith Pryor. 1982. "Applying Educational Theory to Workbook Instruction." In *Theories of Bibliographic Education: Designs for Teaching* (pp. 91–110), edited by Cerise Oberman and Katina Strauch. New York: Bowker.

Bernard, Robert M. et al. 2004. "How Does Distance Education Compare with Classroom Instruction? A Meta-analysis of the Empirical Literature." *Review of Educational Research* 74, no. 3: 379–439.

Berninger, Virginia W., and Todd L. Richards. 2002. *Brain Literacy for Educators and Psychologists.* San Diego: Academic Press.

Beyer, Barry K. 1985a. "Critical Thinking: What Is It?" *Social Education* 49, no. 4: 270–276.

———. 1985b. "Teaching Critical Thinking: A Direct Approach." *Social Education* 49, no. 4:297–303.

Bibliothèques de l'Université Paris-Sorbonne. "biblioparis4's Bookmarks on Delicious." Available: http://delicious.com/bibliparis4 (accessed November 30, 2008).

Bigge, Morris L. and S. Samuel Shermis. 1999. *Learning Theories for Teachers,* 6th ed. New York: Harper Collins.

Biggs, John B. 1999a. *Teaching for Quality Learning at the University.* Buckingham, Great Britain: Open University Press.

———. 1999b. "What the Student Does: Teaching for Enhanced Learning." *Higher Education Research and Development* 18, no. 1: 57–75.

Birch, Tobeylynn, Emily Bergman, and Susan J. Arrington. 1990. "Planning for Library Instruction in Special Libraries." In *The LIRT Instruction Handbook* (pp. 91–106), edited by May Brottman and Mary Loe. Englewood, CO: Libraries Unlimited.

Birmingham Public Library. *Placing a Hold . . . So Easy, but Can a Caveman Do It?* (December 20, 2008). Available: www.youtube.com/watch?v=jddYPQkyFvM&feature=related (accessed December 25, 2008).

Bishop, Simon. 2006. "Using Analogy in Science Teaching as a Bridge to Students' Understanding of Complex Issues." In *Overcoming Barriers to Student Understand: Threshold Concepts and Troublesome Knowledge* (pp. 182–194). London: Routledge.

Bjorner, Susanne. 1991. "The Information Literacy Curriculum: A Working Model." *IATUL Quarterly* 5, no. 2: 150–160.

Black, Leah and Denise Forro. 1999. "Humor in the Academic Library: You Must Be Joking! Or, How Many Academic Librarians Does It Take to Change a Lightbulb?" *College & Research Libraries* 60, no. 2 :165–172.

Blackboard (2008). Available: www.blackboard.com (accessed December 27, 2008).

Blake, Tim K. 2005. "Journaling: An Active Learning Technique." *International Journal of Nursing Education Scholarship* 2, no. 1, Article 7. Available: www.bepress.com/ijnes/vol2/iss1/art7 (accessed December 24, 2008).

Blakey, Elaine and Sheila Spence. 1990. "Thinking for the Future." *Emergency Librarian* 17, no. 5: 11, 13–14.

Bligh, Donald A. 2000. *What's the Use of Lectures?* San Francisco: Jossey-Bass.

blip.tv. "Homepage" (2008). Available: http://blip.tv (accessed December 25, 2008).

Bloglines. "Homepage" (2008). Available: www.bloglines.com (accessed December 27, 2008).

Bloom, Benjamin Samuel. 1956. *Taxonomy of Educational Objectives: The Classification of Educational Goals. Handbook 1: Cognitive Domain. Handbook 2: Affective Domain.* New York: McKay.

———. 1981. *All Our Children Learning: A Primer for*

Parents, Teachers, and Other Educators. New York: McGraw-Hill.

Bloom, Benjamin Samuel, George F. Madaus, and J. Thomas Hastings. 1981. *Evaluation to Improve Learning*. New York: McGraw-Hill.

Blowers, Helene. "Learning 2.0" (May 2, 2006a). Available: http://plcmcl2-about.blogspot.com (accessed December 28, 2008).

———. "Web 2.0 Meets Information Fluency: Evaluation" (September 20, 2006b). Available: http://joycevalenza.edublogs.org/2006/09/20/web-20-meets-information-fluency-evaluation (accessed December 23, 2008).

Blum, H. Timothy and Dorothy Jean Yocom. 1996. "A Fun Alternative: Using Instructional Games to Foster Student Learning." *Teaching Exceptional Children* 29, no. 2: 60–63.

Bober, Christopher, Sonia Poulin, and Luigina Vileno. 1995. "Evaluating Library Instruction in Academic Libraries: A Critical Review of the Literature 1980–1993." *Reference Librarian* 24, no. 51/52: 53–71.

Bodi, Sonia, 1988. "Critical Thinking and Bibliographic Instruction: The Relationship." *Journal of Academic Librarianship* 14, no. 3: 150–153.

———. 1990. "Teaching Effectiveness and Bibliographic Instruction: The Relevance of Learning Styles." *College & Research Libraries* 51, no. 2: 113–119.

———. 2002. "How Do We Bridge the Gap Between What We Teach and What They Do?" *Journal of Academic Librarianship* 28, no. 3: 109–114.

Boettcher, Jennifer. 2006. "Framing the Scholarly Communication Cycle." *Online* 30, no. 3:24–26.

Boisselle, Juliet, Susan Fliss, Lori Mestre, and Fred Zinn. 2004. "Talking Toward Techno-pedagogy: Information Literacy and Librarian Collaboration—Rethinking Our Roles." *Resource Sharing and Information Networks* 17, no. 1/2: 123–136.

Bonk, Curtis J. and Charles R. Graham. 2006. *The Handbook of Blended Learning*. San Francisco: Pfeiffer.

Bonn, George. 1960. *Training Laymen in the Use of the Library*. Volume 2, pt. 1 of *The State of the Library Art*, edited by Ralph R. Shaw. New Brunswick, NJ: Rutgers University Press.

Bonwell, Charles C. 1996. "Enhancing the Lecture: Revitalizing a Traditional Format." In *Using Active Learning In College Classes: A Range of Options for Faculty* (pp. 31–44), edited by Tracey E. Sutherland and Charles C. Bonwell. San Francisco: Jossey-Bass.

Bonwell, Charles C. and Tracey E. Sutherland. 1996. "The Active Learning Continuum: Choosing Activities to Engage Students in the Classroom." In *Using Active Learning In College Classes: A Range of Options for Faculty* (pp. 3–16), edited by Tracey E. Sutherland and Charles C. Bonwell. San Francisco: Jossey-Bass.

Boruff-Jones, Polly D. and Amy E. Mark. 2003. "Information Literacy and Student Engagement: What the National Survey of Student Engagement Reveals About Your Campus." *College & Research Libraries* 64, no. 6: 480–493.

Bostick, Sharon Lee. 1992. *The Development and Validation of the Library Anxiety Scale*. PhD dissertation. Detroit: Wayne State University.

Boud, David, ed. 1988. *Developing Autonomy in Student Learning*, 2nd ed. London: Kogan Page.

Boyd, Angela. "Paper Handouts" (February 25, 2007). Electronic bulletin board. Available: http://lists.ala.org/wws/arc/ili-l (accessed July 14, 2008).

———. "Re: [ili-l] Analogies in ILI." Personal e-mail (June 23, 2008).

Boyd, Danah M. and Nicole B. Ellison. 2008. "Social Network Sites: Definition, History, and Scholarship." *Computer-mediated Communication* 13, no. 1: 210–230. Available: www3.interscience.wiley.com/cgi-bin/fulltext/117979376/PDFSTART (accessed December 27, 2008).

Boyd, Robert. "Anthropology 7 Class Web Site" (1997a). Fall session, UCLA College of Letters and Science. Available: www.sscnet.ucla.edu/classes/fall97/anthro7 (accessed December 25, 2008).

———. "Fossil Flash Cards" (1997b). Fall session, UCLA College of Letters and Science. Available: www.sscnet.ucla.edu/classes/fall97/anthro7/new/flashcard.pl?quiz=fossils (accessed December 25, 2008).

Bradford, Peter, Margaret Porciello, Nancy Balkon, and Debra Backus. 2006–2007. "The Blackboard Learning System: The Be All and End All in Educational Instruction?" *Journal of Educational Technology Systems* 35, no. 3: 301–314.

Brandon, David. P. and Andrea B. Hollingshead. 1999. "Collaborative Learning and Computer-supported Groups." *Communication Education* 48, no. 2: 109–126.

Bransford, John, Sean Brophy, and Susan Williams. 2000. "When Computer Technologies Meet the Learning Sciences: Issues and Opportunities." *Journal of Developmental Psychology* 21, no. 1: 59–84.

Bransford, John D., Ann L. Brown, Rodney R. Cocking, and National Research Council. 1999a. *How People Learn: Bridging Research and Practice*. Washington, DC: National Academies Press.

———, eds. 1999b. *How People Learn: Brain, Mind, Experience and School*. Washington, DC: National Academies Press.

Brasley, Stephanie. 2006. "Building and Using a Tool to Assess Info and Tech Literacy." *Computers in Libraries* 26, no. 6/7: 44–48.

Brazzeal, Bradley. 2006. "Research Guides as Library Instruction Tools." *Reference Services Review* 34, no. 3: 358–367.

Breeding, Marshall. 2008. "Winning the Competition for Attention on the Web." Computers in Libraries 28, no. 6: 31–33.

Breivik, Patricia Senn. 1985. "Putting Libraries Back in the Information Society." *American Libraries* 16, no. 1: 723.

Breivik, Patricia Senn and E. Gordon Gee. 1989. *Information Literacy: Revolution in the Library*. New York: Macmillan.

———. 2006. *Higher Education in the Internet Age: Libraries Creating a Strategic Edge*. Westport, CT: American Council on Education and Praeger Publishers.

Brewer, Michael and ALA OITP. "Digital Copyright Slider" (2007). Available: http://librarycopyright.net/digitalslider (accessed December 25, 2008).

Brey-Casiano, Carol. 2007. "From Literate to Information Literate Communities Through Advocacy." *Public Library Quarterly* 25, no. 1/2: 181–190.

Brier, David and Vicky Lebbin. In press. "'Next Slide, Please': An Analysis and Conversation on the Uses and Misuses of Microsoft PowerPoint at Library Instruction Conferences." In *Proceedings of the Thirty-fifth Annual LOEX Library Instruction Conference*, May 3-5, 2007, San Diego, CA.

Briggs, Laura E. and James M. Skidmore. 2008. "Beyond the Blended Librarian: Creating Full Partnerships with Faculty to Embed Information Literacy in Online Learning Systems." In *Using Technology to Teach Information Literacy* (pp. 87–106), edited by Thomas P. Mackey and Trudi E. Jacobson. New York: Neal-Schuman.

Brigham Young University. "iLink BYU Online Catalog" (2005). Available: http://catalog.lib.byu.edu/uhtbin/cgisirsi/OzWx3DqnDW/LEE/129440338/60/548/X (accessed December 4, 2008).

British Library and JSIC. "Information Behaviour of the Researcher of the Future" (January 11, 2008). Available: www.twine.com/_b/download/1y8bplft-4x/b0bsl79jx59rwtw7lr978psshbdk7tsxlb1w4wlpmfhprmt/1y8bplft-4x/b0bsl79jx59rwtw7lr978psshbdk7-tsxlb1w4wlpmfhprmt/gg_final_keynote_11012008.pdf (accessed December 22, 2008).

Brookfield, Stephen D. 1994. "Adult Learners: Motives for Learning and Implications for Practice." In *Teaching and Learning in the College Classroom* (pp. 137–149), edited by Kenneth A. Feldman and Michael B. Paulsen. Needham Heights, MA: Ginn Press.

Brookfield, Stephen. 1995. *Becoming a Critically Reflective Teacher*, 1st ed. The Jossey-Bass Higher and Adult Education Series. San Francisco: Jossey-Bass.

Brooklyn Public Library. "Events Calendar" (2008). Available: www.brooklynpubliclibrary.org/calendar/EventList.do (accessed December 28, 2008).

Brosnan, Mark. 1998a. "Avis Sets Sights on Technophobes." *Travel Trade Gazette UK & Ireland* (September 2): 45.

_______. 1998b. *Technophobia: the Psychological Impact of Information Technology*. London; New York: Routledge.

Brottman, May and Mary Loe, eds. 1990. *The LIRT Library Instruction Handbook; Information for a New Age: Redefining the Librarian*. Englewood, CO: Libraries Unlimited.

Brown, Cecelia and Lee R. Krumholz. 2002. "Integrating Information Literacy Into the Science Curriculum." *College & Research Libraries News* 63, no. 2: 111–123.

Bruce, Christine. 1997. *The Seven Faces of Information Literacy*. Adelaide, Australia: Auslib Press.

———. 2000. "Information Literacy Programs and Research: An International Review." *Australian Library Journal* 49, no. 3: 209–218.

Bruce, Christine and Philip Candy. 2000. "Information Literacy Programs: People, Politics and Potential." In *Information Literacy Around the World* (pp. 3–10), edited by Christine Bruce and Philip Candy. Wagga Wagga, New South Wales: Centre for Information Studies, Charles Sturt University.

Bruner, Jerome S. 1963. *The Process of Education*, 2nd ed. New York: Random House.

———. 1966. *Toward a Theory of Instruction*. Cambridge, MA: Belknap Press of Harvard University.

BUBL LINK. "Catalogue of Internet Resources" (2007). Available: http://bubl.ac.uk (accessed December 27, 2008).

Budd, John M. 2007. "The Spellings Commission: Challenges to Higher Education and Academic Libraries." *portal: Libraries and the Academy* 7, no. 2: 137–146.

Bui, Khanh Van T. 2002. "First Generation College Students at a 4 Year University: Background Characteristics, Reasons for Pursuing Higher Education, and First-year Experiences." *College Student Journal* 36, no. 1: 3–11.

Bundy, Alan. 2002. "Essential Connections: School and Public Libraries for Lifelong Learning." *Australian Library Journal* 51, no. 1: 47–70.

Burger, Leslie. 2008. "All Seasons and All Reasons." *American Libraries* 39, no. 3: 45–48.

Burhanna, Kenneth J. 2006. "Collaboration for Success: High School to College Transitions." *Reference Services Review* 26, no. 4: 509–519.

Burke, Gerald, Carol Anne Germain, and Lijuan Xu. 2005. "Information Literacy: Bringing a Renaissance to Reference." *portal: Libraries and the Academy* 5, no. 3: 353–370.

Burkhardt, Joanna. 2007. "Assessing Library Skills: A First Step to Information Literacy." *portal: Libraries and the Academy* 7, no. 1: 25–49.

Burkhardt, Joanna, Mary C. Macdonald, and Andree J. Rathemacher. 2003. *Teaching Information Literacy: 35 Practical Standards-based Exercises for College Students*. Chicago: ALA.

Burlington County (NJ) Library System. "Research & Information Center." Available: http://explore.bcls.lib.nj.us/index.php (accessed December 27, 2008).

Burnett, Sara and Simon Collins. 2007. "Ask the Audience! Using a Personal Response System to Enhance Information Literacy and Induction Sessions at Kingston University." *Journal of Information Literacy* 1, no. 2. Available: http://

ojs.lboro.ac.uk/ojs/index.php/JIL/article/view/AFP-V1-I2-2007-1/11 (accessed December 27, 2008).

Burton, John K., David M. Moore, and Susan G. Magliaro. 2004. "Behaviorism and Instructional Technology." In *Handbook of Research in Educational Communications and Technology* (pp. 3–36), edited by David H. Jonassen. Mahwah, NJ: Erlbaum.

Byerly, Gayla, Annie Downey, and Lilly Ramin. 2006. "Footholds and Foundations: Setting Freshmen on the Path to Lifelong Learning." *Reference Services Review* 34, no. 4: 589–598.

Cahoy, Ellysa Stern. 2004. "Put Some Feeling Into It!" *Knowledge Quest* 32, no. 4: 25–28. Available: www.ala.org/ala/aasl/aaslpubsandjournals/kqweb/kqarchives/vol32/32n4cahoy.pdf (accessed December 23, 2008).

Calderhead, Veronica. 1999. "Partnerships in Electronic Learning." *Reference Services Review* 27, no. 4: 336–343.

California Clearinghouse on Library Instruction, North. "Welcome" (2005). Available: http://ic.arc.losrios.edu/~ccli (accessed December 22, 2008).

California Community Colleges, Board of Governors. "An Information Competency Plan for the California Community Colleges" (1998). Available: www.santarosa.edu/~kathy/ICC/bog98-9.pdf (accessed December 22, 2008).

California School Library Association. 1997. *From Library Skills to Information Literacy: A Handbook for the 21st Century*, 2nd ed. San Jose, CA: H. Willow Research and Publishing.

California School Library Association. Standards Taskforce. 2004. *Standards and Guidelines for Strong School Libraries*. Sacramento: California State Library Association.

California State University. "CSU Information Competence Project" (2007). Available: http://library.csun.edu/infocomp/project/index.html (accessed December 22, 2008).

California State University. Information Competence Assessment. "Phase Two Summary Report" (2002) Available: www.csupomona.edu/~kkdunn/ICassess/phase2summary.htm (accessed September 12, 2007).

California State University, San Marcos Library. "CSUSM General Education Website." Available: www2.csusm.edu/ge (accessed December 22, 2008).

Callison, Daniel. 1998. "Authentic Assessment." *School Library Media Activities Monthly* 14, no. 5: 42–43.

Cameron, Lynn. 2004. "Assessing Information Literacy." In *Integrating Information Literacy Into the Higher Education Curriculum* (pp. 207–236), edited by Ilene Rockman. San Francisco: Jossey-Bass.

Campbell, Jerry D. 2006. "Changing a Cultural Icon: The Academic Library as a Virtual Destination." *Educause Review* 41, no. 1: 16–30.

Camtasia Studio. "Screencast Software" (2008). Available: www.techsmith.com/camtasia.asp (accessed December 25, 2008).

Candy, Phil. 1990. "How People Learn to Learn." In *Learning to Learn Across the Life Span*, (pp. 30–63), edited by Robert M. Smith et al. San Francisco: Jossey-Bass.

———. 2000. "Reaffirming a Proud Tradition: Universities and Lifelong Learning." *Active Learning in Higher Education* 1, no. 2: 101–125.

Canfield, Marie P. 1972. "Library Pathfinders." *Drexel Library Quarterly* 8, no. 3: 287–300.

Carlile, Heather. 2007. "The Implications of Library Anxiety for Academic Reference Services: A Review of the Literature." *Australian Academic and Research Libraries* 38, no. 2: 129–147.

Carnevale, Dan. 2000. "Survey Finds 72% Rise in Number of Distance-education Programs." *Chronicle of Higher Education* 46, no. 18: A57–A58.

Carr, Sarah. 1999. "U. of Nebraska's Class.com Hooks Up with a Kentucky School." *Chronicle of Higher Education* (October 22): A56.

Carroll, John M. and Hans van der Meij. 1996. "Ten Misconceptions About Minimalism." *IEEE Transactions on Professional Communication* 39, no. 2: 72–86.

Carspecken, Phil and Michael Apple. 1992. "Critical Qualitative Research: Theory, Methodology, and Practice." In *The Handbook of Qualitative Research* (pp. 507–554), edited by Margaret D. Le Compte, Wendy L. Millroy, and Judith Preissle. New York: Academic Press.

Carter, Elizabeth W. 2000. "Doing the Best You Can with What You Have: Lessons Learned From Outcomes Assessment." *Journal of Academic Librarianship* 28, no. 1: 36–41.

Carter, Henry V. 2007. "Why the Technology, Education and Copyright Harmonization Act Matters to Librarians: Two Cheers for the TEACH Act." *Journal of Interlibrary Loan, Document Delivery & Electronic Reserve* 18, no. 1: 49–56.

Case, Eddie, Ron Stevens, and Melanie Cooper. 2007. "Is Collaborative Grouping an Effective Instructional Strategy? Using IMMEX to Find New Answers to an Old Question." *Journal of College Science Teaching* 36, no. 6: 42–47.

Caspers, Jean S. 1998. "Hands-on Instruction Across the Miles: Using a Web Tutorial to Teach the Literature Review Research Process." *Research Strategies* 16, no. 3: 187–197.

Castellan, N. John Jr. 1993. "Evaluating Information Technology in Teaching and Learning." *Behavior Research Methods, Instruments, & Computers* 25, no. 2: 233–237.

CBiffle. "Power Teaching Critical Thinking: AMAZING STUDENT ENGAGEMENT!" (May 7, 2008). Available: www.teachertube.com/viewVideo.php?video_id=41378 (accessed November 23, 2008).

Centre for Information Literacy Research. "Facebook" (2008). Available: www.facebook.com/group.php?gid=8531548789 (accessed December 23, 2008).

Chartered Institute of Library and Information Professionals. "Information Literacy Definition" (2008). Available: www.

cilip.org.uk/policyadvocacy/informationliteracy/definition/default.htm (accessed September 15, 2008).

Chatto, Calmer D. 2000. "Reference Services: Meeting the Needs of International Adult Learners." *Reference Librarian* 33, no. 69/70: 349–362.

Chau, May Ying. 2002–2003. "Helping Hands: Serving and Engaging International Students." *Reference Librarian* 38, no. 79/80: 383–393.

Chayefsky, Paddy. 1976. *Network*. Produced by Howard Gottfried and directed by Sidney Lumet. Motion Picture. 120 min. Metro-Goldwyn Mayer/United Artists.

Chickering, Arthur W. and Stephen C. Ehrmann. 1996. "Implementing the Seven Principles: Technology as Lever" (October 1996). Available: www.tltgroup.org/programs/seven.html (accessed December 27, 2008).

Chickering, Arthur W. and Zeldo F. Gamson. 1987. "Seven Principles of Good Practice in Undergraduate Education." *AAHE Bulletin* 39, no. 7: 1–6.

Childers, Cheryl D. 1996. "Using Crossword Puzzles as an Aid to Studying Sociological Concepts." *Teaching Sociology* 24, no. 2: 231–235.

Christian, Gayle R., Caroline Blumenthal, and Marjorie Patterson. 2000. "The Information Explosion and the Adult Learner: Implications for Reference Librarians." *Reference Librarian* 33, no. 69/70: 19–30.

Chudnick, Steve. "Analogies." Personal e-mail (June 25, 2008).

Churchwell, Charles D. 2007. "The Evolution of the Academic Research Library During the 1960s." *College & Research Libraries* 68, no. 2: 104–105.

Cibbareli, Pamela R. 1998. "Guidelines for Successfully Teaching the Internet." *Information Outlook* 19, no. 1: 2–11.

Clark, Jennifer. 2008. "PowerPoint and Pedagogy: Maintaining Student Interest in University Lectures." *College Teaching* 56, no. 1: 39–45.

Clark, Richard E., and David F. Feldon. 2005. "Five Common but Questionable Principles of Multimedia Learning." In *Cambridge Handbook of Multimedia Learning* (pp. 97–115), edited by Richard E. Mayer. Cambridge, MA: Cambridge University Press.

Clark, Ruth C. and David Taylor. 1994. "The Cause and Cure of Worker Overload." *Training* 31, no. 7: 40–43.

Classroom Instruction in Facebook. "Facebook" (2008). Available: www.facebook.com/group.php?gid=2416166855 (accessed December 23, 2008).

Clement, John. 1983. "A Conceptual Model Discussed by Galileo and Used Intuitively by Physics Students." In *Mental Models* (pp. 325–340), edited by Dedre Gentner and Albert L. Stevens. Hillsdale, NJ: Lawrence Erlbaum Associates.

Clinchy, Blythe McVicker. 1994. "Issues of Gender in Teaching and Learning." In *Teaching and Learning in the College Classroom* (pp.115–125), edited by Kenneth A. Feldman and Michael B. Paulsen. Needham Heights, MA: Ginn Press.

Clobridge, Abby and David Del Testa. 2008. "The World War II Poster Project: Building a Digital Library Through Information Literacy Partnerships." In *Using Technology to Teach Information Literacy* (pp. 51–64), edited by Thomas P. Mackey and Trudi E. Jacobson. New York: Neal-Schuman.

Clusty. "Search Engine" (2008). Available: www.clusty.com (accessed December 23, 2008).

CMLEA. 1994. *From Library Skills to Information Literacy: A Handbook for the 21st Century*. Castle Rock, CO: H. Willow Research and Publishing.

Coffman, Steve. 1998. "What If You Ran Your Library Like a Bookstore?" *American Libraries* 29, no. 3: 40–44.

Cohen, Laura and Trudi Jacobson. "Evaluating Web Content" (January 2008). Available: http://library.albany.edu/usered/eval/evalweb (accessed December 23, 2008).

Colborn, Nancy Wooton and Rosanne M. Cordell. 1998. "Moving From Subjective to Objective Assessments of Your Instruction Program." *Reference Services Review* 26, no. 3/4: 125–137.

College & Research Libraries. 1939–. Chicago: ALA.

Collins, Linda J. 2007. "Livening Up the Classroom: Using Audience Response Systems to Promote Active Learning." *Medical Reference Services Quarterly* 26, no. 1: 81–88.

CommonCraft. "Explanations in Plain English" (2007). Available: www.commoncraft.com (accessed December 27, 2008).

Communications in Information Literacy. 2007–. Available: www.comminfolit.org/index.php/cil (accessed December 22, 2008).

Computers for Communities. "Homepage." (2008). Available: http://computers4communities.org (accessed December 22, 2008).

Conrad, Rita-Marie and J. Ana Donaldson. 2004. *Engaging the Online Learner*. San Francisco: Jossey-Bass.

Conservapedia. "The Trustworthy Encyclopedia." Available: www.conservapedia.com/Main_Page (accessed November 23, 2008).

Conteh-Morgan, Miriam. 2002. "Connecting the Dots: Limited English Proficiency, Second Language Learning Theories, and Information Literacy Instruction." *Journal of Academic Librarianship* 28, no. 4: 191–196.

Cook, Kim N., Lilith R. Kunkel, and Susan M. Weaver. 1995. "Cooperative Learning in Bibliographic Instruction." *Research Strategies* 13, no. 1: 17–25.

Cooper, James and Pamela Robinson. 1998. "Small Group Instruction in Science, Mathematics, Engineering, and Technology: A Discipline Status Report and a Teaching Agenda for the Future." *Journal of College Science Teaching* 27, no. 6: 383–388.

Cooper, Mark N. "Disconnected, Disadvantaged, and Disenfranchised: Explorations in the Digital Divide." Washington, DC: Consumer Federation of America (2000). Available: www.consumersunion.org/pdf/disconnect.pdf (accessed December 29, 2008).

Cooper, Robert and Robert E. Slavin. 2001. "Cooperative Learning Programs and Multicultural Education: Improving Intergroup Relations." In *Multicultural Education: Issues, Politics and Practices* (pp. 15–33), edited by Farideh Salili and Rumjahn Hoosain. Greenwich, CT: Information Age Publishing.

Copperstein, Susan E. and Kocevar-Weidinger. 2004. "Beyond Active Learning: A Constructivist Approach to Learning." *Reference Services Review* 32, no. 2: 141–148.

Corbeil, Joseph Rene and Maria Elena Valdes-Corbeil. 2007. "Are You Ready for Mobile Learning?" *Educause Quarterly* 30, no. 2: 51–58.

Corcoran, Fran and Dianne Langlois. 1990. "Instruction in the Use of Library Media Centers in Schools." In *The LIRT Instruction Handbook* (pp. 77–88), edited by May Brottman and Mary Loe. Englewood, CO: Libraries Unlimited.

Corno, Lyn and Ellen B. Mandinach. 1983. "The Role of Cognitive Engagement in Classroom Learning and Motivation." *Educational Psychologist* 18, no. 2: 88–108.

Cornwall, Malcolm. 1988. "Putting It Into Practice: Promoting Independent Learning In a Traditional Institution." In *Developing Autonomy in Student Learning* (pp. 242–257), edited by David Boud. London: Kogan Page.

Costa, Arthur L. and Bena Kallick. 2000. "Learning Through Reflection." In *Assessing and Reporting Habits of Mind* (pp. 15–28), edited by Arthur L. Costa and Bena Kallick. Alexandria, VA: Association for Supervision and Curriculum Development.

Cote, Joseph A., James McCullough, and Michael Reilly. 1985. "Effects of Unexpected Situations on Behavior–Intention Differences: A Garbology Analysis." *Journal of Consumer Research* 12, no. 2: 188–194.

Courts, Patrick L. and Kathleen H. McInerney. 1993. *Assessment in Higher Education: Politics, Pedagogy and Portfolios*. Westport, CT: Praeger.

Cox, Christopher and Elizabeth Blakesley Lindsay. 2008. *Information Literacy Instruction Handbook*. Chicago: ALA, ACRL.

Craver, Kathleen W. 1986. "The Changing Instructional Role of the High School Library Media Specialist: 1950–1984." *School Library Media Quarterly* 14, no. 4: 183–191.

Creative Commons. "Homepage" (2008a). Available: http://creativecommons.org (accessed December 25, 2008).

———. "License Your Work." (December 23, 2008b). Available: http://creativecommons.org/about/license (accessed December 29, 2008b).

Crews, Kenneth. "Distance Education and the TEACH Act." ALA. Available: www.ala.org/Template.cfm?Section=Distance_Education_and_the_TEACH_Act&Template=/ContentManagement/ContentDisplay.cfm&ContentID=25939 (accessed December 25, 2008).

Critical Thinking: Unfinished Business. 2005. Edited by Christine M. McMahon. San Francisco: Jossey-Bass.

Cross, K. Patricia. 1998. "Classroom Research: Implementing the Scholarship of Teaching." *New Directions for Teaching and Learning* 75: 5–12.

Cruickshank, Donald R., Deborah Bainer Jenkins, and Kim K. Metcalf. 2003. *The Act of Teaching*, 3rd ed. New York: McGraw-Hill.

Cuban, Larry. 1986. *Teachers and Machines: The Classroom Use of Technology Since 1920*. New York: Teachers College Press, Columbia University.

Culturgrams. 2008. Provo, UT: Brigham Young University, eMSTAR Inc.

Cummings, Lara Ursin. 2007. "Bursting Out of the Box: Outreach to the Millennial Generation Through Student Services Programs." *Reference Services Review* 35, no. 2: 285–295.

Cunningham, April and Alison Carr. 2008. Research as a Cognitive Process. In *SCIL Works 2008: Putting Theory Into Practice—The Why Behind Instructional Strategies*. Claremont, CA: SCIL.

Cunningham, Jim. 1999. "Ten Ways to Improve Your Web Site. *College & Research Libraries News* 60, no. 8: 614–615, 628.

Cunningham, Sheila and Bernadette Swanson. "Library Instruction/Marketing Posters" (2006). Available: http://trc.ucdavis.edu/instruction/posters (accessed December 24, 2008).

CUNY Graduate Center. "Research by Subject or Program" (2008). Available: http://library.gc.cuny.edu/subsplus/subjects/subjects.php (accessed December 27, 2008).

Curry, C. Lyn. 2000. "Facilitating Adult Learning: The Role of the Academic Librarian." *Reference Librarian* 33, no. 69/70: 219–231.

Curtis, Donnelyn. 1995. "Writing for Information Literacy Training." In *Teaching Electronic Information Literacy: A How-To-Do-It Manual* (pp. 41–56), edited by Donald A. Barclay. New York: Neal-Schuman.

Curtis, Ruth V. and Charles M. Reigeluth. 1984. "The Use of Analogies in Written Text." *Instructional Science* 13: 99–117.

Curzon, Susan. "Information Competence" (1995). Available: http://library.csun.edu/susan.curzon/corecomp.html (accessed September 12 2007).

———. 2002. "Introducing the CSU Information Competence Initiative." *Libraries@CalState: Newsletter of the California State University Libraries* 1, no. 1: 1–2.

———. 2004. "Developing Faculty–Librarian Partnerships in Information Literacy." In *Integrating Information Literacy Into the Higher Education Curriculum: Practical Models for Transformation* (pp. 29–45), edited by Ilene Rockman. San Francisco: Jossey-Bass.

Curzon, Susan and Lynn Lampert, eds. 2007. *Proven Strategies for Building an Information Literacy Program*. New York: Neal-Schuman.

Dagher, Zoubeida R. 1995. "Review of Studies on the Effectiveness of Instructional Analogies in Science Education." *Science Education* 79, no. 3: 295–312.

Dalsgaard, Christian and Mikkel Godsk. 2007. "Transforming Traditional Lectures Into Problem-based Blended Learning: Challenges and Experiences." *Journal of Open and Distance Learning* 22, no. 1: 29–42.

Damast, Alison. "Be True to Your Cyberschool." *Business Week*, April 19, 2007. Available: www.businessweek.com/bschools/content/apr2007/bs20070419_375162.htm (accessed December 27, 2008).

D'Andrade, Hugh. "Library of Congress on DMCA, Copyright Law Troubles. San Francisco: Electronic Frontier Foundation (July 17, 2008) Available: www.eff.org/deeplinks/2008/07/library-congress-dmca-copyright-law-troubles (accessed December 25, 2008).

Darwin, Charles. 1859. *On the Origin of the Species by Means of Natural Selection*. London: J. Murray.

Daugherty, Alice. "Re: Analogies in IL." Personal e-mail (June 25, 2008).

Davis, Will. "Change the World BIO 300 Assignment." (2007). Available: http://web.arc.losrios.edu/~library/faculty/alt_assigns/altassign.htm#WDavis (accessed December 23, 2008).

de Jong, Ton. 2005. "The Guided Discovery Principle in Multimedia Learning." In *The Cambridge Handbook of Multimedia Learning* (pp. 215–228), edited by Richard E. Mayer. Cambridge, MA: Cambridge University Press.

DeCandido, GraceAnne A. 1999. "Bibliographic Good vs. Evil in *Buffy the Vampire Slayer*." *American Libraries* 30, no. 8: 44.

Decoding the Disciplines: Helping Students Learn Disciplinary Ways of Thinking. 2004. Edited by David Pace and Joan Middendorf. New Directions for Teaching and Learning, no. 98. San Francisco: Jossey-Bass.

Dede, Chris. 2005. "Planning for Neomillennial Learning Styles." *Educause Quarterly* 28, no. 1. Available: http://connect.educause.edu/Library/EDUCAUSE+Quarterly/PlanningforNeomillennialL/39899 (accessed December 27, 2008).

Deitering, Ann-Marie. "Critical Glanceability" (September 19, 2008). Available: http://info-fetishist.org/2008/09/19/criticalthinking (accessed December 29, 2008).

DeLorenzo, Ron. 1999. "When Hell Freezes Over: An Approach to Develop Student Interest and Communication Skills." *Journal of Chemical Education* 76, no. 4: 503.

Dembo, Myron H. 1988a. *Applying Educational Psychology in the Classroom*, 3rd ed. New York: Longman.

———. 1988b. *Teaching for Learning: Applying Educational Psychology in the Classroom*. Santa Monica, CA: Goodyear.

Dempsey, Beth. 2004. "Cashing in on Service." *Library Journal* 18, no. 1: 38–41.

DeMulder, Elizabeth K. and Kimberly K. Eby. 1999. "Bridging Troubled Waters: Learning Communities for the 21st Century." *American Behavioral Scientist* 42, no. 5: 892–901.

Denman, Mariate. 2005. "How to Create Memorable Lectures." *Speaking of Teaching* 14, no. 1: 1–5.

Dervin, Brenda and Patricia Dewdney. 1986. "Neutral Questioning: A New Approach to the Reference Interview." *RQ* 25, no. 4: 506–513.

Desai, Christina M. and Stephanie J. Graves. 2008. "Cyberspace or Face-to-Face: The Teachable Moment and Changing Reference Mediums." *Reference & User Services Quarterly* 47, no. 3: 242–255.

Dewald, Nancy. 1999a. "Transporting Good Library Instruction Practice Into the Web Environment: An Analysis of Online Tutorials." *Journal of Academic Librarianship* 25, no. 1: 26–32.

———. 1999b. "Web-based Library Instruction: What Is Good Pedagogy?" *Information Technology and Libraries* 18, no. 1: 26–31.

Dewald, Nancy et al. 2000. "Information Literacy at a Distance: Instructional Design Issues." *Journal of Academic Librarianship* 26, no. 1: 33–44.

Dewey, John. 1915. "The School and Social Progress." In *The School and Society* (pp. 3–28), edited by John Dewey. Chicago: University of Chicago Press.

———. 1916. *Democracy and Education*. New York: Macmillan.

Dewey, Melvil. 1876. "The Profession." *American Library Journal* 1:6.

Diaz, David P. and Ryan B. Cartnal. 1999. "Students' Learning Styles in Two Classes: Online Distance Learning and Equivalent On-campus." *College Teaching* 47, no. 4: 130–136.

Dick, Walter W., Lou Carey, and James O. Carey. 2005. *The Systematic Design of Instruction*, 6th ed. Boston: Pearson/Allyn & Bacon.

Digital Divide Network. "About the Digital Divide Network." Available: www.digitaldivide.net/about (accessed December 22, 2008).

DiMartino, Diane and Lucinda R. Zoe. 2000. "International Students and the Library: New Tools, New Users, and New Instruction." In *Teaching the New Library to Today's Users: Reaching International, Minority, Senior Citizens, Gay/Lesbian, First Generation, At-risk, Graduate and Returning Students, and Distance Learners* (pp.17–43), edited by Trudi E. Jacobson and Helene C. Williams. New York: Neal-Schuman.

Discovery Education. "Puzzlemaker" (2008). Available: http://puzzlemaker.discoveryeducation.com (accessed December 28, 2008).

Dixon, Mary. "Using an Encyclopedia Scavenger Hunt" (2006). Available: www.informationliteracy.org/plans/view/211/back/0 (accessed December 23, 2008).

DOAJ. "Directory of Open Access Journals" (2008). Available: www.doaj.org (accessed December 23, 2008).

Dodge, Bernie. "WebQuest." (October 29, 2000a). Available: http://webquest.org/index.php (accessed December 22, 2008).

———. "A WebQuest About WebQuests" (September 10, 2000b). Available: http://edweb.sdsu.edu/WebQuest/webquestwebquest-es.html (accessed December 27, 2008).

Dods, Richard. 1997. "An Action Research Study of the Effectiveness of Problem-Based Learning in Promoting the Acquisition and Retention of Knowledge." *Journal for the Education of the Gifted* 20, no. 4: 423–437.

Dogpile. "Search Engine" (2008). Available: www.dogpile.com (accessed December 23, 2008).

Doherty, William A. and Cleborne D. Maddux. 2002. "An Investigation of Instruction and Student Learning Styles in Internet-based Community College Courses." *Computers in the School* 19, no. 3/4: 22–32.

Dolphin, Philippa. 1990. "Evaluation of User Education Programmes." In *User Education in Academic Libraries* (pp. 73–89), edited by Hugh Fleming. London: Library Association.

DomainTools. "Whois Lookup and Domain Suggestions." Available: www.domaintools.com (accessed December 23, 2008).

Donovan, Judy. 2006. "Active Learning Online: Increased Student Involvement and Impact on Academic Achievement." Research paper presented at National Education Computing Conference. July 4–7, San Diego.

Doolittle, John H. 1995. "Using Riddles and Interactive Computer Games to Teach Problem-solving Skills." *Teaching of Psychology* 22, no. 1: 33–36.

Dorner, Daniel G. and G.E. Gorman. 2006. "Information Literacy Education in Asian Developing Countries: Cultural Factors Affecting Curriculum Development and Programme Delivery." *IFLA Journal* 32, no. 4: 281–293.

Downing, Karen. 2000. "Instruction in a Multicultural Setting: Teaching and Learning with Students of Color." In *Teaching the New Library to Today's Users: Reaching International, Minority, Senior Citizens, Gay/Lesbian, First Generation, At-risk, Graduate and Returning Students, and Distance Learners* (pp. 47–70), edited by Trudi E. Jacobson and Helen C. Williams. New York: Neal-Schuman.

Downing, Karen and Joseph Diaz. 1993. "Instruction in a Multicultural/Multiracial Environment." In *Learning to Teach: Workshops on Instruction* (pp. 37–45), edited by Learning to Teach Task Force. Chicago: ALA.

Doyle, Christina S. 1996. "Information Literacy: Status Report From the United States." In *Learning for Life* (pp. 39–48), edited by Di Booker. Adelaide, Australia: University of South Australia Library.

Doyle, Christina S. and ERIC Clearinghouse on Information & Technology. 1994. *Information Literacy in an Information Society: A Concept for the Information Age*. Syracuse, NY: ERIC Clearinghouse on Information & Technology Syracuse University.

Driscoll, Amy and Swarrup Wood. 2007. *Developing Outcomes-based Assessment for Learner-centered Education*. Sterling, VA: Stylus.

Driscoll, Marcy Perkins. 1994. *Psychology of Learning for Instruction*. Boston: Allyn & Bacon.

Dudley, Miriam. 1978. *Library Instruction Workbook*. Los Angeles: University of California Library.

———. 2000. "History of BIS." Interview by Esther Grassian. March 26, 2000.

Duncan, Jennifer and Wendy Holliday. 2008. "The Role of Information Architecture in Designing a Third-generation Library Web Site." *College & Research Libraries* 69, no. 4: 301–318.

Dunn, Rita S. 2000. "Capitalizing on College Students' Learning Styles: Theory, Practice, and Research." In *Practical Approaches to Using Learning Styles in Higher Education* (pp. 3–18), edited by Rita S. Dunn and Shirley Griggs. Westport, CT: Bergin and Garvey.

Dunn, Rita S. and Shirley Griggs. 2000. "Practical Approaches to Using Learning Styles in Higher Education." In *Practical Approaches to Using Learning Styles in Higher Education* (pp.19–32), edited by Rita S. Dunn and Shirley Griggs. Westport, CT: Bergin and Garvey.

Eadie, Tom. 1990. "Immodest Proposals: User Instruction for Students Does Not Work." *Library Journal* 115, no. 17: 42–45.

Earlham College. "Homepage" (2008). Available: www.earlham.edu (accessed December 22, 2008).

Eble, Kenneth Eugene. 1988. *The Craft of Teaching: A Guide to Mastering the Professor's Art*, 2nd ed. The Jossey-Bass Higher Education Series. San Francisco: Jossey-Bass.

Eco, Umberto. 1983. *The Name of the Rose*. San Diego: Harcourt, Brace, Jovanovich.

EDEN. "European Distance and e-Learning Network." Available: www.eden-online.org/eden.php (accessed December 27, 2008).

Educause Learning Initiative. "7 Things You Should Know About. . . " (2008a). Available: www.educause.edu/ELI7Things/7495?bhcp=1&time=1225774460 (accessed December 28, 2008).

———. "7 Things You Should Know About Second Life" (June 11, 2008b). Available: http://connect.educause.edu/Library/ELI/7ThingsYouShouldKnowAbout/46892 (accessed December 29, 2008).

EFF. "Unintended Consequences: Seven Years Under the DMCA." San Francisco: Electronic Frontier Foundation (April 2006). Available: www.eff.org/files/DMCA_unintended_v4.pdf (accessed December 25, 2008).

———. Available: www.eff.org (accessed December 25, 2008).

———. "ELI Resources" (2008c). Available: www.educause.edu/ELIResources/10220 (accessed December 29, 2008).

"eGames Generator." Available: https://egames.clsllc.com (accessed December 28, 2008).

Eisenberg, Michael. 2007. Teaching Information Literacy:

Context, Context, Context. In *Proven Strategies for Building an Information Literacy Program*, edited by Susan Curzon and Lynn Lampert. New York: Neal-Schuman.

Eisenberg, Michael and Robert E. Berkowitz. 1990. *Information Problem-solving: The Big Six Skills Approach to Library & Information Skills Instruction, Information Management, Policy, and Services* (pp. 163–175). Norwood, NJ: Ablex.

———. "The Big6: Information Skills for Student Achievement" (2008). Available: www.big6.com (accessed December 22, 2008).

Eisenberg, Michael, and Michael Brown. 1992. "Current Themes Regarding Library and Information Skills Instruction: Research Supporting and Research Lacking." *School Library Media Quarterly* 20, no. 2: 103-109.

Elhoweris, Hala, Gowri Parameswaran, and Negmeldin Alsheikh. 2004. "College Students Myths About Diversity and What College Faculty Can Do." *Multicultural Education* 12, no. 2: 13–18.

Eliot, Andrew J. and Markus A. Maier. 2007. "Color and Psychological Functioning." *Current Directions in Psychological Science* 16, no. 5: 250–254.

Elliot, Andrew J. et al. 2007. "Color and Psychological Functioning: The Effect of Red on Performance Attainment." *Journal of Experimental Psychology: General* 136, no. 1: 154–168.

Elliott, Stephen N., Thomas R. Kratochwill, Joan Littlefield Cook, and John F. Travers. 2000. *Educational Psychology: Effective Teaching, Effective Learning*, 3rd ed. Boston: McGraw-Hill.

Ellis, Lisa A. 2004. "Approaches to Teaching Through Digital Reference." *Reference Services Review* 32, no. 2: 103–119.

Ellis, R.A., G. Marcus, and R. Taylor. 2005. "Learning Through Inquiry: Student Difficulties with Online Course-based Material." *Journal of Computer Assisted Learning* 21: 239–252.

El Mansour, Bassou and Davison M. Munpinga. 2007. "Students' Positive and Negative Experiences in Hybrid and Online Classes." *College Student Journal* 41, no. 1: 242–248.

Elmborg, James. 2004. "Literacies Large and Small." *International Journal of Learning* 11, no. 10: 1235–1239.

———. 2006. "Critical Information Literacy: Implications for Instructional Practice." *Journal of Academic Librarianship* 32, no. 2: 192–199.

Elmira College. "SubjectsPlus" (June 25, 2008). Available: www.gtlsubjects.net/subsplus/subjects (accessed December 27, 2008).

Emmett, Ada and Judith Emde. 2007. "Assessing Information Literacy Skills Using the ACRL Standards as a Guide." *Reference Services Review* 35, no. 2: 210–229.

Emmons, Mark and Wanda Martin. 2002. "Engaging Conversation: Evaluating the Contributions of Library Instruction to the Quality of Student Research." *College & Research Libraries* 63, no. 6: 545–560.

Encyclopaedia Britannica. "Fatally Flawed: Refuting the Recent Study on Encyclopedia Accuracy by the Journal *Nature*" (March 2006). Available: http://corporate.britannica.com/britannica_nature_response.pdf (accessed December 23, 2008).

Encyclopedia of Library and Information Science, vol. 25 (p. 66). 1978a. New York: Marcel Dekker.

Encyclopedia of Library and Information Science, vol. 25 (p. 449). 1978b. New York: Marcel Dekker.

Engeldinger, Eugene. 1988. "Teaching Only the Essentials: The Thirty-minute Stand." *Reference Services Review* 16, no. 4: 47–50, 96.

Envisioneer Express. "3D Building Design & Project Viewer." Available: www.envisioneerexpress.com (accessed December 24, 2008).

Erickson, Frederick. 2007. "Culture in Society and Educational Practices." In *Multicultural Education: Issues and Perspectives* (pp. 33–61), edited by James A. Banks and Cherry A.M. Banks. Hoboken, NJ: Wiley.

Estabrook, Leigh, Evans Witt, and Lee Raine. "Information Searches That Solve Problems." Washington, DC: Pew Internet & American Life Project (December 30, 2007). Available: www.pewinternet.org/PPF/r/231/report_display.asp (accessed December 22, 2008).

ETS. "ICT Literacy Assessment: Do Your Students Have the ICT Skills They Need to Succeed?" (2004). Available: www.ets.org/ictliteracy (accessed November 14, 2007).

———. "iSkills Assessment Tour" (2008). Available: www.ets.org/portal/site/ets/menuitem.1488512ecfd5b8849a77b13bc3921509/?vgnextoid=1ebb0e3c27a85110VgnVCM10000022f95190RCRD&vgnextchannel=34b4a79898a85110VgnVCM10000022f95190RCRD (accessed December 24, 2008).

Eve, Juliet, Margo de Groot, and Anne-Marie Schmidt. 2007. "Supporting Lifelong Learning in Public Libraries Across Europe." *Library Review* 56, no. 5: 393–406.

Everquest. Available: http://everquest.station.sony.com (accessed December 28, 2008).

Evidence-based Library and Information Practice. 2006–. University of Alberta Learning Services. Available: http://ejournals.library.ualberta.ca/index.php/EBLIP (accessed December 22, 2008).

Facebook. "Homepage" (2008). Available: www.facebook.com (accessed December 8, 2008).

Facione, Peter A. "Critical Thinking: A Statement of Expert Consensus for Purposes of Educational Assessment and Instruction." Newark, DE: American Philosophical Association (1990). Available: http://eric.ed.gov/ERICWebPortal/contentdelivery/servlet/ERICServlet?accno=ED315423 (accessed December 29, 2008).

Facione, Peter A. and Noreen C. Facione. "Holistic Critical Thinking Scoring Rubric" (1994). Available: https://www.

aacu.org/meetings/pdfs/criticalthinkingrubric.PDF (accessed December 23, 2008).

Fallon, Sean. "Solar Powered 'Sticker Lamps' Offer Paper Thin Illumination." Gizmodo (October 27, 2008). Available: http://gizmodo.com/5069451/solar-powered-sticker-lamps-offer- paper+thin-illumination (accessed December 27, 2008).

Farber, Evan Ira. 1974. "Library Instruction Throughout the Curriculum: Earlham College Program." In *Educating the Library User* (pp. 145–162), edited by John Lubans, Jr. New York: Bowker.

———. 1993. "Bibliographic Instruction at Earlham College." In *Bibliographic Instruction in Practice: A Tribute to the Legacy of Evan Ira Farber* (pp. 1–14), edited by Larry Hardesty, J. Hasteiter, and D. Henderson. Ann Arbor, MI: Pierian Press.

———. 1995a. "Bibliographic Instruction, Briefly." In *Information for a New Age: Redefining the Librarian* (pp. 24–33), edited by ALA Library Instruction Round Table. Englewood, CO: Libraries Unlimited.

———. 1995b. "Plus ca Change?" *Library Trends* 44, no. 2: 430–438.

———. 2007. *College Libraries and the Teaching/Learning Process: Selections From the Writings of Evan Ira Farber*, edited by David Gansz. Richmond, IN: Earlham College Press.

Fargo, Lucile F. 1939. *The Library in the School*. Chicago: ALA.

Farkas, Meredith G. 2007. *Social Software in Libraries*. Medford, NJ: Information Today.

———. 2008. "In Practice." *American Libraries* 39, no. 9: 45.

Farmer, Lesley S.J. 1999. "Making Information Literacy a Schoolwide Reform Effort." *Book Report* 18, no. 3: 6–8.

———. 2002. "Harnessing the Power of Information Power." *Teacher–Librarian* 29, no. 3: 20–24.

———. 2007. "The School Library Media Teacher as Information Literacy Partner." In *Proven Strategies for Building an Information Literacy Program* (pp. 279–294), edited by Susan Curzon and Lynn Lampert. New York: Neal-Schuman.

Feeley, Jim. "Lights! Camera! Vodcast!" *Wired* 14, no. 5 (May 2006). Available: www.wired.com/wired/archive/14.05/howto.html (accessed December 26, 2008).

Feinberg, Jonathan. "Wordle" (2008). Available: http://wordle.net (accessed December 26, 2008).

Felder, Richard M. and Rebecca Brent. 1996. "Navigating the Bumpy Road to Student-centered Instruction." *College Teaching* 44, no. 2: 43–47.

Fenwick, Tara J. 2000. "Expanding Conditions of Experiential Learning: A Review of the Five Contemporary Perspectives of Cognition." *Adult Education Quarterly* 50, no. 4: 243–272.

Fialkoff, Francine. 2008. "The Borders Concept." *Library Journal* 133, no. 5: 8.

Fick, Gary. "ILI Analogies." Personal e-mail (June 23, 2008).

Fields, Anne M. 2006. "Ill-structured Problems and the Reference Consultation: The Librarian's Role in Developing Student Expertise." *Reference Services Review* 34, no. 3: 405–420.

Fink, Deborah. 1989. *Process and Politics in Library Research*. Chicago: ALA.

Fink, L. Dee. 2003. *Creating Significant Learning Experiences: An Integrated Approach*. San Francisco: Jossey-Bass.

Finkelstein, Ellen. "PowerPoint Tips" (2008). Available: www.ellenfinkelstein.com/powerpoint_tip.html (accessed December 27, 2008).

Fisher, Karen E., Joan C. Durrance, and Marian Bouch Hinton. 2004. "Information Grounds and the Use of Need-based Services by Immigrants in Queens N.Y.: A Context-based, Outcome Evaluation Approach." *Journal of the American Society for Information Science and Technology* 55, no. 8: 754–766.

Fister, Barbara. 1990. "Teaching Research as a Social Act: Collaborative Learning and the Library." *RQ* 29, no. 3: 505–509.

———. 2002. "Fear of Reference." *Chronicle of Higher Education* 48, no. 40: B20.

Five Colleges of Ohio. "Flow of Information" (2000). Available: http://collaborations.denison.edu/ohio5/infolit/a1flow (accessed December 23, 2008).

Fjallbrant, Nancy. 1988. "Recent Trends in Online User Education." *IATUL Quarterly* 2, no. 4: 228–236.

Fjallbrant, Nancy and Ian Malley. 1984. *User Education in Libraries*. London: Clive Bingley.

Fleck, Margaret et al. 2002. "From Informing to Remembering Ubiquitous Systems in Interactive Museums." *Pervasive Computing* 1, no. 2: 13–21.

Fletcher, J. D. and Sigmund Tobias. 2005. "The Multimedia Principle." In *The Cambridge Handbook of Multimedia Learning* (pp. 117–134). Cambridge, MA: Cambridge University Press.

Flickr. "Photo Sharing" (2008). Available: www.flickr.com (accessed December 25, 2008).

Ford, Donna Y. and J. John Harris. 1999. *Multicultural Gifted Education*. New York: Teachers College Press.

Formist. "Homepage." Available: http://formist.enssib.fr/rubrique.php3?id_rubrique=4 (accessed December 22, 2008).

Foster, Nancy Fried and Susan Gibbons, eds. "Studying Students: The Undergraduate Research Project at the University of Rochester" (2007). Available: http://docushare.lib.rochester.edu/docushare/dsweb/View/Collection-4436 (accessed December 27, 2008).

Fox, Richard. 1995. "Development and Learning." In *An Introduction to Teaching: Psychological Perspectives* (pp. 55–71), edited by Charles Desforges. Oxford, England: Blackwell.

Francis, Mary. "Analogies." Personal e-mail (June 24, 2008).

Franklin, Lori. 2006. "Never Too Young to Learn: Website Evaluation as Elementary." *Library Media Connection* 24, no. 4: 39–41.

Frederick, Peter J. 1981. "The Dreaded Discussion: Ten Ways to Start." *Improving College and University Teaching* 29, no. 3: 109–114.

———. 1986. "The Lively Lecture." *College Teaching* 34, no. 1: 45–50.

Freedman, Janet L. and Harold A. Bantly. 1982. *Information Searching: A Handbook for Designing & Creating Instructional Programs,* rev. ed. Metuchen, NJ: Scarecrow Press.

Freeman, Kyri. "Re: Re: Instruction Session Handouts/Packets" (August 26, 2008). Electronic bulletin board. Available: ILI-L@ala.org (accessed August 26, 2008).

Freilberg, H. Jerome and Amy Driscoll. 2005. *Universal Teaching Strategies*. Boston: Allyn & Bacon.

Freire, Paulo. 2002. *Pedagogy of the Oppressed.* New York: Continuum.

Frick, Elizabeth. 1975. "Information Structure and Bibliographic Instruction." *Journal of Academic Librarianship* 1, no. 4: 12–14.

———. 1990. "Qualitative Evaluation of User Education Programs: The Best Choice?" *Research Strategies* 8, no. 1: 4–13.

Friedman, Lia G. and Melissa Morrone. "The Sidewalk Is Our Reference Desk: When Librarians Take to the Streets" (2008). In *World Library and Information Congress: 74th IFLA General Conference and Council*, August 10–14, Quebec, Canada. Available: www.ifla.org/IV/ifla74/papers/158-Friedman_Morrone-en.pdf (accessed January 3, 2009).

friendofdarwin's Darwin Poster (June 25, 2007). Available: www.youtube.com/watch?v=f_iJb2AeL4U (accessed December 26, 2008).

Fritsch, H. 2001. "Distance Education." In *International Encyclopedia of the Social and Behavioral Sciences* (pp. 3781–3784). Amsterdam: Elsevier.

Frogg, Piper. 2007. "A Dozen Tips for Diverse Classrooms." *Chronicle of Higher Education* 54, no. 9: B12.

Fry, Thomas K. and Joan Kaplowitz. 1988. "The English 3 Library Instruction Program at UCLA: A Follow-up Study." *Research Strategies* 6, no. 3: 100–108.

Fryer, Wesley A. "Writing Webpages with Wesley: Web Authoring Concepts/Basic Terms" (August 5, 2001). Available: www.wtvi.com/html/www2.html (accessed December 26, 2008).

Gagnon, G.W. and M. Collay. 2001. *Designing for Learning: Six Elements in Constructivist Classrooms*. Thousand Oaks, CA: Corwin Press.

Gaines, Lawrence S. and Robert D. Coursey. 1974. "Novelty Experiencing, Internal Scanning, and Cognitive Control." *Perceptual and Motor Skills* 38, no. 6: 891–898.

Gaitan, Concha Delgago. 2006. *Building Culturally Responsive Classrooms*. Thousand Oaks, CA: Corwin Press.

Gallucci, Kathy. 2006. "Learning Concepts with Cases." *Journal of College Science Teaching* 36, no. 2: 16–20.

Gao, Hong et al. 2007. "A Review of Studies on Collaborative Concept Mapping: What Have We Learned About the Technique and What Is Next?" *Journal of Interactive Learning Research* 18, no. 4: 479–492.

Garfield, Bob. 1992. "Freberg." *Advertising Age* 63, no. 3: 52.

Garner, Pamela W. 2008. "The Challenge of Teaching for Diversity in the College Classroom When the Professor Is the 'Other.'" *Teaching in Higher Education* 13, no. 1: 117–120.

Garner, R. L. 2006. "Humor in Pedagogy: How Ha-Ha Can Lead to Aha!" *College Teaching* 54, no. 1: 177–180.

Garrett, Jeffrey. 2007. "Subject Headings in Full-text Environments: The ECCO Experiment." *College & Research Libraries* 68, no. 1: 69–81.

Gartner Group Intraweb. "Hype Cycles" (2008). Available: http://gartner.library.ucla.edu (accessed December 28, 2008).

Gatten, Jeffrey N. 2004. "Student Psychosocial and Cognitive Development: Theory to Practice in Academic Libraries." *Reference Services Review* 32, no. 2: 157–163.

Geck, Caroline. 2006. "The Generation Z Connection: Teaching Information Literacy and the Newest Net Generation." *Teacher-Librarian* 33, no. 3: 19–23.

Gelmon, Sherril B. 1997. "Intentional Improvement: The Deliberate Linkage of Assessment and Accreditation." In *Assessing Impact: Evidence and Action—Presentations From the 1997 AAHE Conference on Assessment and Quality* (pp. 51–65), edited by AAHE. Washington, DC: American Association for Higher Education.

Gentner, Dedre, Jeffrey Loewenstein, and Leigh Thompson. 2003. "Learning and Transfer: A General Role for Analogical Encoding." *Journal of Educational Psychology* 95, no. 2: 393–408.

Georghiades, Petros. 2002. "Making Children's Scientific Ideas More Durable." *Primary Science Review* 74: 24–27.

———. 2004. "Making Pupils' Conceptions of Electricity More Durable by Means of Situation Metacognition." *International Journal of Science Education* 26, no. 1: 85–99.

Germain, Carol Anne, Trudi E. Jacobson, and Sue A. Kaczor. 2000. "A Comparison of the Effectiveness of Presenting Formats for Instruction: Teaching First-year Students." *College & Research Libraries* 61, no. 1: 65–72.

Gerstenmaier, J. and H. Mandi. 2004. "Constructivism in Cognitive Psychology." In *International Encyclopedia of the Social and Behavioral Sciences* (pp. 2654–2659). Available: www.sciencedirect.com/science?_ob=MiamiImageURL&_imagekey=B7MRM-4MT-09VJ-1R-1&_cdi=23486&_user=4423&_check=y&_orig=search&_coverDate=10%2F18%2F2004&view=c&wchp=dGLbVzW-zSkWW&md5=64d3d3263be83dc

c2d3892bfe1b64d4a&ie=/sdarticle.pdf (accessed, July 5, 2008).

Ghaphery, Jimmy and Dan Ream. 2000. "VCU's My Library: Librarians Love It. . . . Users? Well, Maybe." *Information Technology and Libraries* 19, no. 4: 186–190.

Gibson, Craig. 1992. "Accountability for BI Programs in Academic Libraries: Key Issues for the 1990's." *Reference Librarian* no. 38: 99–108.

———. 2008. "The History of Information Literacy." In *Information Literacy Handbook* (pp. 10–23), edited by Christopher N. Cox and Elizabeth Blakesley Lindsay. Chicago: ALA, ACRL.

Gilchrist, Debra. 1997. "To Enable Information Competency: The Abilities Model in Library Instruction. In *Programs That Work: Papers and Sessions Material Presented at the 24th National LOEX Library Instruction Conference* (pp. 19–33), edited by Linda Shirato. Ann Arbor, MI: Pierian Press.

Giles, Jim. 2005. "Internet Encyclopedias Go Head to Head." *Nature* 438: 900–901.

Gilton, Donna L. 1994. "A World of Difference: Preparing for Information Literacy Instruction for Diverse Groups." *Multicultural Review* 3, no. 3: 54–62.

Ginman, Mariam and Sara von Ungern-Sternberg. 2003. "Cartoons as Information." *Journal of Information Science* 29, no. 1: 69–77.

Given, Lisa. 2000. "Envisioning the Mature Re-entry Student: Constructing New Identities in the Traditional University Setting." *Reference Librarian* 33, no. 69–70: 79–83.

Glasser, William. 1992. *The Quality School: Managing Students Without Coercion,* 2nd ed. New York: Harper Perennial.

Gliffy. "Online Diagram Software" (2008). Available: www.gliffy.com (accessed December 24, 2008).

Glitz, Beryl. 1998. *Focus Groups for Libraries and Librarians.* New York: Forbes.

Gold, Helen E. 2005. "Engaging the Adult Learner: Creating Effective Library Instruction." *portal: Libraries and the Academy* 5, no. 4: 467–481.

Goldenstein, Cheryl et al. "TIP: Tutorial for Information Power." Laramie: University of Wyoming (2008). Available: http://tip.uwyo.edu (accessed December 23, 2008).

Google. Available: www.google.com (accessed December 27, 2008).

Google Blogger. 2008. Available: https://www.blogger.com/start (accessed December 29, 2008).

Google Image Labeler. 2007. Available: http://images.google.com/imagelabeler (accessed December 5, 2008).

Google Image Search. 2008. Available: http://images.google.com (accessed December 27, 2008).

Google Reader. 2008. Available: https://www.google.com/accounts/ServiceLogin?hl=en&nui=1&service=reader&continue=http%3A%2F%2Fwww.google.com%2Freader (accessed December 27, 2008).

Google Scholar. 2008. Available: http://scholar.google.com (accessed December 27, 2008).

Google SketchUp. 2008. Available: http://sketchup.google.com/product/gsu.html (accessed December 24, 2008).

Google SketchUp for Education. 2008. Available: http://sketchup.google.com/customers/education.html (accessed December 24, 2008).

Google Talk. 2008. Available: www.google.com/talk (accessed December 27, 2008).

Google Trends. 2008. Available: www.google.com/trends (accessed December 30, 2008).

Gooler, Dennis B. 1990. "Changing the Way We Live in the Information Age." In *Learning to Learn Across the Life Span* (pp. 307–328), edited by Robert M. Smith. San Francisco: Jossey-Bass.

Gordin, Douglas N. et al. 1996. "Using the World Wide Web to Build Learning Communities in K–12." *Journal of Computer Mediated Communication* 2, no. 3. Available: http://jcmc.indiana.edu/vol2/issue3 (accessed December 24, 2008).

Gordon, Rachel Singer and Michael Stephens. 2006. "Tech Tips for Every Librarian." *Computers in Libraries* 26, no. 5: 34–35.

Gordon-Murnane, Laura. 2006. "Social Bookmarking, Folksonomies, and Web 2.0 Tools." *Searcher* 14, no. 6: 26–38.

Gorman, Michael. 1991. "Send for a Child of Four! Or Creating the BI-less Academic Library." *Library Trends* 39, no. 3: 354–362.

Gould, Ted. 1977. *6 Ways to Ask a Reference Question.* Videotape, 6 min. Produced and directed by Ted Gould. Davis: University of California.

Grabowski, Stanley M. 1980. "What Instructors Need to Know About Adult Learners." *National Society for Performance and Instruction Journal* 19, no. 1: 15–16.

Gradowski, Gail, Loanne Snavely, and Paula Dempsey, eds. 1998. *Designs for Active Learning.* Chicago: ALA.

Grafstein, Ann. 2002. "A Discipline-based Approach to Information Literacy." *Journal of Academic Librarianship* 28, no. 4: 197–204.

Grant, Carl and Christina Sleeter. 1993. "Race, Class, Gender and Disability in the Classroom." In *Multicultural Education: Issues and Perspectives* (pp. 48–67), edited by James A. Banks and Cherry A.M. Banks. Boston: Allyn & Bacon.

———. 2007. "Race, Class, Gender and Disability in the Classroom." In *Multicultural Education: Issues and Perspectives* (pp. 63–83), edited by James A. Banks and Cherry A.M. Banks. Hoboken, NJ: Wiley.

Grassian, Esther. 1993. "Setting Up and Managing a BI Program." In *Sourcebook for Bibliographic Instruction* (pp. 59–73), edited by Katherine Branch and Carolyn Dusenbury. Chicago: ALA.

———. "Thinking Critically About World Wide Web Resources" Los Angeles: University of California Los Angeles

(1995). Available: www2.library.ucla.edu/libraries/college/11605_12337.cfm (accessed December 23, 2008).

———. 1998. "alt.help.I.can't.keep.up! Support for the 'Electronically Challenged.'" In *Finding Common Ground: Creating the Library of the Future Without Diminishing the Library of the Past* (pp. 136–139), edited by Cheryl LaGuardia and Barbara A. Mitchell. New York: Neal-Schuman.

———. 2004a. "Building on Bibliographic Instruction: Our Strong BI Foundation Supports a Promising IL Future." *American Libraries* 35, no. 9: 51–53.

———. 2004b. "Do They Really Do That?" *Change* 36, no. 3: 22–27.

———. "Information Literacy: Wilder Makes (Some Right, But) Many Wrong Assumptions." Librarians Association of the University of California. Opinions (2005). Available: www.ucop.edu/lauc/opinions/literacy.html (accessed December 22, 2008).

———. "Find UCLA Library Books" (September 27, 2006). Available: www2.library.ucla.edu/pdf/col_findbooks.pdf (accessed December 26, 2008).

_____. 2008a. "Ideas and Strategies for Incorporating Information Literacy Into Your Classroom" UCLA College Library. Available: http://www2.library.ucla.edu/libraries/college/10374_11837.cfm (April 16, 2009).

———. "Summary: Responses to Analogies Query" (July 2, 2008b). Electronic bulletin board. Available: ILI-L@ala.org (accessed, July 2, 2008).

———. "Thinking Critically About Web 2.0 and Beyond" (2008c). Available: www2.library.ucla.edu/libraries/college/11605_12008.cfm (accessed December 23, 2008).

———. "Wikipedia, YouTube, IL 9 20 08" (September 20, 2008d). Available: www.slideshare.net/estherg/wikipedia-you-tube-il-9-20-08-presentation (accessed November 23, 2008).

———. "Wikipedia, YouTube & Information Literacy" (September 9, 2008e). Available: www.slideshare.net/estherg/wikipedia-youtube-information-literacy-presentation (accessed November 23, 2008).

Grassian, Esther and Susan E. Clark. 1999. "Internet Resources: Information Literacy Sites: Background and Ideas for Program Planning and Development." *College & Research Libraries News* 60, no. 2: 78–81, 92.

Grassian, Esther, Catherine Marley Haras, and Billy Pashaie. In press. "Teaching in a Tea House." In *Proceedings of the Thirty-fifth Annual LOEX Library Instruction Conference*, May 3–5, 2007, San Diego, CA.

Grassian, Esther and Joan Kaplowitz. 2001. *Information Literacy Instruction: Theory and Practice*. New York: Neal-Schuman.

———. 2005. *Learning to Lead and Manage Information Literacy Instruction*. New York: Neal-Schuman.

———. Forthcoming. "Information Literacy Instruction." In *Encyclopedia of Library and Information Science*, edited by Marcia J. Bates and Mary Maack. Oxford, England: Taylor & Francis.

Grassian, Esther and Michael Oppenheim. "Internet Resources: Information Literacy Sites: Background and Ideas for Program Planning and Development—An Update." (September 2005) Available: http://wikis.ala.org/acrl/index.php/Information_Literacy_Sites (accessed December 22, 2008).

Grassian, Esther and Rhonda B. Trueman. 2007. "Stumbling, Bumbling, Teleporting and Flying. Librarian Avatars in Second Life." *Reference Services Review* 35, no. 1: 84–89.

Grassian, Esther, Rhonda B. Trueman, and Patricia Clemson. 2007. "Stumbling, Bumbling, Teleporting and Flying . . . Librarian Avatars in Second Life: Selected Bibliography." *Reference Services Review* 35, no. 1: 90–97.

Grassian, Esther and Diane Zwemer. "Hoax? Scholarly Research? Personal Opinion? You Decide!" (2008). Available: www2.library.ucla.edu/libraries/college/11605_12006.cfm (accessed December 22, 2008).

Grassian, Esther et al. "BICO Task Force: Final Report." UCLA Library, Information Literacy Program (September 30, 2005). Available: http://repositories.cdlib.org/uclalib/il/04 (accessed December 28, 2008).

———. "Road to Research" (2008). Available: www.sscnet.ucla.edu/library (December 23, 2008).

Gratch-Lindauer, Bonnie. 2003. "Selecting and Developing Assessment Tools." In *Assessing Student Learning Outcomes for Information Literacy Instruction* (pp. 22–39), edited by Elizabeth Fuseler Avery. Chicago: ALA.

———. 2005. "Information Literacy Student Behaviors: Potential Items for the National Survey of Student Engagement." *College & Research Libraries News* 66, no. 10: 715–718.

———. 2007. "The Role of Assessment." In *Proven Strategies for Building an Information Literacy Program* (pp. 257–277), edited by Susan Curzon and Lynn Lampert. New York: Neal-Schuman.

———. 2008. "Information Literacy-related Student Behaviors: Results From the NSSE Items." *College & Research Libraries News* 68, no. 7: 432–441.

Gratch-Lindauer, Bonnie and Amelie Brown. 2004. "Developing a Tool to Assess Community College Students." In *Integrating Information Literacy Into the Higher Education Curriculum* (pp. 165–206), edited by Ilene Rockman. San Francisco: Jossey-Bass.

Gray, Tara and Laura Madson. 2007. "Ten Easy Ways to Engage Your Students." *College Teaching* 55, no. 2: 83–87.

Gray, Terry A. "Mr. William Shakespeare" (April 27, 2009). Available: http://shakespeare.palomar.edu/ (accessed April 28, 2009).

Greenbaum, Thomas L. 1998. *The Handbook for Focus Group Research*, 2d ed. Thousand Oaks, CA: Sage Publications.

Greenfield, Louise W. 1987. "Publication Sequence: The

Use of a Conceptual Framework for Library Instruction to Students in Wildlife and Fishery Management." In *Conceptual Frameworks for Bibliographic Education* (pp. 166–179), edited by Mary Reichel and Mary Ann Ramey. Littleton, CO: Libraries Unlimited.

Greenhill, Kathryn [SL: Dumont, Emerald]. "Steps to Research." Murdoch University Library, Western Australia. Available: http://slurl.com/secondlife/Murdoch%20University/221/159/23 (accessed January 6, 2009).

Gresham, Keith and Debra Van Tassel. 2000. "Expanding the Learning Community: An Academic Library Outreach Program to High Schools." *Reference Librarian* 32 no. 67–68: 161–173.

Gribas, Cyndy, Lynn Sykes, and Nick Dorochoff. 1996. "Creating Great Overheads with Computers." *College Teaching* 44, no. 2: 66–68.

Gross, Bertran W. 1997. "Intercultural Communication Competencies: A Strategy for a Multicultural Campus." In *Strategies for Promoting Pluralism in Education and the Workplace* (pp. 21–29), edited by Lynne Brodie Welch, Betty Jane Cleckley, and Marilyn McClure. Westport, CT: Praeger.

Gross, Grant. "Tech Companies, One Economy Launch Broadband Program." *PC World*, April 8, 2008. Available: www.pcworld.com/businesscenter/article/144281/tech_companies_one_economy_launch_broadband_program.html (accessed December 22, 2008).

Gross, Tina and Arlene G. Taylor. 2005. "What Have We Got to Lose? The Effect of Controlled Vocabulary on Keyword Searching Results." *College & Research Libraries* 66, no. 3: 212–230.

Grossman, Herbert. 1990. *Trouble-free Teaching: Solutions to Behavior Problems in the Classroom*. Mountain View, CA: Mayfield.

Gullikson, Shelley. 2006. "Faculty Perceptions of ACRL's Information Competency Standards for Higher Education." *Journal of Academic Librarianship* 32, no. 6: 583–592.

Gust, Kara J. 2006. "Teaching with Tiffany's: A Go-lightly Approach to Information Literacy Instruction for Adult and Senior Learners." *Reference Services Review* 34, no. 4: 557–569.

Gutierrez, Carolyn and Jianrong Wang. 2001. "A Comparison of an Electronic vs. Print Workbook for Information Literacy Instruction." *Journal of Academic Librarianship* 27, no. 3: 208–212.

Hacker, Donald J., John Dunlovsky, and Arthur C. Graesser, eds. 1998. *Metacognition in Educational Theory and Practice*. Mahwah, NJ: Lawrence Erlbaum Associates.

Hackman, J. Richard. 1998. "Why Teams Don't Work." In *Theory and Research on Small Groups* (pp. 24–31), edited by R. Scott Tindale, et al. New York: Plenum Press.

Hahn, Karla L. 2008. "Two New Policies Widen the Path to Balanced Copyright Management." *College & Research Libraries News* 69, no. 7: 398–400.

Hainer, Eugene. 1998. "Information Literacy in Colorado Schools." *Colorado Libraries* 24, no. 4: 5–9.

Hake, Richard R. 1998. "Interactive-engagement versus Traditional Methods: A Six-thousand Student Survey of Mechanics Test Data for Introductory Physics Courses." *American Journal of Physics* 66, no. 1: 64–74.

Hall, Edward Twitchell. 1966. *The Hidden Dimension*. New York: Doubleday.

———. 1976. *Beyond Culture,* 1st ed. Garden City, NY: Anchor Press.

Hall, Patrick. 2002. "Not All Sources Are Created Equal: Student Research, Source Equivalence, and the Net." *Internet Reference Services Quarterly* 7, no. 4: 13–21.

Hall, Vernon C., Johanna Bailey, and Christopher Tillman. 1997. "Can Student-generated Illustrations Be Worth Ten Thousand Words?" *Journal of Educational Psychology* 89, no. 4: 677–681.

Halpern, Diane E. and Milton D. Hakel. 2003. "Applying the Science of Learning to the University and Beyond." *Change* 33, no. 4: 436–441.

Halualani, Rona Tamiko, Anu S. Chitgopekar, Jenifer Huynh Thi Ahn Morrison, and Patrick Shaou-Whea Dodge. 2004. "Diverse in Name Only? Intercultural Interaction at a Multicultural University." *Journal of Communication* 54, no. 2: 270–286.

Hanley, Jennifer. "Boolean Logic Is Yummy!" (2006). Available: www.informationliteracy.org/plans/view/292/back/0 (accessed December 23, 2008).

Hansen, Edmund J. and James A. Stephens. 2000. "The Ethics of Learner-centered Education: Dynamics That Impede the Process." *Change* 32, no. 1: 41–47.

Hanson, Michele G. 1995. "Joining the Conversation: Collaborative Learning and Bibliographic Instruction." *Reference Librarian* 24, no. 51/52: 147–159.

Harada, Violet and Ann Tepe. 1998. "Pathways to Knowledge." *Teacher Librarian* 26, no. 2: 9–15.

Hardesty, Larry. 1995. "Faculty Culture and Bibliographic Instruction: An Exploratory Analysis." *Library Trends* 44, no. 2: 339–367.

———. 1999. "Reflections on 25 Years of Library Instruction: Have We Made Progress?" *Reference Services Review* 27, no. 3: 242–246.

———, ed. 2007. *The Role of the Library in the First College Year*. Columbia, SC: University of South Carolina, National Resource Center for the First Year Experience and Students in Transition.

Hardesty, Larry and John Mark Tucker. 1989. "An Uncertain Crusade: The History of Library Use Instruction in a Changing Educational Environment." In *Academic Librarianship Past, Present, and Future; a Festschrift in Honor of David Kaser* (pp. 97–111), edited by John Richardson, Jr., and Jinnie Y. Davis. Englewood Cliffs, NJ: Libraries Unlimited.

Harnad, Stevan et al. 2004. "The Access/Impact Problem and the Green and Gold Roads to Open Access." *Seri-*

als Review 30, no. 4. Available: http://eprints.ecs.soton.ac.uk/10209/1/impact.html (accessed December 25, 2008).

Harris, Francis Jacobson. 2003. "Information Literacy in School Libraries: It Takes a Community." *Reference & User Services Quarterly* 42, no. 3: 215–223.

———. 2006. "Blogging and the Media Specialist." *Learning & Leading with Technology* 33, no. 8: 32–33.

Haynes, Margot. "Re: Badke Article on Wikipedia" (March 8, 2008). Electronic bulletin board. Available: ILI-L@ala.org (accessed March 10, 2008).

Haynie, Nancy Ann. 1994. "Wundt, Wilhelm." In *Encyclopedia of Psychology* (p. 178), edited by Raymond J. Corsini. New York: John Wiley and Sons.

Heath, Shirley B. 1996. *Way with Words: Language, Life and Work in Communities and Classrooms*. Cambridge, England: Cambridge University Press.

Heintzelman, Nicole, Steve Kronen, Courtney Moore, and Joyce Ward. 2007. "Cybertorials: Teaching Patrons Anytime, Anywhere." *Public Libraries* 46, no. 2: 12–14.

Heller-Ross, Holly. 2000. "Information Literacy for Interactive Distance Learners." In *Teaching the New Library to Today's Users: Reaching International, Minority, Senior Citizens, Gay/Lesbian, First Generation, At-risk, Graduate and Returning Students, and Distance Learners* (pp. 191-219), edited by Trudi E. Jacobson and Helene C. Williams. New York: Neal-Schuman.

Hensley, Randall Burke. 2004. "Curiosity and Creativity as Attributes of Information Literacy." *Reference & User Services Quarterly* 44, no. 1: 31–36.

———. 2007. "Getting to Goals: New Influences on the Role of Goals in Active and Sustainable Information Literacy Programs." In *Proven Strategies for Building an Information Literacy Program* (pp. 3–11), edited by Susan Curzon and Lynn Lampert. New York: Neal-Schuman.

Hensley, Randall Burke and Elizabeth Hanson. 1998. "Question Analysis for Autobiography." In *Designs for Active Learning* (pp. 55–56), edited by Gail Gradowski, Loanne Snavely, and Paula Dempsey. Chicago: ALA, ACRL.

Heward, William L., Sara Ernsbarger Bicard, and Rodney A. Cavanaugh. 2007. "Educational Equality for Students with Disabilities." In *Multicultural Education: Issues and Perspectives* (pp. 329–367), edited by James A. Banks and Cherry A.M. Banks. Hoboken, NJ: Wiley.

Hickson, Joyce and Michael Baltimore. 1996. "Gender Related Learning Styles: Patterns of Middle School Pupils." *School Psychology International* 17, no. 1: 59–70.

Higgs, Joy. 1988. "Planning Learning Experiences to Promote Autonomous Learning." In *Developing Autonomy in Student Learning* (pp. 40–58), edited by David Boud. London: Kogan Page.

Hilliard, Asa G. 1992. "Behavioral Style, Culture and Teaching and Learning." *Journal of Negro Education* 61, no. 3: 370–377.

Himmel, Ethel and William J. Wilson. 1998. *Planning for Results: A Public Library Transformation Process: The Guidebook*. Chicago: ALA.

Hinton, Andrew. "Architectures for Conversation (ii): What Communities of Practice Can Mean for IA (and UX in general, for that matter)" (May 6, 2007). Available: www.slideshare.net/andrewhinton/architectures-for-conversation-ii-what-communities-of-practice-can-mean-for-information-architecture (accessed December 27, 2008).

Hoekman, Robert, Jr. 2007. *Designing the Obvious*. Berkeley, CA: New Riders.

Hoffner, Courtney and Elisa Slater. "English 110 LibGuide." Los Angeles: Loyola Marymount University (2007). Available: http://libguides.lmu.edu/content.php?pid=10084 (accessed September 27, 2008).

Hofstadter, Douglas R. 2000. "Analogy as the Core of Cognition." In *The Best American Science Writing 2000* (pp. 116–144), edited by James Gleick. New York: HarperCollins.

Hofstede, Geert. 1986. "Cultural Differences in Teaching and Learning." *International Journal of Intercultural Relations* 10, no. 3: 301–320.

———. 2000. *Culture's Consequences: Comparing Values, Behaviors, Institutions and Organizations Across Nations*, 2nd ed. Thousand Oaks, CA: Sage.

Hollingsworth, Jeana. "Analogies in ILI." Personal e-mail (Jun 23, 2008).

Holmes, John. 2000. "Just in Case, Just in Time, Just for You: User Education for the Re-entry Student." In *Teaching the New Library to Today's Users: Reaching International, Minority, Senior Citizens, Gay/Lesbian, First Generation, At-risk, Graduate and Returning Students, and Distance Learners* (pp. 127–144), edited by Trudi E. Jacobson and Helene C. Williams. New York: Neal-Schuman.

Honan, Mathew. "Advertisers Paid Me to Blog About Them. Is That So Wrong?" Wired 16, no. 2: 58 (January 18, 2008). Available: www.wired.com/techbiz/it/magazine/16-02/ps_payperpost (accessed December 23, 2008).

Honey, Peter and Alan Mumford. "Honey-Mumford Learning Styles Questionnaire—LSQ." Available: www.peterhoney.com (accessed December 22, 2008).

Hoon, Peggy E. "The TEACH Toolkit." Raleigh: North Carolina State University (2002). Available: www.lib.ncsu.edu/dspc/legislative/teachkit/resources.html (accessed December 25, 2008).

Houlson, Van. 2007. "Getting Results From One-shot Instruction: A Workshop for First-year Students." *College and Undergraduate Libraries* 14, no. 1: 89–108.

Hovius, Beth. 2006. "Public Library Partnerships Which Add Value to the Community: The Hamilton Public Library Experience." *IFLA Journal* 32, no. 3: 214–223.

Howard, Sheila. 1983. "Library Use Education for Adult University Students." CLJ 40, no. 2: 149–155.

Howe, Neil and Bill Strauss. 2000. *Millennials Rising: The Next Great Generation*. New York: Vintage.

Huang, Jie and Susan Russell. 2006. "The Digital Divide and

Academic Achievement." *Electronic Library* 24, no. 2: 160–173.

Huba, Mary E. and Jann E. Freed. 2000. *Learner-centered Assessment on College Campuses*. Boston: Allyn & Bacon.

Hunt, Earl and James W. Pellegrino. 2002. "Issues, Examples, and Challenges in Formative Assessment." *New Directions for Teaching and Learning* 89: 73–85.

Hunter, Madeline. 1985. *Mastery Teaching: Increasing Instructional Effectiveness in Secondary School, College and University*. El Segundo, CA: TIP.

Hurley, Tina, Nora Hegarty, and Jennifer Bolger. 2006. "Crossing a Bridge: The Challenges of Diversity and Delivering a Pilot Information Literacy Course for International Students." *New Library World* 107, no. 1226/1227: 302–320.

Hutchins, Elizabeth O., Barbara Fister, and Hris Huber MacPherson. 2000. "Changing Landscapes, Enduring Values: Transition From Bibliographic Instruction to Information Literacy." *Journal of Library Administration* 36, no. 1/2: 3–19.

Iannuzzi, Patricia. 1998. "Faculty Development and Information Literacy: Establishing Campus Partnerships." *Reference Services Review* 26, no. 3–4: 97–102, 116.

———. 1999. "We Are Teaching, But Are They Learning: Accountability, Productivity and Assessment." *Journal of Academic Librarianship* 28, no. 4: 304–305.

IATUL. 1970. *Educating the Library User: Proceedings of the 4th Triennial Meeting*, edited by C.M. Lincoln. Loughborough, England: Loughborough University of Technology Library.

Iding, Marie K. 1997. "How Analogies Foster Learning From Science Texts." *Instructional Science* 25, no. 4: 233–253.

IFLA. "Information Literacy Resource Directory" (2007) Available: www.ifla.org/VII/s42/index.htm (accessed September 15, 2007).

———. "Information Literacy Section" (October 23, 2008). Available: www.ifla.org/VII/s42/index.htm (accessed December 22, 2008).

______. "Round Table on User Education" (2002). Available: http://web.archive.org/web/20020601205023/http://www.ifla.org/VII/rt12/rtued.htm (accessed April 14, 2009).

IFLA. High Level Colloquium on Information Literacy and Lifelong Learning. "The Alexandria Proclamation on Information Literacy and Lifelong Learning" (2005). Available: www.ifla.org/III/wsis/BeaconInfSoc.html (accessed September 15 2008).

IFLA and UNESCO. "Public Library Manifesto" (1994). Available: www.ifla.org/VII/s8/unesco/eng.htm (accessed December 22, 2008).

———. "School Library Manifesto" (2006). Available: www.ifla.org/VII/s11/pubs/manifest.htm (accessed December 22, 2008).

———. "InfoLit Global." Available: www.infolitglobal.info (accessed December 23, 2008).

InfoLit iSchool. University of Sheffield. Available: http://slurl.com/secondlife/Infolit%20iSchool/113/189/21/ (accessed: December 22, 2008).

Information Literacy Instruction Through Social Software. "Facebook" (2008). Available: www.facebook.com/group.php?gid=6301621235 (accessed December 23, 2008).

Indiana University–South Bend. "Boolean Operators" (May 29, 2007). Available: www.youtube.com/watch?v=vube-ZcJFk4&feature=related (accessed December 28, 2008).

Ingram, Dorothy S. 2000. "The Andragogical Librarian." *Reference Librarian* 33 no. 69/70: 141–150.

Inhelder, Bärbel and Jean Piaget. 1958. *The Growth of Logical Thinking From Childhood to Adolescence: An Essay on the Construction of Formal Operational Structures*. London: Routledge & Kogan Paul.

Insight Assessment. "California Critical Thinking Disposition Inventory (CCTDI)" (2008a). Available: www.insightassessment.com/test-cctdi.html (accessed December 23, 2008).

———. "California Critical Thinking Skills Test (CCTST)" (2008b). Available: www.insightassessment.com/test-cctst.html (accessed December 23, 2008).

Inspiration. "The Essential Visual and Thinking Tool" (2008). Available: www.inspiration.com/productinfo/inspiration/index.cfm (accessed December 23, 2008).

International Symposium on Wearable Computers. "Homepage" (2008). Available: http://iswc.net (accessed December 23, 2008).

Internet Archive. "Wayback Machine." Available: www.archive.org/index.php (accessed December 27, 2008).

"Internet Public Library: Blogs." Available: www.ipl.org/div/blogs (accessed December 27, 2008).

Internet Public Library: Pathfinders. Available: www.ipl.org/div/pf (accessed December 24, 2008).

Internet World Stats. "Usage and Population Statistics" (2008). Available: www.internetworldstats.com/stats.htm (accessed December 25, 2008).

Irvine, Jacqueline J. 2003. *Educating Teachers for Diversity; Seeing with a Cultural Eye*. New York: Teachers College Press.

Irwin, Kate. 2007. "Note: Copyright Law—Librarians Who Teach: Expanding the Distance Education Rights of Libraries by Applying the Technology, Education, and Copyright Harmonization Act of 2002." *Western New England Law Review* 29: 875–914.

Ithaca College Library. "SubjectsPlus." Available: www.ithacalibrary.com/subsplus (accessed December 27, 2008).

Jackson, Lydia and Julia Hansen. 2006. "Creating Collaborative Partnerships: Building the Framework." *Reference Services Review* 34, no. 4: 575–588.

———. In press. "A Community without Walls—Testing the Waters." In *Proceedings of the Thirty-Fifth Annual*

LOEX Library Instruction Conference, May 3-5, 2007, San Diego, CA.

Jackson, Susan. 1995. "Information Literacy and Public Libraries: A Community Based Approach." In *Information for a New Age: Redefining the Librarian* (pp. 35–45), edited by LIRT Fifteenth Anniversary Task Force. Englewood, CO: Libraries Unlimited.

Jacobs, Heidi L.M. 2008. "Information Literacy and Reflective Pedagogical Praxis." *Journal of Academic Librarianship* 34, no. 3: 256–262.

Jacobs, Susan Kaplan, Peri Rosenfeld, and Judith Haber. 2003. "Information Literacy as the Foundation for Evidence-based Practice in Graduate Nursing Education: A Curriculum-integrated Approach." *Journal of Professional Nursing* 19, no. 5: 320–328.

Jacobsen v. Katzer. 535 F.3d 1373 (Fed. Cir. 2008).

Jacobson, Trudi E. 2004. "Meeting Information Literacy Needs in a Research Setting." In *Integrating Information Literacy Into the Higher Education Curriculum* (pp. 133–164), edited by Ilene Rockman et al. San Francisco: Wiley & Sons.

———. 2008. "Motivation." In *Information Literacy Instruction Handbook* (pp. 73–83), edited by Christopher N. Cox and Elizabeth Blakesley Lindsay. Chicago: ALA, ACRL.

Jacobson, Trudi E. and Carol Anne Germain. 2004. "A Campus-wide Role for an Information Literacy Committee." *Resource Sharing and Information Networks* 17, no. 1–2: 111–121.

Jacobson, Trudi E. and Beth L. Mark. 1995. "Teaching in the Information Age: Active Learning Techniques to Empower Students." *Reference Librarian* 24, no. 51–52: 105–120.

Jacobson, Trudi E. and Helene C. Williams, eds. 2000. *Teaching the New Library to Today's Users: Reaching International, Minority, Senior Citizens, Gay/Lesbian, First Generation, At-risk, Graduate and Returning Students, and Distance Learners.* New York: Neal-Schuman.

Jacobson, Trudi E. and Lijuan Xu. 2002. "Motivating Students in Credit-based Information Literacy Courses: Theories and Practice." *portal: Libraries and the Academy* 2, no. 3: 423–441.

Jaffee, David. 2007. "Peer Cohorts and the Unintended Consequences of Freshman Learning Communities." College Teaching 55, no. 2: 65–71.

James Madison University. "Go for the Gold." Harrisonburg, VA: James Madison University (2008a). Available: www.lib.jmu.edu/gold/default.aspx (accessed December 22, 2008).

———. "Library Skills Test." Harrisonburg, VA: James Madison University (2008b). Available: www.jmu.edu/assessment/resources/prodserv/instruments_ilt.htm (accessed September 12, 2008).

Janes, Joseph. 2008. "Internet Librarian." *American Libraries* 39, no. 9: 44.

Jansen, Amy. 2003. "The Special Library Context." *Reference & User Services Quarterly* 42, no. 4: 315–316.

Jehlik, Theresa. 2004. "Information Literacy in the Public Library." *Nebraska Library Association Quarterly* 35, no. 4: 7–13.

Jeng, Ling Hwey. "Reference Questions." Electronic bulletin board. Available: cala@csd.uwm.edu (accessed June 13, 2000).

Jenkins, John M. and Deborah L. Bainer. 1994. "Common Instructional Problems in the Multicultural Classroom." In *Teaching and Learning in the College Classroom* (pp. 127–135), edited by Kenneth A. Feldman and Michael B. Paulsen. Needham Heights, MA: Ginn Press.

Jiao, Qun G. and Anthony J. Onwuegbuzie. 2004. "The Impact of Information Technology on Library Anxiety: The Role of Computer Attitudes." *Information Technology and Libraries* 23, no. 4: 138–144.

Jiao, Qun G., Anthony J. Onwuegbuzie, and Art A. Lichtenstein. 1996. "Library Anxiety: Characteristics of 'At-risk' College Students." *Library and Information Science Research* 18, no. 2: 151–163.

Jing. "Screencast Software" (2008). Available: www.jingproject.com (accessed December 25, 2008).

Johnson, Anna Marie, Sarah Jent, and Latisha Reynolds. 2007. "Library Instruction and Information Literacy 2006." *Reference Services Review* 35, no. 4: 584–640.

Johnson, Anna Marie, and Phil Sager. 1998. "Too Many Students, Too Little Time: Creating and Implementing a Self-Paced, Interactive Computer Tutorial for the Libraries' Online Catalog." *Research Strategies* 16 no.4:271–84.

Johnson, David W., Roger T. Johnson, and Karl A. Smith. 2007. "The State of Cooperative Learning in Postsecondary and Professional Settings." *Educational Psychology Review* 19, no. 1: 15–29.

Johnson, Dolores. 1997. "What's Love Got to Do with It: Strategies for Teaching in Multilingual and Multicultural Classrooms." In *Strategies for Promoting Pluralism in Education and the Workplace* (pp. 107–113), edited by Lynne Brodie Welch, Betty Jane Cleckley, and Marilyn McClure. Westport, CT: Praeger.

Johnson, Doug and Michael Eisenberg. 1996. "Computer Literacy and Information Literacy: A Natural Combination." *Emergency Librarian* 23, no. 5: 12–16.

Johnson, Genevieve. 2008. "The Relative Learning Benefits of Synchronous and Asynchronous Text-based Discussion." British Journal of Educational Technology 39, no. 1: 166–169.

Johnson, Laurence F., Alan Levine, and Rachel S. Smith. "Horizon Report." Austin, TX: New Media Consortium (January 30, 2008). Available: www.nmc.org/pdf/2008-Horizon-Report.pdf (accessed December 28, 2008).

Johnson, Susan and Jim Cooper. "Quick Thinks: The Interactive Lecture" (2007) Available: http://amps-tools.mit.edu/Tomprofblog/archives/2007/09/818_quickthinks.html (accessed May 6 2008).

Johnston, Bill and Sheila Webber. 2005. "As We May Think: Information Literacy as a Discipline for the Information Age." *Research Strategies* 20, no. 3: 108–121.

Jonassen, David H. 1997. "Instructional Design Models for Well-structured and Ill-structured Problem-solving Learning Outcomes." *Educational Technology Research and Development* 45, no. 1: 65–94.

———. 2000. "Revisiting Activity Theory as a Framework for Designing Student-centered Learning Environments." In *Theoretical Foundations of Learning Environments* (pp. 89–121), edited by David H. Jonassen and Susan M. Land. Mahwah, NJ: Erlbaum.

Jonassen, David, Johannes Strobel, and Joshua Gottdenker. 2005. "Model Building for Conceptual Change." *Interactive Learning Environment* 13, no. 1/2: 15–37.

Journal of Academic Librarianship. 1975–. Ann Arbor, MI: Mountainside Publishing.

Journal of Information Literacy. 2007–. Loughbrough, England: Loughbrough University Library. Available: http://jil.lboro.ac.uk/ojs/index.php/JIL/index (accessed December 22, 2008).

Juettemeyer, Tricia. 2007. "Re: Examples of Inaccurate Wikipedia Entries?" Electronic bulletin board (March 8, 2007). Available: ili-l@ala.org (accessed February 8, 2008).

Julien, Heidi. 2005. "Education for Information Literacy: A Global Perspective." *Journal of Education for Library and Information Science* 46, no. 3: 210–216.

Julien, Heidi and Cameron Hoffman. 2008. "Information Literacy Training in Canada's Public Libraries." *Library Quarterly* 78, no. 1: 19–41.

Jumpchart. "Website Planning." Available: www.jumpchart.com (accessed December 14, 2008).

Juznic, Primoz, Maja Blazic, Tanya Mercum, and Barbara Plesterjak. 2006. "Who Says That Old Dogs Cannot Learn New Tricks?" *New Library World* 107, no. 1226/1227: 332–345.

Kabagarama, Daisy. 1997. *Breaking the Ice: A Guide to Understanding People From Other Cultures*, 2nd ed. Boston: Allyn & Bacon.

Kafai, Yasmin B. and Mitchell Resnick, eds. 1996. *Constructionism in Practice: Designing, Thinking and Learning in a Digital World*. Mahwah, NJ: Erlbaum.

Kagan, Jerome. 1966. "Reflection–Impulsivity: The Generality and Dynamics of Conceptual Tempo." *Journal of Abnormal Psychology* 71, no. 1: 17–24.

Kaleba, Kermit. 2007. "Businesses Continue to Push for Lifelong Learning." *T & D* 61, no. 6: 14.

Kalin, Sally and Loanne Snavely. 2001. "Strategies to Make the Library an Instructional Partner on Campus." In *Library User Education: Powerful Learning, Powerful Partnerships* (pp. 18–23), edited by Barbara I. Dewey. Lanham, MD: Scarecrow Press.

Kalyuga, Slava. 2007. "Expertise Reversal Effect and Its Implications for Learner-tailored Instruction." *Educational Psychology Review* 19, no. 4: 509–539.

Kamhi-Stein, Lia and Alan Stein. 1998. "Teaching Information Competency as a Third Language: A New Model for Library Instruction." *Reference & User Services Quarterly* 38, no. 2: 173–179.

Kapitzke, Cushla. 2001. "Information Literacy: The Changing Library." *Journal of Adolescent and Adult Literacy* 44, no. 4: 450–456.

———. 2003. Information Literacy: "A Positivist Epistemology and a Politics of Outformation." *Educational Theory* 53, no. 1: 37–53.

Kaplowitz, Joan. 1986. "A Pre and Post-test Evaluation of the English 3 Library Instruction Program at UCLA." *Research Strategies* 4, no. 1: 11–17.

———. 1995. *Evaluating Bibliographic Instruction: Issues and Influences*. Unpublished Manuscript.

———. 2008. "The Psychology of Learning: Connecting Theory to Practice." In *Information Literacy Instruction Handbook* (pp. 26–49), edited by Christopher N. Cox and Elizabeth Blakesley Lindsay. Chicago: ALA.

Kaplowitz, Joan and Janice Contini. 1998. "Computer-assisted Instruction: Is It an Option for Bibliographic Instruction in Large Undergraduate Survey Classes?" *College & Research Libraries* 59, no. 1: 19–27.

Kartoo. "Web Browser." Available: www.kartoo.com (accessed December 1, 2008).

Katz, Irvin R. 2007. "ETS Research Finds College Students Fall Short in Demonstrating ICT Literacy: National Policy Council to Create National Standards." *College & Research Libraries News* 68, no. 1. Available: www.ala.org/ala/mgrps/divs/acrl/publications/crlnews/2007/jan/ets.cfm (accessed March 26, 2009).

Kazakoff-Lane, Carmen. "Re: Video Tutorials and ANTS" (June 3, 2008). Electronic bulletin board. Available: ili-l@ala.org (accessed July 14, 2008).

Kazdin, Alan E. 1994. *Behavior Modification in Applied Settings*. Pacific Grove, CA: Brooks/Cole.

Keefe, James W. 1982. "Assessing Student Learning Styles: An Overview." In *Student Styles and Brain Behavior* (pp. 43–53), edited by National Association of Secondary School Principals. Reston, VA: NAASP.

———. 1987. *Learning Style: Theory and Practice*. Reston, VA: National Association of Secondary School Principals.

Keefer, Jane A. 1993. "The Hungry Rat Syndrome: Library Anxiety, Information Literacy and the Academic Reference Process." *RQ* 32, no. 3: 333–339.

Keller, John M. 1987. "Strategies for Stimulating the Motivation to Learn." *Performance and Instruction Journal* 26, no. 8: 1–7.

Kellough, Richard D., Noreen G. Kellough, and Eugene C. Kim. 1999. *Secondary School Teaching: A Guide to Methods and Resource: Planning for Competence*. Upper Saddle River, NJ: Merrill.

Kelly, George. 1963. *A Theory of Personality: The Psychology of Personal Constructs*. New York: W.W. Norton and Company.

Kelly, Mary and Holly Hibner. 2005. "Teaching Computers to Seniors: What Not to Do." *Public Libraries* 44, no. 3: 151–155.

Kennedy, James R., Jr. 1974. *Library Research Guide to Religion and Theology: Illustrated Search Strategy and Sources*. Ann Arbor, MI: Pierian Press.

Kent State University. "Project Sails." Kent, OH: Kent State University (2008). Available: https://www.projectsails.org/index.php?page=home (accessed September 12, 2008).

Kentucky Department of Education. 1995. *Online II: Essentials of a Modal Library Media Program*. Louisville: Kentucky Department of Education.

Kern, M. Kathleen. 2006. "Get to Know Your Gadget Guy or Gal: Tips From an Accidental Library Technologist on Staying Current." *Reference & User Services Quarterly* 46, no. 2: 12–15.

Keyser, Marcia W. 2000. "Active Learning and Cooperative Learning: Understanding the Difference and Using Both Styles Effectively." *Research Strategies* 17, no. 1: 35–44.

Kida, Thomas. 2006. *Don't Believe Everything You Think: The 6 Basic Mistakes We Make in Thinking*. Amherst, NY: Prometheus Books.

Kim, Sara et al. 2006. "A Conceptual Framework for Developing Teaching Cases: A Review and Synthesis of the Literature Across Disciplines." *Medical Education* 40: 867–876.

King, Alison. 1993. "From Sage on the Stage to Guide on the Side." *College Teaching* 41, no. 1: 30–35.

Kipnis, Daniel G. and Gary M. Childs. 2004. "Educating Generation X and Generation Y; Teaching Tips for Librarians." *Medical Reference Services Quarterly* 23, no. 4: 25–33.

Kirkpatrick, Donald. 1998. *Evaluating Training Programs: The Four Levels*. San Francisco: Berret-Koehler.

Kirton, Jennifer and Lynn Barham. 2005. "Information Literacy in the Workplace." *Australian Library Journal* 54, no. 4: 365–376.

Kiss, Jemima. 2008. "Web 3.0 Is All About Rank and Recommendation" (February 4, 2008). Available: www.guardian.co.uk/media/2008/feb/04/web20?gusrc=rss&feed=media (accessed November 19, 2008).

Kivel, Andy. 2003. "Institutionalizing a Graduation Requirement." In *Assessing Student Learning Outcomes for Information Literacy Instruction* (pp. 193–200), edited by Elizabeth Fuseler Avery. Chicago: ALA.

Kleinman, Glenn M. 2000. "Myths and Realities About Technology in K–12 Schools." In *The Digital Classroom: How Technology Is Changing the Way We Teach and Learn* (pp. 7–15), edited by David T. Gordon. Cambridge, MA: Harvard Education Letter.

Klingberg, Susan. 2005. "Information Checklist: A Resource for Inter-segmental Collaboration." *Reference Services Review* 34, no. 4: 484–490.

Knapp, Patricia B. 1956. "A Suggested Program of College Instruction in the Use of the Library." *Library Quarterly* 26, no. 3: 224–231.

———. 1966. *The Monteith College Library Experiment*. Metuchen, NJ: Scarecrow.

Knight, Lorrie A. 2003. "Assessing Student Learning Through the Analysis of Research Papers." In *Assessing Student Learning Outcomes for Information Literacy Instruction* (pp. 201–206), edited by Elizabeth Fuseler Avery. Chicago: ALA.

———. 2006. "Using Rubrics to Assess Information Literacy." *Reference Services Review* 34, no. 1: 43–55.

Knowles, Malcolm Shepherd. 1980. *The Modern Practice of Adult Education: From Pedagogy to Andragogy*, rev. and updated. New York: Cambridge, the Adult Education Company.

———. 1996. "Andragogy: An Emerging Technology for Adult Learning." In *Boundaries of Adult Learning* (pp. 82–97), edited by Richard Edwards, Ann Hansen, and Peter Raggatt. London: Routledge.

Ko, Susan and Steve Rossen. 2004. *Teaching Online: A Practical Guide*, 2d ed. Boston: Houghton-Mifflin.

Kobelski, Pamela and Mary Reichel. 1981. "Conceptual Frameworks for Bibliographic Instruction." *Journal of Academic Librarianship* 7, no. 2: 73–77.

Köhler, Wolfgang and Ella Winter. 1925. *The Mentality of Apes*. New York: Harcourt Brace.

Kolb, David A. 1976. *Learning Styles Inventory: Technical Manual*. Boston: McBer.

———. 1984. *Experiential Learning: Experience as the Source of Learning and Development*. Englewood Cliffs, NJ: Prentice-Hall.

Kolb, David A. and Ronald Fry. 1975. "Toward an Applied Theory of Experiential Learning." In *Theories of Group Processes* (pp. 237–256), edited by Cary Cooper. London: Wiley.

Kolbert, Elizabeth. 2008. "What Was I Thinking?" *New Yorker* 84, no. 2: 77–79.

Kools, Marieke et al. 2006. "The Effect of Graphic Organizers on Subjective and Objective Comprehension of a Health Education Text." *Health Education & Behavior* 33, no. 6: 760–772.

Koppi, A.J., J.R. Lublin, and M.J. Chaloupka. 1997. "Effective Teaching and Learning in a High-tech Environment." *Innovations in Education and Training International* 34, no. 4: 245–251.

Kotter, Wade R. 1999. "Bridging the Great Divide: Improving Relations Between Librarians and Classroom Faculty." *Journal of Academic Librarianship* 25, no. 4: 244–303.

Kounin, Jacob S. 1970. *Discipline and Group Management in Classrooms*. New York: Holt, Rinehart and Winston.

Kozma, Laszlo. "WikipediaVision (beta)" (2009). Available: www.lkozma.net/wpv/ (accessed April 23, 2009).

Kraemer, Elizabeth, Dana Keyse, and Shawn Lombardo. 2003. "Beyond These Walls: Building a Library Outreach

Program at Oakland University." *Reference Librarian* 39, no. 82: 5–17.

Kraemer, Elizabeth W. et al. 2007. "The Librarian, the Machine, or a Little of Both: A Comparative Study of Three Information Literacy Pedagogies at Oakland University." *College & Research Libraries* 68, no. 4: 330–342.

Kroenke, Kurt. 1984. "The Lecture: Where It Wavers." *American Journal of Medicine* 17, no. 3: 393–396.

Kruger, Justin and David Dunning. 1999. "Unskilled and Unaware of It: How Difficulties in Recognizing One's Own Incompetence Lead to Inflated Self-assessments." *Journal of Personality and Social Psychology* 77, no. 6: 1121–1134.

Kuhlthau, Carol Collier. 1981. *School Librarian's Grade-by-Grade Activities Program: A Complete Sequential Skills Plan for Grades K–8*. West Nyack, NY: Center for Applied Research in Education.

———. 1985. "A Process Approach to Library Skills Instruction." *School Library Media Quarterly* 13, no. 1: 35–40.

———. 1988. "Developing a Model of the Library Search Process: Cognitive and Affective Aspects." *RQ* 28, no. 3: 232–242.

———. 1989. "Information Search Process: A Summary of Research and Implications for School Library Media Programs." *School Library Media Quarterly* 17, no. 1: 19–25.

———. 1990. "Information Skills for an Information Society: A Review of Research." *Information Reports and Bibliographies* 19, no. 3: 14–26.

———. 1991. "Inside the Search Process: Information Seeking from the User's Perspective." *Journal of the American Society for Information Science* 42, no. 5: 361–371.

———. 1993. *Seeking Meaning: A Process Approach to Library and Information Services, Information Management, Policy, and Services*. Norwood, NJ: Ablex.

———. 2004. *Seeking Meaning*, 2nd ed. Westport, CT: Libraries Unlimited.

Kupersmith, John. 1984. "The Graphic Approach: Don't Do This! Don't Do That!" *Research Strategies* 2, no. 4: 185–187.

———. 1987. "The Graphic Approach: 'Library Anxiety' and Library Graphics." *Research Strategies* 5, no. 1: 36–38.

Kwon, Nahyun. 2008. "A Mixed-methods Investigation of the Relationship Between Critical Thinking and Library Anxiety Among Undergraduate Students in Their Information Search Process." *College & Research Libraries* 69, no. 2: 117–131.

Kwon, Nahyun, Anthony J. Onwuegbuzie, and Linda Alexander. 2007. "Critical Thinking Disposition and Library Anxiety: Affective Domains on the Space of Information Seeking and Use in Academic Libraries." *College & Research Libraries* 68, no. 3: 268–278.

Kyle, Pat. 2008. "Re: Re: Career Day" (April 14, 2008). Electronic bulletin board. Available: infolit@ala.org (accessed April 14, 2008).

Ladd, Paula A. and Ralph Ruby, Jr. 1999. "Learning Style and Adjustment Issue of International Students." *Journal of Education for Business* 75, no. 6: 363–367.

Lage, Maureen L., Glenn J. Platt, and Michael Treglia. 2000. "Inverting the Classroom: A Gateway to Creating an Inclusive Learning Environment." *Journal of Economic Education* 3, no. 1: 30–43.

LaGuardia, Cheryl, Michael Blake, Lawrence Dowler, Laura Farwell, Caroline M. Kent, and Ed Tallent. 1996. *Teaching the New Library: A How-To-Do-It Manual for Planning and Designing Instructional Programs*. New York: Neal-Schuman.

Lampert, Lynn. 2003. "Marketing/Teaching Information Literacy for Special Populations." Paper read at SCIL Open House, January 17, at California State University Fullerton.

———. 2005. "Getting Psyched About Information Literacy: A Successful Faculty–Librarian Collaboration for Educational Psychology and Counseling." *Reference Librarian* 43, no. 1: 5–23.

Lance, Keith. 2002. "What Research Tells Us About the Importance of School Libraries." *Teacher-Librarian* 39, no. 1: 76–78.

Lance, Keith and David Loertscher. 2003. *Powering Achievement: School Library Media Programs Make a Difference*. San Jose: H. Willow Research and Publishing.

Lance, Keith, Marcia J. Rodney, and Christine Hamilton-Pennell. 2005. *Powerful Libraries Make Powerful Learners*. Canton: Illinois School Library Media Association.

Lanir, Joel, Kellogg S. Booth, and Leah Findlater. 2008. "Observing Presenters' Use of Visual Aids to Inform the Design of Classroom Presentation Software." In *Proceedings of the Twenty-sixth Annual SIGCHI Conference on Human Factors in Computing Systems* (pp. 695–704). Florence, Italy, April 5–10, 2008. Available: http://portal.acm.org/ft_gateway.cfm?id=1357165&type=pdf&coll=GUIDE&dl=GUIDE&CFID=38394676&CFTOKEN=98273868 (accessed December 24, 2008).

Laslett, Robert and Colin Smith. 1984. *Effective Classroom Management: A Teacher's Guide*. London: Croom Helm.

Last.fm. "Music Service" (2008). Available: www.last.fm (accessed December 28, 2008).

Lau-Bond, Jennifer and Jacob Jeremiah. "Library Research Tutorial." Roosevelt University Library (2008). Available: http://rulibrarydl.pbwiki.com (accessed December 24, 2008).

Lawson, Stephen. "T-shirt Helps Find Hotspots." *PC World*, October 7, 2007. Available: www.pcworld.com/article/138139/tshirt_helps_find_hotspots.html (accessed December 27, 2008).

Learning Times. Available: www.learningtimes.org/index.php (accessed December 27, 2008).

Lee, Kathryn. 2006. "Online Collaborative Case Study Learning." *Journal of College Reading and Learning* 37, no. 2: 82–100.

Lee, Wynetta Y. 2001. "Toward a More Perfect Union: Reflecting on Trends and Issues for Enhancing Academic Performance of Minority and Transfer Students." *New Directions for Community Colleges* 114: 39–44.

Lenn, Katy. 2000. "Seasoned Students." In *Teaching the New Library to Today's Users: Reaching International, Minority, Senior Citizens, Gay/Lesbian, First Generation, At-risk, Graduate and Returning Students, and Distance Learners* (pp. 173–187), edited by Trudi E. Jacobson and Helene C. Williams. New York: Neal-Schuman.

Levine, Tamar and Smadar Donitsa-Schmidt. 1998. "Computer Use, Confidence, Attitudes, and Knowledge: A Causal Analysis." *Computers in Human Behavior* 14, no. 1: 125–116.

Lewis, Hedwig. 2000. *Body Language: A Guide for Professionals*. Thousand Oaks, CA: Sage.

Lexington Public Schools Libraries. "How Do I Know if I've Found Good Information on the Web?" (2000). Available: http://lps.lexingtonma.org/Libdept/elem.lib./eleval.html (accessed December 23, 2008).

Li, Suzanne. 1998. "Library Services to Students with Diverse Language and Cultural Backgrounds." *Journal of Academic Librarianship* 24, no. 2: 139–143.

LibGuides. "Web 2.0 for Libraries 2.0" (2008). Available: www.springshare.com/libguides (accessed December 24, 2008).

"Library Cartoons: An Annotated Bibliography" (January 11, 2008). Available: http://pw1.netcom.com/~dplourde/cartoons/index.html (accessed December 25, 2008).

LibraryThing. Available: www.librarything.com (accessed July 4, 2008).

Lichtle, Marie-Christine. 2007. "The Effect of an Advertisement's Colour on Emotions Evoked by an Ad and Attitude Towards the Ad." *International Journal of Advertising* 26, no. 1: 37–62.

Liedtke, Michael. "Portals Return to Search for Niche." *Los Angeles Times*, October 19, 2000, section C.

"Lifelong Learning Conference" (2008). Available: http://lifelonglearning.cqu.edu.au/2008 (accessed December 22, 2008).

LII. "Librarian's Internet Index" (2008). Available: http://lii.org (accessed December 23, 2008).

Liles, Jeff 2007. "Librarian Readiness and Pedagogy." In *Proven Strategies for Building an Information Literacy Program* (pp. 113–131), edited by Susan Curzon and Lynn Lampert. New York: Neal-Schuman.

LILi. "Lifelong Information Literacy" (2008). Available: www.library.ucla.edu/libraries/college/10645.cfm (accessed December 22, 2008).

Lin, Poping. 1994. "Library Instruction for Culturally Diverse Populations: A Comparative Approach." *Research Strategies* 12, no. 3: 168–173.

Lindstrom, Joyce and Diana D. Shonrock. 2006. "Faculty–Librarian Collaboration to Achieve Integration of Information Literacy." *Reference & User Services Quarterly* 46, no. 1: 18–23.

LinkedIn. "Business Networking" (2008). Available: www.linkedin.com (accessed November 30, 2008).

Linn, Robert L. and Norma Gronlund. 2005. *Measurement and Assessment in Teaching*, 9th ed. Upper Saddle River, NJ: Prentice Hall.

Linux. "Linux Online!" (2008). Available: www.linux.org (accessed December 27, 2008).

LION. "Library Information Literacy Online Network" (2008). Available: http://liontv.blip.tv (accessed December 26, 2008).

Lipkind, Erin. "Biographies of Native American Leaders" (May 5, 2008). Available: http://questgarden.com/31/94/4/060726232615 (accessed December 24, 2008).

Lippincott, Joan K. 1987. "End-user Instruction: Emphasis on Concepts." In *Conceptual Frameworks for Bibliographic Education* (pp. 183–191), edited by Mary Reichel and Mary Ann Ramey. Littleton, CO: Libraries Unlimited.

———. 2002. "Developing Collaborative Relationships: Librarians, Students and Faculty Creating Learning Communities." *College & Research Libraries News* 63, no. 3. Available: www.ala.org/ala/mgrps/divs/acrl/publications/crlnews/2002/mar/developingcollaborative.cfm (accessed March 26, 2009).

Liu, Shu. 2008. "Engaging Users: The Future of Academic Library Web Sites." *College & Research Libraries* 69, no.1:6-27.

Liu, Ziming. 1993. "Difficulties and Characteristics of Students From Developing Countries." *College & Research Libraries* 54, no. 1: 25–31.

Lloyd, Anne Maree. 2006. "Information Literacy Landscapes: An Emerging Picture." *Journal of Documentation* 62, no. 5: 570–583.

Loe, Mary and Betsy Elkins. 1990. "Developing Programs in Library Use Instruction for Lifelong Learning: An Overview." In *The LIRT Library Instruction Handbook* (pp. 6–8), edited by May Brottman and Mary Loe. Englewood, CO: Libraries Unlimited.

LOEX. "Clearinghouse for Library Instruction" (2005). Available: www.emich.edu/public/loex/loex.html (accessed December 22, 2008).

———. "Instruction Resources: Tutorials" (2007a). Available: www.emich.edu/public/loex/search.php?cat=3 (accessed December 24, 2008).

———. 2007b. *Uncharted Waters: Tapping the Depths of Our Community to Enhance Learning*. Available: http://public.csusm.edu/acarr/loex/index.html (accessed December 22, 2008).

———. "Instruction Resources" (2008). Available: www.emich.edu/public/loex/resources.php (accessed September 12 2008).

LOEX of the West. "To Fabulous Las Vegas 2008." Available: www.library.unlv.edu/conferences/loexw/history.html (accessed April 20, 2008).

Logan, Debra Kay. 2008. "Putting Students First." *American Libraries* 39, no. 1/2: 56–59.

Lombardo, Shawn V. and Cynthia E. Miree. 2003. "Caught in the Web: The Impact of Library Instruction on Business Students' Perceptions and Use of Print and Online Resources." *College & Research Libraries* 64, no. 1: 6–22.

Long, Cindy. 2008. "Mind the Gap: It's a High-speed, High-def, Wi-Fi World. But Not for Everybody." *NEA Today* 26, no. 6: 24–31.

Longstreet, Wilma S. 1978. *Aspects of Ethnicity: Understanding Differences in Pluralistic Classrooms*. New York: Teachers College Press.

Lonsdale, Ray and Chris Armstrong. 2006. "Role of the University Library in Supporting Information Literacy in UK Secondary Schools." *Aslib Proceedings* 58, no. 6: 553–569.

Lorence, Daniel and Heeyoung Park. 2008. "Report of Racial and Digital Disparities in Web-based Health Information." *International Journal of Healthcare Technology and Management* 9, no. 1: 39–44.

Lorenzen, Michael. 2001a. "Active Learning and Library Instruction." *Illinois Libraries* 83, no. 2: 19–24.

———. 2001b. "A Brief History of Library Information in the United States of America." *Illinois Libraries* 83, no. 23: 8–18.

———. 2003. "International Bibliographic Activities in the 20th Century: A Literature Review." *MLA Forum* 2, no. 1. Available: www.mlaforum.org/volumeII/issue1/InternationalBib.html (accessed May 25, 2008).

———. "Information Literacy Land of Confusion" (November 2, 2008). Available: www.information-literacy.net (accessed November 16, 2008).

Lorenzo, George and Charles Dziuban. "Ensuring the Net Generation Is Net Savvy" (White Paper) (2006). Available: http://connect.educause.edu/Library/ELI/EnsuringtheNetGenerationI/39340 (accessed September 8, 2008).

Lowman, Joseph. 1995. *Mastering the Techniques of Teaching*, 2nd ed. The Jossey-Bass Higher and Adult Education Series. San Francisco: Jossey-Bass.

Lowyck, Joost and Johanna Poysa. 2001. "Design of Collaborative Learning Environments." *Computers in Human Behavior* 17, no. 4: 507–516.

Lubans, John Jr., ed. and comp. 1983. *Educating the Public Library User.* Chicago: ALA.

Luke, Allan and Cushla Kapitzke. 1999. "Literacy and Libraries: Archives and Cybraries." *Pedagogy, Culture & Society* 7, no. 3: 467–491.

Lukowicz, Paul. 2008. "Guest Editorial: Wearable Computing and Artificial Intelligence for Healthcare Applications." *Artificial Intelligence in Medicine* 42, no. 2: 95–98.

Lynch, Clifford A. 1998. "Recomputerizing the Library: New Roles for Information Technology in a Time of Networked Information." In *Re-creating the Academic Library: Breaking Virtual Ground* (pp. 3–22), edited by Cheryl LaGuardia. New York: Neal-Schuman.

Lynda.com. "Online Training" (2008). Available: www.lynda.com (accessed December 26, 2008).

MacDonald, Gina and Elizabeth Sarkodie-Mensah. 1988. "ESL Students and American Libraries." *College & Research Libraries* 49, no. 4: 425–431.

MacDonald, Mary C. 2008. "Program Management." In *Information Literacy Instruction Handbook* (pp. 113–137), edited by Christopher N. Cox and Elizabeth Blakesley Lindsay. Chicago: ALA. ACRL.

Macey, Richard. "Speak to the Collar, the Shirt's Playing Its Own Tune." *Sydney Morning Herald*, October 27, 2007. Available: www.smh.com.au/news/technology/speak-to-the-collar-the-shirts-playing-its-own-tune/2007/10/26/1192941339431.html (accessed December 27, 2008).

Mackey, Thomas P. and Trudi E. Jacobson. 2008. *Using Technology to Teach Information Literacy*. New York: Neal-Schuman.

Mackey, Thomas P. and Jean McLaughlin. **2008**. "Developing Blog and Wiki Communities to Link Student Research, Community Service, and Collaborative Discourse." In *Using Technology to Teach Information Literacy* (pp. 5–28), edited by Thomas P. Mackey and Trudi E. Jacobson. New York: Neal-Schuman.

Macklin, Alexis Smith. 2008. "Problem-based Learning." In *Information Literacy Instruction Handbook* (pp. 56–65), edited by Christopher N. Cox and Elizabeth Blakesley Lindsay. Chicago: ALA. ACRL.

Maehl, William. 2003. "Lifelong Learning." In *Encyclopedia of Education* (pp. 1480–1483), edited by James W. Guthrie. New York: Macmillan Reference USA.

Mager, Robert Frank. 1997a. *Goal Analysis: How to Clarify Your Goals so You Can Actually Achieve Them,* 3rd, completely rev. ed. Atlanta: Center for Effective Performance.

———. 1997b. *How to Turn Learners On—Without Turning Them Off: Ways to Ignite Interest in Learning,* 3rd, completely rev. ed. Atlanta: Center for Effective Performance.

———. 1997c. *Making Instruction Work, or, Skillbloomers: A Step-by-Step Guide to Designing and Developing Instruction That Works,* 2nd, completely rev. ed. Atlanta: Center for Effective Performance.

———. 1997d. *Measuring Instructional Results, or, Got a Match?: How to Find Out if Your Instructional Objectives Have Been Achieved,* 3rd, completely rev. ed. Mager Six-pack. Atlanta: Center for Effective Performance.

———. 1997e. *Preparing Instructional Objectives: A Critical Tool in the Development of Effective Instruction,* 3rd ed. Atlanta: Center for Effective Performance.

Magi, Trina J. 2003. "What's Best for Students? Comparing the Effectiveness of a Traditional Print Pathfinder and a Web-based Research Tool." *portal: Libraries and the Academy* 3, no. 4: 671–686.

———. "Business Research Assistant" (November 12, 2007). Available: http://library.uvm.edu/guides/subjectguides/BIZ (accessed December 24, 2008).

Magolda, Marcia B. Baxter. 2006. "Intellectual Development in the College Years." *Change* 38, no. 3: 50–54.

Maki, Peggy. 2002. "Developing an Assessment Plan to Learn about Student Learning." *Journal of Academic Librarianship* 28, no. 1–2: 8–13.

———. 2004. *Assessing for Learning: Building a Sustainable Commitment Across the Institution*. Sterling, VA: Stylus.

Mallonee, Barbara C. 1981. "A Pitch for Collaborative Learning: Discovering a Paragraph Heuristic." Unpublished. ERIC document ED218642.

Maness, Jack M. "Library 2.0 Theory: Web 2.0 and Its Implications for Libraries" (June 2006). Available: www.webology.ir/2006/v3n2/a25.html (accessed December 23, 2008).

Mann, Thomas. 1993. *Library Research Models: A Guide to Classification, Cataloging, and Computers*. New York: Oxford University Press.

———. 2007. "The Peloponnesian War and the Future of Reference, Cataloging, and Scholarship in Research Libraries" (June 13, 2007). Available: www.guild2910.org/Pelopponesian%20War%20June%2013%202007.pdf (accessed December 23, 2008).

Manning, Maryann and Gary Manning. 1996. "Art in Reading and Writing." *Teaching Pre K-8* 26, no. 6: 90–91.

Manuel, Kate. 2002. "Teaching Information Literacy to Generation Y." *Journal of Library Administration* 36, no. 1/2:195–217.

Marcum, Deanna. 2005. "The Future of Cataloging" (January 16, 2005). Available: www.loc.gov/library/reports/CatalogingSpeech.pdf (accessed November 30, 2008).

Marcus, Sandra and Sheila Beck. 2003. "A Library Adventure: Comparing a Treasure Hunt with a Traditional Freshman Orientation Tour." *College & Research Libraries* 64, no. 1: 23–44.

Maricopa County Community College. "Information Literacy" (1994). Available: www.mcli.dist.maricopa.edu/ocotillo/report94/Report94.html (accessed December 22, 2008).

Mark, Beth L. and Trudi E. Jacobson. 1995. "Teaching Anxious Students Skills for the Electronic Library." *College Teaching* 43, no. 1: 28–31.

Markey, Karen and Pauline A. Cochrane. 1981. *Online Training and Practice Manual for ERIC Data Base Searchers,* 2d ed. Syracuse, NY: ERIC Clearinghouse on Information Resources.

Markey, Karen et al. 2005. "Testing the Effectiveness of Interactive Multimedia for Library-user Education." *portal: Libraries and the Academy* 5, no. 4: 527–544.

Markoff, John. "Entrepreneurs See a Web Guided by Common Sense." *New York Times*, November 12, 2006. Available: www.nytimes.com/2006/11/12/business/12web.html (accessed November 22, 2008).

———. "A Software Secretary That Takes Charge." *New York Times*, December 14, 2008. Available: www.nytimes.com/2008/12/14/business/14stream.html?_r=1&scp=1&sq=software%20secretary%20that%20takes%20charge&st=cse (accessed December 15, 2008).

Martin, Melissa. "Medical Information on the Internet." San Diego Public Library. Available: www.sandiego.gov/public-library/catalog-databases/medical.shtml (accessed December 23, 2008).

Martyn, Margie. 2007. "Clickers in the Classroom: An Active Learning Approach." *Educause Quarterly* 30, no. 2: 71–74.

Marzano, Robert J., Ronald S. Brandt, Carolyn Sue Hughes, Beau Fly Jones, Barbara Z. Presseisen, Stuart C. Rankin, and Charles Suhor. 1988. *Dimensions of Thinking*. Alexandria, VA: Association for Supervision and Curriculum Development.

Marzano, Robert J., Debra Pickering, and Jay McTighe. 1993. *Assessing Student Outcomes: Performance Assessment Using the Dimensions of Learning Model*. Alexandria, VA: Association for Supervision and Curriculum Development.

"Mashup Awards" (2008). Available: http://mashupawards.com (accessed December 9, 2008).

Maslow, Abraham H. 1954. *Motivation and Personality*. New York: Harper.

———. 1987. *Motivation and Personality*, 3rd ed. New York: Harper and Row.

Mason, Lucia. 1994. "Analogy, Metaconceptual Awareness and Conceptual Change: A Classroom Study." *Educational Studies* 20, no. 2: 267–291.

Maughan, Patricia D. 2001. "Assessing Information Literacy Among Undergraduates: A Discussion of the Literature and the University of Berkeley Assessment Experience." *College & Research Libraries* 62, no. 1: 71–85.

MavericksPlan. "Floor Plan Design Software" (January 21, 2006). Available: www.mavericksplan.com/mavericks/default.aspx (accessed December 24, 2008).

Maxwell, Alexander. 2007. "Ban the Bullet-point! Content-based PowerPoint for Historians." *History Teacher* 41, no. 1: 39–54.

Maybee, Clarence. 2006. "Undergraduate Perceptions of Information Use: The Basis for Creating User-centered Student Information Literacy Instruction." *Journal of Academic Librarianship* 32, no. 1: 79–85.

Mayer, Richard E. 1979. "Can Advance Organizers Influence Meaningful Learning?" *Review of Educational Research* 49, no. 2: 371–383.

———. 2002. "Cognitive Theory and the Design of Multimedia Instruction." *New Directions for Teaching and Learning* 89: 55–71.

———. 2003. "The Promise of Multimedia Learning: Using the Same Instructional Design Methods Across Different Media." *Learning and Instruction* 13, no. 2: 125–139.

———. 2004. "Should There Be a Three-strikes Rule Against

Pure Discovery Learning? The Case for Guided Methods of Instruction." *American Psychologist* 59, no. 1: 14–19.

———, ed. 2005a. *Cambridge Handbook of Multimedia Learning*. New York: Cambridge University Press.

———. 2005b. "Cognitive Theory of Multimedia Learning." In *The Cambridge Handbook of Multimedia Learning* (pp. 31–48), edited by Richard E. Mayer. New York: Cambridge University Press.

———. 2005c. "Principles for Managing Essential Processing in Multimedia Learning: Segmenting, Pretraining, and Modality Principles." In *The Cambridge Handbook of Multimedia Learning* (pp. 169–182), edited by Richard E. Mayer. New York: Cambridge University Press.

———. 2005d. "Principles for Reducing Extraneous Processing in Multimedia Learning: Coherence, Signaling, Redundancy, Spatial Continuity, and Temporal Contiguity Principles." In *The Cambridge Handbook of Multimedia Learning* (pp. 183–200), edited by Richard E. Mayer. New York: Cambridge University Press.

Mayer, Richard E. and Roxanne Moreno. 2003. "Nine Ways to Reduce Cognitive Load in Multimedia Learning." *Educational Psychologist* 38, no. 1: 43–52.

Mazer, Joseph P., Richard E. Murphy, and Cheri J. Simonds. 2007. "I'll See You On 'Facebook': the Effects of Computer-mediated Teacher Self-disclosure on Student Motivation, Affective Learning, and Classroom Climate." *Communication Education* 56, no. 1: 1–17.

McCarthy, Patrick and Gregory Heald. 2003. "Integrated Information Literacy Impact Study." In *Assessing Student Learning Outcomes for Information Literacy Instruction* (pp. 216–222), edited by Elizabeth Fuseler Avery. Chicago: ALA.

McCormick, Mona. 1983. "Critical Thinking and Library Instruction." *RQ* 22, no. 4: 339–342.

McDaniel, Sarah. 2007. "Defining Information Literacy: Conceptual Models and Practice." In *Proven Strategies for Building an Information Literacy Program* (pp. 13–27), edited by Susan Curzon and Lynn Lampert. New York: Neal-Schuman.

McDermott, I.E. 2007. "Escaping Ugly: Graphic Design Aids for Untrained Librarians." *Searcher* 15, no. 5: 12–16.

McGrath, Peter. 1999. "Potholes on the Road Ahead." *Newsweek* (September), 20: 78.

McGregor, Joy. 1999. "How Do We Learn?" In *Learning and Libraries in an Information Age* (pp. 25–53), edited by Barbara K. Stripling. Englewood, CO: Libraries Unlimited.

McGuiness, Claire. 2006. "What Faculty Think: Exploring Barriers to Information Literacy Development in Undergraduate Education." *Journal of Academic Librarianship* 32, no. 6: 573–582.

McKeachie, Wilbert James. 1986. *Teaching Tips: A Guidebook for the Beginning Teacher,* 8th ed. Lexington, MA: D.C. Heath.

———. 1994. *Teaching Tips: A Guidebook for the Beginning College Teacher*, 9th ed. San Francisco: New Lexington Press.

———. 1999. *Teaching Tips: Strategies, Research and Theory for College and University Teachers*, 10th ed. Boston: Houghton-Mifflin.

McKibbon, Shelley. "Using Analogies to Get the Message Across" (April 2, 2008). Available: http://libguides.library.dal.ca/data/files/2983/Analogies.pdf (accessed December 23, 2008).

McLaughlin, James A., Lih-Cheng Chen Wang, and William A. Beasley. 2008. "Transforming the College Through Technology: A Change of Culture." *Innovative Higher Education* 33, no. 2: 99–109.

Mediavilla, Cindy. 2001. *Creating the Full-service Homework Center in Your Library*. Chicago: ALA.

———. 2003. "Homework Helpers." *School Library Journal* 49, no. 3: 56–59.

Meebo. "Instant Messaging Service" (2008). Available: www.meebo.com (accessed December 29, 2008).

MeeboMe. "Instant Messaging Service" (October 5, 2008). Available: www.meebome.com (accessed December 29, 2008).

Mellinger, Margaret and Jane Nichols. "Subject Search Disconnect: Or How Do Our Users Want to Search for Subject Information." *Oregon Library Association Conference*. Salem, Oregon, April 12, 2006. Available: http://hdl.handle.net/1957/1642 (accessed December 27, 2008).

Mellon, Constance A. 1986. "Library Anxiety: A Grounded Theory and Its Development." *College & Research Libraries* 47, no. 2: 160–165.

———. 1987. *Bibliographic Instruction: The Second Generation*. Littleton, CO: Libraries Unlimited.

Meola, Marc. "Can (Political) Blogs Be Trusted?" (June 27, 2007). Conference Blogging, Information Literacy, Authority. ACRLog. Available: http://acrlblog.org/2007/06/27/can-political-blogs-be-trusted (accessed December 23, 2008).

MERLOT. "Multimedia Educational Resource for Learning and Online Teaching" (2008). Available: www.merlot.org/merlot/index.htm (accessed December 24, 2008).

Merriman, Joyce. 2006. "Patient Information Handouts are Useful Education Tools." *American Family Physician* 73, no. 4: 572.

Messick, Samuel. 1978. "Personality Consistencies in Cognition and Creativity." In *Individuality in Learning* (pp. 4–22), edited by Samuel Messick. San Francisco: Jossey-Bass.

Mestre, Lori. 1998. "Structuring a Session with Questions." In *Designs for Active Learning* (pp. 50–51), edited by Gail Gradowski, Loanne Snavely, and Paula Dempsey. Chicago: ALA. ACRL.

———. 2006. "Learning Styles in an Online Environment." *Reference & User Services Quarterly* 46, no. 2: 27–32.

Metros, Susan E. and Kristina Woolsey. 2006. "Visual Literacy:

An Institutional Imperative." *Educause Review* 41, no. 3: 80–81.

Meyers, Chet and Thomas B. Jones. 1993. *Promoting Active Learning: Strategies for the College Classroom,* 1st ed. The Jossey-Bass Higher and Adult Education Series. San Francisco: Jossey-Bass.

Meyers, Noel M. and Duncan D. Nulty. 2008. "How to Use (Five) Curriculum Design Principles to Align Authentic Learning Environments, Assessment, Students' Approaches to Thinking, and Learning Outcomes." *Assessment & Evaluation in Higher Education* 1–12.

Mezick, Elizabeth M. 2007. "Return on Investment: Libraries and Student Retention." *Journal of Academic Librarianship* 33, no. 5: 561–566.

Mi, Jia and Cathy Weng. 2008. "Revitalizing the Library OPAC Interface, Searching and Display Challenges." *Information Technology and Libraries* 27, no. 1: 5–21.

Michigan Library Consortium. "Machinima: MLC in Second Life" (November 6, 2007). Available: www.youtube.com/watch?v=q3FXzXgmvqw (accessed December 24, 2008).

Microsoft. "Microsoft and One Laptop per Child Partner to Deliver Affordable Computing to Students Worldwide" (May 15, 2008a). Available: www.microsoft.com/presspass/press/2008/may08/05-15MSOLPCPR.mspx (accessed December 22, 2008).

Microsoft. "PowerPoint" (2008b). Available: http://office.microsoft.com/en-us/powerpoint/default.aspx (accessed December 26, 2008).

Middle States Commission on Higher Education. 2006. *Characteristics of Excellence in Higher Education: Eligibility Requirements and Standards for Accreditation.* Philadelphia: Middle States Commission on Higher Education.

Milam, Peggy. 2004. "A Road Map for the Journey." *Library Media Connection* 22, no. 7: 20–23.

Miller, George A. 1956. "The Magic Number Seven, Plus or Minus Two: Some Limits on Our Capacity for Processing Information." *Psychological Review* 63, no. 2: 81–97.

Miller, Patty. 1999. "The Hurried Student: NHCTC Library Finds Many Ways to Help Their Busy Users." *Community and Junior College Libraries* 8, no. 2: 63–69.

Millet, Michelle S. and Sue Samson. 2003. "The Learning Environment: First-year Students, Teaching Assistants, and Information Literacy." *Research Strategies* 19, no. 2: 84–98.

Milwaukee Public Library. Available: www.mpl.org (accessed April 11, 2008).

Mindomo. "Online Mind Mapping Software" (2008). Available: www.mindomo.com (accessed December 5, 2008).

Miri, Barak, David Ben-Chaim, and Uri Zoller. 2007. "Purposely Teaching for the Promotion of Higher-order Thinking Skills: A Case of Critical Thinking." *Research in Science Education* 37, no. 4: 353–369.

MIT. "MIT OpenCourseWare" (2008). Available: http://ocw.mit.edu/OcwWeb/web/home/home/index.htm (accessed December 27, 2008).

Mitchell, Eleanor and Stephanie Brasley. 2001. "Information Competency Continuum: A University, K–12 Collaboration." In *Library User Education: Powerful Learning, Powerful Partnerships* (pp. 248–255), edited by Barbara I. Dewey. Lanham, MD: Scarecrow Press.

Mizrachi, Diane. 2004. "Information Literacy in Sociology at UCLA." *Academic Exchange Quarterly*. Available: http://findarticles.com/p/articles/mi_hb3325/is_/ai_n29148993 (accessed March 30, 2009).

———. 2008a. "LITE Bites." Available: www2.library.ucla.edu/libraries/college/10373.cfm (accessed December 24, 2008).

———. 2008b. "LITEBite 6: The Librarian of Oz." Available: www.youtube.com/watch?v=pcI-ufMhrv8 (accessed December 24, 2008).

———. Forthcoming. "Library Anxiety." In *Encyclopedia of Library and Information Science,* edited by Marcia J. Bates and Mary Maack. New York: Taylor & Francis.

Mizrachi, Diane and Jaclyn Bedoya. 2007. *Reference Services Review* 35, no. 2: 249–256.

Mizrachi, Diane and Snunit Shoham. 2004. "Computer Attitudes and Library Anxiety Among Undergraduates." *International Information & Library Review* 36: 29–38.

Moeckel, Nancy and Jenny Presnell. 1995. "Recognizing, Understanding and Responding: A Program Model of Library Instruction Services for International Students." *Reference Librarian* 24, no. 51–52: 309–325.

Montgomery, Kathleen. 2002. "Authentic Tasks and Rubrics: Going Beyond Traditional Assessments in College Teaching." *College Teaching* 50, no. 1: 34–39.

Moodle. Available: http://moodle.org (accessed December 24, 2008).

Moore, Deborah, Steve Brewster, Cynthia Dorroh, and Michael Moreau. 2002. "Information Competency Instruction in a Two Year College: One Size Does Not Fit All." *Reference Services Review* 30, no. 4: 300–306.

Moran, Barbara B. 1990. "Library/classroom Partnerships for the 1990's." *College & Research Libraries News* 51, no. 5: 511–514.

Moreno, Roxana and Richard Mayer. 2007. "Interactive Multimodal Learning Environments. Special Issue on Interactive Learning Environments: Contemporary Issues and Trends." *Educational Psychology Review* 19, no. 3: 309–326.

Morgan, David. 1997. *Focus Groups as Qualitative Research,* 2d ed. Thousand Oaks, CA: Sage Publications.

Morgan, Nigel and Linda Davies. 2004. "Innovative Library Induction—Introducing the 'Cephalonian Method.'" *SCONUL Focus* 32: 4–8. Available: www.sconul.ac.uk/publications/newsletter/32/2.rtf (accessed December 23, 2008).

Morse, Janice M. and Peggy-Anne Field. 1995. *Qualitative*

Research Methods for Health Professionals, 2nd ed. Thousand Oaks, CA: Sage.

Moseng, Christopher. 2007. "The Failures and Possible Redemption of the DMCA Anticircumvention Rule-making Provision." *Journal of Technology Law & Policy* 12, no. 2: 333–374.

MOUSE, Inc. "Homepage" (August 6, 2008). Available: www.mouse.org (accessed December 22, 2008).

Moyer, Jessica. "Re: First Year Library." Electronic bulletin board. (September 11, 2006). Available: ili-l@ala.org (accessed September 24, 2008).

Mudrock, Theresa. "Engaging Students in the Game of Research." *Perspectives* 43, no. 9 (December 2005). Available: www.historians.org/perspectives/Issues/2005/0512/0512tea1.cfm (accessed December 23, 2008).

Muller, Derek A. et al. 2007. "Conceptual Change Through Vicarious Learning in an Authentic Physics Setting." *Instructional Science* 35: 519–533.

Multnomah County Library. "Homework Center" (2008). Available: www.multcolib.org/homework/index.html (accessed December 22, 2008).

Munro, George and Allen Slater. 1985. "The Know-how of Teaching Critical Thinking." *Social Education* 49, no. 4: 284–292.

Murphy, Deborah et al. "UCSC's NetTrail" (2004). Available: http://nettrail.ucsc.edu (accessed December 23, 2008).

Murray, Bridget. 2002. "What Psych Majors Need to Know." *Monitor on Psychology* 33, no. 7. Available: www.apa.org/monitor/julaug02/psychmajors.html (accessed March 30, 2009).

Murray, Janet. 2001. "Teaching Information Literacy Skills to Students with Disabilities: What Works." *School Libraries Worldwide* 7, no. 2: 1–16.

Murray, Mary T. "Summary: Teaching a 1-credit Class." Electronic bulletin board (June 6, 2008). Available: ili-l@ala.org (accessed 23 July 2008).

Museum of Media History. *EPIC 2015* (November 30, 2007). Available: www.youtube.com/watch?v=OQDBhg60UNI (accessed December 26, 2008).

NACOL. "National Standards of Quality for Online Courses" (2007). Available: www.inacol.org/resources/nationalstandards/NACOL%20Standards%20Quality%20Online%20Courses%202007.pdf (accessed December 27, 2008).

Nahl, Diane. 1999. "Creating User-centered Instructions for Novice End-users." *Reference Services Review* 27, no. 3: 280–286.

Naidu, Som. 2005. "Editorial." *Distance Education* 26, no. 3: 279–280.

Najjar, Lawrence J. 1998. "Principles of Educational Multimedia User Interface Design." *Human Factors* 40, no. 2: 311–324.

Nardi, Bonnie A. and Vicki L. O'Day. 1999. *Information Ecologies: Using Technology with Heart.* Cambridge, MA: MIT Press.

Nas, Sjoera. "Creative Commons License Upheld in Dutch and Spanish Courts." EDRI-gram no. 4.6 (March 29, 2006). Available: www.edri.org/edrigram/number4.6/ccdecisions (accessed December 25, 2008).

NASA Glenn Science and Engineering Library. "NASA Glenn SciTech Guides." Available: http://nasa-grc.libguides.com (accessed December 27, 2008).

Nashua Public Library. "Free Computer Workshops" (December 17, 2008). Available: www.nashualibrary.org/ComputerClasses.htm (accessed December 23, 2008).

Nashville Public Library. "Teen Web" (2008). Available: www.library.nashville.org/teens/teenweb.asp (accessed November 30, 2008).

National Center for Education and the Economy. 2007. *Tough Choices or Tough Times: The Report of the New Commission on the Skills of the American Workforce.* San Francisco: John Wiley & Sons.

National Commission on Excellence in Education. 1983. *A Nation at Risk: The Imperative for Educational Reform*: Washington, DC: National Commission on Excellence in Education.

National Council for the Accreditation of Teacher Education. 2002. *Professional Standards for the Accreditation of Schools, Colleges, and Departments of Education*, 2002 Edition. Available: www.ncate.org/documents/unit_stnds_2002.pdf (accessed August 2007).

National Framework. "*The Scottish Information Literacy Project.*" Glasgow Caledonian University (2007). Available: www.caledonian.ac.uk/ils/framework.html (accessed September 12, 2008).

Natowitz, Allen. 1995. "International Students in United States Academic Libraries: Recent Concerns and Trends." *Research Strategies* 13, no. 1: 4–16.

NCAT. "The National Center for Academic Transformation" (2005a). Available: www.thencat.org (accessed December 27, 2008).

———. "Program in Course Redesign" (2005b). Available: www.thencat.org/PCR.htm (accessed December 27, 2008).

NCSU Libraries. "Endeca at the NCSU Libraries." Available: www.lib.ncsu.edu/endeca (accessed December 23, 2008).

Neelameghan, A. and Greg Chester. 2006. "Environmental Knowledge and Marginalized Communities: The Last Mile Connectivity." *Webology* 3, no. 1. Available: www.webology.ir/2006/v3n1/a24.html (accessed March 30, 2009).

Neeley, Teresa Y. 2002. *Sociological and Psychological Aspects of Information Literacy in Higher Education.* Lanham, MD: Scarecrow Press.

———, ed. 2006. *Information Literacy Assessment: Standards-based Tools and Assignments.* Chicago: ALA.

Nelson, Craig E. 1994. "Critical Thinking and Collaborative Learning." *New Directions for Teaching and Learning* 59: 45–58.

Nelson, Sandra. 2001. *The New Planning for Results: A Streamlined Approach*. Chicago: ALA.

NetNewsWire. "Newsgator" (2008). Available: www.newsgator.com/INDIVIDUALS/NETNEWSWIRE (accessed December 27, 2008).

NetSupport School. "Classroom Management" (2008). Available: www.netsupportschool.com (accessed December 27, 2008).

NeverWinter Nights. "Community Site" (2008). Available: http://nwn.bioware.com (accessed December 28, 2008).

New England Association of Schools and Colleges—Commission on Institutions of Higher Education. *Standard 7: Library and Information Resources, Standards for Accreditation* (2001). Available: www.neasc.org/cihe/standards.pdf (accessed August 13, 2007).

New Media Consortium. "Conference" (2008). Available: www.nmc.org/keyword/conference (accessed December 27, 2008).

New Media Consortium and Educause. "2008 Horizon Report: Horizon Report Metatrends" (2008). Available: http://horizon.nmc.org/wdata/xdocs/Horizon-Metatrends.pdf (accessed December 27, 2008).

New York Public Library. Available: www.nypl.org (accessed April 11, 2008).

New York Public Library, Brooklyn Public Library, and Queens Library. "Homework Help" (2005). Available: http://homeworkNYC.org (accessed August 23, 2007).

Newby, Timothy J. 1995. "Instructional Analogies and the Learning of Concepts." *Educational Technology Research and Development: ETR&D* 43, no. 1:5–18.

NFIL. "National Forum on Information Literacy" (December 3, 2008a). Available: www.infolit.org/index.html (accessed, December 22, 2008).

———. "What Is Information Literacy?" (December 3, 2008b). Available: www.infolit.org (accessed December 30, 2008).

NFIL, UNESCO, and IFLA. "Beacons of the Information Society: The Alexandria Proclamation on Information Literacy and Lifelong Learning" (2005). Available: www.ifla.org/III/wsis/BeaconInfSoc.html (accessed December 22, 2008).

Nichols, James, Barbara Shaffer, and Karen Shockey. 2003. "Changing the Face of Instruction: Is Online or In-class More Effective?" *College & Research Libraries* 64, no. 5: 378–388.

Nichols, Janet W. 1999. "Building Bridges: High School and University Partnerships." *NASSP Bulletin* 83, no. 3: 75–81.

Nicol, David J. and Debra Macfarland-Dick. 2006. "Formative Assessment and Self-regulated Learning: A Model and Seven Principles of Good Feedback Practice." *Studies in Higher Education* 31, no. 2: 199–218.

Niederhauser, Dale S. and Trish Stoddart. 2001. "Teachers' Instructional Perspectives and Use of Educational Software." *Teaching and Teacher Education* 17, no. 1: 15–31.

Nielsen, Jakob. "Usability as Barrier to Entry" (November 28, 1999a). Available: www.useit.com/alertbox/991128.html (accessed December 27, 2008).

———. "When Bad Design Elements Become the Standard" (November 14, 1999b). Available: www.useit.com/alertbox/991114.html (accessed December 27, 2008).

———. 2000a. *Designing Web Usability*. Indianapolis: New Riders Publishing.

———. "Jakob Nielsen's Alertbox: End of Web Design" (July 23, 2000b). Available: www.useit.com/alertbox/20000723.html (accessed December 27, 2008).

———. "The Mud-throwing Theory of Usability" (April 2, 2000c). Available: www.useit.com/alertbox/20000402.html (accessed December 27, 2008).

———. "How Little Do Users Read?" (May 6, 2008a). Available: www.useit.com/alertbox/percent-text-read.html (accessed December 26, 2008).

———. "Site Map Usability" (August 12, 2008b). Available: www.useit.com/alertbox/sitemaps.html (accessed December 26, 2008).

———. "Jakob Nielsen's Website." Available: www.useit.com (accessed December 24, 2008).

Nimmer, David. 2000. "A Riff on Fair Use in the Digital Millennium Copyright Act." *University of Pennsylvania Law Review* 148, no. 3: 673–742.

Noble, David F. "Digital Diploma Mills: The Automation of Higher Education." *First Monday: Peer-reviewed Journal on the Internet* 3, no. 1 (1998a). Available: http://web.archive.org/web/20050901133756/http://www.firstmonday.dk/issues/issue3_1/noble (accessed December 27, 2008).

———. "Digital Diploma Mills, Part II: The Coming Battle Over Online Instruction: Confidential Agreements Between Universities and Private Companies Pose Serious Challenge to Faculty Intellectual Property Rights" (1998b). Available: http://web.archive.org/web/20080126050442/http://communication.ucsd.edu/dl/ddm2.html (accessed December 27, 2008).

———. "Digital Diploma Mills, Part III: The Bloom Is Off the Rose" (November 1998c). Available: http://web.archive.org/web/20071230035607/http://communication.ucsd.edu/dl/ddm3.html (accessed December 27, 2008).

Norgaard, Rolf. 2003. "Writing Information Literacy: Contributions to a Concept." *Reference & User Services Quarterly* 43, no. 2: 124–130.

———. 2004. "Writing Information Literacy in the Classroom." *Reference & User Services Quarterly* 43, no. 3: 220–226.

Norlin, Dennis A. 1992. "We're Not Stupid You Know: Library Services for Adults with Mental Retardation." *Research Strategies* 10, no. 2: 56–68.

Norman, Donald A. 1983. "Some Observations on Mental Models." In *Mental Models* (pp. 7–14), edited by Dedre

Gentner and Albert L. Stevens. Hillsdale, NJ: Lawrence Erlbaum Associates.

North Central Association of Colleges and Schools. "Standards." Available: http://ncahigherlearnngcommission.org (accessed November 20, 2007).

North West Commission on Colleges and Universities. "Standards." Available: www.nwccu.org/index.htm (accessed November 20, 2007).

Northfield Mount Hermon (MA) School Library. "LibGuides—Northfield Mount Hermon School." Available: http://libguides.nmhschool.org (accessed December 27, 2008).

Notess, Greg R. 2006. "The Terrible Twos: Web 2.0, Library 2.0, and More." *Online* 30, no. 3: 40–42.

November, Alan. "Information Literacy Resources" (2008). Available: http://novemberlearning.com/index.php?option=com_content&task=category§ionid=5&id=27&Itemid=85 (accessed December 23, 2008).

Novey, Levi T. and Troy E. Hall. 2006. "The Effect of Audio Tours on Learning and Social Interaction: An Evaluation at Carlsbad Caverns National Park." *Science Education* 91: 260–277.

Nowakowski, Fran. 2008. "Analogies." Personal e-mail. 25 Jun 2008.

NSSE. "National Survey on Student Engagement" (2008). Available: http://nsse.iub.edu/index.cfm (accessed December 22, 2008).

Oakleaf, Megan. 2007. "Using Rubrics to Collect Evidence for Decision-making: What Do Librarians Need to Learn?" *Evidence-based Library and Information Practice* 2, no. 3: 27–42.

Oatman, Eric. 2006. "Overwhelming Evidence." *Library School Journal* 52, no. 1: 56–59.

Oberg, Dianne. 1999. "A Community of Learning for the Information Age." In *Learning and Libraries in the Information Age* (pp. 299–323), edited by Barbara K. Stripling. Englewood, CO: Libraries Unlimited.

Oberman, Cerise. 1980. *Petals Around a Rose: Abstract Reasoning and Bibliographic Instruction: A Paper*. Chicago: ACRL.

Oberman, Cerise and Rebecca A. Linton. 1982. "Guided Design: Teaching Library Research in Problem Solving." In *Theories of Bibliographic Education* (pp. 111–134), edited by Cerise Oberman and Katina Stauch. New York: Bowker.

Oberman, Cerise and Katina Strauch. 1982. *Theories of Bibliographic Education; Designs for Teaching*. New York: Bowker.

Oblinger, Diana and James Oblinger. "Educating the Net Generation." *Educause* (2005). Available: www.educause.edu/educatingthenetgen/5989 (accessed December 27, 2008).

O'English, Lorena and Sarah McCord. 2006. "Getting Into the Game: Partnering with a University Athletics Department." *portal: Libraries and the Academy* 6, no. 2: 143–153.

Office of Economic Co-operation and Development. 1996. *The Knowledge-based Economy*. Paris: OECD.

O'Hanlon, Nancy. 2007. "Information Literacy in the University Curriculum: Challenges for Outcomes Assessment." *portal: Libraries and the Academy* 7, no. 2: 169–189.

Olgren, Christina. 2000. "Learning Strategies for Learning Technologies." *New Directions for Adult and Continuing Education* 88, no. 1: 7–16.

Olsen, Erica. "Librarian Avengers" (November 29, 2007). Available: http://librarianavengers.org/about-2 (accessed December 25, 2008).

Olson, Susan. 2008. "Re: Re: Re: Career Day." Electronic bulletin board (April 14, 2008). Available: infolit@ala.org (accessed April 14, 2008).

Omaha Public Library. Available: www.publiclibrary.org/events/computer.html (accessed April 11, 2008).

"Online Learning Booms as More States Expand and Plan Initiatives." 2007. *Electronic Education Report* 14, no. 6: 4–6.

Onwuegbuzie, Anthony J. 1998. "The Relationship Between Library Anxiety and Learning Styles Among Graduate Students: Implications for Library Instruction." *Library and Information Science Research* 20, no. 3: 235–249.

Onwuegbuzie, Anthony J., Qun G. Jiao, and Sharon L. Bostick. 2004. *Library Anxiety: Theory, Research, and Applications*. Lanham, MD: Scarecrow Press.

"Open Source Web Design" (2008). Available: www.oswd.org (accessed December 26, 2008).

Open University. Available: www.open.ac.uk (accessed December 27, 2008a).

———. "Information Literacy Toolkit." Available: www.open.ac.uk/iltoolkit/index.php (accessed December 27, 2008b).

Oregon State University Libraries. "Library a la Carte." Available: http://alacarte.library.oregonstate.edu (accessed December 24, 2008).

———. "Get Help with a Class" (2004a). Available: http://ica.library.oregonstate.edu/course-guides (accessed December 27, 2008).

———. "Get Help with a Subject" (2004b). Available: http://ica.library.oregonstate.edu/subject-guides (accessed December 27, 2008).

O'Reilly, Tim. "What Is Web 2.0: Design Patterns and Business Models for the Next Generation of Software" (September 30, 2005). Available: www.oreillynet.com/lpt/a/6228 (accessed November 19, 2008).

Orme, William A. 2004. "A Study of the Residual Impact of the Texas Information Literacy Tutorial on the Information Seeking Ability of First Year College Students." *College & Research Libraries* 65, no. 5: 205–215.

Osland, Joyce S. and Allen Bird. 2000. "Beyond Sophisticated Stereotyping: Cultural Sensemaking in Context." *Academy of Management Executive* 41, no. 1: 65–79.

O'Sullivan, Carmel. 2002. "Is Information Literacy Relevant

in the Real World?" *Reference Services Review* 30, no. 1: 7–14.

Oswald, Debra. "Peanut Butter & Jelly Analogy." Personal e-mail (July 3, 2008).

Oswald, Tina A. and Martha Turnage. 2000. "First Five Minutes." *Research Strategies* 17, no. 3: 347–351.

Owusu-Ansah, Edward K. 2007. "Beyond Collaboration: Seeking Greater Scope and Centrality for Library Instruction." *portal: Libraries and the Academy* 7, no. 4: 415–429.

Oxford English Dictionary, 2nd ed. 1989. Oxford: Clarendon Press.

Pace, David. 2004. "Decoding the Reading of History: An Example of the Process." In *Decoding the Disciplines: Helping Students Learn Disciplinary Ways of Thinking* (pp. 13–21), edited by David Pace and Joan Middendorf. New Directions for Teaching and Learning, no. 98. San Francisco: Jossey-Bass.

Paglia, Alison and Annie Donahue. 2003. "Collaboration Works: Integrating Information Competencies Into the Psychology Curriculum." *Reference Services Review* 31, no. 4: 320–328.

Paige, Kathy. 1996. "Panel Session." In *Learning for Life: Information Literacy and the Autonomous Learner* (pp. 13–22), edited by Di Booker. Adelaide, Australia: University of South Australia Library.

Paivio, Allan. 1973. "Picture Superiority in Free Recall: Imagery or Dual Coding?" *Cognitive Psychology* 5, no. 2: 176–206.

Pallis, J.M. 1997. "K–8 Aeronautics Internet Textbook." In *The World Wide Web as a Medium of Instruction: What Works and What Doesn't. Proceedings of the March Learning Technologies Conference* (pp. 18–25). NASA Dryden Flight Research Center, March 18–20, 1997. Edwards, CA: NASA. NASA Report CD–3358.

Palmer, Parker J. 1998. *The Courage to Teach: Exploring the Inner Landscape of a Teacher's Life*, 1st ed. San Francisco: Jossey-Bass.

Papastergiou, Marina. 2006. "Course Management Systems as Tools for the Creation of Online Learning Environments: Evaluation From a Social Constructivist Perspective and Implications for Their Design." *International Journal on E-Learning* 5, no. 4: 593–622.

Pappas, Marjorie. 1998. "Designing Authentic Learning." *School Library Media Activities Monthly* 14: 29–31, 42.

———. 2000. "Managing the Inquiry Learning Environment." *School Library Media Activities Monthly* 16, no. 7: 27–30, 36.

———. 2007. "Tools for the Assessment of Learning." *School Library Media Activities Monthly* 23, no. 9: 21–25.

Pappas, Marjorie and Ann Tepe. 1997. *Pathways to Knowledge (TM). Follett's Information Skills Model*, 3rd ed. McHenry, IL: Follett Software.

Parker, Roger C. 2006. *Looking Good in Print*. Scottsdale, AZ: Paraglyph Press.

Partnership for 21st Century Skills. "A Report and Mile Guide for 21st Century Skills" (2003). Available: www.21stcenturyskills.org (accessed September 8, 2008).

———. "Homepage" (2008). Available: www.21stcenturyskills.org (accessed December 22, 2008).

Patton, Michael Quinn. 1980. *Qualitative Evaluation Methods*. Beverly Hills: Sage.

Pavlov, Ivan Petrovich. 1927. *Conditioned Reflexes*. New York: Dover.

———. 1928. *Lectures on Conditioned Reflexes*. New York: International Publishers.

Pawley, Christine. 2003." Information Literacy: A Contradictory Coupling." *Library Quarterly* 73, no. 4: 422–452.

PayPerPost (2008). Available: http://payperpost.com (accessed December 27, 2008).

PBwiki. "Productivity Software" (2008). Available: http://pbwiki.com (accessed December 27, 2008).

Peacock, Judith. 2007. "Beyond the Fashionable: Strategic Planning for Critical Information Literacy Education." In *Proven Strategies for Building an Information Literacy Program* (pp. 29–53), edited by Susan Curzon and Lynn Lampert. New York: Neal-Schuman.

Pearson, Debra and Beth McNeil. 2002. "From High School Users College Students Grow: Providing Academic Library Research Opportunities to High School Students." *Knowledge Quest* 30, no. 4: 24–28.

Pederson, Sarah. 2003. *Learning Communities and the Academic Library.* National Learning Communities Project Monograph Series. Olympia, WA: The Evergreen State College, Washington Center for Improving the Quality of Undergraduate Education in cooperation with the American Association for Higher Education and the Association of College and Research Libraries.

Penn, Mark J. and E. Kinney Zalesne. 2007. *Microtrends: The Small Forces Behind Tomorrow's Big Changes*. New York: Twelve.

Perez, Sarah. "Why Gen Y Is Going to Change the Web" (May 15, 2008). Available: www.readwriteweb.com/archives/why_gen_y_is_going_to_change_the_web.php (accessed December 27, 2008).

Perraut, Anne Marie. "American Competitiveness in the Internet Age" (2006). Available: www.infolit.org/meetings/InfoLitsummit16Oct2007B.pdf (accessed February 7, 2008).

Perry, William Graves. 1981. "Cognitive and Ethical Growth: The Making of Meaning." In *The Modern American College* (pp. 76–116), edited by Arthur W. Chickering. San Francisco: Jossey-Bass.

———. 1988. "Different Worlds in the Same Classroom." In *Improving Learning: New Perspectives* (pp. 145–161), edited by Paul Ramsden. London: Kogan Page.

Peterson-Lugo, Billie. 2006. "Tech Talk: Web 2.0" (December 2006). *LIRT News* 29, no. 2: 8–10.

Petherbridge, Donna and Diane Chapman. "Upgrading or Replacing Your Learning Management System: Implications for Student Support" (Spring 2007). *Online Journal of Distance Learning Administration* 10, no. 1. Available: www.westga.edu/~distance/ojdla/spring101/petherbridge101.htm (accessed December 24, 2008).

Petress, Ken. 2004. "Critical Thinking: An Extended Definition." *Education* 124, no. 3: 461–466.

Petruzzi, Tony and Mary Frances Burns. 2006. "A Literacy Center Where? A Public Library Finds Space to Promote and Provide Family Learning Activities." *Public Library Quarterly* 25, no. 1/2: 191–197.

Pew Internet & American Life Project. "Information Searches That Solve Problems" (December 30, 2007). Available: www.pewinternet.org/PPF/r/231/report_display.asp (accessed December 22, 2008).

———. "Demographics of Internet Users" (July 22, 2008a). Available: www.pewinternet.org/trends/User_Demo_7.22.08.htm (accessed December 27, 2008).

———. "Latest Trends" (2008b). Available: www.pewinternet.org/trends.asp (accessed December 25, 2008).

Philbin, Marge, Elizabeth Meier, Sherri Huffman, and Patricia Boverie. 1995. "A Survey of Gender and Learning Styles." *Sex Roles* 32, no. 7–8: 485–494.

Phipps, Shelley E. 1980. "Why Use Workbooks? Or, Why Does the Chicken Cross the Road? and Other Metaphors, Mixed." *Drexel Library Quarterly* 16, no. 1: 41–53.

PIA Information Services. "DepEd Chief Pushes for More Resources for ICT in Basic Education" (September 6, 2006). Available: www.pia.gov.ph/default.asp?m=12&fi=p060906.htm&no=40 (accessed December 22, 2008).

Piaget, Jean. 1952. *The Origins of Intelligence in Children,* 2nd ed. New York: International Universities Press.

———. 1954. *The Construction of Reality in the Child*. New York: Basic Books.

Piaget, Jean and Bärbel Inhelder. 1969. *The Psychology of the Child*. London: Routledge & K. Paul.

Picasa. "Photo-organizing Software" (2008). Available: http://picasa.google.com (accessed December 24, 2008).

Picasso, Vicki and Debbie Booth. "InfoSkills Tutorial" (October 24, 2007). Available: www.newcastle.edu.au/services/library/tutorials/infoskills/index.html (accessed December 23, 2008).

Picciano, Anthony G. and Jeff Seaman. "K–12 Online Learning: A Survey of U.S. School District Administrators." Sloan Consortium (2007). Available: www.sloan-c.org/publications/survey/pdf/K-12_Online_Learning.pdf (accessed December 27, 2008).

Pillsbury, Ralph T. 2006. "Making Learning a Never-ending Story." *Science Scope* 30, no. 4: 22–26.

Pinchbeck, B.J. "Homework Helper" (2007). Available: http://bjpinchbeck.com (accessed December 29, 2008).

Pink, Daniel H. 2007. "Pecha Kucha: Get to the PowerPoint in 20 Slides Then Sit the Hell Down." *Wired* 15, no. 9 (August 21, 2007). Available: www.wired.com/techbiz/media/magazine/15-09/st_pechakucha (accessed December 26, 2008).

Pinto, Maria, Andres Fernandez-Ramos, and Vinciane Doucet. 2008. "Measuring Students' Information Literacy Skills Through Abstracting: Case Study from a Library and Information Science Perspective." *College & Research Libraries* 9, no. 2: 132–154.

Pithers, R.T. and Rebecca Soden. 2000. "Critical Thinking in Education: A Review." *Educational Research* 42, no. 3: 237–249.

Pittman, Kim M. 1999. "Student-generated Analogies: Another Way of Knowing?" *Journal of Research in Science Teaching* 36, no. 1: 1–22.

PLoS. "Public Library of Science" (2008). Available: www.plos.org (accessed December 23, 2008).

Pomerantz, Jeffrey. 2005. "Collaboration as the Norm in Reference Work." *Reference & User Services Quarterly* 46, no. 1: 45–55.

portal: Libraries and the Academy. 2001–. Baltimore: Johns Hopkins University Press.

Postman, Neil and Charles Weingarten. 1971. *Teaching as a Subversive Activity*. New York: Delacorte Press.

Powis, Chris and Jo Webb. "Start with the Learner." CILIP: Chartered Institute of Library and Information Professionals (2005). Available: www.cilip.org.uk/publications/updatemagazine/archive/archive2005/janfeb/webbpow.htm (accessed July 31 2008).

Prange, Laurie. 2007. "Freeware/Shareware to Create Building Map." Electronic bulletin board (March 29, 2007). Available: ILI-L@ala.org (accessed July 14, 2008).

Prensky, Marc. 2001. *Digital Game-based Learning*. New York: McGraw-Hill.

———. 2007. "Changing Paradigms: From 'Being Taught' to 'Learning on Your Own with Guidance'" *Educational Technology* 47, no. 4: 64.

———. 2008. "Students as Designers and Creators of Educational Computer Games: Who Else?" *British Journal of Educational Technology* 39, no. 6: 1004–1019.

Price, Thomas. "Buried Treasure: A WebQuest in Optimization" (March 10, 2008). Available: http://questgarden.com/61/79/2/080305092401 (accessed December 14, 2008).

Princeton Public Library. "Class Calendar" (December 2008). Available: http://princetonlibrary.org/research/techcenter/classes.html#completelist (accessed December 27, 2008).

Purdue, Jeff. 2003. "Stories, Not Information: Transforming Information Literacy." *portal: Libraries and the Academy* 3, no. 4: 653–662.

Purdue University. "Purdue Opens New Chapter in National Information Literacy" (2005). Available: http://news.uns.purdue.edu/html3month/2005/050930.Celebrate.library.html (accessed December 22, 2008).

Quible, Zane K. 1998. "A Focus on Focus Groups." *Business Communication Quarterly* 61, no. 2: 28–37.

Quick Takes. "Inside Higher Ed" (February 7, 2006). Available: www.insidehighered.com/news/2006/02/07/qt (accessed December 22, 2008).

Rabine, Julie and Catherine Cardwell. 2000. "Start Making Sense: Practical Approaches to Outcomes Assessment in Libraries." *Research Strategies* 17, no. 4: 319–335.

Rader, Hannelore B. 1990. "Bibliographic Instruction or Information Literacy?" *College & Research Libraries News* 51, no. 1: 18–20.

———. 1991. "Information Literacy: A Revolution in the Library." *RQ* 31, no. 1: 25–29.

———. 1993. "From Library Orientation to Information Literacy: Twenty Years of Hard Work." In *What Is Good Instruction Now?: Library Instruction for the 90s* (pp. 25–28), edited by Linda Shirato. Ann Arbor, MI: Pierian Press.

———. 2003. "Information Literacy: A Global Perspective." In *Information and IT Literacy: Enabling Learning in the 21st Century* (pp. 24–42), edited by Allan Martin and Hannelore B. Rader. London: Facet Publishing.

———. 2004. "Building Faculty–Librarian Partnerships to Prepare Students for Information Fluency: The Time for Sharing Information Expertise Is Now." *College & Research Libraries News* 65, no. 2: 74–90.

"Radical Reference" (April 17, 2008). Available: www.radicalreference.info (accessed January 3, 2009).

Ragains, Patrick. 1997. "Evaluation of Academic Librarians—Instructional Performance: Report of a National Survey." *Research Strategies* 15, no. 2: 159–175.

Ramsden, Paul. 1988. "Studying Learning: Improving Teaching." In *Improving Learning: New Perspective* (pp. 13–31), edited by Paul Ramsden. London: Kogan Page.

Rankin, Virginia. 1988. "One Route to Critical Thinking." *School Library Journal* 34, no. 1: 28–31.

Rawlings, Hunter R. III. 2007. "Information, Knowledge, Authority, and Democracy." Keynote address presented at the 151st ARL Membership Meeting in Washington, DC, October 10, 2007. Available: www.arl.org/bm~doc/mm-f07-rawlings.pdf (accessed April 14, 2008).

Rayner, Stephen and Richard Riding. 1997. "Toward a Categorisation of Cognitive Styles and Learning." *Educational Psychology* 17, no. 1–2: 5–27.

Ready, Sandy, Marvin E. Wiggins, Sharon Lee Stewart, Katherine Jordan, and Kathy Sabol. 1990. "Library Instruction in Academic Libraries Including Graduate, Four-year and Two-year Institutions." In *The LIRT Instruction Handbook* (pp. 21–46), edited by May Brottman and Mary Loe. Englewood, CO: Libraries Unlimited.

Ream, Dan and Lucretia McCulley. 2007. "Who Do You Trust? Wikipedia and the Authority of Anonymous Strangers." ACRL National Conference Presentation, Baltimore.

Reed, Shannon L. and Kirilka Stravreva. 2006. "Layering Knowledge: Information Literacy as Critical Thinking." *Teaching Literature, Language, Composition and Culture* 6, no. 3: 435–452.

Reference Services Review. 1973–. Ann Arbor, MI: Pierian Press.

Reichel, Mary and Mary Ann Ramey, eds. 1987. *Conceptual Frameworks for Bibliographic Education: Theory Into Practice*. Littleton, CO: Libraries Unlimited.

Reidling, Ann Marlow. 2004. *Learning to Learn: A Guide to Becoming Information Literate in the 21st Century*, 2nd ed. New York: Neal-Schuman.

Reinhardt, Stephen. "Library OPACs & Mobile-Friendly Features." Userslib.com. (August 10, 2008) Available: http://userslib.com/2008/08/10/library-opacs-mobile-friendly-features (accessed December 27, 2008).

Renkl, Alexander. 2005. "The Worked-out Examples Principle in Multimedia Learning." In *The Cambridge Handbook of Multimedia Learning* (pp. 229–246), edited by Richard E. Mayer. New York: Cambridge University Press.

Research Strategies. 1983–2005. Ann Arbor, MI: Mountainside Publishing.

Resta, Paul and Therese Laferriere. 2007. "Technology in Support of Collaborative Learning." *Educational Psychology Review* 19: 65–83.

Rethlefsen, Melissa L. 2007. "Tags Help Make Libraries Del.icio.us" (September 15, 2007). Available: www.libraryjournal.com/article/CA6476403.html (accessed November 30, 2008).

Richards, John P. 1978. "Instructional Psychology: From Behavioristic to Cognitive Orientation." *Improving Human Performance Quarterly* 7, no. 3: 256–266.

Riddle, John S. and Karen A. Hartman. 2000. "But Are They Learning Anything? Designing an Assessment of First Year Library Instruction." *College and Undergraduate Libraries* 7, no. 2: 59–69.

Ridgeway, Trish. 1989. "Integrating Active Learning Techniques into the One-hour Bibliographic Instruction Lecture." In *Coping with Information Illiteracy: Bibliographic Instruction for the Information Age* (pp. 33–42), edited by Glenn S. Mensching and Teresa B. Mensching. Ann Arbor, MI: Pierian Press.

Riding, Richard and Indra Cheema. 1991. "Cognitive Styles: An Overview and Integration." *Educational Psychology* 11, no. 3: 193–215.

Rio Salado College. "Critical Thinking Rubric" (2008). Available: www.rio.maricopa.edu/distance_learning/critical_think_rubric.shtml (accessed December 23, 2008).

Roberson, Donna. "Meet the Immigrants" (June 14, 2004). Available: www.lubbockisd.org/webquests/MeetImmigrants (accessed December 23, 2008).

Roberts, Anne F. and Susan Griswold Blandy. 1989. *Library Instruction for Librarians*, 2nd rev. ed. Library Science Text Series. Englewood, CO: Libraries Unlimited.

Robertson, Mark. 2006. "Re: Stephen Colbert v. Wikipedia." Electronic bulletin board..(August 9, 2006). Available: ili-l@ala.org (accessed 8 Feb 2008).

Robinson, Otis. 1880. "Rochester University Library—Administration and Use." *U.S. Bureau of Education, Circular of Information* no. 1880: 15–27.

Rockman, Ilene. 2002. "Strengthening Connections Between Information Literacy, General Education and Assessment Efforts." *Library Trends* 51, no. 2: 185–198.

———. 2003a. "Creating the Teachable Moment." In *Musings, Meanderings and Monsters Too* (pp. 58–64), edited by Martin H. Raish. Lanham, MD: Scarecrow Press.

———. 2003c. "Integrating Information Literacy Into the Learning Outcomes of Academic Disciplines." *College & Research Libraries News* 64, no. 9: 612–615.

———. 2004a. "Conclusion: Continuing the Dialogue." In *Integrating Information Literacy Into the Higher Education Curriculum* (pp. 237–250), edited by Ilene Rockman. San Francisco: Jossey-Bass.

———, ed. 2004b. *Integrating Information Literacy Into the Higher Education Curriculum*. San Francisco: Jossey-Bass.

———. 2004c. "Introduction: The Importance of Information Literacy." In *Integrating Information Literacy Into the Higher Education Curriculum* (pp. 1–28), edited by Ilene Rockman. San Francisco: Jossey-Bass.

———. 2004d. "Successful Strategies for Integrating Information Literacy Into the Curriculum." In *Integrating Information Literacy Into the Higher Education Curriculum* (p. 66), edited by Ilene Rockman. San Francisco: Wiley & Sons.

———. "Viewpoint: Why ICT Assessment Is Needed Now." (2004e) Available: www.compus-technology.com/print.asp?ID=17733 (accessed October 7, 2007).

Rockman, Ilene and Gordon W. Smith. 2005. "Information and Communication Technology Literacy: New Assessments for Higher Education." *College & Research Libraries News* 66, no. 8: 587–589.

Rogers, Carl R. 1969. *Freedom to Learn: A View of What Education Might Become*. Columbus, OH: C.E. Merrill.

Rogers, Carl R. and H. Jerome Freiberg. 1994. *Freedom to Learn*, 3rd ed. Toronto: Maxwell Macmillan Canada.

Rogers, Curtis. "Flickr Class at SC State Library" (2007). Available: www.flickr.com/photos/curtisrogers/489935451 (accessed December 27, 2008).

Roland, David. 1997. *The Confident Performer.* Sydney: Currency Press.

Rosenzweig, Roy. 2006. "Can History Be Open Source? Wikipedia and the Future of the Past." *Journal of American History* 93, no. 1: 117–146.

Rosinki, Phillipe and Geoffrey N. Abbott. 2006. "Coaching From a Cultural Perspective." In *Evidence-based Coaching Handbook: Putting Best Practices to Work for Your Clients* (pp. 255–275), edited by Dianne R. Stober and Anthony M. Grant. New York: Wiley.

Rotter, Julian B. 1971. "External Control and Internal Control." *Psychology Today* 51, no. 1: 37–42, 58–59.

———. 1975. "Some Problems and Misconceptions Related to the Construct of Internal Versus External Control of Reinforcement." *Journal of Consulting and Clinical Psychology* 43, no. 1: 56–67.

Rovai, Alfred P. 2004. "A Constructivist Approach to College Learning." *Internet and Higher Education* 7, no. 2: 79–93.

Rovai, Alfred P. and Hope M. Jordan. 2004. "Blended Learning and Sense of Community: A Comparative Analysis with Traditional and Fully Online Graduate Courses." *International Review of Research in Open and Distance Learning* 5, no. 2: 1–13.

Royer, Regina and Jeffrey Royer. 2004. "Comparing Hand Drawn and Computer Generated Concept Mapping." *Journal of Computers in Mathematics and Science Teaching* 23, no. 1: 67–81.

"RSS Specifications." Available: www.rss-specifications.com/what-is-rss.htm (accessed April 28, 2009).

Rua, Robert J. 2008. "After-school Success Stories." *American Libraries* 39, no. 10: 46–48.

Rubick, Kate. 2007. "Conservapedia." Electronic bulletin board (March 8, 2007). Available: ili-l@ala.org (accessed February 8, 2008).

Russell, Catherine. 2007. *Schirmer Encyclopedia of Film*, vol. 4. S.v., "Video." New York: Schirmer Reference, pp. 303–307.

Russell, Thomas L. 1999. *The No Significant Difference Phenomenon: As Reported in 355 Research Reports, Summaries and Papers.* Raleigh: North Carolina State University.

———. "No Significant Difference Phenomenon" (2008). Available: www.nosignificantdifference.org (accessed December 24, 2008).

Ruth, Stephen. 1997. "Getting Real About Technology-based Learning: The Medium Is NOT the Message." *Educom Review* (September–October): 32–37.

Rymaszewski, Michael et al. 2007. *Second Life: The Official Guide*. Indianapolis: Wiley.

Sakai. "Sakai CLE" (2008). Available: http://sakaiproject.org (accessed December 27, 2008).

Salili, Farideh and Rumjahn Hoosain. 2001. "Multicultural Education: History, Issues and Practices." In *Multicultural Education: Issues, Policies, and Practices* (pp. 1–13), edited by Farideh Salili and Rumjahn Hoosain. Greenwich, CT: Information Age Publishing.

Sanburn, Lura. 2005. "Improving Library Instruction: Faculty Collaboration." *Journal of Academic Librarianship* 31, no. 5: 477–481.

Sanchez, Irene M. 2000. "Motivating and Maximizing Learning in Minority Classrooms." *New Directions for Community Colleges* 112: 35–43.

Sanders, Judith A. and Richard L. Wiseman. 1994. "The Effects of Verbal and Nonverbal Teacher Immediacy on Perceived Cognitive, Affective and Behavioral Learning in the Multicultural Classroom." In *The College Classroom* (pp. 623–639), edited by Kenneth A. Feldman and Michael B. Paulsen. Needham Heights, MA: Ginn Press.

San Diego State University. "SDSU Second Life Pioneers." Available: http://slurl.com/secondlife/Meadowbrook/226/103/23/?title=SDSU%20Second%20Life%20Pioneers (accessed March 1, 2008).

Santa Monica Public Library. Available: www.smpl.org (accessed April 11 2008).

Sarkodie-Mensah, Kwasi. 1998. "Using Humor for Effective Library Instruction Sessions." *Catholic Library World* 68, no. 4: 25–29.

———. 2000. "The International Student on Campus: History, Trends, Visa Classification, and Adjustment Issues." In *Teaching the New Library to Today's Users: Reaching International, Minority, Senior Citizens, Gay/Lesbian, First Generation, At-risk, Graduate and Returning Students, and Distance Learners* (pp. 3–16), edited by Trudi E. Jacobson and Helene C. Williams. New York: Neal-Schuman.

Saunders, Laura. 2007. "Regional Accreditation Organizations' Treatment of Information Literacy: Definitions, Collaboration, and Assessment." *Journal of Academic Librarianship* 33, no. 3: 317–326.

Savery, John R. 2006. "Overview of Problem-based Learning: Definitions and Distinctions." *Interdisciplinary Journal of Problem-based Learning* 1, no. 1: 9–20.

Scales, B. Jane and Elizabeth Blakesley Lindsay. 2005. "Qualitative Assessment of Student Attitudes Toward Information Literacy." *portal: Libraries and the Academy* 5, no. 4: 514–526.

Scales, B. Jane, Greg Matthews, and Corey M. Johnson. 2005. "Compliance, Cooperation, Collaboration and Information Literacy." *Journal of Academic Librarianship* 31, no. 5: 229–235.

Schaeffer, S.J. (Sandy) III. "De-coupling Course Management from the LMS/CMS." *Campus Technology* (January 9, 2008). Available: http://campustechnology.com/articles/57220 (accessed November 29, 2008).

"School Libraries—Blogging Libraries" (2008). Available: www.ipl.org/div/blogs (accessed December 27, 2008).

"School Libraries Work!" Available: www2.scholastic.com/content/collateral_resources/pdf/s/slw3_2008.pdf (accessed February 28, 2008).

Schrock, Kathy. "Critical Evaluation Surveys and Resources" (2008a). Available: http://school.discoveryeducation.com/schrockguide/eval.html (accessed December 23, 2008)

———. "Kathy Schrock's Guide for Educators" (2008b). Available: http://school.discoveryeducation.com/schrockguide (accessed November 11, 2008).

Schroeder, Robert. "Active Learning with Interactive Whiteboards." *Communications in Information Literacy* 1, no. 2 (2007). Available: www.comminfolit.org/index.php/cil/article/viewArticle/Fall2007AR2/50 (accessed December 23, 2008).

Scitikus, Tom T. and Manka M. Varghese. 2007. "Language Diversity and Schooling." In *Multicultural Education: Issues and Perspectives* (pp. 297–325), edited by James A. Banks and Cherry A.M. Banks. Hoboken, NJ: Wiley.

Scocco, Daniel. "Top 25 Web Design Blogs" (2008). Available: www.dailyblogtips.com/top-25-web-design-blogs (accessed December 26, 2008).

Scriven, Michael. 1973. "The Methodology of Evaluation." In *Educational Evaluation: Theory and Practice* (pp. 60–104), edited by Blaine Worthen and James Sanders. Belmont, CA: Wadsworth.

Search-Cube. "Web Browser" (October 31, 2008). Available: www.search-cube.com (accessed December 29, 2008).

SearchMe. "Web Browser" (2008). Available: www.searchme.com (accessed December 29, 2008).

Seattle Public Library. Available: www.spl.org (accessed April 11, 2008).

Second Life. "Virtual World." Available: http://secondlife.com (accessed December 27, 2008).

SEOmoz. "SEOmoz's Web 2.0 Awards" (2008). Available: www.seomoz.org/web2.0 (accessed December 28, 2008).

Seton, Jo and Ninette Ellis. 1996. "Information Literacy for International Postgraduate Students." In *Learning for Life* (pp. 39–48), edited by Di Booker. Adelaide, Australia: University of South Australia Library.

Severiens, Sabine and Geert Ten Dam. 1997. "Gender and Gender Identity Differences in Learning Styles." *Educational Psychology* 17, no. 1–2: 79–93.

Shade, Barbara J., Cynthia A. Kelly, and Mary Oberg. 1997. *Creating Culturally Responsive Classrooms*, 1st ed, *Psychology in the Classroom*. Washington, DC: American Psychological Association.

Shade, Barbara J. and Clara A. New. 1993. "Cultural Influences on Learning: Teaching Implications." In *Multicultural Education: Issues and Perspectives* (pp. 317–331), edited by James A. Banks and Cherry A.M. Banks. Boston: Allyn & Bacon.

Shaffer, Gary. 2006. "Stop the Presses! A Hip New After-school Program Has Turned Kids Into Modern-day Jimmy Olsens and Lois Lanes." *School Library Journal* 52, no. 7: 38–39.

Shankar, Viswanath. "CMS and LMS—A Comparison" (February 20, 2007). Available: www.contentmanagementnews.com/contentmanagementnews-82-20070220CMSandLMSAComparison.html (accessed November 29, 2008).

Shapiro, Jeremy L. and Shelley K. Hughes. 1996. "Information Literacy as a Liberal Art: Enlightenment Proposals for a New Curriculum." *Educom Review* 31 (March–April). Available: www.educause.edu/pub/er/review/reviewarticles/31231.html (accessed December 22, 2008).

———. 2001. "The World Wide Web, the Reorganization of Knowledge, and Liberal Arts Education." *Educational Technology* 41, no. 10: 12–16.

Sharkey, Jennifer. 2006. "Toward Information Fluency: Applying a Different Model to an Information Literacy Course." *Reference Services Review* 34, no. 1: 71–85.

Sharma, Shikha. 2006. "From Chaos to Clarity: Using the Research Portfolio to Teach and Assess Information Literacy Skills." *Journal of Academic Librarianship* 33, no. 1: 127–135.

Shavelson, Richard J. and Leta Huang. 2003. "Responding Responsibly to the Frenzy to Assess Learning in Higher Education." *Change* 35, no. 1: 10–19.

Shaw, Sue. 2008. "Engaging a New Generation of Graduates." *Education + Training* 50, no. 5: 367–378.

Sheridan, Jean. 1986. "Andragogy: A New Concept for Academic Librarians." *Research Strategies* 4, no. 4: 156–167.

———. 1990. "The Reflective Librarian: Some Observations on Bibliographic Instruction in the Academic Library." *Journal of Academic Librarianship* 16, no. 1: 22–26.

Shirato, Linda. 1999. "LOEX and Library Instruction." *Reference Services Review* 27, no. 3: 214–218.

Shonrock, Diana D., ed. 1996. *Evaluating Library Instruction: Sample Questions, Forms, and Strategies for Practical Use*. Chicago: ALA. LIRT.

Shores, Louis. 1970. *Library-College USA: Essays on a Prototype for an American Higher Education*. Tallahassee, FL: South Pass Press.

Silberman, Mel. 1996. *Active Learning: 101 Strategies to Teach Any Subject*. Boston: Allyn & Bacon.

Simba Information. "E-rate Marks 10 Years of Funding Telecommunications Services for Schools." *Electronic Education Report* (June 6, 2007). Available: www.fundsforlearning.com/index2.php?option=com_content&do_pdf=1&id=893 (accessed December 22, 2008).

SIMILE. "Studies in Media and Information Literacy Education." 2001–. Toronto, Canada: University of Toronto Press. Available: www.utpjournals.com/simile/simile.html (accessed December 22, 2008).

Simmons, Michelle Holschuh. 2005. "Librarians as Disciplinary Discourse Mediators: Using Genre Theory to Move Toward Critical Information Literacy." *portal: Libraries and the Academy*. 5, no. 3: 297–311.

Simon, Kenneth. "Re: [ili-l] Analogies in ILI. "Personal e-mail (June 23, 2008).

"SKILLS Act Gives High Marks to School Librarians." 2007. *American Libraries* 38, no. 7: 15.

Skinner, B.F. 1938. *The Behavior of Organisms*. New York: Macmillan.

———. 1968. *The Technology of Teaching*. New York: Appleton-Century-Crofts.

———. 1974. *About Behaviorism*. New York: Knopf.

———. 1983. *A Matter of Consequences*. New York: Knopf.

———. 1984. "The Shame of American Education." *American Psychologist* 39, no. 9: 947–954.

Skoglund, Christine. 2003. "The Public Library Context." *Reference & User Services Quarterly* 42, no. 4: 313–314.

Slavin, Robert E. 2006. *Educational Psychology: Theory Into Practice,* 8th ed. Boston: Allyn & Bacon.

Slideshare. "Presentation Software" (2008). Available: www.slideshare.net (accessed December 24, 2008).

Sloan, Robin and Matt Thompson. *EPIC 2015*. Available: www.albinoblacksheep.com/flash/epic (accessed December 24, 2008).

Small, Ruth V., Jaime Snyder, and Katie Parker. 2008. *New York State's School Libraries and Library Media Specialists: An Impact Study*. Syracuse, NY: Center for Digital Literacy, Syracuse University.

Smalley, Topsy. "Information Competency in the California Community Colleges"(2008). Available: www.topsy.org/infocomp.html (accessed December 22, 2008).

Smith, Felicia A. 2007. "Games for Teaching Information Literacy Skills." *Library Philosophy and Practice* 9, no. 2: 1–12. Available: www.webpages.uidaho.edu/~mbolin/f-smith.pdf (accessed December 28, 2008).

Smith, Terry C. 1991. *Making Successful Presentations: A Self-teaching Guide*, 2nd ed. New York: Wiley.

SnagIt. Okemos, MI: TechSmith (2008). Available: www.techsmith.com (accessed, December 24, 2008).

SnapNDrag. "Screen Capture Software." Available: www.yellowmug.com/snapndrag (accessed December 25, 2008).

SnapzProX. Rochester, NY: Ambrosia Software, Inc. (2008). Available: www.ambrosiasw.com/utilities/snapzprox (accessed December 25, 2008).

Snavely, Loanne. 1998. "Teaching Boolean Operators in a Flash Using a Deck of Cards." In *Designs for Active Learning* (pp. 114–116), edited by Gail Gradowski, Loanne Snavely, and Paula Dempsey. Chicago: ALA, ACRL.

———. 2004. "Making Problem-based Learning Work: Institutional Challenges." *Libraries and the Academy* 4, no. 4: 521–531.

Snavely, Loanne and Natasha Cooper. 1997. "The Information Literacy Debate." *Journal of Academic Librarianship* 23, no. 1: 9–14.

Snyder, Judith. "Non-technical Website Guidelines" (2008). Available: www.customwebhelp.com/non-technical-website-guidelines.shtml (accessed December 26, 2008).

Soldat, Alexander S., Robert C. Sinclair, and Melvin C. Mark. 1997. "Color as an Environmental Processing Cue: External Affective Cures Can Directly Affect Processing Strategy Without Affecting Mood." *Social Cognition* 15, no. 1: 55–72.

Somerville, Mary, Lynn Lampert, Kathy Dabbour, Sallie Harlan, and Barbara Schader. 2007. "Toward Large Scale Assessment of Information and Communication Technology Literacy: Implementation Considerations for the ETS ICT Literacy Instrument." *Reference Services Review* 35, no. 1: 8–20.

Sonntag, Gabriela. 2007. "In Search of Excellence: Qualities for a Teaching Model." In *Proven Strategies for Building an Information Literacy Program* (pp. 133–145), edited by Susan Curzon and Lynn Lampert. New York: Neal-Schuman.

Sonntag, Gabriela and Yvonne Meulemans. 2003. "Planning for Assessment." In *Assessing Student Learning Outcomes for Information Literacy Instruction* (pp. 6–21), edited by Elizabeth Fuseler Avery. Chicago: ALA.

"SOS for Information Literacy" (2006). Available: www.informationliteracy.org (accessed December 22, 2008).

Sourceforge.net. "Open Source Software" (2008). Available: http://sourceforge.net (accessed December 25, 2008).

Southern Association of Colleges and Schools. "Standards." 2007. Available: www.sacscoc.org (accessed November 20, 2007).

Spalding, Steve. "How to Split an Atom: How to Define Web 3.0" (July 14, 2007). Available: http://howtosplitanatom.com/news/how-to-define-web-30-2 (accessed December 27, 2008).

SPARC. "The Scholarly Publishing and Academic Resources Coalition" (2008). Available: www.arl.org/sparc/about/index.shtml (accessed December 23, 2008).

Sparks-Langer, Georgea. 2000. *Teaching as Decision Making*. Upper Saddle River, NJ: Prentice-Hall.

"Special Libraries—Blogging Libraries" (December 16, 2008). Available: www.blogwithoutalibrary.net/links/index.php?title=Special_libraries (accessed December 27, 2008).

Spellings, Margaret. "A Test of Leadership: Charting the Future of U.S. Higher Education" (2006) Available: www.ed.gov/about/bdscomm/list/hiedfuture/reports/final-report.pdf (accessed December 30, 2008).

Spiteri, Louise F. 2007. "The Structure and Form of Folksonomy Tags: The Road to the Public Library Catalog." *Information Technology and Libraries* 26, no. 3: 13–25.

Spitzer, Kathleen L., Michael Eisenberg, Carrie A. Lowe, and ERIC Clearinghouse on Information & Technology. 1998. *Information Literacy Essential Skills for the Information Age*. Syracuse, NY: ERIC Clearinghouse on Information & Technology, Syracuse University.

Staedter, Tracy. "'Bionic Lens' Adds Computing Power to Sight." *Discovery News*, Discovery Channel (February 5, 2008). Available: http://dsc.discovery.com/news/2008/02/05/bionic-contact-lens.html (accessed December 9, 2008).

Staley, Shannon M. 2007. "Academic Subject Guides: A Case Study of Use at San Jose State University." *College & Research Libraries* 68, no. 2: 119–139.

Stanford University. "Copyright and Fair Use Center" (2008). Available: http://fairuse.stanford.edu (accessed December 25, 2008).

Stemler, Steven E., Julian G. Elliott, Elena L. Grigorenka, and Robert Sternberg. 2006. "There Is More to Teaching than Instruction: Seven Strategies for Dealing with the Practical Side of Teaching." *Educational Studies* 32, no. 1: 101–118.

Sternberg, Robert and Elena L. Grigorenka. 2002. "The Theory of Successful Intelligence as a Basis for Instruction and Assessment in Higher Education." *New Directions for Teaching and Learning* 89: 45–53.

———. 2004. "Successful Intelligence in the Classroom." *Theory Into Practice* 43, no. 4: 274–280.

Stevens, Charles H., Marie P. Canfield, and Jeffrey J. Gardner. 1973. "Library Pathfinders: A New Possibility for Cooperative Reference Service." *College & Research Libraries* 34, no. 1: 40–46.

Stevens, Christy R., and Patricia J. Campbell. 2006. "Collaborating to Connect Global Citizenship, Information Literacy, and Lifelong Learning in the Global Studies Classroom." *Reference Services Review* 24, no. 4: 536–566.

Stewart, Darlene L. 1993. *Creating the Teachable Moment*. Blue Ridge Summit, PA: Tab Books.

Stoffle, Carla J. 1998. "Literacy 101 for the Digital Age." *American Libraries* 29, no. 1: 46–48.

Stoffle, Carla J., Alan E. Guskin, and Joseph A. Boisse. 1984. "Teaching, Research, and Service: The Academic Library's Role." In *Increasing the Teaching Role of Academic Libraries* (pp. 3–14), edited by Thomas Kirk. San Francisco: Jossey-Bass.

St. Olaf College. "Research Practices Survey—Information for Faculty" (2008). Available: www.stolaf.edu/offices/ea/Assessment/ResPracSur/FacultyInfo.htm (accessed November 1, 2008).

Stover, Mark and Steven D. Zink. 1996. "World Wide Web Home Page Design: Patterns and Anomalies of Higher Education Library Home Pages." *Reference Services Review* 24, no. 3: 7–20.

St. Paul (MN) Public Library. "Homework Help" (2008). Available: www.stpaul.lib.mn.us/homework (accessed, December 22, 2008).

Strife, Mary L. 1995. "Special Libraries and Instruction: One on One Public Relations." *Reference Librarian* 24, no. 51–52: 415–419.

Stripling, Barbara K. 1996. "Quality in School Library Media Programs: Focus on Learning." *Library Trends* 44, no. 3: 631–656.

———. 2007. "Assessing Information Fluency: Gathering Evidence of Student Learning." *School Library Media Activities Monthly* 23, no. 8: 25–29.

Stripling, Barbara K. and Judy M. Pitts. 1988. *Brainstorms and Blueprints: Teaching Library Research as a Thinking Process*. Englewood, CO: Libraries Unlimited.

Stronck, David R. 1983. "The Comparative Effects of Different Museum Tours on Children's Attitudes and Learning." *Journal of Research in Science Teaching* 20, no. 4: 283–290.

Stull, Andrew T. and Richard E. Mayer. 2007. "Learning by Doing versus Learning by Viewing: Three Experimental Comparisons of Learner-generated versus Author-provided Graphic Organizers." *Journal of Educational Psychology* 99, no. 4: 808–820.

"StumbleUpon" (2008). Available: www.stumbleupon.com (accessed November 22, 2008).

Suchy, LeAnn. 2007. "Re: Examples of Inaccurate Wikipedia entries?" Electronic bulletin board (March 8, 2007). Available: ili-l@ala.org (accessed 8 Feb 2008).

Sullivan, Patrick. 2004. "Developing Freshman-level Tutorials to Promote Information Literacy." In *Integrating Information Literacy Into the Curriculum* (pp. 71–91), edited by Ilene Rockman. San Francisco: Jossey-Bass.

SUNY. 2000. "Information Literacy Initiative Overview." Available: www.sunyconnect.suny.edu/ili/iliover.htm (accessed April 14, 2009).

SUNY Buffalo. "Distance Learners Help Guide." Available: http://ublib.buffalo.edu/libraries/help/distance.html (accessed December 28, 2008a).

———. "Library Skills Workbook." Available: http://ublib.buffalo.edu/libraries/workbook (accessed December 31, 2008b).

"Supermarket Psych-out." 1999. *Tufts University Health & Nutrition Letter* 16, no. 1: 1.

Suprenant, Thomas T. 1981. "Library Instruction: A Column of Opinion: A Second Opinion," edited by Carolyn Kirkendall. *Journal of Academic Librarianship* 6, no. 6: 346.

Sutherland, Naomi and C.M. Winters. 2001. "The A, B, Z's of Bibliographic Instruction: Using Real-life Analogies to Foster Understanding." *Reference Librarian* 73: 293–308.

Svinicki, Marilla D. 1994. "Practical Implications of Cognitive Theories." In *Teaching and Learning in the College Classroom* (pp. 275–282), edited by Kenneth A. Feldman and Michael B. Paulsen. Needham, Heights, MA: Ginn Press.

Svinicki, Marilla D. and Barbara A. Schwartz. 1988. *Designing Instruction for Library Users: A Practical Guide*. New York: M. Dekker.

Swanson, Troy. 2004. "Implementing a Critical Information Literacy Model." *portal: Libraries and the Academy* 4, no. 2: 259–273.

Sweller, John. 2005. "The Redundancy Principle in Multimedia Learning." In *The Cambridge Handbook of Multimedia Learning* (pp. 159–168), edited by Richard E. Mayer. New York: Cambridge University Press.

Swensen, Rolf and Suzanne Garrison-Terry. 1994. "Dispelling the 'Old Green Spinach': Impressions of Bibliographic Instruction in Europe." *Research Strategies* 12, no. 2: 94–114.

Tag, Sylvia. 2004. "A Library Instruction Survey for Transfer Students: Implications for Library Services." *Journal of Academic Librarianship* 30, no. 2: 102–108.

Tagliacozzo, R. and M. Kochen. 1970. "Information-seeking Behavior of Catalog Users." *Information Storage and Retrieval* 6, no. 5: 363–381.

Talab, R.S. 2007. "Distance Education Public Domain, Free, and 'Fair Use' Resources: A Webliography." *TechTrends* 61, no. 6: 9–11.

Talbot, Janet Frey, Rachel Kaplan, Frances E. Kuo, and Stephen Kaplan. 1993. "Factors That Enhance Effectiveness of Visitor Maps." *Environment and Behavior* 25, no. 6: 7–25.

"Talking with Don Norman." *Educom Review* 34, no. 3 (1999). Available: http://connect.educause.edu/Library/Abstract/TalkingwithDonNorman/41089 (accessed December 25, 2008).

Tallent-Runnels, Mary K. et al. 2006. "Teaching Courses Online: A Review of the Research." *Review of Educational Research* 76, no. 1: 93–135.

Tancheva, Kornelia, Camille Andrews, and Gail Steinhart. 2007. "Library Instruction Assessment in Academic Libraries." *Public Services Quarterly* 3, no. 1/2: 29–56.

Tapscott, Don and Anthony D. Williams. 2006. *Wikinomics: How Mass Collaboration Changes Everything*. London, England: Penguin Books.

Tayeb, Monir. 2001. "Conducting Research Across Cultures: Overcoming Drawbacks and Obstacles." *International Journal of Cross-cultural Management* 1, no. 1: 91–108.

Taylor, Marilyn. 1987. "Self-directed Learning: More Than Meets the Observer's Eye." In *Appreciating Adults Learning: From the Learner's Perspective* (pp. 179–196), edited by David Boud and Virginia Griffin. London: Kogan Page.

TeacherTube. "Instructional Videos" (2008). Available: www.teachertube.com (accessed December 23, 2008).

Teaching Information Literacy Skills to Social Sciences Students and Practitioners: A Casebook of Applications. 2006. Edited by Douglas Cook and Natasha Cooper. Chicago: ALA. ACRL.

"Techlistmania." 2008. *American Libraries* 39, no. 1/2: 31.

Technology, Education, and Copyright Harmonization Act of 2002. Public Law 107-273, 107th Congress (November 2, 2002). Available: www.copyright.gov/legislation/pl107-273.html (accessed December 25, 2008).

"Technology News." 2008. *American Libraries* 39, no. 9: 42–43.

Technorati. Available: http://technorati.com (accessed December 27, 2008).

TechTerms.com. "Mashup." (2008a). Available: www.techterms.com/definition/mashup (accessed December 29, 2008).

TechTerms.com. "Widget" (2008b). Available: www.techterms.com/definition/widget (accessed December 29, 2008).

Tempelman-Kluit, Nadaleen. 2006. "Multimedia Learning Theories and Online Instruction." *College & Research Libraries* 67, no. 4: 364–369.

Tennant, Mark. 2006. *Psychology and Adult Learning*. London: Routledge.

Tennant, Roy. 1997. "Web Sites By Design: How to Avoid a 'Pile of Pages.'" Syllabus (August): 49–50.

Thomas, Nancy Pickering. 2004. *Information Literacy and Information Skills Instruction: Applying Research to Prac-*

tice in the Library Media Center, 2nd ed. Westport, CT: Libraries Unlimited.

Thompson, Christen. 2003. "Information Illiterate or Lazy: How College Students Use the Web for Research." *portal: Libraries and the Academy* 3, no. 2: 259–268.

Thompson, Glenn J. and Barbara R. Stevens. 1985. "Library Science Students Develop Pathfinders." *College & Research Libraries News* 46, no. 5: 224–225.

Thompson, Helen M. and Susan A. Henley. 2000. *Fostering Information Literacy: Connecting National Standards, Goals 2000, and the SCANS Report, Information Literacy Series*. Englewood, CO: Libraries Unlimited and its division Teacher Ideas Press.

Thompson, Spenser. 2003. "Information Literacy Meeting of Experts." In *Meeting sponsored by the U.S. National Commission on Libraries and Information Science (NCLIS) and the National Forum on Information Literacy (NFIL) with the support of the United Nations Education, Scientific, and Cultural Organization (UNESCO)*. Prague, the Czech Republic: NCLIS.

Thorndike, Edward L. 1913. *Educational Psychology*. New York: Teachers College, Columbia University.

Thorpe, S.J. and M.J. Brosnan. 2007. "Does Computer Anxiety Reach Levels Which Conform to DSM IV Criteria for Specific Phobia?" *Computers in Human Behavior* 23: 1258–1272.

Thousand Oaks (CA) Library. "Homework Help" (December 17, 2008). Available: www.tol.lib.ca.us/databases/db_subhw.html (accessed December 22, 2008).

.______. "Learning @ Your Library." (March 20, 2009). Available: www.tol.lib.ca.us/classes/latlib.html (accessed April 21, 2009)

Thunder Bay (Ontario) Public Library. "Internet Links" (2008). Available: www.tbpl.ca/internal.asp?id=283&cid=333 (accessed November 30, 2008).

Tiberius, Richard and Ivan Silver. "Guidelines for Conducting Workshops and Seminars That Actively Engage Participants" (2001). Available: www.aadprt.org/training/workshops/Guidelines_for_Conducting_Workshops_and_Seminars.pdf (accessed December 23, 2008).

Tillay, David, Linda Nelson, and Scott Hopgood. "Survivor Student Web Site Rubrics" (December 28, 2002). Available: http://ed.fnal.gov/lincon/w01/projects/survivor/rubricswebpage.htm (accessed December 23, 2008).

Tipton, Roberta and Patricia Bender. 2006. "From Failure to Success: Working with Underprepared Transfer Students." *Reference Services Review* 34, no. 3: 389–404.

TLT Group. "Low Threshold Applications and Activities" (September 27, 2008a). Available: www.tltgroup.org/ltas.htm (accessed December 24, 2008).

———. "Seven Principles: Collection of Ideas for Teaching and Learning with Technology" (September 27, 2008b). Available: www.tltgroup.org/seven/Library_TOC.htm (accessed December 27, 2008).

———. "Rubrics." Available: www.tltgroup.org/resources/Flashlight/Rubrics.htm (accessed September 12, 2008).

Todd, Russ and Carol Collier Kuhlthau. "Student Learning Through Ohio School Libraries: The Ohio Research Study" (2004). Available: www.oelma.org/studentlearning (accessed December 22, 2008).

Tolman, Edward Chace. 1932. *Purposive Behavior in Animals and Men*. New York: The Century Co.

Tompkins, Heather. 2003. "The Academic Library Context." *Reference & User Services Quarterly* 42, no. 4: 314–315.

———. 2007. "Freeware/Shareware to Create Building Map." Electronic bulletin board (April 2, 2007). Available: ILI-L@ala.org (accessed July 14, 2008).

Topping, Keith J. 2005. "Trends in Peer Learning." *Educational Psychology: An International Journal of Experimental Educational Psychology* 25, no. 6: 631–645.

Tosa, Yukiko and Thomas Long. 2003. "Teaching Library Research Skills: Online and at the Library." *PNLA Quarterly* 68, no. 1: 14–15.

Town, J. Stephen. 2003. "Information Literacy: Definition, Measurement, Impact." In *Information and IT Literacy: Enabling Learning in the 21st Century* (pp. 51–65), edited by Allan Martin and Hannelore B. Rader. London: Facet.

Trail, Mary Ann, Carolyn Gutierrez, and David Lechner. 2006. "Reconsidering a Traditional Instruction Technique: Reassessing the Print Workbook." *Journal of Academic Librarianship* 32, no. 6: 632–640.

Train, Briony and Judith Elkin. 2001. "Branching Out: A Model for Experiential Learning in Professional Practice." *Journal of Librarianship and Information Science* 33, no. 2: 68–74.

Tucker, John Mark. 1980. "User Education in Academic Libraries: A Century in Retrospect." *Library Trends* 28: 9–27.

Tufte, Edward R. 1983. *The Visual Display of Quantitative Information*. Cheshire, CT: Graphics Press.

———. "PowerPoint Is Evil: Power Corrupts. PowerPoint Corrupts Absolutely." *Wired* 11, no. 9 (September 2003). Available: www.wired.com/wired/archive/11.09/ppt2.html (accessed December 24, 2008).

Turner, Diane. 1993. "What's the Point of Bibliographic Instruction, Point-of-Use Guides and In-house Bibliographies?" *Wilson Library Bulletin* 67, no. 5: 64–68.

Turro, Mireia Ribera. 2008. "Are PDF Documents Accessible?" *Information Technology and Libraries* 27, no. 3: 25–43.

Tushnet, Rebecca. 2006. "My Library: Copyright and the Role of Institutions in a Peer-to-Peer World." *UCLA Law Review* 53, no. 4: 977–1029.

Twigg, Carol A. "Who Owns Online Courses and Course Materials? Intellectual Property Policies for a New Learning Environment." The Pew Learning and Technology Program (2000). Available: www.center.rpi.edu/Monographs/Whoowns.html (accessed December 25, 2008).

———. 2003. "Improving Learning and Reducing Costs: New Models for Online Learning." *Educause Review* 43, no. 1 (2003). Available: www.educause.edu/ir/library/pdf/erm0352.pdf (accessed December 27, 2008).

Twitter. "Social Network" (2008). Available: http://twitter.com (accessed December 27, 2008).

Tyckoson, David A. 2000. "Library Service for the First Generation College Student." In *Teaching the New Library to Today's Users: Reaching International, Minority, Senior Citizens, Gay/Lesbian, First Generation, At-risk, Graduate and Returning Students, and Distance Learners* (pp. 89–105), edited by Trudi E. Jacobson and Helene C. Williams. New York: Neal-Schuman.

———. 2007. "That Thing You Do." *Reference & User Services Quarterly* 47, no. 2: 111–113.

Tyler, Ralph Winfred. 1976. *Educational Evaluation: New Roles, New Meanings*. Chicago: University of Chicago Press.

UCLA Biomedical Library. 2007. "Dissecting a Database" (September 2007). Available: www2.library.ucla.edu/pdf/dissecting_database.pdf (accessed December 12, 2008).

UCLA College Library. "How to Narrow or Broaden Your Topic" (1997). Available: www.library.ucla.edu/libraries/college/11605_11640.cfm (accessed December 23, 2008).

———. "Session Evaluations" (April 2, 2004). Available: www.library.ucla.edu/libraries/college/services/evaluations.htm (accessed December 5, 2008).

UCLA Library. "Google Scholar vs. PsycINFO" (2005). Available: www2.library.ucla.edu/googlescholar/exercise.cfm (accessed December 23, 2008).

"U.K. Clearinghouse for Materials Related to Education of Library Users." 1977. *Information Hotline* 9, no. 10: 3.

Uncyclopedia "The Content-free Encyclopedia That Anyone Can Edit" (November 5, 2008). Available: http://uncyclopedia.wikia.com/wiki/Main_Page (accessed November 23, 2008).

UNESCO. "Increasing Information Literacy of Afghan Women" (June 8, 2007). Available: http://portal.unesco.org/ci/en/ev.php-URL_ID=25154&URL_DO=DO_TOPIC&URL_SECTION=201.html (accessed December 22, 2008).

———. "Information for All Programme (IFAP)" (December 19, 2008a). Available: http://portal.unesco.org/ci/en/ev.php-URL_ID=1627&URL_DO=DO_TOPIC&URL_SECTION=201.html (accessed December 22, 2008).

———. "Information Literacy." (2008b). Available: www.unesco.org/webworld/en/information-literacy (accessed February 19, 2008).

———. "Training-the-Trainers in Information Literacy" (December 6, 2008c). Available: http://portal.unesco.org/ci/en/ev.php-URL_ID=25623&URL_DO=DO_TOPIC&URL_SECTION=201.html (accessed December 22, 2008).

UNESCO and IFLA. "An International State-of-the-Art Report" (May 2007). Available: www.infolitglobal.info/docs/UNESCO_IL_state_of_the_art_report_-_Draft070803.doc (accessed December 22, 2008).

Unger, Harlow G. 1996. *Encyclopedia of American Education*. S.v., "Metacognition." New York: Facts on File.

Universidad Autonoma de Ciudad Juarez. "Encuentro de Desarrollo de Habilidades Informativas" (2008). Available: www.uacj.mx/dhi (accessed December 22, 2008).

University of Auckland. *Boolean Operators* (April 8, 2008). Available: www.youtube.com/watch?v=Os6VdXOwKCo (accessed December 26, 2008).

University of British Columbia. "Ancient Spaces: Antiquity Comes Alive" (2007). Available: http://ancient.arts.ubc.ca (accessed December 28, 2008).

University of California. California Digital Library. "Inside CDL: Instructional Materials" (2008). Available: www.cdlib.org/inside/instruct (accessed December 24, 2008).

University of California Commission on General Education. "General Education in the 21st Century: A Report of the University of California Commission on General Education" (April 1, 2007). Available: http://repositories.cdlib.org/cshe/CSHE-7-07 (accessed December 24, 2008).

University of Minnesota. "Assignment Calculator" (August 23, 2006). Available: www.lib.umn.edu/help/calculator (accessed December 27, 2008).

University of Pennsylvania. 2005. "PennTags" (2005). Available: http://tags.library.upenn.edu/help (accessed November 30, 2008).

———. *Weigle Information Commons Music Video* (June 25, 2008). Available: www.youtube.com/watch?v=4z4Z717yD08 (accessed December 24, 2008).

University of South Florida. "Distance Learners" (2008). Available: www.lib.usf.edu/public/index.cfm?Pg=DistanceLearners (accessed December 27, 2008).

University of Victoria Libraries. "Research Help: Subject Guides" (2008). Available: http://webapp.library.uvic.ca/subsplus/subjects/index.php (accessed December 27, 2008).

USAC. "Schools and Libraries Program—USAC" (2008). Available: www.usac.org/sl (accessed December 22, 2008).

U.S. Census Bureau. "Population: Immigration" (2007). Available: www.census.gov/population/www/socdemo/immigration.html (accessed March 18, 2008).

U.S. Department of Commerce and National Telecommunications and Information Administration. 1999. "Falling Through the Net: Defining the Digital Divide." Washington, DC: U.S. GPO.

U.S. Department of Education. 1991. *America 2000: An Education Strategy*, rev. ed. Washington, DC: U.S. Department of Education.

U. S. Department of Education. Institute of Education Sciences. IES National Center for Education Statistics. 2007.

"Fast Facts: Is Participation in Adult Learning Increasing?" Available: http://nces.ed.gov/fastfacts/display.asp?id=89 (accessed April 27, 2009).

U.S. Department of Justice. "ADA Home Page: Information and Technical Assistance on the Americans with Disabilities Act." Available: www.usdoj.gov/crt/ada (accessed March 18, 2008).

U.S. Department of Labor. Secretary's Commission on Achieving Necessary Skills. 2000. *What Work Requires of Schools: A SCANS Report for America 2000*. Washington, DC: GPO.

U.S. Library of Congress. "The Library of Congress' Photostream" (2008). Available: http://flickr.com/photos/library_of_congress (accessed November 23, 2008).

U.S. National Academy of the Sciences. "Being Fluent with Information Technology: Executive Summary" (1999). Available: http://books.nap.edu/openbook.php?record_id=6482&page=1 (accessed December 22, 2008).

U.S. National Library of Medicine and National Institutes of Health. "MedlinePlus" (December 26, 2008). Available: http://medlineplus.gov (accessed December 27, 2008).

U.S. NCLIS and NFIL. "The Prague Declaration" (2003). Available: www.infolit.org/International_Conference/PragueDeclaration.pdf (accessed December 22, 2008).

Utah State Office of Education. 1996. *Library Media Information Literacy Core Curriculum for Utah Secondary Schools*. Salt Lake City: Utah State Office of Education.

Valenza, Joyce Kazman. 2003a. *Power Research Tools, Learning Activities & Posters*. Chicago: ALA.

———. 2003b. "Spreading the Gospel of Information Literacy: A Schoolwide Initiative." *Knowledge Quest* 32, no. 1: 49–50.

Van Cleave, Kendra. 2007. "Collaboration." In *Proven Strategies for Building an Information Literacy Program* (pp. 176–190), edited by Susan Curzon and Lynn Lampert. New York: Neal-Schuman.

van der Meij, Hans and Ard W. Lazonder. 1993. "Assessment of the Minimalist Approach to Computer User Documentation." *Interacting with Computers* 5, no. 4: 355–370.

van Dijk, Jan A.G.M. 2006. "Digital Divide Research, Achievements and Shortcomings." *Poetics* 34: 221–235.

Veldof, Jerilyn. 2006. *Creating the One-shot Library Workshop: A Step-by-Step Guide*. Chicago: ALA.

Vella, Jane. 2000. *Learning to Listen. Learning to Teach,* 2nd ed. San Francisco: Jossey-Bass.

Viewzi. "Web Browser" (2008). Available: www.viewzi.com (accessed December 29, 2008).

Villano, Matt. "Sign of the Times." *Campus Technology*, April 24, 2006. Available: http://campustechnology.com/mcv/resources/solutioncenters/center/Presentation/article/?id=40831&msid=6 (accessed December 24, 2008).

Virkus, Sirje. "Information Literacy in Europe: A Literature Review." *Information Research* 8, no. 4 (2003). Available: http://informationr.net/ir/8-4/paper159.html (accessed December 22, 2008).

VisiBone. "Web Designer's Color Reference Poster" (2008). Available: www.visibone.com/color/poster4x.html (accessed December 27, 2008).

VoiceThread "Group Conversation" (2008). Available: http://voicethread.com/#home (accessed December 9, 2008).

"Volcanoes Online." ThinkQuest. Available: http://library.thinkquest.org/17457 (accessed December 28, 2008).

Von Holzen, Roger. 2005. "The Emergence of a Learning Society." *The Futurist*: 24–25.

Vrasidas, Charalambos and Marina S. McIssac. 2000. "Principles of Pedagogy and Evaluation for Web-based Learning." *Educational Media International* 37, no. 2: 105–111.

Vygotsky, Lev S. and Michael Cole. 1978. *Mind in Society: The Development of Higher Psychological Processes*. Cambridge: Harvard University Press.

W3C. "Policies Relating to Web Accessibility" (August 25, 2006a). Available: www.w3.org/WAI/Policy (accessed September 20, 2008).

———. "Web Accessibility Evaluation Tools: Overview" (March 17, 2006b). Available: www.w3.org/WAI/ER/tools (accessed September 1, 2008).

———. "Evaluating Web Sites for Accessibility: Overview" (2008). Available: www.w3.org/WAI/eval/Overview.html (accessed December 27, 2008).

W3Schools. "HTML Links" (2008). Available: www.w3schools.com/HTML/html_links.asp (accessed December 26, 2008).

Waelchli, Paul. 2007. "Librarians' Sport of Choice: Teaching Information Literacy Through Fantasy Football." *College & Research Libraries News* 69, no. 1: 10–15.

Walker, Billie E. 2006. "Using Humor in Library Instruction." *Reference Services Review* 34, no. 1: 117–128.

Walker, Donna E. 1998. *Strategies for Teaching Differently: On the Block or Not*. Thousand Oaks, CA: Corwin.

Wallis, Jake. 2003. "Cyberspace, Information Literacy, and the Information Society." *Library Review* 54, no. 4: 218–222.

Walter, Virginia. 2007. "Information Literacy: A New Role for Public Libraries?" In *Proven Strategies for Building an Information Literacy Program* (pp. 297–307), edited by Susan Curzon and Lynn Lampert. New York: Neal-Schuman.

Wang, Rui. 2006. "The Lasting Impact of a Library Credit Course." *portal: Libraries and the Academy* 6, no. 1: 79–92.

Warlick, David F. 2004. *Redefining Literacy for the 21st Century*. Worthington, OH: Linworth.

Warmkessel, Marjorie Markoff and Frances M. Crothers. 1993. "Collaborative Learning and Bibliographic Instruction." *Journal of Academic Librarianship* 19, no. 1: 4–7.

Warren, Leslie A. 2006. "Information Literacy in Community Colleges: Focusing on Learning." *Reference & User Services Quarterly* 45, no. 4: 297–303.

Warren, Scott J., Mary Jo Dondlinger, and Saha A. Barab.

2008. "A MUVE Towards PBL Writing: Effects of a Digital Learning Environment Designed to Improve Elementary Student Writing." *Journal of Research on Technology in Education* 4, no. 1: 113–140.

Washington State University. Center for Teaching, Learning & Technology. "Guide to Rating Critical and Integrative Thinking" (2006). Available: http://wsuctproject.wsu.edu/ctr.htm (accessed December 23, 2008).

Watson, John B. and Rosalie Rayner. 1920. "Conditioned Emotional Reactions." *Journal of Experimental Psychology* 3, no. 1: 1–14.

Way, Tom. "Dihydrogen Monoxide in the Dairy Industry." Available: www.dhmo.org/milk.html (accessed December 23, 2008).

"Web Browser Extensions" (September 16, 2008) Available: www.libsuccess.org/index.php?title=Web_Browser_Extensions (accessed December 29, 2008).

Webber, Sheila and Stuart Boon. "Information Literacy Weblog." Available: http://information-literacy.blogspot.com (accessed December 22, 2008).

Webber, Sheila and Bill Johnston. 2000. "Conceptions of IL: New Perspectives and Implications." *Journal of Information Science* 26, no. 6: 381–397.

WebQuest.org (2007). Available: www.webquest.org/index.php (accessed December 24, 2008).

WebWhacker. "Offline Browser" (2008). Available: www.bluesquirrel.com/products/webwhacker (accessed December 27, 2008).

Wehmeyer, Lillian Biermann. 1996. "Teaching Online Search Techniques Your Students Can Use." *Syllabus* 10, no. 2: 52–56.

Weidenbenner, Jeni Venker. 2003. "The School Library Context." *Reference & User Services Quarterly* 42, no. 4: 314.

Weil, Michelle M. and Larry D. Rosen. 1997. *Technostress: Coping With Technology @Work @Home @Play*. New York: Wiley & Sons.

Weimer, Mary Ellen. 2002. *Learner-centered Teaching: Five Key Changes to Practice*. San Francisco: Jossey-Bass.

———. 2003. "Focus on Learning. Transform Teaching." *Change* 35, no. 5: 49–54.

Weinberger, David. 2007. *Everything Is Miscellaneous: The Power of the New Digital Disorder*. New York: Henry Holt and Co.

Weiner, Bernard. 1995. *Judgments of Responsibility: A Foundation for a Theory of Social Conduct*. New York: Guilford Press.

Wenzler, John. "LibraryThing and the Library Catalog: Adding Collective Intelligence to the OPAC." Workshop on Next Generation Libraries. CARL North Information Technology Interest Group (September 7, 2007). Available: http://online.sfsu.edu/~jwenzler/research/LTFL.pdf (accessed December 23, 2008).

Wergin, Jon F. 1988. "Basic Issues and Principles in Classroom Assessment." *New Directions for Teaching and Learning* 34: 5–17.

Wertheimer, Max. 1912. "Experimental Studies of the Perception of Movement." *Zeitschrift fur Psychologie* 61, no. 2: 161–265.

Westbrook, Lynn. 1993. "Evaluation." In *Learning to Teach: Workshops on Instruction* (pp. 71–76), edited by Learning to Teach Task Force. Chicago: ALA.

———. 1997. "Qualitative Research." In *Basic Research Methods for Librarians* (pp. 143–163), edited by Ronald R. Powell. Greenwich, CT Ablex.

———. 2006. "Mental Models: A Theoretical Overview and Preliminary Study." *Journal of Information Science* 32, no. 6: 563–579.

Western Association of Schools and Colleges. "Standard 2" (2001). Available: education.berkeley.edu/accreditation/pdf/WASC_Handbook.pdf (accessed December 22, 2008).

West's Encyclopedia of American Law. 1998 ed. S.v., "Copyright." Singapore: Cengage Gale.

Wetpaint. "Free Web Hosting Service" (2008). Available: www.wetpaint.com (accessed December 4, 2008).

White, Charlie. "Zink Pocket Printer: iPhone Companion?" (January 30, 2007). Available: http://gizmodo.com/gadgets/gadgets/zink-pocket-printer-iphone-companion-232549.php (accessed December 27, 2008).

Whitfield, Patricia, Beverly J. Klug, and Patricia Whitney. 2007. "Situative Cognition: Barriers to Teaching Across Cultures." *Intercultural Education* 18, no. 3: 259–264.

"Why Blue M&M's Make You Drowsy." *Forbes* 159, no. 9: S82, 1997.

Wiggins, Grant. 1996. "Practicing What We Preach in Designing Authentic Assessment." *Educational Leadership* 54, no. 1: 18–25.

———. 1997. "Feedback: How Learning Occurs." In *Assessing Impact: Evidence and Action—Presentations from the 1997 AAHE Conference on Assessment and Quality* (pp. 31–39), edited by AAHE. Washington, DC: American Association for Higher Education.

———. 1998. *Educational Assessment: Designing Assessments to Inform and Improve Student Performance*. San Francisco: Jossey-Bass.

WikiMatrix. "Wiki Choice Wizard." Available: www.wikimatrix.org/wizard.php (accessed December 27, 2008).

Wikipedia. "The Free Encyclopedia." Available: http://wikipedia.org (accessed December 27, 2008).

Wilcoxson, Lesley and Michael Prosser. 1996. "Kolb's Learning Style Inventory (1985): Review and Further Study of Validity and Reliability." *British Journal of Educational Psychology* 66, no. 3: 247–257.

Wilder, Stanley J. 2003. *Demographic Change in Academic Librarianship*. Washington, DC: Association of Research Libraries.

———. 2005. "Information Literacy Makes All the Wrong

Assumptions." *Chronicle of Higher Education* 51, no. 18: B13.

Williams, Genevieve. "Unclear on the Context: Refocusing on Information Literacy's Evaluative Component in the Age of Google" (2007) Available: http://libr.unl.edu:2000/LPP/williams.htm (accessed November 13, 2007).

Williams, Lisa. 2005. "Federated Searching: Simplicity or Mass Confusion?" *LIRT News* 28, no. 2: 3.

Williams, Peter. "Against Information Literacy." 2006 Available: www.cilip.org.uk/publications/updatemagazine/archive/archive2006/july/williams.htm (accessed September 15, 2008).

Williams, T. Craig, and Hyder Zahed. 1996. "Computer-based Training Versus Traditional Lecture: Effect on Learning and Retention." *Journal of Business & Psychology* 11, no. 2: 297–310.

Williams, Tracy. "Re: Analogies in ILI." Personal e-mail (June 25, 2008).

Willingham, Daniel T. 2007. "Critical Thinking: Why Is It So Hard to Teach?" *American Educator* 31, no. 2: 8–19.

Wilson, A. Paula. 2005. *100 Ready-to-Use Pathfinders for the Web*. New York: Neal-Schuman.

Wilson, Ellen Knowlton. "Re: [ili-l] Analogies in IL." Electronic bulletin board. (June 23, 2008). Available: ILI-L@ala.org (accessed July 5, 2008).

Wilson, Lizabeth A. 1992. "Changing Users: Bibliographic Instruction for Whom?" In *The Evolving Education Mission of the Library* (pp. 20–53), edited by Betsy Baker and Mary Ellen Litzinger. Chicago: ALA.

———. 2001. "Information Literacy: Fluency Across and Beyond the University." In *Library User Education: Powerful Learning, Powerful Partnerships* (pp. 1–17), edited by Barbara I. Dewey. Lanham, MD: Scarecrow Press.

WILU. "Workshop on Instruction in Library Use." Available: www.yorku.ca/wilu2007 (accessed December 22, 2008).

Wimba. "People Teach People" (2008). Available: www.wimba.com (accessed December 29, 2008).

Winn, William. 2004. "Cognitive Perspectives in Psychology." In *Handbook of Research in Educational Communications and Technology* (pp. 79–112), edited by David H. Jonassen. Mahwah, NJ: Erlbaum.

Wisconsin Association of Academic Librarians. "Information Literacy Competencies and Criteria for Academic Libraries in Wisconsin" (1998). Available: www.wla.lib.wi.us/waal/infolit/ilcc.html (accessed December 22, 2008).

Witkin, Herman A. 1978. "Cognitive Style in Academic Performance and in Teacher–Student Relations." In *Individuality in Learning* (pp. 38–72), edited by Samuel Messick. San Francisco: Jossey-Bass.

Witkin, Herman A., Carol A. Moore, Donald R. Goodenough, and Patricia W. Cox. 1977. "Field-dependent and Field-independent Cognitive Styles and Their Educational Implications." *Review of Educational Research* 47, no. 1: 1–64.

Wong, Gabrielle, Diana Chan, and Sam Chu. 2006. "Assessing the Enduring Impact of Library Instruction Programs." *Journal of Academic Librarianship* 3, no. 4: 384–395.

Woodard, Beth S. 2003. "Technology and the Constructivist Learning Environment: Implications for Teaching Information Literacy Skills." *Research Strategies* 19, no. 2: 181–192.

Woodruff, Allison et al. 2001. "Electronic Guidebooks and Visitor Attention." In *Proceedings of the 6th International Cultural Heritage Informatics Meeting (ICHIM '01)* (pp. 437–454). Pittsburgh: A&MI Publishing.

Woods, Kathleen G. 1990. "Planning an Instructional Program in a Public Library." In *The LIRT Instruction Handbook* (pp. 49–74), edited by May Brottman and Mary Loe. Englewood, CO: Libraries Unlimited.

WordPress. "Open Source Blogging." Available: http://wordpress.com (accessed December 29, 2008).

World Lecture Hall. Center for Instructional Technologies, University of Texas at Austin (January 28, 2008). Available: http://web.austin.utexas.edu/wlh/index.cfm (accessed December 24, 2008).

Wright, Carol. "Information Literacy & You." Pennsylvania State University Libraries (2008). Available: www.libraries.psu.edu/instruction/infolit/andyou/infoyou.htm (accessed December 23, 2008).

WriteMaps. "Sitemap Software" (2008). Available: http://writemaps.com (accessed December 27, 2008).

Wrubel, Laura and Kari Schmidt. 2007. "Usability Testing of a Metasearch Interface: A Case Study." *College & Research Libraries* 68, no. 4: 292–311.

WSIS. "World Summit on the Information Society" (2008). Available: www.itu.int/wsis/index.html (accessed December 22, 2008).

XeroxCorp. "Xerox Second Life: Machinima Avatar" (April 10, 2007). Available: www.youtube.com/watch?v=gjVkIEDJWpw (accessed November 22, 2008).

Yaghi, Hussein M. and Mary Bentley Abu-Saba. 1998. "Teachers' Computer Anxiety: An International Perspective." *Computers in Human Behavior* 14, no. 2: 321–336.

Yi, Hua. 2005. "Library Instruction Goes Online: An Inevitable Trend." *Library Review* 54, no. 1: 47–58.

York County Community College. "Active Learning Techniques for Library Instruction." (December 4, 2007). Available: www.yccc.edu/library/activeLearning/active_learning.htm (accessed December 23, 2008).

Young, Rosemary M., and Stephena Harmony. 1999. *Working with Faculty to Design Undergraduate Information Literacy Programs*. New York: Neal-Schuman.

Young, Timothy G. 2007. "The Young Visitors: Introducing Children to the Research Library Through Exhibition Tours." *College & Research Libraries News* 68, no. 4: 235–238.

YouTube. "Video Web Site" (2008). Available: www.youtube.com (accessed July 14, 2008).

Zemsky, Robert and William F. Masy. "Thwarted Innovation:

What Happened to e-Learning and Why." A Final Report for The Weatherstation Project of the Learning Alliance at the University of Pennsylvania in cooperation with the Thomson Corporation. Philadelphia: The Learning Alliance at the University of Pennsylvania (2004). Available: www.cedma-europe.org/newsletter%20articles/misc/ThwartedInnovation%20(Jun%2004).pdf (accessed December 27, 2008).

Zhang, Li, Erin M. Watson, and Lara Banfield. 2007. "The Efficacy of Computer-assisted Instruction Versus Face-to-Face Instruction in Academic Libraries: A Systematic Review." *Journal of Academic Librarianship* 33, no. 4: 478–484.

Zimmerman, Barry J. 1990. "Self-regulated Learning and Academic Achievement: An Overview." *Educational Psychologist* 25, no. 1: 3–17.

Zoho. "Apps for Your Business Needs" (2008). Available: www.zoho.com (accessed December 29, 2008).

Zurkowski, Paul G. 1974. *The Information Service Environment: Relationships and Priorities*. Washington, DC: National Commission on Libraries and Information Science.

Zwemer, Diane. "Flow of Information." UCLA College Library (2000). Available: www2.library.ucla.edu/libraries/college/11605_12028.cfm (accessed December 23, 2008).

Index

Page numbers followed by the letter "f" indicate figures.

D

J

K

L

M

U

V

Y

Z

About the Authors

Esther S. Grassian received an MLS from UCLA in 1969. Since then, she has served in a variety of reference and instruction positions in the UCLA College Library. Her working title was first "Reference Librarian," then "Reference/Instruction Librarian," followed by "Electronic Services Coordinator," "Instructional Services Coordinator," "Information Literacy Outreach Coordinator," "Interim Head," and "Information Literacy Librarian." Her titles reflect both her involvement with reference, instruction, and technology in an undergraduate library and the development of the modern library instruction/bibliographic instruction/information literacy movement.

She has also held various elected and appointed positions in information literacy–related organizations, including serving as a member of the first Association of College Research Libraries' (ACRL) Institute for Information Literacy Advisory Board, as well as Chair of the ACRL Instruction Section and Chair of the California Clearinghouse on Library Instruction, South (now called SCIL). She was also a member of the UCLA Library's Information Literacy Initiative Steering Committee for several years, beginning with its inception in 2001.

Her publications include the first edition of *Information Literacy Instruction: Theory and Practice* (2001), *Learning to Lead and Manage Information Literacy Instruction* (2005), and the "Information Literacy Instruction" article for the forthcoming *Encyclopedia of Library and Information Science*, all co-authored with Joan R. Kaplowitz. She also wrote "Thinking Critically About World Wide Web Resources" (www.library.ucla.edu/libraries/college/11605_12337.cfm), "Thinking Critically About Web 2.0 & Beyond" (www2.library.ucla.edu/libraries/college/11605_12008.cfm), "Information Literacy: Wilder Makes (Some Right, But) Many Wrong Assumptions" (www.ucop.edu/lauc/opinions/literacy.html), and "Building on Bibliographic Instruction" (2004), as well as chapters in *The Sourcebook for Bibliographic Instruction* (1993) and in *Learning to Teach* (1993).

Esther has led workshops and spoken at programs at the local, state, and national levels in real life (RL), and in the three-dimensional virtual world of Second Life (SL) on a variety of topics, including how to teach one-shot sessions, how to reach out to faculty/teachers and parents for IL, how to use Wikipedia, Google, and YouTube for ILI, and how to teach critical thinking about information tools and materials.

She taught UCLA's four-credit "Library and Information Resources" undergraduate course seven times in the mid-1980s and, in 1989, co-proposed (with Joan R. Kaplowitz) a four-credit course for graduate students in the UCLA Department of Information Studies. The course title, "User Education/Bibliographic Instruction: Theory and Technique," was changed to "Information Literacy Instruction: Theory and Technique," again reflecting the changing nature of this field. Esther and Joan have alternated teaching this course since 1990. In addition, Esther proposed, developed, and has taught two one-credit undergraduate information literacy courses at UCLA in the Honors Department and in the English Composition Department.

In 1995, she was named Librarian of the Year by the Librarians Association of the University of California, Los Angeles, for her efforts at incorporating information literacy into the UCLA academic curriculum and for her work at developing and implementing Internet training programs for UCLA staff and users. In 2004, she and Joan R. Kaplowitz were honored to receive an ACRL Instruction Section Publication Award for the first edition of *Information Literacy Instruction: Theory and Practice.*

Joan R. Kaplowitz has a Doctorate in Psychology as well as a Master's in Library Science. She retired in 2007 after 23 years as a librarian at UCLA. Dr. Kaplowitz worked at UCLA since graduating from UCLA's Library and Information Science program in 1984. She began her career as a reference/instruction librarian and was later Educational Services Coordinator and Head of Public Services at the Education and Psychology Library. She ended her UCLA Library career as the Head of the Research, Instruction and Collection Services division at the UCLA Louise M. Darling Biomedical Library in June 2007.

Dr. Kaplowitz was heavily involved in information literacy instruction at the local, state, and national levels for her entire career and continues to be active in this area even though she has retired from the UCLA Library system. During her early years at UCLA she taught several sections of UCLA's undergraduate course "Library and Information Resources." In 1989, she collaborated with UCLA's Esther Grassian to propose and develop the UCLA graduate library program's course "Information Literacy Instruction: Theory and Technique." She and Ms. Grassian have alternated presenting this course since its inception in 1990. Although she has retired from the library, Dr. Kaplowitz is continuing to teach this course. Dr. Kaplowitz was also part of the faculty development team for Association of College and Research Libraries' Institute for Information Literacy's Immersion Program and taught in six of the programs between 1999 and 2004.

Dr. Kaplowitz was awarded several Librarians' Association of the University of California research grants in support of her research and publication endeavors. She held office in the American Library Association's New Members Round Table and the California Clearinghouse on Library Instruction (now know as SCIL or the Southern California Instruction Librarians group). Dr. Kaplowitz was also involved with the American Library Association's Committee on Accreditation and served on several ad hoc teams reviewing ALA accreditation for several graduate library programs.

From 2001 to 2003, Dr. Kaplowitz was a member of the UCLA Library's Information Literacy Initiative's steering committee and remained on that body when the Initiative became a full-fledged program. She remained involved until her retirement in 2007.

Dr. Kaplowitz has published and made numerous presentations on various topics such as the psychology of learning and cognitive styles, assessment in information literacy, student-centered learning, and mentoring within the profession. She is the co-author (with Ms. Grassian) of the first edition of *Information Literacy Instruction: Theory and Practice* (2001), which received the ACRL Instruction Section's Publication of the Year award, and *Learning to Lead and Manage Information Literacy Instruction* (2005). The Neal-Schuman Company published both books.

Dr. Kaplowitz and Ms. Grassian are currently writing the "Information Literacy Instruction" section for the next edition of the *Encyclopedia of Library and Information Science*. Dr. Kaplowitz was the author of the chapter on the Psychology of Learning in the 2008 *Information Literacy Handbook* published by the Instruction Section of the Association of College and Research Libraries. She recently made presentations for the UCLA's Department of Information Studies in the area of student learning outcomes, active learning, and assessment and for the California State University at Los Angeles Library on active learning and Learner-centered Teaching. Dr. Kaplowitz was awarded UCLA Emerita status in 2008 and continues to be involved in the UCLA Department of Information Studies program. Her Web site, Transform Your Teaching, can be found at www.joankaplowitz.com.